CANADA:
Its Regions and People

Canada and Canadians are currently at crossroads. Their hard-earned self-identity as constituting a distinct people, a nation-state in the political sense of the term, is now facing serious competition from other, often more basic, senses of individuals and collective identity based on language, culture, territory, religion, gender, ethnicity, social class, and religion. Whether or not Canada survives and thrives as a nation-state into the twenty-first century will depend largely on the outcome of this struggle over competing identities.

If the past is an indication of the future, the ten chapters of this rather unorthodox book lead us to the conclusion that Canadians will confront and overcome, yet once again, this age-old challenge with imagination and determination. The structure of this book, which combines chapters on regions, provinces, time periods and themes with a general overview, was quite deliberate. This book was conceived primarily for non-Canadian students, involved in Canadian studies programmes, who are seeking historical background on a wide-range of topics. Most students come to the study of Canada through their interest in contemporary Canadian literature, visual arts, music, sociology, geography, political science, government policy, trade or economics. Most of these disciplines or topics take for granted that their students possess a general basic knowledge of Canada's past. Their practitioners offer their analyses and draw conclusions which often do not make much sense to the non-Canadian students who lack a basic knowledge of Canada's past.

The editors of this book felt that this problem could be overcome if we offered Indian students interested in Canadian studies a book on Canadian history. All of the contributors are from Canada and are well known specialists in their respective sub-fields of Canadian history. Each of them presents, from his or her particular vantage point, a comprehensive overview of their chosen subject matters.

Michael D. Behiels is a professor in Canadian history in the University of Ottawa. A few of his recent works are: *Prelude to Quebec's Quiet Revolution. Liberalism versus Neo-nationalism, 1945-1960* (1985); *Quebec since 1945: Selected Readings* (1987); *The Meech Lake Primer. Conflicting Views of the 1987 Constitutional Accord* (1989).

K.S. Mathew is a professor and head of the department of history in the Pondicherry University, India. He is also the director of the U.G.C. Centre for Canadian Studies. As a Fellow of the Shastri Indo-Canadian Institute he worked in Ottawa University for familiarising himself with Canadian history in 1990. Besides, he worked in Wisconsin (USA), Ottawa (Canada), and Bordeaux (France) universities as visiting professor/fellow for a semester each. He has brought out several books and research articles on Maritime history of India.

CANADA:

Its Regions and People

Editors

Michael D. Behiels

and

K.S. Mathew

Munshiram Manoharlal
Publishers Pvt. Ltd.

ISBN 81-215-0803-7
First published 1998

© 1998, Centre for Canadian Studies,
Department of History, Pondicherry University

Typeset, printed and published by
Munshiram Manoharlal Publishers Pvt. Ltd.,
Post Box 5715, 54 Rani Jhansi Road, New Delhi 110 055.

Contents

Contributors

Cornelius J. Jaenen,
Department of History,
Ottawa University,
Ottawa, Canada.

Michael J. Piva,
Department of History,
University of Ottawa,
Ottawa, Canada.

Ernest Forbes,
Department of History,
University of Fredericton,
Fredericton, Canada.

Peter Baskerville,
Department of History,
University of Victoria,
Victoria, Canada.

Jean Burnet,
Ontario Historical Society,
Toronto, Canada.

R. Douglas Francis,
Department of History,
University of Calgary,
Calgary, Canada.

Linda Kerr,
Department of History,
University of Alberta,
Edmonston, Canada.

Wendy Mitchinson,
Department of History,
University of Waterloo,
Waterloo, Canada.

Michael D. Behiels,
Department of History,
University of Ottawa,
Ottawa, Canada.

Editors

K.S. Mathew,
Department of History,
Pondicherry University,
Pondicherry, India.

Michael D. Behiels,
Department of History,
Ottawa University,
Ottawa, Canada.

Introduction

Canada, in every respect, is a highly diversified and multifaceted country, home to thirty million citizens who share, in relative prosperity and harmony, a vast and varied expanse of geography comprising half a continent bordering on three oceans. The forging of a Canadian people out of such a vast array of human and geographic diversity has been an arduous challenge. The setbacks in this process of building a stable and prosperous Canadian citizenry, one which remains socially and linguistically diverse yet politically united, have been, and continue to be, as numerous as the many shared achievements.

Nonetheless, Canadians have attained what has eluded citizens of many older, more established nation-states, that is, political unity within socio-cultural and linguistic diversity. Despite the continued threat of secession by the majority French-speaking community of the province of Quebec, all Canadians share a sense of Canadian political identity and citizenship. Canadians are, quite rightly, very proud of, and eager to display to the world at large, their sense of shared political identity whenever they travel abroad or entertain international visitors at home. This is a remarkable achievement given the many obstacles that had to be overcome. Many countries look to Canada as a model for the twenty-first century as the world truly evolves into a shrinking global village thanks to instantaneous communications and rapid mass transportation by air.

As a modern nation-state, Canada was created by the British Parliament in 1867. Some one hundred and thirty years later, it is still perceived by people worldwide as a very young and developing country. What is often not fully appreciated is the fact that Canada has a much older history, one stretching back to the days before the arrival of the Europeans in the sixteenth century when numerous Aboriginal communities roamed over every region of North America. After a long period of demographic and social decline thanks to an imposed economic and political marginalization, Canada's various Aboriginal communities, including the Natives, the Inuit, and the Métis, are now growing in size and their leaders are seeking various forms of self-government within the Canadian federation. These communities have a long yet largely unexplored pre-contact history that remains to be deciphered and told.

Although European contact with North America goes back several centuries, the first permanent European settlers in the region that eventually became Canada were French colonists and fur traders. The process began in the early 17th century with the Acadian settlements in the Maritime region of present day Nova Scotia, Prince Edward Island, and New Brunswick. These were followed by numerous French settlements along the magnificent St. Lawrence River and its many tributaries. As contacts with the various Aboriginal communities were made and alliances formed through fur trading and missionary activities, French settlements eventually spread into the heart of the continent all the way to the Gulf of Mexico via the Mississippi River and westward to the impressive Rocky Mountains bordering the western plains region via the great lakes and the majestic lakes and rivers of northern Canada.

With the defeat of New France by the British forces in the battle of the Plains of Abraham in 1759 and the subsequent Treaty of Paris in 1763, the French colonies of North America, except for the Islands of St. Pierre and Miquelon located off the coast of Newfoundland, were integrated into the British American colonial empire. When the thirteen British American colonies overthrew their British rulers in the American Revolution of 1776-83, British North America was reduced to the colonies of Old Quebec and Nova Scotia as well as the vast territory known as Rupert's Land in the North-west controlled by the Hudson Bay Company. It was out of this conglomeration of multi-cultural, multi-religious, and multi-lingual British North American colonies that the semi-autonomous Dominion of Canada was forged between The Constitution Act, 1791 and The British North American Act, 1867.

Prior to the outbreak of the Great War in 1914, the territory of Canada expanded to include the western plains all the way to the Pacific Ocean and to the Arctic Ocean all across the northern hemisphere. Selling its immense natural resources into a European market, Canada developed into a semi-industrial nation-state with three expensive transcontinental railways binding the communities of the various regions together. Emulating its southern neighbour's frenetic expansion in the post civil war years, Canada opened its doors to waves of immigrants from the United Kingdom, the United States, and northern, central, and eastern continental Europe while deliberately keeping out Asians and Blacks. The Great War of 1914-18, and the subsequent social upheaval and economic recession, helped forge Canadians into a people, understood in the political sense of the term. In many ways, modern Canada came of age during the Great War as thousands of soldiers fortunate enough to return home turned their backs on the jingoistic and self-serving

British Empire. As Canadian society continued to urbanize, industrialize, and become increasingly integrated into the United States economy, an inclusive liberal Canadian nationalism supplanted the exclusive conservative British-Canadian nationalism that had enticed thousands upon thousands of British Canadians into the Great War and left the country terribly divided, despondent, and disillusioned.

In the mid-1920s, Canadian political leaders, in cooperation with the leaders of several other semi-autonomous British colonies, forced British authorities into transforming the archaic and anti-democratic British Empire into a British Commonwealth of autonomous nation-states. In 1931, with the Statute of Westminster, Canada was formally recognized as an independent nation-state. In the interim it had established diplomatic legations in London, Washington, Paris and Tokyo hoping to enhance its trading prospects while avoiding any direct responsibilities in international crises. This was not an easy task given the continuing deep linguistic, cultural, and class divisions between English-speaking and French-speaking Canadians. The maturation of Canada as an independent nation was hindered further when the largely middle-class prosperity of the 1920s quickly vanished with the onslaught of the Great Depression of the 1930s. The important socio-economic transformations of the previous decade ground to a halt. Meanwhile Canadians in all regions experimented with a range of political ideologies, from the right-wing populism and nationalism to Fabian socialism and communism, in search of solutions to the difficult structural economic and political problems created by rise of monopoly capitalism, the collapse of international trade, and an overly-rigid federal system that had failed to address the urgent needs of its citizens.

The Second World War and the return of international trade, beginning with the United States, accelerated the urbanization, secularization, and industrialization of Canadian society, especially in the two central provinces of Quebec and Ontario. A very large influx of European displaced persons, refugees, and immigrants, which lead eventually to the liberalization of Canada's exclusionary immigration policies in the 1960s, contributed immensely to the maturation of the Canadian society by accentuating the democratization of its overly deferential and elitist political culture. Canada evolved, somewhat belatedly, into a liberal-democratic, social welfare nation-state, one capable and willing to meet the basic, social and economic needs of all its peoples.

These developments also propelled Canada into playing a modest but significant role in international affairs through the many agencies of the United Nations, the North Atlantic Treaty Organization, the British

Commonwealth of Nations, and eventually the Organization of Francophone states. With the support and assistance of countries like India, Canada developed, and put into practice, the concept of peacekeeping as a means of ensuring that localized conflicts did not evolve into a full-scale war between the two competing superpowers, the United States and the Soviet Union. All of these developments contributed to the formation of a sense of shared Canadian citizenship as Canada moved toward the celebration of its centenary in 1967. This sense of shared citizenship was symbolized by a very distinctive flag, the red maple leaf on a white background with two red borders, and the adoption of a national programme of universal health insurance known as medicare.

A prolonged period of post-war prosperity, coupled with the development of provincial economies and the modernization of provincial political institutions and bureaucracies propelled by that of Quebec, allowed Canadians the luxury of opening the pandora's box of constitutional reform. Canada's political leaders undertook the challenge of Canadianizing the The British North American Act, 1867, finding an acceptable amending procedure, adding the Canadian Charter of Rights and Freedoms, and setting in motion the difficult process of restructuring the federation. This constitutional renewal process ran parallel to, and was often at odds with, yet another profound social transformation sweeping through Canadian society at all levels. This transformation was fuelled by rapid technological innovation and global economic change; by marvellous educational opportunities open to all citizens on the basis of merit; by mass immigration from all parts of the world; by significantly enhanced participation of women in higher education and throughout the work force; and finally, by a democratization of Canada's increasingly pluralistic and diversified political culture.

After several unsuccessful attempts, The British North America Act, 1867 was patriated in 1982 and the Canadian Charter of Rights and Freedoms along with a complicated series of amending formulas based on the principle of the equality of the provinces were added to the Constitutional framework. Many of the provincial premiers, led by a succession of nationalist/separatist premiers of Quebec, were critical of, or rejected outright, The Constitution Act, 1982. They demanded further constitutional reforms which would increase significantly provincial jurisdictional powers and fiscal resources, diminish the scope of the Charter and grant Quebec special constitutional status as the homeland of Canada's Francophone minority. The vast majority of Canadians, comprising all regions, social classes, ethnocultural communities, official language minorities, Aboriginal communities, religious groups, and civil liberties organization, rejected two formal attempts by the dominant political and economic elites to weaken the Canadian nation-state by creating an even more decentralized confederation of provinces or by granting Quebec either special constitutional status or a bi-national, Quebec-Canada confederation.

Canada and Canadians are currently at another crossroads. Their hard-earned self-identity as constituting a distinct people, a nation-state in the political sense of the term, is now facing serious competition from other, often more basic, senses of individual and collective identity based on language, culture, territory, religion, gender, ethnicity, social class, and religion. Whether or not Canada survives and thrives as a nation-state into the twenty-first century will depend largely on the outcome of this struggle over competing identities. Will Canadians, as they managed to do so successfully in the past, continue to believe in and practice a policy of unity in diversity by accepting the principle of multiple and mutually supportive identities?

If the past is any indication of the future, the ten chapters of this rather unorthodox textbook lead us to the conclusion that Canadians will confront and overcome, yet once again, this age-old challenge with imagination and determination. The structure of the textbook, which combines chapters on regions, provinces, time periods, themes with a general overview, was quite deliberate. The textbook was conceived primarily for non-Canadian students, involved in Canadian studies programmes, who are seeking historical background on a wide-range of topics. Most students come to the study of Canada through their interest in contemporary Canadian literature, visual arts, music, sociology, geography, political science, government policy, trade, or economics. Most of these disciplines or topics take for granted that their students possess a general basic knowledge of Canada's past. Their practitioners offer their analyses and draw conclusions which often do not make much sense to non-Canadian students who lack a basic knowledge of Canada's past.

The editors of this textbook, felt that this problem could be overcome if we offered Indian students interested in Canadian studies a textbook in Canadian history that was printed in India and therefore more readily accessible at a reasonable cost. All of the contributors who graciously agreed to participate in this project, are well-known specialists in their respective sub-fields of Canadian history. Each of them presents, from his or her particular vantage point, a comprehensive overview of their chosen subject matters. Students can choose to read the textbook from cover to cover or use it as a handy reference tool when seeking background information on a wide range of topics. The editors wish to take this opportunity to thank each of the nine historians for their respective contributions as well as for their patience while this project found its way ever-so-slowly to fruition. We also wish to thank the Shastri Indo-Canadian Institute for a seminar grant part of which was advanced to the publisher as grant-in-aid for the publication of this book. We hope this book will prove useful to the students pursuing their studies in Canadian subjects especially in the identified centres of Canadian programmes in India.

We would like to place on record our indebtedness to Dr. M. Manicakam and L. Pandidurai who helped us in reading the final proof and prepared the index. Our thanks are due to Munshiram Manoharlal Publishers, New Delhi for the prompt execution of the work to coincide with the 14th International Conference on Canadian Studies hosted by the Centre for Canadian Studies in the Department of History, Pondicherry University in January 1998.

MICHAEL D. BEHIELS
K.S. MATHEW

1

New France to 1760

CORNELIUS J. JAENEN

The French were the first Europeans to establish permanent settlements and extend their sovereignty over the vast expanse that would become modern Canada. The French colony, known as Nouvelle France, comprised three regions: Acadia, which included the modern provinces of Nova Scotia, New Brunswick and Prince Edward Island, to which was appended the base of Placentia in southern Newfoundland, Canada proper, which consisted of the arable lands of the St. Lawrence valley and the *Pays d'en haut,* or upper country of the Great Lakes basin, to which in the eighteenth century was appended the *Mer de l'Ouest,* the far western region stretching onto the great central plains, or Prairies as they are commonly called today. In other words, New France at its greatest extent included most of the populated regions of modern Canada with the exception of the Pacific coastal region. The importance of this vast overseas colony should not be exaggerated, however, because it was, apart from the well populated shores of the St. Lawrence river between the island of Montreal and the Island of Orleans just below Quebec (Canada) and the eastern shores of the Bay of Fundy (Acadia), a vast colonial claim without extensive settlement. In essence, there were two distinct regions—the restricted area of French colonization in the lower St. Lawrence valley and along the shores of the Bay of Fundy, and the extensive ancestral lands of various Amerindian nations where the French established a few trading posts, military forts and mission stations.

First Encounters

Initial French encounters with this 'New World' were the result of the overseas expansion of Western European fishing and marine hunting enterprises. Breton, Norman and Basque fishermen from French Atlantic ports frequented Newfoundland waters in the late fifteenth century in search of cod to supply the markets of protein-starved Catholic countries where the religious calendar had over 150 days abstinence from meat and dairy products. The earliest documentary record of French participation is 1504, but we know also that four years later Amerindian captives were brought to France as proof of having visited the 'new lands', and by 1510 the Norman and Breton fishermen were keeping the Rouen market well stocked with cod. By the 1570s, the French were the most numerous in this international enterprise, this in spite of the wars of religion raging at home at the time. One eye-witness in 1578, reported that the French had almost 200 vessels on the fishing banks, or equal to that of the Spanish, Portuguese, English and Basques combined. The profits of this private enterprise were divided up usually with one-half to the victualler, one-quarter to the owners of the vessel, and the remaining quarter to the master and crew. Some merchants began to buy fishing vessels and become their own victuallers, thus realizing an even greater profit. The partners took care to have their contracts drawn up before a notary because losses at sea and spoilage could become matters of controversy. The cod fishery continued to bring in greater profits than any other enterprise in New France.[1]

Cod fishing was seasonal life abroad was unpleasant on an often stormy ocean, but the rewards were attractive and the environment was generally healthy. There was little scurvy, for example, and the death rate was considerably lower than on royal vessels engaged in the southern or oriental trade. The young men who worked for several years on these fishing expeditions were seasoned sailors as well and they were eagerly recruited for the royal navy. Consequently, the fishery was promoted by the Crown as a 'nursery of seamen'.

In the late sixteenth century, the French began to exploit the walrus rookeries on the coasts and islands of the Gulf of St. Lawrence. They drove out most of the Portuguese and Basques who had preceded them. The walrus, huge marine animals sometimes called the morse, lived and travelled in herds and were slaughtered in large numbers when they rested along sandy beaches and rocky shorelines. Their tusks provided prized ivory, their hides were made into ropes, and their blubber was turned into oil.[2]

Whaling was another popular enterprise which provided much of the oil for the lamps of Europe and *baleen,* or whalebone, for the bolstering of dresses. Although the Basques dominated whaling activities off Labrador, where they established an impressive station at Boetes [Red Bay], the

---

[1]The standard work on the cod fishery is still Harold A. Innis, *The Cod Fisheries. The History of an International Economy,* Toronto, 1978.

[2]A popular but well informed account of walrus hunting is Farley Mowat, *Sea of Slaughter,* Toronto, 1985.

French controlled activities in the Gulf of St. Lawrence.[3]

The catching of cod and the hunting of marine animals along the Atlantic seaboard led to another economic pursuit which encouraged the French to penetrate into the interior of the continent. Charter contracts began to refer to 'fish, oils, fat, merchandise and other goods' which fishing vessels brought back from north-eastern North America. These other goods were luxurious furs, hides and skins obtained in barter with Amerindians. A contract dated 1580, for example, 'for pursuit of whales and trade with the Natives', indicated that the fur trade was developing as a portable sideline. It was no surprise to Jacques Cartier, as he approached the new-found-lands in 1534, that aboriginal hunters "set up a great clamour and made frequent signs to us to come on shore, holding up to us furs on sticks".[4]

The initial contacts had been made by private entrepreneurs with no official backing from the Crown, from the nobility, or from religious institutions. The motives were clearly economic and the profits did not accrue immediately to the privileged orders in French society. As the fishery led to the development of the fur trade, another unusual characteristic of these initial contacts emerged. Many, probably the majority, of the entrepreneurs belonged to the *Religion prétendue réformée,* as Protestantism was then labelled. Calvinism and Lutheranism were religious minorities in France, but their influence and economic activity in bourgeois circles of France's Atlantic ports outweighed their numerical strength.

Protestant Colonization

The first French Protestant project for the establishment of a colony in the Americas was tied to Jacques Cartier's third voyage. Cartier had been commissioned in 1534 by King Francis I, who envied the Spanish discovery of New World Treasures, "to discover certain islands and lands where it is said that a great quantity of gold and other precious things are to be found". Thus it was that Cartier contacted Micmac and Laurentian Iroquois peoples, with whom he bartered, along the shores of the Gulf of St. Lawrence already frequented by the fishing fleets. He returned the following year to explore the St. Lawrence valley as far inland as the island of Montreal. In

[3]The whaling operations became known through the research of Selma Barkham in Spanish archival respositories, beginning in 1972, and since then through marine archaeological work by Robert Grenier of Parks Canada and Professor James A. Tuck of Memorial University of Newfoundland. A good overview is available in George M. Story, *Early European Settlement and Exploration in Atlantic Canada,* St. John's, 1982, pp. 41-65.

[4]The citations relating to these early French voyages are found in H.P. Biggar, ed., *The Voyages of Jacques Cartier,* Ottawa, 1924, pp. 49-56.

1541, he was again commissioned to "enter deeper into these lands, to converse with the peoples found there and live among them, if need be" in preparation for the arrival of settlers under the command of Jean-François LaRocque de Roberval, a Lutheran nobleman from southern France. Cartier believed he had discovered gold and diamonds (which later proved to be only iron pyrites and mica chips), therefore he hurried back to France, leaving Roberval's settlers without the benefit of his experience in establishing a colony in 1542. Roberval's party soon built an elaborate headquarters with "two strong towers situated on a small mountain in order to prevail against the barbarity of the inhabitants". Besides the hostility of the Laurentian Iroquois whose villages dotted the shores of the St. Lawrence river, the colonists had to contend with an outbreak of scurvy and a particularly cold winter in which even the wine froze in the casks. The colonists ran short of supplies and Roberval had some difficulty in maintaining order among mutinous settlers. Many were hardened criminals, chosen as one wag said 'by the best judges in France', who had been released from prison on the promise to relocate in the colony. The survivors returned to France in 1543.

Colonies were established in 'Florida' in the 1550s, and in the Bay of Rio de Janeiro, Brazil, in the 1560s, but both proved to be failures. The Spaniards destroyed the former, and the Portuguese destroyed the latter. Thus Protestant interest in colonial ventures received a serious setback. Neither the Crown nor private entrepreneurs showed much enthusiasm for overseas colonization during the rest of the sixteenth century.[5]

Acadian Beginnings

Nevertheless, another Protestant entrepreneur, Pierre Gua de Monts, received a trade monopoly from King Henry IV in 1603 for the entire north Atlantic seaboard from present-day Maine to the Arctic circle, in exchange for the promise to establish sixty colonists each year and promote Catholic missionary work among the aboriginal peoples. De Monts, organized an association of merchants from several cities under the direction of a Dutch shareholder, Cornelius de Bellois, to finance a joint Protestant-Catholic expedition. Among those recruited was the geographer Samuel de Champlain. Three vessels carrying artisans, soldiers and peasants, accompanied by two Catholic priests and a Protestant pastor, sailed into the Bay of Fundy, where

---

[5]There is as yet no definitive work on French Protestantism in the Americas. Useful are Cornelius J. Jaenen, "The Persistence of the Protestant Presence in New France, 1540-1760", *Proceedings of the Second Meeting of the Western Society for French History,* Austin, 1975, and Marc-André Bédard, *Les Protestants en Nouvelle-France,* Québec, 1978.

the first settlement was planted on Dochet Island. The site proved disastrous—unsheltered in the stormy winter months and lacking fresh water—so in the spring of 1604 the survivors moved across the Bay of Fundy to the Annapolis valley (Nova Scotia), where Port Royal was established as a permanent base.[6] When Jean de Poutrincourt was left in charge of local affairs for the de Mont's company, good relations were established with the Micmac inhabitants. This may be ascribed to the avoidance of French settlement on Micmac campsites and respect for their seasonal migrations, the mutually satisfying barter of European manufactured goods for peltries, and the evolving Micmac association with Catholicism following the conversion of a respected chieftain, Membertou, and his family.

In 1611, the Marquise de Guercheville bought out the interest of the merchant association in Port Royal. Under her protection, Jesuits arrived to assume responsibility for missionary work. Friction developed between the fur trade interests and missions, but this was short-lived because Samuel Argall captured the barely defended outpost in 1613 in the interests of the Virginia Company, which announced a rival claim to all the Atlantic seaboard. Most of the French colonists withdrew inland to live among the Micmacs. The Scottish colony, called Nova Scotia, was neither prosperous nor stable as it faced incursions of the French and Micmacs.

In 1632, by the terms of the Treaty of Saint-Germain-en-Laye, the colony was returned to France. But internal dissension replaced external threat. Under the rule of the Company of New France, established in 1627, Acadia was divided into two sectors. The La Tour family administered the western section from its headquarters at Fort Sainte-Marie on the Saint John river (New Brunswick today) and the d'Aulnay family administered the eastern section from Port Royal. However, there was no definition of the limits of their authority, of their share of expenses and profits of the fur trade, or of the boundaries of their territory. Bitter feuding resulted and was not resolved until a fortunate marriage between the heads of the two families in 1653.

Alternating sovereignty between England and France over Acadia, a border country between two competing imperial powers, throughout the seventeenth century—thirteen changes in total—did not contribute to any firm attachment on the part of the relatively isolated and self-sufficient Acadians to either Crown. They held tenaciously to their salty marshland farms and orchards, their herds, their fishery, and their friendly trade and intercourse with the Micmacs and some Anglo-American colonists to the south. Salutary neglect by France bred independence of spirit and indomitable

---

[6]The early history of Acadia is covered in John G. Reid, *Acadia, Maine and New Scotland: Marginal Colonies in the Seventeenth Century,* Toronto, 1971.

self-reliance. In the absence of regularly constituted parishes, seigneurial control of land compulsory militia service and family networks bound them together and provided them with a community identity.[7]

Founding of Canada

In 1600, Pierre de Chauvin, a Protestant naval captain, established an annual encounter at Tadoussac, at the mouth of the Saguenay river, for the exchanges related to the fur trade with Algonkian hunting bands. In 1608, Samuel de Champlain, working in the interests of the de Monts' association, established a permanent base, or *habitation,* at the 'point of Quebec', roughly the site of the Laurentrain Iroquois village of Stadacona, where Cartier and Roberval had wintered. From this beachhead, the small French colony traded with the Algonkian and Huron nations, and also joined them in war against their Iroquois enemies.

The founding of Quebec as the headquarters for Canadian Operations had many consequences. The St. Lawrence river naturally led the French to move westwards into the hinterland as they pursued the fur trade with the Native peoples, and as they developed agricultural settlement. Quebec was inland, however, and trans-Atlantic communication with France was cut off during the long winter season. Moreover, Champlain had had little choice in supporting his trading partners in an ongoing inter-tribal war between the Hurons/Algonkians and the Five Nations Iroquois. This enmity of the Iroquois would almost destroy the colony on more than one occasion, until peace was eventually concluded with them in 1701.[8]

Company of New France

In 1627, Louis XIII's first minister, Cardinal Richelieu decided to end the rivalries that had characterized the various associations of merchant-entrepreneurs interested in the trade of New France. He organized a charter company of over one hundred nobles and bourgeois, the Company of New France, commonly called the One Hundred Associates, and assigned them the property of the colony with the right to create large estates called *seigneuries*[9] therein, the right to set up its administrative structure, and the

---

[7]The emergence of an Acadian identity is developed in Naomi Griffiths, *The Acadians: Creation of a People,* Toronto, 1973.

[8]The standard work on this early period remains Marcel Trudel, *The Beginnings of New France, 1524-1663,* Toronto, 1973.

[9]The estate granted by the Company of New France, and after 1663 directly by the Crown, was known as a seigneury. The landowners or seigneurs, who theoretically had been members of the two privileged orders or *états*—the nobility and clergy—kept a portion of the estate known as the *domain* for their own personal use. The larger portion was granted to *censitaires,* farmers who owned their plots but who paid annual dues to the seigneur in perpetuity.

exclusive control over all commerce. Modelled somewhat on the Dutch East India Company, the company of New France differed from it in one important respect. It was saddled with the obligation to bring out a prescribed number of settlers annually, to finance their establishment, to maintain the requisite number of artisans and soldiers to launch a successful colony, and to support the Catholic missionaries in their efforts to convert the Native peoples and to serve the spiritual needs of the colonists.

The company suffered many serious reverses, ranging from the capture of its first supply fleet in 1628, an Anglo-Huguenot occupation of Canada from 1629 to 1632, to Iroquois incursions marked by a triumphant destruction of the Huron confederacy on which the Jesuit missions and company's fur trade relied. Also, the company was unable to overcome its inability to attract immigrants to what was, according to travel and missionary accounts, an apparently inhospitable northern country.

Nevertheless, during its administration of New France, from 1627 to 1663, the Company of New France did see some progress. In 1634, a second town Trois Rivières, was founded at the mouth of the St. Maurice river. It was a popular meeting place for Native traders bringing down their furs from the northern hunting territories, so an annual trade fair was organized there. Five years later, the first nursing and teaching sisters arrived to establish their institution in Quebec, and the first steps were taken to attach the missions to a metropolitan see. In 1642, a third town, Montreal, was founded and it soon became the commercial hub of the colony. By 1659, Sulpician secular clergy had arrived to assume the seigneury of the whole island of Montreal and launch their native missionary and educational work. A bishop had also arrived, although a diocese had not yet been erected. The company had granted a number of seigneuries, hoping that wealthy landowners would recruit farmers and artisans to exploit their holdings. A few nobles did attempt to populate their seigneuries, but it was only the Jesuits, the Sulpicians and the women's religious communities that were successful immigration agents.

Utopian Experiments

The 'discovery' of the Americas and its hitherto unknown inhabitants had inclined those of mystical bent to surmise that, now that 'the remainder of Adam's descendants' had been found, the end of the world could not be far off.[10] Accordingly, it was a time for renewed missionary activity to bring all of the world under Christian dominion. The early seventeenth century in France was also a period of spiritual revival. New religious orders sprang up,

[10]See "France's America and Amerindians: Image and Reality", *History of European Ideas,* VI, 4 (1985), 405-20 for more information on early concepts of the colonial experience.

home and foreign missions were undertaken, and devout lay men and women organized cells of the Company of the Holy Sacrament throughout the realm to impose rigorous moral and religious standards on society. New France felt the full impact of this *dévotisme* in its formative period.

The Jesuit missionaries enjoyed both official protection and generous financial support when they began their missionary work among the Micmacs of Acadia in 1611, and among the Algonkian and Huron peoples of Canada in 1625. Among the sedentary agricultural Hurons along Georgian Bay in the *pays d'en haut,* or 'upper country', they laid the foundations of what was to become a New Jerusalem of converted aborigines untainted by the vices of Europe. Zealous visionaries saw in the North American forests the possibility of a regained Garden of Eden ushering in the second advent of Christ. Mother Marie de l'Incarnation, superior of the Ursulines who taught Native girls at their Quebec monastery, envisaged the aboriginal neophytes as a 'church of the apostolic age'. The native distaste for regimented schooling soon brought her to more realistic objectives. European-origin diseases took on epidemic proportions in Native villages and encampments, to the extent that there was catastrophic depopulation and demoralization among the survivors. The Jesuits in Huronia also abandoned their idealistic dreams as they faced opposition from within the community from staunch adherents of traditional aboriginal religion, and from outside the community from the Iroquois who in 1949-50 defeated and dispersed the Huron people.

Meanwhile, near their headquarters at Quebec, the Jesuits had obtained a bequest which enabled them to set aside land and funds for a *réduction,* or what came to be called a Native reserve in later times. The objective was to induce nomadic hunting bands of Algonkian nations to take up residence on the seigneury of Sillery and become agriculturalists. The aim was to christianize and 'francize', convert and civilize, heathen 'wanderers' and turn them into docile, francophone, Catholic peasants. The initial plan underwent considerable adaptation, until the seigneuries granted to missionaries for the express purpose of assimilating Amerindians, modelled on a Paraguayan experiment and known as *réductions,* became virtual refuges for persecuted native Christian converts and segregated communities in which they were shielded from the alcohol and immorality of the colonial towns. Nearly all the people who continued to live on the seven *réductions*—Hurons, Iroquois, Abenaki—were sedentary agriculturalists, who proved to be very effective allies of the French in the colonial wars.[11]

---

[11]For more detailed information see "Problems of Assimilation in New France, 1603-45", *French Historical Studies,* IV, 3 (1966): 245-89, also republished in J. M. Bumsted, ed., *Canadian History before Confederation. Essays and Interpretations,* Georgetown, 1972, pp. 58-77.

In 1642, the Société de Notre-Dame pour la Conversion des Sauvages, inspired and sustained by the *dévot* network in France, launched another utopian enterprise on the island of Montreal. The founding of Ville-Marie professed as its objective the building of an ideal community, but its directors were astute entrepreneurs who recognized the potentialities of the site as a trade and communications centre situated in the most fertile agricultural belt of the Laurentian lowlands. This town dedicated to the Virgin Mary soon lost its otherworldly trappings and became the rather secular centre for business and military matters.

Mgr Laval, the first colonial bishop, who arrived in 1659, belonged to the same visionary group. He quickly set up a seminary, in which he hoped to train an aboriginal diocesan clergy. He refused to have an episcopal palace constructed, preferring to live with the clergy of his seminary in what he believed to be the practice of the church in the first centuries of the Christian era. In violation of the practice of the Gallican church (Roman Catholic Church in France), Laval wanted the tithes collected centrally at the seminary from whence he could have them redistributed to the parishes and missions according to their perceived needs. All his attempts to create a Christian utopia came to nought as revivalistic fervour waned in France and Louis XIV intervened directly to dampen the fires of austere and aggressive religiosity. Louis XIV expected his subjects to profess his Catholic religion, but he did not think they should resort to excessive zealousness.

Introduction of Royal Government

Leaving colonization largely in the hands of private entrepreneurs, a charter company and religious institutions did not provide satisfactory results. By the 1660s there were complaints from the few colonists themselves about their insecurity *vis-à-vis* Iroquois threats, the lack of control over trading activities and the brandy traffic among Native peoples, the slow pace of settlement and the uncertainty about legal rights and procedures. In 1661, Louis XIV had decided to rule without a first minister, so it was no surprise that two years later he revoked the charter of the Company of New France and brought the colony under his personal rule. It must be remembered, of course, that this absolutism was not tyrannical despotism, tempered as his personal intervention was by the Court, the tribunals, the bureaucracy, and the colonial administration that would be put in place in an isolated overseas possession far from the close scrutiny of Versailles.

The colonial government was patterned on French provincial administration. At its head, representing the King, was a Governor-General, who was in-charge of military matters, external affairs and relations with the

Amerindians. He was seconded by local governors in each of the three towns—Quebec, Trois Rivières, Montreal—and in Acadia (Isle Royale after 1713) and eventually at New Orleans in Louisiana. The Intendant was in-charge of finances, law and order, and he was assisted by sub-delegates in each of the aforementioned regions. The Intendant also presided the meetings of the Sovereign Council, which was a court of appeal, a deliberative council which issued local ordinances, and chancery which registered and proclaimed royal edicts to give them force of law in the colony. The Bishop joined the Governor and Intendant on this council, but his participation was soon restricted to occasional interventions to protect the privileges of the clergy. The councillors were appointed by the Crown and the directors of the *Compagnie des Indes Occidentales,* created in 1664 and given the monopoly of the fur trade. Governor and Intendant reported to the King and, after 1669, usually through the Minister of Marine and Colonies in Versailles. In 1674, the royal prerogative asserted itself more forcefully by rescinding all administrative powers of the *Compagnie des Indes Occidentales,* by giving all sovereign councillors royal commissions, and by concurring with the creation of a diocese encompassing all North America north of the Spanish possessions.

This very centralized system of government was not without redeeming features. Royal instructions in 1663 explained that "the general spirit of government ought to lean in the direction of gentleness, it being dangerous to employ severity against transplanted peoples, far removed from their prince [and his enforcement officers]". This policy, defined as *paternalism,* was reiterated on several occasions. In 1686, for example, the Intendant was reminded to "pay heed to all the complaints and needs of the inhabitants", so that they "enjoy complete tranquillity among themselves and increase in numbers".[12] The King as head of church and state expected to be obeyed in all matters, but he also accepted that he was responsible for the welfare of his subjects. Paternalism as practised in New France, meant that the colonists received free land on request and they were exempt from the heavy burden of taxation that fell on their metropolitan counterparts.

Although France had no parliamentary government, the Estates-General not having met since 1614, in New France the colonial notables were represented, though not elected, on the Sovereign Council at Quebec. Governor Frontenac was remained that "it is good that every man speak for himself, and that none speak for all", following metropolitan practice.

[12]These policy statements are found in Margaret Conrad et al., *History of the Canadian Peoples,* vol. I: *Beginnings to 1867,* Toronto, 1993, pp. 139-41 and are based on the administrative correspondence of the French régime found in the National Archives of Canada, Ottawa, MG 1, series C11A and B.

Nevertheless, consultative assemblies were called by Governor and Intendant to deal with contentious issues such as brandy trafficking, Iroquois incursions, trade restrictions, parish boundaries, food shortages and statute labour for repairing roads and bridges. Merchants organized *bourses,* or chambers of commerce, in Montreal and Quebec from 1700 onwards to regulate matters of common concern. The parish provided an opportunity for democratic expression because through its elected council, the *fabrique,* it owned and controlled its temporal assets, including the church building, presbytery, cemetery, and sometimes a parish school. The Sovereign Council, in deliberating the appropriateness of royal edicts and declarations to the colonial situation, did not hesitate to influence the Governor and Intendant to respond to Versailles indicating what amendments were desired before implementing the law. Orders from Versailles often reflected the desires and opinions of colonial administrators. Contrary to what historians believed decades ago, there was no heavy-handed despotic oppression.[13]

Immigration Projects

In spite of the favourable conditions just cited, far fewer French chose to emigrate to New France than to the Antilles. Approximately 12,000 immigrants came to New France and settled permanently between 1600 and 1750. Early literary sources stressed the harsh climate, isolation and dangers of Native attacks, so that Canada had a 'bad press' from the outset! The lack of success of the sixteenth century colonization projects may have had some influence as well. And yet, in the absence of any strong attraction to come to Canada or Acadia, and in the absence of any strong factors pushing people out of the mother country (let us remember that Huguenots when persecuted fled, and were not driven out), France pumped money, materials and men into a comparatively unprofitable colony. New France, as we have seen, was first claimed for economic exploitation and for reasons of state. By the beginning of the eighteenth century, it would be maintained, not for its economic returns, but for strategic reasons and national glory.

The state intervened to support colonization because private enterprise had not succeeded in populating the colony. Indentured labourers nearly always tried to return to France at the termination of their contracts. As early as 1647 craftsmen were encouraged to emigrate by the promise that

[13]A brief but useful overview of government administration in William J. Eccles, *The Government of New France,* Ottawa, 1968, Historical booklet no. 18. More analytical is André Vachon, "The Administration of New France", in *The Dictionary of Canadian Biography,* vol. II: *1701-70,* Toronto, 1969, pp. xv-xxv. The DCB is an excellent tool because the biographies are all placed into their historical context.

after six years in the colony they would be accredited masters of their trade. Captains of vessels bound for the colony were compelled to bring out colonists, the number being determined by the tonnage of the vessel. A subsequent prohibition to take on invalids, mentally deranged, wayward sons, children and aged men would seem to indicate some fraud on the part of a number of individuals. More successful were the inducements offered to officers and soldiers, sent out to defend the colony, to settle permanently. About 25 per cent of the troops sent out before 1715 remained in Canada. The officers were offered free seigneurial estates, while the soldiers were allotted plots on these seigneuries along with material assistance and the promise of brides, the *filles du roi* recruited in the hospices of French cities and provided with dowries from the royal treasury. This influx of 850 women did much to redress the gender ratio of the population: male preponderance fell from 300 per cent in 1630 to 25 per cent in 1681. In the eighteenth century, an estimated 20 per cent of soldiers sent to the colony remained as permanent settlers. By mid-eighteenth century, the number of women exceeded the number of men.

The state intervened further through forced immigration and through demographic legislation. New France was never a penal colony, yet from the first venture by Roberval in 1542 there were always some undesirables sent out to Canada. It is evident that among the *filles du roi* there were the unemployed 'vagrants' and prostitutes, in addition to the unfortunate orphans, foundlings and children seized from Protestant families deemed to be a burden on the religious institutions which sheltered them. After 1718, the number of penal deportees increased, upwards of seven hundred according to one document. They were mostly salt smugglers, counterfeiters and poachers, and since there was no opportunity to practise their misdemeanours in the colony, they were soon regarded as men of initiative who were quickly rehabilitated. Black slaves, imported mostly for domestic service by religious institutions and military and bourgeois households, constituted another element in forced immigration.

Much has been made of the demographic legislation put in place in the late seventeenth century, but it appears to have had little direct bearing on the increasing birth rate and overall population of Canada. Fathers whose daughters were not married by the age of 16 and whose sons were still bachelors at the age of 19 were subjected to a number of penalties and losses of privileges in the 1670s. Still, the church registers indicate that young people generally married at a more advanced age than this legislation required. Family allowances were provided for a family of ten children 'living and not in holy orders' and for families of twelve children 'living and not in holy order', but the royal treasury stopped payment within ten years so that very few ever qualified. Natural increase, attributable to a high fertility rate and a comparatively healthy population resulted in a population increase from 15,000 in 1700 to 50,000 in 1750 in Canada. This population also became more and more rural with the passage of time, and the Montreal region slowly began to catch up to the Quebec region. By 1750 the colony had moved away from its initial cod fishing and fur trading economy, which required little permanent settlement, to a subsistence agricultural colony with a stable population base.

Economic Theory and Policy

Economic theory in the sixteenth century France, on the eve of the colonization of New France, has been defined as bullionist and populationist. In other words, economic power was equated with the accumulation of gold and silver, especially through a favourable balance of trade with Spain which had grown rich on the precious metals of Central and South America. There was also the conviction that the world's population, like the amount of bullion, was fixed, therefore one nation's increase in population meant a decrease in the demographic strength of its potential competitors.

In the mid-seventeenth century to this economic theory were added concepts which were protectionist, nationalist and state interventionist. Jean-Baptiste Colbert in the 1660s encouraged the development of French metropolitan commerce and industry through state subsidies, the granting of monopolies and high protective tariffs against foreign imports. The Colbertian system was very nationalistic, therefore highly favoured by Louis XIV, because it was designed to increase the power and prestige of France internationally and to make her self-sufficient domestically. Colonies were viewed as producers of primary resources, raw materials for metropolitan manufacture, and as markets for the manufactured goods of the mother country.[14]

These economic theories and practice, and state policies, were eventually called mercantilist. *Mercantilism* was never a coherent and well-defined policy, and appears to have existed largely in the minds of economists and historians attempting to bring some coherent order to their understanding of the colonial period. Nevertheless, governments in the pursuit of their short-term fiscal needs adopted a general set of principles, not always strictly observed, which characterized the relationship of the European colonizing

[14]Apart from general works on French mercantilism, readers will find William J. Eccles, *Canada under Louis XIV, 1663-1701*, Toronto, 1964 which provides a clear picture of how the Colbertian policies also favoured colonial development.

powers, whether France, England, or Spain, and their overseas possessions and trade counters. In addition to the concepts mentioned above, European powers tried to impose a closed imperial system by forbidding their colonies to trade with foreigners, discouraging colonial manufacturing, and requiring trade to be carried on metropolitan ships manned by metropolitan crews. French business interests came to support most of these policies when they organized their Council of Commerce in 1700.[15]

New France did not fit well into the mercantilist concept for a number of reasons. Firstly, its resources, or *staples* as economist Harold Innis called them, fish and furs initially, did not require a large number of European producers or investors in the colony. Secondly, fish required no manufacturing and furs stimulated the Paris hat-making industry and little else. Thirdly, a small colonial population meant a very restricted market for French manufactures. Finally, its natural markets seemed to be the Antilles and New England and these were theoretically out of bounds according to mercantilist dogma.

The clearest enunciation of the mercantilist thesis is found in Pont-chartrain's instructions as Minister of Marine to the Intendant at Quebec in 1706: "In general, it is not proper for manufacturing to establish itself in that country because that would only be done to the detriment of those manufactures in France; rather you must proceed so that the raw materials of Canada pass to France to be manufactured. That must be the general practice, nevertheless, one must not prevent some enterprises from becoming established, especially for the needs of the poor people."[16] Were there exceptions to the 'general practice', and if so precisely what deviations from dogma? Colonial saw mills, grist mills, tar works, small boat-building enterprises which did not compete with metropolitan industry were tolerated. There were also state-sponsored enterprises, such as the royal shipyards at Quebec and the Forges St. Maurice near Trois Rivières. There was limited inter-colonial trade between Quebec and Louisbourg and the French Antilles, especially when certain commodities could not on occasion be supplied from France. There were also officially prohibited 'leaks' between the French and British trade systems, notably illicit trade between Montreal and Albany, and between Louisbourg and New England ports. These infractions of the rules enabled goods to pass between two supposedly closed imperial systems to the immediate advantage of the colonials in each case. There were attempts to prevent such international intercourse but local interests, especially the

---

[15]Dale Miquelon, *New France, 1701-1744: A Supplement to Europe,* Toronto, 1987.

[16]Paul W. Bennett et al., *Canada. A North American Nation,* Toronto, 1989, p. 139, citing from the official correspondence in National Archives of Canada.

Montreal merchant community and the military establishment at Louris-
bourg, resisted imposition of imperial policy.

Mercantilist restrictions on colonial initiatives have often been blamed for
economic retardation, especially in North American historiography. This
may be attributed to an espousal of the frontier thesis, which opposed frontier
or colonial vitality and innovation to metropolitan external controls, and to
an ideology of capitalistic private enterprise. In the case of New France, the
Minister of Marine explained in 1699 that "it produces nothing of great value
in spite of the infinite expenditure we incur there" and concluded that given
its small population, isolation, and geographical and climatic conditions its
economy remained in 'the state of infancy'. This 'infant economy' required
state intervention to stimulate growth, external investment for development,
etc.—all economic realities which would long continue to characterize the
'northern approach' to North American colonization.

Critics of mercantilist regulation have tended to ignore the advantages the
system provided for New France. The metropole had to buy and dispose of
all the primary products of the colony. This provided France with a major
problem in 1696, because there was a glut of furs on the Rouen market and
the Parisian hatters were over-supplied. Yet alliance and friendly intercourse
with the Amerindian suppliers required that outlets be found for the furs they
wished to exchange in order to acquire European manufacture. The metropole
also had to supply the colony with the manufactures, foodstuffs and armaments
it required. This was sometimes difficult, especially in the competition with
English and Dutch manufacturers in the Amerindian trade. Native barterers
became very skilful in judging the relative quality of cloth, guns, utensils and
ornaments. It was the metropolitan suppliers also, not colonial merchants,
who bore the major costs of insurance, transport risks, and fluctuations in
market prices. It was the administration in Versailles, not Quebec, that had
to undertake naval construction and armament, provide shipping and
defence against piracy and foreign aggression. One need but consider the
huge expenditure undertaken for the construction of the large fortress at
Louisbourg on Isle Royale (Cape Breton), or at Fort de Chartres in the
Illinois country, to appreciate the advantages that imperial policy could
provide the colony.

Staples Economy

Since investment and managerial skills generally came from the exterior,
where the markets were located, it is not surprising that metropolitan French
entrepreneurs, not Canadian colonials, also reaped a large share of the
benefits of colonial enterprises. The obvious problem with a staples economy

was that the colony only slowly developed a bourgeoisie, opportunities for investment, and local industries. The fur trade illustrated the problem.[17]

In the fur trade, Canadians were really middlemen between Native producers and primary manufacturers, on the one hand, and metropolitan investors, marketers and final manufacturers, on the other hand. It had developed, as we have seen, as a sideline of the fishery and by the early seventeenth century the French decided to concentrate on it in their exploitation of the northern approaches to the continent. Family groups and townspeople organized themselves into associations to strengthen their capital and lessen personal risks. It was out of these merchant associations, granted monopolies by the Crown, that a national commerce emerged. The Company of New France (1627) and the Company of the Indies (1664) had the export monopoly of furs, but the colonists enjoyed the right to trade with the Amerindians and with each other.

In 1681 the officials at Quebec imposed a system of *congés,* or trading permissions, to bring some semblance of order in the competitive trade with which abuse in the liquor traffic and fraud were increasingly associated. These licences were suppressed in 1696, when there was a glut of furs on the metropolitan market, but they were restored in 1716 to normalize relations with Native tribes of the hinterland following the end of prolonged European wars. The importance of the Amerindians in this trade cannot be overemphasized. The French increasingly were under pressure to provide trade goods in the quantities and of the quality demanded by the Native peoples, and also to increase the presents which were given at formalized rituals of alliance, friendship and exchange. The commanders at military posts in the hinterland were given responsibility for the conduct of the trade in their vicinity. This tended to emphasize the relationship between commerce and military alliance in Amerindian minds, as well as in the eighteenth century French colonial policy. Furthermore, it invited the participation of the military in the trade itself.[18]

The fur trade did not result in the accumulation of huge fortunes in Canada. It did provide a reasonable standard of living for importers and retailers in Montreal in particular, some employment and income to voyageurs and *coureurs de bois,* and a means of cementing good relations with the

[17]The seminal work on the Canadian 'staples' (raw materials) trade remains Harold A. Innis, *The Fur Trade in Canada,* Toronto, 1956. A useful commentary on his research is W. J. Eccles, "A Belated Review of Harold Adams Innis, The Fur Trade in Canada", *Canadian Historical Review,* LX, 4 (1979), 419-41.

[18]W.J. Eccles, "The Social, Economic and Political Significance of the Military Establishment in New France", *Canadian Historical Review,* LII, 2 (1971), 1-22.

Native nations of the hinterland. Extension into the hinterland, however, did not provide for a broad-based economy, so that the thesis of the fur trade as 'the life-blood of the colony' is somewhat utopian. The fur trade stimulated three metropolitan industries: hat-making, textiles, and distilling. Mercantilist ideology forbade the establishment of these industries in Canada. In fact, permission to open a hat-making establishment was specifically forbidden to a group of Montreal petty investors. It did not rob Canada of a great industry because there was no viable market for it and it undoubtedly saved these local entrepreneurs from bankruptcy. Apart from rough homespuns for everyday wear, better and cheaper textiles came from France. And distilling in Canada would have no hope of competing with the Dutch operations in western France.

Canada had its own exotic staple which caused quite a flurry in metropolitan circles involved in a lucrative trade with China in the mid-eighteenth century. Jesuit missionaries in Manchuria described the plant ginseng which was in great demand for its supposed aphrodisiac, tonic and restorative properties. Missionaries in Canada realized that it grew wild in the forests along the St. Lawrence valley. Canadian ginseng appeared on the Canton market in 1721, but the boom in exports began in 1747 and reached its peak in 1752, when the mark up reached 1200 per cent. Merchants in La Rochelle were told by agents of the Company of the Indies to buy up the roots at any price because the Chinese market was unlimited. 'Excessive rapaciousness', as one observer of colonial development opined, undermined the trade. Canadians of all classes, including the slaves of the women's religious orders, reaped the roots, often immature, dried them hastily and improperly in ovens and stoves, and then were shocked when Cantonese buyers refused to accept any more Canadian ginseng.[19]

Agriculture

Agriculture seemed a more stable basis for a transplanted European settlement than the exploitation of the resources of the fishing grounds and the forests. It would assure colonists a degree of self-sufficiency and when developed to the point that wheat and flour were exported it could become commercial. However, the full agricultural potential of the Laurentian valley was realized only very slowly. 'Making land', the clearing of the forests and draining of swampy river flats, were both arduous work and time-consuming. The colonists possessed few efficient tools and implements and had very few draught animals. In general, it took a family about 5 years to

[19]Brian Evans, "Ginseng: Root of Chinese-Canadian Relations",*Canadian Historical Review*, LXI, 1 (1985), 1-26.

clear and break three hectares of land, which was the minimum necessary to feed themselves and their animals.[20]

It is not known how many colonists had any experience of farming in France before emigrating, and even if they had, they would have inherited very backward farming practices. Crop rotation, manuring, weed control and the regulation of the breeding of their herds and flocks were matters they seemed oblivious of, if we are to believe the directives the Intendants issued to improve their production. In Acadia, on the other hand, the colonists who were evidently familiar with wetlands reclamation constructed an intricate system of high dikes to prevent the Bay of Fundy tides, which reached a height of 14.7 meters at the top of Minas Basin, inundating their fields with seawater, and of high brush and sod dams on rivers and creeks, as close to the sea as possible, to prevent the draining of fresh water from inland during low tides. The climate of Canada was generally unfavourable compared to the regions of France from which the majority of them came. There were only 115 frost-free days per year at Quebec, for example, and the winters were unusually cold and the summers unusually hot. Caterpillars and grasshoppers managed to destroy more than one harvest every decade. The fertile belt of the Laurentian valley was also generally narrow, except at its widening near the island of Montreal. The lack of supply centres and markets proved to be a serious handicap once surpluses were produced.

The land-holding system of New France was known as *seigneurialism,* or the traditional organizational pattern of the mother country wherein the privileged orders were granted estates by the Crown. These seigneurs populated their estates with *censitaires,* or copyholders, who owned their plots but they and their successors were bound in perpetuity to pay annual dues to the seigneur. It meant that the privileged orders exploited the labour of their subordinates, although in the early decades of implantation in New France it was a very non-oppressive system.

The seigneurial system was introduced into the colony by the Company of New France not only to provide a rational and legal framework for land-holding with which Frenchmen were familiar but also as a method of colonization because seigneurs required censitaires to provide them with an income. It was expected by some to provide a system of social and state control. It did provide Canada with a basic land survey system, running along both banks of the St. Lawrence river, then with successive *rangs* behind the river-front concessions. It did not favour the development of towns or service centres, so that by 1760 there were still only three towns,

---

[20]There is still no definitive study of agriculture in the colony, although many aspects of farm production are touched upon in R. Cole Harris, *The Seigneurial System in Canada,* Madison, 1966.

six nucleated villages and 4 hamlets between the islands of Montreal and Orleans. The Custom of Paris required equal division of half the property between all the children, male and female, on the death of the parents. This would have resulted in excessively small holdings had families not worked out strategies to avoid too much subdivision of land. In the end, the seigneurial system had two important consequences for the future development of Canada: firstly, it provided a framework for a class structure in which the seigneurs increasingly asserted their rights and privileges; secondly, the seigneurial tract had become virtually fully occupied by the end of the French régime so that it became a closed area of francophone population.[21]

The survey system itself was unique to the Laurentian environment. Instead of the circular village-centred three field system common to feudal Europe, the Canadian survey lines were laid out in trapezoidal parallelograms running back from the St. Lawrence at a 45 degree angle towards the north-west on the north shore of the river. There were, by way of exception, three circular seigneuries owned by the Jesuits near the town of Quebec. The strip survey meant that each family farm had about 150 metres of river frontage and ran back between two parallel lines towards the higher ground, a distance about ten times its width. The advantages of such a survey were numerous in a colony of new settlement. Rapid and cheap surveying was possible, although there might later be some dispute about the upper limits of the concession. Unlike in the traditional European pattern, the plots were adjacent to the homestead. Each family enjoyed privacy, yet it was not too distant from neighbours. Most important, there was common access to the river, which was the chief means of transport and communication, and the source of water, fish and marine animals. There was no immediate need to build roads and bridges to maintain colonial communications. The long strip farms also had the advantage of cutting across the gain of the land and its soil belts, so that a censitaire possessed a variety of soils and vegetation associations. A typical pioneer farm on the shores of the St. Lawrence river would have marshlands providing fodder for animals, rich heavy soils for growing cereals, upland meadows for grazing, and on the backside of the concession a wood lot with stone suitable for building.

The drawbacks, as already intimated, were that towns were slow to develop in such a settlement pattern. The church found it difficult to service the scattered population and to locate parish churches where they were accessible to sufficient numbers of people capable of supporting a resident curate. The seigneurs also found lack of concentrated settlement

[21]A rapid overview is provided in Marcel Trudel, *The Seigneurial Régime*, Ottawa, 1956, Historical Booklet no. 6.

around the manorhouse which meant that their social and political leadership role did not develop as rapidly as they had hoped. Another problem, which emerged in time, was that once all the river lots were taken up, a second and third range had to be opened up. These farms did not enjoy access to the waterfront and new roads were required. Riverine settlements, beginning along the St. Lawrence, then spreading to the Richelieu, St. Maurice and eventually Ottawa rivers gave access to enemies as well as friends. The Iroquois invasion route from Lake Champlain down the Richelieu river, or down the St. Lawrence from Lake Ontario, became deeply engraved in the memory of seventeenth century colonists.

This pre-industrial peasant society differed from that of the mother country in a number of respects, yet the ultimate objectives of seigneurialism were the same on both sides of the Atlantic. The censitaires or copyholders insisted on being called *habitants* (a term which originally meant a permanent settler as opposed to a sojourner or *hivernant*) rather than *paysan* (peasant) which was considered demeaning. There were few social distinctions throughout much of the seventeenth century because some seigneurs were almost as poor as their censitaires. They did not even exercise all of their banal rights—the exclusive right to operate and charge for the use of a grist mill, winepress and bake-oven. Nor could they speculate on land because land was free in the colony, there being neither a purchase price nor state taxes attached to it, and it was abundant throughout most of the French régime. In 1711, the Edicts of Marly required seigneurs to cede land to all applicants, and required censitaires to till their concessions and live on them. In 1741 the Crown seized some seigneuries which had not been developed. If seigneurs were willing and sufficiently wealthy to build a stone church and endow the parish, they would be honoured as its patron founder with a special pew, first access to the sacraments and remembered in congregational prayers in perpetuity. Few availed themselves of the honour. Nor were they accorded many administrative privileges—these going usually to the captains of the militia. The militia itself was organized by parishes, not seigneuries, so that only a few seigneurs were also militia captains.

By the eighteenth century, the seigneurial system began to take on more of its class orientation. Banal mill rights were exacted more regularly, and new contracts with censitaires often reserved the fish, timber and building stone to the seigneur. As land had come into production, seigneurial revenues increased and permitted the building of some handsome manorhouses and the social distinctions associated therewith. The oldest seigneuries still retained the characteristics of a typical peasant society with its local networks of marriage and business relations and land acquired largely through inheritance from the descendants of the original habitants. But, beginning with third generation and second rang settlement, new marriage patterns and new communities emerged which were more related to locality than to family. Excessive sub-division of land was avoided by donation among living heirs, and farm income was supplemented through seasonal employment not only in the fur trade, as in the seventeenth century, but also in saw mills and lumber camps, and through wage labour in the towns.

Two historical myths required examination. The first holds that society in New France was egalitarian and that seigneurs enjoyed few privileges and enjoyed only meagre revenues from their estates. This historical interpretation is the result of a prolongation of early settlement experiences typical of the mid-seventeenth century into the mid-eighteenth century. This approach seeks to fit New France into the frontier thesis, enunciated in nineteenth century American history, whereby pioneer settlers moving westwards across the continent created an individualistic, democratic and egalitarian society. American westward expansion also brought conflict with aboriginal inhabitants whose lands were seized. In New France there was no such moving frontier of settlement, but containment within the Laurentian lowlands remained characteristic of the entire French régime. Society remained communitarian, authoritarian and class conscious. If seigneurs had enjoyed no privileges or profits, it is inconceivable that the eighteenth century colonial merchants and military officers would have purchased seigneuries, or that after the conquest British merchants and officers would have done likewise. Secondly, the administrative system has been depicted as one of checks and balances in which the Intendant protected the rights of the censitaires against greedy or power-hungry lay and clerical seigneurs. In fact, the Intendants were not great arbiters protecting the underdogs of society. Rather, their first concern was to maintain the established power structure and social order and to brook no insubordination. The lower classes were seen as the source of all social disturbances and therefore had to be held in their 'proper place' where it had pleased God to put them!

Commerce and Industry

New France began as a commercial counter, not as a colony of agricultural settlement. Nevertheless, its eventual development tended to move away from the earlier emphasis on commercial exploitation. The new orientation was favoured by those who espoused the religious ideology of agriculturalism, especially in a French context where so much of commerce and finance had been in the hands of Protestants or Jews for a brief period.

Historians have long presumed that mercantilist restrictions were to be blamed for the slow economic development of New France. However, another order of considerations is required to reach a more valid explanation of this retardation. The optimum conditions for the development of the Canadian and Acadian economies would have included a sizeable pool of producers and consumers, capital for investment, skilled labourers, access to large markets, a variety of resources which were in great demand, good transportation and communication systems, and favourable geographic location and climatic conditions. New France possessed none of these! There were few incentives for either metropolitan or colonial entrepreneurs to invest or inaugurate commercial and industrial ventures.

The first Intendant, Jean Talon, had a dream of building a self-sufficient colony along the lines of the Colbertian plan for France itself. But he soon ran into opposition from mercantilist theorists—colonies existed for the benefit of the mother country, not to become powerful states in their own right! This somewhat stifled his efforts, but in the long term it also saved the colony from the complete collapse of non-viable enterprises. There was a limited success for his schemes for the growing of hemp and flax, for tarworks and mining. Hemp, flax and tar all supplied the royal navy but soon succumbed to products of better quality and lower price in the mother country. There was little demand for Cape Breton coal, the age of steam not having arrived as yet, and the great copper and iron deposits around Lake Superior remained too distant and unproven for development. The stimulation Talon gave to the construction of small fishing and transport vessels did result in the colony supplying local demands.

The success of colonial private enterprise in building vessels for the Gulf of St. Lawrence fishery, the Labrador whaling operations and river barge transportation in the colony encouraged a project to build ships of the line for the French navy. In 1732, the Ministry of Marine began offering a bounty of three livres per ton for every vessel built in the colony. About 8 to 10 vessels qualified for the bounty each year thereafter. The colonists having neither the necessary capital for investment in the large naval project nor the required skilled labour force, and tradition in France favouring state enterprise for such a large defence contract, it was decided in the 1730s to establish royal shipyards at St. Charles, near Quebec. Construction began in 1731. In the 1740s ten warships were launched and two more in the 1750s. In total, at least 230 vessels of several sizes and types were built at Quebec and another 75 at Louisbourg. Small establishments turned out 14 vessels, including four armed naval vessels, on Lake Ontario, one on Lake Erie and one on Lake Superior. The major naval project failed, however, because it proved too costly to import skilled workers from France and the vessels themselves proved to be of inferior quality and had to be replaced in short order. Their unskilled work was done by well-paid colonial seasonal day labourers while the skilled workers from France were under naval jusrisdiction, poorly housed in shanties, relatively ill-paid, and required to work even in inclement weather. Inevitably, friction arose between the two groups, until in 1741 the French workers organized the first strike in Canadian history. The workers soon yielded to threats of the full impact of naval discipline but their contracts soon came to an end for other reasons than poor working conditions. The enterprise had been ill-conceived in terms of both location and processing. The St. Charles river proved to have either too shallow water at some seasons or a dangerously swift current at other seasons. On launching, vessels were known to have struck botton, and on one occasion to actually have keeled over. There were no proper facilities for drying and storing the lumber so much of the stock deteriorated. Also the oak and pine of the adjacent forests, and this included even the Lake Champlain region, were found unsuitable for the construction of large war ships. The state concluded that the high costs and the unsatisfactory product of this colonial enterprise were unwarranted. France turned to Baltic lumber for domestic construction or bought its vessels from the Dutch thereafter.[22]

A second state venture proved little more successful. In the 1730s, Poulin de Francheville opened bog ironworks on the St. Maurice river just north of Trois Rivières to manufacture forged iron stoves, cauldrons, pots, axeheads, small tools and implements. François-Antoine Cugnet purchased the struggling plant in 1735 and within three years had it in full-blown operation, thanks, in good measure, to a state subsidy of 100,000 livres. In 1743 the operations went into bankruptcy, although Cugnet was still personally solvent. The state then assumed ownership of what was deemed to be an important industry for the colony, thereby setting a pattern of state intervention to maintain a viable northern economy. There were marginal profits from time to time, but the ventures into steel-making and cannon founding in 1747, for example, were no more successful than the shipbuilding venture. Once again, as in the case of the shipyards, the limited success was attributable to poor location and management. The plant itself was poorly

---

[22]The authoritative work on this subject is Jacques Mathieu, *La Construction navale royale à Québec, 1739-1759*, Québec, 1971.

organized, there was no good road linking the mine, limestone quarry and foundry, and water levels provided an irregular supply of power. Skilled labourers and machines had to be imported from France at considerable expense, and even the local unskilled workers demanded a high wage. The major failing was probably the absence of competent managerial skills. This did not improve quickly because at the British conquest, the government continued to operate the ironworks, with no greater profits than under French administration.[23]

In terms of transportation, the Canadians were able to adapt Amerindian technology and manufacture snowshoes and progressively longer birchbark canoes able to carry greater quantities of goods. They were also innovative and developed an efficiently designed and constructed sleigh, the *carriole,* that could glide over 120 kilometers of deep snow in one day pulled by the same horse. For summer transportation, they developed an equally efficient light carriage, the *calèche,* that could reach remarkable speeds.[24]

Trade in France was regulated by the craft guilds, but as already stated the lock-step progression from apprentice to journeyman to eventual achievement of mastery was bypassed early in efforts to populate the colony. Tradesmen organized themselves into religious fraternities honouring their respective patron saints. This became such a social vehicle for boisterous and ostentatious celebrations that the clergy sought to control the rivalry that developed between the various artisanal groups. When the roofers in Montreal tried to obtain a royal decree recognizing their exclusive control over their trade they met with a negative response. Both the general population and the colonial administration were opposed to the monopolistic self-regulation which artisanal guilds represented. Canadians in general wanted to be free to change occupations whenever they wished, and to pursue any chosen task without external controls. Survival in a pioneering community had fostered such self-sufficiency and flexibility of occupation as habitants usually built their own houses, its crude furniture and their implements and tools. The "Jacques of all trades, but master of none" was the honoured handyman as opposed to a highly skilled specialist. The colonial administration was intent on excluding all forms of organized control groups, such as guilds, and leave arts, trades and crafts open to all colonists.[25]

[23]Michel Gaumond, *Les Forges de Saint-Maurice,* Québec, 1968.

[24]Raymond Douville and J.D. Casanova, *Daily Life in Early Canada,* London, 1968.

[25]The best analysis of Canadian economic development in the period is still Jean Hamelin, *Economie et société en Nouvelle-France,* Québec, 1960. On artisanal regulations see Peter N. Moogk, "In the Darkness of a Basement: Craftsmen's Associations in Early French Canada", *Canadian Historical Review,* LVII, 4 (1976), 399-439.

As far as commerce was concerned, the war economy and its associated supply trade was a great financial boost to the colony, especially after 1744, although the benefits were not widely shared. Troops brought in money and provided semi-skilled labour in many cases. Large sums were spent on fortifications and their upkeep, on maintaining military posts throughout the upper country, on supplying the colonial militia, and on presents to the Native allied nations. The war industries in France profited the most, of course, but the supply trade still permitted twenty-two inhabitants of Canada to become millionaires by 1760. This supplying of the war effort from 1744 through to 1760 was organized by the Intendant François Bigot into a so-called *Grande Société* of colonial entrepreneurs dealing with select suppliers, notably the Gradis firm in Bordeaux which involved both Jews and Protestants. That a royal official should profit from his public office was not only legal at the time, but also it was expected in a system where salaries were comparatively modest. The system was changed in 1759, during a fiscal reform in France, and so it was that Bigot and associates were brought to trial in France on charges of fraud and embezzlement which were defined after the fact.[26]

Social and Political Control

Pioneer colonial societies are often considered to be freewheeling, even lawless, communities where justice is sometimes taken in hand by the populace. Two aspects of life in New France might be interpreted as fitting such a pattern of behaviour: the persistence of the activities of unlicensed traders, the *coureurs de bois,* in the hinterland; and outbursts of popular revolts in settled areas.

In the 1680s the Governor and Intendant began issuing licences, called *congés,* to traders leaving Montreal to go into the upper country of the Great Lakes basin to barter European manufactured goods for the peltries of Native hunters. The system was designed to control the number of young men leaving the settlements each season, to prevent illicit trading with Anglo-Americans, and to reduce the amount of brandy offered to the Amerindians. Church and state officials decried the number of unlicensed operators in the upper country and threatened these wood-rovers with heavy penalties unless they returned to the settlements. It was held that these *coureurs de bois* debauched the Native peoples, abandoned their European

[26]Guy Frégault, *The War of the Conquest,* Toronto, 1969, adopts a 'nationalist' French Canadian stance in condemning France and her colonial officials for the fall of Canada to the British. A different view is presented in Ian K. Steele, *Guerillas and Grenadiers: The Struggles for Canada, 1689-1760,* Toronto, 1969.

manners and morals, hindered the work of the missionaries through their immorality and their insolent mockery of the priests, and retarded the development of the colony by their failure to take up a farm and found a family. In reality, most of them returned after a few years to the settlements where they made an important contribution. The few years a young man spent in the hinterland represented a means of supplementing income for the family farm. In the upper country, living with Amerindians, they had learned to speak a native language, how to travel and survive in the wilderness, and how to wage effective guerilla warfare. They usually returned with some of the profits of the fur trade which aided them in establishing their own independent farm household. The liaisons established with Amerindian peoples, and the knowledge gained from their experience in the upper country, served them well as militiamen.

Governor Denonville, among others, complained of a general degeneration of civilized standards in New France. He complained of the insubordination of the common people, the permissive upbringing of the children, and the drunkenness and foul language commonly met within the towns. The youth in rural parishes were so undisciplined that he even upbraided a gang of youths, the Chevaliers, who rode about on gaudily decorated steeds disturbing the peace, somewhat in the brazen fashion of a modern day American motorcycle gang. Teenagers bundled shamelessly under heavy horsehide robes in the unheated churches in winter, while the older men retired to the rear of the church to smoke and "swear the Holy Name of God and of the Blessed Virgin" during the sermons. These descriptions fit the image of a frontier society.[27]

Although all collective action for redress of grievances was forbidden, there were public protests and demonstrations in the colony from time to time. These outbursts were directed against such matters as excessively high salt prices, bread shortages, arbitrary levies for fortifications, restrictive artisanal regulations, and unpopular alterations in parish boundaries. These were protests against economic hardships which should not have occurred in a well-managed colony, it was believed, or against actions which should have been preceded by consultation with the community. The colonists protested not against the established order but against what was perceived to be mismanagement and misguided policies to the detriment of the common good. During the final war for the conquest of the colony, the women of Quebec stormed the Governor's residence demanding the withdrawal of an

<hr/>

[27]The nature of colonial society in the measure that it deviated from the utopian model that the clerico-nationalist writers long upheld is described in Cornelius J. Jaenen, *The Role of the Church in New France,* Toronto, 1976.

order that butchers sell equal amounts of beef and horsemeat to their customers. Unlike their metropolitan counterparts, they abhorred the thought of eating horsemeat, saying it was unchristian to do so, and adding that 'the horse is the friend of man'.[28]

The popular conviction that state officials deserved respect and commanded obedience only in so far as they discharged their duties properly may have arisen from the multiplicity of regulations which governed all aspects of life. The General Regulations of 11 May 1676, issued by the Sovereign Council, are an example of this bureaucratic zeal. The regulations designated the time, place and nature of the public market in Quebec, the official control of the accuracy of all weights, scales and measures, the inspection of inns, the inspection of cargo entering or leaving the port, etc. There were elaborate building codes providing for fire walls, access to roofs, and maintenance of latrines and privies, also fire regulations which required that stoves and heaters be set in chimneys and forbidding smoking or carrying a lighted torch on the street. The regulations required butchers to dispose of waste in the river, bakers to sell bread of the prescribed weight and at the set price, innkeepers to observe the restricted hours of operation and not extend credit. There were clauses prohibiting 'vagabondage', prostitution, begging, swearing, blaspheming, and holding Protestant services.

Courts and Legal Procedure

At the pinnacle of the judicial system was the Intendant. He supervised the entire court system and procedure, interpreted the Custom of Paris as this civil law applied in the colony, presided the sessions of the Superior Council, and channelled any appeals that were taken to France. He supervised the notaries who drew up official documents, last wills and testaments, inventories of goods upon decease, and the like, as well as the surveyors who measured out concessions and set property boundaries. There were no lawyers in New France, and there was no police force. The Baron de Lahontan, a severe critic of many aspects of colonial society, observed that justice might not be any less tainted than in metropolitan France "but at least if it is sold, it is much cheaper" because "we do not pass through the squeezing of the lawyers, the grasp of attorneys, nor the claws of clerks; that vermin has not yet affected Canada".[29]

The Sovereign Council of Quebec, established in 1663, was the high court and after 1726 it became almost exclusively a court of appeal, as its name

[28]Terence Crawley, "Thunder Gusts: Popular Disturbances in Early French Canada", *Historical Papers, 1979,* Ottawa, 1979, 11-31.

[29]Cited in André Vachon, "Le Notaire en Nouvelle-France", *Revue de l'Université Laval,* X, 3 (1955-56), 235.

change to Superior Council indicated. It met in the Intendant's palace, usually on Mondays, to hear cases from anywhere in the colony. There were no fees, but fines were levied if an appeal was judged to be unfounded, a nuisance, or an insult to the dignity of the court. This was deemed necessary because the colonists were unusually fond of litigation when it did not involve them in onerous expense.

The next level of justice was the royal courts in four principal centres whose judges were named by the Crown on the advice of the colonial Governor and Intendant. The lowest level of courts consisted of seigneurial courts, which the Crown tried gradually to suppress. The Sulpician clergy, however, managed to exercise their seigneurial rights of justice over their seigneuries around Montreal throughout the French regime. The church enjoyed the privilege of its own ecclesiastical court, the *Officialité*, which tried all cases involving the clergy and canon law. Appeals from the church court were heard in the Superior Council, and eventually could go to the King's privy council. In one celebrated case, involving the Sulpician curate Fénélon, brother of the famous archbishop in France, accused of preaching an Easter sermon in 1674 attacking abuses in gubernatorial power, the appeals went through all the acrimonious stages imaginable until it eventually reached Versailles. The solomonic royal decision was that the civil authorities should show more respect to the clergy and the standards they upheld, but the priest was exiled from the colony. No direct attack on established civil power would be tolerated, not even from a subservient national church.

France did not have a unified system of civil law, currency, or even of standard weights and measures in the seventeenth century. In 1664, Louis XIV ordered that the Custom of Paris, a collection of civil procedures dating from 1510, be applied in New France. It underwent a number of changes in its application to the colonial setting so that by the end of the French régime it was popularly known as Canadian customary law. One important feature was the regulation of inheritance rights inasmuch as it protected the property of women.

In criminal matters, the courts followed the procedures set forth in France by ordinances of 1498 and 1539, which were eventually codified in the Great Criminal Ordinance of 1670. Criminal procedure almost seemed to assume the guilt of the accused, until the latter could prove innocence. Accusations and witnesses were heard privately, the accused was subjected to interrogation without knowledge of what charges had been made, and only later was there revelation of the nature of the charges and testimonies, and confrontation of the accused and plaintiffs. Trial was by judge, and when the evidence was only circumstantial he would acquit the accused. Before proceeding to a sentence in a criminal charge, the law required the confession of the accused. If necessary, this was obtained through the procedure known as the *question,* the painful application of pegs which bruised the legs to refresh an accused's memory! Justice in the colony was less harsh than in many other jurisdictions in the seventeenth and eighteenth centuries. There was no capital punishment for witchcraft as in New England, or for stealing a loaf of bread as was common in Europe.

In the absence of a police force, the local militia carried out such operations as hunting down criminals and making arrests. The executioner was hated by almost everyone, therefore the position was usually filled by offering a stay of execution to a condemned person in return for taking on the job. Judges in the colony were reluctant to impose the severe local punishment of cutting out the tongue for blasphemy, hanging and quartering for counterfeiting, and branding with a *fleur-de-lis* on the cheek for a first conviction of selling brandy to the Native peoples. Besides capital punishment for crimes against the state and persons, there was a category of infamous crimes which carried such penalties as public humiliation on a wooden horse, the stocks or pillory. Sometimes there was an additional loss of civil rights, even exile and banishment from the town or parish. More frequent were pecuniary sentences involving fines payable to charity and confiscation of property.[30]

Slavery existed in the colony and appears to have been regulated by the *Code Noir* of 1685, although this was never officially proclaimed in Canada or Acadia. In 1709 regulations were issued for domestic slavery in Canada by the Intendant, in line with provisions of the Code. Louisiana, where plantation slavery existed, adopted the Code in 1724. The *Code Noir* was humane compared to practices at the time: slaves were encouraged to marry, family units could not be broken up, children were to be given a rudimentary education, all were to be instructed in the Catholic religion, and all had the right to take their masters to court (although none dared to do so). There were no slave rebellions as in the Antilles. Slavery was confined largely to the urban centres of Montreal, Quebec, Trois Rivières, Louisbourg and Detroit as the chief slave-owners were religious communities, military officers, civil administrators, and bourgeois merchants.[31]

---

[30]For the nature of French law in New France see legal historian Douglas Hay, "The Meanings of the Criminal Law in Quebec, 1764-1774", in Louis A. Knafla, ed., *Crime and Criminal Justice in Europe and Canada,* Waterloo, 1981, pp. 77-110.

[31]For a brief summary of the situation in New France see Marcel Trudel, "Ties that Bind", *Horizon Canada,* 18 (1985), 422-27.

Family Life

All societies in their nascent stage place great influence on family and kinship relations. In Acadia, for example, it remained virtually the sole institution as neither the seigneurial system, the parish system, nor the militia system became implanted before the British conquest of that region in 1710. Acadians became a close-knit society of kinship groups, many of which had good relations through inter-marriage and trade with the Micmac and Maliseet peoples. The same general pattern of relationships could be found in Canada, but there other institutional networks also lay claim to local and regional loyalties and associations. In general, colonial families differed from those in the mother land with respect to earlier marriages, higher levels of fecundity and lower mortality rates. The average age of death in the mid-eighteenth century in France was 67, in Canada 57; this great difference has been attributed to an early immigrant population that was particularly robust and the relatively slow spread of epidemic diseases in a sparsely populated colony. Probably better nutrition, better sanitation and healthier outdoor activities than in French urban centres had some impact on colonial well-being.

In the mid-eighteenth century, a typical 'completed' Canadian family would consist of a father just over forty years of age, a mother in her late thirties, and about eight children, ranging in age from 14 years to a few weeks old. This profile takes into account the average age of marriage for women at about 22 and about 27 for men, the spacing of births about every 23 months, and an infant mortality rate of about 246 out of every 1000 during the first year of life. Most adults were married, and there was a marked tendency for widows and widowers to remarry. In short, the colonists were fond of the married state. The number of religious, who were bound by vows of chastity, were strictly limited by the state. The *coureurs de bois* were usually young bachelors who might enter into temporary liaisons with Native women and father *Mètis* children in the hinterland, but they nearly always returned to the settlements to take up family life.[32]

Marriage ceremonies left little doubt about the purpose of matrimony being the procreation of children. In addition to the required wedding in the parish church, custom decreed that the priest should bless the nuptial bed where children would be conceived and as the service book said, "remember that your wedding bed will some day be your death bed, from whence your souls will be sent before God's tribunal".[33]

[32]John F. Bosher, "The Family in New France", in R. Douglas Francies and Donald B. Smith, eds., *Readings in Canadian History: Pre-Confederation,* Toronto, 1990.

[33]Cornelius J. Jaenen, *The Role of the Church in New France,* Toronto, 1976, p. 140.

Class distinctions in family relations were important as members of the local élite formed a kinship network. The lower classes, particularly the rural habitants, often ran into church and state rules restricting consanguineous marriages. It has been argued that women enjoyed a 'favoured' position in the colony through protection of their rights of inheritance, marriage contracts and possession of property. They certainly had a wider range of economic opportunities open to them than was common at the time in the English colonies. Nevertheless, if women with economic status seemed equal to men, society was still patriarchal. Married women who conducted such business transactions as buying property or selling slaves did so with their husband's express permission. Fathers could assign their daughters' dowries without the consent of their wives. Men were the legal heads of the household. The only way a woman could protect herself from an abusive husband or one who wasted the family fortune on alcohol and mistresses was to appeal to the royal courts for a separation of goods and persons, and this was granted only in particularly notorious cases. Just as a woman rarely won a case against her husband, so domestic servants, apprentices and slaves rarely dared to charge their masters or mistresses. It was the widows who acquired more power and authority than married women to conduct business, make contracts, and serve as legal witnesses. Children were legally minors until the age of twenty-five, and as such required the permission of their parents to marry (just as a soldier of any age required the permission of his officer to marry), and their inheritance was managed by legal guardians.

Children were an economic asset as they grew older and contributed to the work force and some times income of the farm or urban working class household. But very young children, the handicapped and large numbers of children placed a strain on family resources. Merchant families in Montreal, Quebec and Louisbourg might view children as carrying on the family business or inheriting a bureaucratic position, and daughters as making a 'good marriage' permitting upward social mobility. A noble family in the colony saw the likelihood of its children carrying on the family tradition in the military, ecclesiastical or bureaucratic arena, and unlike in France also in the commercial sphere. Since a number of the colonial nobility were not wealthy, they saw great advantage if a daughter married into the bourgeoisie and so 'regilded the family coat of arms'.[34]

In the absence of any concept of childhood development, children were perceived and even dressed as miniature adults. The church taught that at the

[34]Peter Moogk, "Les Petits Sauvages: The Children of Eighteenth Century New France", in Joy Parr, ed., *Childhood and Family in Canadian History*, Toronto, 1982, pp. 17-43.

age of seven they had become fully responsible for all moral and ethical decisions and were to be treated as such. They were shown little affection, life expectancy being so precarious. Missionaries were surprised at the affection Amerindians showed to their children, the permissive manner in which they raised them, and the apparent harmony that existed in long-houses and villages. Royal officials often complained that the colonists were becoming too indulgent in raising their children, were unconcerned about their education, and did not impose the required standards of respect for superiors and authority. In the face of high infant mortality rates, the church comforted parents with the assurance of the salvation of all baptized infants. Popular belief transformed these 'holy innocents' into angels.

Education and Literacy

From the earliest times, the colony made some form of instruction available to both Amerindian and settlers' children. There were only modest opportunities to obtain formal schooling and these were dominated by religious institutions. Not surprisingly, French models were employed. This was of great importance because some significant strides were made in the field of pedagogy in the seventeenth century France. French had started to replace classical Latin as a language of instruction in elementary schools, education of girls began to be considered, and reading and writing emerged as prominent subjects. Teacher training institutions known as 'normal schools' were founded to transform teaching from an occupation to a profession. Elementary Free schools known as *petites écoles* were organized to provide instruction for the children of the poor in order to promote social order, reduce crime and begging, and inculcate religious morality. All of these innovations found expression in New France.

The challenges educators faced in the colony often seemed insurmountable. Communities of religious women and the male missionaries all attempted to lure Amerindian children into schools in order to 'civilize' and convert them. Their efforts brought few tangible results as very few Native students remained more than a few months in the restrictive authoritarian atmosphere of a colonial school with its foreign curriculum and strange values.

Children of the lower classes had few opportunities to acquire any formal instruction, unless from a parish priest or an itinerant schoolmaster, until the secular Sisters of the Congregation began opening *petites écoles* in parishes around Montreal and at Louisbourg. The bishops did not favour extensive education for girls and frowned on secular women's communities (which the state supported), preferring them cloistered, and so the girls at the Congregation school in Montreal were condemned on one occasion for pretentious dress consisting of "headgear with several lace folds and coiffures supported by more than a single ribbon-century". They were obviously copying their mothers and older sisters, not their religious instructors.

Elitist communities, such as the Jesuits and Ursulines, were obliged in the colonial context to modify their objectives and approaches. Great intellectuals became language students themselves, and offered rudimentary instruction to any who would listen in the vulgar tongue. In dealing with Amerindians, whether children or adults, they found that instruction through music, through carefully selected paintings and games was most effective.

The Intendant Jacques Raudot advised the Minister of Marine and Colonies in 1717 that the colonists had copied the permissive child-rearing practices of the 'savages', that the youth were ignorant and undisciplined, and therefore it was important to "establish school masters in all regions, who besides the instruction they would give them, would teach them early in life to be obedient". Itinerant school masters did appear from time to time in rural parishes but the clergy soon convinced the state authorities to discourage the practice because most were retired soldiers of allegedly little learning and dubious morals. In the towns, well-to-do families might hire a tutor from the mother country. Some parishes also hired single, male lay teachers but these usually married and moved on to more remunerative employment after a few years.

Organized and generalized schooling, therefore, did not exist in New France. Most habitants felt no pressing need for literacy. The population was too dispersed to justify schools in many areas, and the chronic shortage of resident clergy did not help in providing even rudimentary religious instruction to all children. The quality of education offered by the Jesuits in their college, by the Sulpicians in Montreal, or the Ursulines in Quebec, was equal to that offered in comparable institutions elsewhere. In 1701, Antoine Forget introduced the most advanced pedagogical approaches in the Sulpician school at Montreal. These included the class method rather than individual study, streaming of pupils according to ability, and the establishment of a good rapport between teacher and pupils to facilitate learning. On the other hand, the atmosphere remained very serious as silence was imposed and hand gestures were used to communicate, and all playful and exuberant behaviour resulted in severe reprimand.

As in most pre-industrial societies, the majority of adult colonists were illiterate. This was especially evident in rural areas and among the lower stratum of society, the written word being more in evidence in urban centres where educational, administrative and religious institutions were concentrated. Unlike the general pattern of much higher illiteracy among women than men in the seventeenth and eighteenth centuries, in rural New France there was little gender difference in terms of signature literacy. About 10 per cent of men were able to sign the marriage register compared to 11 per cent for women. In urban areas the literacy rate was much better as 46 per cent of grooms could sign the register and 37 per cent of brides could do so. There was a cultural bias against providing much education for girls, but it would appear that there was also a bias against providing boys with much 'book learning' compared to practical learning by doing. Bishop Dosquet complained in the 1740s that the number of schools and teachers did not keep pace with an increasing population, that educational standards were in decline, and there was a growing public indifference towards education. These trends were seen as part of the process of 'canadianization' of society, the declining proportion of literate metropolitan subjects. On the other hand, there was a decline in the urban areas of the male literacy rate after 1750 attributable to the arrival in the colony of regular soldiers from France, many of whom were barely literate.

There were several good libraries in the colony, either technical or religious in terms of their holdings. The Sulpicians lent books to those who were interested. Royal officials were responsible for enforcing the censorship imposed by the Crown and the church, but Protestant polemical books and banned novels found their way into the colony from time to time. In succession, between 1665 and 1749, the Jesuits, the Sulpicians and the botanizing governor La Galissonière asked for a printing press for Quebec, but permission was never granted. It is doubtful that there was a sufficiently large reading public to warrant such a venture. In any case, Versailles argued that allowing a colonial press would cut into the profitable metropolitan monopoly and would increase the dangers of disseminating offensive works.[35]

Social Welfare

Louis XIV took his role as 'father' of his nation accountable to God for the welfare of his subjects seriously. To Intendant Champigny in 1686 he gave instructions "to pay heed to all the complaints and needs of the inhabitants, and respond to them as best as possible, so that they live together in harmony". In the seventeenth century the number of butchers, bakers and millers was regulated, as were the quality and price of their consumer goods. When the Intendant proposed to remove price controls, the King insisted that they should be maintained for 'the well-being of the country'. The Sovereign Council called a consultative assembly on the matter and when

[35]Roger Magnuson, *Education in New France*, Montreal, 1992.

popular will sided with the King price controls were maintained throughout the French régime.[36]

Personal misfortune or a crop failure could leave some colonists destitute. But some colonists found the work required to 'make land' too arduous and came to Quebec to beg. With an increase in the number of beggars in the town of Quebec in 1677, the Sovereign Council ordered them back to their rural communities. In 1683 another group of beggars were ordered back to their abandoned farms. These were classified as the 'undeserving poor' who merely avoided hard work. But when more beggars appeared in 1688, the Intendant and Sovereign Council studied the circumstances which had driven them to become mendicants and then drafted a regulation setting out the terms of social assistance to the 'deserving poor'. The objective of this social legislation was to put an end to the annoyance caused in the city by the presence of beggars, to provide work for those who were fit, and to prevent any subject from starving to death. In the three main towns, *Bureaux des Pauvres* staffed by the local parish priest and three directors were to be organized to supervise social assistance and supervise community work.

The chronically indigent who could not be cared for by relatives soon became a subject of further state action. In 1698 the Charron Brothers, a secular lay association, opened an almshouse near Montreal which they operated until 1727, at which time the Sisters of Charity assumed control. Public funds aided in its support as did fines from the royal courts. In 1692, Bishop Saint-Vallier endowed an almshouse for both men and women near Quebec, the Hôpital Général, which operated its own farm and workshops where the able-bodied poor were set to work at a minimum wage. The institution was designed not just to dispense charity but also to implement social policy.

In 1736 the Crown assumed financial responsibility for the care of abandoned illegitimate infants, known henceforth as the 'King's children', which were placed first with wet-nurses and then in foster homes. These children were, as charges of the Crown, to be treated legally as those of legitimate birth. This was a particularly humane approach for the times.

All of the chief towns had a hospital which, although instituted to treat military, naval and administrative personnel extended free hospital care to all colonists. The high quality of medical care afforded qualified them for state subsidies. There were also urban dwellers who organized pre-paid medical insurance plans and engaged the services of master surgeons in Montreal and Quebec. Hospitalization and medical care were superior to that found in

---

[36] William J. Eccles almost depicts New France as an embryonic 'welfare state' in *Essays on New France*, Toronto, 1987.

most colonial situations. New France can be credited with having pioneered in some areas of social welfare legislation. Poverty had never been regarded as a sin by the church, but as an opportunity for the more fortunate to practice charity. The state, however, regarded poverty as a misfortune and socially undesirable. There was, therefore, a community obligation to eradicate its manifestations. It was not assumed that society would have beggars, unemployed, homeless and unattended sick. There was a social responsibility for the state itself to provide funds and personnel and to organize community initiatives to meet these challenges.

Role of the Church

The religious situation is best summarized in the statement that the state was religious and the church was national. The Roman Catholic church in New France drew its strength not only from the universal character of that segment of Christianity but also from the fact it was the King's religion and in that respect enjoyed many exclusive privileges and rights. It alone could lawfully engage in missionary work in the colony after 1627, it administered the educational and social welfare institutions for the state, and it had a monopoly on religious publication. The colonial church was also in a position of dependency on the state inasmuch as the Crown controlled the nomination of its bishop and the constitutions and membership of all religious communities. It was clearly part of the Gallican establishment for as Intendant Dupuy wrote in 1728, "The church is in the state, and not the state in the church."[37]

In the first decades of colonization, before the introduction of royal government in 1663, the church wielded unusually important influence in political and social matters. This changed as the colony became more populated and state institutions were introduced. The decline in clercial influence may also be attributed to the waning of the activities in the colony of members of the religious zealots, the *dévots,* after the suppression of the Company of the Holy Sacrament in France by Louis XIV in 1664. The puritanical teachings associated with the Jansenist heresy, which caused some anxiety in official circles in the mother country, never took root in New France. But the colonial church, though middle-of-the-road orthodox in doctrine, did attempt to impose rigourist practices, characterized by 'little compassion or concession'. Three of the colonial bishops were particularly

[37]"Church-State Relations in Canada, 1604-1685", Canadian Historical Association, *Annual Report,* 1967, Ottawa, 1967, 20-40. The situation described in Canada in *The Role of the Church in New France,* Toronto, 1976 is the same in Louisbourg according to A.J.B. Johnson, *Religion in Life at Louisbourg,* Montreal, 1984.

concerned about the supposed 'decline' in morality and religiosity in the colonial setting. Saint-Vallier set high standards for religious teaching and practice in his service book and catechism, published at the beginning of the eighteenth century. Bishop Dosquet, later in the century, tried to upgrade educational standards and the code of clerical behaviour. The last bishop of the French régime, Pontbriand, was very concerned about the low entrance requirements for admission of colonial candidates to the seminary and the priesthood.

The parish was neither the centre of community social life nor of education during the French colonial period. Clerical historians of the late nineteenth and twentieth century have woven webs of nationalistic (almost racist) utopianism by assigning religious motivations to the dominant role in colonial society. Early immigration was not as selective as they pretended, nor was colonial society 'purified' of the evils rampant in the mother country. The colonial church never did overcome the problems posed by disorders connected with the fur trade, the slow development of parishes, the scarcity of clergy, and excessive alcohol consumption by both colonists and Native peoples.

At the popular level, most colonists conformed outwardly to the pious practices associated with Catholicism: they recited the rosary in their homes, said grace before and after meals, usually attended mass when the church was not too distant, and observed the fasts and feasts as prescribed. They loved the pomp and ceremonials of various high holidays but could also show disrespectful scorn of admonishing sermons and attempts to curb the exuberance of youth. They joined religious fraternities and sodalities, but this religiosity did not lead them to make generous bequests to the church, or to pay their tithes and parochial dues joyfully.

The young men who did choose to enter holy orders gravitated to the secular diocesan seminary rather than to the Jesuits and Sulpicians with their higher educational standards and stricter discipline. Most of the religious vocations came from the artisan class in the towns, not from the rural peasantry. Young women also showed a preference for the secular religious communities which afforded direct contact with the colonists over the cloistered orders. By the end of the French régime the ratio of clergy to the general population was in steep decline. This crisis of religious vocations would become even more serious in the early decades of British rule.

Military Ethos

Throughout the seventeenth century New France was engaged in warfare for its very survival. There was a relatively long period of peace from 1713 to

1744, and then the imperial wars once again overshadowed all activities. The intermittant wars with the Iroquois confederacy began in 1609 and did not end until the Treaty of Montreal in 1701, when France and her native allies came to an agreement to recognize Iroquois neutrality in the contest for empire. The wars of Louis XIV ended with the Treaty of Utrecht in 1713 and proved disastrous for the colony. Colonials had actually overrun much of English Newfoundland, carried out successful frontier raids into New York and New England, and had taken possession of the Hudson Bay Company posts. But France's loss of the European conflict saw a restoration of all the gains made in North America and the cession to Britain of Acadia, except Cape Breton and Isle-Saint-Jean (Prince Edward Island). The Acadians now became British subjects.

This prevalence of war in the first century of colonial development resulted in the growth of a military tradition, as well as of a military élite. The troops sent to Canada in the 1660s to deal with Iroquois menace were *troupes de la Marine,* the independent companies of fifty men commanded by a captain who had been organized to guard the harbours and naval bases as well as overseas posts. Unlike in the regiments of regular ground forces, commissions could not be purchased in the Marine companies, and promotion depended on merit, or proven ability, and seniority. In 1684, when there were six vacancies in the officer corps, Governor Denonville asked that these be given to the unemployed youth of colonial noble families. The experiment proved so successful that soon most of the officers were recruited in Canada as they almost invariably had experience of the country and of Native relations. It was widely acknowledged that they made ideal commanders for frontier skirmishing. The waiting list of candidates grew long, so in 1753 it was ordered that only the sons of serving officers could apply. An élitist group of some eighteen families emerged to create a virtual military caste system. The marine soldiers were still sent out from France on tours of duty under Canadian officers. In Louisbourg both the soldiers and the officers came from France.

In 1669 a colonial militia force was organized for home defence and incursions into enemy territory when required. All males between the ages of 16 and 60, with the exception of the nobility and clergy, were required to report at regular intervals for training and to respond quickly when called out either for a military operation or for aid to the civil power. Auxiliary services could include freighting goods, construction work, and scouting activities. Aid to the civil power included the enforcement of law and order in local communities, searching for and arresting criminals, and the carrying out of public works projects. The militia was organized by parishes under the command of a captain. The captain of the militia was the local representative of the state responsible for such duties as reading out all public announcements, requisitioning grain in times of famine, supervising statue labour and parish building projects. This assignment of state duties to captains of militia, who for the most part, came from upwardly mobile bourgeois families, was also a means of restricting the influence of the clergy and the seigneurs. Militia service was compulsory and not remunerated, although each militiaman was equipped with a musket, powder, shot, bedroll, and in winter campaigns also with over-clothing. The Canadian militia soon gained the reputation of being ferocious and effective frontier fighters, who having adopted many of the characteristics of Amerindian guerilla warfare were much feared by the Anglo-American colonists.

In the two final colonial wars, the War of the Austrian Succession, 1744-48, and the Seven Years' War, 1754-60, the regular ground troops from the Ministry of War, the *troupes de terre*, played the principal role. British and French navies and regular regiments faced each other in engagement conducted along the lines of European conventional warfare. Both Louisbourg and Quebec were subjected to long sieges, in 1578 and 1759 respectively, before surrendering. The Canadian militia and allied Native warriors provided valuable assistance in the initial stages of the campaign, but became frustrated as warfare became increasingly European in command, strategy, tactics and battle plan. In the end, most historians now agree, New France was conquered by superior British forces, both navel and military, not by any failure in command, bravery, or defence strategy.[38]

French-Amerindian Relations

Eighteenth century British military observers believed that the main advantage the French enjoyed in North America was a successful relationship with the Amerindians. This had long assured them of the support of Native allies in their military encounters and frontier skirmishes with the Anglo-American colonists and their British backers. This largely successful friendship and cooperation was the result of a number of elements which together made up the context of contact, not the result of any innate superior French national characteristics.

The French built their relationship with the Amerindian nations on a number of basic practices. They benefited from having a consistent, unitary and centralized policy in dealing with the Native nations. The Governor-General spent each summer at Montreal, away from his capital at Quebec, in order to meet with Native leaders from the hinterland, to renew alliances,

[38]George F.G. Stanley, *New France: The Last Phase, 1744-1760,* Toronto, 1968.

regulate conditions of trade, and most important—to distribute the annual presents sent by the King. A consistent element in policy was the avoidance of authoritarian overbearing and a pretension to rule these independent nations. The French extended their claim to and exploitation of the continent without any extensive implantation of colonists. The French never signed any treaties of land surrender with Native nations, nor felt any need to do so. They recognized the native occupation and ownership of the interior of the vast continent, and took care to obtain permission to erect forts, build mission stations, and establish trading posts on Native lands. In 1716, orders were issued to concede no seigneuries in the upper country beyond the island of Montreal. There was no alienation of Native lands to provide for French colonial settlements.[39]

The military relationship was one of alliance, not of incorporation of Native fighting units as auxiliaries of a French army. Just as the Amerindian nations were independent (although claimed to be under French protective sovereignty) and self-governing, so they were recognized as having their own military organization, distinctive objectives in warfare, unique strategies and tactics, and their own code of behaviour relative to actual engagements and the treatment of prisoners. French officials adopted Native protocol in their encounters with Amerindian leaders and delegates were generous in gift-giving on ceremonial occasions, and never imposed their policies or laws on them. French and Amerindian societies were very different, each having some positive things to learn from the other. Neither saw the other as its ideal; yet neither saw the other as completely worthless.

Legacy of Conquest

In 1759, Quebec, the fortified capital of New France was forced to capitulate after a three-month siege and naval bombardment. The following summer, three British armies converged on Montreal, after the fall of most of the interior military posts and the collapse of the Amerindian alliance system. The commercial centre of the colony was unable to withstand a siege therefore a capitulation was arranged in September 1760. The colony was under military occupation and military rule for three years. The definitive Treaty of Paris in 1763 ceded New France to the British Crown, and in 1764 a civil government was established.

---

[39]Cornelius J. Jaenen, "The Uniqueness of the French Relationship with Canada's Native Peoples, 1504-1763", in Aparnu Basu, ed., *Imperialism, Nationalism and Regionalism in Canadian and Modern Indian History,* New Delhi, 1989, pp. 1-29; also, "French Sovereignty and Native Nationhood during the French Régime", in J.R. Miller, ed., *Sweet Promises. A Reader on Indian-White Relations in Canada,* Toronto, 1991, pp. 18-42.

The immediate British policy was to attempt to reconcile the 'new subjects', Canadians and Amerindians, to British rule. It was soon realized that British and French societies had some common characteristics, so that the British régime would also be the continuation of what has been called an 'ancien régime society'. Two French régime institutions survived the conquest and took on added significance under the new rulers—the church and the seigneurial system. The Roman Catholic Church continued to provide religious, educational and welfare services, and began to play an important role in the formation of the ideology of the conquered population. The seigneurial tract was fully occupied and provided a region of homogeneous population which British immigrants could not penetrate. So there arose the concept of two charter groups, the descendants of the two European colonizing powers. The British began to introduce their organizational framework but had to make many concessions to the already established social order. These 'concessions' established a principle of duality in the colony. In other words, under British rule—especially after the success of the American Revolution—the society which had taken root along the banks of the St. Lawrence entrance to the continent could continue to evolve, albeit within a different and often alien context. New Frances lived on the Quebec and through this new expression of itself, sometimes referred to as the 'French fact', would influence the development of the whole of Canada.

BIBLIOGRAPHY

Early Colonisation
Dickason, Olive P. *The Myth of the Savage and the Beginnings of French Colonialism in the Americas*. Edmonton: University of Alberta Press, 1984.
Eccles, W.J. *France in America*. Toronto: Fitzhenry & Whiteside, 1973.
Hoffman, Bernard G. *Cabot to Cartier*. Toronto: University of Toronto Press, 1961.
Jaenen, Cornelius J. *Friend and Foe: Aspects of French-Amerindian Cultural Contact in the Sixteenth and Seventeenth Centuries*. New York: Columbia University Press, 1976.
Reid, John G. *Acadia, Maine and New Scotland: Marginal Colonies in the Seventeenth Century*. Toronto: University of Toronto Press, 1971.
Trigger, Bruce G. *Natives and Newcomers: Canada's "Heroic Age" Reconsidered*. Montreal: McGill-Queen's University Press, 1985.
Trudel, Marcel. *The Beginnings of New France, 1524-1663*. Toronto: McClelland & Stewart, 1973.

Church and Missions

Jaenen, Cornelius J. *The Role of the Church in New France.* Toronto: McGraw-Hill Ryerson, 1976.

—. *The French Relationship with the Native Peoples of New France.* Ottawa: Indian and Northern Affairs Canada, 1984.

Johnston, A.J.B. *Religion in Life at Louisbourg, 1713-1758.* Montreal: McGill-Queen's University Press, 1984.

Jones, Elizabeth. *Gentlemen and Jesuits.* Toronto: University of Toronto Press, 1986.

Mealing, S.R., ed. *The Jesuit Relations and Allied Documents.* Ottawa: Carleton University Press, 1990.

Upton, L.F.S. *Micmacs and Colonists: Indian-White Relations in the Maritime Provinces, 1713-1867.* Vancouver: University of British Columbia Press, 1979.

Administration and Law

Dubé, Jean-Claude. *Les Intendants de la Nouvelle France.* Montréal: Fides, 1984.

Eccles, W. J. *Canada under Louis XIV, 1663-1701.* Toronto: McClelland & Stewart, 1964.

—. *The Canadian Frontier, 1534-1760.* Albuquerque: University of New Mexico Press. 1974.

Knafla, Louis, ed. *Crime and Criminal Justice in Europe and Canada.* Waterloo: Wilfrid Laurier University Press, 1981.

Lachance, André. *Crimes et criminels en Nouvelle-France.* Montreal: Boréal Express, 1984.

Miquelon, Dale. *New France, 1701-1744: A Supplement to Europe.* Toronto: McClelland & Stewart, 1987.

—. *The First Canada to 1791.* Montreal: McGill-Queen's University Press, 1994.

Stanley, George F.G. *New France: The Last Phase, 1744-1760.* Toronto: McClelland & Stewart, 1968.

Agriculture and Commerce

Bosher, J.F. *The Canadian Merchants, 1713-1763.* London, 1668.

Dechêne, Louis. *Habitants and Merchants in Seventeenth Century Montreal.* Montreal: McGill-Queen's University Press, 1992.

Griffiths, Naomi. *The Acadians. Creation of a People.* Toronto: McGraw-Hill Ryerson, 1973.

Hamelin, Jean. *Economie et Société en Nouvelle-France.* Québec: Presses de l'Université Laval, 1960.

Harris, R.C. *The Seigneurial System in Early Canada*. Madison: University of Wisconsin Press, 1966.

Heidenreich, Conrad and Ray, Arthur J. *The Early Fur Trades. A Study in Cultural Interaction*. Toronto: University of Toronto Press, 1976.

Innis, Harold A. *The Fur Trade in Canada*. Toronto: University of Toronto Press, 1970.

—. *The Cod Fisheries. The History of an International Economy*. Toronto: University of Toronto Press, 1978.

Lunn, Alice Jean E. *Développement économique de la Nouvelle France, 1713-1760*. Montréal: Presses de l' Université de Montréal, 1986.

Rich, E.E. *Montreal and the Fur Trade*. Montreal: McGill University Press, 1966.

Society and Culture

Douville, Raymond and Casanova, Jacques. *Daily Life in Early Canada*. London: Oxford University Press, 1968.

Eccles, W. J. *Essays on New France*. Toronto: Oxford University Press, 1987.

Greer, Allan. *Peasant, Lord, and Merchant: Rural Society in Three Quebec Parishes, 1740-1840*. Toronto: University of Toronto Press, 1985.

Griffiths, Naomi. *The Contexts of Acadian History, 1686-1784*. Montreal: McGill-Queen's University Press, 1992.

Lachance, André.*La Vie urbaine en Nouvelle-France*. Montréal: Boreal, 1987.

Magnuson, Roger. *Education in New France*. Montreal: McGill-Queen's University Press, 1992.

Mathieu, Jacques. *La Nouvelle-France, Les Français en Amérique du Nord, XVIe-XVIIIe si ècles*. Québec: Presses de l'Université Laval, 1991.

Parr, Joy, ed. *Childhood and Family in Canadian History*. Toronto: University of Toronto Press, 1982.

Peyser, Joseph E. *Letters from New France. The Upper Country, 1686-1783*. Urbana: University of Illinois Press, 1992.

Zoltvany, Yves F. *The French Tradition in North America*. Toronto: Fitzhenry & Whitesides, 1972.

Military Events and Conquest

Dickason, Olive P. *Louisbourg and the Indians, 1713-1760*. Ottawa: Parks Canada, 1976.

Frégault, Guy. *The War of the Conquest*. Toronto: Oxford University Press, 1969.

Griffiths, Naomi. *The Acadian Deportation: Deliberate Perfidy or Cruel Necessity?* Toronto: Copp Clark, 1969.

Jones, Dorothy V. *License for Empire. Colonialism by Treaty in Early America.* Chicago: University of Chicago Press, 1982.

Leach, Douglas E. *The Northern Colonial Frontier, 1607-1763.* Toronto: Holt, Rinehart & Winston, 1966.

Miquelon, Dale, ed. *Society and Conquest: The Debate on the Bourgeosie and Social Change in French Canada, 1700-1850.* Toronto: Copp Clark, 1977.

Steele, Ian K. *Guerillas and Grenadiers: The Struggle for Canada, 1689-1760.* Toronto: Ryerson Press, 1969.

White, Richard. *The Middle Ground: Indians, Empires, and Republics in the Great Lakes Region, 1650-1815.* Cambridge: University Press, 1991.

Historiography

Gagnon, Serge. *Quebec and its Historians. The Twentieth Century.* Montreal: Harvest House, 1984.

Hamilton, Roberta. *Feudal Society and Colonization. The Historiography of New France.* Gananonque: Langale Press, 1988.

Jaenen, Cornelius J. "Canada during the French Régime", in D.A. Muise, ed., *A Reader's Guide to Canadian History. I: Beginnings to Confederation.* Toronto: University of Toronto Press, 1982, pp. 31-43.

Miquelon, Dale. *Society and Conquest. The Debate on the Bourgeosie and Social Change in French Canada, 1700-1850.* Toronto: Copp Clark Pitman, 1977.

2
British North America to 1867

PETER BASKERVILLE

INTRODUCTION

This article provides a general overview of economic, social and political developments in British North America from 1763 to 1867. These are traditional dates: the one signals the passing of Quebec from France to England; the other the transformation of the British colonies into a nation called Canada. Historians have made a great deal of both dates: book shelves bend under the weight of analyses of the Conquest and of Confederation. Clearly, both have importance and their significance is not lost sight of in the following chapter. Yet there is a tendency, in survey histories especially, for writers to generalize too cavalierly about the impact of these events. The truth is that for many of the people who lived in British North America in these one hundred years, neither happening was of much importance. Moreover, each event affected different groups of people in different ways. This last point is especially important. British North American colonists were a diverse lot. Natives, of course, as article details, were not colonists at all. Moreover, even within Quebec, the Conquest affected people in markedly differential ways. Colonial societies were shaped and split by region, class, gender, ethnicity and religion. These overlapping tensions gave form and meaning to life in the pre-Confederation era. The following discussion centres on those tensions in an attempt to illustrate the stresses and challenges experienced by those who lived in a North America over which a common name had yet to be placed.

I. THE LATE EIGHTEENTH CENTURY

Britain's American empire changed dramatically in the latter half of the eighteenth century. In February 1763, the Treaty of Paris ended the French-British War and ceded to the British France's North American territory. England already controlled Nova Scotia, Newfoundland fishing settlements, and, via the Hudson's Bay Company, a wide expanse of land in the northern interior. In addition, of course, the thirteen American colonies to the south remained under British control. By 1791, this British American Empire was altered once again. The thirteen southern colonies had successfully fought for independence during the American Revolution of 1775. While Britain maintained control of her northern colonies, the form of the control had undergone significant change. By the 1790s, five northern colonies—upper Canada, Lower Canada, Nova Scotia, New Brunswick and Prince Edward Island—had been granted locally elected assemblies overseen by appointed councils. Two others—Cape Breton and Newfoundland—continued to be ruled without representative government and a vast western territory remained under nominal control of the Hudson's Bay Company.

The second half of the eighteenth century witnessed three massive and forced movements of people in North America. The Acadian deportations of the 1750s uprooted a stable and pacific farming community. A second bloodier and more prolonged uprooting concerned the subjugation and pushing out of American natives by white settlers. The third forced migration took place during and immediately following the American Revolution when some 80,000 to 100,000 Loyalists fled the United States. While nearly half went to England and the British West Indies, the rest went north: 35,000 moved to the Maritimes, 2,000 settled in central Quebec and some 7,500 entered the country of the Mississauga natives, 'this', as one disgruntled Loyalist termed the area north of Lake Ontario, 'American Siberia'. From the perspective of the evolution of British Imperial policy as well as from the vantage point of those who lived in North America, the closing years of the eighteenth century represented a time of tumultuous change. A closer consideration of that era is, therefore, warranted.

Quebec

It is an understatement to say that in 1763 Britain did not possess a finely drawn blueprint for the governance of her newly acquired American territories. Indeed, such a policy only slowly emerged, often in reaction to events in North America. Yet British sensitivities to North American events were conditioned by particular social, economic and political traditions within England. The Royal Proclamation of October 1763 provides an excellent example of how Imperial policy resulted from the complex interplay of North American events and British sensitivities.

It has been aptly noted that Britain had a policy for war, but not for peace. A decentralized and devisive Imperial bureaucratic structure made the creation of any coherent policy for administering the new land extremely problematic. Even as various bureaucratic agencies vied for control of the process, events in North America precipitated a series of ill-considered solutions that were embodied in the Royal Proclamation of 1763. The so-called Pontiac uprising of 1763-65 provided the catalyst. The curtailment of trade with Western natives, who were long accustomed to French trade and gift-giving, sparked and armed uprising nominally under the control of Pontiac, an Ottawa chief from the Detroit area. Commencing in the spring of 1763, the western natives captured nine British forts, caused one to be. evacuated and besieged two others. While brutally repressed—Pontiac formally made peace in 1765—the uprising sent immediate shock waves to distant London, England. Deeply fearing any potential alliance between the French in Quebec and the western natives, British policy-makers hived Quebec off from what became known as a large block of Indian territory to the west and south. The British forbade white settlement in that area and stipulated that natives could sell land only to the British government. Such a territorial definition could be seen by the natives to guarantee their independence and traditional rights to lands, and, indeed, the Proclamation has become one of, if not the, most important basis of aboriginal land title in Canadian law today.

But the Proclamation Act attempted to deal with more than discontented natives. The boundary delimitation was also meant to encourage the northward movement of an increasingly expansive population in the southern thirteen colonies. By denying further westward expansion, Imperial administrators assumed that the colonists would begin to move north and eventually—sooner rather than later, it was hoped—outnumber the 75,000 or so French-speaking settlers in Quebec. In anticipation of that happening, the Proclamation Act provided for the granting of an elected assembly in Quebec, 'as soon as possible', even while denying Roman Catholics the right to participate in administrative and judicial positions. Quebec, in other words, was to become a province just like all the others, with a complete set of British institutions including British civil and criminal law. Such a policy ignored realities in Quebec and in the thirteen colonies, but emerged logically from eighteenth century Whig notions as to the proper arrangement of political and social organizations. The Glorious Rebellion of 1688 coloured that thinking. 1688 taught that protestants must reign supreme and that such a rule must be carried out through representative institutions and via British legal models. Such a policy emerged from a commitment to abstract principle untempered by an acknowledgement of North American realities.

Undoubtedly, Imperial administrators were encouraged by the earlier example of New Englanders moving north to assume land vacated by the deported Acadians in the Maritime region. In the 1750s, 7,500 Acadians had been ruthlessly shunted aside to make way for the New Englanders. No one suggested that ten times that number could be removed from Quebec. Similarly, however, few realized that the westward minded colonists from the thirteen colonies would virtually ignore the Proclamation, and, rather than trekking north, would continue to move west. Moreover, the French in Quebec did not show any willingness to adopt British law and worship in an alien church. In fact, the Capitulation of 1760 had guaranteed Canadians their traditional property rights. As a result, British administrators in Quebec were handed a proclamation that was unenforceable.

Quebec's first British Governor, Brigadier-General James Murray faced the prospect of granting an elected assembly which would be enjoyed by only some 400 or so British merchants who had followed the army to Quebec. For Murray, as for others of his class—the officer and landowning class—merchants were 'the scum of the earth'. 'Country gentlemen', one Lord affirmed (to the general applause of Parliament)

> ... were undoubtedly the best and most respectable objects of the confidence of the people ... they had the greatest stake in the country after all and were the most deeply interested in its welfare: because let what happen, men of business and manufacturers could go and get their living elsewhere; but a country gentleman could not quit his native country, because he could not carry his estate with him.[1]

This perspective, in addition to relegating merchants and industrialists to a low social rank, also conditioned thinking on emigration. British policy-makers believed that the English should stay and farm at home: "... there ought to be no temptation ... to quit their native soil, to increase colonies at the expense of their country". Protestant help, therefore, could not be looked far from Britain and was not forthcoming from the southern colonies. For Murray to rule according to the imperatives of his class upbringing and the dictates of Imperial policy he would have to have been, as one historian put it, 'a deity'. He fell short of such stature and, amidst some controversy, lost his post in 1768.

His successor, Guy Carleton, shared Murray's sensibilities and struggled with the same problems. By the early 1770s, however, British policy-makers were beginning to appreciate the weaknesses of the Proclamation Act. This understanding emerged separate from the events which led to the American Revolution of 1775. Rather, Imperial administrators gradually came to

---

[1] Cited in Pierre Tousignant, "Problematique pour une nouvelle approache de la constitution de 1791", *Reveue d'historie de l'amerique français,* 27 (1973), 204-5.

realize that foreign territories—as defined by religion, legal customs and language—like Quebec and India, could only be ruled effectively through the cultivation of local collaborators. Effective collaborators had to have deep roots in colonial societies. British protestant merchants in Quebec did not fill that bill. On the other hand, French Canadian seigneurs, the traditional land holding elite in New France, and the French Roman Catholic clergy seemed ideal for the task at hand.

Pressured by Carleton, the Imperial Government passed the Quebec Act of 1774, an act designed to ensure British control of Quebec by working with, or better still, through loyal collaborators of good colonial standing. Some moves had already been made in this direction. In 1766, Jean Olivier Briand, the former grand vicar of Quebec, had been appointed the official leader of Quebec's Catholics. As well, Carleton, like Murray before him, refused to call an assembly despite pressure from the anglo-merchants. The Quebec Act solidified and extended these initiatives. Territorially, New France was restored; Quebec and the Indian Territory as defined in 1763 became the new Quebec. The colony was to play much the same role as it had prior to the Conquest: curb the expansion of the thirteen colonies and act as an outlet for the trade in furs in an attempt to maintain native alliances. French civil law was reintroduced (British criminal law was retained). Catholics were allowed to hold judicial and administrative positions, a decision fundamental to the success of the collaborative policy. Equally important, the Act guaranteed the rights of seigneurial tenure and religious toleration. Finally, it allowed the province to be ruled by a Governor-General and an appointed Council.

The Quebec Act attempted to come to grips with a complex set of problems. It demonstrated a sensitivity on the part of Imperial administrators to the realities of Quebec and North America which stood in dramatic contrast to the attitudes which informed the Proclamation Act of 1763. But as immediate and longer term events would demonstrate, the Imperial vision remained clouded by deeply held social biases, biases which blurred the real nature of seigneurial and church relations with the people of Quebec. Consistent with their own landed background, Imperial policy-makers assumed that the seigneurs were the effective rulers in New France. Such a view completely overlooked the role played by intendants, by militia captains (who were themselves habitants) and by the tradition of consultative assemblies. So, too, the British overemphasized the power exercised by the Catholic Church. In the pre-Conquest era, the Church had not been able to control in any effective way the social behaviour of the habitant class. Nor did it succeed in doing so in the letter half of the eighteenth century.

Compared to Quebec, it is generally assumed that Britain's other North

American possessions were somehow less or foreign in nature and thus easier to govern. As the historian Jack Bumsted has reminded us, such an assumption underlines one of the primary Canadian myths, that of the concept of two founding peoples, a notion that has received much political support in modern Canada with the promotion of bilingualism and biculturalism. As with all myths, however, the idea of two founding peoples oversimplifies a more complex reality. In the later eighteenth century, cultural diversity characterized British North America, especially outside of Quebec. Moreover, the myth of two founding peoples contains within it other potent but highly problematic assumptions. To what extent can one define a nation or a colony or an empire simply in terms of language, or culture or religion? To assume that one can do so overlooks differences based on social class, on gender, and on colour.

These differences often cut across ethnic, religious and cultural groupings. In fact, the collaborative initiative pursued by Britain in Quebec foundered on the basis of group differentiation. The habitants were unwilling to follow the dictates of the seigneurs, just as they were unwilling to abide wholeheartedly with the strictures of the Catholic Church. The habitants had long evinced a culture, a set of behaviours distinct from that of other groups within Quebec. In some areas on Sunday, the tavern rivalled the church as a meeting place. At times, priests required 'bouncers' to maintain discipline during sermons. Habitants had a long tradition of resisting tithe collections and seigneurial exactions. This is not to conclude that the habitants were completely independent from other groups or classes in Quebec. It is to suggest, however, that a common language, religion and ethnic background did not, in late eighteenth century Quebec, make a homogeneous society.

The West

One can, in fact, argue that Britain's North American possessions outside of Quebec were even more diverse and certainly not capable of being subsumed under one simple linguistic or cultural designation. In the north-west, as one of the following chapters clearly outlines, the native population was composed of many different nations, each of which possessed its own culture and internal divisions. On the far west coast, for example (an area now called British Columbia), there were at least twenty-four separate native nations and within some of those there existed different linguistic groupings. Pushed by Montreal-based fur traders, the Hudson's Bay Company was only just beginning to leave the Hudson's Bay and explore the vast western interior. The explorations of the Hudson's Bay trader, Samuel Hearne, excited the curiosity of the experienced explorer, Captain James Cook, who in 1776 set sail from England in search of the fabled North West passage. In so doing, he charted much of the north west coast and traded with natives in the Nootka sound region. Indeed, it would be decades before permanent trading posts were established in that area and even then, those posts would be staffed until well into the nineteenth century by a mixture of Sandwich Islanders, local natives, Metis, Scots, British, and Quebec-born traders.

The Maritime Region

The expulsion of the Acadians did not result in homogeneous Maritime society. Indeed, in the mid-1760s some 2,600 Acadians were still resident in Nova Scotia and throughout the period more returned to swear an oath of allegiance to the Crown and attempt to re-establish their shattered lives. In the place of many Acadians, the Crown had attracted via subsidies and free land about 8,000 protestant New Englanders and about 1,500 protestant Germans. Many of them had assumed well-tended Acadian farms, most notably in the Bay of Fundy region. About half of the 13,500 people in Nova Scotia in 1767 were from the southern colonial seaboard region. The rest were Irish, German, English and Scottish. About 20 per cent of the population were Catholics and the rest were Protestant. The presence in Halifax, the colony's major centre, of an Anglican church, a Congregational chapel and a Dutch meeting house aptly indicates the diversity of its populations. When it is realized that within England, Wales, Ireland and Scotland, in this period, there lived many culturally, linguistically and regionally diverse peoples, and that the same held true for the regions from which the American born moved to Nova Scotia, the full scope of the diversity of the colonial population can be appreciated.

Local rather than regional economics typified this area and accentuated the fragmented character of social development. Outside of Halifax, many scattered settlements of from 250 to 800 people farmed, fished and engaged in some lumbering. Some 3,000 people resided in Halifax, the region's primary urban centre, a place which had benefited from British military presence during the Seven Years War, but whose economy languished following the end of conflict. An elected assembly, granted in 1758, was dominated by a close knit clique composed of merchants and British bureaucratic placemen, most of whom resided in Halifax (those elected from outlying areas often never attended), and many of whom (including the Lieutenant-Governor Michael Franklin) owned much land throughout the colony.

The placement of large blocks of land in the hands of wealthy and loyal subjects stood at the heart of imperial policy for the control and development of its North American possessions outside of Quebec. The classic example of this policy occurred in 1767 with the partitioning of the Island of St. John (renamed Prince Edward Island in 1798) into 67 lots of 20,000 acres each and their allocation by lottery to about 50 well-connected British residents. The absentee landowners were allowed ten years to settle one protestant person on each 200 acres of their property. In fact, Catholics from the Scottish highlands were the first to arrive and by the mid-1770s 1300 people resided on the Island, most of whom rented land from absentee owners and struggled to make a living.

It is often argued that those who settled in these colonies achieved a degree of economic, political and social freedom that they could never have obtained in the class-bound and status-oriented societies on the other side of the Atlantic. This version of the frontier thesis—that the wilderness environment acted as a levelling influence—requires major qualification. Close studies of the small settlements outside of Halifax, townships such as Horton, Annapolis and Amherst, have concluded that from the time of initial settlement about one-fifth of the farmers owned well over half of the improved and improvable land. The larger landowners dominated development in their regions. Economic stratification and social differentiation, rather than homogeneous and egalitarian societies characterized maritime development in North America in the late eighteenth century. And, it should be emphasized, Imperial administrators rested content with that state of affairs, believing that collaboration could be effectively achieved by working with large landowners and, when necessary, wealthy merchants.

Yet it would be wrong to conclude that Imperial policy for the controlled development of its North American maritime region was an unmitigated success. Control presented little problem in this period; development, however, proved more difficult to achieve. The colonial government rarely balanced its books and after 1767 depended on an annual £5,000 grant from the British Parliament in order to operate. British military and naval expenditures exceeded that amount. Even then, the colony's debt reached £20,000. Lacking a dominant staple product, the colony's economy proceeded via a series of fits and starts. Given the area's economic marginality, potential settlers sought greener fields with the result that Nova Scotia and the Island of St. John became financial burdens on the British public purse, a fact which rankled many including Edmund Burke: 'Good God!' he exclaimed from his Parliamentary seat, "What sum the nursing of that ill-thriven, hard-visaged, and ill-favoured brat, has cost to this wittol nation."

Newfoundland
The cod fishery dominated Newfoundland's development. Unlike its

Maritime counterparts, Newfoundland was a money-maker. British merchants argued that the cod fishery was more valuable than all of Spain's gold and silver holdings in the Americas. Moreover, in Imperial eyes, Newfoundland had great strategic worth. Throughout the eighteenth century, the British government supported the migratory fishery in order to provide skilled sailors for their navy. To realize that objective, Imperial policy-makers discouraged year long residency on Newfoundland: able bodied seamen were needed at home, not on the rocky outcrops of the Newfoundland coast. As a result, no one could legally own land in the colony. Nor were the institutional trappings of a structured society provided.

Despite this studied neglect an inshore fishery run by fishers who 'wintered' on the island had taken a strong hold by the 1760s. Over 7,000 people lived year round in the colony by the early years of that decade. West County merchants from England supplied these fishers with provisions and contracted with them to purchase their catch. Yet by the late-1760s, West County merchants, encouraged by British authorities and facilitated by the construction of larger ocean-going vessels, began to fish off the Grand Banks and to lessen direct ties with Newfoundland residents. Larger catches and the return home in the winter of more fishers nicely served Imperial ends. As with much else in Britain's North American Empire, however, the American Rebellion of 1755 would transform that evolving structure.

Rebellion and British North America

The turmoil attendent on the rebellion of Britain's Thirteen American colonies had direct repercussions to the north. The war with Britain rendered Newfoundland's migratory fishery fraught with risk and expense. American privateers patrolled the Grand Banks and raided fishing vessels. This led to the virtual end of the yearly migration to the banks. These privateers, small but armed New England vessels, raided, as well, coastal communities in a form of naval guerilla warfare throughout the Maritime region. By the later years of a war which only ended in 1783, Nova Scotian communities had begun to retaliate in kind. Some local merchants profited from the spoils of war but many more residents suffered from higher food costs, and from the disruption wrought on an already marginal economy. Through it most Nova Scotians struggled to survive rather than plotted for one or other side. Many seemed to have found some solace, if not security, in the religious teachings of a revivalist preacher, Henry Alline. Stressing an individualist relationship with spiritual concerns seemed appropriate to many Nova Scotians confused by discordant community conflict. From this spiritual quest, a unique sense of Nova Scotian identity, an identity separate from both Britain and the southern colonies, gradually emerged.

The American Revolution provided the first indication of the weaknesses underlying the Quebec Act. Habitants generally resisted calls to form local militias. The aggressive acts of American invaders—the British regulars evacuated Montreal and withstood an American siege at Quebec in the winter of 1775-76—forestalled any widespread support for the thirteen colonies. Threats of excommunication by Bishop Briand may also have helped to quiet any tendency on the part of the habitants to support openly the Americans. But, despite the best attempts of the clergy and the seigneurs, most habitants seemed to have remained apathetic or, at best, lukewarm supporters of British rule. Britain remained in control of Quebec thanks more to the military inefficiency exhibited by the thirteen colonies than to any support from the French Canadian habitants. This first attempt at ruling via collaboration left much to be desired.

The Revolution had an immediate impact on the region north and west of Quebec, an area known as the *pays d'en haut*. It represented the first major test of British native policy since the Pontiac uprising. Continued control of military posts in native territory at Carleton Island (off Kingston), Niagara, Detroit and Michilimackinac was crucial to British hopes of victory. From them, garrisons further to the west and south could be provisioned; offensives into New York, Pennsylvania and Ohio and Illinois territories could be staged. To them could be attracted Indian allies and British supporters from both the northern and southern regions. Success depended largely on the attitude of the local Natives. Carleton, and after 1778 his successor as British Commander-in-Chief, Frederick Haldimand, realized this and redoubled their efforts in provisioning and providing presents to Natives on the north shore of Lake Ontario and the upper St. Lawrence. Similarly, through the Northern Indian Department, under the administration of Sir John Johnson, whose wife Molly Brandt was an influential Mohawk, every attempt was made initially to guarantee the neutrality and ultimately to attract the active support of the Six Nations Iroquois in northern New York.

By the late 1770s, activity in the north, especially at Niagara, had become quite intense. The defeat of General Burgoyne and his force of 7,000 British regulars at Saratoga, New York, in October 1777, altered British strategy. Further major offensives using regular troops in that area were not possible. Instead, the British relied on guerilla activity carried out by loyal volunteers and, whenever possible, Native allies. A provincial corps of Loyalists and Natives from the Seneca of the Six Nations, raised and commanded by John Butler, staged a series of devastating guerilla raids out of Niagara following 1777. These successes attracted more support for the Loyalists' cause. The raids also provoked retaliation. Under Major-General John Sullivan, an American force of 5,000 swept through the Six Nations' territory late in 1779. With much of their homeland laid waste, some 5,000 Iroquois retreated to Niagara, swelling the ranks of the 'loyal'.

Hardpressed to provision such large numbers, Haldimand instituted a policy with fateful consequences for the local Mississauga people. He ordered the Lake Ontario garrisons to begin to cultivate their own food. Not so disinterested members of the Northern Indian department and military stationed at Niagara (including Butler and some of his relatives) eagerly advised Haldimand that the best agricultural land lay on the west side of the Niagara River under Mississauga control. For three hundred suits of clothing, supplies which the British intended to give away anyway, the Mississauga, in May 1781, ceded valuable land to the Crown. It was the first of many such cessions.

Under the smokescreen of war, the foundations for a colony not yet established were being put in place. Contracts for provisioning and supplying both Native allies and the army provided considerable economic opportunity for a nascent merchant community. But to succeed merchants had to be of a special sort. Strong military contacts were one necessary prerequisite. But that by itself was not sufficient. John Butler is a case in point. Extremely successful in attracting Iroquois support and engineering guerrilla raids, Butler aspired to a more comfortable sinecure. Haldimand considered Butler for the vacant post of superintendent of the Northern Indian Department but concluded that he was too 'deficient in education and liberal sentiments'. The point was clear for those who chose to read it. To make it, whether as a merchant, dependent on military contracts for success, or as a bureaucrat, breeding, respectability and the proper social bearing were the *sine qua non*. Just as the mechanism for the divestiture of Indian lands had been put into operation during the Revolutionary War, so too had the ground rules for the investiture of Upper Canada's future élite been laid.

The guerilla-like offensives waged from the northern posts, although successful, were not sufficient to alter the war's overall course. When the French entered on the side of the Americans in 1778, the line of battle became tremendously extended and British resources correspondingly stretched. Gains, when made, often could not be held. To the chagrin of the northern Loyalists, who, after all, had themselves lost few battles, the British called a halt to further military action in April 1782. Fearing retribution from the victors, many of those Americans who had supported the British trekked north in search of a safe heaven.

The Loyalists

Loyalists were those Americans who supported the British or at least did not actively support those Americans who rebelled. Most Loyalists would have stayed in the United States had they experienced forgiveness, rather than vindictiveness. Loyalists moved because it was not safe to stay. In the early years of the war, visible British supporters, generally members of an office holding elite dependent on Imperial backing, fled the country, some settling in the Maritime region, most going to Britain. An older historiography keyed on the background and activities of this elite and from them generalized about the Loyalist experience as a whole. More recent research has exposed the weakness of such an elite-centred focus. By the closing years of the conflict, the movement north had intensified many times over. The ultimate forced migration was a polyglot mixture of classes, races, ethnic backgrounds and, very likely, motivations.

"Strange is the collection of people here", one contemporary observed of the Loyalists in the *pays d'en haut* in 1784. And so they were. Most of the 7,500 or so were farmers generally from northern New York State. Five hundred, however, were black slaves whose elite Loyalist masters used every means possible to keep them from claiming their freedom. An additional 2,100 were Iroquois and other natives who had supported the British. Most Loyalists had little wealth and possessed only modest education (many were illiterate). Over 50 per cent had been born outside of the Thirteen Colonies, often of German, Irish or Scots (Gaelic speaking) background. Indeed, the typical Loyalist in the up-country had only been in America for about ten years and, therefore, had scarcely time to become part of an American consensus on any issue. European, not American, attitudes coloured perceptions and underlay decisions. In one sense, these immigrant Loyalists had already been uprooted and looked for stability and continuity, not rebellion and change. Thus to the extent that they 'decided' anything—more often than not their local landlord would decide the issue for them—they opted for continuity under the Crown, a decision at root more psychological than ideological in nature.

Similar diversity characterized the much larger Loyalist flow into the Maritimes: "(A) collection of all nations, kindreds, complexions and tongues assembled from every corner of the globe and till lately equally strangers to me and each other", one Annapolis Valley resident of Nova Scotia ruefully commented. As in the *pays d'en haut,* most migrants possessed modest wealth, although somewhat fewer were from an agrarian background and more were American born. Religion spanned the protestant spectrum. One-tenth, or over 3,000, were black, most often runaway slaves from

Virginia or South Carolina. Loyalism cut across social and economic lines: the resulting mix could probably be taken as a mirror image of the society from which they were forced to leave.

It may indeed be that the Loyalists were more committed to Empire than those who had settled in British North America before them. Certainly, an older historiography made much of that apparent characteristic. Some have argued that the Loyalist attachment to the Crown represented one of the seminal building blocks of an evolving British North American identity. In the nineteenth century, Loyalist associations were formed to commemorate that event. Yet Governor Parr of Nova Scotia had his doubts. In his opinion, "the generality of those who came [to Shelburne, Nova Scotia] were not much burthened with Loyalty, a spacious name which they made use of". Certainly their apparent support of the British cause did not result in unquestioning obedience. Despite concerted efforts on the part of British administrators to settle Loyalists in specific areas, high transiency rates characterized the settlement process. Two-thirds of the people in some townships in the *pays d'en haut* either failed to take up their allotted land or moved within a year. Shelburne, a town of 10,000 in the mid-1780s, had less than 1,000 people ten years later. Almost half of Nova Scotia's black Loyalists, having suffered unrelenting discrimination—in Shelburne in 1784, for example, whites "Drove the Negroes out the Town"—left for Sierra Leone in 1792. In the Maritimes, Loyalists clashed with established elites over control of the best land and over the quest for place and preferment at Halifax, the region's major centre. Many such Loyalist aspirants were forced to settle in hinterland regions where they began to forge a rural centred opposition to counteract the Halifax clique's political control. In part, because of this dispute, in 1784 a second colony, New Brunswick, was carved out of the original Nova Scotia, a colony where, in the eyes of the Loyalists, at least, a society "The Envy of the American States" could be created. Yet even here, political fighting with established elites at Saint John and the capital, Fredericton, occurred regularly.

Even in the *pays d'en haut,* where no established elite existed; where the British administrators scurried quickly to purchase for pittances huge blocks of land from the Mississauga natives in order to provide free land for westward moving Loyalists; where half-pay allotments to disbanded officers or their widows plus payment of Loyalist claims for damages and losses due to their alleged support of the British plus free supplies amounted to an outlay on the part of the Crown of over £1,000,000 by 1787; Loyalists proved to be a disputatious lot. Since the up-country was under the administrative control of Quebec, there was, of course, no assembly and the seigneurial land holding system was in place. Accordingly, Loyalists petitioned for a freehold system, no taxes and an elected assembly. As in Nova Scotia and New Brunswick, Loyalists couched their demands on the rhetoric of the 'country party' opposition which had emerged in England in the eighteenth century, a critique which focused on excessive centralization of power and the enjoyment of such power by 'corrupt' and self-satisfying cliques and oligarchies protected by appointed governors and their councils. Loyalists, in other words, came more often to oppose than support the existing colonial power structures, structures set in place by no less than Imperial administrators acting on behalf of the Crown itself.

It would be very wrong, however, to conclude from the nature of Loyalist political and social demands that they were at all radical in the sense of wishing to overturn constituted authority and to establish something new. Their goal was, rather, to achieve a place of respect and power within that realm. The Loyalists, and most especially the Loyalist elite, were steadfast supporters of a hierarchically structured society. When Loyalists petitioned for an assembly or for financial compensation, they routinely stressed their devotion 'to His Majesty's Interest' and their willingness 'to sacrifice their Lives and their Properties in defence of his Crown'. What they desired, they claimed, was only the re-establishment of past prerogatives and institutions, a demand which conveniently overlooked the fact that most had never enjoyed many of the prerogatives. Nevertheless, by couching their demands in terms of restoration and recreation, they presented a conservative visage and, in the process, helped to manufacture the Loyalist myth, so celebrated by an older historiography. In their fundamental objective, they stood as one with Imperial administrators in the *pays d'en haut,* and with the established ruling cliques in Nova Scotia and New Brunswick. They proposed no new recipe for change; they simply desired a larger piece of the existing pie.

What we know of the experience of one oft-ignored Loyalist group underlines the conservative nature of Loyalist society. During the Revolution, Loyalist women achieved what the historian Janice Potter-MacKinnon has termed 'remarkable' accomplishments. Many women left behind with their families while their husbands went to fight on behalf of the British or simply went north to escape vilification and possible imprisonment by the Patriots, did not sit timidly awaiting rescue. Some acted as British spies. Others sheltered and provisioned Loyalist raiding parties. Almost all had to perform the traditional male role of household head and see to financing and outfitting the household. More telling, they had often to carry out negotiations with Patriots in order to be given the right to leave for British North America. And often most demanding they had, sometimes pregnant and with a young family, to make a dangerous trek through enemy territory in inclement conditions in order to reach refugee camps in New York or asylum in British-held territory to the north.

To what extent were these 'loyal' women recognized and rewarded for their activity? The Loyalist vision, as Potter-MacKinnon succinctly put it 'Left no place for [these] women and their accomplishments'. They lived in a patriarchal society: men were the decision-makers and women and children were the followers. Within such a context, affection was possible: men were expected to be benevolent good providers; in return for which women were expected to be deferential and obedient. A married woman became a *femme covert,* a person with no legal identity separate from her husband. To reward women for their at times heroic activity during the Revolution, then, would be an explicit recognition that women could function on a level of equality with men. For the patriarchal Loyalist elite, such a notion was not simply untenable; it was unthinkable. So strongly entrenched was this relationship that even for Loyalist women, such a notion may have been equally difficult to conceive. When Loyalist widows, for example, petitioned for compensation they adopted 'the language of enfeeblement'. No matter how heroic their accomplishments had been, those achievements had to be and almost invariably were downplayed or even omitted. In their place were pleas for support based on their status as 'a poor helpless woman', 'a Feeble Woman', a woman without a man to protect her. And, as if to underline the rhetoric of submissiveness and subordination employed by Loyalist women, the all-male adjudicators of Loyalist claims awarded, on a proportional basis, much more to men than to women.

Women's subordination reflected a wider pattern of structured inequality throughout British North America. Far from acting as an assimilative force, the Loyalist migration had, in many ways, accentuated the reality of social diversity in Britain's northern colonies. The Quebec Act had signalled Britain's recognition that such diversity could not be eradicated. The American Revolution underlined the necessity for demonstrating respect and recognition for colonial needs and sensibilities. Within these constraints, Imperial administrators opted for the maintenance of bounded diversity.

Land grants and compensation payments were designed to preserve and enhance social differentiation. Thus the higher one's military rank the more land the officer and his family members received. Awards for the compensation of losses incurred during the Revolution reflected one's social and economic standing prior to the conflict. In the *pays d'en haut* attempts were made to settle enlisted men in townships where their commanding officers resided, in order to better exercise social control.

Concerted attempts were made to establish a dominant church, that of the Church of England. Anglican bishops were provided for Nova Scotia in 1787 and the Canadas in 1793. The Constitutional Act of 1791, which established two colonies out of Quebec, Upper and Lower Canada, provided that one-seventh of each township be set aside for the maintenance 'of a Protestant clergy'. While the Act did not clearly state that such an arrangement was for the particular benefit of Anglicans, many then and later assumed that such was the case. The fact remained, however, that Anglicans were outnumbered not only by other Protestants, but most significantly by Roman Catholics. Roman Catholics were the majority in Lower Canada, Cape Breton, Prince Edward Island, close to one-half in Newfoundland and sizeable minorities in the other colonies. Thus Catholics were given limited recognition and rights—more than Catholics received in England at that time. The Constitutional Act allowed Catholics to vote in the Canadas as they could following 1789 in Nova Scotia. Other colonies were slower in granting such rights: Prince Edward Island only did so in 1830. Moreover, only in the Canadas could Catholics actually sit in the Assembly in this period. Imperial representatives granted only what they considered to be necessary to maintain social order. Equality was never their goal.

Similar principles underlay the establishment of new political structures in this period. Loyalists in the up-country argued forcefully for an elected assembly. Since it was costing Britain over £100,000 per year to administer that region and since the passage of the self-denying ordinance of 1778 had made it illegal for Britain to tax her colonies unless they had representatives in the British parliament—an unthinkable prospect—Imperial authorities willingly concurred. They would grant the region a locally elected assembly with the right to tax and the responsibility of meeting its own fiscal needs. In order to protect the up-country English from being assimilated by the French, Quebec was split into two colonies and an assembly was provided for each. While the franchise was quite liberal—even women could vote in Lower Canada until the 1830s—the powers of the Assembly were deliberately constrained. In the interests of social stability and control, assemblies were to be balanced by a colonial equivalent of a House of Lords, and, no less significantly, by a suitable representative of the ruling monarch. A proper governmental system had to include elements of the monarchy, the aristocracy and the democracy or common people.

Upper Canada received a Lieutenant Governor (and Lower Canada a Governor-General) who, acting as the Crown's representative, could withhold or reserve Royal assent to any legislation. He also appointed both the

Executive Council, whose appointees sat at his pleasure and offered him advice and appointed members of the legislative council, the 'upper' section of the bicameral legislature. Members of the legislative council numbered at least seven and, like members of the British House of Lords, were to hold their seats for life. The Assembly, the 'lower' section of the bicameral legislature, consisted of no more than sixteen representatives elected for no longer than four-year terms. To become law, legislation had to pass through both the elected assembly and the appointed legislative council. It had, next, to receive the Lieutenant Governor's assent, followed, within two years, by the Crown's confirmation. This was a complex structure, one which left considerable control in the hands of Imperial administrators in England and one which over time and with special focus on the powers of the two councils, especially their control of patronage, generated much debate and dissatisfaction in both the Canadas.

Colonial Economies

In economic affairs, colonies existed to serve the Imperial needs of the Mother Country. Some have called this mercantilism, a doctrine which allocated to colonies the role of supplying raw material to the heartland and receiving manufactured goods in return. The desire for Imperial self-sufficiency underlay the mercantilist doctrine. A series of Navigation Laws set controls to the colony's trading rights and restricted foreign nations from participating in colonial trade. This system spawned a particular type of colonial business elite. Throughout the Atlantic ports wholesale merchants became the 'co-ordinators of colonial commerce'. Within the protected free trade zone of the British Empire, colonial merchants shipped what they could and imported as much as possible. Following 1775, however, the Maritime economy survived primarily via British military spending and after 1783 from Loyalist compensation and half-pay pensions for officers (the latter two payments may have amounted to £ 475,000 between 1783 and 1800). In theory, the Imperial Government provided protection for the Maritimes in the West Indies trade. In practice those colonies, despite the beginnings of a shipbuilding industry in New Brunswick and some signs of commercial agriculture, could not generate the resources to satisfy West India's needs. As a result, in 1783 the British government allowed the United States to ship, in British boats, American commodities to the Indies. In these years, the Newfoundland fishery emerged as the brightest spot in the Atlantic economy.

At Quebec, despite the sudden existence of a new Imperial market, competition from British merchants and political bias, French fur traders/

merchants persisted at the level they had enjoyed before the Conquest until the late 1770s. They often worked as partners with British traders, who benefited from their superior understanding of and experience in the local trade. A second influx of British merchants, this time from the south following the passage of the Quebec Act and the American Revolution, tipped the scale firmly in favour of British control in this sector. The Quebec Act gave to the Quebec Governor control over the Ohio Valley and the northern interior. Albany fur traders, in competition with Montreal, took note and began to move their operations north to Montreal to more effectively deal with the new administrative order. The consolidation of the Montreal fur trade in the hands of the Scots-run North West Company by the end of the 1780s spelled the end of significant French managerial/mercantile involvement. Some have viewed this as the triumph of *laissez-faire* capitalism, of the British Protestant ethic, over French Catholic, Old World pre-capitalist values. The gradual nature of change up to the eve of the American Revolution does not, however, support such an argument. The fact is that those merchants who moved north after 1775 tended to be better capitalized than those *in situ* and British as well as French merchants fell victim to the new arrivals.

Because of their established contacts in England, British merchants gradually took control of the import-export trade. Yet even in this sector, some French merchants persisted successfully capitalizing on contacts with French Huguenot merchants in London. Although as with all generalizations, significant exceptions exist, one can conclude that the Conquest did tend to funnel French business activity into the countryside: Francophone merchants increasingly acted as the gatekeepers between rural and urban Quebec; Anglophone merchants performed a similar function between urban Quebec and the wider world. Some have seen this process as further example of the decapitation of the French bourgeois class and its replacement by a politically-connected British entrepreneurial group. If export activities are held to be the main determinants of economic growth, then, the Francophone bourgeoisie was indeed decapitated. Yet, such a perspective is unduly restrictive. It trivializes the significance of economic activity in non-export oriented business endeavour. Rural Francophone merchants would become the seedbed for the emergence in Lower Canada of a group of business-mind politicians who in the second quarter of the nineteenth century would help lead that colony into the era of steam, of industrial capitalism, of Confederation.

Mention has already been made of the merchants' emergence to power in the up-country region during the Revolutionary War. While one should be cautious about attributing too much power to this group—individuals within the merchant class failed far more often than they succeeded and the longevity of even those who enjoyed success was far from guaranteed—it is nevertheless the case that merchants, relative to their number in society, were substantially overrepresented in the law courts and land boards of this period. By the late 1780s, several powerful and interlocking mercantile ventures centred at Detroit, Niagara and Kingston and linked to old fur-trading families at Montreal and to military establishments at their respective localities, had emerged to positions of economic and, increasingly, administrative control. The Cartwrights of Kingston, the Hamiltons of Niagara and the Askins of Detroit all linked to the Todds and McGills of Montreal, headed the list. They played the leading role in adapting local institutions to the reality of local colonial conditions, especially to the reality of local economic conditions. Rarely learned in the complexities of British common law procedure, the merchants opted instead for informality, simplicity and economy. These attitudes reflected mercantile ideas in New York and, to an extent, in England too.

In addition to administering the courts, the merchants were the courts heaviest users. They tended to be the initiators of suits at the other end of which were often retired Loyalist officers struggling to maintain payments. Merchants also tended to centralize court activities at Niagara, Kingston and Detroit thus making it impossible for rural settlers to enjoy equal ease of access. The general result was the strengthening and solidifying of merchant endeavours throughout the old Mississauga territory.

The movement north of well capitalized and experienced fur traders from Albany ushered in an era of intense and bitter mercantile conflict in the far north-west. By 1779, Hudson's Bay traders complained that north of Lake Superior, Montreal 'pedlars are in every hold and corner where there are any Indians to be found'. Indeed by the 1790s it seemed that the fur trade had been firmly grasped by one enterprise operating out of Montreal, the North West Company, the result of a series of mergers of nine smaller competing partnerships. Despite the fact that the Hudson's Bay Company had set up fifty-nine posts in the western interior by 1798, the North West Company shipped about five times the value of fur each year. Competition between the two companies and by the mid-1790s a second Montreal-based enterprise, the XY Company, grew increasingly brutal, with bloodshed common. All three firms distributed copious amounts of alcohol in order to attract native traders. Violence intensified as a result.

The fight for fur also increased exploration of the far west. Members of the North West Company were particularly active in exploring overland routes to the Pacific. In 1790 Spain and Britain had stopped just short of armed conflict off the Pacific slope. By 1793, after several false starts, Alexander Mackenzie reached the Ocean via the Bella Coola River. The route, however, proved too arduous for the commercial fur trade. It took the renewed effort of two other North West traders, Simon Fraser and David Thompson, to establish a land-based fur trade on the Pacific slope, a feat they accomplished between 1805 and 1814.

II. FRAGMENTS OF EMPIRE: THE PATTERN OF ECONOMIC EXPANSION, 1791-1867

In 1790 some 250,000 people, scattered in isolated regional enclaves, marked the British presence in North America. Most lived east of the Ottawa River: 60 per cent in Lower Canada, 35 per cent in Atlantic Canada and 4 per cent in Upper Canada. By the middle of the nineteenth century the population had increased, due both to a high birth rate and a high-rate of immigration, to over 2.5 million. By 1851, 40 per cent lived west of the Ottawa River, most of whom lived in Upper Canada, 35 per cent resided in Lower Canada and 25 per cent in Atlantic Canada. By 1871, the population had increased at a slower rate to just over 3.7 million. Nor did the percentage distribution change dramatically: 2 per cent lived west of Ontario (Upper Canada); 43 per cent lived in Ontario; 30 per cent lived in Quebec (Lower Canada); and 25 per cent resided in Atlantic Canada.

Two waves of immigration followed that of the Loyalists: the first was a steady stream of Americans, often called late Loyalists, who moved north into the Maritimes, the Eastern Townships of Lower Canada and especially into Upper Canada in the years before the War of 1812. This was followed by a massive movement of people out of the British Isles. In England the end of the Napoleonic Wars in 1815 initiated an extended period of deflation, unemployment and depression. As a result, between 1815 and 1850, 960,000 set sail for British North America: about one-half stayed there, most of the rest continuing on to the United States. Of those who set sail, some 60 per cent were Irish, 20 per cent English and 20 per cent Scottish. Most immigrants left in search of better economic prospects. They hoped to find what was called 'a poor man's country'; a region where land was affordable and hard work would suffice to ensure at least a modest independence.

Were they successful? It is tempting to view the pioneer period with nostalgia, as an era somehow simpler, more stable and more orderly than our complex present. Such a perspective, while common, is unfortunate. It belittles the harsh realities of the living conditions which many British North American settlers encountered. It may well be that the move from the Old World to the New resulted in improved prospects for some. A closer look, however, suggests that for many others violence, poverty and harsh living conditions were the norm. Nor should this be surprising. One has only to recall the hierarchical social and political structure which existed in all of the BNA colonies at the close of the eighteenth century. In each of those colonies the power of the established elites touched the lives of the common settlers in, admittedly, uneven and often inconsistent ways. While that power could be at times evaded, it could never be completely ignored. This was even more the case in the economic sector. In each of the colonies, and in some more than others, an economic elite linked closely to Britain exerted great influence over the pace and character of economic growth. All did not benefit equally from economic development. Social and economic gradations were intense and commonplace. To 'make it', to succeed in British North America, one had to please the proper people. Birthplace, ethnicity, gender, colour and class counted and conditioned one's expectations, behaviour and rewards.

The degree to which the immigrants, their families and the families of the settlers already present in 1790 realized their aspirations is explored in the following section. While a central focus on the lived experience of the settlers is common, the section itself is organized on regional lines. This permits a clearer appreciation of regional differences especially in an era where economic, social and political links between the colonies were minimal. Eventually, these colonies came together in 1867 to form a nation called Canada. But to see the first sixty-seven years of the nineteenth century as an inexorable march towards confederation is to overlook established regional, economic and social distinctions. Put more positively, it is only by exploring those distinctions that one can come to understand the strengths and weaknesses of Confederation itself.

During the first two-thirds of the nineteenth century, staple exploitation, many historians have argued, dominated economic activity in British North America. The extraction and sale to external markets of fish, fur, timber and wheat both fuelled and set limits to economic growth. Mercantilist policies imposed by Great Britain, policies which discouraged economic diversification within British North America, encouraged staple extraction. Too great a reliance on the explanatory power of the staple/mercantilist perspective, however, leads to a blurring of regional differences and to an understating of human agency. In reality, colonial economies did develop at different rates in this era. Colonies within British North America were endowed with different sets of natural resources. Moreover within each colony local business elites had some influence (however bounded by material and Imperial constraints) over the pace and nature of economic growth.

Fur in the West, 1790-1869

If any region was dominated by the exploitation of one staple, the area which would become known as Western Canada stands out. Indeed for much of the period under review that region was governed by a fur trading company, the Hudson's Bay Company, with its headquarters in London, England. An examination of the western fur trade sheds light on the changing nature of the fur business in a pre-industrial era; underlines the variety of responses made to economic opportunities posed by the trade in fur; and unveils the bitter corporate rivalries that characterized early expansion and which belie the myth of a peaceful frontier. In short, such a study lays bare the nature of European expansion across Native territories in what was to become Canada's west.

Between 1800 and 1820 the North West Company (NWC) and the Hudson's Bay Company (HBC) vied for control of the western fur trade. This competition intensified during the era of the Napoleonic Wars, between France and Britain in Europe, and during the War of 1812, between Britain and the United States in North America. These wars disrupted traditional fur trade markets; made it difficult to hire employees at cheap wages and occasioned a sharp increase in the cost of provisions and trade goods. Of crucial importance of both companies, traditional stocks of beaver, the only fur which retained a high demand in Europe, also began to decline dramatically.

The Hudson's Bay Company reacted by undertaking a major managerial and structural reorganization. In many ways the HBC began to follow the lead of its larger rival, the NWC. A profit sharing system similar to that of the NWC was introduced. Traditionally the HBC had recruited employees from the Orkney Islands, off Scotland's northern coast; now the Company began to hire workers from the St. Lawrence parishes in the heart of its rival's domain. Secret plans to expand into the still fur rich and North West controlled Athabasca region, and to set up an agricultural colony at Red River, astride the NEC's main transport system, were set in motion. The father of the latter scheme, the Scottish peer, philanthropist, and HBC director, Lord Selkirk, saw the colony as a way to assist poor Scottish agriculturists, while the remainder of the HBC's board believed that the projected colony could provide cheap labour and food and help meet one of the original conditions of the Company's charter, that of western colonization.

Bloody competition ensued. New posts were built and new personnel hired. Battles broke out in the Red River colony which had been set up by some 200 settlers from Ireland and Scotland. When Selkirk's agent banned the export of pemmican—dried buffaloo meat supplied to the North West Company traders by Metis, or half-breed, hunters—the Metis, encouraged by the North West Company, engaged the colony's Governor, Robert Semple, in battle, killing him and twenty of his men. Bloody encounters also took place in the Athabasca region. 'Bully-boys' employed by both sides harassed natives and rival traders. The Nor'Westers adopted an official policy not to assist 'Hudson's Bay servants … in case of starvation'. One Nor'Wester expressed 'exultation' when 'no less than 15 men, 1 clerk with a woman and child died of starvation going up Peace River'. Both companies attempted to acquire furs destined for and prepaid by their rivals. Both suffered large financial losses due to depredation by the other. North West Company connected judges and sympathetic juries in Upper and Lower Canada consistently thwarted Selkirk's attempts to enlist legal help in what had become the waging of a private war for control of the North West fur trade.

Both sides differed large financial losses. Pressured by the Colonial office, the two companies reluctantly merged in 1821: the Hudson's Bay Company retained its name, but 32 of the 53 trading partners were old Nor'Westers. Of more importance, the merger ended Montreal's century long link to the fur trade. Provisions, goods and furs now flowed only through Hudson's Bay: 'the fur trade', lamented one old Nor'Wester, 'is forever lost to Canada'. Nevertheless the Hudson's Bay Company, as had the North West Company before it, continued to recruit poor peasants from 'voyageur parishes' in Lower Canada. At both the managerial and labourer levels, the Hudson's Bay Company benefited from the North West Company's experiences. At strategic moments, the Hudson's Bay Company appropriated some of the best elements of its rival's strategy and structure. Indeed, this was one key to the Hudson's Bay Company's success.

The Merger ended what George Simpson, soon to be the Company's main North American manager, termed the era of 'Prize fighting'. Economy and retrenchment followed: by 1825 operating posts numbered 45, down from 109 in 1821 and employees numbered 900 down from about 2000 at the time of the merger. Post activities became routinized and more centrally directed. While Chief Traders and post Factors did meet annually with Simpson at Red River, the latter had, one Chief Trader complained, 'everything cut and dry for us'. Although the profit sharing system remained, these men were increasingly treated less as partners and more as employees.

At the lower ranks, Simpson felt it was advisable "to have about an equal proportion of (Mixed-Blood, Irish and Scottish workers) which will keep up a spirit of competition and enable us to deal with them on such terms as may be considered necessary and proper." A racially mixed work force would, he hoped, weaken collective resistance and increase managerial control. There were, however, even in an era of monopoly, real limits to the control Simpson could achieve over his work force. While some Chief Traders believed that "[R]egular hours of work were as essential in the wilds as in business city marts and factories", such aspirations to clocklike efficiency were seldom realized. Natural rather than factory time conditioned work rhythms throughout the fur trade. Seasonal constraints set bounds to work possibilities. Moreover, much work occurred free of direct supervision: hunting, cutting and carting firewood, and transporting fur, for example. In this context, attempts to introduce factory type discipline met with limited success and significant opposition in the form of strikes and mutinies.[2]

Controlling Native employees proved particularly troublesome. For many Natives, like those who operated the transport brigades to York Factory, Company employment was not a necessity: traditional foraging, fishing and hunting, and for some, even farming, could and did provide viable alternatives. "'Tis a perfect plague," one Chief Factor lamented "...knowing that [they know] they have it in their power to distress you." Native trappers and traders, people who did not consider themselves employees, were even more difficult to control. Some historians have argued that the Company used credit to keep these trappers and traders on a tight leash. Yet it is more probably the case that Native traders had during the competitive era become used to credit giving (both rivals had willingly granted credit in their attempts to enlist Native support) and, in the face of HBC resistance, demanded its continuance. In fact, the existence of free land and free resources set severe constraints on the HBC's ability to control Native traders. Only when land and resources were securely under private control could wage labour be bought and sold and could credit make trappers and traders beholden to the HBC. One should not conclude, however, that Natives had the HBC on a string. The HBC did, after all, control provisions. Native desire for, or even dependence on, these provisions, gave to the HBC its power. The Company agreed to continue credit-giving in monopoly conditions because it could alter markups on provisions to compensate for poor of lazy hunters. Good hunters paid the debts of poor hunters. Only in competitive situations—i.e., when more than one company offered supplies—could credit be of economic benefit of Native traders.

Simpson also took steps to minimize the possibility of competition. He attempted to trap bare 'frontier' areas, like the Snake River country, south of the Columbia River. This tactic would, he hoped, discourage American

[2]Michael Payne, *The Most Respectable Place in the Territory,* Ottawa, 1989, 51-64.

trappers from proceeding north where he implemented a policy of selected conservation in, what would become, British Columbia and the prairies. This frontier policy sacrificed profits in order to protect more controlled and managed resources from outside competitors.

Effective on the coast, the policy enjoyed only mixed results in the Red River country. In 1836 the HBC had taken formal control of the small and struggling settlement at Red River. The Company virtually appointed the governing council; the local chief factor became the colony's governor; the Company exerted strong influence over the court system; and the settlers depended on the Company as an outlet for their produce. Red River seemed a company town *par excellence*.

At Red River, however, a potentially bicultural people resisted such dominance. French-speaking mixed-bloods were especially aggressive. They recalled with pride their battles in the competitive era. They were, in fact, essential to the colony's existence. They provided settlers with food from the buffalo hunt when crops failed; protected the settlement from Sioux attacks; manned the transportation system on which the fur traders depended; engaged in subsistence farming; and, increasingly traded freely in fur, resisting the Hudson's Bay Company's attempts to control them. In the process they affirmed and reaffirmed their own implicit claims to territorial suzerainty.

Many Metis seized the opportunity to trade with Americans at Pembina, seventy miles south of Red River. The HBC attempted to convict three 'free traders' in 1849, but the court, fearing open rebellion, acquitted all three. Throughout the 1850s American competition escalated backed by a network of rail and steamship lines which linked Pembina to New York and facilitated the swift acquisition of trade goods and the influx of itinerant competitors. In the face of this intense competition, the Company's charter, Simpson complained in 1857, was 'almost a nullity'. Moreover, as white settlers from the Canadas began to move westward in the late 1850s and early 1860s, Metis dissatisfaction escalated at Red River. Even English-speaking mixed-bloods, hitherto relatively peaceful and supportive of the HBC, began to engage in forms of civil disobedience. The HBC looked on, impotently, as rifts widened within the Red River community. In 1863, the Company's London directors, in fact, sold the corporation to a group of financiers more interested in land speculation than fur trading. In 1869 the Company sold much, but far from all, of its western land to the recently-created Dominion of Canada, thus ending yet another phase in the Europeanization of Western British North America.

Arrested Transition: The Economies of the Atlantic Region, 1790-1867

As in the west, staple extraction dominated the economy of the Maritime region. The export of fish, wood and coal provided the region with exchange to purchase food and manufactured imports from abroad. British mercantilist policy encouraged a form of enclave industrial development where supplies were imported and end products exported. Colonial inputs were discouraged. Economic linkages within the colonial region were difficult to facilitate. Merchants stood at the centre of this economy, an economy, as one historian has put it, "never … more than the sum of its constituent parts." Ironically, only at the level of labour could that economy be characterized as integrated. Many, if not most, miners, wood workers and fishers also farmed. Staple industry co-existed with farm enterprise. Occupational pluralism became a way of life for rural dwellers, a culture of work handed down from one family generation to the next.

The lumber industry emerged within the mercantile system. The closing of the Baltic, England's main source of timber, in 1807 by Napoleon forced England to institute a sliding protective tariff which guaranteed easy access for colonial timber. Although the Baltic opened after 1815, that preference was maintained until the early 1840s. New Brunswick's exports of ton timber increased from 5,000 tons in 1805 to 417,000 tons in 1825, averaging off to 200,000 tons annually until the 1840s. Commencing in the 1830s and continuing throughout the 1840s and 1850s, trade in lumber and deals to the United States gradually surpassed the export of ton timber to Great Britain, as the British began to dismantle its official policy of mercantilism.

In the early years of the nineteenth century, Saint John merchants extended lines of credit to numerous country storekeepers and brokers who, in turn, outfitted part-time lumberers. These men wintered in the woods and delivered their timber in the spring. By mid-century, several large companies dominated the timber sector. Wage labourers supplanted 'independent' contractors. The consolidation of timber operations in the hands of several wholesale merchants marked a step away from decentralized economic relations. Yet, at the same time, the wood workers toiled on a seasonal basis and depended on other jobs to survive the rest of the year. In this sense, the lumber industry remained nestled within and dependant upon a pre-industrial social and economic milieu. Moreover, throughout the pre-confederation era, the lumber sector experienced boom and bust swings dictated by external demand, swings so severe that even some of the wealthiest of lumber entrepreneurs fell victim to them.

The existence of significant shipbuilding in the Maritime region, might, at first glance, seem to belie the assertion that no integrated industrial development emerged in this period. Between 1815 and 1860, Prince Edward Island, New Brunswick and Nova Scotia manufactured 212 million tons of shipping, about half of which was exported to the United Kingdom. Yet the evolution of that industry stands as a central example of the ambivalent nature of Atlantic business enterprise, one which developed under the protective umbrella of the mercantile system. Colonial ship owners could sell their vessels duty free on the British market. They could sell their goods in a British market protected by preferential duties. By virtue of the Navigation Acts, which kept foreign shipping out of most colonial trade routes, they enjoyed privileges as general carriers. Small wonder that most major merchants in the important Atlantic ports were also major ship owners.

But few were shipbuilders. For most merchants, ships were adjuncts to a process of commercial exchange. They bought vessels from others to ship goods to and receive goods from others and to sell vessels themselves to others. Consistent with their main aim, merchants also encouraged, via tariff policies, the importing of as many inputs for boat building as possible. Had, for example, all metal imports for New Brunswick ships been manufactured in that province the value of output from the local metal sector would have increased by close to 25 per cent in 1871. The potential for shipbuilding to alter the local economic context was appropriated by merchants with their eyes on exchange, not production value. As well those who worked in the shipbuilding industry for the most part did so on a part-time basis. In this sense, occupational pluralism provided shipbuilders with a bank of cheap labour and little incentive to move towards a more integrated system of production.

Large coal deposits have often acted as catalysts for regional industrialization. Such was not the case in coal-rich Nova Scotia. In 1827, the British government granted the General Mining Association a sixty-year monopoly in Nova Scotia. By the late 1830s, its operations ranked as one of the largest concentrations of industrial workers and industrial investment in British North America: it employed 1,500 workers and had sunk $ 250,000 in investments into the colony. Yet the enterprise fitted well within the staple-focused, mercantile-managed colonial economy. If coal took Nova Scotia to the brink of industrialization in this era, it was industrialization of a truncated sort. Capital, technology, skilled workers and experienced managers were imported from the British Isles. Only unskilled labour was hired locally and, for them, coal mining was simply one of the several jobs needed to maintain a living. Little linkages or diversification occurred outside of export oriented coastal enclaves. Profits and products were exported. Not until the late 1850s could colonial entrepreneurs set up competing mines.

Between 1793 and 1815 international warfare undermined Newfoundland's migratory fishery. By 1820 most of the major fish merchants resided in St. John's, not in England. Large British firms, nevertheless, continued to dominate. The fishery also remained dependant on shifting external demand, growing international competition and the availability of the natural resource. Measured on a per capita basis, the export of fish fluctuated 'around a declining trend' for much of the nineteenth century.

Merchants took full advantage of this context. Many refused to pay cash for fish, preferring, instead, to remit 'in goods'. The so-called truck system—the payment for produce by high-priced goods—reduced real wages and exploited isolated outpost families, for whom few other economic alternatives, save migration, existed. In Nova Scotia, too, although fish was the primary export, fishers themselves were, according to one contemporary "the most wretchedly poor of any class in the whole province".

At mid-century, over one-half of all people in Nova Scotia and New Brunswick farmed. Some, especially those who settled earliest, profited from sales to lumbering camps and in some communities the local farmer, not the local merchant, stood at the top of the economic and social pyramid. Recent studies have emphasized the variety of farming conditions across the region. Most often, however, those who farmed did so on a part-time basis and lived within, in a social and economic sense, highly stratified communities. From these communities, owners of staple-exploiting enclave industries tapped a rural proletariat at minimal cost to themselves.

Railway construction is often equated with industrial growth. By 1866 only 218 miles of track had been constructed in New Brunswick and only 147 miles in Nova Scotia. In both communities, merchants had been divided over the need for railways. Many continued to invest in and profit from seaward activity—ships and shipping. Others, especially those most closely associated with coal mining in the later 1850s, pressed for railways. In both colonies these pressures led to state backing for some construction and in New Brunswick the state actually owned and operated one line. Those most involved in Maritime railway development were, as we shall see in a subsequent chapter, those most sympathetic to a larger political and economic union with the Canadas.

*   *   *

It is often alleged that control by an exterior state accounted for the pattern of economic development in this period. Yet it is interesting to note that even as British mercantile policies began to recede in the 1840s—timber preferences dropped dramatically in 1841, the Corn laws were ended in 1846 and the Navigation Law repealed in 1849—few maritime merchants moved to support local industrial production. In Nova Scotia and in New Brunswick, tariffs continued to facilitate the import of manufactured goods. In Nova Scotia, industrial growth lagged dramatically in this period of relatively weak external state control. In 1850 that colony's industrial output compared favourably with that of Upper Canada. Twenty years later it generated less than half as much industrial product and imported twice the per capita value of manufactured goods. In New Brunswick, as the mercantile system disintegrated, the dominant mercantile elite began to split: some continued to espouse traditional policies, others, pressured and influenced by a growing artisanal sector, pushed for, and in some cases, implemented tariffs to protect local production. Partly as a result, some economic diversification took place. Certainly in comparison to Nova Scotia, by 1870, New Brunswick boasted a more dynamic manufacturing base: while the former imported just under half of its manufactured goods, New Brunswick imported just under one-third of those items. The relative strength of mercantile elites is clearly only part of the explanation for this contrast in development. More historical work is needed on this question before a comprehensive explanation can be reached. Nevertheless, at this stage, one further point is appropriate: even within the Atlantic region, a region dominated by various forms of staple enterprise, differential development occurred. One must, therefore, be wary of generalizing about *an* Atlantic economy.

Lower Canada: Economic Change 1790-1867

A traditional historiography has emphasized the role played by urban, usually anglophone, entrepreneurs involved in externally directed, staple-dominated trades in setting the pace for economic growth. While there can be no doubting the importance of such entrepreneurial activity, this traditional focus is, none the less, too narrow. It overlooks the emergence and importance of locally oriented economic activity, business pursuits often promoted and managed by Francophone entrepreneurs resident in smaller rural centres. Rural-urban or city-country economic interrelations went far towards influencing economic and business development in Lower Canada in the years leading up to Confederation.

Rural Enterprise: 1790-1867

As in other BNA colonies, the large majority of nineteenth century Lower Canadians lived in rural areas. As late as 1871 one-half of all per capita commodity income came from the rural sector. Yet, it is often argued that the rural economy was a troubled one throughout much of the pre-confederation era. Lower Canadian wheat production did decline: at the turn of the century it represented up to 70 per cent of field crop output; by 1844 it represented less than 15 per cent. Because, over 80 per cent of rural dwellers were French, some scholars have suggested that poor French Canadian farming habits contributed to an agricultural crisis. More careful analysis has demonstrated that variations in output within English-French farming groups were more dramatic than any differences between them. Infestations of wheat midge and the Hessian fly coupled with increased competition from Upper Canada's richer agricultural land are more persuasive reasons for declining wheat production. Indeed, in this period, the north-east United States as well as BNA's north-east was being overshadowed by production from a developing western interior.

The notion of rural crisis has itself been reviewed critically. The decline of wheat production relative to total crop output is, some historians suggest, only one side of the story. Transformation and diversification rather than decline marked Lower Canadian farm output. Increased production of potatoes, corn, tobacco, barley, peas and hemp reflected 'modernization', a rational response by French Canadian habitant farmers to changing market opportunities. Studies of peasant wills suggest that average habitant household wealth increased in the first thirty-five years of the nineteenth century. Regional studies have shown that a majority of farmers produced for markets; they were, in other words, consumer not subsistence oriented. Many habitants, in fact, loaned as well as borrowed money. These studies have also pointed to significant rural stratification in Lower Canada. All habitants were not equal. Economic growth and social differentiation took place in rural regions.

Yet, perhaps, the most significant finding of recent rural studies is the perpetuation at the top of the economic and social pyramid of a traditional rural elite: the church, the seigneurs and rural merchants. The question then becomes to what extent did the continuance of a traditional elite, especially accompanied by the old seigneurial rights and land-holding structure, stand in the way of swifter economic development. For many historians, the answer is that seigneurs and the Catholic Church blocked capitalistic economic development. The transition from a subsistence peasant household production to a more commercial/mercantile and even industrial system of production occurred, it is argued, more slowly and unevenly in Lower, than in Upper Canada, due to the persistence of a 'feudal' elite.

Most rural Lower Canadians did live on seigneuries. And seigneurs did take advantage of their rights, increasing their rents and dues by some 36 per cent between 1790 and 1831. Even seigneurs like the leader of reform-minded political party, Louis Joseph Papineau, did not hesitate to take his settlers to court for non-payment of dues. Increasingly in the nineteenth century the seigneurial system benefited one group at the expense of a larger group. Yet the group who benefited was not all of a piece. As early as 1800, some two-thirds of all seigneurs were of bourgeois origins and half of them were English. Many of these men (and some women) conceived of their seigneuries as more than simply rent producing territories. Some established what have been called industrial villages on their seigneuries. Barthélemy Joliette, to give only one example, operated a distillery, flour, saw, shingle, carding and fulling mill complex at a village he called, appropriately enough, Industrie! In the late 1840s, he even built a twelve-mile railway to transport his products to market.

Enterprise such as this provided opportunities for part-time artisanal labour from coopers, carters and blacksmiths and thereby acted as spurs for economic diversification in rural areas. In fact, as early as 1831 about 12 per cent of those who lived in the St. Lawrence seigneurial lowlands did not farm. This represented about 40,000 people, nearly equal to those who lived in the three largest cities, Montreal, Quebec and Trois Riviérès. Some 1,300 units of production (if a grist and saw mill operated in the same building, each was counted separately) existed in 1831 and this number had doubled by 1851.

Clearly, the rural economy of the seigneurial lowlands encompassed much more than farming. The somewhat diversified structure of that economy followed a pattern similar to that of some European countries and of neighbouring New England where decentralized industrial growth preceded full scale industrialization. Following 1850 Lower Canada's agricultural sector diversified in a way similar, as we shall see, to that of Upper Canada. Railway development and the Reciprocity Treaty of 1854 with the United States (a trade treaty which facilitated the free exchange of a wide range of natural products) sparked trade in cattle, horses, butter, cheese, wool and sawn lumber. Yet Lower Canada's total agricultural output lagged relative to Upper Canada's. By 1870 income per Lower Canadian (the Quebec) farm was only about two-thirds of the average Upper Canadian (then Ontario) farm. The relative lack of cash available to Lower Canadian farm households may indeed have negatively affected the rate of rural economic diversification and industrial growth. Industry was much more prevalent in rural Upper Canada and that industry, by almost any indice, out performed its Lower Canaditan counterpart. A richer agricultural sector created a more dynamic local market for the consumption of manufactured items. By 1870 Upper Canada/Ontario's lead in industrial output and diversification over Lower Canada/Quebec had been established. It was a lead which held constant for over the next half a century.

As in the Maritimes, British preferential duties provided a major impetus to the export of Lower Canadian timber and lumber. Between 1805 and 1810, shipping out of the port of Quebec, the major export point for lumber products on the St. Lawrence, increased from 170 to 661 vessels and tonnage increased fivefold. Tariff reductions in the 1820s and 1840s did not seriously affect this trade. Not until the 1870s did an era of sustained decline in the British squared timber trade begin. By the late 1850s a second forestry enterprise, trade in sawn lumber to local and American markets exceeded in value that of the squared timber sector. By that decade, more trees remained available for cutting into planks, deals and boards than for squared timber. For over seventy-five years Lower Canada/Quebec's export sector was dominated by forestry products.

As in the Maritimes, many of those who worked in the woods did so on a part-time basis. One Lower Canadian lumber entrepreneur explained to a Parliamentary Committee in 1821 that only a 'very few' worked full-time in the forestry business. Most farmed in the summer. "[F]requently many farmers procure a small quantity [of wood] which he exchanges for rum and clothes and provision, and all the necessaries that he requires, with the merchant, who, in the country, retails out different things which are imported into Canada...."[3] Lumber merchants such as William Price took full advantage of his workers. Employees were paid in vouchers or tokens redeemable only at the company's store or head office. If they were ill too often they were fined five shillings per day. Work days extended from "dawn until nightfall: the men must", Price's manager instructed a foremens, "leave the yard before daybreak in order to be at their site as soon as it is light enough to work, and they shall not leave the site until it is too dark to continue." Price, who controlled immense timber reserves and the best mill sites in the Saguenay and Lake St. Jean region of Quebec, also did his best to discourage the development of any economic endeavour not firmly tied to his enterprise. The attempt by a concerned Oblate priest to establish an agricultural colony outside of Price's control was thwarted when Price successfully appealed to the priest's superiors for his recall. One historian characterized this episode as but one example of the tactics used by the "champions of clerical-capitalist collusion in the Saguenay".

Some rural regions for a time developed within an business environment of farm and forest. For, very few of these areas, however, did much mixed enterprise result in sustained development. Rather systematic exploitation of forests with little thought for the region's future bequeathed to local colonists a heritage of not much more than bare subsistence.

[3]Richard Reid, ed., *The Upper Ottawa Valley to 1885*, Toronto, 1900, 87.

Urban Economies

The Staple thesis with its emphasis on export oriented production would not have predicted that much rural enterprise was locally oriented and exhibited significant diversification. For similar reasons, the staple thesis fails to capture the nature of urban development in this period. Montreal, for example, did not suffer following the decline of the fur trade. Rather craft industries, small manufacturing, construction, sawmilling and shipbuilding emerged. Between 30 and 40 per cent of urban household heads were crafts-workers in the pre-1841 era. Women, who represented 25 per cent of the urban work force in 1841 (and one-third in 1871) worked in the leather and needle trades and as prostitutes, teachers, domestics, nurses and innkeepers.

Local and regional markets attracted British as well as French merchants. The Bank of Montreal, which commenced operations in 1817 and was chartered in 1822 is a case in point. British import-export merchants, men with extensive international contacts, often forged in the fur trade era, dominated the Board of Directors. Indeed, before 1835 only 10 per cent of directors were Francophones. Yet the bank did underwrite local commodity production as well as shipbuilding, distillery and construction activity, loaning to Francophone and Anglophone businessmen. Many of the Francophone *petite bourgeoisie,* however, felt overlooked by Lower Canada's dominant bank and, accordingly, founded six 'French' banks between 1835 and 1875, which, by the latter year commanded assets of some eighteen million dollars. Yet even those banks reflected the complexity of Montreal's and Lower Canada's business community: only seven of the twelve founding directors of the Banque de Peuple, for example, were French and Bank's manager was American.

Being certainly significant financial institutions, the French banks were smaller than their English counterparts. They also tended to be more locally and regionally oriented, whereas the operations of most English banks tended to a provincial and after Confederation national orientation. In part, this reflects a structure which began to evolve following the Conquest when Francophone businessmen began to focus more on local trade while British merchants appropriated the export sector. Before 1841, in both Quebec and Montreal, the majority of merchants and general business people were English. Only in the area of law were Francophones better represented. Moreover, in this period 75 per cent of government salaries, 80 per cent of government pensions and 99 per cent of government contracts went to Anglophones. Clearly ethnicity conditioned one's chances of succeeding within Lower Canada's evolving urban economy.

Canal and railway construction favoured Montreal over all of its Lower

Canadian urban rivals. By 1871 Quebec possessed about 1,235 kilometres of railway but almost none ran on the North Shore, an area that Quebec city considered to be its hinterland. The Grand Trunk, the largest railway in Upper and Lower Canada, reflected Montreal's interests: it tied that city to the developing Upper Canada and led directly to increased trade in sugar, tea, coffee, cotton and hardware. Similarly, the initiatives of those who adhered to the dreams of the Empire of the Saint Lawrence, the notion that Montreal could dominate the trade of not simply Upper Canada but of the American midwest as well—one of the reasons for the early promotion of the Grand Trunk Railroad itself—had little to offer to Quebec City. The construction of the Lachine Canal in the late 1840s did not assist in the realization of that dream. It did, however, result in increased hydraulic power, a potential quickly exploited by Montreal entrepreneurs. By 1871 forty-four industrial enterprises abutted the canal.

Outside of Montreal, Quebec City, Sherbrooke and Hull, little significant manufacturing occurred in Lower Canada by 1871. Three-quarters of Lower Canada's urban dwellers lived in Montreal and Quebec in 1871 and those two cities accounted for 52 per cent (Montreal, alone, counted for 43 per cent!) of the province's total value of industrial output. This stands in marked contrast to the pattern of development in Upper Canada where the two largest cities, Toronto and Hamilton, contained under 25 per cent of the province's urban population in 1871 and generated only 18 per cent of the province's total industrial output. This contrast reinforces the point raised in the analysis of the rural economy: Lower Canada's relatively underdeveloped rural agricultural regions did not provide as rich a local base on which to develop a dispersed and diversified industrial economy.

The role played by the continuance of the seigneurial system and its so-called 'feudal' elite in the context of this relatively slow transition, is, however, less clear. Agricultural growth was hampered more by poor land and harsh climate than by system of tenure and taxes. Yet economic prerogatives did accrue more to some than others. Even after the abolition of seigneurial tenure in 1854, the traditional elite continued to enjoy a favoured position: the government liberally indemnified seigneurs for the loss of seigneurial rights; habitants could purchase land, but only at an upset price few could afford; as late in 1935, 60,000 Quebec farmers continued to pay a rent to the last seigneur's heirs. The cancelling of all hidden dues did facilitate increased commercial and industrial activity, but such development continued for the most part firmly in the hands of those accustomed to control. In a sense, a form of gentlemanly capitalism, not unlike that which emerged in Great Britain in the nineteenth century, where much commercial and some industrial enterprise developed under the control of traditional land-owning elites, characterized rural development in Lower Canada. The persistence of a traditional social structure did not preclude all economic change, growth and diversification. It may well have contributed, however, to a more imbalanced and uneven rate of growth.

Upper Canada

On average, Upper Canada possessed better agricultural land than her sister colonies to the east. The export of agricultural and wood products, the output of staple industries, certainly proved important to the colony's development. Yet that economy was far from staple dominated. Although often ignored by historians, the colony's buoyant local market facilitated significant commercial-industrial growth.

The Rural Economy

Most Upper Canadians farmed for a living. As late as 1870, farm output comprised slightly less than 60 per cent of the province's per capita commodity income. As we have already noted, average income per farm exceeded that for Lower Canadian and Maritime farmers. Diversification of farm output commenced at an early stage of the colony's history: between 1819 and 1822 one farmer recorded in his diary that he produced 39 different crops on his farm! A dynamic local (as opposed to export-directed) economy facilitated the production and sale by farmers of firewood, pork, hides, hay, ashes, as well as wheat. Fluctuation in external demand for wheat did not lead directly to boom and bust in the colony's economy (a scenario which a staple model would predict.) While wheat was a major cash crop, its cultivation in 1803 required only 50 per cent of the land under tillage, and the export portion took up only 20 per cent of tilled land. Moreover, lumber products rivalled wheat as export earners: the value of timber and wood exports from the St. Lawrence-Great Lakes region equalled in value wheat and flour exports between 1815 and 1840.

The dismantlement of the mercantile system in the 1840s did not adversely affect Upper Canada's growth. By 1850 at least half of Upper Canada's wheat 'export' went to other British North American colonies. The local economy absorbed significant output from the lumber sector. The 1854 Reciprocity Treaty with the United States facilitated trade in a wide range of natural products, a trade flow which had commenced before the Treaty and which continued after the Treaty's abrogation in 1866. Agricultural diversification intensified: by 1871 wheat comprised less than one-quarter of tilled land; mixed farming, dairy and livestock production assumed increased importance.

A study of farm income in 1861 has concluded that most farm families could live adequately without recourse to off-farm work; only 16 per cent of Upper Canada's farms produced less than they consumed. Moreover, the older the farmer the more land he owned and tilled. These findings stand in dramatic contrast to the situation in the Maritimes and Lower Canada. For those who could afford to acquire land, farming in Upper Canada offered a reasonable return. Yet, it should be noted, farming was far from a quick route to wealth. In 1861 most farmers owned more acres than they tilled. Increasing the amount of acreage farmed was a slow labour intensive process. As agricultural ladder may indeed have been in place, but it took generations to ascend to the upper rungs. And for all those who persisted and succeeded, many others dropped out. Even in the wheat-rich of Peel County, 62 per cent of all freeholders there in 1861 had left by 1871. Transiency marked even relatively wealthy rural regions, where some moved on 'picked', as one lamented, 'as bare as a bird's ass'.

The Commercial Economy

For much of the period under review, merchants stood at the centre of Upper Canada's economy. A system of long credit, settled in terms of goods and/or cash, underlay rural enterprise. Local merchants obtained goods on twelve month credit from urban wholesalers. Up to roughly the 1850s urban wholesalers practised a general business in order to protect themselves from fluctuation in any particular commodity and imported, generally from Great Britain, on a similar twelve month credit basis. Rural and urban merchants in Upper Canada, while vulnerable to bankruptcy, were none the less better off than the farmers on whom they depended for business. Yet their control was less than that exercised by Atlantic region merchants. Prices were sensitive more to general market conditions than to the exercise of local arbitrary exploitation. Competition made it very difficult to exercise such control: by 1846 at least 160 Upper Canadian villages possessed two or more stores. Itinerant hawkers and pedlars fanned out across the colony. Wholesalers competed in urban centres. Farmers did not hesitate to shop around.

If constricted, merchant power was none the less formidable. Many amassed large lots of land: the Baby and Askin families, for example, long time fur traders and merchants, owned about two-thirds of the land patented by speculators in the Western District of Upper Canada in 1815. Merchants dominated the colony's major financial institution, the Bank of Upper Canada. From the outset, they sat on the appointed legislative and executive councils, the presumed preserve, it will be recalled, of the gentry. As in Lower Canada, a form of gentlemanly capitalism characterized early Upper Canadian growth, or as one contemporary critic complained, 'a closed borough' *modus operandi* controlled economic affairs. A relatively small number of patrician/ merchants promoted canal construction in the 1820s, founded banks and even attempted to, in the 1830s, underwrite railroad development.

By the 1830s it was becoming increasingly difficult for a few to dominate. Developing urban places like Hamilton, Toronto, London, Cobourg, Port Hope, Kingston and Port Stanley vied for trade and economic power. From the 1830s onwards, merchants dominated city councils. Paralleling a similar development in England, the municipal sate offered local merchants opportunities to expand and consolidate local economic power. Elected politics at the provincial level reflected the growth of regionally focused business elites. Before 1830, just under two-thirds of members of the house of assembly had been farmers. Those elected in the 1830s who pursued only a commercial business career outnumbered by a two to one margin those who only farmed. While most Upper Canadians farmed, their political leaders were fast becoming urban oriented, businessmen on the make.

This trend intensified in the 1850s. By 1852 the government had put in place financial legislation which facilitated large scale borrowing abroad. Municipal governments and railroad corporations were allowed to borrow with the backing of the provincial government. Thanks in part to this enabling legislation over 1,400 miles of track was laid down in Upper Canada in the 1850s. The Great Western and the Grand Trunk roads designed to link American routes on the eastern seaboard and New York State with Michigan lines to Chicago, accounted for just under 60 per cent of that mileage.

From the outset the provincial government assumed it would never have to exercise its role as guarantor. Events dictated otherwise. By 1859, acting under the Municipal Loan Fund Act, business leaders in twenty Upper Canadian centres had borrowed 7.3 million dollars: some 1.2 million dollars of which was overdue. By the early 1860s both Toronto and Hamilton had amassed three million dollar debts outside of government guarantees. In all cases, the provincial government had to take steps to save those municipalities from bankruptcies. In the wake of this borrowing, municipalities curtailed urban services, cutting back on clean water, sanitation, social assistance and fire protection expenditures, thus lowering the quality of life, especially for the urban poor, in this era.

Railway companies also defaulted on government-backed loans. An amount of one hundred million dollars was invested in Canadian railways in the 1850s, seventy million of which went to Upper Canada. By the late 1850s, the colony's three largest railroads petitioned the government for relief. By the end of the decade, about 50 per cent of government revenue went to meet interest on debt due mostly on account of railway borrowings. By that time government and private finances were well on the way to being indistinguishable.

In the 1850s both the state and large private businesses were grappling with dramatic structural change. Both railways and the government were beginning to professionalize and systematize their respective operations: to apply the method of the counting house and factory to their respective spheres. Managerial change and the implementation of a more bureaucratic procedure proceeded in a symbiotic, interconnected and parallel manner in the public and private spheres. Indeed, British investors were swift in sending to the Canadas skilled British managers who, the investors hoped, would upgrade managerial control and operating systems. The Canadian state acted in a complementary fashion. The government passed legislation which pushed railroad management in the direction of more centralized and regimented control of labour and general operations. For a time the state's railway board employed a small staff of engineers to inspect and upgrade railway company procedures in these areas. The state also directly managed the reconstruction of one bankrupt railway and set general operating procedures for that road the following twenty years.

It is important to emphasize that the mid-century was significant transitional period in terms of the restructuring of state and business enterprise. The push for development capital emerged from within the colony and paralleled similar initiatives from nearby American states. The financial rules were set, to a surprising extent, by local political and merchant promoters. Once foreign capital reached the colony, British financiers held only a very limited control over its expenditure. While many local merchants and businessmen profited personally, they were unable to manage effectively capital expenditures during the construction era and managerial processes during the early operational period. Railway accidents were common and labour strife escalated in this period. A combination of state labour legislation, managerial regulation and on-site inspection and the importing of British managers helped to stabilize matters. Internal state procedures were also reorganized to better meet the demands of an emerging industrial sphere and an increasingly complex international financial structure. The beginnings of an independent commercial policy, signalled by the implementation of a tariff structure that did not simply or solely favour British imports was part and parcel of these changes. So, too, was the setting up of an internal audit system. In all of this, the state did not act as an independent broker, balancing the competing interests of labour, business and general populist concerns within the contours of market economy. In the pre-Confederation era, the business sector (while often divided amongst itself) had few real rivals to contest its political influence. Local politicians and entrepreneurs (who were often, but not always the same people) along with British merchant bankers were, in effect, exploring new terrain. Out of that exploration emerged a more modern bourgeois state, one which predated and provided the context for Confederation.

Railways contributed to industrial growth. They created demand for manufactured items and facilitated the expansion of local markets. In fact, Upper Canadian railways became themselves effective industrial producers: two of the largest three industrial companies in Upper Canada/Ontario in 1870 were railways. They were the first large integrated—manufacturing, transportation, communication—industrial corporations to operate in the Canadas. In 1861 the Great Western employed over 2,000 people and the Grand Trunk over 3,100. Railway were at the vanguard of managerial and corporate change. There were, however, in the Canadian context, very few imitators. Only six of the largest sixty industrial firms were incorporated in 1870. Most were partnerships or sole proprietorships and, in many of those cases, kin relations played significant roles in managing the company. This traditional organizational structure was required in an era where transport and communications made it necessary to trust people you knew in running farflung business enterprises. By 1860, however, railway and telegraph lines rendered such reliance less necessary. Centralized corporate management was now more possible, yet such structures emerged only slowly.

Nor by 1870 had many industries followed railways into the age of steam. Only 26 per cent of all establishments used other than hand power and of those only 10 per cent used steam. Those that did were certainly the largest and combined they employed about one-half of one province's workers and produced about three-quarters of value added output. Yet all industrial sectors contained a mix of craftshops, power-driven factories and manually-generated manufacturers. By 1870 Upper Canada/Ontario's total industrial production was about 50 per cent greater than that of its closest rival, Lower Canada/Quebec. Yet if that province's industrial structure presaged its future, it also exhibited many links to its past. It was truly on the cusp of the industrial revolution.

III. ELITE RULE AND THE EMERGENCE OF DISSENT: POLITICS AND POWER, 1791-1840

For much of the period before 1840, factions within the upper ranks of society vied for political control in Britain's North American colonies. Most political struggle centered on small group of elitist leaders. Yet in all colonies, dissent, often local in origin and sporadic in behaviour, tested the limits of elitist control. In two of those colonies—Upper and Lower Canada—that dissent erupted into open rebellion before 1840.

Upper Canada

Upper Canada's political elite represented an uneasy balance between commerce and administration, and British ideals and North American practice. The colony's first Lieutenant Governor, John Graves Simcoe, had slowly realized that to govern at all he had to rely on commercial men of affairs. There were too few qualified alternatives. Merchants and bureaucrats had to coexist. And so they did. Robert Hamilton, a wealthy merchant in the Niagara region owned one of the finest homes in Upper Canada. Simcoe supped there at ease. Social life in tiny York, the colony's capital, was an incestuous round of balls and suppers. Bureaucrat's wives vied to control the social calendar in the hopes of advancing their husband's fortunes. Sixty per cent of the major appointments made at York between 1803 and 1812 went to members of already established families. A strong proprietary attitude surrounded the issue of office-holding—one could own and bequeath such offices. Such displays of wealth and power led to social closure. Intermarriage, liberal land grants, proper education and conspicuous consumption helped both to solidify the emerging commercial/bureaucratic elite and to separate it from the mass of Upper Canada's settlers.

Yet the elite did not have matters all their own way. Even in the 1790s, elitist political leaders could complain that many of the assembly's rural-backed members "have violent levelling principles which are totally different from the ideas I have educated with". When, at the turn of the century, Imperial administrators, in an attempt to promote a more consolidated settlement process, raised land settlement fees (and in the process padded their own pockets), rural based discontent increased and found a leader in Robert Thorpe, an Anglo-Irishman who was a newly appointed puisne judge of the Court of King's Bench. Frustrated when he did not receive the vacant chief justiceship, Thorpe began to criticize what he termed the oppressive actions of a clique at the centre of power. While on his judicial rounds in the central and western regions, he encouraged jurors to comment on civil affairs. Their criticisms reflected the frustrations of small farmers, Loyalists, and perhaps Irish settlers at current land policy and a perceived Scots hegemony, visible both locally (Hamilton at Niagara) and at York. A duel resulting from one court case over which Thorpe presided in the Niagara District saw a representative of the local Scots 'shopkeeper aristocracy'—as Thorpe labelled them—kill the Irish lawyer and M.L.A. William Weekes.

Thorpe promptly moved into Weekes' house and, notwithstanding his position on the court, successfully contested the vacant seat. In June 1807, another Irishman allied to Thorpe, Joseph Willcocks, fired from his position as Sheriff of the Home District for "general and notorious bad conduct", moved to Niagara and set up Upper Canada's first opposition newspaper, the Upper Canadian *Guardian*.

The new paper was too much for York's bureaucrats and indeed for Niagara's 'shopkeepers'. Thorpe, despite incendiary language, always counselled loyalty to the Crown and never incited rebellion. The merchants and bureaucrats viewed Thorpe as a troublemaker, closing ranks against what one termed a group of 'desperados'. They began, with the assistance of the Scots merchant and postmaster at York, William Allan, to open Thorpe's mail. They finished by having the imperial government suspend Thorpe and the frustrated ex-justice left Upper Canada late in 1807.

Was this a tempest in the proverbial teapot? Were York's administrators merely paranoid? Did the Thorpe affair reflect anything more than a falling out amongst the bureaucratic elite? Certainly petty jealousies and paranoia coloured many of these events. Yet Thorpe also acted as a touchstone for discontent simmering across Upper Canada. Despite the elite's attempts to downplay it, dissent did not disappear with Thorpe's departure. The *Guardian*, lamented one member of the elite, seemed to be in every household in the western district. The composition of the assembly gradually reflected this dissatisfaction. By 1812, under the loose leadership of Willcocks, a broadly reform-oriented group composed of eleven of the assembly's twenty-three members generally voted together, arguing for legislative control of money bills, lower salaries for bureaucrats, lower assessment rates, and easier land regulations.

People voiced dissent through other than simply political forms and institutions. Despite the heavily centralized nature of the court structures and despite the control of the position of local justices of the peace by merchants, settlers did use the courts in their own ways. After 1800, in the eastern (Kingston) district, juries composed of small landowners increasingly overturned judicial decisions or provided lenient sentences in case of conviction, continuing to do so despite being fined by the court for unpalatable decisions. Religion also provided a forum for popular discontent. Methodists, probably the colony's largest religious group, not only resented official preferences given to Anglicans in matters of land, but also seethed at restrictions on their right to conduct marriages. Methodism provided a common meeting ground for Upper Canadians who lived in the rural areas. The communal religious experience enhanced self-worth and helped to create an identity separate from the merchant bureaucratic elite who lived in Kingston, York, and Niagara. Since most Methodists and indeed most rural settlers were from the United States, Methodism provided a focus for a community that, at least potentially, spanned the border. Not surprisingly, Upper Canada's elite looked askance at such goings on. Methodists were regularly unseated when elected to the assembly, simply on the basis of their religion. Suggestive of the links between Methodism and reformism in these early years, Willcocks and his supporters consistently fought motions to unseat Methodist ministers following 1807.

The War of 1812, fought by England and her North American colonies against the United Sates, dealt a solid blow to the emerging Upper Canadian reform movement. Confrontation seemed unlikely following 1794 when Britain ceded her western forts to the United States. The situation changed with the renewal of French-Britain conflict in the early nineteenth century. Believing that the Americans supported France, Britain attacked an American frigate, the *Chesapeake,* in 1807. Britain also began to arm and increase supply allotments to western natives who were fast losing land to the expanding American nation. Harassed on the seas, frustrated on the frontier and enticed by what appeared to be 'easy pickings' in Upper Canada—most of whose settlers had been born in the United States and who, American leaders believed, were secretly awaiting deliverance from British rule—the United States declared war in June 1812.

Senior civil and military personnel shared the perception of a disloyal Upper Canadian population. General Isaac Brock correctly worried more about 'the disposition of the people' than the enemy. The Upper Canadian militia were at least as poorly trained and equipped as their American counterparts. The Assembly consistently blocked attempts to suspend *habeas corpus* and impose a form of military rule. Natives evinced reluctance to provide unequivocal support. Dramatic early victories led by Brock at Detroit and Queenston Heights (where he lost his life) temporarily eased local dissent. The sacking of York in April 1813, however, led to criticism of British tactics. Governor-General Sir George Prevost responded by appointing agents to root out traitors. Many reform leaders, fearing the strengthening of appointed government agencies at the expense of the elected assembly, left the colony, some to fight on the American side.

Poor American tactics—they failed to follow up victories on Lake Erie and never massed an effective attack on Kingston astride the communication lifeline to Montreal—led to a standoff. The Treaty of Ghent, on December 24, 1814, set up commissions to settle naval armaments on the Great Lakes, Maritime fishing rights and sundry boundary disputes. While the war hit

Upper Canada more dramatically than the other colonies, not all Upper Canadian regions were affected equally. The Niagara area suffered much damage and economic dislocation, but the York region profitted from a growing trade in wheat and foodstuffs. As important, York's bureaucratic elite extended its control via the civil-military presence in Upper Canada. Kingston suffered little and profitted substantially from both a legal trade with Lower Canadian suppliers and an illicit trade with American merchants throughout the conflict. Yet cross-border connections tended to be with Americans of conservative Federalist persuasions. Aware that the War was sweeping away the Federalists as a strong political force in the United States, the Kingston elite, like its counterpart at York, determined that the same would not occur in Upper Canada. The war stiffened the elite's resolve to create, on the British North American frontier, a Tory fortress impervious to extreme democratic influence.

A show trial in May 1814 at Ancaster near the Niagara frontier signalled that intent. Dressed in regal robes, judges indicted seventy-one traitors and sentenced seventeen to be hung, drawn and quartered, before finally pardoning nine and hanging eight. This blend of majesty, mercy and brutality characterized the elite's tactics. Few were executed in Upper Canada, but hanging was always a public spectacle.

Between 1818 and 1828 the so-called Family compact, a closely-knit Tory elite with connections in all regions of the colony, gained control of the executive and legislative councils. Their activities alienated many Upper Canadians who, by the end of the 1820s, began to coalesce as "His Majesty's faithful opposition", a phrase only just current in parliamentary circles at London, England. Several issues underlay reform's emergence. In 1817, Americans born in the United States after 1783 were stripped of the vote and the right to own land in Upper Canada. The so-called Alien question simmered throughout the 1820s, as well it might give the large number of American-born living in the colony. In 1822, one American-born was denied the right to sit in the Assembly. Enraged, opponents of the Tories bypassed the Lieutenant Governor and, for the first, but not last time, petitioned directly to England for justice. Much to the Tories' shock, redress was granted and the American-born received equal civil rights.

Even as this directive reached the colony, the powerful local Anglican Bishop, John Strachan, aggressively pushed the prerogatives of the Anglican or what he hoped would be the state church. Already in control of school textbook selections, he lobbied for an Anglican-controlled colonial university. Reformers counteracted his blatantly false statistics on Anglican numeric strength and Methodist weakness by the sending of yet another petition to

England (this one with eight thousand signatures) decrying a 'clerico-political aristocracy'.

A series of other 'outrages' escalated passions. A fiery Scots reformer, Robert Gourlay, canvassed Upper Canadians encouraging them to speak out about all grievances. When Strachan and others attempted to silence him, he called the Bishop a 'monstrous little fool of a person'. Authorities stepped in, and following an eight month term in jail, Gourlay was banished for disturbing the colony's 'tranquility'. Francis Collins, a reform editor was imprisoned for a year on trumped up libel charges initiated by John Beverly Robinson, the powerful Attorney General and the elite's chief spokesperson in the assembly. Another reform editor, William Lyon Mackenzie, had his printing press dumped into Lake Ontario by sons and law students of the elite. Led by a local sheriff and two local magistrates, a band of black-faced and sheet-covered men tarred and feathered a prominent reform opponent.

The elite itself seemed impervious to prosecution. Those involved in the printing press escapade escaped criminal charges and had the civil damages exacted against them paid by public subscription. The ring leaders of the tar and feather incident not only evaded prosecution but were also freed from a separate brutal rape charge. The two magistrates were even appointed to a higher office by the Lieutenant Governor.

Not surprisingly, reform swept the 1824 and 1828 elections. Yet reform ranks lacked unity. Moreover, rural society at large seemed ready still to accept a traditional leadership provided that it could demonstrate acceptable moral standards. A new Lieutenant Governor, Sir John Colborne, took step to do just that. Non Family Compact members received patronage and some social and economic reforms were implemented. In the end, however, Colborne represented only the proverbial calm before the storm.

If violence simmered in the 1820s, it escalated in 1830s. Some four hundred riots occurred throughout British North America before 1850. Some fifty-one of them took place in Upper Canada before 1840, forty-four of them in the 1830s. To contain disaffection (both imagined and real) the colony's elite began to look more and more to state and state-supported institutions. The 1830s marked the beginnings of the rise of the modern institutional state and, in its shadow, the emergence to power of new ruling class. Hospitals, designed to, as one doctor explained 'repress [the] vices' of the sick were constructed alongside state-supported 'house of industry' charged with containing and reforming their inmates so that on release they would fit quietly within a stable society. A 'Lunatic Hospital' was authorized. Intense debate over education set the stage for institutional centralization in the 1840s. The Kingston Penitentiary, the colony's largest public building, opened in 1835. It became society's showcase: its architecture embodied the moral values of the elite; its massive and imposing exterior cowed and impressed.

As well, the Tories took steps to buttress their beleaguered political position. They sought support from two groups of new immigrants. Protestant Irish, often members of anti-Catholic Orange lodges, were organized by unscrupulous Tory placemen and aspiring Tory leaders to intimidate dissent. Between 1830 and 1834 riots against reformers occurred in at least six areas throughout the colony. Physical force increasingly substituted for the rule of law. A second group, the Upper Canadian Methodists, swelled by British immigration and led by a moderate reformer, Egerton Ryerson, moved closer to the Tory camp. The possibility of sharing in clergy reserve money and the right to solemnize marriages, granted in 1831, helped ease tensions and provided the Tories with access to an organized religious body so useful for the management of local elections.

In 1834, however, Reformers proved to be even more adept at local political organization and dominated the assembly much to the chagrin of the newly appointed Lieutenant Governor, Sir Francis Bond Head. The Colonial Office had replaced Colborne in the hope that a more effective system of collaboration would be put in place. Unfortunately, for the Colonial Office, Bond Head did not know the meaning of conciliation. The ensuing deadlock between the reform assembly and the Tory governor resulted in the assembly's dissolution and a violent election in which Bond Head literally led the Tories to victory. All those who had opposed him were stripped of office. In despair many moderate reformers left politics leaving reform leadership open to those of a more radical bent, like William Lyon Mackenzie who in December 1837 led about a thousand ill-armed followers to the colony's capital (renamed Toronto) in an unsuccessful attempt to overthrow the government. A second uprising in western Upper Canada failed as well. Pursued by Loyalist militia, the rebels fled to the United States where some staged a series of border raids in 1838, keeping the colony in a state of tension.

Rebel grievances were intensified by a severe international financial crisis in late 1837 which was itself compounded by Bond Head's refusal to allow banking policies which might have eased the credit crunch. Yet the background of the rebels cannot be distinguished from that of the loyal on economic grounds. Rebels did, however, tend to be more often of American or Scottish rather than English background and to be Presbyterian or Baptist rather than Anglican. These social differences suggest that general Family Compact policies set the context for revolt. Nor should one assume that, because only an ill-organized minority revolted, dissent lacked wider support. When the elite attempted to replicate the show trials of 1814, petitions for clemency flooded into Toronto. Moreover, a small group of moderate men on the make, drawn from both reform and Tory ranks and representing the emerging business-oriented politicians, began to devise a new set of rules for the governing of Upper Canada. They would be aided, somewhat inadvertently, as we shall see, by a Colonial Office intent on repairing the fractured Canadian political system.

Lower Canada

The Constitutional Act of 1791 institutionalized socio-political conflict in Lower Canada. Lower Canadian Anglophones were extremely upset by the separation of Upper and Lower Canada. They were even more enraged by the liberal franchise regulations which permitted most rural dwellers over eighteen (including, until 1834, women) to vote. Nor were they happy that French civil law and the seigneurial system continued in existence. The Catholic Church shared in this unease. Explicit guarantees of legal recognition had not been forthcoming. The confiscation of Jesuit land by the state in the early nineteenth century coupled with a sharply declining ratio of priests to population added to their discomfort. Throughout this period a weakened Catholic Church sought allies even as a beleaguered, primarily urban, Anglophone elite struggled to persist and preserve their social, economic and political power.

Before 1791, English and French merchants and some French professionals—lawyers, surveyors and doctors—had petitioned for an elected assembly. After 1791 these groups went their own ways. French merchants and professionals sought support in rural areas, from which many had themselves emerged. There they found an independent-minded rural based habitant class. From the time of New France habitants had demonstrated what has been termed a 'culture of solidarity'. Habitants were active participants in parish affairs setting limits to the power of priests and at times engaging in pointed disputes over the placement of local churches. Local self-management of the parish was a right closely held by rural habitants. Habitants also set limits to appropriate marriage marches via charivaris, a common feature of rural village behaviour. Similarly, in other matters relating even to criminal as well as civil law, habitants were far from passive. Often habitants would set up their own informal processes for the settlement of disputes by arbitration, bypassing the professional judiciary. Folk law, whereby communities ostracized rather than jailed petty criminal offenders, set powerful bounds to acceptable action. In this context, Francophone professionals and merchants had to cultivate rural support, they could not command it. They drew strength from as much as gave strength to habitant needs and desires.

Anglophone merchants responded by gravitating towards the governor who appointed members to the executive and legislative councils. By 1805 political power had become increasingly fractured along ethnic lines: English in the appointed councils and French in the elected assembly. English bureaucrats, merchants and a few Francophone seigneurs dominated the councils; Francophone middle and agrarian based classes took control of the assembly. By 1804, a new English newspaper, the *Quebec Mercury* challenged the governor to 'unfrenchify' the colony. A French newspaper, *Le Canadien,* soon responded in kind. That paper's editor, and assembly leader, Pierre Bedard, looked to British constitutional arguments to defend and acquire power for the assembly. He wanted the assembly to control the civil list—the government's payroll—and to manage all government patronage. When Bedard's *Parti canadienne* attempted to expel two Anglophone assembly members in 1809, the new governor, Sir James Craig (1807-11) dissolved the assembly. In 1810 he shut Bedard's paper down, jailing the editor and twenty of his co-workers on flimsy charges of 'treasonous practice'. As in Upper Canada, so too in Lower Canada, British appointed rulers suffered little dissent. In Lower Canada, unlike in the upper colony, ethnic differences rendered such suffrage even more fragile and gave a sharper edge to political disputes.

Divergence on economic matters was less clear-cut. Francophone leaders certainly resented the control by English speculators of some two million acres of Eastern Township land, territory set apart from the seigneurial system in the hopes of attracting American and British immigration to Lower Canada. It is true, too, as we noted in an earlier chapter, the Anglophone and Francophone merchant classes focused on different economic sectors: the former profited from external trade in wheat, lumber and fur; the latter specialized in a growing local and regionally-based rural and small urban economy. Yet common interests existed. As early as 1791 French and English bourgeois were active purchasers of seigneuries, each group owning about one-third of the St. Lawrence lowland seigneuries, and many oversaw much economic diversification on their land. Banks were supported by both groups. Moreover, in the 1790s and in the 18730s the assemblies and the councils were at one on many matters relating to economic development. In this regard, it is useful to note that the assembly and the councils and no difficulty in passing legislation designed to 'discipline' an emerging urban industrial work force and thus strengthen the power and economic well-being of a nascent class of industrial employers. On one major fiscal matter, however, significant and ultimately telling divergence did exist. The export oriented Anglophone merchants used their power in the councils to veto assembly proposals to tax imports to pay for jails, roads and canals. They advocated, instead, a tax on land. Such a proposal was simply politically stupid. The *Parti canadienne* adroitly used this cry for a land tax to rally habitant support and solidify opposition to the English party.

Out of this complexity, three points should be underlined. The first is that ethnic difference facilitated by structures put in place in 1791 and intensified by a patronage system which systematically favoured one group at the expense of the other made agreement between the contending elites increasingly difficult. The second point to note is that neither elitist political group could operate independently of their base of support. For the *Parti canadienne* that base was a rural peasantry long steeped in activism and solidarity at the parish level. For the English or bureaucratic party that support rested ultimately at the level of the Colonial office, the overriding ambition of which was to put in place collaborators, loyal to be sure, but effective as well. Finally, the contending groups reflected in various ways the pressures of a changing rural and urban economy. If the extremes in each camp would never see eye to eye on how best to channel change, eventually moderates would. As events transpired, however, it would take a rebellion before those moderates could command events.

As in Upper Canada, the War of 1812 stilled dissent in Lower Canada. Lower Canadians successfully turned back half-hearted attacks in 1812 and 1813 by New England militiamen. The Catholic Church made the most of these victories by proclaiming loudly its allegiance to the British Crown in its time of need. And the loyal were rewarded: an annual salary for the Bishop in 1813; a place on the legislative council in 1817; and official legal recognition of the Bishopric in 1818 gave to the Church needed institutional strength. But if the Church could be conciliated, it remained to be seen whether it could be an effective contender for the support of the rural people.

It was clear that the Church's major rival in that domain, the *Parti canadienne*, renamed the *Parti patriote* in 1826, would not be conciliated. By 1827 that party held over 90 per cent of the assembly's seats and was led by a charismatic lawyer-seigneur, Louis Joseph Papineau. Through his charisma, Papineau focused habitant grievances against the English and reflected the frustration felt by the Francophone professional class which faced increasing competition from an Anglophone professional class and had systematically been denied government preferment. By 1830, Papineau had begun to advocate American, republican institutions, renouncing the

British parliamentary, conciliar model. Papineau and his party also attempted to undermine Church control of parish schools, a not entirely successful attempt which earned the party the Church's lasting enmity. The *Parti patriote* in effect was emerging along the lines of a European liberal nationalist movement and like its European counterpart it was subject to similar divisive strains and internal contradictions. Thus, for, example, Papineau could advocate political democracy even while defending the ancient régime and its institutions. He remained a very exacting seigneur who expected his habitants to pay their dues or suffer consequences.

The Anglophone party dug in its heels. In 1812 under Governor-General Lord Dalhousie its leaders attempted for a second time (the first was in 1812 under Craig) to reunite the Canadas, raise electoral qualifications and abolish French as an official language. Fifty thousand French Canadians signed petitions opposing the initiative and the Colonial Office quickly dropped the matter. The Colonial Office, in fact, became increasingly conciliatory, even allowing, in 1830, the assembly to control Crown revenue. While too much for the Anglophone party, for the *Parti patriote* it was a case of too little, too late. By the end of the 1820s, that party had renounced all British Institutions. Riots and death occurred in 1832 at an election in Montreal. Strikes escalated. British immigrants brought cholera (10,000 Lower Canadians died in 1834 and 1836) and patriote supporters accused the Governor-General of bringing in the sick to spread disease throughout the colony!

The *patriotes* swept the 1834 election and immediately passed the Ninety-two Resolutions advocating American republican institutions and the Governor's impeachment, along with other incendiary items. Eighty thousand signatures accompanied the Resolutions to London. English and French began to coalesce into armed factions. Doric Clubs, Legions and Rifle corps for the British and the *Fils de la Liberté*, echoing French revolutionary organizations of the 1790s, for the French. Newly-appointed Governor-General, Lord Gosford failed to conciliate the contending factions. Early in 1837, the Colonial Secretary, Lord John Russell, threw down the gauntlet: his Ten Resolutions flatly denied all *patriote* demands and he threatened to reunite the colony with Upper Canada should dissent persist.

By November 1837, street battles had erupted in Montreal. In many rural parishes in the Montreal district, pressure was put on local office holders to resign their commissions. Those who did became heroes; those who persisted in office were increasingly terrorized by the local population. *Patriote* leaders built on this groundswell of rural opposition. The result was full-scale war in rural villages to the south and north of Montreal. Two thousand British regulars put down a *patriote* uprising at St. Denis. In December at St. Eustache, fifty-eight *patriotes* died. By the middle of the month, the revolt had been quelled: Papineau and other rebel leaders having fled to the safety of the United States. In February, November and December of 1838, armed rebels crossed the border only to meet defeat each time.

The Rebellion suffered from a vacillating leadership under Papineau, from some contradictory economic and social goals—some supported and others opposed the seigneurial system—and from firm clerical resistance. Yet some nine thousand Lower Canadians participated in the revolt. Many more had signed petitions supporting some of the more radical of the *patriote*'s demands. When it is realized that rebel support came mostly from the Montreal region—the lumber regions of Quebec and the Ottawa Valley were relatively calm—the concentration of rebel support could have led to dramatic results. A traditional explanation for such activity in the Montreal plains stresses agricultural crisis and rural poverty. Yet the most radical activity, in fact, occurred in the three wealthiest parishes in Lower Canada: St. Denis, St. Charles and St. Eustache. The traditional interpretation does not take into account the differential nature of wealth in the Montreal countryside and the significant diversification of economic endeavour concentrated in that region. Rebel participation reflected and emerged from this complex social and economic environment. Parish traditions tended to be the strongest where the economy permitted some degree of activity beyond that of the wearying search for subsistence. 'Urban villages' were the centres of rural revolt. Local merchants and professionals angered by being shut out of economic and government preferment organized but did not create rural opposition on the Montreal plains. As in Upper Canada, so too in Lower Canada, its results would ultimately favour a moderate group, a group well connected to both rural and urban Lower Canada and a group not averse to working with like-minded leaders from the upper colony.

The Atlantic Region

In important ways, political development in the Atlantic region paralleled that in the Canadas. Family Compacts, often fragile alliances of bureaucrats and merchants, dominated political affairs. Political disputes, escalating in the 1820s and 1830s, centred on control of colonial finances, the distribution of power between appointed councils and elected assemblies, and religious/ educational issues. As in the Canadian colonies, appointed Lieutenant Governors attempted to maintain political order, non-party government and British control. In important ways, nevertheless, these similarities were tempered by local geographic, ethnic and economic differences.

A Period of Calm: 1791-1820

Such differences were most evident in the case of Newfoundland. That colony had limited institutional means available for the political expression of social and economic discontent. A year long resident Lieutenant Governor was not appointed until 1818 and an elected assembly was not granted until 1832. Before 1812 one reformer, William Carson, did protest the lack of an assembly, but the only result was the loss of his government job. In Prince Edward Island, by 1812, a precursor to a political party known as the 'Loyal Electors', did control the local assembly. The Lieutenant Governor branded such a party 'unconstitutional' and in 1813 suspended the assembly not allowing it to meet again until 1818. The 'Loyal Electors' were, in fact, not very radical. Led by a lawyer and land agent, D.B. Palmer, they did not argue for land reform or for the granting of civil and political rights to Catholics, who had none.

Prior to 1812 political conflict also arose in New Brunswick. Regional leaders, a loose combination of merchants, religious dissenters and early landowners did argue for increased power to the assembly and less control for the appointed councils which tended to be dominated by appointees from Fredericton and Saint John. As in Prince Edward Island, however, this early conflict resembled more a battle between the 'ins' and the 'outs' than any difference rooted in major social and economic change. As Nova Scotia suggests, such differences, while small in principles, could nonetheless result in violent and fractious disputes. Similar to New Brunswick, regional leaders vied for control against a Halifax-dominated appointed council. Despite disunity among the opposition, violence at the polls and even the threat of duels between rival candidates testify to the seriousness with which some contended for political position.

The War of 1812, as in the Canadas, quieted reform impulses. For the Atlantic region, the War of 1812 brought prosperity. Newfoundland gained great local control of the fisheries, thanks to British warships. Nova Scotia merchants became or financed privateers who captured American ships and cargoes. Smuggling proved equally rewarding. Since military demands were few, public displays of British patriotism were common. Elite attitude, values and the British connections were reinforced.

The Emergence of Reform, 1820-42

During this era of deepening social and economic stratification, elite political leaders took measures to contain and co-opt emerging populist dissent. If elite dominance was not irreparably undermined, neither was populist pressure completely co-opted.

The economic downturn following 1815 severely affected Newfoundland outport residents. When, in 1820, two Irish Catholic outport fishermen received twelve and fourteen lashes for failure to pay debts, 180 Irish merchants in St. John's signed a petition for redress. Following Carson's arguments, they began to push for an elected assembly as a panacea for social and economic ills. The Colonial Office reluctantly granted their wishes in 1832, only, however, under the assumption that a local legislature would now have to incur the costs of running the colony, thus saving the Crown money.

Divisions quickly emerged between Irish and English and outport residents and St. John's merchants. Religious conflict accentuated these divisions. Although one-half of the population was Irish and Catholic, the Church of England enjoyed special privileges in matters of religion and schooling. A new Catholic Bishop, Michael Fleming, Irish born and follower of the Irish nationalist Daniel O'Connell, brought twenty-one young Irish priests to the colony in the 1830s. He participated openly in public elections, precipitating violence, mob intimidation of a protestant newspaper editor and the calling out of the militia by the Lieutenant Governor to maintain peace. In fact, violence was not limited to sectarian issues. Outport resident protested the truck system and in one outport, Conception Bay, at least thirty separate instances of violent protest took place in the 1830s. By the late 1830s, one historian has concluded, a class struggle was taking place in Newfoundland. Protestant merchants at St. John's moved against this wide ranging, but loosely unified protest. Admitting that representative government was probably a mistake, they asked the colonial Office for assistance: that office suspended the constitution in 1841 and the following year enacted the Newfoundland Act which provided for a more restricted franchise and an assembly composed of both elected and appointed members. It remained to be seen whether the new assembly could completely contain sectarian and class violence.

Populist protest also emerged in Prince Edward Island. Angered by the strict enforcement of an imperial land tax known as the 'quitrent', small resident landowners and leaseholders were on the verge of open rebellion in 1823. By the mid-1820s three political factions contended for political control: a declining but powerful aristocratic elite which had the Lieutenant Governor's support; an emerging middle-class group which favoured general economic growth; and a rural-based populist group which espoused rural equality and 'peoples rights'.

The issue of escheat sharply illustrates the division between these groups. Under escheat, lands not appropriately developed by proprietors could be returned to the Crown. The aristocratic party opposed any such measure. The middle-class faction advocated a limited escheat levied against those who, by doing nothing, blocked general economic growth. William Cooper, leader of the Escheat Party, desired an end to all proprietorial-based control and a general redistribution of land to resident tenant farmers. In part because Catholics, who represented one-half of the Island's population, were granted voting rights in 1829, Cooper's party gained wide support in the early 1830s. By 1838 it controlled 75 per cent of the assembly's seats and rural tenants began to meet quitrent collectors with force. Yet the Colonial Office ignored Cooper and the appointed council blocked all radical reform initiated by the Escheat group. A conciliatory Lieutenant Governor met some of the worst grievances. In 1842 the party went down to defeat and disbanded soon after. But it did leave a legacy: subsequent political parties could ignore the issues which Cooper triumphed only at their peril.

Populist expression seemed more inhibited in New Brunswick. In part this reflected the enforcement of the most severely restricted franchise act in British North America. Geography also played a role: discrete communities with localized issues led to factionalism, not to party groupings. Disputes over road and bridge building money dominated assembly deliberations. The Imperial appointment of Thomas Baillie as commissioner of Crown Lands in 1824, however, introduced a new discordant element into New Brunswick politics. Ambitious and arrogant, Baillie, via a rigorous system of land tax collection and new programme for Crown land sales (80 per cent of New Brunswick land was Crown owned), challenged both the assembly, which had no control over land revenue, and leading timber operators, who, accustomed to the cheap existing leasehold system, correctly feared that the sale of land and increased rent would benefit a few large, monopolistically oriented lumber barons. Disadvantaged timber merchants gained control of the assembly in the 1830s and waged legislative war on Baillie. Comparable in policy to the middle class reformers on Prince Edward Island, the group gained assembly control of Crown lands in 1837. Harmony ensued while the assembly spent £133,000 more than it collected between 1837 and 1842. Many middle class reformers grew uneasy about such expenditures. How to harness and centralize economic development, became for them, as it did for similar reform groups in other British North America colonies, the next political challenge.

As in New Brunswick, Nova Scotia's geography led to the growth of scattered settlement. Accordingly, local issues took priority. Not until the 1830s did issues of general concern emerge. A combination of a declining economy, a rigid Lieutenant Governor determined to maintain direct British hegemony and the entry into the reform stage of the mercurial Joseph Howe provided the necessary spark. Howe, a moderate reform newspaper editor, brilliantly defended himself from public charges of libel in 1835. A year later, he entered the assembly as a forthright opponent of the Halifax elite's control of the council. Sir Colin Campbell, the Lieutenant Governor, steadfastly refused all requests for broadening the council's membership and for making the council (he created a second one with a similarly restricted membership) more accountable to the assembly. His obstinance seemed all the more unreasonable when compared to the conciliatory measures being granted in neighbouring New Brunswick. While decrying the rebellious outbursts in the Canadas, Nova Scotia reformers, nonetheless, petitioned the Colonial Office for Campbell's recall. Yet three thousand Nova Scotians counter-petitioned on Campbell's behalf and he persisted in office until 1840. And while the Reformers won the 1840 election, unity within the reform ranks was minimal: Howe, an active campaigner for Speaker of the Assembly only won the position by two votes, some four or five apparent reformers having voted for the Tory candidate. Clearly in Nova Scotia, sectional and regional pressures continued to triumph over any sense of party discipline.

Throughout the Atlantic region, the Colonial Office and colonial politicians experimented with ways to construct political institutions which allowed participation of a wider number while maintaining real control in the hands of a central few. In the 1840s, in that region as well as in the Canadas, it gradually became clear that a system known as responsible government offered one possible avenue towards such a goal.

IV. CONFRONTING CHANGE: POLITICS AND SOCIETY, 1838-64

The Merging of the Canadas

John Lampton, the Earl of Durham, a British emissary charged with resolving the Canada problem, disembarked at Quebec in June 1838 in full ceremonial dress astride a white horse and accompanied by an orchestra. For Durham, the Lower Canadian conflict was simply racial in origin (conveniently ignoring the fact that some Anglophones had actively participated alongside the *patriotes* during the Rebellion) and for him the solution, too, was simple: assimilate the French. Union with Upper Canada would, he argued, 'elevate' the French from a 'hopeless inferiority'. No French Canadian could accept Durham's racial slurs. But eventually some could and did accept the main threat of the rest of his programme.

He believed that the assembly should initiate public policy and appoint "the persons by whom that policy was to be administered". Many moderate reformers in the Canadas, like Robert Baldwin, thought that this meant responsible government: a system which required that the executive be chosen from and reflect the political composition of the elected assembly.

The executive council would become the equivalent of a modern Cabinet. By linking the executive council to the assembly, Durham did not intend to increase the power of the latter at the expense of the former. In fact, he continued to allocate a great deal of power to the Lieutenant Governor. That person was expected to govern in 'harmony' with the assembly. The individuals who sat on the executive council and had assembly seats would see to the efficient running of political affairs. Political parties would not be encouraged. Councillors would act as individuals, not as party representatives. By linking the executive council to the assembly, then, Durham attempted to deepen the former's power and give to the council the credibility necessary to administer an increasingly complex economic and social state.

Durham's myopia concerning the governor's powers, party development, and assimilation was shared by many in the Colonial Office. Following Durham, a succession of governors were sent over to rule according to the principle of harmony with the governor in the conductor's seat. Neither Durham nor the Colonial Office, however, constructed the ultimate rules of the game. Within the Canadas, Durham's sketch formed the basis for a more comprehensive blueprint, a game plan devised by an emerging set of moderate, business oriented, conservative and reform politicians from Upper and Lower Canada.

*   *   *

In Lower Canada, an appointed Special Council ruled between 1838 and 1841. By initiating changes to seigneurial tenure; constructing state-run asylums; funding, under church control, a school system; generally strengthening central control of the countryside; and sanctioning the Act of Union in February 1841, which reunited Upper and Lower Canada as one political unit, the Council set the stage for the emergence to power of the moderate wing of the Lower Canadian elite. In Upper Canada, Durham and his successor as Governor-General, Charles Poulett Thomson (Lord Sydenham), conciliated Upper Canada's tory-dominated assembly by the promise of a 1.5 million pound sterling loan from Great Britain. Consistent with Durham's desire to assimilate the French, Canada East (the old Lower Canada) received only as many seats (42) in the new assembly as Canada West (the old Upper Canada) even though Canada East had 200,000 more people. Debt was merged, although Canada West owed thirteen times that owed by Canada East. English became the only official language and the capital was at Kingston, a stronghold of Anglo-Saxon loyalism.

Clearly the deck seemed stacked in favour of Canada West and in favour of the British Canadians over the French Canadians. Yet the attempt to govern according to the notion of harmony undercut the policy of assimilation and instead strengthened the tendency towards dualism. Almost all contenders for political power agreed on the need for a strong central executive. Disagreement focused on which component of the executive branch would have primary authority: the council or the governor. Already in close correspondence, politicians like Robert Baldwin and Francis Hincks from Upper Canada and Louis La Fontaine, a lawyer and *patriote* from Lower Canada believed that executive councillors should be the central actors in political administration. The gulf between the governor and the emerging reform group was no less significant over the issue of duality. Sydenham clearly hoped that the Union would be a crucible wherein the French could be effectively subdued and assimilated. Yet to achieve greater reform party strength, Baldwin and Hincks were ready to stand by La Fontaine in the latter's attempt to bend the Union towards the goal of *la survivance,* the retention and enrichment of French culture in Lower Canada.

While Sydenham resisted the recognition of any alliance between reformers, even he, to govern effectively, had to acknowledge that the Union's two sections, Canada East and Canada West, possessed separate languages, religions, civil law codes, judicial systems and forms of land tenure. He and his successors (he died in late 1841) as Governor-General (there were three in the space of four years) instituted what was, in effect, a dual administrative structure. As early as 1843 each section had its own law officer, crown land commissioner, provincial secretary, and superintendent of education. Far from moving towards a unitary government system, the Colonial Office's representatives were setting the administrative foundation for the emergence of a federal or dual government structure.

The Colonial Office was not pleased. A new Governor, Sir Charles Metcalfe, arrived in April 1843 with orders to resist further erosion. Instead, recognizing that assimilation and harmony were incompatible, Metcalfe repealed restrictions on the official use of French, approved Montreal as the new seat of government and sponsored a general amnesty for most rebels. He stood firm, however, on the issue of executive control. So, too, did the reformers, who had long since become tired of trusting governors. In a bitter and violent election (1843), reform went down to defeat in Canada West but their French Canadian allies, under La Fontaine, swept the lower province. The Hincks-Baldwin determination to ally with La Fontaine paid dividends. Although shut out of power by the dying Metcalfe, the Reformers tightened their party organization and triumphed in the election of 1847.

The La Fontaine-Baldwin government in 1847 was the first true party government to exercise power in the Canadas. It marked the first of a long line of bifurcated ministries representing at the highest political level the reality of linguistic duality. The transferral of power was, in the context of the Canadas' turbulent and violent political past, suitably symbolized by the passage of the Rebellion Losses Bill in 1849. This bill promised to compensate those French Canadians who had suffered property damage in the rebellion. Coming on the heels of the repeal of the Navigation Acts and the seeming abandonment by Britain of loyal colonists, it aroused the frustrated fury of old compact tories and Anglo merchants in Montreal. When Lord Elgin, the Governor-General, signed the legislation over Tory cries, some like Samuel P. Jarvis, an elder Toronto Tory, prayed "they would ... string him up as a caution to other traitor governors". Others did more than wish. They burned the Parliament Buildings in Montreal. They pelted Elgin with rotten eggs and tomatoes. But even Tory vigilantism could not turn the clock back. By 1850 the seeds of Canada's modern political system had been well sown.

Not that Baldwin and La Fontaine would be around long to reap the rewards. Their attempt to resolve cultural and political issues were only partly successful. The Rebellion Losses Bill was not the only issue to spark opposition. Religious and educational matters were also contentious. Throughout the 1840s Catholic-Protestant conflict overlay much political activity. The Catholic Church became more closely devoted to the Pope, more aggressive in asserting its primacy over the state and more energetic in establishing devotional societies at the popular level, a combination of initiatives known as Ultramontanism. Schooling was often at the centre of this tension. In Lower Canada, state financed and church-run elementary schools increased dramatically in numbers as did religious communities which were the main source of teachers. In an attempt to head off anger and anxiety in protestant Canada West, Baldwin and La Fontaine passed a secular public schools act and created a secular university. They did, however, permit the establishment of separate Catholic public schools if a sufficient number of locals so desired.

To many protestants in the Canadas and, indeed, in the Maritimes, fear of Catholic hegemony was fanned by the influx of Irish Catholic occasioned by the potato famines in Ireland in the late 1840s (between 1846 and 1851, 200,000 British subjects, two-thirds from Ireland migrated to the Canadas). In the context of schooling, however, Protestant and Catholic teachings shared a commitment to capitalist development and bourgeois led growth. Ignace Bourget, the powerful Bishop of Montreal, for example, instituted a modern curriculum with less Latin and a greater focus on trade and farming. Similar to the aims of middle-class businessmen in other colonies, Lower Canadian Catholic clergy took the lead in the crusade for temperance: only sober, prudent, thrifty and industrious habitants could compete effectively in the modern world. Despite Protestant-Catholic and French-English enmity, the schooling system of each of the Canadas espoused similar ends, ends very compatible with those of the political elite.

Yet opposition soon emerged. In 1849 violent uprisings against compulsory schooling and school taxes occurred in many Lower Canadian rural areas, where rural families often resented increased taxes and compulsory schooling because it interfered with work on the farm. Even in Canada West, the state-sponsored educational system proved less effective than its proponents had hoped. Local school boards, due to entrenched customs and financial restraint, only slowly, if at all, adopted the state's slate for proper school texts. At some schools, students set up underground libraries, the books of which were more widely circulated and read than those from the official libraries. The religious and ethnic background of local teachers, not curriculum, often dictated whether rural families would send their children to school. Moreover, increased educational costs gradually made it more difficult for other than the children of middle-class families to progress through the upper grades of the public educational system.

At a broader level, a small group known as the Rouges argued for the complete separation of church and state in Canada East and the implementation of a secular education system. These views were espoused with greater militancy and enjoyed wider support in Canada West where 'reformers', known as Clear Grits, opposed any religious teaching in schools, advocated the end of all official privileges for the French language and, when the census of 1851 revealed that Upper Canadians outnumbered Lower Canadians, pushed for representation by population in place of equal representation by section.

Baldwin and La Fontaine's control of the political agenda was further weakened by their reluctance to sponsor measures designed to promote the colony's economic growth. Over such issues as support for railways and legislation which would facilitate the legal rights of chartered companies, even in the era of manufacturing, Hincks and other more economically aggressive politicians began to part company with Baldwin and La Fontaine. In 1851, Hincks, in alliance with Augustus-Norbert Morin, a lawyer-politician from Canada East, took over the reform party. Yet fissures continued to widen within the reform alliance. If Hincks and Morin conciliated many business-conservative interests—like the old tory Allan MacNab who proclaimed that 'All my politics are railroads'—they failed to pacify Clear Grit fears concerning religious and language issues. When Hincks became involved in a series of unsavoury financial scandals, there was, in Canada

West, an opposition movement, led by a rising reformer and owner of the widely-read Toronto *Globe,* George Brown, ready to capitalize on his errors in judgement.

The resultant split in the Upper Canadian section of the old Baldwin-La Fontaine party led to a watershed in Canadian political history. The election of 1854 saw a realignment of political groups. French Canadian reformers led by Morin and Georges-Etienne Cartier, an ex-*patriote* and a lawyer for the Grand Trunk railway, joined with an Upper Canadian conservation group composed of some old tories like MacNab and young moderate conservative leaders like the lawyer, businessman, John A. Macdonald. This alliance of moderate conservatives from Upper Canada and moderate reformers from Lower Canada supplanted the old grouping of Upper Canadian reformers with their Lower Canadian counterparts and remained the norm in central Canadian politics from 1854 until 1896. It represented the triumph of common economic goals over religious and ethnic differences.

This political interplay occurred at a level above the lived reality of most Upper and Lower Canadians. In Canada East, out-migration to New England states where work in mills and factories seemed more available marked the beginning of what would become a serious exodus of people in the later nineteenth century. In Montreal and in Toronto, skilled and unskilled workers found it more difficult to own homes as the period progressed. Increasingly, too, different economic groups began to live in separate city districts. Families at the lower end of the economic scale tended to have more children than those at the upper level hoping to increase the family's work force in order to survive. Similar workplace, residential and family experience helped create a sense of working-class consciousness, a consciousness forged also on the canals and railroads of the 1840s and 1850s. At least sixty-one strikes occurred in Lower Canada between 1843 and 1879. Forty strikes led by skilled workers protesting the introduction of machinery and demanding higher wages took place in Upper Canada in 1853 and 1854. On railroads, strikes were, as one Great Western railroad engineer reminisced, as regular as the 'croaking of the frogs'. In both Canadas, unions were formed by moulders, tailors, joiners, machine workers, printers, firemen and others. A new set of class distinctions began to develop with the emergence of industrial capitalism in the 1850s.

Political parties, also in an emerging state, did not reflect these nascent social and economic groupings, Politics catered to upper and middle class values and needs. Legislation restricting worker rights and enhancing employer's power was common in this period. Voting rights dependant on the dollar value of property owned or rented severely restricted the franchise for the urban poor at the municipal as well as colonial level. Even as economic needs of many were ignored or curtailed by political leaders, Macdonald and his Lower Canadian allies, Cartier and Alexander Tilloch Galt, a politician, land speculator and businessman from the Eastern Townships, brought the Union to the brink of financial collapse. As we have noted earlier, by 1857 railroads and municipalities began to default on government guaranteed loan repayments. A wider tax base and the acquisition of richer resources to finance past and underwrite continued economic expansion appeared to be the only feasible answer. In 1858 Galt, especially, pushed for a wider union of all British North American colonies. The British Colonial Office considered the idea to be premature and shelved it, but not long enough to gather dust. The Union's increasingly shaky and tangled financial situation prevented that from occurring.

The reshaping of politics which took place in 1854 resulted in more than the emergence of bourgeois party and the Union's near financial collapse. It also led to the virtual collapse of the Union's political structure. This occurred because a majority of Upper Canadians refused to accept cultural differences and rejected a party based on the primacy of business. They rallied instead around George Brown and the *Globe*'s incendiary if not racist and bigoted leadership. Brown and his Clear Grit followers hoped to relegate Catholics and French to a segregated position. Arguing that too much of Upper Canada's cultural legislation, like that relating to schools, had been created by Lower Canadian votes and capitalizing on Upper Canada's larger population. Brown centered his platform on the principle of representation by population. Not surprisingly, this simple but powerful appeal found little support in the Lower Province. Brown also correctly sensed a growing restlessness in rural areas as good farmland became less easily available and he began to proclaim the benefits of westward expansion, adroitly tapping the latent imperialism within Upper Canadians. Finally, Brown began to espouse a form of federation within which he hoped to contain and subordinate the French and the Catholics. In a series of elections following 1858, reformers dominated the Upper Canadian polls and the moderate reform/conservatives (the blue party as they came to be called) controlled Lower Canada. John A. Macdonald's conservative party allied with the blue party in Canada East led by George Cartier while the Brownite reformers sought but failed to consolidate an alliance with reform Rouge Lower Canadians who were themselves very suspicious of working closely with English-speaking protestants. The result was political deadlock: a recurring situation of equality among political opponents. By 1864 political deadlock and near bankruptcy had created an environment conducive to further political change and the fashioning of a new constitutional arrangement.

Politics and Society in the Atlantic Region 1841-64

The impact of Durham's report extended beyond the Canadas. As in the Canadas, colonial Political elites in the Atlantic region moved towards establishing political parties, creating a stronger locally rooted executive and expanding the state's role in social and economic policy. In varying degrees within each of the Atlantic colonies, sectarian strife and class conflict provided the context for such change.

Religion certainly played an important role in the lives of Atlantic people. The arrival of Irish famine migrants in the mid-1840s sparked Orange (Protestant) and Catholic Irish conflict. Orange lodges grew dramatically in that decade in New Brunswick. Sectarian violence in Saint John led to the creation of a professional police force. Urban justice tended to favour white Protestants over other ethnic groups; Catholic Irish rioters were generally more severely dealt with than were their Protestant antagonists. Similar sectarian conflict occurred in Halifax and throughout Newfoundland. Nor were such divisions only evident in the region's largest cities: St. John's Halifax and Saint John, the latter by far the largest with 38,800 residents. Religion was no less important in the countryside. Yet, as in the city, so in the country, various churches sent different and often conflicting messages. If one Calvinist Presbyterian minister could justify a potato famine in Cape Breton as God's punishment for "unthriftiness and offensive indolence", and a Catholic priest defend proprietors' rights against those of Prince Edward Island tenants, other evangelical preachers were more sympathetic to the poor and critical of the elite. While the impact of religion was profound, that impact was in complex ways constrained and influenced by matters of ethnicity (especially Irish) and class.

While some historians have labelled the twenty years before Confederation a 'Golden Era' in Atlantic Canada, such a description is inappropriate. Farming output in Nova Scotia and New Brunswick fell short of feeding the region. In some Nova Scotia regions, one-half of farm families produced less than was necessary to feed their families. In 1861 in six New Brunswick districts, 62 per cent of all farms were worth less than $500; 12 per cent were worth over $2,000. Relatively few Atlantic Canada residents flourished during the so-called 'Golden Era'. In Newfoundland, over 90 per cent of the population struggled to survive in fishery; some 2 per cent, mainly merchants, enjoyed a more affluent lifestyle. In Nova Scotia in 1871, 10 per cent of the families owned 81 per cent of the wealth. Social-economic stratification marked the Atlantic area. Small wonder that many began to leave the

region—in the decade of the 1860s, 13,000 more people left than arrived—
seeking employment in New England mills or lumber camps. Many others
took solace in religion, 'to us', as the unemployed head of one family on the
move confided to his diary "a guide and a light to pass through/this Dark
vale of Sorrow".

Newfoundland politics most dramatically reflected sectarian and class
issues. Yet in the midst of conflict, a local political culture began to emerge,
one which in some ways began to bridge religious, ethnic and class divisions.
Lieutenant Governor Frederic Harvey used the power available to him
under the imposed constitution of 1842 (the so-called Newfoundland Act)
to encourage such development. In other Atlantic region colonies (and in
the Canadas too), elite politicians hoped that local state sponsored educational
systems would calm dissent via the instilling of obedience, regularity and
allegiance to appropriate cultural and political symbols. Newfoundland's
relatively small middle class made it difficult to raise money to support such
a system. Moreover, the nature of the colony's household economy rendered
widespread participation doubtful. Girls helped mothers at home and in the
curing of fish. Boys went with their fathers in the fishing boats. Few of either
sex attended school after the age of eleven or twelve. As a result, Harvey
looked to other means. He supported the newly founded Native's Society,
composed of middle class Newfoundlanders who saw the Island as their
home and the monarch as their leader; temperance organizations, which
preached total abstinence in drink and moderation in all other pursuits; and
literary societies and mechanics institutes designed to ameliorate intemperate
and radical attitudes. He also sponsored many public displays of loyalty to
the Queen and England attended by all classes, religions and ethnic groups.

But divisions persisted. By 1847 the Colonial Office bowed to pressure
to reinstate the assembly and conciliar system and in 1855 the colony was
granted responsible government. Splits appeared in the dominant reform-
Catholic party during the 1850s. Fear of Protestant ascendency mounted
when the 1857 census revealed that Catholics were outnumbered 64,000 to
55,000. Riots and deaths punctuated the election of 1861. When the dust
settled even extreme leaders began to advice moderation. Over the next
several years, Conservatives and Reformers began to reach out to Catholics
and Protestants respectively thus helping to diffuse the violent sectarian
nature of Newfoundland politics.

The intertwining of class and religion as co-determinants of political
behaviour is nicely illustrated by a study of Prince Edward Island's politics
in the pre-Confederation era. By the late 1840s, a reform group led by
George Coles, a local merchant and manufacturer, focused on responsible

government as the best means of achieving reform unity and, perhaps, of allowing the beleaguered tenants, the majority of Prince Edward Islanders, some power in the political arena. A reluctant Colonial Office granted responsible government in 1851 but remained determined to protect the rights of absentee landowners. The passage of the Free Education Act (the first colony in the British Empire to do so), the widening of the franchise (1855) and the implementation of the Land Purchase Act (1853) did promise significant benefit for rural dwellers. But the Reform policy of gradualism, compensation and resale to tenants in the end accomplished little: in 1861 squatters and tenants comprised 60 per cent of all landowners.

Their conservative opponents were equally ineffectual concerning the land issue. They did, however, cynically manipulate Protestant-Catholic enmity (55 per cent of the colony were Protestant and 45 per cent were Catholic) to their political advantage. They seized on some ill-advised comments by a Roman Catholic bishop concerning *Bible* reading in the state school system to avert attention from the land problem and to vault to power in 1859. In the early 1860s, the Conservatives referred the land issue to a Commission. Frustrated residents organized the Tenants League and began to advocate civil disobedience. Conservatives and Reformers, too, looked to the Confederation issue of the mid-1860s as yet another way to ignore fundamental social and economic grievance. It was an all too common juxtaposition: matters of religion and nationalism were used by a political elite to blunt and forestall more radical economic and social reform.

Political events in New Brunswick underline how responsible government was both a movement towards democracy and a measure for the centralization of power. While the executive council possessed direct links to the assembly as early as 1838, a party system had not been put in place, some holding ministerial positions did not sit on the council and the assembly, not the council, controlled the all important financial matters. Assembly members were content with this system, some, in fact, correctly arguing that responsible government would limit their control over financial appropriations and, in that sense, could be seen as an infringement on their individual democratic rights.

By the early 1850s a small faction of middle class, commercially oriented politicians did argue for responsible government and the executive's right to initiate money bills. Like the bourgeois oriented party which emerged in the Canadas, reformers under the leadership of a local banker, Smauel Tilley, believed in a relatively activist government, a form of government which required, they argued, more centralized control of money matters. They extended the franchise, but only a little; consolidated financial control in the executive's hands; provided financial support for railroad construction; and enacted a Prohibition Act. The latter proved impossible to enforce and caused their resignation and the election of the old conservatives virtually on a one-plank platform of repeal of prohibition. After acting on that plank, the conservatives lost control of the assembly and in 1857 the Reformers were re-elected and retained power for the following eight years.

In New Brunswick, party groupings solidified over the temperance issue. In this process women, although they could not vote, were active. Their petitions and pressure in favour of temperance pushed the reformers to pass the ill-fated Prohibition Act in the first place. As in her sister colonies, religion, too, underlay political choices. Most voted on the basis of the moral teachings of their religion. Anglicans and Presbyterians supported the conservative anti-temperance slate; Methodists and Baptists voted reform; Catholics, traditionally pro-reform, had great difficulty on the temperance issue and, where possible, voted a non-party ticket.

In 1847, Nova Scotia became the first British North American colony to form an 'administration based on party'. By 1849 the dominant Reform party had transformed the executive council into a cabinet of minister and had doled out substantial amounts of patronage at the expense of conservative supporters. The assembly did retain some control over money bills so centralization of power occurred more slowly in Nova Scotia than in the Canadas. The Reform governments of the 1850s (the opposition held power only briefly in the latter part of the decade) were conservative in their social policy and, as in New Brunswick and the Canadas, active in economic measures. Railroads received strong support, and by 1864 per capita indebtedness had increased by more than tenfold. As in the Canadas, a development-minded administration had mortgaged the colony's future.

Joseph Howe, the pre-eminent reformer in Nova Scotia in this period, closely resembled George Brown of Upper Canada. Both men were editors of major newspapers situated in the most dominant and expanding urban centre in their provinces. Both reflected the attitudes of the expansive urban, commercial/industrial elite of their cities. Both opposed universal male franchise. Both exhibited strong anti-Catholic attitudes. In Brown's case, this prevented him from heading a Canadian administration for longer than two days. In Howe's case, it led to the overthrow of the Reformers in 1857 after he had publicly vilified Catholics and advocated the formation of a Protestant party to safeguard society from the 'Papists'. In all of this, Howe and Brown and the reformers who followed them exhibited many of the beliefs of mid-Victorian British liberalism. Responsible government co-existed comfortably with such elitist, sectarian and anti-democratic views.

For their part, the Nova Scotia Conservatives, under the leadership of Charles Tupper, shared many of the reformers' elitist and anti-democratic views. Like the Conservatives in the Canadas, however, Tupper and his followers were more willing to bury sectarian hatches and concentrate instead on facilitating economic growth, which for Tupper meant the construction of railroads which would link Nova Scotia to the Canadian interior and, in the process, open up markets for his colony's rich coal mines and provide a stimulus for local industrial development.

By the eve of Confederation, many Maritime politicians had gained valuable experience in the financing and management of railways in the context of public enterprise, and many of them also had begun to shift from a seaward, export oriented development policy to a landward continentally-focused entrepreneurial agenda. Some had even argued loudly and long, but unsuccessfully, for an Intercolonial railroad which would link major Atlantic ports, like Halifax, to the developing continental interior. When Canadian political leaders, frustrated by political deadlock and beset by bankruptcy, began to advocate a larger union and to look to Atlantic region leaders for support and assistance, politicians like Tupper and Tilley were willing to listen.

V. THE SEARCH FOR ECONOMIC AND POLITICAL INTEGRATION: CONFEDERATION, 1864-67

A number of external concerns, both continental and imperial, added to the pressure for change arising from within British North America. The American Civil War excited much fear and concern in the Canadas. In a widely reproduced speech, Thomas D'Arcy McGee, a Montreal politician, put it succinctly:

> They [the Americans] coveted Florida and seized it; they coveted Louisiana and purchased it ... Canada was the first ambition of the American confederacy and never ceased to be so.[4]

Late in 1861 Americans boarded a British ship, the *Trent*, to arrest two Confederate diplomats. England demanded an apology. The Toronto *Globe* thought the American act was "one of the most absurd and stupid ... which history records". In response, the Canadian government created a provincial Department of Defence and, in a move which could only give the Americans confidence, began to parade its underequipped, underpaid, undertrained and understaffed militia. The Trent Affair was followed by several other

[4] P.B. Waite, *The Life and Times of Confederation, 1864-67,* Toronto, 1990, 87.

cause célèbres over the next three years culminating in the threat of attacks on various British North American centres by Fenians—a group of Irish nationalists who believed the best way to harm Britain was through her colonies. These threats (more imagined than real) were adroitly used by pro-Confederationists, in the Canadas and in the Maritimes, to put down internal opposition. Defence demanded British North American unity. To oppose this was to be pro-American and anti-British. The War of 1812 and the border raids of 1838, still alive in many Canadian memories, provided the historical context for such rhetoric.

American aggression coupled with the Canadian Colony's troubled political situation concerned Imperial administrators. The movement from a formal to informal empire signalled by the dismantlement of the old mercantile system and the granting of responsible government in the 1840s, did not mean the end of the British Imperial tradition. Rather it meant the continuation of British rule through a collaborative structure within which the interests of a local Canadian elite, of British colonial administrators and of Imperial investors intersected. Important merchant banks situated in the City of London had been involved in Canadian governmental finance since the mid-1830s. Two of them, Glyn, Mills & Co. and the Baring Brothers, began to extend their official relationship as the government's London financial agents to include increasingly large investments in Canadian railway development. The local colonial government via Hincks' financial guarantees facilitated this investment. Local financial institutions, especially the colony's official resident bank, the Bank of Upper Canada, also played important roles. Imperial investors looked to these financial institutions for support in the implementation of their colonial investment programmes. When the London financial market became tight, those institutions were expected to provide interim financing. By the mid-1850s, the Canadian government, Canadian railroads, Canadian banks and London financiers were bound together in a web of interrelated investment activity.

Under this structure, the imperial government exercised an indirect role. The movement towards informal empire, of course, made this inevitable. Ever cost conscious, imperial administrators happily stepped back both from direct involvement in colonial politics and from the financing of railways and other colonial entrepreneurial activity. At the same time the Colonial Office continued to guard zealously its remaining prerogatives, the main one being the setting of the timing for the ensuing stages of devolution. Control of the agenda, however, depended on the acquiescence of loyal colonial collaborators. And since the cultivation of such support could only be achieved indirectly via the suasion of the Governor-General and/or the assistance of private financiers in the City of London, the maintenance of imperial prerogatives became a difficult and tension-filled endeavour.

These difficulties were impressed on Imperial administrators, when in the face of potential American aggression the Canadian government refused to spend what the Colonial Office considered to be a sufficient sum on defence. This failure coupled with recent tariff increases against British as well as American manufactured goods and by the apparent refusal of Canadian governments to provide sufficient funds for the construction of an Intercolonial railroad linking the Maritimes with central Canada, made Imperial administrators and London financiers receptive to proposals for restructuring the British North American colonial system.

The Coalition of 1864, in the Canadas, nicely represented the interests of the various components of the colonial/imperial governing structure. George Brown's initiative and his willingness to join John A. Macdonald, Georges Etienne Cartier and Alexander T. Galt to seek a solution to the debilitating political/constitutional problems besetting the Union have been correctly interpreted as statesmanship on his part. Without doubt, the Union's political problems required some such burying of political hatchets if a viable solution was to be found and implemented. Statesmanship, however, facilitated this coalescence of political antagonists. When viewed in non-political terms, the Coalition of 1864 represents the merging of two hitherto separate groups of the Anglo-Canadian business elite. John A. Macdonald, supported by Alexander Galt, Thomas D'Arcy McGee, and Georges Cartier represented that sector of business and finance associated with the Grand Trunk Railroad and Montreal. Georges Cartier, tied through family with the Bank of Montreal, entered full-time politics with the backing of the money he made as solicitor for the Grand Trunk Railroad. McGee, traditionally considered a prophet and cheerleader of Confederation, was linked to prominent Montreal business families like the Molsons and Ogilvies as well as the Grand Trunk. Alexander Galt had long been associated with large land companies and with the Grand Trunk. John A. Macdonald and his law partner, Alexander Campbell, sat on the boards and represented many Upper Canadian financial institutions: institutions which were often active in railroad financing. Charles John Brydges, the Grand Trunk's general manager, and Macdonald were fast friends and confidants throughout the 1860s. This group, centred on the Grand Trunk, desired eastward expansion via the Intercolonial. Through the activities of the Grand Trunk's president, an experienced British railway manager, Edward Watkin, the railroad was also closely tied to the Hudson's Bay Company and thus open as well to the prospect of westward expansion. In addition, the Colonial Secretary, the Duke of Newcastle, had been actively working with Watkin to raise financial capital to purchase from the Hudson's Bay Company a right of way to the Pacific Coast.

George Brown, on the other hand, represented the industrial and financial leaders of Toronto, Montreal's rival, as well as the more prosperous rural sections of Upper Canada. Due to the increased shortage of good Upper Canadian land, these interests pressed for westward expansion to the uncharted prairies. While Brown, through the *Globe,* incessantly attacked the Grand Trunk for sloppy construction and financial mismanagement, he was far from adverse to all railroads. In fact, he was a public supporter of the Grand Trunk's main rival, the Great Western.

Complementary and at times overlapping business interests formed one thread which helped to bind the coalition together. A second point of inter-section related to common attitudes on the issue of democracy. Macdonald and Brown opposed the notion of political equality, distrusted the ability of the mass and favoured privilege for the propertied. In 1870 Macdonald, then Prime Minister of Canada, introduced an amendment to a proposed federal statute which would have established a straight income qualification of $400 a year for the right to vote. His amendment stipulated that day labourers should be excluded, even though they might make $400 a year because, as the Prime Minister put it: "they had no abiding interest in the country". He felt that popular appeals on matters as important as Confederation would "subvert the principles of the British constitution" and would be 'an obvious absurdity'. This elitist view was inherent in Macdonald's determined desire for a strong central government. If we keep the local or provincial governments weak 'we shall have', he asserted at one of the conferences leading to Confederation, "a strong and lasting government under which we can work out constitutional liberty as opposed to democracy and be able to protect by having a powerful central government". Minority rights, not majority rule, was an abiding concern of many of the Fathers. Which minorities were to receive protection? One that seemed to be excluded was of course, the day labourer and, in general terms, the poor. Another was the Indian. Macdonald was quite clear on this point when he wrote to the electoral returning officer of the district of Algoma in Ontario in October 1867.

> I drew the clauses relating to Algoma in the Union Act, but I really forgot all about the Indians. Had they occurred to my mind I should certainly have excluded them.

The returning officer, taking his master's cue, refused to accept the vote of any Indian in the subsequent election. "Classes and property should be represented as well as numbers", Macdonald commented during the Confederation debates. And through the appointed Upper House or Senate, the North American version of the British House of Lords, Macdonald hoped to achieve his ends. In connection with the establishment of the Senate, he argued that "the rights of the majority ought to be protected and the rich are always fewer in number than the poor."

George Brown was at one with Macdonald in his aversion to democracy. In the United States Brown pointed out:

the balance of power is held by the unreasoning ignorant mass, to swing them is the grand aim of the contest and as truth, character, statesmanship, honest policy and fair argument would be thrown away upon them, both parties by consent—nay of necessity—resort to other expedients.[5]

These other expedients were left to the lurid imagination of his audience. It is not surprising then that this successful businessman and large landowner could number among his political supporters some of the richest and most powerful of the city of Toronto's business and social elite. The pro-Confederation forces in the Canadas were united by geography—centred on the St. Lawrence-Lake Ontario transportation corridor—by business, commercial and social interests and by common economic and political problems. That elite became the moving force behind Confederation.

Members of the Canadian coalition acted with despatch. The coalition itself had only been formed in June 1864: in September of that year the Canadians arrived uninvited at Charlottetown where they took over a conference originally scheduled for the discussion only of Maritime Union. Here they presented their broader conception: a federation of British North America. Their attitudes and actions take on, in fact, a quasi-imperialist hue. Especially is this true of the exuberant Brown. On approaching Charlottetown for the first conference, Brown wrote to his wife:

About noon we came to an inlet which we entered, and running up for some miles what appeared to be a river but was in fact but an inlet of the sea, amid most beautiful scenery, we came suddenly on the Capital City of the Island. Our steamer dropped anchor magnificently in the stream and its man-of-war cut evidently inspired the natives with huge respect for their big brothers from Canada. I flatter myself we did that well.... Having dressed ourselves in the correct style, our two boats were lowered man-of-war fashion—and being each duly manned with four oarsmen

[5]B.W. Hodgins, "Democracy and the Ontario Fathers of Confederation," in E. Firth, ed., *Profiles of a Province*, Toronto, 1967, pp. 83-91.

and a boatswain, dressed in blue uniform, hats, belts, etc., in regular style, we pulled away for shore and landed like Mr. Christopher Columbus who had the precedence of us in taking possession of portions of the American continent.

At Charlottetown the Canadians sketched the broad picture: a strong central government and weak local governments, an appointed Upper House, a debt equalization scheme and subsidy programme were put across at least in principle and accepted by a majority of those present.

The details were hammered out at Quebec. In the words of the Confederate opponent:
They went [up to Quebec] taking with them several ladies who, they knew, are always in favor of union. They had nice times going up and nicer after they got there; all they did was in secret, confidential.... They had a fat time, dinners balls champagne suppers and when surrounded with such influences did they form a new Empire. After sitting 16 days the wonderful creature [Confederation] made its appearance.[6]

The Canadians had prepared the draft resolutions for each day's agenda. The secretary was John A. Macdonald's brother-in-law. The Chairman was Étienne Taché from Lower Canada and all the major introductory speeches were made by Canadians. The Canadians were reluctant to compromise on any of their stated ends. Should peripheral areas such as Prince Edward Island and Newfoundland fail to agree—so be it. They could be attracted later. Seventy-two resolutions were produced at Quebec and these became the backbone of the new constitution. The Quebec scheme, slightly modified at London in 1866-67, was then enacted into law by the Imperial parliament as the British North America Act.

In keeping with their attitudes towards democracy, none of the Canadian elite suggested that the electorate should be consulted on the Confederation scheme. Instead, a special session of the assembly was called to discuss the issue. During the Confederation debates, the central Canadian elite made quite clear what the rule of the Maritimes and the west would be in the new nation. As Galt put it, the Maritimes would supply minerals, coal, fish and an opening to the sea, the Canadas would supply manufactured goods and eventually the west would supply wheat. And as George Brown somewhat more aggressively stated,

the proposal is that our farmers and manufacturers and mechanics shall carry their wares unquestioned into every village of the Maritime Provinces

---

[6]P.B. Waite, *The Charlottetown Conference,* CHA Booklet, #15, Toronto, 1966.

and they shall with equal freedom bring their fish and their coal and their West India produce to our 3 millions of inhabitants.[7]

The question as to who were to be the hewers of wood and drawers of water was an easy one for the Upper Canadian elite to answer: everyone but them.

Not surprising, Maritime proponents of confederation faced a rocky road. Political supporters clearly were reluctant to test public opinion on the Confederation issue in any formal way. In Nova Scotia, Joseph Howe emerged as a strong and energetic opponent, but the assembly under conservative control and aided by the Lieutenant Governor and, very likely, money from Canadian railroad interests, managed in 1866 to overturn a negative vote of the previous year. In New Brunswick, events were even more chaotic. In 1865 Tilley reluctantly acceded to an election and lost. Whether the election can be interpreted as a clear-cut referendum on Confederation is doubtful, but many New Brunswickers made that claim then and since. As in Nova Scotia, railway money and colonial office influence exercised via the Lieutenant Governor facilitated the resignation of an already divided government and the re-election in April 1866 of the pro-Confederates led by Tilley. In both Prince Edward Island and Newfoundland, similar support seemed less forthcoming. Nor from the perspective of the Canadas and the Colonial Office were either of these colonies absolutely essential for Confederation. Prince Edward Island would join in six years. Newfoundland would join in eighty-three years.

Both because of the dominance of the Canadian delegates at the conferences leading to Confederation and the problems experienced by Maritime politicians in putting Confederation in place, many have overlooked the extent to which maritime leaders did, in fact, exercise agency in the negotiations leading to union. Fittingly, the issue of the Intercolonial railroad illustrates well the shrewdness exhibited and the success realized by the Maritime leaders. The debate over the Intercolonial was more than simply a sub-text at conferences. As Samuel Tilley put it, "We won't have the Union unless you give us the Railway". Tilley pushed successfully for the right to increase the colony's debt before Confederation, and for the right to borrow money at a lower rate of interest pending the assumption of debt by the new Canadian government. The representatives from Canada could hardly complain: their debt far overshadowed that of the Maritimes. Even George Brown, a strong advocate of westward, not eastward expansion, realized that an Intercolonial route was necessary in order to achieve Confederation. These concessions

[7]Ibid.

allowed Tilley to raise money immediately for local railroad construction and thus to go some way toward pacifying opposition. Charles Tupper, from Nova Scotia, also pushed for debt increases. Together they made certain that one of the clauses passed at the Quebec Conference promised the building by the new government of an Intercolonial railway.

The British North America Act

The British North America Act has been subjected to many and different interpretations. One of the most recurring is the claim that confederation was in some way a Compact or a Treaty, and that from this Compact a bilingual and bicultural nation emerged. It is important to note, however, that the three conferences that led to Confederation were not organized along ethnic and cultural lines. Rather they were meetings of provinces, each province was given one vote and the Canadas, since for administrative purposes they were organized into two divisions, were given two votes. Their primary purpose was not to enter into a bilateral cultural agreement. In fact, the main object the Canadians had was to entice the Maritimes into a larger union and, in the process, convince them that a strong central government was a necessity. Maritime, not French, delegates objected most frequently.

From the evidence available, ethnic and cultural matters occupied only a minor part of the proceedings. Although some very precise resolutions were passed, it is difficult to interpret them as the harbingers of a bicultural or bilingual nation. Section 133 of the British North America Act deals with language. It very clearly states that English and French should have equal status in the federal parliament (printed or oral), in the courts of Canada (pleas and written) and in the legislature and courts of Quebec. All this is very precise and limited. Also the Canadian government, according to the British North America Act, did not need to write any of its publications other than those emanating from parliament in any language other than English. There is no evidence that the French Canadian delegates were dissatisfied with these restrictions.

The most divisive of all cultural issues considered by the Fathers was not language, but education for the religious minorities. The problem of education for minorities at the time of Confederation was always presented from the religious viewpoint, not the linguistic. Although it became a critical problem within a generation of Confederation, language was not an important educational issue in the 1860s. All guarantees given, education involved not nationality or language, but religion. Religious guarantees did not represent a disadvantage to the Anglo-Saxon minority of Quebec which was at the time of Confederation all but identical with the Protestant minority. English-speaking Quebecers, albeit only about one-quarter of the population of Quebec, exercised power out of all proportion to their number. They controlled industry, commerce and finance especially in the Montreal, Quebec and Eastern Township areas. And they were both jealous of their privileged positions and fearful of any change which might undermine that situation. Alexander Galt, their major spokesman, hived some twelve electoral districts to guarantee English Protestant dominance. He also attempted to obtain better protection for the schools of the Protestant Quebec minority.

The Quebec Conference had given the right to control education to the provinces "saving the rights and privileges which the Protestant and Catholic minority in both Canadas may possess as to their denominational schools at the time when the union goes into operation." This was narrow in two ways: no mode of appeal was set down and it excluded New Brunswick and Nova Scotia. At London, Galt proposed that the rights of the Catholic minority as existed in law concerning education in the Maritimes be included and that all religious minorities in all provinces be granted the right to appeal to the central government against any law of a provincial legislature that prejudicially affected their educational interests. Such were the educational guarantees as written in the British North America Act.

It must be emphasized that the British-Canadians in Lower Canada were satisfied because they were virtually all Protestants. But what of the French Canadians in other provinces? Why did the French Canadian delegates from Quebec not fight for their rights? There are at least two answers to this important question and both are somewhat complicated. Proponents of the Compact idea accept the fact that the specific rights to language were embodied in Section 133. They also accept the fact that the problem of education was debated in a religious not linguistic form. They nevertheless continue to maintain that Confederation was a compact in the sense of an unstated moral commitment, a gentleman's agreements, a product of the spirit of comradeship and trust that permeated the Confederation movement. In this sense, then, the compact adherents argue, the French Canadian delegates just assumed and trusted that the rights of their countrymen in the other provinces would be protected. In support of this, isolated comments from various Fathers are trotted out which indicate their desire to extend the spirit of the Union period into the Confederation era. According to these Fathers, the Union period was one of mutual good feeling and trust between the races and was an era in which both French and English rights were fully and equally guaranteed. Yet one should be wary of taking these statements out of context. Religious riots were all too common and the following temperate comment by Brown in 1859 is typical of the Upper Canadian reform view of the French Canadian Roman Catholics of Lower Canada:

> Conceding to the French the credit which their political conduct earned
> before the present union [of 1841], we are obliged to hold them
> accountable for many of the anomalies and much of the wrong which
> now disgrace the system. They have evinced no forebearance, no
> generosity, no justice ... under the union....

The exultation felt by George Brown at the close of the Quebec Conference
probably adequately catches the 'spirit' of the Union period. 'All right!!!' he
wrote to his wife,

> Conference through at six o'clock this evening—constitution adopted—
> a most creditable document—a complete reform of all the abuses and
> injustice we have complained of!! Is it not wonderful? French Canadianism
> entirely extinguished![8]

But even if one accepts the fact that some sort of harmony did exist, it is
still possible to claim that the extent of this harmony was adequately
encompassed by Section 133 of the BNA Act. By it, Quebec, formerly lower
Canada, would continue to have control over its language within its
boundaries. Confederation guaranteed that. George Brown and his Upper
Canadian reform followers, believing that the French would no longer be
able to interfere with their rights, willingly accepted this.

The answer then to the initial question of why the French Canadian
delegates did not fight for the language rights of their compatriots in the
other provinces is not the one given by Compact theorists. Rather as far as
most Quebec Francophones were concerned, there were no French Canadians outside Quebec—as Cartier put it in 1866, "Upper Canada is inhabited
by only one race; the same is not true of Lower Canada." Or as Hector
Langevin, a French Canadian proponent of Confederation, said in 1865,
"Upper Canada has a homogeneous population professing different religions." The 75,000 French-speaking Canadians in Upper Canada were
ignored. So too were the Acadians: according to one historian, during the
whole debate on the Quebec resolutions in the Canadian legislature the
Acadian expulsion by the British was mentioned only twice. The little
protection they did receive was as Catholics not as French-speaking Canadians.

Why this rather near-sighted view on the part of the French Canadians?
At least part of the reason seems to lie in the defensive mentality possessed by
many Quebecers at the time of Confederation. Few expressed any overt

---

[8]J.M.S. Careless, *Brown of the Globe, Statesman of Confederation, 1860-80,* Toronto, 1963, p.
171.

desire to expand their language and institutions to the north-west for example. Led by the clergy and some French bourgeois who were closely tied to the Anglo business structure, the French instead hoped to colonize, via provincially-owned railroads, the northern reaches of Quebec. This business-Catholic elite seemed to fear too great a French-Canadian emigration, already underway to the New England States, and seemed consciously to accept the notion that the French fact had its best chance for survival on the North American continent within the boundaries of Quebec. To dilute or siphon off their strength in Quebec could therefore be potentially disastrous.

There is another variation to the Compact theory—and this is the one most often used by provinces to extract power from the federal government. The Compact theorists claim that a confusion quickly arose between region and race. Once races became equated with regions, the idea of a pact between races became transformed into the idea of a pact between provinces. According to the extreme version of this theory, a number of sovereign provinces met, delegated certain enumerated, i.e., listed powers to a central government and retained all other powers for themselves. The result was continuous struggle for power which in constitutional terms has hinged on the relative strengths of the enumerated powers in Section 91 of the British North America Act which lists, following the general catch-all statement: "peace, order and good government", the powers available to the central government and those in Section 92 which list the supposedly exclusive powers of the provincial legislatures.

It is generally accepted that Macdonald and most of the Fathers desired a strong central government. Certainly such a desire is in line with the interpretation of motivations offered earlier. The economic interests desired a strong central government for without it the attainment of loans and capital from abroad to finance railroads, etc., would be extremely difficult. Similarly the problems of defence would be compounded without a strong central administrative authority. Macdonald summed this attitude up when he wrote the following to a friend late in 1864:

> If the Confederation goes on, you, if spared the ordinary age of man will see both local powers and governments absolved in the general power. This is as plain to me as if I saw it accomplished.

Quite clearly then, the classic meaning of federalism as coordinate sovereignties was not Macdonald's idea. A better way to describe his nation is 'quasi-federalism'.

A second point which the Compact theorists often overlook is simply that the provinces thought they could guarantee regional equality and local interests not through the concept of delegated or enumerated powers, but through the appointed Upper Chamber, the Senate. The major rationale for the Senate's existence and the major reason that the Maritimes and Quebec agreed with the principle of weak provincial governments was that they thought their rights could be protected by the concept of equal regional representation in the Senate. Each of Quebec, Ontario and the Maritimes were allowed twenty-four representatives. The third and most damning argument against the idea that the provinces were somehow sovereign entities similar to the American States a century earlier who had coalesced in a treaty form, is that this notion is simply historically and legally incorrect. The British North America Act was a legislative creation not a treaty which emerged from the deliberations of sovereign powers. In fact, the British North American colonies and then Canada, after 1867, did not and would not have treaty-making powers for some years to come.

Nevertheless, despite the best intentions of the Fathers, the British North America Act did contain seeds of future problems. While Section 93 of the British North America Act did set up the central government as the final guardian of minority rights in education, Section 92 gave to the provinces exclusive control over all civil rights. Also the provinces were given exclusive rights over provincial 'property', a stipulation which seemed to conflict with the federal government's supposed control over Public Debt and Property. The Act, then, embodied contradictions, contradictions that ambitious provincial premiers and disgruntled anti-confederates strove to exploit, often successfully, in the years following 1867.

BIBLIOGRAPHY

The Late Eighteenth Century

Bumsted, J. *Understanding the Loyalists.* Sackville, 1986.

Griffiths, Naomi. *Acadian Deportation.* Toronto, 1968.

Historical Atlas of Canada, vol. I. Toronto, 1993.

Lawson, Philip. *The Imperial Challenge: Quebec and Britain in the Age of the American Revolution.* Kingston, 1989.

Paquet, G., and Wallot, J.P. *Patronage et Pouvoir dans le Bas-Canada, 1794-1812.* Montreal, 1973.

Potter-MacKinnon, Janice. *While the Women Only Wept: Loyalist Refugee Women.* Montreal, 1993.

Wynn, Graham. "A Region of Scattered Settlements and Bounded Possibilities: Northeastern America, 1775-1800," *Canadian Geographer,* 31 (1987), 319-38.

Fragments of Empire: The Pattern of Economic Expansion, 1791-1867
Baskerville, P. *The Bank of Upper Canada.* Ottawa, 1987.

Brown, J. *Strangers in Blood: Fur Trade Company Families in Indian Country.* Vancouver, 1980.

Courville, S., and Seguin, N. *Rural Life in 19th Century Quebec.* CHA Historical Booklet #47, 1989.

Greer, A., and Radforth, I. *Colonial Leviathan: State Formation in Mid-19th Century Canada.* Toronto, 1992.

Historical Atlas of Canada, The Land Transformed, 1800-1891, vol. 2. Toronto, 1993.

Inwood, Kris, ed. *Farm, Factory and Fortune: New Studies in the Economic History of the Maritime Provinces.* Fredericton, 1993.

McCalla, Doug. *Planting the Province: The Economic History of Upper Canada, 1784-1870.* Toronto, 1993.

Ommer, Rosemary. *From Outpost to Outpost: A Structural Analysis of the Jersey Gaspé Cod Fishery, 1767-1886.* Montreal, 1991.

Ouellet, Fernand. *Economic and Social History of Quebec, 1760-1850.* Montreal, 1966.

Pannekoek, F. *The Fur Trade and Western Canadian Society, 1670-1870.* CHA Historical Booklet #43, Ottawa, 1987.

Paquet, G., and Wallot, J.P. *Lower Canada at the Turn of the Century: Restructuring and Modernization.* CHA Historical Booklet #45, 1988.

Payne, Michael. *"The Most Respectable Place in the Territory": Everyday life in the Hudson's Bay Company Service, York Factory, 1788-1870.* Ottawa, 1989.

Ronald Rudin. *Banking en français: The French Banks of Quebec, 1835-1925.* Toronto, 1985.

Salée, Daniel. "Seigneurial Landownership and the Transition to Capitalism in Nineteenth Century Quebec", *Quebec Studies,* 12 (1991), 21-32.

Samson, Daniel, ed. *Contested Countryside: Rural Workers and Modern Society in Atlantic Canada, 1800-1950.* Fredericton, 1994.

Schulze, David. "Rural Manufacture in Lower Canada: Understanding Seigneurial Privilege and the Transition in the Countryside", *Alternate Routes,* 7 (1984), 134-67.

Van Kirk, Sylvia. *"Many Tender Ties": Women in the Fur Trade Society, 1670-1870.* Toronto, 1980.

Wilson, Bruce G. *The Enterprises of Robert Hamilton: A Study of Wealth and Influence in Early Upper Canada, 1776-1812.* Ottawa, 1983.

Wynn, Graham. *Timber Colony: A Historical Geography of Early 19th Century New Brunswick.* Toronto, 1981.

Elite Rule and the Emergence of Dissent: Politics and Power, 1791-1840
Beck, J.M. *Joseph Howe,* vols. 1 and 2. Montreal, 1982-83.
Brown, I. "The Origins of the Asylum in Upper Canada, 1830-39", *Canadian Bulletin of Medical History,* I (1984), 37-58.
Buckner, Phil. *The Transition to Responsible Government: British Policy in British North America.* Westpoint, 1985.
Craig, G. *Upper Canada: The Formative Years.* Toronto, 1966.
Dictionary of Canadian Biography, vols. 4-8. Toronto, 1980s and 1990s.
Greer, Allan. *The Patriots and the People: The Rebellions of 1837 in Rural Lower Canada.* Toronto, 1993.
Johnson, J.K. *Becoming Prominent: Regional Leadership in Upper Canada, 1791-1841.* Kingston, 1989.
McCann, P. "Culture, State Formation and the Invention of Tradition, Newfoundland, 1832-1855", *Journal of Canadian Studies,* 23, 1988.
Ouellet, F. *Lower Canada, 1791-1840: Social Change and Nationalism.* Toronto, 1980.
Read, Colin. *The Rising in Western Upper Canada, 1837-38.* Toronto, 1982.
Read, C., and R.J. Stagg, *The Rebellion of 1837 in Upper Canada.* Toronto, 1985.
Romney, Paul. *Mr. Attorney: The Attorney General for Ontario in Court, Cabinet and Legislature, 1791-1899.* Toronto, 1986.

Confronting Change: Politics and Society, 1838-1864
Careless, J.M.S. *The Union and the Canadas: The Growth of Canadian Institutions, 1841-57.* Toronto, 1967.
—, ed. *The Pre-Confederation Premiers: Ontario Government Leaders, 1841-1867.* Toronto, 1980.
Dictionary of Canadian Biography, vols. 5-12. Toronto, 1980s and 1990s.
Monet, Jacques. *The Last Cannon Shot: A Study of French Canadian Nationalism, 1837-50.* Toronto, 1969.
Noel, S.J.R. *Patrons, Clients, Brokers: Ontario Society and Politics, 1791-1876.* Toronto, 1990.
Ormsby, W.G. *The Emergence of the Federal Concept in Canada, 1839-45.* Toronto, 1969.
Prentice, A. et al. *Canadian Women: A History.* Toronto, 1988.
Romney, P. *Mr. Attorney: The Attorney General for Ontario in Court, Cabinet and Legislature, 1791-1899.* Toronto, 1986.
Stewart, G.T. *The Origins of Canadian Politics: A Comparative Approach.* Vancouver, 1986.

The Search for Economic and Political Integration: Confederation, 1864-67

Baker, William M. *Timothy Warren Anglin, 1822-96: Irish Catholic Canadian.* Toronto, 1977.

Beck, J. Murray. *Joseph Howe: The Briton Becomes a Canadian, 1848-1873.* Kingston and Montreal: McGill-Queen's University Press, 1983.

Bonenfant, Jean-Charles. *The French Canadian and the Birth of Confederation.* Ottawa, 1966.

Buckner, Phillip. "The Maritimes and Confederation: A Reassessment", *Canadian Historical Review,* 71 (1990), 1-30.

Creighton, Donald. *Dominion of the North: A History of Canada.* Toronto, 1944.

—. *John A. Macdonald: The Young Politician.* Toronto, 1952.

—. *John A. Macdonald: The Old Chieftain.* Toronto, 1955.

—. *The Road to Confederation: The Emergence of Canada, 1863-1867.* Toronto, 1964.

Groulx, Lionel. *La Confédération canadienne, ses origines.* Montreal, 1918.

Lower Arthur, R.M. *Colony to Nation: A History of Canada.* Toronto, 1946.

Martin, Ged, ed. *The Causes of Canadian Confederation.* Fredericton: Acadiensis Press, 1990.

Morton, W.L. *The Critical Years: The Union of British North America, 1857-1873.* Toronto, 1964.

Muise, D.A. "The Federal Election of 1867 in Nova Scotia: An Economic Interpretation", *Collections of the Nova Scotia Historical Society,* 36 (1968), 327-51.

Pryke, Kenneth G. *Nova Scotia and Confederation, 1864-1871.* Toronto, 1979.

Ryerson, Stanley B. *Unequal Union: Confederation and the Roots of Conflict in the Canadas, 1815-1873.* Toronto, 1968.

Trotter, R.G. *Canadian Federation, Its Origins and Achievement: A Study in Nation Building.* Toronto, 1924.

Waite, P.B. *The Life and Times of Confederation, 1864-67.* Politics, Newspapers, and the Union of British North America. Toronto, 1962.

Weale, David, and Harry Baglole. *The Island and Confederation: The End of an Era.* Summerside: Williams & Crue, 1973.

Whitelaw, William Menzies. *The Maritimes and Canada Before Confederation.* Toronto, 1934.

3

Canada's Atlantic Provinces after Confederation

Ernest Forbes

Confederation has been called an unequal union. This was particularly obvious in the comparison of populations of the four tiny prospective Atlantic provinces—Nova Scotia (388,000), New Brunswick (286,000), Newfoundland and Labrador (147,000), and Prince Edward Island (94,000)—with those of the two large central provinces—Ontario (1,621,000) and Quebec 1,192,000—at the time of the initial federation. The gap later widened with the rise of dominant industrial metropolises in each of the two larger provinces. Such great discrepancies might not have mattered had the provincial governments disappeared into a complete legislative union as some Confederates had proposed. There each citizen would, theoretically at least, have had equal influence and shared evenly in the benefits of government. Nor would it have been so serious, perhaps, had the constitution provided the equal representation for strong autonomous provinces at one level of the legislature, which other Confederates favoured. But the constitution outlined in the British North America Act of 1867 fell somewhere in between. The provinces remained as rallying points for local interests and loyalties. With the failure of the Senate to emerge as an effective guardian of provincial concerns, those of the larger provinces clearly dominated in the central government. The Atlantic provinces would not only lose the struggle to protect contemporary interests but would find the rules of the game increasingly skewed against them as the constitution continued to evolve. Thus the first hundred and thirty years of confederation were for the Atlantic provinces highlighted by struggles to resist declining economic and political influence in the union which they all eventually joined.

Some years ago historian Del Muise hypothesized a major economic division between a traditional 'wood, wind and water' economy in the Atlantic region and a newly emerging economy based on coal, steam and steel. The contrast was particularly visible in the province of Nova Scotia. The participants in the old economy had sold their agricultural products, timber, fish and ships in international markets including Great Britain, the United States and the West Indies. The carrying trade, which featured substantial merchant marines in both Nova Scotia and New Brunswick and linkages to local banks and insurance companies was also part of the traditional economy. Their economic orientation tended to produce a world-view favouring international trade, low tariffs and modest governments which would allow maximum competitiveness in world markets. Meanwhile, a new economy was beginning to take shape as Maritimers began to contemplate the industrial advantages of having the only coal resources in eastern British North American. Mining promoters, foundrymen, and other manufacturers had begun to call for governments to take the lead in railway development and were willing to face with equanimity the taxes, in the form of tariffs, which these would require. Indeed, some saw the tariffs as affording necessary protection while the colonies developed their own infant industries. Thus, confederation found proponents of the old economy suspicious of and hostile to a union with protectionist Canada while proponents of the new tended to favour confederation as leading to the railway and industrial development which they favoured.

While the economic division alone offers a simplistic explanation of the region's response to confederation, it can be useful in suggesting broad trends in popular attitudes. Many in the traditional industries in Nova Scotia did oppose confederation. Agricultural, shipbuilding and timber interests did come out against the union. Nova Scotia Confederates picked up substantial support in counties such as Cumberland, Pictou and Cape Breton, where coal resources suggested potential, for industrial development in continental milieu. As the key source of industrial energy, coal was the 'black gold' of the nineteenth century. The incipient new economy provided a base for support for Confederates led by Cumberland County's Charles Tupper. The Anti-confederates, led by Joseph Howe, initially prevailed, reflecting the relatively greater strength of traditional economic interests. But the American threat, British pressure and the promise of a better deal than the Quebec Resolutions led the Nova Scotia legislature to reverse its position to favour confederation before the end of 1866.

New Brunswickers, whose economy was dominated by the timber trade were initially even more hostile to confederation. Unable to persuade the legislature to accept the scheme in 1865, Confederate leader Samuel Leonard Tilley called an election on the issue and suffered a disastrous defeat. Only the difficulties of his opponents, the threat of Fenian invasions and vigorous interference from the British government enabled him to reverse the verdict at the polls the following year.

Prince Edward Islanders, heavily dependent on agriculture, too gave a response reflective of economic interest. Dependent upon the traditional economy and fearing that Great Britain might simply annex their island to the new union, they were most vocal in their opposition. They rejected the Quebec Resolutions and declared that there never could be a scheme for union which would fit the island's needs. But as the years went by Confederates there moved obliquely in committing the island to the construction of an expensive railway system which left farmers the dubious choice between entering confederation or facing a massive increase in taxation. Thus in 1873 the Island province formed with New Brunswick and Nova Scotia a region of small provinces which shared an ocean boundary and the interests which went with it—a region which increasingly became known as simply 'the Maritimes'.

That Newfoundland, a large rugged island where the codfishery ruled supreme, had shown any interest in Confederation was surprising. Its interest is usually explained in terms of the series of natural disasters which had disrupted the fisheries in the early 1860s and by the Protestant merchant community's fear of the potential radicalism of Irish Catholic fishermen. There seemed little potential economic advantage for Newfoundlanders in the new union. They had no railway debts and their principal fish markets were in Britain, the West Indies and Europe. Their population was heavily concentrated on the side of the island most distant from North America. As a contemporary folksong declared "Our face is towards Europe, Our back's to the Gulf, Come near at your peril Canadian wolf!" Charles Fox Bennett, the proprietor of a tin mine, mobilized the anti-confederates in 1870 in an election victory which determined that Newfoundland would remain a Dominion separate from Canada within the British Empire.

On entering Confederation the Maritimes pushed to secure the economic benefits which the Confederates had envisioned. Most important was the construction of the Intercolonial Railway which would link the region with the markets of central Canada. This had been a part of the Confederation agreement and was spelled out in the British North America Act. Its construction proceeded by government contract and gave a powerful patronage lever for the confederates in constructing a federal Conservative party in the region. Completed in 1876, the railway also served as an engine of economic development in the communities along the line.

Proponents of the new economy were quick to ally themselves with protectionists in central Canada. In 1870 Nova Scotia politicians had negotiated a deal with their Ontario counterparts for protective tariffs on coal, wheat and flour. Billing it as retaliation against American protectionism which would serve to develop national sentiment within the country, the sponsors of the new legislation called it their National Policy. In the face of manufacturers' opposition, the legislation was soon repealed but the name endured for the protectionist policies of the Conservatives. These suddenly became more popular in the face of American dumping practices during the economic depression which began in 1873 and persisted through most of the decade.

The Macdonald government's National Policy of protective tariffs, introduced by finance minister S.L. Tilley in 1879, restored the 50 cents a ton coal tariff, the duty on wheat and flour, and introduced a series of frankly protectionist *ad valorem* tariffs on manufactured goods produced in Canada. The new tariffs, railway construction and the opening up of the west to rapid settlement have traditionally been treated by Canadian historians as forming part of a coherent programme to develop an integrated national economy.

With Tilley in the finance portfolio and Charles Tupper as minister of railways, the Maritimes were well situated to benefit from the new programme. While 50 cents a ton may not seem like much protection on coal, introduced at a time when a ton of coal sold for 79 cents at the pithead, it was substantial. Since coal was a heavy and bulky commodity, one would expect industry to come to the coal rather than vice versa. For the first few years of the new programme, that seemed to be the case. As Bill Acheson has pointed out "The Maritimes by 1885 ... with less than one-fifth of the population ... contained eight of twenty-three Canadian cotton mills—including seven of the nineteen erected after 1879— three of five sugar refineries, two of seven rope factories, one of three glass works, both of the Canadian steel mills and six of the nation's twelve rolling mills."[1] As well as seeking tariff changes designed to make their industries competitive, Maritime manufacturers sought freight rate changes which would make their goods more competitive in central Canadian markets. Tupper was favourably disposed and the government-operated railway, which did not have to show a profit or resort to public markets to raise capital, often found it both politically and economically expedient to lower rates to attract or maintain industry in the region.

Maritimers sought to further consolidate their industrial position in Canada through participation in the Canadian Pacific Railway. This was by no means automatic. Though calling it a transcontinental railway, the Macdonald government initially planned to terminate the line at Montreal. Only the financial difficulties encountered by the builders near the end of construction in 1885 gave the Maritime caucus of the governing Conservative

[1]T.W. Acheson, *Acadiensis,* vol. 1, no. 2 (Spring, 1972), pp. 3-28.

Party enough leverage to force its extension by a 'Short Line' from Montreal through Maine to Saint John, New Brunswick.

While business boomed along the railways connecting industrial town—from Sydney westward through New Glasgow and Halifax and northward through Amherst and Moncton to Saint John—traditional 'outports', such as Pictou and Guysborough in Nova Scotia, Shediac and Hillsborough in New Brunswick and Summerside and Murray Harbour in Prince Edward Island appeared to be in a lingering depression. Much of their problems of job losses and a mass exodus were related to the decline of the 'old economy'. The wooden shipbuilding industry which was scattered through the outports of the region initially met the challenges from iron hulled vessels by building larger and faster ships and seeking out the less travelled routes in which they could still compete. The 1880s saw that industry's collapse in the Maritimes. The wood trade too declined as the more accessible timber was consumed. The slump in the West Indies' economy lessened its ability to absorb the Maritimes' agricultural products, fish and timber. Meanwhile, the protective tariff made most Canadian producers less competitive in international markets.

One can hardly blame former anti-confederate politicians, such as James Fraser of Guysborough County, who, as they witnessed the decline of activity in their ports and a general exodus of population from their communities, began to say 'We told you so!'. They attributed most economic problems to confederation and the National Policy and called for the Maritime provinces' secession from confederation and union in a separate Dominion within the British Empire. In the mid-1880s, Fraser pushed hard for the separatist option within the ruling Nova Scotia Liberal party. But the representatives of the new industrial towns, although unhappy with the financial terms of Confederation, saw union as essential to their industrial future. Liberal premier and former anti-confederate W.S. Fielding skilfully united both factions in a campaign for a re-negotiation of financial terms with the federal government. Demanding either better terms or secession the Fielding administration increased their share of the popular vote in the provincial election of 1886 by a whopping 13 per cent.

Despite Fielding's apparent mandate for separation, the Macdonald-led federal government refused to negotiate. Fielding soon found that his options were limited. The Maritime union which was supposed to accompany secession proved impossible of achievement. In New Brunswick, Premier A.G. Blair, whose province was the principal beneficiary of the recently begun CPR Railway extension was cool to the plan. In Prince Edward Island, where people traditionally feared any scheme which might smack of

annexation or lead to the loss of their local legislature, the Liberal leader
wanted nothing to do with Fielding's proposal and Conservative Premier
W.W Sullivan failed to answer his letters. Meanwhile, the federal Conservatives, while making no public concessions to the Maritimes, empowered
former Nova Scotian premier, Sir John Thompson, the province's senior
cabinet minister, to work quietly behind the scenes with concessions on
patronage, freight rates and other issues. In the federal election of 1887
secession appeared to be soundly defeated as the Conservatives won 14 of 21
seats.

On Prince Edward Island in 1887 W.W. Sullivan launched an appeal to
the British throne regarding the alleged failure of the federal government to
honour promises in the confederation agreement. His primary concern was
winning additional finances but his strongest evidence of the federal
government's delinquency involved its failure to provide 'continuous
communication' in ferry service between the Island and mainland, especially
during the winter months. An embarrassed federal government promised to
look into the matter and the Island government eventually received a small
payment of $20,000 a year in compensation for claims outstanding.

By their dramatic actions Fielding and Sullivan had won small victories.
But their need to resort to such tactics suggested the weakness of the smaller
provinces' influence in the daily workings of the federal system and boded ill
for their protection of economic interests in the long term.

Newfoundland, meanwhile, faced its own tough choices. With a narrowing
of profits from the fisheries offering a limited base for a growing population,
the Conservatives under the leadership of William Whiteway became the
focus of those calling for a diversification of the economy through a kind of
National Policy featuring the construction of a railway across the island from
Port aux Basques to St. John's. While the merchants and other exponents of
the traditional economy decried the cost and accurately predicted that the
burden of the debt involved would ultimately fall on the fisheries, they failed
to develop a popular alternative. Whiteway's party won the election and
began construction on the railway in 1881. By the mid-1890s the railway was
nearing completion. It had encouraged mineral, timber and pulp and paper
developments, but the income generated would not pay operating expenses
much less a return on capital invested. Certainly the promised diversification
did not enable Newfoundland's two banks to survive the crisis in the fisheries
which saw both close their doors by the end of 1894. This crisis caused
Newfoundland politicians to again approach the Canadian government
about the possibility of Confederation. The latter's lack of enthusiasm did
not encourage drastic action by the Newfoundlanders, who now saw Canada

as villain standing in the way of much coveted reciprocal trade agreements with the United States. Canadian Banks moved into the vacuum allowing the smaller Dominion to recover its solvency and maintain its political independence.

The social milieu in the Atlantic colonies resembled that of the rest of British North America with similarities more striking than differences and both tending to date from original patterns of settlement. As elsewhere in British North America, religion was an important determinant. Weekly church services gave ideological leadership and were supported by a variety of auxiliary activities including Sunday schools, prayer meetings and missionary societies. The Atlantic region was about one-third Catholic—26 per cent of Nova Scotians, 36 per cent of New Brunswickers, 42 per cent of Prince Edward Islanders and 46 per cent of Newfoundlanders. The Maritimes had four major Protestant denominations—Anglican, Presbyterian, Methodist and Baptist with concentrations related to ethnicity and original patterns of settlement. Presbyterians were prominent in Scottish communities in eastern Nova Scotia. Baptists dominated in the west and were common in New Brunswick's Saint John River Valley—areas whose settlers tended to come from the United States. Here too Methodists were well represented although their greatest density was on the Chignecto isthmus—which included the town of Sackville—originally settled by English Yorkshiremen. Anglicans were common in the capital cities and the Saint John River Valley. In Newfoundland, the Protestants were divided between Anglicans and Methodists and were dominant in the outports north of Conception Bay.

Ethnic and religious diversity was both reflected in and consolidated by divisions in higher education in the Maritimes. Acadia University in Wolfville served the Baptist community, Mount Allison at Sackville the Methodists. King's College in Windsor had an Anglican affiliation. A college of the same name in Fredericton had emerged as the University of New Brunswick without losing its Anglican and Loyalist traditions. Saint Mary's university in Halifax was an Irish Catholic institution and Saint Francis Xavier University in Antigonish served the needs of Scottish Catholics. Scottish Presbyterians tended to embrace the publicity supported Dalhousie University. On Prince Edward Island two colleges, a Catholic Saint Dunstan's and a Protestant Saint Andrew's allowed Islanders to take the first year or two of university instruction close to home, a privilege denied to Newfoundlanders until the establishment of Memorial College there in 1925.

That such duplication of effort stood in the way of the development of a modern university in the region was apparent to those involved. Efforts at cooperation in the 1870s failed. The Carnegie Foundation, the American

philanthropic organization to whom the Maritime colleges frequently
appealed for funds, proposed in 1921 a concentration of the different
denominational colleges in a single university at Halifax and offered generous funding for the transition. Saint Francis Xavier was the first to refuse,
giving the others an excuse to back out. In the end only King's College, its
buildings recently ravaged by fire, took up the Foundation's offer and moved
its operations to the Dalhousie campus.

Although not without their own controversies, the Protestants in the
nineteenth century shared a common *Bible* and were strongly influenced by
movements for evangelical reform. They cooperated in a variety of reform
organizations such as the Sons of Temperance and the Woman's Christian
Temperance Union. They also shared a common suspicion of Catholics, not
only because of doctrinal differences—symbolized in a different version of
the *Bible*—but also because of their hierarchical organization which seemed
to divert loyalties outside the country. Catholics on the other hand saw
Protestant efforts at non-sectarianism as aggression against them. They
assumed a defensive posture in organizing their own temperance, philanthropic and reform organizations and were particularly suspicious of Protestants' efforts to establish public systems of education.

Newfoundland in the 1860s acted to defuse religious tensions by
channelling educational monies into three denominational school systems
and by an informal proportional representation of Catholics and Protestants
in their political parties. Nova Scotia adopted a single public school system
in 1863, which was ameliorated for the Catholics through informal agreements
regarding school board representation, the participation of religious orders,
such as the Sisters of Charity, in classroom teaching, after school religious
instruction and, in areas of Catholic concentration such as Halifax, *de facto*
separate Catholic schools. On Prince Edward Island, questions of religious
instruction in the teachers' college and in the public schools polarized
politics from the 1850s through the 1870s. Thereafter, Island politicians
developed a series of informal compromises similar to those prevailing in
Nova Scotia.

New Brunswick leaders seemed to learn nothing from their neighbours'
experiences. The government of George King followed the Common Schools
Act of 1871 with regulations effectively barring religious instruction from the
classroom and the participation of Catholic teaching orders. New Brunswick
Catholics, mainly Irish and Acadian in origin, resolved to maintain their own
schools and refused to pay the new taxation. Their appeal to the federal
government to disallow the provincial legislation met delay and the eventual
decision of the Macdonald government not to intervene.

One of their protests erupted into violence in Caraquet after a small rump of Protestants used the Catholics' refusal to pay the new taxes to challenge the election of parish officers. The resort of some Acadians to intimidation led to a show of force by an Anglophone militia early in 1875, which resulted in one fatality on each side and nine Acadians being charged with murder. Only then did the New Brunswick government negotiate with the Catholic bishops the kind of compromises which their neighbours had already worked out. These allowed after school instruction, religious order classroom participation and some *de facto* Catholic schools. Such compromises did not end controversies over the role of religion in public education. These surfaced periodically throughout the next half century, sometimes given impetus by the anti-Catholic Orange Order or even, on occasion, by the Ku Klux Klan.

Religious controversy often went hand in hand with ethnic tensions. Acadians moved into the land opened for settlement by the railway construction in Northern New Brunswick and showed a greater resistance to emigration during the decline of the outports. They steadily increased their proportion of New Brunswick's population, even gaining majorities in several of the northern counties and prominence in the industrial and railway centre of Moncton. From the 1860s to the 1900s the Acadian share of New Brunswick's population went from 15 to 27 per cent and peaked at 33 per cent by 1931. They had also assumed majority status within the Catholic Church in the province.

Naturally enough the Acadians sought the political and cultural recognition which their numbers appeared to warrant. And just as naturally Anglophones viewed with dismay their reduction to minority status in local communities and the apparent cultural aggression of the newcomers. Although sometimes discouraged by an Irish-dominated hierarchy, Acadian leaders sought the bilingual schools through which their language might be preserved. Their establishment of Saint Joseph College in 1864 helped train an emerging leadership including the politicians P.A. Landry and Pascal Poirier. Imbibing the nationalistic currents of that age, they in turn embraced the Evangeline myth popularized by an American poet, H.W. Longfellow, in an epic poem of that name. In 1881 they organized at Memramcook the first of a series of Acadian national conventions. These chose a series of national symbols distinct from the Quebecois, including a flag, a national anthem and a national day of celebration. Meanwhile, they pushed for greater recognition of their nationality within the two major political parties and the Catholic Church. Although their organizations, such as the Assomption Society which arranged their conventions and the Mutual Assomption

Society, an insurance company, which after 1903 provided an economic base for their operations, were regional, most of their political gains—first federal cabinet minister (1878), first Senatorship (1885), first Bishop (1911) and first premier (1923)—came in New Brunswick, where their numbers made them a potent political force.

Gender was also an important source of social division. Prevailing attitudes as to the different roles for men and women in the Atlantic colonies had hardened into an ideology often characterized by the term 'separate spheres'. Rooted in their biological differences men and women were supposedly designed to play different social roles. Women's was a nurturing role through the raising of children and looking after the home. Theoretically, they had no business in the work places outside the home and needed only the education which would make them effective wives and mothers. This ideology influenced legislation in all four colonies, which denied voting and property rights to women as well as access to public office. Reality, however, differed from theory as the need for survival, the support of family income and other motives drew women into a variety of occupations, including domestic service, prostitution, teaching, nursing and the operation of their own businesses. By the end of the century work as secretaries, factory workers and store clerks had replaced domestic service as the chief employment of female labour.

The prevailing ideology was never without challenge from women in the region. Methodist women demanded access to higher education and were admitted to Mount Allison University in the 1850s. Although Mount Allison was initially regarded as a kind of finishing school for daughters of the upper classes, some, such as Grace Annie Lockhart, who graduated with a Bachelor's of Science and English Literature degree in 1875, took full advantage of the supposedly more practical courses intended for the men. The Baptists also admitted women to Acadia about the same time. Baptist women in the Maritime pioneered the development of separate women's missionary societies in Canada, a movement which quickly spread to other denominations and regions. Halifax in the 1870s witnessed a lively exchange of pamphlets on the role of women in the churches. The 1880s saw the importation from the United States of an exclusively female temperance organization known as the Woman's Christian Temperance Union. With branches in most Maritime centres and a reported membership in excess of 1500 the WCTU emerged as a key feminist organization. Not only did it lead the campaign for women's voting rights but it deliberately trained its membership in parliamentary procedure so that they would have the confidence to assume the public role which they believed should be theirs.

As elsewhere in North America the 1890s proved a critical decade for feminist activity in the Maritimes. In 1893 the National Council of Women established branches in both Halifax and Saint John. Although units of the Dominion Women's Enfranchisement Association appeared by 1894, the movement was spearheaded in both cities by the WCTU. In Nova Scotia and New Brunswick compliant legislatures had voted women the franchise in municipal politics on the same property qualification as men. Nova Scotia women almost secured the provincial franchise in 1893 when a bill to remove any mention of gender from the act passed second reading by two votes. But then came the backlash. J.W. Longley, the Attorney General, who feared the revolutionary changes in the relations of men and women implicit in the feminist movement, stalled the legislation until members had gone home near the end of the session and defeated it. The Catholic hierarchy also came out against the movement which it too saw as revolutionary in its implications and a threat to family life. Although the feminists worked hard in a political campaign to carry the enfranchisement legislation—amassing petitions of more than ten thousand signatures in support in both Nova Scotia and New Brunswick—they had the fatal weakness of having to depend on others for their political influence. The politicians backed away from the issue and majorities against the feminists mounted throughout the remainder of the decade. Some feminists, such as Edith Archibald of Halifax, consciously shifted their attention to the social causes of the progressive movement. They re-emphasized a maternal feminist rhetoric which justified a greater role by women in public life in terms of the separate spheres ideology and the special role that women could play in 'mothering' society through their support of social reform.

Social reform became the slogan of the next two decades as North Americans began to critically examine the *laissez-faire* principles to which they had paid at least lip-service in the previous century. In a new wave of optimism Atlantic residents joined in the discussion of ways of restructuring society to eliminate poverty, disease, alcoholism, class exploitation and other social problems of the day. Some of the most vigorous discussions emerged within the churches. An element within the Protestant denominations combined a renewed evangelical thrust with a re-interpretation of Christianity as a social religion. Christ was concerned not just to save individual Christians, declared the Nova Scotia Methodist Conference in 1907, but 'came to save society.'[2] Christ's teachings contained the blueprints for the realization of His Kingdom on earth. Not only was social reform possible, but its achievement was a Christian duty.

[2]*Minutes of the Nova Scotia Conference of the Methodist Church,* 1907, p. 78.

The theoretically revolutionary ideology of the social gospel emerged first among Methodists and Baptists and gradually won a dominant voice within the Presbyterian and Anglican denominations. As Joanne Veer has pointed out, it had an early supporter in the WCTU whose membership was exposed to these ideas through their American leaders, such as Francis Willard, and found in the movement the intellectual justification for their own activities. Between 1909 and 1911 the Protestant denominations established Moral and Social Reform Councils in each of the three Maritime provinces. Their goal was the re-organization of society on Christian principles. Catholics, whose response to the new ideas found expression in a Papal encyclical, *Rerum Novarum,* which denounced the abuses of *laissez-faire* capitalism and called for the Church to play a greater role in their amelioration, cautiously sent observers.

The term 'reform' spanned a broad spectrum of goals and emphases. On the left were socialists such as the journalist, Martin Butler, or the school teacher and lay preacher H.H. Stuart, who believed that the restructuring of society on Christian principles would automatically lead to a democratic socialist state. Although proportionally as numerous as in the rest of the country, socialists and their organizations remained on the fringe of the mainstream political movements in the region. On the right were those for whom the new ideology simply provided another rationale for the pursuit of traditional moral reform causes, such as the banning of liquor. The majority seemed to fit the classic progressive stance of seeking through legislation to gradually ameliorate the abuses of the capitalist system while encouraging the weaker elements of society—labourers, farmers, and fishermen—to protect themselves in the organization of trade unions and cooperatives and through a more direct involvement in politics.

Progressive reform in the Maritimes was framed against the background of continuing industrialization. By the turn of the century coal mines and the iron and steel industry were organized into two large corporations. Funded within the region, the Nova Scotia Steel and Coal Corporation had foundries and rolling mills in the Trenton-New Glasgow area of Pictou County and blast furnace in Sydney Mines. A Boston entrepreneur, Henry Whitney, developed the Dominion Coal Company whose subsidiary, the Dominion Iron and Steel Company (DISCO) operated a major steel plant at Sydney. The two corporations, Scotia and Dosco, shared more than two dozen mines in Nova Scotia and were organized to continue the manufacturing process from the basic coal and iron ore to the marketing of products such as steel rails, barbed wire, and railway cars. In 1895 the steel mills escaped their reliance on inadequate local resources of iron ore with the opening of a large iron mine on Bell island near St. John's Newfoundland. By 1905 Nova Scotia produced some six million tons of coal annually, about half of which was consumed locally, and accounted for fifty-five per cent of Canada's production of pig iron.

While capitalization in mineral development in the Maritimes approximated half of the Canadian total, and manufacturing output peaked during the Great War, the Maritimes' economy was less healthy than production totals seemed to indicate. Much of the industry in the region fell victim to metropolitan takeovers. Lacking a single metropolis of their own and scattered through the region's towns in the dispersed pattern of the earlier shipbuilding industry, the often family-owned businesses of the Maritimes proved sitting ducks for takeovers by competitors from central Canada. One after another the textile mills, sugar refineries, and rope and glass factories fell prey to outside control. This sometimes meant immediate closure as the local markets were served from central Canada. More common was the continued operation of the local plants; but without subsequent expenditure on modernization, closure was only delayed until some future recession.

Metropolitan trends also saw the centralization of financial institutions in central Canada. Here the ambitions of local entrepreneurs sometimes proved the culprit, as, for example, when the Bank of Nova Scotia absorbed other banks within the region and then went on to take over institutions in Ontario. But with success came the transfer of headquarters to Toronto in 1900 to be closer to the centre of operations. Thereafter its role tended to be that of the collector of investment capital within the Maritimes and its export westward, where returns seemed to be more certain.

The regional economy was also shaken by changes in fundamental policies, which had originally helped in the industrialization of the region. With Ontario wanting to develop a steel industry using coal imported from the United States, the National Policy was breached and the Maritimes lost its advantage in having the only coal resources in eastern Canada. The fifty cents a ton tariff on coal failed to rise with inflation. In 1887 anthracite coal was placed on the free list. In 1907 the tariff on bituminous coal, was rebated when imported for 'the smelting of metals'. In 1914 this clause was changed to 'the melting of metals'.[3]

At the same time the Maritimes began to lose their special relationship with the Intercolonial Railway. With the growth of western Canada and its development of a strong regional grievance at its higher railway freight rates relative to central Canada, the still lower rates on the Intercolonial appeared

---

[3]"Memorandum of successive changes in tariffs item 1049 ...", Papers to the Advisory Board on Tariffs and Taxation, vol. 8, ref. 3, NAC.

an embarrassing anomaly. Railway interests were particularly concerned as they faced new competition or looming bankruptcy resulting from the over-expansion of the Laurier era. The Conservative federal government of Robert Borden, whose support came largely from Ontario and the West, under the guise of more 'business like' management began the process of eliminating the Intercolonial's pro-active role in regional development. It cancelled special rates and levelled up standard rates in and from the region. In 1917 Prime Minister Borden ordered the Intercolonial to be treated for rate-making purposes like any other railway under the Board of Railway Commissioners and included it in the combination of bankrupt lines called the Canadian National Railways. Maritime producers saw their long-haul rates shoot up about 50 per cent and those with special rates, such as the sugar refineries, for example, saw their transportation cost more than double.

Such blows to the Maritime economy were hardly noticed in the abnormal conditions created by war. Business boomed as Maritime industry strained to produce the required munitions. Scotia became expert in the production of high quality shell casings and for a time DISCO produced the ship's plate required for a modern shipbuilding industry. In the latter stages of the war the price of agricultural products, fish and timber sky-rocketed, giving many Maritimers a taste of unprecedented prosperity. The boom continued into the first half of 1920, when prices suddenly plummeted. This marked the beginning of a general recession which turned into a lingering economic depression in the Maritimes.

The buoyant economy fuelled the optimism and rising expectations of the progressive era as Maritimes anticipated the new and better society that would emerge from a period of reconstruction after the war. The war brought the reform movement to a climax as the major denominations came up with platforms or agendas which included such planks as prohibition, equal pay for men and women, the eight hour days, profit sharing for workers, slum clearances, inspections of food in stores, public hydro, and campaigns against diseases such as tuberculosis. They also called for the elimination of traditional party loyalties and the limitation of 'big business' control of governments. The region saw its share of political scandals as progressive muckrakers sought to 'expose business' role.

The reformers could claim some victories. At the outset of the war, Halifax feminists had organized a meeting to plan their participation in the war effort. Georgina Pope, daughter of a prominent Prince Edward Island family, who had commanded a contingent of nurses during the Boer War suggested focusing their efforts through the Red Cross. This they did, virtually monopolizing the executive positions in the most important voluntary organization supporting Canada's military. Responsibilities ranged from knitting stockings to the outfitting of hospital ships, the support of Canadian prisoners of war and the succour of victims of wartime disasters. Their activities acquired a front line urgency after the collision of TNT and gasoline laden ships in Halifax harbour levelled the north end of the city leaving more than 1600 dead and another nine thousand injured.

Women in Nova Scotia and New Brunswick gained the vote in time for the post-war elections. In Nova Scotia and Prince Edward Island they secured the right to run for public office. Women in the two larger provinces apparently exerted their new-found power in the referendums for prohibition which passed by more than two to one majorities. Nova Scotian governments showed their concern for the new voters in a promise of commissions to investigate mothers' allowances and minimum wages for women workers. But women's influence soon proved less than they and their opponents had expected. While gaining access to the ballot, women were still denied admission to the informal 'back room' meetings where key decisions were made in each of the traditional parties. Here, as elsewhere in Canada, despite occasional protests, women were shepherded into separate auxiliaries whose duties seemed to be fund raising, refreshments, and rubberstamping the decisions taken by the males. Two women did gain nominations in the Nova Scotia election of 1920, both in constituencies where their party stood little chance of victory. Having failed to perform miracles, they quickly became part of the mythology that women could not win in the Maritimes.

Maritime governments failed to deliver mother's allowances and other progressive promises primarily because they were short of money. In surrendering their customs duties at the time of confederation the Maritime colonies had given up a substantially larger percentage of their income than had the colony of Canada. Nova Scotia and New Brunswick had gradually overcome embarrassing deficits through expanding revenues from coal mining and timber resources, only to discover along with the other provinces after the turn of the century that popular aspirations for roads, social services, and assistance to business far outstripped their finances. With Ontario and Quebec suspicious of any federal initiatives which might tap revenues concentrated in their metropolises, the Canadian government followed a policy of *ad hoc* deals with particular provinces. In creating the new Prairie provinces of Alberta and Saskatchewan in 1905, for example, the federal government used the absence of crown land as an excuse to channel much-needed funds to the new governments. Manitoba demanded and was granted comparable funding. In 1906 a settlement was reached with the remaining provinces which saw the Maritimes with substantially smaller grants on a per capita basis than even the large central provinces. Later commentators have criticized Maritime governments for accepting such an unfavourable settlement but their acute shortage of funds and declining political representation undermined their bargaining position. Their relative penury was reflected in the westward migration of their teachers, who could double their salaries on the Prairies.

Newfoundlanders too shared in a period of industrialization as they turned to outside capital for the more rapid development of their economy. Most spectacular was the infamous Reid deal by which the colony surrendered their railway, ferry service, and six thousand square miles of land to a former Canadian bridge builder in return for a million dollars and a commitment to operate the railway. While the Liberal opposition played upon the progressives' suspicion of big business' involvement with government, their policies in office included a modified Reid agreement and in 1905 an arrangement with a subsidiary of the British Harmsworth Corporation to develop a pulp and paper industry in Grand Falls. Together with France's relinquishment of its claims to joint fishing rights on Newfoundland's West Coast and the opening the Wabana iron mine on Bell Island, these developments allowed Newfoundlanders to share in the optimism of the period.

Newfoundland's most spectacular expression of progressivism came with the organization of the Fishermen's Protective Union (FPU). Under the dynamic leadership of William Coaker, former telegrapher and pioneer farmer, the FPU evolved a comprehensive programme of reform which emphasized the orderly marketing of fish, the fishermen's escape from merchant credit, greater emphasis on popular education and new programmes of social welfare. The movement spread rapidly in the largely Protestant villages from Bonavista south to Conception Bay but faltered against the sharp hostility of the Catholic Church in St. John's and the southern Avalon Peninsula. Coaker and his supporters won eight seats in the election of 1913.

The outbreak of war in 1914 brought outpourings of nationalistic and imperial sentiment throughout the region. Commitment to the war effort gradually focused on conscription and a Union government pledged to its support. The major deviation came from the Acadians whose elite broke with the rank and file to support conscription. The war's end would see a resulting long term transfer of Acadian loyalties from Conservatives to Liberals in federal politics.

The Canadian government used the moral authority gained from the needs of war to assert its emergency constitutional powers through the War Measures Act. It invoked this legislation for a variety of interventionist pieces of legislation including the nationalization of railways, prohibition (which would remain in place for those provinces whose people voted to retain it in referenda after the war) and a national tax on incomes.

Politics followed a remarkably similar pattern in Newfoundland as Coaker entered a coalition government with the ruling People's party in support of the war effort. Newfoundland's casualties on a per capita basis had been about double those of Canada. With enlistments faltering by 1917 the Union government imposed conscription. While in Canada French Canadians saw conscription directed against them, in Newfoundland Irish Catholics saw themselves as the targets. Coaker's support of conscription and prohibition further ensured that the FPU would be unlikely to expand into Catholic communities. With the dismantling of the Union Government in 1919, however, Coaker was invited into a revitalized Liberal government under the leadership of Richard Squires. As Minister of Fisheries he was able to introduce the government marketing board which had been key part of the FPU's platform. Unfortunately his timing could not have been worse as fish prices sky-rocketed for much of the first year and plummeted the second. Coaker became disillusioned with what he regarded as the lack of loyalty on the part of his followers and largely abandoned the FPU agenda

The close of the war saw Maritimers briefly diverge from their two-party political tradition. In 1918 a committee of New Brunswick farmers called a convention to promote an occupational organization patterned after the United Farmers of Ontario. The United Farmers of New Brunswick set out to organize farmer cooperatives and to contest federal and provincial elections. Similar organizations appeared the next year in Nova Scotia and early in 1919, T.W. Caldwell won the Carleton-Victoria by-election for the newly formed Progressive party. Shortly thereafter this Manitoba dominated organization sent George Chipman, an ex Nova Scotian, to the Maritimes to establish there a subsidiary to his *Grain Growers Guide*. The *United Farmers' Guide* became the official organ of both the political movement and its economic institutions, the New Brunswick Cooperatives and the United Fruit Companies of Nova Scotia.

The Westerners used their control of the *Guide* to push a Prairie agenda on issues such as freight rate equalization and tariff reductions which soon became disillusioning to their hosts. The United Farmers of Nova Scotia won seven seats in the provincial election of June 1920. By October secret deals with the old line parties in New Brunswick tended to undercut claims of nine seats won in that province. By 1921 the political wing of the movement was largely a hollow shell with the local cooperative organizations wanting to dump the Manitoba-dominated *Guide*. It stayed alive, however, until after the federal election. Only Calwell managed to win a seat and this by a greatly reduced majority. By this time many Maritimers were seeking to express concerns of region as well as occupation and for this had found the Prairie-dominated Progressive Party singularly unsuitable.

The United Farmers were helped in forming the official opposition in Nova Scotia in 1920 by the loose cooperation of four independent labour candidates. Labour organizational activity reached a climax in the Maritimes immediately after the war. The region's most important union, which included several thousand coal miners, dated from the formation of the Provincial Workmen's Association in 1879. The PWA effectively lobbied governments for favourable legislation including a coal mines regulation act, although stopping short of the strikes which in that period labour so seldom won. With the advent of the big international corporations as mine operators, some miners, such as the Scottish-born J.B. McLachlan, began to push for affiliation with an international union—specifically the United Mine Workers of America. While about half of the miners favoured the UMW, almost as many remained loyal to the older union executive. A bitter strike for union recognition in 1909 lasted almost a year and, with the corporations and provincial government siding with the PWA, resulted in a crushing defeat for the UMW. But then with the outbreak of the war, a federal government seeking labour peace at all costs negotiated a coalition between the two unions called the Amalgamated Mine Workers of Nova Scotia. By 1919 McLachlan had won over the membership to form District # 26 of the United Mine Workers of America.

Promoted by American Federation of Labour organizers, union membership in the Maritimes grew at a rate roughly proportional to the national average—approximating 10,000 or about 10 per cent of the total in Canada at the beginning of the war and rising to about 40,000 by 1919. Organization had been stimulated by the ideologies of socialism and progressivism which had encouraged the work force to look for a better deal after the war. But it was also driven by the workers' need to raise wages undercut by inflation. One of the organizers, C.C. Dane, a radical socialist originally from Australia, had tended to ignore the AFL's policies on craft unions in organizing workers in Cumberland and Pictou Country areas in the Nova Scotia Federation of Labour. In May of 1919 when workers in the metal traders went on strike in Amherst it was the Federation which led the workers of the community in a general sympathy strike whose causes, timing, and duration roughly paralleled the more famous Winnipeg General Strike of the same year. So too did the purge of the radicals by the craft unions, the suppression of the Nova Scotia Federation of Labour and the rapid decline of union membership during the recession of the early 1920s.

The major exception to the decline of the labour movement in the region involved the coal miners. In 1920 the Dominion Coal Company and its steel producing subsidiary, joined together with the Nova Scotia Steel and Coal Company and Halifax Shipyards in a new corporation known as the British Empire Steel Corporation (Besco). Seeking to maintain profits in the recession and burdened by the additional bonus or 'watered stock' issued in the amalgamation, Besco demanded that the workers accept a wage reduction of about one-third. This the miners staunchly rejected and became increasingly radical in their rhetoric and policies. J.B. McLachlan, who joined the Communist party shortly after its 1921 launching in Canada, headed the radical slate which the miners elected in 1922. McLachlan launched a 'hundred per cent strike'—refusing to feed the horses or to maintain the pumps which kept the mines from flooding—in 1922 and the following year brought the miners out on strike in sympathy with the steel workers whose own strike had been compromised by the government's deployment of the militia at the corporation's request. International UMW president John L. Lewis used the strike while a legal contract was in force as an excuse to suspend the radical executive. Meanwhile, the provincial government in a late night raid whisked McLachlan out of Cape Breton for a trial in Halifax where he was convicted of the charge of 'seditious libel' and sentenced to two years in Dorchester penitentiary.

The elimination of the miners' radical leadership did not lessen their resolve. They resisted a wage cut with a month long strike in 1924 and again with a five month strike in 1925 which saw national relief organizations aiding the strikers who had lost their credit in the company stores. The strike ended only after a clash between miners and company police had left one miner dead and several injured and the army once again patrolling the mining areas.

A newly-elected Conservative government, which was less closely allied with the corporation, appointed a royal Commission headed by a British lawyer and industrialist Sir Andrew Rae Duncan. Duncan won the miners' confidence in a series of public hearings and they agreed to accept a 10 per cent cut in their wages. Behind the scenes an intransigent Besco management was forced out and in 1928 the corporation received a facelifting reorganization with its name changed to the Dominion Steel Company (Dosco).

While contemporaries tended to attribute conflict in the coal mines to the ideologies of communism or capitalism, to some Maritimers the conflict was symptomatic of what was happening to the regional economy as a whole. Adverse government decisions in matters such as tariffs and freight rates had severely undercut industry in the region. Besco was fighting to maintain its profits and the miners their standard of living. Neither succeeded. The year 1919 saw the emergence of a regional protest movement under the slogan 'Maritime Rights'. In the optimism of a progressive era, Maritimers believed that through unity, organization and agitation they could redress the balance in political power which had swung so decisively against their region. In that year the regional Boards of Trade, hitherto divided by the fierce rivalry between Halifax and Saint John, reorganized for the more effective defence of the region. Propagandists churned out pamphlets attempting to give their claims regarding such issues as the Intercolonial's freight rates, the role of Halifax and Saint John as Canada's winter ports and provincial subsidies a constitutional validity by rooting them in the promises forming a part of the confederation agreement. The next few years saw conferences, studies, and mass delegations to Ottawa as Maritimers sought to educate the rest of Canada as to their rights. At the same time the depth of regional discontent was reflected in wholesale swings in electoral support, first to the Liberals in the provincial and federal elections of 1920 and 1921 and, when they failed to deliver, to Conservative Maritime Rights candidates in the elections of 1925. Finally, with the Liberals seeking to regain credibility in the region in the election of 1926, Mackenzie King promised a royal commission to investigate Maritime claims and added the pledge that he would implement its recommendations.

Once again Duncan was invited to Canada to head a Royal Commission on problems in the Maritimes. His report was a masterly exercise in the art of the possible as he directed attention away from issues which might tend towards separation or arouse opposition in the more populous provinces while proposing solutions which drew the region more closely into the national economy. These included the restoration of lower Maritime freight rates with federal compensation for the railways, immediate increases to bring Dominion-provincial subsidies in the Maritimes closer to the national level, a general re-thinking of the whole subsidy system to take account of the industrial concentration since confederation, the inclusion of Halifax and Saint John in an existing subsidized funding programme for national ports, and transportation subsidies on coal and coke in lieu of the tariffs which these had once enjoyed under the National Policy. The King government implemented a scaled down version of the more prominent of Duncan's recommendations—including a 20 per cent subsidized reduction in rates on goods moving to central Canada and an increase in Dominion-provincial subsidies to all the three provinces.

Maritime leaders set out to use the implementation of the Duncan Report to reverse the image of economic stagnation which their propaganda had tended to encourage. By declaring that the region had solved its basic problems and was about to boom, they hoped to attract their share of investment capital in the buoyant economic conditions of the later 1920s. To a degree they were successful as new investment in port development, pulp and paper and tourist hotels in both New Brunswick and Nova Scotia led to a brief construction boom by 1929. The initial success of this switch to optimism no doubt explains their continued efforts to pretend that their economy was still healthy after several years into the depression. These efforts during the 1930s did not attract much capital and the myth of relative Maritime prosperity later gave an excuse for federal governments to skimp on relief assistance in the region.

While the Maritimes were largely ignored as a location for American branch plants coming to Canada in the 1920s, it did develop a new industry which was often financed with American capital. This was the rum-running industry. Prohibition came to the United States at the beginning of 1920 at about the same time that most of the Canadian provinces, including the Maritimes, voted to continue it. With the fishing industry stagnating in the low prices of the postwar recession, Maritime fishermen, including the owners of more than half of the Lunenburg schooner fleet, leased their boats to American syndicates engaged in smuggling liquor into the United States. Such activities did not necessarily break Canadian laws. The large central Canadian distilleries produced liquor for export. This they shipped to the little islands of Saint Pierre and Miquelon off the coast of Newfoundland, which were part of France. From there or from the rum-producing Caribbean islands, the former fishing vessels carried the liquor to just outside the American twelve mile limit. There they joined many other vessels in what came to be known as 'rum-row' as they awaited the fast motor launches of the American crime syndicates, who actually smuggled the liquor into the United States.

As fishing schooners became outfitted with diesel engines or were replaced by craft custom-built for the trade, some Maritimers undertook the more hazardous adventure of landing the liquor directly in the United States. The most famous incident involved the *I'm Alone*, a rum-runner operating out of Shelburne, Nova Scotia, which the American coast guard intercepted close to the twelve mile limit and chased it more than one hundred miles out to sea before sinking it with machine gun fire. Having evolved the techniques for supplying their thirsty neighbours to the south it was not long before they applied them at home. Liquor was easily smuggled into the many bays and coves of the region where it was distributed by local gangs to the many retail outlets known as bootleggers, speakeasies or blind pigs. These were often staffed by widows with children for whom no other employment was available.

The industry also contributed to the evolution of the police forces in the region. Municipalities and provincial governments hired temperance inspectors whose prosecution of first offenders suggested that they were more interested in the collection of fines than in actually closing down the industry. In 1926 the federal government organized a 'preventive force' with marine and land-based divisions and these two joined in the game of cops and robbers that characterized the region during this decade. The industry was eventually shut down by the abandonment of prohibition by revenue hungry provincial governments who saw the money to be made in a government monopoly of liquor sales. New Brunswick adopted 'government control' in 1927, Nova Scotia followed suit in 1929. Prince Edward Island kept prohibition in place and became a final refuge for rum-runners until 1948.

The depression of the 1930s hit hardest those countries and regions most dependent on the production of raw materials. Manufacturers could usually cut back production enough to maintain something close to basic prices. Unorganized primary producers tended to increase production as prices declined leading to gluts, panic and destitution. As a region dependent on products of agriculture, fishery and forest the Maritimes was one of the harder hit regions. Not fully recovered from the depression of the 1920s, its figures for per capita income declined to levels only slightly above those of wheat-growing Saskatchewan.

The results of the power inequities between the smaller and larger provinces and their impact on an evolving Canadian constitution became particularly apparent during the depression. The fathers of confederation had failed to anticipate the importance of automobile roads, health services and social welfare needs when they assigned them to the provincial governments. By the turn of the century it was clear that only the federal government had the resources for the programmes required in each of these areas. But a federal scheme which redistributed money for such programmes either on the basis of need or population was not to be popular with government in the central provinces, who jealously guarded the inflated tax bases created by their metropolitan centres. Thus the federal government used the power of its much greater revenues to merely offer to match the expenditures of the provinces in road building and social programmes. A matching grants programme for road construction early in the 1920s left peripheral smaller provinces having to skew expenditures in this direction to participate. With proportionately more elderly within their borders, they simply could not afford to participate in the old age pension scheme launched by the federal government in 1927.

Perhaps most vicious of all was the federal scheme for funding relief during the depression by demanding one-third in matching grants from both municipal and provincial governments. The municipalities whose inhabitants most desperately needed help, such as the northern countries of New Brunswick for example, could not afford their share and the smaller provinces lacked the resources to pay it for them or to participate in a long-term relief programme. Thus most of the federal monies for relief went to the wealthier provinces. Had the approximately six hundred and fifty million spent on relief by the federal government during the depression simply been assigned on the basis of population, the Maritimes' share would have been about 10 per cent or sixty-five million. As it was, they actually received only about fifteen million. Similarly when old age pensions were finally introduced to the Maritimes by mid-decade they were for smaller amounts, with tougher means tests and with proportionately fewer Maritimers than other Canadians in their age group receiving them. This meant that the destitute in the region were much more dependent upon *ad hoc* relief from church and other philanthropic organizations. While these struggled to meet the need, destitution and malnutrition claimed their victims in the region.

As it became clear that the Duncan Commission had not solved the region's problems, some residents sought to revive the protest tradition of the previous decade. The Maritime Transportation Committee, which with the help of an expert had pressed the region's case for lower rates before the Duncan Commission, had evolved into a permanent body playing both an advocacy and advisory role for Maritime shippers. In 1931 it suffered a narrow defeat before the courts which ruled that the 20 per cent reduction of the Maritime Freight Rates Act did not apply to competitive rates, thus undercutting much of what they thought they had won in the previous decade.

In 1934 the Nova Scotia government appointed a royal commission headed by Harry Jones of Leeds University to assess the impact of the tariff upon the Maritime region. Jones, a free trader, was seconded by Harold Innis, an economic nationalist from Toronto, as to the negative regional impact of the tariff. Both found the solution in compensation to the region through additional revenues which allow the smaller provinces to assist local industry. Meanwhile, New Brunswick elected a Liberal government pledged to demand the region's rights under the confederation compact. Ironically, A.P.

Paterson waded into the national constitutional debate just in time to provide King with the excuse that provincial rights under the constitution prevented greater federal activity in the matter of relief. Although neither approach won concessions during the depression, the studies commissioned gave the region a clearer understanding of its problems and suggested solutions which were accepted in part by the 1937 federal Royal Commission on Dominion-Provincial Relations (Rowell-Sirois Commission).

Maritimes also responded more directly to the depression through new organization. When the UMW accepted wage cuts and mine closures the miners organized a rival Amalgamated Mine Workers Union which walked the knife edge between radical protest on one side and an impossible-to-win strike on the other. Timber workers and stevedores on the Miramichi organized a new farmer-labour union demanding fairer wages as the depression eased its grip ever so slightly on their industries. Radicals organized unions among the unemployed in all three provinces. Before the end of the decade governments in New Brunswick and Nova Scotia had respectively introduced legislation providing for a fair wage officer in the former and compulsory union recognition in the latter.

The most spectacular of the new organizational efforts became known as the Antigonish movement. In an apparent response to the papal encyclical *Rerum Novarum,* Saint Francis Xavier University had, at the turn of the century, developed a model farm to bolster the economy in eastern Nova Scotia and its professors were involved in pioneer cooperative organization. In the 1920s they had begun programmes in adult education while fostering pride in Scottish culture. By the 1930s they had developed a technique of organization sometimes characterized as the Antigonish way. Beginning with a study group, members of a community would be encouraged to assess their economic problems and to find solutions which they might implement themselves. These could take the form of cooperative canning and marketing of lobsters, the grading of fish, cooperative creameries, milk delivery systems or the cooperative construction of housing. If lack of capital was a problem, a new credit union might be the solution. When a federal royal commission on the fisheries in the region in 1928 recommended cooperative organization as helpful, the King government appointed Father M.M. Coady as an organizer for the United Maritime Fishermen. Coady also participated in a summer school at the University where those interested were invited to a short course in cooperative organization. The movement spread through eastern Nova Scotia, Prince Edward Island and North and Eastern New Brunswick. Before the end of 1938 a spokesman for the movement claimed an involvement of 50,000 including forty-two stores, ten fish-processing plants, seventeen lobster canneries, one hundred and forty credit unions and twenty-three hundred and ninety study clubs.

The report of the Rowell-Sirois Commission appeared to finally address some of the inequities in the Canadian constitution which had intensified during its first sixty years of evolution. The report noted the inability of the smaller provinces to fund social and educational programmes—per capita expenditures on health and education in New Brunswick and Prince Edward Island were about half the national average—and proposed the maintenance of certain minimum standards in provincial services through the country. It recommended that the federal government take responsibility for old age pensions and a new programme of insurance for the unemployed. At the same time the poorer provinces would be bolstered on an ongoing basis by a system of adjustment grants assessed on the basis of fiscal need. Unfortunately for the smaller provinces a 'catch 22' prevailed. The Canadian constitution had become skewed against the smaller provinces because the interests of the larger prevailed politically. How could the smaller provinces now gain the political influence to force the implementation of the recommendations of the royal commission? One after another the larger and richer provinces objected to the Commission's findings and the federal government quickly dropped the issue.

If the depression hit the Maritimes hard it struck even harder at Newfoundland even more dependent upon primary production and exports. This colony, which had paralleled Canada's rise to Dominion status, had been in financial difficulties even before the depression arrived. Newfoundland's wartime expenditures had greatly inflated a debt initially incurred in railway expenditures. Even with a partial revival in the price of fish in the later 1920s, the island's governments were accumulating deficits at the rate of more than two million dollars a year. They had also been plagued by political scandals. In 1924 Premier Squires was reported to be taking bribes from Besco and was eventually prosecuted for income tax evasion. The opposition leader of a so-called reform party promised changes to help the fishermen but when implemented these proved to be a series of tax and tariff adjustments at the fishermen's expense. Before the end of 1928 Squires and the Liberals were back in power and would have to face the apparently hopeless task of dealing with the depression. With their premier involved in another political scandal in 1931 Newfoundlanders turned again to the reform party under A.B. Morine who looked for help to the British government.

Had Newfoundland been a small independent country which could not meet the interest on its debt, it might have defaulted, declared bankruptcy and used whatever tax revenues it had for the provision of government services. But this was not an option for a British Dominion whose default might undermine the credit status of the British Empire. In 1932 the British persuaded the Canadian banks to carry the Newfoundland deficit with another loan while a commission of two Canadian bankers under the leadership of the British Amulree investigated its problems. The commission recommended the suspension of the Newfoundland government and its replacement by a commission of civil servants. Taking advantage of contemporary and past political scandals, it justified this radically undemocratic departure, not only on the grounds of Newfoundland's financial deficits, which were real enough, but also on the much more dubious grounds of its political immorality.

From 1934 to 1949 Newfoundland was ruled by a commission of government consisting of the British Governor presiding over six British appointed civil servants, three of whom were from Great Britain and three native Newfoundlanders. Historians have tended to write approvingly of the Commission's administrative skills, although deploring their political insensitivity in such actions as dispersing the contents of the National museum or carving up the legislature for offices. Certainly the Commission did not solve the problem of unemployment which rose steadily through the decade. And while the dispensation of relief may have been less erratic than in the Maritimes, the amounts handed out in the form of molasses, corn meal and a few other staples were insufficient to prevent the spread of diseases associated with malnutrition.

It has been said that the First World War ruined Newfoundland and the Second saved it. Newfoundland's mid-north Atlantic location made it of critical importance in the war which broke out in the fall of 1939. The United States found a way to help Britain and further its own interests by trading destroyers for military bases on Newfoundland and Labrador. Canadians too sent in garrisons for the defence of air force installations in Gander and Botwood and constructed a large base at Goose Bay, Labrador. With twenty thousand jobs created in base construction and the resurgence in prices of fish, iron ore, pulp and timber, Newfoundland was soon solvent again, giving its surplus to Great Britain in the form of interest free loans. While solvency was supposed to trigger a return to responsible government status, Newfoundland accepted the British decision that this could best be dealt with after the war.

For the Maritimes too the war meant an end to the chronic unemployment of the depression as local residents jointed the armed forces or found work at home or in central Canada. But the war was something of a disaster for Maritime industry. The King government planned to use the war to industrialize Canada. Controlled by a ministry of munitions and supply and heavily subsidized by the federal government, industrial development went first to central Canada. By the time industry was booming there, expansion into the Maritimes seemed to be limited by shortages of men and machinery. British technical advisors in Canada saw decisions to locate ship's construction and repair up the St. Lawrence River, which was frozen over in the winter months, as 'largely political'. Dosco's President Arthur Cross discovered to his horror that C.D. Howe appeared to have a plan for the industrialization of Canada based on post-war needs which did not include the Maritimes. Cross' proposals to reopen the ship's plate mill and to modernize steel production were stalled by Howe while the government channelled its money into a ship's plate mill for Stelco in Hamilton and into the modernization of Algoma at Sault St. Marie. While the steel shortages following the Americans' entry into the war and the German submarines' closure of the Saint Lawrence did force some belated investment in the Maritimes by the fall of 1942, expansion there tended to be limited and temporary. Maritime industry came out of the war with its machinery worn from heavy wartime production only to find its central Canadian competitors outfitted with greatly expanded and modernized plants financed by the federal government. The gap continued to widen as the federal government channelled funds to these favoured industries to help them retool for civilian production. A plan to add a strip mill for Dosco's production of the sheet steel needed for modern consumer goods in the Maritimes was rejected by the federal government.

The regional image also took a beating during the war. Halifax emerged as a naval headquarters, a staging area for service personnel going overseas and from 1942 the major shipping repair centre. The civilian population more than doubled with military dependents and workers and their families. To these might be added at any given time several thousand military personnel. These competed for a shrinking housing base, consumer goods distributed on the basis of the much smaller previous census and limited schools, hospitals, transportation and recreational facilities. The federal war cabinet discussed Halifax's problems on several occasions, but beyond a plan to remove 'unnecessary' elements of the population did little to alleviate the situation. The end of war in Europe touched off celebrations in Halifax which turned into a raid on the liquor stores by civilian and service personnel and the wholesale plundering of Halifax shops. Central Canadian news-papers added insult to injury by blaming the local residents' lack of hospi-tality for the riots. For the quarter of a million Canadians who passed through this port city, 'the Maritimes', as represented by wartime Halifax, would not be remembered with fondness.

In 1946 Great Britain arranged for the election of a Newfoundland national convention to decide the future of the colony. The British did not want to retain responsibility for the island, especially after the Commission government had put forward an expensive plan for future economic development. They favoured Newfoundland joining the Canadian confederation, a solution attractive to Canada after the war had shown the island's strategic importance and possibility of American interest. All agreed that the Newfoundlanders would have to decide their own fate, through the ballot, although the British and Canadians would work to make the confederation option attractive. Led by Peter Cashin, those calling for a simple return of responsible government dominated the convention. But the confederates had an effective propagandist in Joseph Smallwood whose experience as a journalist and radio broadcaster and engaging personality more than compensated for his relative lack of direct political experience. The confederates secured the appointment of a delegation to Canada to explore the terms of a possible union and when the convention left the confederation option off the referendum ballot, mobilized a letter writing campaign which justified the British intervention in making it one of the three options offered. In the first vote in 1948, confederation came a close second to responsible government. In the second, with the commission government option removed, confederation received a narrow majority.

In negotiations with Newfoundland, some Canadian leaders expressed fears of Maritime jealousy. There had been no such expressions from the Maritimes, but politicians were acutely conscious of the Rowell-Sirois recommendations, which set out the need for constitutional reform, if the smaller provinces were to maintain basic levels of social services and provide necessary infrastructure for modern industry. Since the centrally-dominated government had no intention of implementing these recommendations, it was difficult to see how Newfoundland could be admitted on terms that would allow it to function as a viable province without making similar concessions to the other provinces. The terms finally agreed upon implicitly recognized two levels of educational and social services within the country. After a series of declining special grants to the new province, a royal commission would investigate what further assistance might be necessary to bring Newfoundland's social services up to the level not of the country as a whole but to that prevailing in the three Maritime provinces. The terms of union also extended to Newfoundland the rate reductions of the Maritime Freight Rates Act and brought an offer of membership in the newly re-named Atlantic Provinces Transportation commission. The Confederate organization merged smoothly with the federal Liberal party and Smallwood was appointed provincial premier. Smallwood and his followers took full credit for the extension of Canadian social programmes to the Island. Thereafter they followed an ambivalent strategy of trying to improve their position within confederation, at times pressing their special needs upon the federal government while at others cooperating with the Maritimes in matters of more general concern.

During the first decade after the Second World War the gap in living standards and government services between the rich and poor provinces continued to widen. The term regional disparity, most often used in comparing the Maritimes to the central provinces, but also applied to prairie provinces such as Saskatchewan, became common usage. The Rowell-Sirois report and the many studies which had accompanied it remained in the libraries to educate a new generation on the worsening problems of the Canadian constitution. Governments had rejected the proposals of the commission only to begin to introduce them piecemeal. Family allowances, a monthly payment to mothers for each child, was introduced as a direct federal programme without requiring matching grants from the provinces. So too was the system of unemployment insurance, although this scheme omitted the seasonal workers in farming, lumbering and fisheries such predominated in the Atlantic Provinces. By 1951 the means test had disappeared from the programme of old age pensions which was converted from a matching to a federally-funded programme. Federal governments remained adamant in their continued rejection of the Rowell-Sirois recommendation that subsidies to the provinces to be based on fiscal need, but in practice made slightly larger per capita financial settlements with desperate provincial administrations. Not until the 1957 election of the Conservative federal government led by John Diefenbaker, a long time resident of Saskatchewan, did the central provinces tacitly consent to special grants for the Atlantic provinces.

The drive to overcome regional disparity, which became one of the preoccupations of government from the late 1950s through the 1960s and 1970s originated first in the poorer regions. Local governments involved the private sector in the regional protest through organizations such as the Atlantic Provinces Economic Council and conducted a series of governmental and privately sponsored studies of the region's problems. These yielded many of the proposals which governments and their newly-created developmental agencies later agreed to support. Federal development programmes, such as the Agricultural and Rehabilitation and Development Agency (ARDA), established in 1961, began to channel funds into the region for rural development. An Atlantic Development Board (ADB) sought ways to both strengthen existing industries and to attract new ones to the region. Provincial governments also turned to a professional bureaucracy in both enunciating and trying to implement their own development programmes and retained consultants such as UNB's economist William Y. (Bill) Smith. Buoyant regional and national economies in the early 1960s encouraged the belief that economic disparity could be checked, if not overcome.

New Brunswick in particular was rendered optimistic, not only by increasing revenues from fisheries and forests, but by new discoveries of a large ore body of zinc and other non-ferrous metals in northern part of the province. For the first time provincial governments had the money, thanks to a system of transfer payments based on fiscal need, to offer industry the kind of infrastructure routinely provided by the larger provinces. As highway building and hydro development went forward the provinces were able to alleviate some of the internal disparity in social and educational services which had been aggravated by their revenue shortages.

The changes in the lives of ordinary people in New Brunswick were so spectacular as to be collectively referred to as the 'Equal Opportunity' revolution. Lacking the revenues to maintain traditional services, much less keep up with the more centralized bureaucratic reforms of the other provinces, Maritime governments had often pushed back upon the local municipalities the responsibilities which they could not afford themselves. Education, hospitals, the relief and health care of the indigent, and magistrates' courts were all municipal responsibilities. While such services might be reasonably effective in an industrialized community such as Saint John, they were usually antiquated and seriously deficient in rural areas, especially in the poverty-stricken northern counties. In 1958, for example, a family on welfare in Saint John might receive $125 per month, a similar family in Chatham, Northumberland County $25 and in Gloucester County $8. Students in Saint John might attend a relatively modern high school with well-qualified teachers. In Albert County the modern 'frills' of home economics and 'Industrial Arts' were missing and the teachers minimally qualified. In Kent county more than seven hundred teachers had little or no teacher's training and the schools had to close at Christmas when the School Board ran out of money. The more buoyant revenues of the mid-1960s allowed the government of Louis Robichaud to sweep away this chaotic system in a series of reforms which made services to people the responsibility of the provincial government, abolished county governments and reduced the municipal governments which remained to providers of services for property such as water, sewers and police. These dramatic changes were further enhanced by federal grants for hospitals and higher education which allowed the province to announce a rationalization of universities based upon the idea of a major English university at Fredericton, a comparable French university at Moncton and a system of loans and bursaries which would allow a much greater percentage of the population to attend both. Similar if less sweeping changes characterized the other Atlantic provinces, whose economies also benefited from the extension of the unemployment insurance programme to include seasonal workers.

By 1968 federal efforts at overcoming regional disparity were consolidated under the Department of Regional Economic Expansion (DREE). The department helped in the development of infrastructure and provided industrial incentives for industries located in the poorer regions. Transportation again became part of the strategy for industrializing the Atlantic provinces as the subsided rate reductions were extended to trucking and increased on items selected for their positive impact on regional development.

Perhaps most remarkable through the period of the 1960s and the 1970s was Ontario's continued support for efforts to help the Atlantic Provinces. Part of their motivation was undoubtedly patriotism as national enthusiasm peaked with the celebrations of Canada's hundredth birthday in 1967. The wealthier provinces too were kept on side with larger portions of the federally-collected income tax while the poorer provinces received in addition larger per capita equalization grants based on a formula indicative of fiscal need. By the mid-1980s almost half of the Atlantic Provinces' provincial revenues originated with the federal government and the region also gained a comparable amount from the hidden transfers contained in payments to individuals and industry. But Ontario leaders had begun to realize that their region was among the chief beneficiaries of the expansion of the Maritime economy. By now the Maritimes was so closely integrated with its metropolis in southern Ontario that it provided a captive market for that province's manufacturing, financial and marketing institutions. A dollar transferred to the Atlantic Provinces one week was likely to find its way back to Ontario the next. Indeed as a study of Canada's trade patterns in 1979 later revealed, the Atlantic Provinces had a huge trade deficit with Ontario which was met partly through its own surplus in international trade and partly through the transfer payments. Thus through the taxing power of the central government Canada finally, it seemed, had solved the problem of a constitution which was 'national' for business purposes but 'provincial' in the provision of social services. Canada had developed a national economy which seemed to effectively accommodate its Atlantic Provinces. In the constitutional discussions leading up to the ratification of the Canadian constitution, the region's leaders worked hard to secure formal acceptance of the *de facto* constitutional changes which the fiscal transfers represented. This goal ultimately eluded them, although they did secure recognition of the equalization principle in a section of the Constitutional Act of 1982 not binding upon national and provincial legislatures.

With the recession of the early 1980s neo-conservative economists called for Canada's abandonment of the national economy as part of a necessary adjustment to the emergence of a global economy. Commissioned by the government of Ontario, T.J. Courchene prepared a blueprint of a decentralized federation with a less interventionist central government. The Atlantic Provinces, he suggested, could get by without the hidden transfers of Canada's social programmes. These could be scaled back or responsibility for them transferred to the provinces leaving the region to depend on direct equalization payments alone. Courchene had earlier argued that it was dangerous for governments to interfere with the working of economic laws in the region. If wages were allowed to fall people would either leave, thus saving on welfare costs, or stay, thus providing a pool of cheap labour which would attract new industry. It was an attractive theory for those seeking a rapid re-orientation of the Canadian economy, although local residents wondered why equalization theory had never seemed to work for the region during the many decades before there were any federal social programmes to inhibit it.

Driven by ideology and increasing deficits, governments moved rapidly to re-orient the economy along the lines recommended by their economists. The Macdonald Commission of 1985 contained much of the Courchene blueprint while the Neilsen Task force devoted seventeen volumes to the identification of government services, many affecting the Maritimes, which could be cut back or eliminated.[4] Transportation subsidies to the Maritimes were reduced and the railways given the green light to abandon lines in the region. Unemployment insurance, and federal payments for health and education were repeatedly scaled back. Meanwhile, equalization payments were 'capped' so that payments to the smaller provinces became less dependent on their need and more upon the degree of economic buoyancy in the wealthier provinces.

Critical from an Atlantic Provinces' perspective was the free trade deal with the United States. The region had become closely integrated with a national economy and especially its Ontario metropolis. Ontario could readily tolerate a system of fiscal transfers as long as the money returned

---

[4]T.J. Courchene, *Economic Management and the Division of Powers,* vol. 67, prepared for the Royal Commission on the Economic Union and Development Prospects, Toronto, 1986.

home. With the borders open to American manufacturing, merchandising and financial institutions, the existing system of transfers could not function for long. A majority in the Atlantic Provinces voted against the free trade deal in the election of 1988, but the Brian Mulroney government which proposed it, won a majority of seats elsewhere in the country.

Atlantic Canadians faced other critical decisions in the matter of constitutional revisions proposed in the Meech Lake Agreement of 1987 and in the later Charlottetown Accord. The constitutional revisions demanded by the Quebec government seemed in line with the decentralized blueprint promoted by neo-conservative academics. Yet the opting out provisions in federal programmes seemed to threaten that government's role in redistributing funds to the poorer provinces. But the separation of Quebec suggested an even greater threat. All four Atlantic premiers initially accepted Meech, although the newly elected Liberal governments of Frank McKenna in New Brunswick and Clyde Wells in Newfoundland apparently sought to use their acceptance of the agreement as a bargaining chip in their dealings with the federal government. Thus, they inadvertently put in train the series of events leading to the defeat of the agreement and the orgy of constitution-making which culminated in the ill-fated Charlottetown Accord.

The outstanding feature of the region's recent history has been the dismantling of hard fought gains in social programmes, fiscal transfers and assistance for regional development. After their successes of the 1960s and 1970s, the Atlantic Provinces seemed to abandon their regional defences, which had been based in part upon the cultivation of a protest tradition. The degree of unity which had characterized both the Maritime Rights movement and the later so-called Atlantic Revolution largely disappeared in the 1980s and 1990s. Thinking it was about to escape its 'have not' status once and for all, through Labrador hydro developments and control of its offshore oil and fisheries, Newfoundland went its own way in the 1980s only to encounter a series of defeats in the courts and the eventual destruction of its cod fisheries. The Maritime provinces did not do much better, failing to defend regional interests before the MacDonald Commission and dividing over free trade and Meech Lake.

Regional consciousness has declined in the Atlantic Provinces during the last two decades. The later Howard Darling in the early 1970s characterized Maritime sensitivity on transportation issues as 'pavlovian'. Almost two decades later the Director of the Atlantic Provinces Transportation Commission remarked that they only 'went public' as a 'last resort'. When forced to that extremity in 1995 by the federal government's elimination of the transportation subsidy, they discovered that few ordinary people still understood its significance. The most successful politicians in the region, such as Premier Frank McKenna of New Brunswick, wasted little time on regional defences. Making virtue of the necessity created by dwindling transfers, he led the country in scaling back social, educational and health programmes at the provincial level. This has made him the darling of the Ontario press while giving the appearance at home of a prudent anticipation of the inevitable. Meanwhile at the federal level the region's senior representative in the cabinet, Doug Young, has taken the lead in attacking as a wasteful anachronism the regional transportation subsidies dating from the award of the Duncan Commission. While these politicians continue to ride the crests of ideological currents and press approval, the long-term costs for the Atlantic economy of what amount to basic constitutional changes are still to be calculated.

For the Atlantic Provinces confederation has been an unequal union. The interests of the larger provinces have dominated both in the making of policy and in constitutional change. This initially contributed to the economic decline of the region and led to a blatant disparity in government services. Nevertheless, farsighted and vigorous leadership supported by an informed public has done much to ameliorate such trends especially in educating the dominant provinces regarding the extent to which their interests coincided with the well being of the rest of the country. Indeed the constitutional accommodation of the Atlantic Provinces in the 1960s and 1970s almost seemed to defy political gravity. But the changes of the past decade show how vulnerable the region really was. With changing ideologies, the delicately-forged interdependence of Canadian provinces and regions suddenly became a deplorable 'dependency'. Even before the Quebec referendum of 1995, the Atlantic Provinces have been effectively cast adrift to work out their own salvation within the global economy.

BIBLIOGRAPHY

General Texts

Daigle, Jean, ed. *Acadians of the Maritimes: Thematic Studies.* Moncton: Centre d'Études acadiennes, 1982.

Forbes, E.R. *Challenging the Regional Stereotype: Essays on the 20th Century Maritimes.* Fredericton: Acadiensis Press, 1989.

—, and D.A. Muise, eds. *The Atlantic Provinces in Confederation.* Toronto and Fredericton: University of Toronto Press and Acadiensis Press, 1993.

Hiller, J.K., and P. Neary, eds. *Newfoundland in the Nineteenth and Twentieth Centuries. Essays in Interpretation.* Toronto: University of Toronto Press, 1980.

Pryke, Kenneth G. *Nova Scotia and Confederation, 1864-74.* Toronto: University of Toronto Press, 1979.

Reid, John G. *Six Crucial Decades: Times of Change in the History of the Maritimes.* Halifax: Nimbus, 1987.

The Economy

Alexander, David. *The Decay of Trade: An Economic History of the Newfoundland Saltfish Trade, 1935-1965.* St. John's: ISER, 1977.

Bickerton, James P. *Nova Scotia, Ottawa, and the Politics of Regional Development.* Toronto: University of Toronto Press, 1990.

Forbes, E.R. *The Maritimes Rights Movement, 1919-1927: A Study in Canadian Regionalism.* Montreal and Kingston: McGill-Queen's University Press, 1979.

Ryan, Shannon. *Fish Out of Water: The Newfoundland Saltfish Trade, 1814-1914.* St. John's Breakwater Book, 1986.

Sager, Eric W. *Seafaring Labour: The Merchant Marine of Atlantic Canada, 1820-1914.* Montreal and Kingston: McGill-Queen's University Press, 1989.

—, and Gerald E. Panting. *Maritime Capital: The Shipping Industry in Atlantic Canada, 1820-1914.* Montreal and Kingston: McGill-Queen's University Press, 1990.

Politics

Beck, Murray. *The Politics of Nova Scotia,* vols. I & II. Tantallon: Four East Publications, 1985 and 1988.

Conrad, Margaret. *George Nowlan: Maritime Conservative in National Politics.* Toronto: University of Toronto Press, 1990.

Mackenzie, David. *Inside the Atlantic Triangle: Canada and the Entrance of Newfoundland into Confederation, 1939-1949.* Toronto: University of Toronto Press, 1986.

Neary, Peter. *Newfoundland in the North Atlantic World, 1929-1949.* Montreal and Kingston: McGill-Queen's University Press, 1988.

Noel, S.J.R. *Politics in Newfoundland.* Toronto: University of Toronto Press, 1971.

Social

Calhoun, Sue. *A Word to Say: The Story of the Maritime Fishermen's Union.* Halifax: Nimbus, 1991.

Conrad, Margaret et al., eds. *No Place Like Home: Diaries and Letters of Nova Scotia Women, 1771-1938.* Halifax: Formac, 1988.

Davies, Gwendolyn. *Studies in Maritime Literary History, 1760-1930*. Fredericton: Acadiensis Press, 1991.

Davison, J.D. *Alice of Gran Pré: Alice T. Chaw and Her Grand Pré Seminary, Female Education in Nova Scotia and New Brunswick*. Wolfville: Acadia University, 1981.

Fleming, Berkeley, ed. *Beyond Anger and Longing: Community and Development in Atlantic Canada*. Fredericton: Acadiensis Press, 1988.

Gillespie, Bill. *A Class Act: An Illustrated History of the Labour Movement in Newfoundland and Labrador*. St. John's: Newfoundland and Labrador Federation of Labour, 1986.

Keefer, Janice Kulyk. *Under Eastern Eyes: A Critical Reading of Maritime Fiction*. Toronto: University of Toronto Press, 1987.

McKay, Ian. *The Craft Transformed: An Essay on the Carpenters of Halifax, 1885-1985*. Halifax: Holdfast Press, 1985.

Rawlyk, G.A. *Champions of the Truth: Fundamentalism, Modernism, and the Maritime Baptists*. Montreal and Kingston: McGill-Queen's University Press, 1990.

Scobie, H.H., and John Webster Grant, eds. *The Contribution of Methodism to Atlantic Canada*. Toronto: University of Toronto Press, 1992.

Wilson, R.S., ed. *An Abiding Conviction: Maritime Baptists and Their World*. Hansport: Lancelot Press, 1988.

4

Western Canada Since 1864

R. Douglas Francis

Introduction

Western Canada in 1864 was a vast, still unsettled (except for the native people), isolated, and virgin territory. The area east of the Great Divide of the Rocky Mountains still remained under the aegis of the Hudson's Bay Company. It was known as 'Rupert's Land', loosely defined as all territory whose rivers flowed into Hudson Bay. The area west of the Great Divide was known as the colony of 'British Columbia', 'British' used to distinguish it from 'Spanish' Columbia in South America. This area had only recently, in 1858, been transferred from the Hudson's Bay Company to the British government to ensure that it would not fall into the hands of American expansionists.

Both of these regions still remained essentially in their pristine form. Geographically, Rupert's Land consisted of three sub-regions: the grasslands or prairies (from which the region derives its name) that roll endlessly and often flatly across the southern area from the Red River to the Rocky Mountains and from the international border northward to the valley of the Saskatchewan River; the parkland, an area of gentle hills and valleys, forested especially by aspens and populars, and containing good soil. It runs like an arc over the grasslands from the Red River to the Rockies, following the valleys of the Assiniboine and Saskatchewan rivers, including the North and South branches of the Saskatchewan as they split in a meandering 'Y' formation. Further north lies the boreal forest region, an area heavily forested with spruce and pine trees and consisting of poor soil and numerous rock outcroppings.

These three 'prairie levels' or 'prairie steppes', so-called because they resemble the mounting steps as they rise in elevation, are separated from each other by gentle scarps that appear as long low chains of hills. But all the three areas have been blessed with navigable rivers and river valleys, thus making transportation into and through the region relatively easy. What has been difficult and harsh is the region's climate. A mid-continental region devoid of large bodies of water to moderate temperatures, the region experiences extreme temperatures ranging from +40°C in the summer time to –40°C and colder in the winter. Travellers often comment as much on the weather as on the landscape, for it is the climate that affects the traveller as much as the land itself. In 1864, it was the extreme climate, more than the soil conditions, that led people to question the ability of the region to sustain agricultural settlement.

What tied these three geographical areas together into a single region in 1864—and since that time—has been a common economy and, to an extent, a common culture. In 1864, this region still remained an important fur trading territory. In the parkland and boreal forest areas, beaver furs were of prime importance; in the prairie area, it was the buffalo furs. Most of the fur trapping was done by the native people for European traders who worked for the Hudson's Bay Company. Those furs were exported chiefly by Hudson Bay for markets in Britain. In the case of the buffalo robes, they were sometimes exported via the Great Lakes-St. Lawrence River trade route or even by overland carts to American markets. This external trade within a market economy and industrial capitalism that was shaped by the more dominant European society had already, by 1864, transformed the region. But it was poised at a point of even more dramatic change. Within a decade, Rupert's Land would be transformed from fur trading to agricultural settlement.

West of the Great Divide stood the colony of British Columbia, rich in beauty and natural resources. But it was a region divided geographically into numerous sub-areas that were disconnected by numerous mountain ranges and rivers that were not navigable and that tended to run north and south rather than east and west. This helps to explain in part the difficulty of integrating British Columbia into a transcontinental nation based on an east-west trading axis. Rivers in British Columbia were more a hindrance than an asset to travel. On the other hand, a long coast line and numerous good harbours have made coastal travel, settlement and trade easy. Furthermore, British Columbia's coastal location has made for a moderate climate—at least for those areas where major settlement occurred—and ample rainfall. This in turn has resulted in lush vegetation and rich forested areas. This moderate climate, abundant resources, and natural beauty attracted the first settlers to the region, and has continued to do so since then.

Economics has also tied British Columbia together as in the case of the prairie West. In 1864, it was still the fur trade that prevailed in the region, although it was at a point of decline. Overtrapping was a factor for decline, but so too was the interest of the British government to develop other natural resources in the region such as minerals, coal, salmon, seals, forest and agriculture. These resource developments required permanent settlement, unlike the fur trade that thrived best on sparse settlement.

In the 1850s, the discovery of gold deposits in the Fraser Valley led to a rush of prospectors into the region. Many had come north from California where they had been involved in an earlier gold rush. The British government feared an American takeover of the region, and so decided in 1858 to take the mainland out of the control of the Hudson's Bay Company and to put it under direct control of the British government which could then provide military protection for the region. A year later, in 1859, the government did the same for the colony on Vancouver Island. These two separate colonies— one on the mainland, the other on the Island—were united into the single colony of British Columbia in 1866.

Only two substantial settlements existed in the area by 1864: the Red River Colony at the confluence of the Red and Assiniboine Rivers (present-day Winnipeg); and the colony of British Columbia on Vancouver Island centred at Fort Victoria with a small group spilling over on to the mainland at present-day Vancouver. The Red River Colony consisted chiefly of Métis— mixed blood people, offsprings of intermarriages of native women and fur traders. French Métis constituted approximately half of the roughly 9,000 inhabitants in 1864; English Métis, or the Country-born as they have been called, made up the other half. The fur trade still remained the predominant economic activity of the colony but there was a rudimentary agriculture as well. The Métis had over the years, since the founding of the Red River Colony in 1811 by Thomas Douglas, fifth earl of Selkirk, developed a strong sense of community and a spirit of independence.

The region of present-day British Columbia had been the battleground for four empires in the seventeenth and eighteenth centuries: Russia, Spain, Britain and (later) the United States. By 1864, British control of the area was military, secure under Governor James Douglas. An authoritarian figure (one woman described Governor Douglas a 'a glove of velvet on a hand of steel'),[1] Douglas established British law and order in this frontier society, thus ensuring its continued tie to Britain. Assisting Douglas was Matthew Baillie Begbie, the first judge of British Columbia appointed in 1858. Historian Margaret Ormsby gives this portrait of Begbie: "A Cambridge graduate of considerable intellectual attainment, a man with a natural hauteur, an accomplished teller of anecdotes, and something of a musician, Begbie had

---

[1]Quoted in Jean Barman, *The West Beyond the West: A History of British Columbia,* Toronto, 1991, p. 79.

the distinction of mid and manner so much admired by Douglas."[2] Begbie
followed the British practice of circuit riding, visiting isolated communities
to deal with local problems and dispensing sound justice.

Neither of these colonies of Red River or British Columbia had close
contact with the other British North American colonies to the east of the
lakehead by 1864. Instead they looked southward to neigbouring American
communities for trade and communications. There was, for example, no
direct and easy communication link between the North-West and the other
British North American colonies. The accustomed route was to go through
the United States and then northward into British North America. By 1864,
there had been only one group of some 250 'overlanders' who had made the
arduous and summer-long trek from Canada West (Ontario) to British
Columbia entirely through British territory. Both colonies had a small, if
vocal, minority of British North Americans in them by 1864. But for most
British Columbians and Red River settlers, the United Canadas (the nucleus
of present-day Ontario and Quebec) was a distant and unknown region of
North America with which they had little in common.

Nevertheless, with westward expansion of American and Canadian
settlers into the western regions of the North American continent, the area
of the North-West became important. Prior to 1850, this was not the case.
The North-West was viewed as a cold, hostile, bleak and desolate region,
suitable for fur trading but unfit for human habitation and agricultural
settlement. Robert Montgomery Martin, a Hudson's Bay Company's
employee, neatly summarized a century of opinion on the North-West when
he wrote in 1849 in *The Hudson's Bay Company and Vancouver Island*:

> There are, doubtless, several spots, such as the Red River, adapted in some
> respects for European settlements; but they are like oases in the desert, few
> and far between—and totally inapplicable for extended colonization;
> indeed, at a great many of the posts, not only can no corn be grown, but
> even the potatoe and other crops are cut off by summer frosts, so that the
> rearing and preservation of a sufficient quantity of human food is an
> object of the most anxious solicitude throughout the country. By the
> concession of part of the Oregon country and the Columbia River to the
> United States in 1846, we gave up a fertile and temperate region, south of
> the 49th parallel, capable of yielding abundance of food; and the tract now
> left in the possession of the Hudson's Bay Company will require great
> care and industry to render even the most promising spots productive.[3]

[2]Margaret Ormsby, *British Columbia: A History,* Toronto, 1958, p. 171.
[3]Quoted in R. Douglas Francis, *Images of the West: Changing Perceptions of the Prairies, 1690-1960,* Saskatoon, 1989, p. 11.

After 1850, the region came to be seen in a new, more positive image. This was especially so after the two important scientific expeditions in 1857—the Palliser Expedition sponsored by the British government, and the Hind Expedition, supported by the government of the Canadas. Both expeditions arrived independently at the conclusion that the North-West was an area with great agricultural potential, particularly in the region known as the 'Fertile Belt', being the land stretching in a great arc from the Lake of the Woods along the North Saskatchewan River to the foothills of the Rockies. The North-West held the possibility of being 'a home for millions'.

Now the region became of interest to both Americans and Canadians. Americans saw the region as destined by God to be theirs. As Americans pushed westward, capturing territory from the Spanish, they came to believe that they had a 'manifest destiny' to control the entire North American continent. Canadians also saw the region as a potential hinterland to exploit. The abundant rich agricultural land offered new hope for sons and daughters of Ontario farmers who faced a bleak future since all the good agricultural land in the province had been occupied since the late 1850s. Other Canadians, with an eye to the future, saw a populated North-West annexed to the rest of Canada as a region for east-west trade for the other British North American colonies. For this to occur, the existing British North American colonies needed to act quickly to acquire the North-West.

The desire to acquire Rupert's Land had been one of the major 'causes' of Confederation and the main plank in the platform of the Clear Grits, a party made up chiefly of Upper Canadian farmers and led by George Brown. When Confederation came about in 1867, one of the first tasks of the New Canadian government was to open up negotiations with the Hudson's Bay Company to reach an agreement for purchasing Rupert's Land. The agreement was reached in 1869 when Canada agreed to pay the Hudson's Bay Company 300,000 pounds (approximately $1,500,000) plus allow them to retain one twentieth of the land of the Fertile Belt as well as the land adjacent to their fur trading posts.

The negotiations between the Canadian government and the Hudson's Bay Company had gone on, however, without ever considering, or consulting with, the indigenous population in the region. Even more insulting was the move by the Canadian government to begin surveying the land in preparation to build a railway to the Pacific to link the North-West with the rest of Canada in anticipation that the deal would go through uncontested.

The Métis rose up in resistance. Louis Riel, himself a mixed blood born and raised in the Red River Colony, led the uprising. Riel and his followers captured Fort Garry, the Hudson's Bay Company post and the seat of government. Then they met the newly-appointed Canadian governor, William McDougall, at the American border while he was enroute to Fort Garry to take up residency as the Canadian representative in this new colony. They refused to allow him to enter the country. As a result, the Canadian government was forced to delay the finalization of the deal and to negotiate directly with the Métis.

During the negotiations, a group of bellicose Canadianists in the Red River Colony, led by John Christian Schultz, bent on bringing the region into Canada at any cost, attacked Riel's provisional government. Some of the Canadianists were captured during the skirmish and imprisoned, including the pugnacious Thomas Scott, an Orangeman from Ontario. Riel and his councillors mistakenly decided to execute Scott, apparently in an effort to show the solidarity and strength of the provisional government. What to date had been a local concern that had won Riel and his followers widespread support erupted into a national crisis as Ontarians rallied to Scott's support, elevating him into a political martyr, while Quebeckers backed Riel and the Métis. In response, John A. Macdonald, the Canadian Prime Minister, sent a military expedition under Colonel Garnet Wolseley west to put down the 'insurrection' and to establish a Canadian presence in the region. He feared that American expansionists would use the uprising as pretense for annexing the North-West.

The resistance had run its course by April 1870. In the short run it appeared to be a victory for Riel and his followers. The Canadian government agreed to Manitoba entering Confederation as a province with representation in the Senate and the House of Commons based on the size of the population. Equally important, separate Catholic schools were recognized by law, and both English and French were recognized as official languages in the province. As well, the government guaranteed Métis land titles and federal respect for Indian title. But it was a province 'unlike the others'. Its size was severely curtailed to approximately one hundred miles square, being only the land surrounding the Red River Colony. More importantly its land came under the control of the federal government to be used 'for the purpose of the Dominion'. Here was esta-blished what noted western Canadian historian W.L. Morton calls the initial 'western bias'—western regional dissatisfaction and grievance at central Canadian domination and control, a theme that runs throughout western Canadian history from 1870 to the present.

Patterns of Settlement of the Canadian West

The 'purpose of the Dominion' became agricultural settlement. The government had purchased the West to turn it into an agricultural hinterland to feed the growing urban and industrial centres of central Canada. This required initially a railway to link the region to the rest of Canada, and then immigrants.

First of all, negotiations had to get underway to recognize and extinguish aboriginal title to western lands so that these lands could be available to pioneer settlers. Between 1871 and 1877 the Canadian government negotiated seven Indian treaties, the last one—Treaty Number Seven—being with the Blackfoot Indians of southern Alberta. By these treaties, the native people, possibly unknowingly, relinquished legal title to western lands in return for guaranteed reserve lands, and food and medical assistance in time of famine. In British Columbia, Governor James Douglas had negotiated fairer treaties with the Indians (fourteen of them by 1864) in which the Indians had the right to choose their own land and restrictions were placed on the right to pre-empt Indian land. Unfortunately, Douglas's successor altered the system, and the native people faced greater discrimination. Native people in both British Columbia and on the Prairies became 'wards of the Canadian government' when their territory was incorporated into Confederation and brought under the jurisdiction of the federal Department of Indian Affairs after 1880. In both regions of the West, the government aimed to assimilate the native people into the perceived 'superior' Anglo-Canadian society.

To ensure law and order and thus to prevent the Indian-white wars that plagued the American West, the Canadian government brought into existence the North-West Mounted Police force in 1873. With their red tunics, as symbols of British law and order, they offered a visible alterative to the blue uniforms of American western law enforcers. As the writer Wallace Stegner pointed out: "One of the most visible aspects of the international border [in the West] was that it was a colour line: blue below, red above, blue for treachery and unkept promises, red for protection and straight tongue."[4] The 300 odd force immediately went to work to establish good relations with the native people, to control the American whisky trade in southern Alberta, to aid ranchers and settlers and settle disputes between them, and generally just establish a Canadian presence in the region. The Mounties acquired a reputation of fair play and justice, and have since become an integral part of Canadian—and especially western Canadian—mythology.

The next task was to prepare the region for homesteading. This required surveying the land. The Canadian government decided to adopt the American square township system made up of thirty-six sections of one mile square or

[4]Quoted in R. Doughlas Francis, Richard Jones, and Donald B. Smith, *Destinies: Canadian History Since Confederation,* 2nd edn., Toronto, 1992, p. 62.

640 acres each on the assumption that this would be familiar to American immigrants. Then it passed the Homestead Lands Act of 1872 that provided 160 acres (a quarter-section) of free land to each head of family or twenty-one year old male if he paid a ten dollar registration fee, resided on the land for three years, cultivated 30 acres, and built a permanent dwelling. If he met his obligations on that first quarter-section, it was his, and he could 'preempt', that is to say have first bid on, an adjoining quarter-section for a moderate sum. The government believed that even free land would pay for itself by bringing in immigrants who would need consumer goods, which would in turn generate manufacturing and trade.

To bring potential settlers west and link them to the rest of Canada required a railway. So too did British Columbia's entrance into Confederation. Pressure within the colony of British Columbia to join Canada came from a small but vocal group of Canadianists. Leading the group was Amor de Cosmos (*alias* William Smith) 'Lover of the Universe' who had arrived in British Columbia from Nova Scotia via the California gold rush. He turned to journalism and published the influential Victoria *British Colonist,* through which he became sufficiently well known to be elected to the Vancouver Island legislative assembly in 1863. Here he fought for union of British Columbia with the other British North American colonies, believing this would be to British Columbia's best interest. Supporting him in this behalf was John Robson, also an editor of the New Westminster *British Columbian* and member of the legislature.

In preparation for a larger union with Canada, the two separate West coast colonies—the one centered on Victoria, the other on Vancouver—united into the United Colony of British Columbia in 1866. The colony was heavily burdened with debt accumulated by over extension during the gold rush era. As well the port of Vancouver was eclipsed by the larger and more influential American port of San Francisco.

The West coast colony faced three options in the late 1860: continue as a British colony; join the United States; or unite with Canada. The political elite favoured the first option, but received no encouragement from the British government. Britain was anxious to lessen its colonial obligations by encouraging all of its North American colonies to unite together and be more autonomous. Annexation to the United States was a popular option among the mainland inhabitants, particularly the large number of Americans in the colony. Only a handful of British Columbians seemed to favour union with Canada. Nevertheless de Cosmos and allies created a Confederation League in 1868 to promote their cause. Britian also aided their effort by appointing Anthony Musgrave, a known enthusiast of Confederation of the British

North American colonies during his term as governor of Newfoundland, as the new governor in 1869, upon the death of Governor Frederick Seymour.

Musgrave appointed a three-man delegation to negotiate for British Columbians with the Government of Canada. The negotiations came at a propitious moment. The Canadian government had just successfully acquired the North-West, and negotiated Manitoba into Confederation. Canadian leaders were now anxious to stretch the new nation to the Pacific so as to fulfil the motto of the new Dominion of Canada—*a mari usque ad mare*—meaning 'from sea to sea'. Expecting to bargain hard for their demands, the British Columbian delegation ended up with even more than they had hoped to acquire.

The terms of British Columbia's entrance into Confederation on July 21, 1871 consisted of the following: assumption of the colony's one million dollar debt; implementation of responsible government in the province; undertaking of a public works programme and most significantly, construction of a railroad to be begun within two years of British Columbia's entry into Confederation and completed in ten.

The proposed railway was an ambitious promise. The United States, with ten times the population, had only recently and with great difficulty built its first transcontinental railway. Nor did the politicians realize the difficulties that lay ahead. First of all, they had to find a private company willing and able to undertake the mammoth project and then to map out a viable route through northern Ontario and through the Rocky Mountains. The government agreed to provide assistance in the form of both grants and loans, but not to be responsible for the entire project. Two companies competed for the contract: the Interoceanic Company of Toronto, headed by Senator David Macpherson and backed by British financiers, and the Canadian Pacific Company of Montreal, a consortium under Sir Hugh Allan, president of the Merchant' Bank, with American financial backing. In the end, the government awarded the contract to the Canadian Pacific Company in return for generous financial contributions on Allan's part to the Conservative campaign fund in the election of 1872. The resulting 'Pacific Scandal' forced the Macdonald Conservative government to resign and ended the short-lived Canadian Pacific Company.

After a makeshift period under the Liberal government from 1873 to 1878 when only sections where settlement warranted construction were built as money became available, a newly elected Conservative government in 1878 searched for a new company. The Canadian Pacific Railway Company (CPR), formed by a group of men with heavy investments in the Bank of Montreal and the Hudson's Bay Company—George Stephen, R.B. Angus,

Donald Smith, and several other financiers—came forward to complete the railway. The Company agreed to build an all Canadian transcontinental line within ten years in return for twenty-five million dollars, twenty-five million acres of land consisting of alternative sections of the choicest land on the belt nearly forty kilometres wide on both sides of the track across the prairies, the sections of track already built which amounted to nearly twelve hundred kilometres of track worth an estimated $31 million, exemption from duties on construction materials and taxes on CPR property and its capital stock, and the insertion of a monopoly clause by which no competing line could be built south of the main CPR line until 1900.

What would be the best route to follow? Initially the plan had been to follow the North Saskatchewan River Valley from Winnipeg to the Rockies and then through the Yellowhead Pass to Vancouver. But early on the new company decided on a southerly route through the prairies, including Swift Current, Calgary and the Kicking Horse pass. A number of reasons accounted for this sudden shift: fear that the Northern Pacific, the new American transcontinental that ran from Chicago to Portland, Oregon, would syphon off the trade of the southern prairies; a more optimistic view of the agricultural potential of the grasslands region from John Macoun's scientific expedition in 1880; and the desire to undercut speculators who had bought up land along the proposed northern route in anticipation of making a 'fast buck'.

Construction costs proved to be astronomical, and more than once the CPR Company had to beg the government for more money. In the end, the railway cost the Canadian people a huge sum of money and had raised regional resentments in the Prairie West against this monopoly Company that controlled the everyday life of western farmers, right from the grade of wheat they got at CPR grain elevators, the rail costs to ship their wheat, to the high cost of manufactured goods sent to them over CPR tracks.

British Columbians were relieved to see the 'ribbon of steel' reach the Pacific Coast by 1885, within reason of the promised ten year period. But it shifted the British Columbia economy from a maritime to a continental perspective and tied this West coast province more tightly into the Canadian economy. As well, it made Vancouver an important port city not only for transcontinental trade but as an integral part of an 'old red route to the Orient'—a system of trade through British territory from Britain across the Atlantic Ocean, the North American continent and the Pacific Ocean. In general the CPR 'energized the province's economy', according to Jean Barman in *The West Beyond the West,* by providing a wider market for B.C.'s abundant natural resources.

With the railroad in place, settlement of the West could proceed. But initially, immigration to the West proceeded more slowly than the central Canadian nation builders had hoped. Despite the Canadian government's generous offer of 160 acres of free land to any prospective homesteader, few came. The majority that did come before the turn of the century were migrants from central and eastern Canada who came West because of better opportunities in this virgin territory. In the 1870s so many Ontarians had settled in Manitoba that the region acquired the nickname of 'Rural Ontario West'. Maritimes and English-speaking Quebeckers joined them. These English-speaking Canadians were in a favourable position to dominate the political, economic, social and cultural life of the region, thus ensuring a 'Canadian' perspective in the region. Few French Canadians came West from Quebec, much to the chagrin of French-speaking settlers already in the West; those immigrating from Quebec preferred the close proximity of the New England States or northern Ontario. If they ventured farther afield, they went to the American mid-West, where there was an already sizeable French-speaking population. The Canadian West, by contrast, was pictured, according to historian Robert Painchaud, as a remote region where French Canadians were not welcomed.

Those that came to western Canada from outside the country prior to 1896 were small, often minority, groups, most of them facing persecution elsewhere and thus seeking an asylum in a new land. A group of Russian Mennonites, descendants of the radical Anabaptists of the Reformation era and the followers of Memo Simons (1496-1561), the Reformation leader in the Netherlands, left Russia in the early 1870s, during a period of intense Russification. The Canadian government provided travel assistance in the amount of thirty dollars per adult to 'Mennonite families of good character' and promised them the right to settle in communal villages, or *strassendorf* (such as they had known in Russia), religious freedom, and exemption from military service. The seven thousand Mennonites who came in the 1870s settled on two reserves, one south-east and the others south-west of Winnipeg. The latter reserve was on open prairies; and the Mennonites were the first of the post-Confederation European immigrants to farm prairie land. Jewish immigrants came in the 1880s at the assistance of the Canadian government to escape the Russian pogroms (massacres of Jews). They too settled initially in rural areas of Manitoba as well as present-day Saskatchewan initial communities with such utopian names as 'New Jerusalem'. Few remained in the rural areas, however, choosing instead to become small shopowners, merchants, or labourers in urban centres, particularly Winnipeg. A small group of American Mormons followed their religious leader, Charles Ora Card, into southern Alberta in 1887 to establish Canada's first Mormon community where they could practice without persecution their religious belief in polygamy, or multiple marriages. Their experience in dryland farming in the Utah area served them well in farming the arid Palliser Triangle region of southern Alberta and Saskatchewan. But they soon faced discrimination in Canada over their religious beliefs until in 1890 the church suspended the practice of polygamy.

Also arriving on the Prairies in this initial period of settlement were some two thousand Icelanders. They left their island existence due to a declining fishing trade and infertile land as a result of volcanic ash. They settled on the shores of Lake Winnipeg where they were able to continue their traditional occupations of farming and fishing. They named their settlement 'Gimli', meaning paradise, for, to them conditions seemed ideal. They set up a democratic government and for a brief period established their own 'Republic of New Iceland'. Unfortunately, difficulties beset them from the beginning, including grasshopper plague, inadequate food, and a smallpox epidemic. Despite these setbacks, the original settlement prevailed and even began to prosper by the 1880s.

After 1896, the situation changed dramatically with a great influx of new immigrants into Canada. In that year alone, some 1700 arrived. By 1899 the figure almost tripled to 45,000 and by 1905, reached 150,000. Most of the immigrants went directly to the Prairies. A speaker to the Canadian Club in Winnipeg predicted at the time: "In 40 or 50 years Canada will have a population of 40 to 50 million and Saskatchewan and Alberta will be greater than Ontario in population and Winnipeg will have surpassed Toronto and Montreal."

What had changed by 1896 to account for this tremendous influx of immigrants ? Both 'push' and 'pull' factors played a role in the decision of so many to leave their native land for Canada. The push factors varied as widely as did the migrants themselves. Many left because of limited prospects in their homeland. The Industrial Revolution in Europe had raised the birth rate and lowered the death rate, which led to a larger population. In the countryside, particularly in eastern Europe, relatively poor agricultural land was being divided into smaller parcels to provide for more people. In Galicia, the north-eastern province of the Austro-Hungarian Empire, for example, each peasant family needed about seven hectares for subsistence, yet most farms were only half that size, and some families had to get by on less than a hectare of land. A new class of landless peasants was emerging. To these peasants, the promise of 160 acres of free land seemed like paradise.

In the cities, working-class people lived in cramped quarters in slum areas. To them, free and open land on the prairies offered an escape. The risk was better than the drudgery they now faced. For others, the move was an adventure, a chance to become self-sufficient. This was particularly true of the Americans who moved north and the prosperous British immigrants who came on the advice of friends or relatives already in Canada.

Others, like the Mennonites, Hutterites, and the Doukhobors, came to escape religious persecution. They hoped that in a new homeland they could worship in peace and live free from outside interference. Galician Slavs and Jews faced ethnic persecution in the Austro-Hungarian Empire. Many Asians came to work on the railroads as contract labourers or simply in search of a better way of life. Many immigrants were single men who hoped to make enough money either to return home prosperous or, if they were married, to bring their family to Canada.

The pull factors were equally varied and related to world conditions in general and the Canadian West's attractions in particular. The more rapid growth of international trade after 1896 meant more jobs and greater opportunity to save sufficient money to make the trip. Prosperity also increased demand for raw materials, especially for food for their growing urban population. Western farmers could benefit from a ready market and a high price for Canadian wheat. Increased prosperity also meant declining interest rates and lower freight rates, which in turn resulted in higher profits and a greater opportunity for farmers to borrow money for expansion. Most important of all, Canada benefited from the closing of the Americans frontier after 1890. When the best land—especially well-watered land—in the American West was gone, the Canadian West became the 'last best West'.

Improved farming conditions made the West even more attractive. Better strains of wheat, such as Marquis (discovered by the Canadian plant breeder Charles Saunders in 1909), matured earlier than Red Fife (the first of the hardy strains). This meant that wheat could now be grown in northern areas of Alberta and Saskatchewans without great risk of frost damage. The price of wheat quadrupled between 1901 and 1921, while production increased twentyfold in the same period. Better machinery, such as the chilled steel plough (introduced from the United States), improved harrows and seed drills, and tractors and threshers, also aided western farmers.

By World War I the West was experiencing a mechanical revolution. More land could be brought under the plough in less time and with less effort. Farming now expanded beyond the fertile belt into northern areas such as the Peace River district and into the southern semi-arid region of Palliser's Triangle. Other primary industries, such as coal and lumber production, started to be developed. Secondary industries, such as building and railway construction, led to the development of manufacturing, particularly in

Winnipeg, the largest centre on the Prairies.

Credit for increased immigration must also go to Clifford Sifton, the minister of the Interior in the Laurier government elected in 1896. This 'non-nonsense' Manitoba businessman was the single greatest drive behind the great immigration scheme at the turn of the century. He reorganized his department, bringing it under his direct control. He pressured the Hudson's Bay Company and the Canadian Pacific Railway Company to sell the land that they had in reserve at reasonable rates to prospective settlers. He discontinued the practice of using land grants as incentives to railway promoters. He also simplified the procedures for obtaining a homestead and encouraged settlers to buy adjacent sections.

His most successful technique was mass advertising of the Prairie West. His department produced pamphlets with enticing titles such as *The Wondrous West; Canada: Land of Opportunity; Prosperity Follows Settlement;* and *The Last Best West* which presented an idyllic image of the West with glowing descriptions of the regions soil conditions, climate, transportation facilities, accessibility to markets, and social and cultural facilities. These pamphlets (some one million published a year by 1900) were distributed widely especially in certain targeted areas such as the British Isles and in the American Midwest, where for example, posters about the Canadian West could be found in almost every train station, and brochures available to any number of potential immigrants to Canada. Some of these brochures were also translated into other languages of countries with immigrants considered to be particularly desirable such as Holland, Germany, and the Scandinavian countries.

Between 1896 and 1914 some one and a half million immigrants came to live on the Prairies, increasing the population of the region threefold. Many came from the traditional locations of the British Isles and the United States. But a significant number were 'new immigrants' from western and eastern Europe. They came from such central European countries as Germany, Holland, Denmark, Norway, Sweden, and Finland and from the eastern European areas of Poland, the Ukraine, the Austro-Hungarian Empire and Russia. Some of those who came from eastern Europe belonged to religious minority groups, including a second group of Mennonites, and some 7,000 Doukhobors from Russia where they were being persecuted for their pacifist and religious beliefs during a period of intense Russification, and a group of Hutterites—Anabaptists who came from Russia via the United States where they had been persecuted for their pacifist beliefs and collectivist way of life. Many of the Hutterites settled in southern Alberta and Saskatchewan, while the Doukhobors chose a more northerly location near Yorkton, Saskatchewan until 1905 when they faced local hostility to their radical beliefs and religious protest movements. Subsequently some five thousand of them moved to the Kootenay area of the southern interior of British Columbia, where a sizeable Doukhobors populations still lives today. Here they lived on farms and in houses with up to fifty people each. Other European immigrants often settled together in 'bloc settlements', such as Ukrainians, where they had the assurance and comfort of like-minded neighbours, a common language, and familiar religious and cultural institutions.

Coming to the Canadian Prairies was a strange, exciting and at times frightening experience for immigrants. It meant uprooting oneself from familiar surroundings, family and friends, and social and cultural institutions. Very often immigrants had no idea where they were going, what to expect, and how well they would do. Decisions to leave were often made on the basis of scanty information—a poster image in the local train station, a brief description in a pamphlet, the casual comment of a neighbour, second hand knowledge of others who had gone before them, letters from neighbours or friends who had made the trek earlier. In general, those who left were less well off than those who stayed and were thus more willing to take the risk in hopes of a better life in the New World. Visions of prosperity, contentment, and happiness were certainly a motivating factor.

Once the decision to leave had been made, then came the long journey, first by train to the nearest port—such as Hamburg or Bremen, Amsterdam or Trieste, London or Liverpool—and then by steamship. The trip across the ocean lasted usually ten to twelve days depending on weather conditions. The major ports of entry were usually Quebec or Montreal, but some disembarked at Halifax, Saint John, or Toronto. Next came the overland trip in a 'colonist car' on one of the newly completed rail lines. The 'colonist cars' were miniature ethnic communities, with various nationalities and ethnic groups crowded together in berths with primitive cooking facilities at the end of the car. In these cars, rumours abounded as to how long the trip would take, and what to expect at the other end. Some immigrants had definite destinations in mind, but many others got off on a whim, or on the recommendation of someone else on the train.

Many immigrants alighted first at Winnipeg—'Gateway to the West'— where they stayed temporarily in immigrant halls while applying for a homestead patent at the Immigration Office. This was usually followed by another train ride to the final destination. Alighting from the train, immigrants were met often by local 'hawkers', trying to sell them wares at inflated prices, or by land speculators hoping to make a 'fast buck' by selling them poor land at high price. Supplies had to be acquired and horses or oxen purchased at the nearest town for the overland journey to find one's stake in the ground which marked the boundary of one's homestead site.

Upon arrival, the journey had in a sense only begun for most immigrants. They had to begin a new lifestyle in a strange land. The recollections of Mrs. Johanne Frederiksen of Denmark upon arriving in Nokomis, Saskatchewan with her children on May 13, 1911 was probably characteristic of many immigrants: "You must excuse me [she wrote to her family in Denmark].... It has been difficult just to get food ready three times a day.... When we were set out in the middle of the night in the cold at the last station in a driving snowstorm, we all cried but then my husband was there.... Here it's still so desolate and frightening on the wild prairie. It is like the ocean. We are a tiny midpoint in a circle.... You will...understand that it looks terrifying, more than you can imagine."[5]

Getting established was the first concern. This meant building a house. A settler's first house was usually quite primitive—a tar-papered shack, a one-room log cabin, or, on the open prairies, a sod hut. More pressing was 'breaking the land'—preparing the soil for planting. By luck there would be a crop by Fall, but every prairie farmer leaned the hard way about the vagaries of the weather—hail, early frost, or drought. Once a crop was harvested, then came the negotiating with the CPR for fair grading of the grain at the elevators, the need to haul it to the station, pay the cost of unduly high freight rates, and worry about the price on the grain exchange or in the international market. Making a living farming was a hard, exhausting and precarious existence—a far cry from the idyllic image in the propaganda literature. Many homesteaders never stayed even long enough to complete the three-year residency requirement to qualify for their 'free' land. Disenchanted, they left for jobs in the nearby towns or cities, for work on the railways or in the lumber camps, for a new homestead site elsewhere, or for their home country, admitting defeat. Still, the majority stayed. Some 'weathered the storms', so to speak, and simply 'survived'. Others succeeded from the beginning and prospered. Every one's experience was different, and each settler had his or her own story to tell. Accounts of homesteading in prairie Canada are legendary, and collectively form the 'real' history of prairie settlement. Indeed the 'new immigrants' in the years from 1880 to 1914 were the true pioneering settlers of prairie Canada.

This new and diverse population greatly benefited the region. It provided cultural diversity, thus distinguishing the Prairies from the other regions of the country that tended to have more homogeneous populations. Their

[5]Quoted in Gerald Friesen, *The Canadian Prairies: A History,* Toronto, 1984, p. 255.

numbers also strengthened the political voice of the region by increasing the number of voters and hence the number of seats in the federal Parliament in Ottawa. As well, some of these 'new Canadians' would play an active role in the political and social reform movements on the Prairies in the pre- and inter-war years. Finally, these new immigrants very often formed the backbone of the western Canadian economy, growing the wheat, working in the service industries, or labouring in the mines, on the railroads, or in the factories.

The settlement experience in British Columbia paralleled that of the Prairies with a few notable exceptions. Immigrants began arriving soon after the completion of the CPR in 1885 and the first wave peaked by the outbreak of World War I as it did on the Prairies. But they often came for different reasons. Some came unaware of the very limited agricultural land in the province. Others were seeking a milder climate or work in resource industries. During this period the non-native population of British Columbia increased tenfold to roughly 450,000, thus transforming the province according to historian Jean Barman from a "fragile settler society on the frontier of the western world" to a "self-confident political and social entity."[6] British Columbia continued to have a disproportionately higher percentage of British immigrants in comparison to other ethnic groups than on the Prairies, thus ensuring its continued British nature. Still, for the first time there were more British Columbians born elsewhere in Canada than in Britain, thus making the province more 'Canadian'.

The other major ethnic group out of proportion to those on the Prairie, were Asians. Naturally, British Columbia became the home of thousands of Asians, principally from China and Japan, but some too from India and from what is now considered to be Southeast Asia. Many of the first Chinese immigrants came as indentured labourers, popularly termed 'coolies'. They worked in construction gangs on the railroads or as seasonal workers in the canneries, sawmills or lumber camps. Their pay was consistently a third to a half lower than that given to Europeans doing the same job. Many had come on their own for short periods of time in hopes of making enough money to return home a wealthy individual or to bring over a wife. But low wages curtailed these expectations. Insufficient money also prevented many from striking out on their own. Many ended up in ethnic ghettos in the Chinatowns of Vancouver or Victoria where they worked as house servants or in service jobs for Whites.

Japanese began arriving in the 1890s. Like the Chinese, the majority were single men. They gravitated towards fishing, and preferred living together in such villages as Steveston on the Fraser River or in enclaves in the cities of

[6]Barman, *The West Beyond the West*, p. 129.

Vancouver and Victoria. Some worked at market gardening.

Small numbers of East Indians came. What contemporaries called 'Hindoos' were really Sikhs from the Punjab. They worked mainly in logging which in India was largely a Sikh occupation. The peak years of East India immigration were 1905 to 1908 when an estimated five thousand came.

Ethnic minorities in both the Prairies and British Columbia faced racial discrimination. English-speaking Canadian distrusted the different customs and lamented their distinct languages which they feared would make western Canada like the biblical Tower of Babel, a place with a jumble of languages in which communications broke down. Some feared that the region would lose its British heritage and thus not fit in with the rest of Canada. They also saw the 'foreigners' as an economic threat, taking jobs away from Anglo-Canadians. On the Prairies, the Ukrainians (or Galicians as they were called) faced discrimination because of their tendency to settle together and then maintain their language and customs, thus setting them apart. Doukhobors, Mennonites and Hutterites faced persecution because of their pacifist beliefs, and, in the case of the Doukhobors, because of the looting, burning of their homes, and nude marches of a minority sect called the Sons of Freedom who wanted fellow Doukhobors to return to the Biblical days of the innocence of Adam and Eve. Jews and southern Europeans were criticized for their lack of farming skills and their inability to assimilate.

On the West coast, Asians faced severe discrimination. If the question regarding eastern and southern Europeans was whether, once admitted, they would make good farmers and assimilate, the question regarding Asians was whether they should be allowed into the country at all. In the case of the Chinese, the Canadian government imposed a head tax (money paid on entry) of $ 50 in 1885, which increased to $100 in 1900 and went as high as $ 500 in 1903 as a means to curtail their entry. The head tax effectively reduced overall Chinese immigration, but particularly the number of female immigrants, since many Chinese men were unable to afford to bring to Canada their wife, if they were married, or a future wife, if they were single. (The tax did, however, encourage the importation of 'slave girls', who were brought from impoverished parents in China by Chinese businessmen in Canada to work as domestic servants, or even as prostitutes.) Employers often paid the head tax or brought in Asian males illegally to build the railways and work the mines, because they were industrious and worked for low wages. The fifteen thousand Chinese who worked on the CPR between 1880 and 1885, for example, saved the Company an estimated $ 3.5 million.

Japanese immigrants did not face a head tax, only because Japan was a military ally of Britain and a major trading partner of both Canada and Britain. But the Canadian government succeeded in negotiating an agreement with Japan to restrict immigration to four hundred Japanese annually. The Japanese also faced subtle (and not so subtle) forms of prejudice on an everyday basis such as job discrimination, lower wages than whites, and social ostracism.

As a result of a combined temporary recession and an exceptional annual jump in illegal Asian immigration from two thousand to twelve thousand within a few years, xenophobia reached a fever pitch in 1907. In August of that year an Asiatic Exclusion League formed, and in September organized a protest march through Vancouver's Chinatown. The march turned into a riot in which buildings were damaged and residents assaulted.

A group of East Indians faced overt discrimination when in May 1914 the government of British Columbia refused entry into Vancouver harbour of the *Komagatu Maru* ship carrying 376 Indian passengers abroad. For two months the ship anchored offshore, while government officials deliberated and British Columbians jeered. H.H. Stevens, a Conservative M.P., demanded that Canada be 'pure and free from the taint of other people'. In the end, the *Rainbow*, one of Canada's naval vessels, escorted the Indian vessel out to sea amid cries of 'White Canada forever' and refrains of 'Rule Britannia', and the East Indians were forced to return home.

The causes of racial discrimination on the Prairies and in British Columbia, like elsewhere in Canada, were varied. Some members of the host society felt that immigrants were willing to work for lower wages, thus undermining union solidarity and threatening both jobs and rates of pay. For others, prejudice ran deeper and was more ingrained. Ethnic historian Peter Ward argues in *White Canada Forever* that at the base of racial attitudes in British Columbia was a yearning for a racially pure society. "Heterogeneity would destroy their capacity to perpetuate their values and traditions, their laws and institutions."[7] For these Canadians, racial diversity, or what would late be called 'the Canadian mosaic', was not an asset but a liability, a threat to the very existence of Canada. These Canadians wanted a united country with one language—English—and one culture—British. To achieve this objective meant ethnic minorities had to conform to Anglo-Canadian values. The means to achieve such conformity was through the schools where children would be taught to speak English and renounce their ethnic heritage. Yet, as ethnic historian Howard Palmer has pointed out, there was a basic contradiction in the attitude of the host society to immigrants: they wanted foreigners

[7]Peter Ward, *White Canada Forever: Popular Attitudes and Public Policy toward Orientals in British Columbia,* Montreal, 1978, p. 169.

"to conform and assimilate but then they did everything possible to prevent these new Canadians from assimilating by discriminating against them."[8]

A Booming Hinterland Economy and Political Protest

The years leading up to World War I were boom years full of self-confidence. On the Prairies, wheat farming was lucrative, and yields increasing annually. Quickly the region acquired the reputation of being the 'breadbasket of the nation' and indeed of the British Empire and to a limited extent of the world in the early years of the twentieth century. Wheat farming was the backbone of the western Canadian economy and the wheat economy was the backbone of the Canadian economy. The Prairies had become successfully integrated into a transcontinental Canadian economy, much to the chagrin of many prairie farmers who complained about the federal government's discriminatory high tariffs on imported manufactured food, excessive freight rates on the Prairies, and restrictive policy towards the West as a hinterland to central Canada. Prairie farmers protested against having to buy their manufactured goods and farm equipment in a closed, protected market that benefited central Canadian industrialists and manufacturers while at the same time having to sell their grain on an open, competitive market where the vagaries of world trade prevailed. In the inter-war years, such attitudes led to Prairie protest parties. But prior to the First World War, prairie farmers still believed, and hoped, that they could achieve reform within the existing two-party system.

Parallel developments occurred in British Columbia during this same period. Canadian national parties became the norm in the province, thus tying the province to the nation as a whole. Better communications provided another link, as did the economy. The Canadian national policy was in effect in British Columbia too, where a resource-based economy—similar in nature to that on the Prairies but based on lumber, salmon and minerals rather than wheat—worked to the disadvantage of the local economy by forcing residence of British Columbia to purchase manufactured goods at high protected prices from central Canadian industrialists but to sell their natural resources at lower, competitive international prices.

What muted protest in wesern Canada in the years up to World War I was the booming Canadian economy. There was a ready market for western Canadian natural resources not only in the rest of Canada but in the world at large. Provincial governments grew wealthy, encouraging greater

---

[8]Howard Palmer, "Reluctant Hosts: Anglo-Canadian Views of Multiculturalism in the Twentieth Century," in R. Douglas Francis and Donald B. Smith, eds., *Readings in Canadian History: Post-Confederation*, 3rd edn., Toronto, 1990, p. 199.

intervention in the economy to ensure continued growth. At times, government attitudes became reckless as in the case of timber leases in British Columbia, where the provincial government all but handed over crown land to private lumber companies (often American owned) whose only concern was profits with no regard for conservation or renewal of the forests. The same held true in the salmon fishing industry in the province of British Columbia, where quotas on catches were non-existent or so low and poorly regulated to be meaningless.

Not all inhabitants on the Prairies farmed or even lived in rural areas nor in British Columbia lived in resource towns or in isolated villages. By 1914, one-third (33%) of prairie dwellers lived in a town or city of 1000 people or more. In British Columbia the number of urbanites reached as high as 50 per cent. In both cases, these urban centres functioned as service centres for the surrounding rural communities, providing basic food, clothing professional services and small businesses. Larger cities, such as Kamloops and Kelowna in British Columbia: Medicine Hat in Alberta; Moose Jaw in Saskatchewan; and Brandon in Manitoba emerged along rail lines as supply centres for subregions that encompassed a fifty mile radius. At the top of this urban hierarchy by 1914 were the seven largest cities in the West—Winnipeg, Saskatoon, Regina, Edmonton, Calgary, Vancouver and Victoria, each with its own large hinterland to service with its variety of stores, factories, manufacturing outlets, business officers, government services, health care institutions, universities, and cultural facilities. The relationship between urban and rural communities was one of dependency, and thus one of resentment. Each needed the other to survive, but both resented that dependency role. Even the larger urban centres of the West were dependent on large urban centres outside the region, notably Toronto and Montreal in central Canada, or London, New York, Chicago or San Francisco outside of Canada. This metropolitan/hinterland relationship began early and has remained to today as a distinguishing feather of the economic, political, social and cultural life of the West.

The western Canadian economy of dependency and its manifestation in metropolitan/hinterland tensions was a major factor in the rise of social reform and political protest in the West. Social reform in the West was strongly influenced by the 'Social Gospel' movement, a socially oriented approach to Christianity that developed among many of the Protestant denominations in the West in the early twentieth century. It gave the West a sense of mission to the wider world, and a sense of purpose within the region itself with its aim to create a unified and purified society free of social injustices and moral impurity. The Social Gospel provided an impetus to women suffrage, or the right of women to vote, and prohibition, two social reform movements that were particularly strong in the West. Women first got the right to vote provincially in the province of Manitoba in 1916, quickly followed by Saskatchewan, Alberta and British Columbia, while the prohibitionists saw the earliest results of their efforts on the Prairies. Social gospellers also provided support to improving working and living conditions of the working class and to the trade union movement on the Prairies and in British Columbia.

Labour unrest in the West reached a peak in the immediate post-World War I era. Workers had postponed demands for better wages and improved working conditions as they responded, patriotically to the war effort. But as inflation soared (inflation almost doubled between 1915 and 1919) and unemployment rose with the return of war veterans, workers staged a series of strikes across the country in 1918 and 1919 to seek public attention and to reinforce their demands. The major one took place in Winnipeg in the spring of 1919. On May 1st, the unions of the metal workers' and the builders in the city went on strike. Other Winnipeg union workers, including police officers, fire-fighters, telephone and telegraph operators, and deliverymen, joined them by 15 May, virtually closing down the city. To provide essential services and to regulate the strike, the organizers created a 'General Strike Committee', Business and government officials saw this Committee, with its power to dictate what went on in the city, as a challenge to their own power and as a first step to a Bolshevik State. They countered by creating a 'Citizen's Committee of One Thousand' to maintain public utilities during the walkout.

Fearing that the strike would spread to other centres, the federal government intervened. It sent Arthur Meighen, Minister of Justice and Minister of the Interior, and Gideon Robertson, Acting Minister of Labour, to Winnipeg to review the situation. They arrived already convinced that the strike was a conspiracy. Meighen described the strike leaders (who were mostly British-born) as "revolutionists of varying degrees and types, from crazy idealists down to ordinary themes, with the better part, perhaps, of the latter type". He authorized the Royal North West Mounted Police to arrest ten of the Winnipeg strike leaders on the night of 16 June.

The workers retaliated by holding a silent parade down Main Street to city hall on Saturday, 21 June. During the demonstration, violence erupted between the strikers and the police (hired by the Citizen's Committee of One Thousand to retain the protesters). The mayor of Winnipeg also called in the Mounties to disperse the crowd. During the confrontation one man was killed and another wounded. 'Bloody Saturday', as it became known, ended with the dispersal of the workers and the establishment of military control of the city. By Thursday, 26 June, the strike committee called off the strike, without the workers having gained any of their objectives.

Labour unrest was equally volatile in British Columbia in the post-war period. Indeed, after the war, the Canadian government anticipated that should a general strike occur it would probably be in Vancouver (rather than in Winnipeg), and so arranged for a naval cruiser to be anchored offshore for quick action. Inflation in the province was almost 10 per cent higher than in the rest of Canada, while the unemployment rate was one and a half time greater. As well, there existed socialist cells and parties in the province that thrived on the deplorable working conditions in the resource industries, especially in the mines. Also the movement for One Big Union (OBU), a single union of all workers, was strong in the province. But with the suppression of the Winnipeg strikers, their British Columbian comrades were deferred from similar action. Labour unrest remained into the mid-1920s, as tension between managers and workers continued, and would long remain a hallmark of British Columbian society.

An even more 'revolutionary' change occurred among prairie farmers in the post-war era as they decided to strike out on their own politically to form their own third party committed solely to the interest of farmers. On the Prairies, farmers resented their dependency role: depending on the weather for a successful crop; on eastern-owned companies like the Canadian Pacific Railway Company or the Grain Exchange for the successful marketing of their crops or eastern banks for their loans; on eastern businessmen for their manufactured goods; and on the international market for the sale of their produce. Compounding their problem was the feeling of isolation from their markets in central Canada, Europe or the United States, and powerlessness in the centre of political power in Canada—the federal government in Ottawa. Political and economic decisions that very much affected western Canada were being made by people who did not have a vested interest in the well-being of the region itself.

Western farmers tried a variety of methods to correct this feeling of dependency and powerlessness. They established co-operatives in an effort to regulate and stabilize consumer and marketing prices. Since the majority of prairie farmers grew wheat, grain co-operatives were very popular, including farmer-owned elevators. But local co-operatives had a limited influence in the international market, and even had trouble regulating freight rates or alternating trade practices by powerful companies like the CPR. Prairie farmers concluded that they needed a stronger political voice in Ottawa.

Two possibilities existed: one was for farmers to take control of one of the two existing national parties, the Liberals or the Conservatives, and make it the political voice of farming interests; the other possibility was to begin a new party totally committed to, and controlled by, farmers. Prairie farmers tried both possibilities. Up until 1911, they worked at winning over the Liberal Party under Prime Minister Wilfrid Laurier to their side. But with the defeat of the Liberals in the federal election of 1911 on the policy of reciprocity or free trade with the Americans (which prairie farmers heartily endorsed), prairie farmers became disenchanted with both major parties.

In 1919, a group of disgruntled Prairie members of the Union Party (a loose coalition formed in 1917 by Prime Minister Borden and made up of both Liberals and Conservatives to present a united political effort during World War I) broke rank with the Union government when it refused to lower the tariff. They formed the nucleus of the Progressive Party. It would become apparent that the Progressives were more a protest *movement* than a *party*, out to reform the existing parties rather than to create a new party. When the existing party system proved more entrenched than they had expected, however, these Progressives ran in federal and provincial elections under their new party banner.

The Party's popularity spread rapidly. The Progressive won provincial elections in Alberta in 1921 and in Manitoba in 1922—and even formed a farmer's government in Ontario in 1919—and won the second largest number of seats in the federal election of 1921 with 65 seats, the majority of these seats on the Prairies. But political success came too quickly, and the Progressives could not agree among themselves as to what political role they should play.

The party split between a Manitoba-based wing under Thomas Crerar that wanted to act as a pressure group on the Liberal government to get it to implement policies favourable to farmers, and an Alberta-based wing under Henry Wise Wood that wanted to abolish political parties altogether in favour of a form of 'group government' based on all occupational groups in society. Wood argued that society naturally divided into several economic interest groups, of which the farmers were one and the largest on the Prairies. If each group obtained representation in Parliament, then the laws passed would reflect the interests of all rather than those of the particular group that happened to control the party. Group co-operation would replace party competition.

Unable to resolve their differences, the divided Progressives proved ineffective. They declined the position of official opposition even though, as the second largest party in the House of Commons, they warranted the title.

Then in 1922, Crerar resigned as leader, claiming he could not work with Wise Wood. Robert Forke took over as the new leader, but he had no better luck at uniting the party. One of his alleged followers commented that Forke "does not control one Progressive vote other than his own, and he is not always sure about that". The divisions revealed that the Progressives were more a loose federation of regional groups, with only shallow, insubstantial roots in British Columbia, Quebec, and the Maritimes, and with deep divisions within the two regions of strength—the Prairies and Ontario.

Meanwhile, the minority Liberal government wooed the Progressives by introducing policies that would appeal to western farmers. Prime Minister Mackenzie King lowered the tariff and lowered freight rates to what they had been in the Crow's Nest Pass Act of 1897. Mackenzie King claimed that the Liberals were moving in the same direction as the Progressives, that the Progressives were only 'Liberals in a hurry'.

The Progressives continued to lose political strength throughout the 1920s. Their number of seats went from 65 in the election of 1921 to 24 in the election of 1925 and then to 9 in the election of 1926. By 1930, they were a spent force. In many respects, the progressives had attempted the impossible: to base a party solely on farmers at a time when the rural population was in decline. They had wanted to preserve the family farm, to uphold rural values, and to ensure the political dominance of agricultural interests in a society that was increasingly more urban and industrial. Still, the spirit of the Progressives would live on in the philosophy of populism and in the tradition of western protest, to be taken up by the two new western Canadian-based parties in the 1930s—the Co-operative Commonwealth Federation (CCF), and Social Credit.

In British Columbia during the 1920s, the economy became heavily dependent on foreign markets. A major influencing factor in the shift from a continentally-oriented to an international market was the opening of the Panama Canal in 1914. Now Europe was much closer (in terms of time) as a market for British Columbian national resources such as lumber and minerals as well as Okanagan apples. "At the beginning of the decade", as Jean Barman notes, "some thirty ocean-going ships a month entered the port of Vancouver; by 1929 the number surpassed one hundred."[9] Many of the boats leaving Vancouver harbour carried prairie grain, making this port city a metropolitan centre for its prairie hinterland.

The decade of Twenties changed the cultural fabric of the West. The telephone was possibly the technological invention that revolutionized life

---

[9]Barman, *The West Beyond the West*, p. 238.

on the Prairies by breaking down isolation. Now farm dwellers could talk frequently with their distant neighbours. Social activities could be easily planned, business transacted, and even gossip exchanged on a regular basis. A few prairie farm women benefited from such labour-saving devices as washing machines, electric irons, and refrigerators, but the majority of prairie homesteads still lacked electricity and even indoor running water. More B.C. women succeeded in acquiring these devices during the twenties. In the West in general, popular magazines, mostly imported from the United States, were available through the mail, but on the Prairies, the *Grain Grower's Guide* (1908-28) newspaper was the farmers' 'Bible', offering a variety of quality articles from the marketing of grain to cultural affairs and even a regular women's column. First class Prairie and British Columbian novels were now available, often set in the region itself. On the Prairies, novels by Robert J. Stead, and Frederick Philip Grove were popular, while in British Columbia, Emily Carr's writings were almost as popular as her paintings. More people were able to enjoy these publications as children stayed in school longer to get a better education and the literacy rate of the region increased significantly. Schools and churches were the two important institutions in almost every western Canadian community, and very often were the first community buildings to be built. They served as social gathering centres as much as they did for educational and religious institutions respectively.

Impact of the Great Depression and World War II

The Great Depression of the 1930s was the worst decade in the history of Western Canada. It began with the New York Stock market crash of October 29, 1929—'Black Tuesday'—followed by a world financial collapse. The demand for raw materials and foodstuff was greatly curtailed, and the western Canadian economy grinded to a halt. Unemployment soared in the urban centres, while on the farms, food prices plummeted. Wheat, for example, went from a high of over $ 2.00 a bushel in the late-1920s to .34¢ a bushel by 1932. Some farmers chose to burn their crop rather than to pay the costs of harvesting and marketing it at prices in excess of its value. For the first time the region that had been known as 'the breadbasket of the world' faced food shortage, and the people required handouts. Prairie municipalities that had borrowed money in the prosperous Twenties to expand services to their people and to provide assistance to new business, now faced debts in excess of their tax base along with high interest rates.

On the Prairies, the economic depression was compounded by an agricultural depression. Dust storms, drought, extreme summer and winter temperatures, and plagues of grasshoppers devastated farming. Some farmers 'weathered to storm' so to speak, but many abandoned their farms, already in tax arrears, to move either to northern regions of the Prairie Provinces especially for those in the arid Palliser Triangle area of southern Alberta and Saskatchewan, or west to British Columbia. These prairie itinerants were joined by others from the other regions of the country who 'rode the rods' across the country in search of work. British Columbia was the end of the rail line, both literally and figuratively, and many of the unemployed single men ended up in the seedier areas of B.C. towns and cities or in relief camps, hastily set up by the federal government, where they worked long hours, often at meaningless jobs which social historian James Gray has described as 'boondoggling', for room, board, and a cash payment of initially just over $ 1 a day, then reduced to $ 7.50 a month and finally to .20¢ a day.

Conditions became so deplorable in these 'prison camps', as they became known, that over a thousand of the 'inmates' marched on Vancouver in December 1934 to protest camp conditions. When this failed to have any effect, the camp leaders organized a trek to Ottawa. About a thousand men boarded freight trains in Vancouver on 3 June, 1935. The plan was to pick up additional supporters at each stop along the way, until they reached Ottawa. The 'on-to-Ottawa Trek', as it has become known, was stopped in its tracks when a Royal Canadian Mounted Police force met the trekkers in Regina. In the ensuing Regina Riot, one policeman was killed, many trekkers injured, and about one hundred protest jailed. Only the Trek organizers were allowed to go on to Ottawa to meet with Prime Minister R.B. Bennett. They met an unresponsive prime minister who refused to do anything to meet the workers' demands.

Prime Minister Bennett was being approached by other desperate, ordinary Canadians who were hoping for some temporary financial assistance to get them through another winter or until their next crop could be taken off—any way to avoid the humiliation of having to go on relief or 'the dole', as it was called, and thus succumb to the degradation of a government handout. Some of the letters of these desperate Canadians, from all regions of the country, have been collected and published in a book entitled *The Wretched in Canada,* edited by L. Grayson and M. Bliss. They tell the tale of suffering more poignantly than anything else. The following example, only one of many from western Canadian residents, is illustrative:

I suppose I am silly to write this letter but I haven't anyone else to write to....

We are just one of many on relief and trying to keep our place without being starved out. Have a good 1/2 section not bad buildings and trying to get a start without any money and 5 children all small. Have been trying to send 3 to school and live on $10.00 a month relief for everything, medicine, meat, flour, butter, scribblers. Haven't had any milk for 3 months but will have 2 cows fresh in March sometime. Am nursing a 10 month old baby and doing all the work like cooking, washing, mending on bread and potatoes some days. This is our worst winter as my husband has had to be home to look after outside chores. Other winters he always made some money as we lived in town and I could manage alone.

Am so worried on account of the children as we never have any vegetables except potatoes and almost no fruit and baby hasn't any shoes have kept him in old socks instead but now he is getting so he creeps and pulls them off so often. I would like to get a couple of little pigs this spring. I am sure we can make a go of this place as its good land and doesn't blow if we could just manage until fall. Just had 70 acres in last years and the dry spell just caught it right along with the grasshoppers although we poisoned most of them there were hardly any left by fall. I can't hardly sleep for worrying about it....

Please help me by lending me some money and I will send you my engagement ring and wedding ring as security.... My two rings cost over $100.00 fifteen years ago but what good are they when the flour is nearly all done and there isn't much to eat in the house. In the city I could pawn them but away out here I haven't been off the farm this winter.[10]

Prime Minister Bennett sent five dollars as a gift, a private gesture he made on numerous occasions.

In desperation, people in the West looked to new political parties and new dynamic politicians for solutions. In 1932, J.S. Woodsworth, an ex-Methodist minister, social reformer and political activist, gathered together in Calgary a group of prairie farmers, socialists chiefly from British Columbia, disenchanted liberals, and left wing academics (mainly from the University of Toronto and McGill University) to begin a new party, the Co-operative Commonwealth Federation (CCF), the forerunner of today's New Democratic Party. Democratically based with direct input of party members at annual meetings, and British Fabian socialist in outlook, the Party aimed to become a national party. Most of its political support, however, was in the West, and it made little inroad in the other regions of the country. In the federal election of 1935, the Party won only seven seats, all seven from western Canada (2 in Manitoba; 2 in Saskatchewan; and 3 in British Columbia), even though they got over 10 per cent of the national popular

[10]Quoted in Friesen, *The Canaidan Prairies,* pp. 397-8.

vote. To maintain its support on the Prairies, the Party toned down its socialist policies particularly in terms of promising to nationalize the prairie family farm if elected. The Party won its first provincial election in Saskatchewan in 1944 under its popular Prairie leader T.C. 'Tommy' Douglas, a Prairie evangelist from Saskatchewan and a known social reformer.

In 1935, a second new Prairie protest party of the Depression era arose, this time in Alberta. The Social Credit Party was founded by William 'Bible Bill' Aberhart, a school teacher and later a radio evangelist lay preacher. Initially, Aberhart had rejected social credit theories put forward by the English theories, C.H. Douglas, but as the Depression worsened, he began to introduce social credit ideas into his popular weekly "Voice of the Prairies" bible hour on radio, estimated to have reached over 350,000 people in Alberta, British Columbia, Saskatchewan and even the bordering American states. He argued that the solution to the Depression was for governments to inject more money into the economy in the form of social credit dividends to encourage more purchasing power and thus to revitalize the flagging capitalist economy. His message was so popular that he decided, as late as the spring of 1935, to begin a Social Credit party and to contest seats in the federal and Alberta provincial elections of that year.

Social Credit spread in Alberta like a prairie wild fire. In the provincial election of 1935, the Party swept the province, winning 56 of the 63 seats in the Legislative. The incumbent United Farmers of Alberta (UFA) government (1921-35) was decimated, not winning a single seat. The Social Credit Party had a long 'reign'. It remained in power in Alberta for 36 years, first under Aberhart until his death in 1943, and then under Aberhart's protégé, Ernest Manning until 1968, and for a few years under Harry Strom until the Party's defeat to the Progressive Conservatives in 1971. The Social Credit Party changed over this 36 year period from a radical, more left-of-centre, populist protest party under Aberhart during the Depression years to a conservative, right-of-centre, pro-business party in the prosperous World War II era.

In British Columbia, the charismatic Liberal leader, Duff Pattullo, won the provincial election of 1933 and remained premier of the province throughout the remainder of the Depression until 1941. Pattullo believed that the solution to the Depression was to pour more government money into public works and give some assistance to private industry. His campaign catch-phase was 'socialized Capitalism', and it linked him with the popular New Deal policies of American president Franklin Delanor Roosevelt. Once in power, Pattulo passed a spate of bills reforming taxation, providing some economic assistance to various components of the economy, and restoring social programmes. But he left the chief initiative to the federal government, believing as he did that unemployment relief and economic stimulus were national concerns. These views brought him into conflict with national Liberal Government under William Lyon Mackenzie King, elected in 1935. Pattullo soon became labelled by his opponents as a narrow 'provincial rights' man, whereas in actuality he was, according to historian Margaret Ormsby, 'an enthusiastic nationalist'—a 'British Columbia Canadian'.[11] As early as 1933, Pattullo had informed the Canadian Prime Minister that "we are an empire in ourselves and our hills and valleys are stored with potential wealth which makes us one of the greatest assets of our Dominion." Yet Pattullo was unwilling to surrender provincial powers to the federal government as recommended by the Royal Commission on Dominion-Provincial Relations (or the Rowell-Sirois Commission as it became popularly known after its two chief commissioners) in its *Report*. "It seems obvious", Pattullo wrote at the time, "that surrender by the Provinces of their jurisdiction under the terms of Union, would lead either to disunion or a centralized control." Meanwhile, World War II intervened before the Commission's recommendations could be implemented.

Western Canada distinguished itself in the many men and women who served overseas during the war effort. As well, the region was the major centre for the important British Commonwealth Air Training Plan (BCATP), a programme which eventually trained 130,000 aviators from various Commonwealth countries—nearly half of the Commonwealth airmen during the entire war. Together, the region's involvement in the war effort brought a rapid end to the Depression with its high unemployment. Instead, prosperity rose as the demands for Canadian raw materials and foodstuff once again greatly benefited the West.

But not all western Canadians benefited from the war effort. For Japanese Canadians, the war years were a low time in their experience in Canada. They had come hoping to integrate into Canadian society. By the beginning of the war, most Japanese in British Columbia were Nisei—born in Canada, saw themselves as Canadians first, Japanese second; spoke English; and were well educated. Thus for most, they did not feel a sense of divided loyalty when Japan declared war on the Allied nations and invaded Pearl Harbour in December of 1941.

Many British Columbian Whites, for a long time distrustful of the Japanese and prejudiced against them, believed otherwise. They convinced themselves, or were convinced by others including British Columbian politicians, that Japanese military officers were living in disguise in British

---

[11]Ormsby, *British Columbia: A History*, p. 458.

Columbia as coastal fishermen, and that a Japanese fifth column existed in the coastal province ready to support Japan in an attack on the west coast.

When Canada declared war on Japan, the federal government moved swiftly to seize some twelve hundred fishing boats owned by British Columbians of Japanese descent, and shut down the three Japanese language newspapers and the fifty-nine Japanese-language schools. When this seemed insufficient to satisfy the public outcry against the Japanese in the province, the government then preceded to evacuate the Japanese from the coast to military camps, hastily established for this purpose, farther east in British Columbia and in the rest of Canada. Within the first month, some seventeen hundred Japanese men were sent to camps in Alberta. They were followed by thousands of other men, women and children, making it "one of the greatest forced migrations in Canadian history, second only to the Acadians' expulsion from Nova Scotia" in 1755, according to historian Jean Barman.[12] To this day, the government's decision of total forced evaluation of all Japanese Canadians from the West coast has left a legacy of bitterness. Only recently have those Japanese Canadians who were uprooted received an official Canadian government apology and financial compensation for the indignity and for their personal property that had been taken away from them and sold at the time.

The 'New West' of the Post-World War II Era

A 'New West' emerged in the post-World War II era, one more economically diversified, politically stable, and highly urbanized. World War II marked the end of the era of the wheat economy in the prairie West. Each of the three Prairie Provinces turned to other natural resources upon which to build their economies. Each province found renewed prosperity—Alberta on oil; Saskatchewan on potash and mining; Manitoba on mining and small scale manufacturing. But the old regional unity that had been based on the common wheat economy broke down into provincial divisions, with the three provinces often in conflict over the best policies for the region. Thus in discussing the prairie West in the post-World War II era, it is necessary to discuss each Prairie Province separately. British Columbia also prospered in the years 1945 to 1960 through exploration of its natural resources. It too became more highly urbanized with increasing concentration of population in the Vancouver region. Politically, the province was run by the Social Credit party from 1952 to 1972, thus giving stability to this province too.

Manitoba is the most economically diversified of the three Prairie Provinces with agriculture in the southwest, manufacturing in the urban centres and

[12]Barman, *The West Beyond the West*, pp. 266-7.

especially in Winnipeg, and mining and hydro-electric power in the north. None of these economic activities has emerged, however, to dominate the province's economy, as agriculture does in Saskatchewan, and oil and gas do in Alberta. Exploitation of the West's non-agricultural resources at first generated new markets for Winnipeg manufacturers, but the rise of Calgary and Edmonton meant new competition. Winnipeg suffered, too, from the decline of traditional industries such as meat packing, and from the loss, in the 1960s of Air Canada repair facilities. Agriculture has been the victim of global forces such as intense international competition and subsidy wars, and farm closures and bankruptcies have been numerous. Since the mid-1970s, plant closures and the restructuring of industries such as clothing have resulted in substantial job losses. In general, Manitoba's economy, since World War II, has, according to economist Cy Gonick, continued its 'long-term decline'[13] in relation to the Canadian economy as a whole.

Population-wise, the province has continued a shift from rural to urban living, although not as dramatically as elsewhere on the Prairies, partly because Manitoba was from the beginning a more urbanized province than Saskatchewan and Alberta, with most of that population concentrated in Winnipeg. With a stable but non-expanding economy, Manitoba did not attract much of the post-war immigration. In 1941 the province's population was 730,000; by 1981 it had increased to only 1,026,000. Given that from the beginning of settlement Manitoba had the largest number of Anglo-Saxon immigrants, including Ontarians and English-speaking Quebeckers, of the three Prairie Provinces, its population today is the most homogeneous with only small pockets of ethnic Canadians.

Politically, the province has witnessed few dramatic changes. A Liberal-Progressive coalition party, founded by John Bracken in the early 1920s, ruled the province from 1922 until its defeat over three decades later in 1958. Bracken led the Party through the 1920s and the 1930s until his departure for federal politics in 1942. Then Premier Garson took over until he too left for federal politics in 1948; he was followed by Douglas Campbell who led the Party from 1948 until its defeat in 1958. The party stayed in power by appealing to both urban and rural voters. In essence, the Liberal-Progressive coalition ruled as a non-party, claiming to be above partisan politics. Premier Campbell explained the success of his 'team' by pointing out that it "has eliminated politics from the business of government and … made up for what its lacks in colour by gaining in efficiency."

By the late 1950s, however, a urban-rural split undermined the old

---

[13]Cy Gonick, in Jim Silver and Jeremy Hull, eds., *The Political Economy of Manitoba*, Regina, 1990, p. 25.

coalition, leaving an opening for a renewed Progressive Conservative party to arise under Duff Roblin, grandson of the earlier Manitoba premier R.P. Roblin. Roblin's Conservatives won in the election of 1958, and remained in power until 1969, under Roblin until 1967 and then Walter Weir for the remaining two years. This Progressive Conservative government was more 'progressive' than 'conservative', spending heavily on health, welfare, and education. The government also invested in northern development, developing the mega hydro-electric project on the Nelson River, supporting mining through the INCO at Thompson, and forestry in the Churchill Forest Industry complex at The Pas.

By the late 1960s, Manitobans were ready for a political change. In 1969, they elected the first New Democratic Party (NDP) Government under Edward Schreyer, a Roman Catholic, Ukrainian of a working-class family. The NDP was an urban-based party, supported by both the working class and a rising middle class. The new government adopted major social reforms in order to "open a new way to those who have previously known only disparity and discrimination." Conservative critics denounced the NDP's public automobile insurance plan as too expensive, its higher taxes, and in general, state intervention in the economy, warning Manitobans that the province was moving towards 'state socialism'.

The Conservatives under Sterling Lyon defeated the NDP government in 1977. It proceeded with a programme of restraint and lower taxes, but in 1981 financial cutbacks and economic problems contributed to a return to power of the NDP under Howard Pawley. Pawley's government faced hard economic times—the recession of the 1980s and a backlash from English-speaking Canadians when it tried to extend French language services to its sizeable Franco-Manitoban population. The NDP was defeated in 1988 and a Conservative minority government was formed under premier Gary Filmon. Then in 1990, Filmon won a majority, in part because of his strong criticism of the unpopular Meech Lake Accord, a constitutional package that Westerners saw favouring Quebec over the rest of the provinces in Confederation.

Saskatchewan is still the most rural and agricultural of the three Prairie Provinces, although even here there has been a dramatic shift in population from farms to urban centres and an accompanying shift from farming to a diversified primary extraction economy based more on mineral production, especially potash, petroleum, and uranium. But even in these new economic industries, production is low and profits for the government modest. As a result, the province did not experience an economic boom to the same extent as Alberta or even Manitoba did in the post-war era. Immigration has also been low. Indeed, the greatest concern is out-migration, especially to neighbouring Alberta during boom periods. Agriculture seems to be an 'endangered occupation' even in this, the most rural of provinces. The decade of the 1980s was particularly difficult for Saskatchewan farmers with falling world grain prices, protectionist world markets for agricultural products, drought conditions, and excessively high interest rates. Many long-time Saskatchewan farm families—some dating their family farms back to the early settlement period—have had to sell their farms. Those who have remained have had to change radically their methods of farming to make their farms competitive. This has meant mega-farms of thousands of acres, with sophisticated and very expensive farm equipment, and, in some cases, even computerized production. The days of the quarter-section family farm has disappeared.

The new industries of the Saskatchewan economy—potash, petroleum and uranium—were initially operated by government owned companies established during the lengthy CCF/NDP government days (1944-64, and 1971-82). The government believed in 'planned economic development' and 'social ownership of natural resources'. But the Conservative government, elected in 1982 under Grant Devine, sold a number of these public-owned industries in an effort to boost government revenues to offset a mushrooming provincial debt. In 1991, popular discontent, especially in urban areas, brought the NDP back to power, led by Roy Romanow. The province's dire financial problems have forced the new government to increase taxes and make large spending cuts. This action has provoked discontent, especially among wheat farmers who have demanded emergency cash payments to compensate for low grain prices, and among public-sector unions who wanted a better contract with the government.

Alberta has become the wealthiest and the most urbanized of the three Prairie Provinces. These developments are due to the success of oil and gas, at least up until the 1980s, which replaced agriculture as the main component of the province's economy after World War II. Historians have seen the discovery in 1947 of a massive oil field in the Leduc Valley near Edmonton as the turning point from an agricultural to a fossil fuel economy. This discovery coincided with a growing world demand for fossil fuels. In the 1950s, the Canadian government assisted a private oil company, formed by American and Canadian businessmen, to build a pipeline from Alberta to central Canada and to the northern United states to pump western gas to these export centres. This 'national policy' (compared at the time to the building of the Canadian Pacific Railway) benefited Alberta throughout the 1950s and 1960s, and enabled the province to serge ahead of its sister Prairie

Provinces in wealth and in national influences. The next major economic expansion came in the 1970s with OPEC and the world energy crisis. Along with the importance of oil and gas for national and even international markets came increased financial clout for Alberta, including the relocation of national banks and other corporations to take advantage of the new investment opportunities in the province. Alberta thus has become one of the three 'have' provinces in Canada, along with Ontario and British Columbia. In fact, during the heydays of prosperity in the 1970s, Alberta created a 'Heritage Fund'—billions of dollars of savings from the sale of oil to be used for 'rainy days'.

Those 'rainy days' came quickly. By 1982, the government began borrowing from the Heritage Fund to cover overspending. Albertans began to look for scapegoats for the dramatic reversal. Some Albertans blamed the federal Liberal government. In the late 1970s, it introduced a 'made-in-Canada' oil price that enabled Canadians to buy oil and gas at below world prices. Alberta resented federal price controls which deprived them of billions of dollars of oil revenue. At the same time, the Trudeau government in Ottawa introduced a policy of Canadianizing the oil industry, again against the strong opposition of Albertans. But the real cause for a languishing Alberta economy was a greatly reduced world demand for oil and gas as people implemented energy-saving plans. This resulted in curtailed construction on huge synthetic oil production and heavy oil upgrading projects in northern Alberta. Soon jobless rates matched those of eastern Canadian levels; indeed many unemployed workers who had come West during the boom years of the 1920s, now returned to eastern and central Canada. Real estate values fell sharply. Two major Alberta bank ventures collapsed, though the federal government agreed to finance a costly bailout. Thus far, the Alberta government has held out as the province without a provincial sales tax and instead has attempted to fight the rising debt by heavy cutbacks in public sector and service Jobs. Albertans either long for a return to the 'good old days' or hope for a better tomorrow in 'next year country'.

In the 1980s and early 1990s, Alberta continued to have a predominantly primary resource economy despite major efforts by the provincial government to diversify by supporting secondary manufacturing and small businesses. Primary production has branched out from oil and gas to include timber products (especially pulp and paper), coal, and minerals. But the problem of finding a way to maintain sustained economic growth while protecting the ecology and respecting the rights and needs of the local populace, especially of the native people, remains. There are no easy answers to these complex issues.

The shift from an agricultural to a fossil fuel economy in Alberta has resulted in a corresponding shift from a rural to an urban population. In 1941, over 66 per cent of Albertans lived in rural communities or on farms; in 1991, less than 20 per cent are rural inhabitants. The majority of urbanites live in Calgary and Edmonton, which together account for over 60 per cent of Alberta's total population. These trends have two main implications. First, Edmonton and Calgary have increased their metropolitan dominance over the rest of Alberta. Second, these cities are also major 'players' on the national scene, rivalling Vancouver and Winnipeg and even to a degree Toronto and Montreal as major metropolitan centres of power and influence. Equally, Calgary and Edmonton are sophisticated social and cultural centres with artistic and intellectual achievements such as film production, major publishing companies, and nationally recognized universities. Thus, today the modern Alberta 'cowboy' wears a three-piece suit instead of rawhide pants ('chops'), rides in a sports car instead of on a horse, and works in an office rather than out on the range. Only once a year at Stampede time in Calgary and Klondike Days in Edmonton do Albertans dawn their traditional western garb to perpetuate the myth of the 'good old days' of cowboys and Indians.

Politically, Alberta has always been a one-party province. Albertans have a propensity to vote overwhelmingly for one party for an extended period of time and then to replace that 'dynasty' with a new and equally powerful one. In the post-World War II period, it was the Social Credit Party that enjoyed long years of loyal support among the Alberta electorate. The party succeeded in projecting an image of a grass-roots, rural-based party while at the same time working closely with the business community, especially in the 'oil patch'. It also benefited from the tremendous post war boom in this oil-rich province, simply by being the party in power when the boom began. Social Credit became synonymous with prosperity in the province. But tensions developed beneath the surface: unions resented labour-relations laws with strong antistrike provisions, and many Albertans, particularly the Native people, failed to benefit from the new riches.

Then in 1971, Social Credit was swept out of office and the Party decimated in terms of its electoral base by a new Progressive Conservative regime, particularly strong in urban Alberta. Led initially by the popular premier Peter Lougheed, a member of a well-established Alberta family, the Don Getty, and only recently the afforable Ralph Klein, the Party has stayed in office continuously since 1971. It has done so by changing with the changing times. The Lougheed years were ones of big spending on the assumption that the oil boom would go on forever. When Don Getty took over, his government invested Heritage Fund money in a number of industries which went bankrupt. This bad management along with continual decline in demand for oil and gas led to mushrooming debt. The Klein government has instituted a policy of radical and massive budget cuts designed to eliminate the provincial debt.

British Columbia, like Alberta, experienced a post war economic boom, giving the province the envious nickname 'lotus land' by outsiders. Premier W.A.C. Bennett told the Constitutional Conference in Ottawa in 1969: "With the population of British Columbia growing at twice the rate of the rest of Canada, the presence of British Columbia as an economic region of its own is more obvious as each day passes." This attitude of 'disinterested detachment' as one analyst described it has led some to conclude that 'B.C.' stands for 'Beyond Canada'. Prime Minister Pierre Trudeau once compared British Columbians to villagers who lived at the bottom of a mountain and never climbed to the top to meet those on the other side. And Canadians 'on the other side' see the Rocky Mountains not only as a physical barrier but an intellectual and cultural barrier also, separating this most-westerly province from the rest of Canada.

A number of factors contributed to British Columbia's prosperity. War-torn Europe was badly in need of primary products, such as timber and minerals, from British Columbia. Industrial expansion and urbanization in general and especially throughout North America greatly increased the demand for natural resources. Both the federal and British Columbia government adopted economic strategies that increased the profile of B.C. products internationally. New developments in transportation, such as the building of the Pacific Great Eastern Railroad to Prince George, the Alaska Highway through the heart of British Columbia, and extensive road construction in general boosted the provincial economy and made the transfer of goods more efficient. Mining in the province got a boost when the Aluminium Company of Canada (Alcan) built a large smelter south-east of Prince Rupert at the town of Kitimat, and Consolidated Mining and Smelting, later renamed Cominco, opened up mines at Trail. Alberta oil was piped to the West coast, making fuel more accessible and cheaper.

The new Social Credit government, first elected in 1952, worked closely with business leaders in the province to promote growth in the traditional natural resource industries. Much of the investment capital came from the United States in return for B.C. natural resources, particularly lumber. By 1950 over 84 per cent of B.C.'s lumber exports went south rather than to Britain, the major market up to and including the Depression years. Large integrated multinationals formed, especially during the Social Credit era, to process pulp and paper, shakes and shingles and other byproducts of the forest industry. Hydro-electric power was another important export commodity especially from Columbia and the Peace Rivers. To maintain control over this important source of energy, the Social Credit government 'provincialized' the B.C. Electric Company and amalgamated it with the B.C. Power Corporation to create the B.C. Hydro and Power Authority in 1962.

Mining activities increased as a result of world demand. Japan became a new and important customer especially for copper concentrates and coking coal, and a new port at Roberts Bank, south of Vancouver, was opened up to take coal, once it had arrived by rail from the interior, directly abroad in large bulk carriers. The B.C. government continued to export most of its minerals in raw or semi-processed form, thus depriving the province of badly needed secondary manufacturing. "The value of Canadian products exported from British Columbia shot up five-fold from $675 million in 1952 to $3.3 billion two decades later",[14] Barman notes.

While expanding its export markets, the province continued to develop internally with an even more intense road building programme along with new and improved ferry service between Vancouver and its surrounding islands through the B.C. Ferry Corporation, a creation of the Social Credit government, and better airline service with the beginning in 1941 of Canadian Pacific Airlines, which chose Vancouver as its national headquarters in 1948 because of its strategic location for flights to Pacific Rim countries.

Resource development resulted in a notable population shift. Mining and forestry activities opened up new communities in the interior and in northern British Columbia, such as Fort St. James, Fraser Lake, Elkwood and Sparwood. New regional urban centres emerged such as Prince George which by 1971 had a hinterland extending west to Vanderhoof and Fort St. James and north to Mackenzie, Fort St. John, and Dawson Creek. For the southern interior, the comparable regional urban centre to Prince George was Kamloops, servicing the Kootenay area. But Vancouver became even more entrenched as the major urban centre of the province, spreading out to incorporate adjacent municipalities,

Urban concentration affected other areas as well. Education became more concentrated, resulting in the closure of a number of one or two-room rural schools. Secondary schools grew at an astonishing rate as more children stayed in school longer. Post-secondary education expanded in three directions: the introduction of community colleges, especially in the skilled trades and service industries, in most of the major urban centres in the province; technical colleges, such as the British Columbia Institute of Technology;

[14]Ibid., p. 323.

and new universities, including Victoria University, an outgrowth of Victoria College, in Victoria and Simon Fraser University in Vancouver. Two church-affiliated post-secondary institutions also existed: the Catholic University of Notre Dame (opened in 1950 and closed in 1983 due to financial difficulties) and Trinity Western College, begun by a conservative Protestant group in the early 1960s.

Urban concentration also affected labour unions in the province. Unions became more consolidated and more widespread, making B.C. the most unionized province in Canada, and also consolidated. The largest union was the International Woodworkers of America, followed by the B.C. Federation of Labour. New unions emerged in the burgeoning service industries, such as the B.C. Government Employees' Union and Hospital Employees' Union, and in education with the B.C. Teachers' Federation. B.C. still led the nation in the number of strikes and the intensity of them—an indication of the volatile nature of its resource-based economy.

Politically, the years since World War II have been marked by stability. A coalition government of Liberals and Conservatives formed after the 1941 provincial election under Liberal leader and premier, John Hart, until his resignation in 1947, and his Liberal successor Byron Johnson. By the early 1950s, a new Social Credit Party formed, modelled on that of Aberhart's Alberta Social Credit Party but having its own provincial idiosyncrasies and an equally dynamic leader in W.A.C. 'Wacky' Bennett. A native of the Maritimes, Bennett came West during the Depression years where he entered provincial politics as a Conservative. After losing two bids for the leadership of the Conservative Party, he crossed the floor of the provincial legislature to sit as an independent M.L.A. in 1951. In December of that year, he joined the Social Credit League, and turned it into a party organization. Appealing to religious and protest groups, especially in the rural and hinterland areas of the province, which were feeling resentful at the political monopoly of Vancouver and its business elite, the Party's membership rose from a mere 500 in 1950 to over 8,000 by 1952, enough to enable the Party to win the 1952 provincial election. Once in power, the Party consolidated its electoral base and extended it to include the major urban centres of Vancouver and Victoria as well, thus enabling it to rule the province for the next two decades. Its only serious opposition during this hiatus was the party of the left—the CCF, renamed the New Democratic Party (NDP) in 1961.

By the early 1970s, opposition to the Social Credit regime grew strong enough to dislodge the party. Discontent grew over inflation, unemployment which reached 9 per cent in 1971, and limited expectations as the provincial economy slowed down. Most of all, people were ready for a change. This discontent was sufficient to defeat Social Credit in 1972 and bring in the first B.C. socialist government—an NDP government headed by the flamboyant and pugnacious Dave Barrett, a social worker from a Vancouver working-class family.

The NDP launched a vigorous social and economic programme designed to reorganize social services; to impose a new taxation and royalty structure; to freeze the sale of agricultural land for development; to eliminated discrimination in employment and housing; to give full collective bargaining rights to provincial employees; to draft a new labour code; to introduce rent controls; and to 'provincialize' key services such as the production and marketing of natural gas, and automobile insurance. Such innovative pro-grammes ran into opposition from powerful interest groups in the province such as land developers and the mining and forestry industries, who accused the government of 'legislating by thunderbolt'. They also became victims of a world wide recession that coincided, unfortunately, with the election of the NDP. Rather than curb expectations and spending, however, the NDP government continued to push ahead with its economic programme, increasing the provincial debt from $1.2 billion in 1972 to $3.2 billion by 1975.

In 1975 Barrett called a snap election, hoping to capitalize on the retirement of W.A.C. Bennett after the 1972 election and the political inexperience of Bennett's son, Bill Bennett, who took over the Party's leadership from his father. But Bill Bennett had both a family name and a still powerful party behind him, enabling him to win almost half of the popular vote to become the new provincial premier.

The new Social Credit government was more sophisticated, urban based, and business oriented than was the case under W.A.C. Bennett. Yet it continued to depend, as in the past, on the provinces' natural resources as the chief base of the economy. But these resources—timber, salmon, and minerals—became even more concentrated in a few large multinational corporations, making them highly vulnerable to world demand and an unstable world economy. Just how vulnerable they were, became evident in the early 1980s as another world wide recession played itself out. British Columbians experienced another recession and government cutbacks. The Social Credit government managed to win reelection in 1983 under Bill Bennett. Three years later he retired, and William Vander Zalm, a charismatic, Dutch immigrant, took over as Party leader and premier.

Vander Zalm emphasized privatization of social and other government services, severe restrictions on the powers of unions, and financial restraint. His government also continued to plunder natural resources with little concern for long term conservation. But by the late 1980s, there existed interest groups willing and able to lobby the government to practice restraint in exploiting the province's limited and dwindling natural resources. Particularly vocal were novelists like Bertrand Sinclair who were willing to speak out against the powerful logging companies. "Outside of two or three concerns, logging in B.C. today is an orgy of waste", he wrote. "They're skimming the cream of the forest, spilling half of it." Naturalist Roderick Haig-Brown was equally seething: "A civilization built on foul air and polluted water, on destroyed timber lands overgrazed ranges, exhausted farm lands, on water sucked from one river system to make cheap electricity on another, is too costly and too insecurely based to last."[15] Support for conservation also came from the tourist industry whose livelihood depends on the truth of its slogan of "Beautiful Natural British Columbia". But the tensions between economic growth, which today as always has been based chiefly on the exploitation of natural resources, and conservation, something British Columbians in the past have not been concerned about, will undoubtedly escalate, requiring a greater balance of interest groups in the province than ever before. Carmanah Valley and Clayguot Sound, on Vancouver Island, both containing important stands of old-growth forest, have recently become the subject of exceedingly bitter disputes between conservationists and industrialists. The challenges ahead in the 1990s, whether it's a Social Credit or an NDP government (the NDP won the 1992 election under its leader Michael Harcourt), are great—as they are also for the Prairie Provinces of this region of western Canada.

Conclusion

Western Canada has undergone profound changes since 1864, yet certain common characteristics of the region have prevailed. The region has always been, and continues to be a predominantly resource-based, and thus a hinterland economy. In the case of the Prairie Provinces, that hinterland economy has altered from its initial resource of furs, to wheat, and more recently to oil, gas, potash, timber, minerals and other agricultural products (in addition to wheat). For British Columbia, the shift has been from furs to salmon, timber, and minerals. As historian Jean Barman notes concerning British Columbia: "All that alters are the names of the particular staples being exploited and the ownership of the means of production."[16]

This resource-based economy makes the region dependent on capital from outside the region to develop and market. Initially, much of the capital

---

[15]Quoted in ibid., p. 330.
[16]Ibid., p. 341.

came from Britian, then Canada, and more recently the United States. In times of demand and prosperity, the abundant natural resources of the region have served its people well, providing them with prosperity, but in periods of recession and low demand, this resource economy has proven to be more of a curse than a blessing.

A resource-based economy has also perpetuated a self-fulfilling image of the region as incapable of evolving beyond its primary producing capacity to sustain secondary or even tertiary growth. Despite efforts by western Canadian provincial governments to diversify their economies so as to escape their dependency on vulnerable and limited natural resources, they have not succeeded. This concern can only increase as these resources dwindle and threaten to disappear. How the region will adjust to this critical situation remains a major concern for all those who live in the region.

The region's resource-based economy has also greatly affected the settlement pattern of the region. It has greatly curtailed, for example, settlement in the region. Resource production limits the population necessary in the region to develop it. In the case of the fur trade, settlement was seen as the foe of the forest and the forest was the home of the fur-trading animals on which the fur trade depended. Thus for over a century, the Hudson's Bay Company succeeded in preventing colonies from being established in the region. Wheat production was based on small family farms as opposed to large urban centres, while lumbering and salmon fishing in British Columbia required only lumber camps or small fishing villages respectively.

When urban centres did appear, they consistently became service centres for the rural hinterlands surrounding them, both as supply centres for goods required by the local community and as marketing centres for the local resource. They became one-dimensional towns, whose success or failure was intrically tied to the region's resource economy. Even the larger cities— Winnipeg, Saskatoon, Regina, Edmonton, Calgary, Vancouver and Victoria— were, and continue to be strongly tied to the region's resource economy and languish or prosper accordingly. And like the hinterlands that they service around them, these cities too are hinterlands to larger metropolitan centres outside the region, be it Toronto or Montreal in Canada, or London, New York, Chicago, or San Francisco outside of Canada. Dependency occurs at all levels, linked initially to the region's primary resources.

As well, people in the region have always come from elsewhere. Even the original inhabitants, it is believed, came from Siberia or Outer Mongolia via a land bridge that one existed across the Bering Strait. Later settlers came from the British Isles, the United States, other parts of Canada, and eventually from western and eastern Europe and Asia. They came for a variety of reasons from adventure to job opportunities, and hoped for prosperity. But they were united in their belief that their new home in western Canada would offer them something better than what they left behind. In this respect, the prairie West and British Columbia had at the outset a utopian image that greatly affected how people perceived, and initially responded to, the region. Such idyllic images also fostered the growth of more explicitly utopian settlements in the West than in any other region of the country. This utopian image of the region has, among other things, spurred a host of protest movements and parties. Western Canada was thus the home of a wide variety of social reform movements, and often lead the way in achieving these reform objectives in the nation, such as women's suffrage and prohibition.

The west has also produced strong regional protest movements. Initially, it was the Progressive Party in the 1920s, followed by Social Credit and the Co-operative Commonwealth Federation (CCF) in the 1930s. In British Columbia, it has been the Social Credit and the CCF that have become the parties in power, thus distancing the region from the rest of the country which has tended to vote Liberal and Conservative governments into power.

After World War II, the Prairie Provinces attempted to work within the two traditional parties, giving their loyalty federally mostly to the opposition Conservative party. When this return to the two traditional parties seemed no more satisfying to the region than third parties, the region began in the 1970s to distance itself once again from the rest of the country by producing regional separatist movements/parties, centred mainly in Alberta. What seemed to initiate this new round of regional protest was the feeling once again that the federal government in general and Prime Minister Pierre Trudeau in particular seemed to give little heed to the region's aspirations. Westerners felt that they had little influence on national politics since federal parties depended on Ontario and Quebec for most of their votes. In the heady and prosperous days of the late 1970s, separatist parties arose in Alberta. But the recession of 1981-82 undermined the movement, and the defeat of the Trudeau government in 1984 eliminated the primary focus of western discontent.

The election of a Conservative government under Brian Mulroney with overwhelming support in western Canada in 1984 did not alleviate regional discontent. Falling commodity princes and Ottawa's perceived preoccupation with Quebec provoked new frustration with the Mulroney government. Some Westerners sought increased political power for the region through a revised 'Triple E' Senate—*equal* number of seats for all provinces regardless of population, *elected*, and *efficient*. This hope died with the failure of the Charlottetown Accord, a constitutional reform package in 1993. Westerners then turned to a new regionally-based party, the Reform Party under Preston Manning, son of former Alberta premier, E.C. Manning. Proclaiming that the 'West wants in'—not out of—Confederation, but on an equal and fair basis, the party has condemned the federal government's financial mis-management, its 'Welfare state approach' to meeting social needs, its immigration policy, and its commitment to official bilingualism and multi-culturalism. Underlying all this criticism, according to journalists Sydney Sharpe and Don Braid, is the region's continued hostility to Quebec.

The Reform Party's meteoric rise since 1987 to becoming close to being the second largest party in the House of Commons with 53 seats and a major player in federal politics has given the West a new political voice in Ottawa. Clearly it is a regional party. The fact that the Reform Party's strongest support and base is in the West and to date has had little success in the other regions of the country attests to its regional nature. Also in attacking the other regions of the country—notably Ontario and Quebec—the party shows the continued belief of the region that it has been 'victimized' within Confederation. This too has been a continuing characteristic of the region.

Protest, reform, a hinterland status, isolation and victimization are all part of the reality and the mythology of western Canada. These concepts have taken on a life of their own that have stamped a certain prevailing image on the West over time that has infused its history and its current mentality. For ultimately, the Canadian West is a state of mind—'a region of the mind'—shaped by its history, its literature, and its art. That history is a fusion of fact and fiction, the creative interplay between the two that has always been the source of understanding about the region. It is this mythology, that has both grown out of the past and shaped it, that will also shape the region's future.

BIBLIOGRAPHY

Artibise, Alan F.J., ed. *Town and Country: Aspects of Western Canadian Urban Development*. Regina, 1981.

Barman, Jean. *The West Beyond the West: A History of British Columbia*. Toronto, 1991.

Berton, Pierre. *The Promised Land: Settling the West, 1896-1914*. Toronto, 1984.

Burnet, Jean, and Howard Palmer. *'Coming Canadians': An Introduction to the History of Canada's Peoples*. Toronto, 1988.

Carter, Sarah. *Lost Harvests: Prairie Indian Reserve Farmers and Government Policy*. Montreal, 1990.

Eagle, John. *The Canadian Pacific Railway and the Development of Western Canada, 1896-1914.* Montreal, 1989.

Elliott, David. *Bible Bill: A Biography of William Aberhart.* Edmonton, 1987.

Finkel, Alvin. *The Social Credit Phenomenon in Alberta.* Toronto, 1989.

Fisher, Robin. *Contact and Conflict: Indian-European Relations in British Columbia, 1774-1890.* Vancouver, 1977.

Francis, Daniel. *Battle for the West: Fur Traders and the British of Western Canada.* Edmonton, 1982.

Francis, R. Douglas. *Images of the West: Changing Perceptions of the Prairies, 1690-1960.* Saskatoon, 1989.

Friesen, Gerald. *The Canadian Prairies: A History.* Toronto, 1984.

Gibbins, Roger. *Prairie Politics and Society: Regionalism in Decline.* Toronto, 1980.

Gould, ed. *Logging: British Columbia Logging History.* Saamichton, 1975.

Grayson, L.M., and Michael Bliss, eds. *The Wretched in Canada: Letters to R.B. Bennett 1930-1935.* Toronto, 1971.

Harrison, Dick. *Unnamed Country: The Struggle for a Canadian Prairie Fiction.* Edmonton, 1977.

Jones, David. *Empire of Dust: Settling and Abandoning the Prairie Dry Belt.* Edmonton, 1987.

Laycock, David. *Populism and Democratic Thought in the Canadian Prairie, 1910-1945.* Toronto, 1990.

Macleod, R.C. *The North West Mounted Police and Law Enforcement, 1873-1905.* Toronto, 1976.

Miller, J.R. *Skyscrapers Hide the Heavens: A History of Indian-White Relations in Canada.* Toronto, 1991.

Morton, W.L. *The Progressive Party in Canada.* Toronto, 1950.

Ormsby, Margaret. *British Columbia: A History.* Toronto, 1958.

Owram, Douglas. *Promise of Eden: The Canadian Expansionist Movement and the Idea of the West, 1856-1900.* Toronto, 1980.

Painchaud, Robert. "French-Canadian Historiography and Franco-Catholic Settlement in Western Canada, 1870-1915," *Canadian Historical Review,* 59 (December 1978), 447-66.

Palmer, Howard. *Patterns of Prejudice: A History of Nativism in Alberta.* Toronto, 1982.

Rees, Ronald. *Land of Earth and Sky: Landscape Painting of Western Canada.* Saskatoon, 1984.

Richards, John, and Larry Pratt. *Prairie Capitalism: Power and Influence in the New West.* Toronto, 1979.

Robin, Martin. *The Company Province,* 2 vols. Toronto, 1972.

Roy, Patricia. *A White Man's Province: British Columbia Politics and Chinese and Japanese Immigration, 1858-1914.* Vacouver, 1989.

Sealey, D. Bruce, and Antoine S. Lussier. *The Metis: Canada's Forgotten People.* Winnipeg, 1975.

Sharpe, Sydney, and Don Braid. *Storming Babylon: Preston Manning and the Rise of the Reform Party.* Toronto, 1992.

Stanley, George. *The Birth of Western Canada.* Toronto, 1960.

Taylor, G.W., *Mining: The History of Mining in British Columbia.* Saanichton, 1978.

Thacker, Robert.*The Great Prairie Fact and Literary Imagination.* Albuquerque, 1989.

Thompson, John H. *The Harvests of War: The Prairie West, 1914-1918.* Toronto, 1978.

Turner, Robert D. *West of the Great Divide: An Illustrated History of the Canadian Pacific Railway in British Columbia, 1880-1896.* Victoria, 1987.

Voisey, Paul. *Vulcan: The Making of Prairie Community.* Toronto, 1988.

Ward, Peter. *White Canada Forever: Popular Attitudes and Public Policy toward Oriental in British Columbia.* Montreal, 1978.

5

Quebec Since 1867

MICHAEL D. BEHIELS

Introduction

Linguistic and cultural pluralism have long been the hallmarks of Canada's identity at home and abroad. A crucial dimension to both of these characteristics has been the presence of a strong and dynamic French-speaking community, located in large majority in the province of Quebec, whose roots go back to the very origins of the country in the early seventeenth century. The French were the first Europeans to explore, with the aid of the aboriginal peoples, most of the North American continent all the way to the Rocky Mountains. For settlement purposes, they preferred the territory known as Acadia in the Maritime region and the St. Lawrence river valley which came to be known as the province of Quebec. Following the Seven Years War, 1756-63, the Catholic and French-speaking majority of Quebec was joined by a dynamic minority of British and American settlers and businessmen of various ethnic origins.

The province of Quebec, located between the Laurentians to the north-west and Appalachian Mountains to the south-east and bordered by the Ottawa river on the southwest, is the home of 85 per cent of Canada's over six and a half million citizens of French origin as well as one million English-speaking Canadians of various origins. The vast majority of the other 15 per cent of Canada's Francophones live in the two adjacent provinces of New Brunswick and Ontario, although every province has a small minority of Francophones who continue to maintain their language and culture. Beginning in the 1840s, but especially so after Confederation, Quebec's Francophones have gained increasing control over the social, cultural, political and economic institutions within the province. But this development was often held up by the persistence of their traditional values and institutions as well as by the presence of the small but powerful English-speaking elite which controlled the national economy and the national agenda from its position of dominance in Montreal, long the centre of the

Canadian economy. Over time considerable tension developed between Quebec's Francophone socio-economic classes and their leaders and these English-speaking political and economic elites which controlled the economic, social and political levers of power. Before the later's dominance could be challenged effectively it was necessary for the Francophone society of Quebec to undergo a social and ideological revolution of its own.

Beginning in the 1930s, the Quebec society experienced a widening of the gap between the traditional political class and the clerical elites who defended obsolete and outmoded institutions and value systems, and the rising urban working and lower-middle classes who adhered to the secular permeating much of their society by this time. By the 1960s, this gap was closed momentarily when the emerging new middle class of intellectuals, politicians and bureaucrats modernized Quebec's political, economic and social institutions. By the 1970s the urban working and lower-middle classes bore the brunt of an increasingly nationalistic and secular middle class of militant ideologues, social science professionals, bureaucrats and technocrats whose members used their newly acquired control over the society's educational, social, and health institutions to advance their goal of creating a nationalist state. This new Francophone middle class has used the modernized state to advance its own interests as well as to provide the policies, funding and structures required to create a Francophone bourgeoisie capable of challenging and eventually displacing the Anglophone bourgeoisie of Montreal. In so doing, a fragment of this new middle class acquired the power and the desire to challenge the very fabric of the Canadian federal system.

Since the late 1960s the trend in Quebec historiography has been to down play the distinctive nature of the Francophone society of Quebec since Confederation. Revisionist historians portrayed all of Quebec, including the Francophone community, as a normal, modern, secular, urban, industrial society which was not out of step with the rest of North America. In contrast, the traditional historiography had placed almost exclusive priority on the cultural, linguistic, and religious factors which set the Francophone society apart from its Anglo-Protestant Canadian and American neighbours. In reality, an accurate analysis of the evolution of Quebec society since 1867 must reflect both the distinctiveness and the similarities of the Quebec experience. Because of its relatively limited social structure and shared value system, the Francophone elites were able to retain much of the 'ancien regime' mentality and social institutions. Meanwhile, the economic structure evolved steadily and with it the values and behaviour of thousands upon thousands of urbanite Francophones who were drawn into the new economic structures to earn their living. In short, the process was one involving a complex process of continuity and change and this chapter will emphasize this fascinating dynamic.

Industrial Capitalism and Social Change to 1930

One of the strongest factors behind the creation of the semi-autonomous nation-state, called Canada, in 1867 was the desire of the mercantile and financial capitalists to bring the industrial revolution to the British North American colonies. The construction of the Grand Trunk Railroad in the 1850s from south western Ontario to the south shore of the St. Lawrence across from Quebec City created a financial crisis for the colony of Canada but also served as a catalyst to industrial development. A combination of continued population expansion, a transportation revolution, the modernization of agriculture, the availability of easy credit, and increased urbanization contributed to the establishment of industrial capitalism in Quebec. This great transformation would only be stalled by the Great Depression of the 1930s.

A significant expansion of the population of the provinces of Quebec through continually high levels of natural increase and British emigration ensured a scarcity of good agricultural land. These events set in motion a process of out-migration by the 1850s of French Canadians to the factory towns of New England. Indeed, birth and death rates, which hovered around 40 and 25 per thousand respectively until 1900, fell slowly to 30 and 12 per thousand by the mid-1930s. Quebec's population, comprised of 80 per cent of Francophones to this day, rose from nearly, 1.36 million in 1881 to 2.87 million by 1931.

Immigration and emigration played a significant role in the transformation of Quebec society. Nearly 700,000 immigrants arrived between 1901 and 1931 while nearly a million, many of them Francophones, emigrated to adjacent provinces or to the New England states. Quebec has generally been the choice of settlement for 15 to 20 per cent of all immigrants entering the country since the 1840s. In the mid-to-late nineteenth century, the vast majority of these immigrants were of British or American origin. Initially, most of them settled in the predominantly agricultural Eastern Townships but many then moved into Montreal or farther west after 1900. In the twentieth century, Quebec's British Canadians were joined by large numbers of Italians, Jews as well as a range of western, central and eastern Europeans who chose to settle in the region of metropolitan Montreal where they adopted English as their primary language of education and work. By 1931, these various ethnocultural communities comprised 6 per cent of Quebec's population. Until the 1960s, the Francophone political and clerical elites encouraged their linguistic and social integration into the Anglophone community because they feared the assimilation influence of these immigrants upon their predominately rural and Catholic society. While most of these ethnocultural groups opted for linguistic integration, the bilingual nature of Montreal allowed them to develop and maintain their separate cultural and religious identities to the present day.

At the time of Confederation, agriculture was still the predominant economic activity for 70 per cent of all Quebec's inhabitants. Consequently, the social structure of the society was still not very elaborate. Most people lived and worked on farms and socialized in rural parishes under the watchful eyes of their clergy and the petty bourgeoisie of doctors, lawyers and small businessmen. For the habitants and their families, life was often harsh, if not cruel, and many owed debts to local merchants or their former Seigneurs. Fertile land was in very short supply and many families were having to seek new farms in the Eastern Townships or in the regions of the Laurentian shield, the Lowers St. Lawrence and the Saguenay, all areas where land was not very productive. Indeed, many families sought employment in the factory towns and cities of Quebec or the New England states. Prior to the 1850s, Francophones had been slow to respond to the agricultural crisis pertaining to cereal production brought on by soil exhaustion, poor farming techniques, and the continued subdivision of already small farms. This agricultural crisis was overcome in the decades after 1870 thanks to migration of surplus labour and the production of dairy products, butter and cheese, for the domestic and British markets as well as livestock and hay for the U.S. market. Both markets emerged as a result of the transportation revolution ushered in by steam ships navigating the St. Lawrence and its tributaries and the railways which connected Montreal to the New England states and Europe via the ocean at Portland, Maine. Despite the renewal, most farms remained small and undercapitalized because of the prevailing traditional values, surplus labour, and the shortage of capital to allow progressive farmers to consolidate larger and more efficient farms. Throughout the period, the Catholic Church took the lead in the colonization movement, with crown land and subsidies from the state, which established thousands of Francophone families on farms in remote regions. In these regions, such as the Saguenay, the Outaouais, and Saint-Maurice and Beauce valleys and the Lower St. Lawrence, the land was marginal and agriculture had to be supplemented by employment in the forestry, pulp and paper or mining industries. Ironically, the agro-forestry economy accelerated the proletarisation of the rural class as it provided many of the rural marginal landholders as well as day-labourers with the skills to seek employment off the farms.

With the progressive commercialization of agriculture, villages and regional towns such as Saint-Hyacinthe, south of Montreal, began to spring up throughout rural Quebec. In 1901 there were 24 towns and villages with more than 2,500 people whereas by 1931 there were 44 in this category. Over time, many of these communities attracted small and medium size industries employing the growing surplus rural population. As industrialization progressed to serve the growing Canadian market, agriculture began to lose its dominant position in the provincial economy to manufacturing as illustrated by the decline in employment from 45.5 per cent in 1891 to 19.3 per cent by 1941.

Factors involved in the rise of industrial production included the expansion of the domestic market, the building of the railways and upgrading of the St. Lawrence/Great Lakes seaway, the growth and diversification of commercial and banking institutions, and Quebec government policies. By 1914 all regions of Quebec were served by railroads and Montreal had become home to the central offices and construction/service yards of the Canadian Pacific and Canadian National railroad systems which provided employment to thousands of workers. While these railways linked Quebec to the rest of Canada, they also provided ties into the United States railway systems thereby increasing trade, usually raw materials in return for manufactured products. Water transportation remained vital throughout this period and constant improvements were made to navigation on the St. Lawrence to allow ocean going vessels to reach the port of Montreal, by far the most active trans-shipment centre in Canada. Marine access to Ontario, the American mid-west and the Canadian west was increased dramatically by continued improvements in St. Lawrence and Great Lakes seaway above Montreal. Foreign and domestic manufactured commodities were shipped to points west of Montreal while millions of metric tons of cereal grains, and central Canadian dairy products were shipped to Great Britain and continental Europe.

In this period, Montreal became the centre of Canada's dominant financial institutions which were responsible for accumulating the savings of Canadians from coast to coast and investing those savings through public and private corporations in hopes of turning a profit for their clients and shareholders. The Bank of Montreal and Sun Life dominated the banking and insurance sectors but faced stiff competition from a great many other national, provincial, and regional banks and insurance companies. Indeed, some of Quebec's financial institutions, including an important system of savings co-operatives called *caisses populaires,* were created by a small but very active and successful Francophone middle bourgeoisie to help finance local industry and the modernization of agriculture. One effective way for the dominant institutions to deal with smaller, aggressive competitors was to buy them out. Indeed, during the period 1900-10 and again in the 1920s a process of consolidation took place in both sectors. By 1930, after swallowing up many smaller banks, both the Royal Bank of Canada and the Bank of Montreal each had nearly a billion dollars in assets. Sun Life could boast of assets of $400,000 and 1,500 employees, making it the largest insurance company in the British Empire. The primary role of the Quebec government in the process of industrial expansion was to provide the legal and political framework in which the private sector could thrive without too many constraints. The Quebec government subsidized directly and indirectly the expansion of regional railroads at a cost of $14.5 million by 1896. As well, the government allowed the pulp and paper companies access to the forest resources before granting the denuded land to the farmers. Local municipalities did their best to attract industrial development by granting land and subsidies to railroad companies and up to twenty year tax exemptions to manufacturers.

During the initial stage of Quebec's industrial revolution, 1850-1900, industry relied upon imported coal and hydraulic energy along the Lachine Canal in Montreal to drive the machinery. With the advent of new production and transmission technologies at the turn of the century, Canadian, British and American companies were able to exploit the immense hydro-electric potential offered by the province's four main rivers, the St. Lawrence west of Montreal, the Ottawa and its tributary the Gatineau, the Saguenay and the Saint-Maurice. By 1933, Quebec accounted for nearly 50 per cent of the 8 million horsepower of hydro-electric energy generated throughout Canada. The handful of large private hydro-electric corporations sold 75 per cent of their production to the wood products, pulp and paper, chemical, and aluminium industries. Unlike Ontario where the production and distribution of hydro-electricity was nationalized and sold at cost, Quebec's private companies kept rates artificially high for urban residential consumers and refused to provide service to the rural communities. As a result, the mechanization of home and farms and the development of the electrical appliance manufacturing industry were delayed.

Well over 50 per cent of the manufacturing industries in Quebec were located in Montreal and the surrounding region while the remainder were dispersed among urban centres in the Eastern Townships, Quebec City, and eventually Trois-Rivières. The leading industries were food and beverages, textiles, clothing, wood and wood products, leather primarily for boots and shoes, iron and steel products, transportation equipment, tobacco products, and pulp and paper, and chemical products. The Labour intensive light industries were generally characterized by low wages and poor working conditions and served the domestic market under the protection of a high tariff. The capital intensive heavy industries employed high skilled and high wage workers, mostly from Great Britain, and produced products for both the Canadian and United States markets. Unlike Ontario, Quebec lacked a primary steel production industry and as a result it did not attract, in the 1920s, a share of the highly profitable, high wage automobile industry. Overall, the gross value of production in manufacturing in Quebec quickly surpassed that of agriculture by 1890 and mushroomed from $153 million in 1900 to $ 1.1 billion by 1929, just short of 30 per cent of the total Canadian output. While structural problems persisted, too many low wage jobs, continual high levels of unemployment and a cultural division of labour, Quebec, like Ontario experienced an annual rate growth rate of 5.5 per cent in manufacturing output between 1870 and 1930. Indeed, the economic and social landscape of Quebec, especially in the Montreal region, had been dramatically and irrevocably altered by the arrival of industrial capitalism.

The economic transformation invariably produced an alteration of the existing social structure of the Quebec society. In the pre-industrial, commercial society one could distinguish three social classes. The dominant class or ruling elite was made up of a vanishing aristocracy of French and English-speaking seigneurs, military officers, government leaders and senior officials, Church leaders, and the ascendant Anglo-Canadian commercial bourgeoisie. Then came a secondary social class of consisting of Francophone and Anglophone petty bourgeoisie drawn from the ranks of the liberal professions and small business enterprise often competing for control at the local and regional levels of society. The third class comprised the bulk of the population of farm, village, and urban working class families.

The industrial revolution destroyed what remnants there were of the seigneurial class, undermined the military class, and assured the eventual dominance of the ascendant national Anglo-Canadian mercantile and industrial elites over the economy and, to a considerable degree, over politics and the state. Members of the Anglo-Canadian bourgeoisie—there was only a handful of Francophone bourgeois—used their connections with the British economic and political elites to create substantial fortunes in trade, finance, real estate, transportation, public works projects, and industrial production. Associated with, but distinct from, this big bourgeoisie was a regional middle bourgeoisie, Francophone and Anglophone, comprising entrepreneurs, traders, financiers, and real estate speculators and promoters. Indeed, the Francophone middle bourgeoisie was quite successful in the small- and medium-sized cities and towns, including Quebec City, Sherbrooke and Trois Rivières, where its members established manufacturing enterprises, created small banking institutions, and controlled most of the whole-sale and retail trade and the developing service sector. Indeed, in the two decades before WW I, several dynamic Francophone middle bourgeois managed to build the modern city of Maisonneuve just to the east of Montreal (which annexed it after the war) while other members created extensive real estate and banking networks to serve the agricultural and working-class communities.

In Quebec, by 1867 the Anglo-Canadian bourgeoisie were forced to share control over the state with the Francophone middle and petty bourgeoisie. In turn, the Francophone elites had to share their power with Catholic Church officials and clergy at all levels of the society. How does one account for this complex power-sharing arrangement which characterized Quebec society in this era? Following the failure of the Rebellions of 1837-38, a resurgent Catholic Church, led by ultramontane nationalist Bishops Bourget of Montreal and Laflèche of Trois Rivières, asserted its widespread social control over the rural Francophone population as well as the emerging urban working class. Church leaders talked the moderate Francophone petty bourgeoisie into abandoning the dream of independence for Quebec and to accept British parliamentary democracy in return for a share of political and economic power in the emerging commercial/industrial state. Church officials agreed to support the moderate wing of the Francophone petty bourgeoisie only if they agreed to support the Catholic Church's control over education, health, and social services. This power-sharing agreement allow-ed the Francophone petty bourgeoisie to control Quebec's political institutions at all levels thereby constraining the exercise of the full range of power in the hands of the predominantly Anglo-Canadian bourgeoisie.

Unfortunately, the Francophone political elite, drawn from the ultracon-servative, rural petty bourgeoisie and the urban, liberal middle bourgeoisie, was opposed to creating a strong interventionist and regulatory provincial government capable of addressing some of the socio-economic problems created by industrialization or to pursue aggressively the economic interests of the underdeveloped Francophone bourgeoisie. This decision served the interests of Quebec's Anglo-Canadian bourgeoisie which used its connec-tions abroad and the national state to advance its undisputed control over both the pan-Canadian as well as Quebec economies.

The most distinctive feature of the Quebec society well into the twentieth century was the preponderant presence of, and role played by, the Catholic Church in all aspects of the lives of French-Canadian Catholics from coast

to coast. This overwhelming presence was immediately visible to all new-
.comers, who were confronted with church spires and religious personnel
everywhere they turned and, on many occasions, were witness to the
numerous religious processions and pilgrimages. Thousands of male and
female religious personnel, originating mostly from the rural communities,
permeated all levels of the Francophone society. They administered and
staffed the hundreds of parishes, rural and urban, all the primary schools, the
convents, the classical colleges, the Universities of Laval and Montreal, the
hospitals, and the social service agencies. Every parish had one or more
priests, several brothers and a few nuns. Few if any aspects of the personal and
public lives of Francophones went unsupervised by religious personnel and
sanctions for misbehaviour were usually quick to follow.

This had not always been so. In the 1830s, there was only one priest per
1,834 parishioners and many parishes had no resident priest. The Catholic
Church's overwhelming prevalence by 1900 was the result of a deliberate
strategy adopted after the Rebellions of 1837-38 by its Bishops, especially
Bourget of Montreal. The Church expanded its recruitment of native
Francophone men and women via its classical colleges, convents, noviciates
and seminaries and by inviting a number of religious orders from France to
establish in the province. Between 1850 and 1900, twelve male religious
communities from France moved into Quebec and were joined by twenty-
five female religious communities nine of which originated in France. As a
result of these changes, the number of parishioners per priest declined from
1080 to 510 between 1850 and 1890. By 1900 there were nearly 10,000 nuns
teaching, healing and attending to the poor in the Francophone communities of Quebec. Helping them out in the field of teaching were orders such
as the Christian Brothers. The Church also benefited from the assistance of
lay men and women who laboured in a wide range of philanthropic societies
at the parish and diocesan levels. A consequence of this pervasive clericalisation
of the society was a puritanical, jansenist, conservative mentality which soon
came to characterize most of the social behaviour of Francophone Catholics.
The Church worked hard, but not always successfully, to repress expressions
of sexuality and popular culture and to keep women confined to the home
as mothers and housewives. Most Francophone Catholics came to perceive
their catholicism and their culture as inextricably intertwined. The one
would not survive without the other. The general acceptance of this doctrine
ensured the Church a predominant role in the social arena as well as helping
it to exercise considerable influence over the political class well into the
twentieth century. The Church displayed an ambivalence towards industrial
capitalism and urbanization. Bishops and theologians, on the one hand,

denounced industry's dissemination of liberalism, individualism and secularism. Yet many local priests encouraged controlled industrialization, especially in regional communities, because the jobs created kept Francophone Catholics in Quebec.

One of the most dramatic social by-products of the industrial revolution was the formation of the working class. Indeed, all of the various ruling elites, Francophone and Anglophone, felt threatened by this development and struggled to control the emergence of this new social class, French and English-speaking. This rapidly expanding working class included the skilled artisans (formerly small independent producers), the swollen ranks of the unskilled urban and rural day labourers, and the vast influx of immigrants, first from the British Isles and then after 1896 from all parts of Europe. The working class faced long hours (from 60 to 72 hours per week), of dangerous and unhealthy working conditions, piece work which provided little or no job satisfaction, seasonal and structural unemployment, and wages which, except for very skilled workers, remained below the poverty level until the 1940s. Employers continually undermined the bargaining position of all workers by getting permission from the federal government to import skilled and unskilled workers from abroad and supporting high levels of immigration. As a consequence, many children and single women—married women were discouraged from working outside the home but took in borders or did factory piece work to supplement family income—were forced to join the labour force to supplement family income as domestics, clerks, or labourers in factories. In these sweat shops, they received wages far below those of their male counterparts and were constantly exploited and abused by male workers and their bosses. Even in the relatively safe occupations of teaching and nursing, lay women faced the competition of female religious personnel who worked for less than subsistence salaries.

Living conditions for working class families remained abysmal throughout this entire period. All but a few of the workers rented dilapidated, drafty tenements from ruthless landlords, often French-Canadians, who evicted them every first May so that they could raise the rent, charged the new tenants. Many of the one or two room tenements, located close to the noisy and polluted factories, did not have water and sewer facilities and often housed up to a dozen people. As a result, it was difficult to practice proper hygiene and members of the working class suffered poor health, even premature death, either of which quickly undermined the fragile family economy. Gas or electricity were either not available or too expensive for working class families. They had to cook their food and heat their drafty lodgings using coal or wood stoves, a practice which caused numerous life-threatening fires during the intensive cold of the long winter months. To survive many working families had to rely upon the charitable organisations, social agencies, and hospitals operated by or through the Catholic and Protestant churches and Jewish synagogues. In time, some of the larger municipalities like Montreal and Quebec City established their own system of social and health agencies to supplement those of the private organisations which were soon swamped by the ever expanding demand.

The heated debate which emerged as a result of emergence of the working class did not allow the formation of a strong and united working class movement in Quebec. Instead, the debate lead to the fragmentation of the working-class movement along ethnic, religious, and regional lines. Despite the strong opposition of church leaders, organized labour emerged in the early 1880s with the establishment of locals of the American Knights of Labour in Montreal and Quebec City, locals which included all the workers in an industry or a community regardless of skill, ethnicity or religion. In the Montreal region, Knights of Labour locals were soon challenged by locals of skilled and semi-skilled tradesmen affiliated with the American Federation of Labour and/or the Trades and Labour Congress of Canada. Between 1907 and 1921, under the direct guidance of certain Catholic Church and nationalist leaders, French-speaking, Catholic workers belonging to Knights of Labour, international or national unions were urged to form Catholic unions supervised by priests committed to Catholic social doctrine which eschewed class conflict and recourse to strikes. In 1921, these Catholic unions and centrals formed the *Confédération des travailleurs catholiques du Canada* which preached Catholic social doctrine while being forced to resort to strikes to obtain the right to collective bargaining or improved wages and working conditions in order to attract and retain new unionists. By 1931 the CTCC has 121 locals and 25,000 members. Other trade union locals, consisting of an ethnically diverse membership, were concentrated largely in the Montreal region and remained affiliated with the American Federation of Labour and/or the Trades and Labour Congress of Canada. While the secular unions outnumbered the Catholic ones, institutional fragmentation along ethnic and religious lines seriously weakened both the Quebec and Canadian labour movements because it allowed employers and governments to play one central off against the other. The fragmentation reinforced the growing perception of a hard and fast cultural division of labour whereby Francophone workers saw themselves primarily as an exploited working class while perceiving English-speaking Quebeckers as the exploiting capitalists. This distortion of a much more complicated reality played into the hands of the French-Canadian traditional, clerical nationalists during the

1920s. Rather than addressing the problems within their own society it was easy to blame the Anglo-Canadian elite for the economic inferiority of French-Canadians as individuals and as a community.

Politics and Political Institutions to 1930

Politically, prior to the 1930s Quebec was dominated both federally and provincially by the two national parties, first the Conservative Party and then after 1896 the Liberal Party. By participating in the governing party at the federal level, Quebec's voters and politicians were able to assert considerable influence over the development of the emerging nation/state while defending the prerogatives of their provinces and the needs of its citizens, English- and French-speaking. During the later half of the nineteenth century, Quebec's interests in Ottawa were represented by George-Etienne Carter, A.T. Galt, Adolphe Chapleau, and Hector Langevin, all leading politicians in the cabinets of John A. Macdonald's several Conservative administrations. Cartier played a key role in the negotiations of the Manitoba Act of 1871 which brought the province into Confederation. Quebec's cabinet members were instrumental in ensuring that Quebec benefited from the development of a national economy. As a result of their efforts, the Canadian Pacific Railroad located its national headquarters in Montreal and PM Macdonald passed the National Policy of 1879 providing high tariff protection to Quebec's struggling industries.

Between 1870 and 1896, the Quebec Conservative Party became increasingly fractious. The moderate wing, represented by Chapleau after Cartier's death in 1873, favoured rapid economic expansion, and religious and cultural pluralism. The extremist ultramontane wing, led by Langevin, wanted both levels of government to respect the primacy of the Catholic Church over Quebec's social and cultural policy and institutions. This group denounced the sale of the provincially financed Quebec, Montreal, Ottawa and Occidental railroad on the north shore to the CPR by Chapleau when he was premier. The ultramontane Conservatives were also deeply incensed at PM Macdonald's decision to allow Louis Riel, the French-speaking métis leader of the uprisings of 1869 and 1885, to be hanged in November 1885. By the late 1880s the national Conservative Party lost its majority control over the Quebec electorate. When many of the moderate Conservatives defected to the Laurier Liberal Party in the early 1890s, the opportunity was created for a French-Canadian, Wilfrid Laurier, to lead his party to victory in federal election of 1896.

While the Quebec wing of the Conservative Party was experiencing tensions and divisions, the Quebec wing of the national Liberal party was finding it difficult to develop a broad base of electoral support. Having its origins in the radical, anticlerical, ultranationalist Rouge party of the 1850s and 1860s, leading members of the Quebec Liberal party, such as Wilfrid Laurier and Honoré Mercier, worked very hard to moderate the party's radical image hoping thereby to overcome the staunch opposition of the Catholic Church. In time, their efforts paid off. Wilfrid Laurier became leader of the national Liberal party in 1887 and then Prime Minister in 1896 thanks to a solid base of political support in the province of Quebec. With a solid bastion in Quebec, Laurier's Liberal government remained in office until 1911. His successor in 1919, William Lyon Mackenzie King, would be Canada's longest serving Prime Minister thanks in large part to his solid support in Quebec through the able assistance of French-Canadian lieutenants such as Ernest Lapointe in the 1920s.

In the British North America Act of 1867, there was a division of powers between the newly-created federal government in Ottawa and the provincial governments. In general, the provinces, under section 92, were granted responsibilities associated with local government, such as social, cultural and educational matters, property and civil rights, health and social security, public lands, municipal government, public works of a local nature, and the administration of the courts. Within Quebec most of these responsibilities, especially over social, health and educational, resided in the hands of the Catholic Church. As a result, the governmental structure of the province of Quebec remained far less developed and therefore less interventionist in these areas than in the other provinces.

Following Confederation, successive Conservative and Liberal provincial governments, while supporting the modernization of agriculture, emphasized primarily the industrialisation and urbanization of the province in many direct and indirect ways. One of their major concerns was to create industrial employment for thousands of Quebeckers thereby stemming their migration to the New England states. A policy of very low taxes and royalties, combined with direct and indirect support to business, created an attractive climate for investments in the province. When funds permitted, governments pursued an active involvement in developing the provincial economy via railroad subsidization and construction, by leasing large tracts of public land for forestry and mining developments, and by selling outright or, when forced by public pressure, granting long-term leases on numerous hydroelectric dam sites.

In a deliberate effort to avoid raising taxes, these Conservative and Liberal governments supported the Catholic and Protestant Churches' continued and expanded rule over social welfare, health, and educational institutions.

This policy had the full backing of the socially conservative Anglo-Canadian bourgeoisie and the Francophone middle and petty bourgeoisie all of whom favoured *laissez faire* policies unless, of course, more interventionist economic and social policies stood to benefit them directly. A policy of low taxes and financial incentives to business meant that servicing the provincial debt of $35 million by the end of the century took 36.5 per cent of current revenue. This severely limiting the government's desire or capacity to increase its support for much needed social, health and educational programmes. Even when revenues increased tenfold between 1900 and 1930, mainly from natural resource development and new forms of taxation such as on automobiles, successive Quebec Liberal governments preferred to accumulate surpluses rather than address the socio-educational needs of their citizens. In fact, by 1929 twenty-one per cent of Quebec's budget was for the maintenance of highways while only ten per cent was devoted to education, down from 16 per cent in 1912.

The dominance of the Conservative Party over provincial politics was challenged successfully by Honoré Mercier in the mid-1880s, a former Conservative, turned Liberal, Mercier shrewdly exploited the divisions within the Conservative Party, all of which were magnified by the crisis over the hanging of Louis Riel, to attract a small number of ultramontane Conservatives to support his *Parti National* government following the close election of 1886. Premier Mercier championed the cause of provincial autonomy against Ottawa in search of better financial subsidies and control over judicial patronage. He came to terms with the Catholic Church by settling the Jesuit's Estate Question once the order had returned to the province and by refusing to reinstate the Ministry of Education. On the heels of a political patronage scandal involving the construction of the Baie des Chaleurs railway, an ailing premier Mercier was driven from office in 1891 and the Conservative party returned to power until 1897.

By the turn of the century, the extent of the social problems in Quebec resulting from industrialization and urbanization were so great as to force Liberal provincial governments to intervene. Between 1905 and 1935, Premiers Lomer Gouin and Alexandre Tachereau created employment offices to deal with seasonal workers, a compensation board for injured workers, certification mechanisms for labour unions, conciliation services for labour-management conflicts, accepted a limited old-age pension scheme introduced by the federal government, set up support programmes for the indigent and health boards to regulate municipal and hospital standards of care. To handle this increased responsibility, the provincial bureaucracy was expanded to include ministries of public works, of highways, and municipal affairs as well as a whole series of commissions to supervise everything from the rivers to the sale of alcohol. Pushed by its reform wing and business interests, the Gouin government created a whole range of technical and professional schools funded and administered by the province so as to ensure that the province could meet the growing demand for skilled technicians, engineers, and public and private accountants and managers. Yet, Catholic Church leaders were concerned with this secularisation of education and insisted that religious symbols be placed in the classrooms and religious personnel be given the right to oversee the behaviour of the professors and the students. Indeed, the Catholic Church's determination to defeat any pro-posal for the re-establishment of the Ministry of Education which had been abolished in 1875, ensured the survival of Quebec's increasingly anachronis-tic educational system well into the twentieth century.

In this context of Conservative and Liberal dominance of provincial politics, it was very difficult for third party politics to emerge. Yet a form of non-parliamentary opposition to the Gouin and Taschereau government's did emerge. Initially, opposition came from a generation of young French-Canadian petty bourgeois journalists who formed the *Ligue nationaliste canadienne* in 1903. Their platform included a demand for a bilingual and bicultural Canada independent from Great Britain as opposed to the English-Protestant nation state being advocated loudly and forcefully by the British-Canadian imperialists and nationalists. At the provincial level, the *Ligue nationaliste canadienne* developed a full-scale programme of Catholic social, economic, and political reforms they deemed essential if French-Canadians were going to survive the transition to urbanization and indus-trialization and gain some degree of control over their future development as a society. The movement's titular head was Henri Bourassa, staunch opponent of Canada's involvement in the Boer war, 1899-1900. He broke with the Laurier government on this issue and sat as an independent member of parliament and then moved into provincial politics for a short term to fight the policies of the Gouin government. He was soon drawn back to the national scene. Bourassa founded the nationalist and Catholic daily *Le Devoir* in 1910 to lead the fight against Laurier's Naval Bill of 1910. Bourassa contributed to Laurier's defeat in the election of 1910 by supporting Con-servative and nationalist candidates throughout the province. Bourassa then became the most vocal critic of Prime Minister Robert Borden's Conserva-tive government in World War I for introducing conscription of manpower, for overseas service in 1917.

As a result of the conscription crisis, Arthur Sauvé, leader of the provi-ncial Conservative party, 1916-29, was forced to adopt a strong nationalist critique of Premier Taschereau government's economic and social policies throughout the 1920s. During the 1920s Bourassa's role as nationalist critic was taken over by canon Lionel Groulx who taught French-Canadian history at the Université de Montréal and published *L'Action Française,* a monthly periodical which preached a much more Quebec-centred nationalism than Bourassa had ever envisaged. Canon Groulx and his colleagues denounced the liberalism, secularism, individualism, and materialism that were associated with industrialisation and urbanisation. Groulx dreamt of a day when the vast majority of the French-speaking society of Quebec could embrace with enthusiasm its Catholic, French, and agricultural mission in North America. Indeed, for a short time, canon Groulx and his fellow nationalists preached that French Canadians should prepare to achieve independence for their nationality given that the Canadian federation was on the verge of collapsing under its own internal tensions and contradictions. The influence of Canon Groulx's form of French-Canadian ultramontane, conservative nationalism rarely spread beyond certain circles with the Church and the petty bourgeoisie. As long as prosperity remained, as it did throughout the 1920s, Groulx and his colleagues had little impact on the government of the day.

Economy and Society in Transition, 1930-60

All sectors of Quebec's economy were badly undermined but none was destroyed by the Great Depression of the 1930s. The structural features, both strong and weak, were not dramatically altered in this period as all sectors built upon the achievements of the past, especially once the war got underway. In the manufacturing sector the gross value of production fell from $1.2 billion in 1929 to $604 million in 1933 and the number of employees from 206,580 to 157,481. Light and heavy manufacturing began to recover slowly beginning in 1938, took off during the Second World War, and reached a high of nearly $ 3 billion in output and 424,115 employees, many of them women employed in munitions industries, by 1944. Despite the reinforcement of capital intensive, high wage, heavy industry related to munitions, shipbuilding, and aircraft production during the war, the traditional, low wage, light industries such as food and beverages, clothing, and textile continued to dominate Quebec's economy in terms of employment and value added.

Driven by a rapidly expanding population, the advent of the consumer society, and increased foreign investment and technology, better managed, more specialized and productive manufacturing industries saw their total gross value of production climb to $7 billion by 1961. The region of Montreal accounted for over 70 per cent of all manufacturing while the province of

Quebec produced 30 per cent of the total Canadian output as compared to 50 per cent for Ontario. There was, nonetheless, a perceptible shift in the leading sectors as paper, non-ferrous metal, petroleum and coal and transportation products eventually took the lead over clothing, textiles, leather and tobacco after 1945.

The natural resource sector, namely pulp and paper, lumber, electro-chemical, electro-metallurgy, hydro-electricity, and mining, which had over-expanded in the 1920s, suffered severe curtailment during the 1930s. Hundreds of plants were closed and thousands of workers lost their jobs. Eventually though recovery got underway as the war and post-war booms created an insatiable appetite fore ferrous and non-ferrous metals, pulp and paper and the enormous amounts of electricity to drive the primary manufacturing of aluminium smelting, copper refining and petro-chemical plants. For the first time, improved wages and salaries allowed rural and urban consumers to afford a wide-range of electrical appliances and the electricity to make them run. Government subsidies accelerated the electrification of farms, villages and towns. Hydro-Quebec was formed in 1944 to take over the distribution network of Montreal, Light, Heat and Power in order to make rates cheaper for residential and commercial users. Eventually, Hydro-Quebec designed and built its own production facilities on the Saint Lawrence at Beauharnois, on the Bersimis, and on the Ottawa river allowing it to lower its rates even further.

Mining was another sector that took off dramatically in the 1950s thanks, in part, to the completion of the St. Lawrence Seaway in 1959 and the insatiable appetite and expansion of the American military/industrial complex. The gross value of mineral production grew from a mere $92 million in 1945 to $447 million in 1960. The vast iron ore deposits in northern Quebec at Schefferville on the border with Labrador were extracted by the Iron Ore Company of Canada, a subsidiary of Hollinger Mines of the United States, and shipped to the American iron and steel plants south of the Great Lakes. The same situation prevailed for asbestos, copper and many other minerals that were in strong demand south of the border.

Quebec agriculture, focused mainly on the production of hay and oats, milk and cheese, livestock, as well as fruits and vegetables remained far too labour intensive and under-capitalized until the 1960s. Most farms, which averaged 125 acres, lacking electricity nor gasoline tractors prior to the 1950s, were not well situated to undertake modernization. The primary markets were Quebec's urban centres, Great Britain and the United States. Farm income improved dramatically when oversees demand boomed during World War II. But when both demand and prices fell sharply in the late 1940s, agriculture began a precipitous secular decline never to recover its once dominant place in the hearts and minds of Francophone Quebeckers.

Following over half a century of industrialization and urbanization, a majority of Quebec's citizens, 59 per cent, lived in cities and towns by 1931. This development was arrested for a full decade by the Great Depression as thousands of unemployed and destitute city dwellers were encouraged by government grants of free land and subsidies to return the land to eke out a subsistence living for themselves and their families. The rate of urbanization for Anglophones remained considerably higher than for Francophones prior to 1940. Consequently, agriculture and the rural way of life remained the predominant way of life for a significantly higher proportion of Quebec's Francophones than Anglophones accounting for the perpetuation of the myth of agriculturalism among French-Canadian intellectuals and politicians.

But, marginal agriculture had remained viable only as long as complimentary work was available in the forestry industry. Once the forestry companies turned to intensive mechanization and year round exploitation of their resource base, the long standing link with agriculture was broken and thousands of farm families had no recourse but to abandon their farms. During the 1950s, once this irreversible process gained increasing momentum, both in terms of the total number of agricultural employees and production, the traditional nationalist elites experienced a severe identity crisis. Indeed, the percentage of the labour force employed directly in agriculture declined from 23 to 13 between 1931 and 1951, falling further to 7.5 per cent in 1961 and bottoming out at a mere 2.6 per cent by 1981. Agriculture's contribution to the gross provincial production declined from 20 to 10 per cent between 1929 and 1945 and from 4 to 2 per cent between 1961 and 1981. Thanks to numerous federal and provincial government support programmes, marketing boards, and an aggressive cooperative movement, a successful transition period of modernization and specialization was experienced which ensured the survival of a small but healthy agri-business focused on milk products, poultry, pork, beef, and eggs most of which is intended for consumers in other parts of Canada and the United States.

One of the most significant economic developments, which Quebec has shared with the rest of Canada and North America, has been the continuous expansion of the tertiary or service sector, both private and public, since the Second World War. As metropolitan Montreal's numerous financial and commercial enterprises, insurance and real estate businesses, transportation and communication companies, public and para-public corporations, and the full range of personal and professional services expanded to serve the needs of individual, corporate, and government consumers, they provided increasing levels of employment for both men and women. By 1961 the service sector accounted for 55 per cent of the gross provincial production and employed 52 per cent of the labour force.

The process of urbanization, accompanied by increased education levels, and the emergence of both the consumer ethic and the social welfare state contributed to the growing demand for services in all fields. Initially, many of these white collar jobs required only limited education, paid low salaries and evolved into employment ghettos for women, such as the clerical, secretarial, and communication occupations as well as nursing and teaching. By the 1970s, thanks to higher levels of education and the formation of semi-professional and professional unions, most employees in the public and para-public sectors were well paid and discrimination based on gender or colour was becoming less common. Because of the vested interests of the Catholic Church and the innate conservatism of the petty bourgeoisie political class, the growth of public administration and services came considerably latter in Quebec than in Ontario and other provinces. It was not until the major legislative reforms of Quiet Revolution of the 1960s and 1970s that both employment and salaries in the provincial and municipal administrations as well as in the para-public sectors such as eduction, health and social welfare, expanded dramatically. The growth of professional services to corporations, consisting of accountants, engineers, consultants, lawyers, public relations experts, kept pace with the expansion in the public sector while the numbers people employed by companies, namely hotels and restaurants, providing personal services to individuals expanded every decade.

The social structure of Quebec society remained fairly stable during the Depression but began to evolve quite significantly following the War. As mentioned above the agricultural class saw its aggregate size increase marginally until 1940 and then decline precipitously thereafter. For those choosing to remain on the farms or in rural villages and towns, their standard of living improved steadily after the war thanks to universal health and social welfare programmes, better education for their children, and a range of federal and provincial support programmes aimed at modernizing agriculture and related businesses. These socio-economic developments and the continued political over-representation of rural constituencies in the legislature explain why rural communities continued to exert considerable influence over provincial politics and receive the attendant financial rewards until the reforms of the 1970s.

At the other extreme of the social spectrum was the working class, a class that remained dramatically under-represented in the political structure of the province until well into the 1960s. Indeed, the working class and its attendant labour movement suffered quite dramatically during the Depression era. Hard hit by technological transformation during the 1920s and by the acute shortage of jobs during the Depression, well over half the working-class families continued to live below the poverty line while, at time, up to twenty-five per cent remained dependent upon welfare for much of the decade. Working conditions varied widely from industry to industry but generally they left much to be desired. Working hours were very long, exploitation of women and children remained prevalent in most light industries, benefits were non-existent, and wages declined on average by 40 per cent from their 1929 levels. Living conditions for working class families had improved only marginally since the turn of the century. Most families continued to rent two room tenements with few if any amenities from unscrupulous landlords in well recognized working-class districts of Montreal which continued to have few if any public facilities such as parks, recreation centres or libraries.

World War II precipitated a manpower crisis thereby contributing to improvements on most fronts for working men and women. Despite the strong opposition of the Catholic Church leaders, traditional nationalists, and politicians, increasing numbers of single and married women were enticed into the paid labour force. They were trained in a wide variety of specialized skills to replace men in occupations such as machinists, electricians, and welders, formally closed to them. The three elements of the armed forces had their womens' divisions but their tasks were limited primarily of office work. Unfortunately, women's salaries were a third to a half less than the men's and once the war was over they faced a propaganda barrage calling upon them to give up their jobs for the returning soldiers. As a consequence, the rate of female participation in the labour force increased only 4 per cent to 27 per cent in the 1950s. The situation would alter dramatically over the next twenty years with the female participation rate reaching nearly 50 per cent by 1983. Yet, 60 per cent of these women remained trapped in 'pink ghettos' of clerical and secretarial work, nursing, teaching, sales and service, and textiles and clothing.

The 1950s and 1960s were golden decades for many Quebec workers and their families as employment levels remained relatively high in most regions of the province, and wages, working conditions and benefits improved steadily in nearly all occupations. Workers and their families also had access to publicly funded social security measures such as family allowances, social assistance, unemployment insurance, hospital insurance, medial care, and a fully funded Quebec pension scheme which eliminated many risks and unpredictable expenses. The lack of adequate, affordable housing continued to be a real serious problem for a decade after the war. But, thanks to federal and provincial government housing programmes, both the quantity and quality of accommodation improved substantially over the decades. Overall, the standard of living for the working class improved substantially during these two decades. As a result, working-class families were drawn into the consumer society with all of its attendant advantages, more durable goods such as furniture, appliances, televisions, and even cars, as well as its disadvantages such as increased personal debt and the threat of bankruptcy if prolonged periods of unemployment occurred. On the other hand, the automobile allowed some better-off working-class families to flee their overcrowded working-class districts to join the ranks of the expanding lower middle class filling the developing suburbs.

The Depression momentarily weakened an already fragmented and elitist Quebec labour movement which represented primarily skilled workers comprising less than 10 per cent of the labour force in 1929 and 17 per cent in 1941. Yet, one very significant by-product of the depression was the emergence of industrial unions. Thanks to a bullish war-time economy and a federal government intent on avoiding any labour disruptions to wartime production, the new industrial unions gained quick legal recognition. This new development put considerable pressure on the Catholic Union movement, forcing its leaders to open membership to non-Catholics, to organize along industrial as well as trade lines, and to become more militant in their efforts to recruit workers and to resort to militant strikes in order to achieve acceptable collective agreements for their members with recalcitrant employers. Faced with an anti-labour and anti-social Union Nationale government, this militancy continued after the war and resulted in many strikes throughout the province. One highly symbolic strike occurred in 1949 when 5000 asbestos miners engaged in an illegal walk-out to obtain recognition and a collective agreement which provided better wages and working conditions, as well as a degree of co-management over grievance procedures. While the strike was broken by the provincial government and its police force, it marked the arrival of a more dynamic, more autonomous Francophone labour central which remained only nominally Catholic and became increasingly nationalistic as it grew in strength and confidence. When asked to affiliate with the newly-created Canadian Labour Congress of Labour in 1958, the Francophone union central and its many centrals and affiliates refused for fear of loosing their Francophone identity and provincial autonomy. By 1960, a once cautious and staid Catholic union movement had become one of the most progressive labour organizations in Canada.

Despite the decline in the agricultural class and the sharp rise in the working class, the Catholic Church's influence over the daily lives of Quebec's French- and English-speaking Catholics, comprising approximately 86 per cent of the population, remained strong and pervasive as long as its institutional control remained intact. But, only with considerable difficulty and increasing financial support from the Quebec government was the Catholic Church able to retain its control over education, health, social welfare, and educational institutions which were organized on the parish and diocesan level until the 1960s. Between 1930 and 1945 the number of priests grew from four to five thousand while the female religious orders saw their numbers swell from twenty-five to thirty-five thousand during the same period and to forty-five thousand by 1961. In 1941 there was one religious personnel, priest or nun, for every 87 Catholics, a saturation point which declined slowly in the 1950s and then dramatically and irreversibly thereafter as recruitment flagged and thousands of priests, nuns, and brothers defrocked.

Using the new communication tools such as the radio during the 1930s and 1940s, the Catholic Church undertook an aggressive and well-funded propaganda campaign against what clerics perceived as the rise of communism, an ideology they associated with Eastern European immigrant workers who had joined Montreal's labour force since the turn of the century. Church leader at all levels, speaking and writing through the *Ecole sociale populaire* and numerous Catholic action movements, strongly supported 'back to the land' colonization schemes and proposed the creation of a corporatist and Catholic state. In this way the Quebec society could avoid the worst features of rule by plutocracy or the proletariat.

Strains on the institutional Church emerged first in the field of education which was denominational at all levels. Despite the introduction of free and compulsory education in 1943 for 6 to 13 years old, the school participation rate of 5 to 19 years old for Catholic children remained well below that for Protestant children until the educational reforms of the 1960s. Nearly half of the primary and secondary teachers were nuns, priests or brothers and their salaries were less than half, often less than a third, of the lay teachers whose own salaries were below those of their Protestant counterparts. Even with this form of subsidy and increased funding from the provincial government during the 1950s, local school boards had to face serious financial difficulties in the turn over rate of poorly trained lay women teachers remained very high.

Despite efforts in the 1930s to create a publicly-funded Catholic high school system, equivalent to the one which existed for Protestants, there was little success. Even with the growth of Catholic public secondary schools by the mid-1950s, success was only partial because most graduates of this truncated system did not qualify to enter university. With 38,000 predominantly male students in 1960, the Church controlled and administered system of *Collèges classiques* remained the norm for young men seeking entrance into the priesthood or careers in the liberal professions. Graduates choosing careers in the sciences or social sciences found their preparation inadequate and the universities had to provide some upgrading. Meanwhile, the numerous convents and domestic management schools continued to train mostly middle class young women to be solid, responsible mothers and homemakers.

In the area of higher education, the Church owned and operated the two large Catholic universities, Laval and Montreal. A third, the University of Sherbrooke was created only in 1954 to try and meet the growing demand of post-war, baby-boomers. Quebec's and Montreal's English language community had two universities, McGill and Concordia, and a couple of colleges available for their children. For the longest time both French-language, Catholic Universities lacked faculties of sciences and social sciences. When they acquired Faculties of Science in the 1920s, the Church lacked funds and had to appeal to the provincial and municipal governments for help. When Laval and Montreal created full-time Faculties of Social Sciences in the 1940s and 1950s, the Church's stated intention was to disseminate Catholic theology social doctrine rather than train experts in the secular methodologies of the modern social sciences. Furthermore, university education remained out of reach for the vast majority of French-speaking Catholics prior to the 1960s. While English-speaking McGill University graduated 4,852 students between 1936 and 1945, Laval and Montreal managed only to produce 6,640 graduates. This disturbing pattern intensified during the next decade when McGill produced 12,000 graduates compared to just over 13,000 for Laval and Montreal. In 1960, the university participation rate for Anglophone stood at 11 per cent while that for Francophones was a dismal 2.9 per cent. This disturbing pattern soon convinced many nationalist, and political leaders that the Catholic Church could no longer respond adequately to the expanding educational needs of the Francophone Catholics of Quebec.

Indeed, by the early 1950s there were clear indications that nearly 50 per cent of Montreal's Catholics no longer attended Sunday mass and shopped on religious holidays. There were growing demands from within the Church for greater participation of lay men and women in the administration of Church affairs as well as pressures to have the Church play a more active role in the resolution of many of the pressing social problems created by urbanization and industrialization. Bishop Charbonneau of Montreal was an active proponent of a more liberal Catholic social doctrine and championed the cause of five thousand striking Catholic unionist working in the hazardous Asbestos mining industries of the Eastern townships in 1949. During the same period, in the fields of health and social welfare, the Church's autonomy was undermined with the creation of a ministry of youth and social welfare in 1946 and its increased reliance on provincial government funding. As a result, Church leaders were compromised and refused to speak out against the pervasive and anti-democratic political corruption of the Duplessis government during the 1950s.

The traditional Francophone petty bourgeoisie had their power base in the expanding liberal professions, small business, politics and government at all levels, as well as in the wide variety of Catholic Church institutions. This petty bourgeoisie dominated the political and social life at the parish, villages, town, city, and diocesan levels. The elite espoused an ideology of defensive, conservative nationalism which portrayed the Francophone society of Quebec as exclusively Catholic, predominantly rural, and minoritarian within Canada. Its members supported only limited state intervention and low taxation while staunchly defending the Catholic Church's control over education, social welfare, and health institutions. When the federal Liberal governments of PMs Makenzie King and Louis St. Laurent, in response to the electorate, began the process of creating the social service state with unemployment insurance and family allowance programmes in the 1940s, old-age pensions and hospital insurance in the 1950s, this traditional elite came to the defense of the Catholic Church and the political status quo symbolized by the Union Nationale government of premier Maurice Duplessis. On many social issues the Francophone petty bourgeoisie were supported by all the elements of the middle and upper bourgeoisie of entrepreneurs, real estate developers, industrialists, and financiers.

After World War II, a new generation of middle class professionals, educated primarily in the sciences, social sciences, the media, and business, emerged to propose two alternative visions for the Quebec society. Both the neo-nationalists, led by André Laurendeau and Gérard Filion at *Le Devoir,* and the neo-liberals, led by Pierre Elliott Trudeau and Gérard Pelletier at *Cité libre,* denounced traditional petty bourgeoisie and the clerical class for the undemocratic, anachronistic, conservative, self-serving, and ultimately destructive nature of their nationalism. In its place the middle class neo-nationalists proposed the creation of a strong, interventionist, Francophone-controlled Quebec state responsible for the development of all social service, health, and educational institutions and capable of ensuring full Francophone participation in the economic development of the province via both public and private sectors. The neo-liberals rejected the proposed fusion of the Francophone nationality and a modernized Quebec state. Instead, they called for the creation of secular, democratic and pluralistic economic, social, and political institutions, including the state, which would serve without discrimination all of Quebec's citizens rather than the interests of the Francophone majority and its new middle class.

Political Parties and the Political Process Under Seige, 1930-60

Politically, the Depression brought an end to the stranglehold that the Liberal Party had held over Quebec politics since the Laurier victory in 1896. PM Makenzie King was defeated by the Conservative Party leader, R.B. Bennett in the election of 1930 with the help of some Quebec Conservative MPs. PM Bennett was able to hold the allegiance of Quebec MPs for only one term and the Quebec federal Liberals returned to power under PM King in 1935 where many of them remained until their defeat in the Conservative landslide victory of 1958.

Provincially, premier Taschereau had little trouble winning re-election in 1931 against the populist mayor of Montreal, Camillien Houde. Yet, a weakened national Liberal Party combined with widespread discontent and growing fears of socialism among Quebec's petty bourgeoisie and Church officials set the stage for the re-emergence of a new party. The Union Nationale, formed in 1935, was led by Maurice Duplessis, an ambitious lawyer from Trois-Rivières and former leader of the provincial Conservative party.

Events would not move smoothly for Duplessis. Initially, he faced the emergence of a third party, the *Action Libérale Nationale,* made up of disgruntled, ambitious, and nationalistic young Liberals lead by Paul Gouin, the son of former premier Gouin. In the depths of the depression, the ALN attracted nationalists and clerical leaders who proposed a programme of social restoration based on corporatism, political reforms, colonization and agriculture renewal, labour reforms, state regulation of Anglophone and American monopoly capitalism, and nationalization of hydro-electric companies. Eager to gain access to the Conservative Party's finances and organization, Gouin's ALN agreed to a loose coalition with Duplessis's Conservative for the election of 1935. This coalition, soon baptised the union nationale, reduced the Tashereau government to a minority. Duplessis then asserted his control over the Union Nationale, forced the premier to resign by revealing widespread political corruption, and easily won the election of 1936.

Duplessis' conservative populist Union Nationale represented a shrewd coalition of rural notables and farmers, Church leaders and religious personnel at all levels, a large segment of the urban petty bourgeoisie, and a sizeable proportion of the Francophone working class. When he refused to implement the traditional nationalists' call for the nationalization of hydro-electric companies several militant nationalists left the government. Yet, Duplessis eventually regained much of their support with his vocal defense of provincial autonomy against the federal government's social service state. Duplessis' staunch rejection of the social service state and his refusal to nationalize sectors of the Quebec economy helped him cement a long standing alliance with the Francophone, Anglophone and American business classes. His decision to retain intact the existing social, cultural, religious and political institutions of a society experiencing profound socio-economic changes also endeared him to Catholic Church officials.

Shortly after the outbreak of World War II, the Union Nationale attempted to win re-election in 1939 by portraying itself as the only bulwark against conscription of French Canadians for overseas service. The national Liberal Government saw the Union Nationale as a threat to its war effort and PM King decided to help the provincial Liberal Party of Joseph-Adélard Godbout win office in 1939 by promising French Canadians that there would be no conscription of overseas service and jobs for the unemployed in the wartime supply and munitions factories. Premier Godbout alienated the Catholic Church by granting the vote to women and introducing free and compulsory education, infuriated the nationalists by associating himself too closely with the war effort and by conceding to Ottawa provincial social and taxing powers, and drove away big business by nationalizing Montreal Light, Heat, and Power in 1944. Despite the emergence of yet another nationalistic but reformist third party, the *Bloc Populaire Canadien,* the *Union Nationale* managed to defeated both his rivals and was returned to power in 1944 under Duplessis' leadership.

Thanks to an effective political machine, widespread use of patronage, and a distorted electoral distribution favouring rural constituencies, the Union Nationale won re-election three more times. Premier Duplessis, called *le chef,* retained the premiership until his death in 1959. During his fifteen year rule, Duplessis pursued economic, social, and political policies remarkably similar to those of his predecessor, premier Taschereau. He gave the financial, commercial, and industrial capitalists free rein, issued an open invitation for more foreign investment especially in the natural resource sector. As Attorney General, premier Duplessis adopted a very hard line with the increasingly militant trade union movement, especially the *Confédération des travailleurs catholiques du Canada* and the new industrial unions. Premier

Duplessis steadfastly refused to modernize the provincial bureaucracy. The vast majority of civil servants acquired their positions through patronage and nepotism and over 30 per cent had less than five years of education. The government refused to hire specialists in the various disciplines of the Social Sciences because Duplessis considered intellectuals to be 'eggheads' incapable of contributing anything concrete to government policy or programmes. He granted only limited discretionary funding to hard pressed municipalities, school boards, hospitals, social agencies, technical schools, colleges, and universities, while holding the line on taxes and budgetary deficits.

Premier Duplessis effectively undercut his provincial Liberal opponents by portraying its leader, Georges-Emile Laplame, as a supporter and puppet of the interventionist Liberal Government of Louis Saint-Laurent in Ottawa. Strong and vigorous opposition to Duplessis's autocratic and conservative regime first emerged from among the ranks of organized labour and then from the neo-nationalist and neo-liberal movements which emerged in the 1950s. Much of this non-parliamentary opposition eventually found a political vehicle in a revived Liberal Party lead by Jean Lesage in 1958. It was at that juncture that the Liberal Party incorporated in its electoral platform a shrewd mixture of the social, economic and political reform policies advanced throughout the 1950s by the neo-liberals and neo-nationalists. The sudden death of Duplessis's successor, Paul Sauvé, who had promised major reforms, set the stage for the narrow but significant Liberal victory in June 22, 1960. Jean Lesage and his 'Thunder Team' was well on its way to ushering in an era that would come to be called the Quiet Revolution.

Creating the Modern State, 1960 to the Present

A number of factors have conditioned the demographic evolution of Quebec over the past generation. Coinciding with the rapid demise of the influence of the Catholic Church were the introduction of the birth control pill in the mid-1960s and the abortion clinics in the 1970s. As a result of these and other developments, the birth rate among Quebeckers plummeted from 26.6 per thousand in 1961 to 13.3 per thousand by 1991. The therapeutic abortion rate rose from 1.4 per hundred births in 1971 to over 22 per hundred by 1990. Consequently, Quebec's population, which reached 5.3 million by 1961, a 30 per cent increase over the decade, only managed to achieve the 6.9 million mark thirty years later. With emigration, primarily of Anglophones and Allophones, surpassing all immigration between 1966 and 1986, Quebec's proportion of the Canadian population slipped from 30 to just over 25 per cent by 1991.

Two other characteristics of Quebec's changing demography population include the phenomenon of aging and the decline of the traditional family structure. The precipitous decline in the birth rate when combined with a stable adult mortality rate contributed to raising the average age of Quebeckers from 24 in 1961 to over 32 by 1991. By this time 10 per cent of Quebec's population was over the age of 65. Many of these people, comprised in the majority of middle and upper class women, enjoyed longer and healthier years of retirement most often in private or public institutions. An aging population, of course, required fewer new homes, consumer goods, and some kinds of professional services. All of these factors contributed to increasing the rate of UN employment after 1970 to over 10 per cent where it remained into the 1990s. The decline in religious practices combined with the increase in individualism and the search for equality by women in the 1970s resulted in smaller families with both parents working outside the home. These same factors also produced a dramatic increase in common law marriages, in the divorce rate, and in the formation of single parent families most often headed up by working women. By the 1980s, Montreal's growing homosexual and lesbian communities were also challenging the traditional definition of the family by forming common law marriages and raising adopted or natural children.

A fourth characteristic of Quebec's evolving population has been the emergence of ethnic diversification, especially in metropolitan Montreal. Between 15 and 20 per cent of the 100,000 to 120,000 immigrants arriving in Canada every year since 1961 have chosen to settle in the province of Quebec. The bulk of post-war immigrants came from Britain, Italy, central and eastern Europe, Germany, France, Austria, and Greece. The reform of Canada's immigration law in 1967 opened the door to immigrants from a wide variety of Third World Countries. In the 1970s the Quebec government took a much more active role in the recruitment and settlement of immigrants in the province. It managed to attract French-speaking immigrants from Haiti and Vietnam as well as many others from China, Chili, Portugal, Pakistan and Armenia. By the 1990s the non-British component of Quebec's population exceeded 10 per cent thereby surpassing those of British origin which had dropped to just over 7 per cent. On Montreal Island citizens of French, Jewish, Italian origin remained steady at 57, 4.5, and 8 between 1961 and 1981. Those of British origin declined from 18 to 13 per cent in this period while the percentage of those of all other origins rose from 10 to 17.5 per cent. As in the past, these newly-arrived immigrants quickly organized themselves into ethnocultural communities in well-defined districts of Montreal and its environs. Quebeckers also discovered that the northern regions of their province was home to nearly 50,000 Indians and Inuit. These visible minorities, so-called because of their skin colour, dramatically challenged the bicultural and bilingual identity that Francophones and Anglophones had of the Quebec society and created socio-economic and linguistic tensions that had to be addressed by the politicians and the bureaucrats.

Beginning slowly in the 1960s and gaining momentum thereafter, the Quebec economy experienced significant expansion while undergoing important structural changes at all levels. In the three decades after 1960 the volume of production of goods and services tripled thanks to an 86 per cent increase in the number of workers and a 64 per cent increase in the productivity of those workers. Both these factors explain why the standard of living for each Quebec citizen nearly tripled during this period, that is, an increase of 188 per cent. This remarkable expansion took place despite the slow down of Canadian economy following the international oil crisis of the mid-1970s and the sharp recession of the early 1980s.

Despite this increased prosperity, significant structural changes were underway in all three sectors of the economy. Declining tariffs, increased global competition, the lack of capital to modernize outmoded and inefficient light and heavy industries, contributed to a process of deindustrialization during the 1970s and 1980s. In 1961, nearly 30 per cent of workers were employed in manufacturing which accounted for 30 per cent of the gross provincial production. By the early 1990s, this sector provided employment for fewer than 20 per cent of workers and just over 20 per cent of the gross provincial production. Those manufacturers wishing to survive had to resort to expensive automation, streamlined management, and wholesale horizontal and vertical integration. When forced to make this decision, many companies moved their operations to Ontario or abroad. After the Free Trade Agreement of 1988 with the United States, many of the branch plants of U.S. corporations simply shut down their factories and supplied the Canadian market from their U.S. operations. Such was the case for the clothing and textile manufacturers which fell to 8th and 10th place in terms of value of production by 1982 despite modernization of some plants. On the other hand, the newer industries such as aerospace or pharmaceutical preferred to establish themselves in suburban industrial parks located along the new freeways because they relied on trucking rather than railways for their transportation needs. This development left large segments of old industrial Montreal, Sherbrooke, Quebec, and Trois-Rivières abandoned and dilapidated. The dual development of high technology, automated industries and the deindustrialization of other sectors of manufacturing, created structural unemployment reaching levels well over 10 per cent in many sectors and regions, while increasing the percentage of part-time, low paying, dead ends jobs for a generation of young workers which is better educated than at any time in the past. By 1984 the number of employable young men and women drawing social assistance surpassed 250,000 in the province.

During this period the primary sector comprising Quebec's renewable and non-renewable resources faced some problems and underwent restructuring. Pushed by declining prices and federal and provincial government incentives, farming quickly became a specialized business rather than a way of life. Fewer than 75,000 farmers and farm labourers, constituting less than 3 per cent of the labour force, now operate larger, heavily capitalized and mechanized farms producing a wide range of specialized products including milk, pork, poultry, eggs, and some feed grains for the Canadian and U.S. markets. Similarly, the forest industry became heavily mechanized and greater emphasis was placed on transformation of the lumber into wood and wood products for the construction industry. The pulp and paper industry managed to hold its position in the overall economy but faced stiff competition in the U.S. market, its major outlet. Demand for Quebec's copper, zinc, iron ore and asbestos remained strong in the 1960s but declined, along with prices, in the next two decades as new sources were opened up in Third World countries. The Quebec government tried to encourage the refinement of minerals, especially asbestos, in the province but the attempt proved largely fruitless. The government nationalized the asbestos industry at great expense just as the demand for the highly toxic product collapsed worldwide. The recession of the early 1980s and the worldwide glut of iron ore and steel led to the closure of the Schefferville iron ore complex which had been opened up with great promise in the late 1950s. Thousands of mine workers lost their jobs and the North Shore region's economy plunged into deep recession.

The one real promising natural resource sector was that of hydro-electricity. In the 1960s, the state-run Hydro-Quebec, which incorporated all of the large private hydro-electric companies in 1963, built the magnificent complex at Manicouagan-Outardes and negotiated the purchase of most of the output from the Churchill Falls dam in Newfoundland-Labrador. In the 1970s, Hydro-Quebec undertook the construction of the massive James Bay complex of dams capable of producing huge surpluses of power, much of it destined for the markets of New York and the New England states. Hydro-Quebec's rapid expansion created thousands of jobs for Francophone engineers, planners, technicians, and managers and became a symbol of the wholesale modernization of the Quebec society. By the late 1980s, environmental concerns and a decline in demand both at home and in the United

States resulted in surplus production of electricity and the indefinite delay of the next phase of the James Bay complex.

By the 1990s Quebec can be characterized without too much exaggeration as a post-industrial society. Indeed, the province had experienced one of the fastest growing tertiary sectors in the Western world. In 1961, 54 per cent of the work force was employed in the service sector. Within thirty years, this sector employed 72 per cent of all workers. Much of this expansion can be accounted for by the growth of public and para-public sector jobs. In 1960, Quebec had 7 civil servants for every one hundred people. By 1990, there were 150,333 civil servants mostly located in the region of Quebec City, nearly 23 for every one hundred citizens.

The financial sector grew during these years but just managed to maintain its overall position in terms of employment. While Montreal remained the headquarters for a number of Canada's leading chartered banks, insurance companies and real estate corporations, many of the city's landmark corporations pulled up stakes and transferred the bulk of their operations to Toronto or points further west. By the 1960s, Toronto emerged as the centre of what remained of the national economy as the Canadian economy at all levels became increasingly integrated into the United States economy. Quebec's economic peripherialization within North America encouraged its political and economic leaders to pursue other avenues and roles. Encouraged and supported by successive interventionist Quebec governments in the 1960s and 1970s, the displacement of the Anglo-Canadian financial community opened up room for members of an emerging Francophone bourgeoisie to play an increasing role in the financial sector. Witness the rapidly expanding Francophone bank, the *Banque nationale du Canada,* as well as the giant holding corporation known as the *Mouvement Desjardin* with its lucrative *caisses populaires,* and insurance and investment companies valued at $22 billion in 1984. This process was accelerated by language legislation in the 1970s which made French the official language of Quebec and encouraged through non-coercive measures large corporations to function in the French language for purposes of internal communications as well as with the Quebec public.

The commercial sector, driven by increased personal consumption of durable and non-durable goods, followed the pattern emerging in the rest of North America. Ever and ever larger shopping centres with huge parking facilities and well-known chain stores were built in all of Quebec's major urban centres while the traditional smaller stores located on commercial streets found it difficult to compete in terms of price and convenience for consumers wanting to shop using their automobiles. Montreal remained a major centre for the transportation sector including the Canadian National and Canadian Pacific railroads as well as Air Canada and some regional airlines. Thanks to the arrival of radio in the 1920s and television in the 1950s, the French language division of the Canadian Broadcasting Corporation, called Radio Canada, set up its headquarters in Montreal where it served as the catalyst for the expansion of the entire industry and the social transformation of the entire society. The English- and French-language public networks were soon joined by private networks.

The social transformation of Quebec society followed that of the economic transformation. One of the most startling features was the very rapid decline of the presence and role of the long-established Catholic Church. In large part, a triumphant Catholic Church had sown the seeds of its eventual demise during the 1950s by refusing to modernize its approach to education, health and social welfare. Other pressures emanated from the widespread secularization of the Quebec society associated with the rise of pluralism, liberalism and individualism. The advent of Pope John XXIII and Vatican II also broke the back of the traditionalists within the Church neutralizing their ability to defend the Church's vested interests in what were increasingly perceived to be secular fields. With the advent of the Quiet Revolution of the 1960s and the public's demand for separation of Church and State, the Catholic Church was quickly deprived of its historic control over all educational institutions which nevertheless remained confessional, health and social welfare institutions to an aggressive, secular, interventionist Quebec state run by a bureaucratic middle class. When the Church reasserted its doctrinal opposition to birth control, divorce, and abortion by the late 1960s, it simply drove thousands of Francophone Catholics out of the fold thereby opening the way for a smaller but more conservative and fundamentalist Church.

The rapid decline of the numerous secular functions of the Catholic Church, coupled with the rise of an interventionist provincial state after 1960, dramatically altered the socio-economic context in which the professional, intellectual, political and bureaucratic elements of the petty bourgeoisie functioned and renewed themselves. The dynamic and articulate neo-nationalist component of the new middle class quickly dominated the political process and the rapidly-expanding provincial, regional and local bureaucracies following the election of Jean Lesage's Liberal Government in 1960. The neo-nationalists, in effect, became the motor force of the Quiet Revolution whose social, economic and political goals and ambitions determined for the better part of a generation the provincial and national agendas.

The only effective rival to this new middle class, a dynamic Francophone bourgeoisie, or Quebec Inc. as it came to be called, had its roots in the prosperity of the post-war years and supportive policies of the Lesage government in the 1960s. This Francophone bourgeoisie emerged in the 1970s to gain prominence during the recessions and boom periods of the 1980s and early 1990s. During the 1950s, neo-nationalist historian, Michel Brunet, argued that Francophone Quebec would never become a fully modern society since it lacked a big bourgeoisie. Indeed, while French Canadians formed 30 per cent of the Canadian population in 1950, less than 7 per cent of the Canadian economic elite was French Canadian, Brunet argued that the Conquest of 1760 had destroyed the normal evolution of the colony of New France towards a modern nation/state by decapitating its ruling class, the mercantile bourgeoisie. In his estimation, only independence for Quebec would end the rule of the Anglo-Canadian and American bourgeoisie, allowing the emergence of dynamic Francophone bourgeoisie essential to the survival and development of a secular, democratic, fully mature Francophone nationality.

The flourishing of the once marginalized Francophone bourgeoisie was ironically a product of the expansion and modernization of the Quebec society as well as the deliberate economic, social, and linguistic policies pursued by the neo-nationalist bureaucratic middle class directing the Quebec state after 1960. As mentioned, these policies accentuated the partial withdrawal of the Anglo-Canadian and American bourgeoisie out of Montreal thereby leaving economic space for large Francophone corporations. While approximately 10 per cent of the Canadian bourgeoisie is comprised of Francophones by the 1980s, most of its members are concentrated in Quebec where their influence over the economy and the provincial political agenda grew steadily, especially in the late 1980s before the prolonged recession of the 1990s. In 1990 Francophone bourgeois controlled 41 per cent of all industries with over 1000 employees compared to a mere 13 per cent in 1976. Paradoxically, this important social and political development was achieved, contrary to the separatists' belief, without Quebec having to declare independence.

The expansion of the economy and the emergence of a better educated post-war baby-boom generation, including an increasing percentage of young women, on the labour market gave new vitality to the working class. The decline in primary and secondary jobs and the rapid growth of the service sectors, public and private, changed the nature of work from blue collar to white and pink collar occupations, some of which paid better wages while others demanded fewer skills and paid lower wages. This significant transformation of the working class soon altered the nature of its labour organisations whose membership more than doubled from 400,000 in 1961 to 850,000 in 1984.

By 1960, the CTCC adopted a new name, the *Confédération des syndicates nationaux* (CSN) and its leader, Jean Marchand, backed the Quiet Revolution reforms undertaken by the Liberal Government of Jean Lesage. In return, the Lesage government passed a new labour code in 1964 which allowed thousands upon thousands of public and para-public sector employees to form unions with the right to strike. The vast majority of these unions opted to join the CSN or, in the case of the teachers, the *Centrale de l'Enseignement du Québec* (CEQ). This resulted in two militant Francophone unions to rival the larger multi-ethnic *Fédération des Travailleurs du Québec* (FTQ) which represented private sector international trades and industrial unions. By 1987, 65 per cent of unionists belonged to the CSN, 26 per cent to international unions and 9 per cent to public sector unions. During this period, the unionization of Quebec workers ranged between a low of 30 per cent to a high of 40 per cent, with women constituting 38 per cent by 1987. During the 1970s, in their struggle for the allegiance of Quebec's workers and provoked by their ongoing collective agreement negotiations with various Quebec governments and their desire for profound socio-economic reforms, all three union centrals preached an explosive mixture of separatist nationalism and doctrinaire socialism. In 1972, all three centrals organized a common front general strike against the government which ended in violence, the jailing of the three union leaders, and the departure from the CSN of 30,000 members who created their own central. Militants from all three championed the cause of the separatist *Parti Québécois* which eventually achieved power in 1976. A somewhat diminished Common Front in 1980 managed to extract a generous settlement for Public sector employees just prior to the 1980 referendum on sovereignty-association. Yet, these employees saw their financial gains taken away by the *Parti Québécois* government which they helped re-elect to office in 1981.

The neo-conservative 1980s began with a short, sharp recession and concluded with the prolonged recession of the early 1990s. These conditions have all but destroyed the doctrinaire socialist programmes and project of the three main unions centrals. The FTQ's private sector affiliates grew in strength giving it 42 per cent of the union membership by 1990. Membership in the moderate, independent public sector break away unions rose to 28 per cent while that of the CSN dropped to 19 per cent. Growing government deficits meant that public sector jobs were threatened and these workers and their unions felt the need to elaborate a new relationship with their employer, the state, in order to preserve as many of their jobs as possible. Paradoxically, this conservative socio-economic climate has the CSN's and CEQ's flagging support for the *Parti Québécois* and its dream of a capitalist, independent Republic of Quebec. While initially denouncing the Meech Lake Constitutional Accord of 1987, union leaders blamed English-speaking Canada for its demise in 1990 and joined the Bélanger-Campeau Commission's campaign for a second referendum on Quebecs independence. Accordingly, union leaders campaigned for the defeat of the revised version of the Meech Lake Accord, the Charlottetown Consensus Report, in the national referendum of October 1992 on the grounds that it offered too few powers to Quebec.

Challenging Canadian Federalism: The Politics of Neo-Nationalism and Separatism
Responding to the ideological developments of the 1950s, Premier Lesage's Liberal Party's slogan in the watershed provincial election of June, 1960 was: 'Its Time for Change'. The party's lengthy platform promised significant social, economic, and political reforms during the provincial election of June, 1960. The majority of electors responded by giving his party a slim but significant majority of eight seats in the Legislative Assembly. Phase one of the Quiet Revolution, a process which would engulf the province over the next three decades, got underway thanks to this changing of the political guard. A normally conservative-minded Premier Lesage, a member of Quebec's political establishment, became a belated convert to the ideology of neo-nationalism and its goal of state-building. As a result, he proceeded with determination but with considerable caution on all fronts so as not to alienate the Anglo-Canadian and American big business community. Furthermore, Lesage feared alienating too many of the traditional Liberals and many of the rural, small town voters who remained sceptical of his big city colleagues in cabinet and caucus. He did not want to raise expectations too high so as not to create too many disappointed voters at the next election.

His less-cautious, impatient, reform-minded ministers, such as Paul Gérin-Lajoie and René Lévesque, and many of the newly-appointed deputy ministers often swept the premier along with their enthusiasm and coordination. They set out to fulfil many of the rising expectations of the neo-nationalistic Francophone middle class with the creation of a powerful interventionist state with a modern bureaucracy consisting of Francophone middle class technocrats. This state would replace the Catholic Church and the discredited and outmoded system dominated by political notables and a patronage ridden civil service. Within six years, nearly all the political, bureaucratic, and social institutions of Quebec were completely revamped by the wholesale reshaping of the face of the province. As a result, an increasingly polarized Quebec society experienced three decades of social and political tensions and turmoil, a development which continues to have repercussions well beyond Quebec's borders.

Following a heated debate inside and outside government circles and backed by the recommendation of the Royal Commission on Education presided over by Bishop Parent, the Lesage government broke with the past in 1964 and re-instituted the Ministry of Education led by Paul Gérin-Lajoie and his Deputy Minister, Arthur Tremblay, a neo-nationalist education reformer from Laval University. The Catholic Church's predominant role in education came to an unceremonious end. The new ministry's function was to finance and administer a fully integrated public system comprising primary, secondary and technical schools as well as community colleges and universities. The Lesage government had moved quickly in 1961 to sign an agreement with the Federal Government whereby the province would receive additional corporate tax points in lieu of direct federal grants to Quebec universities. This additional revenue spurred on the government's commitment to reform. Denominationalism at the primary and secondary levels, much to the chagrin of the secular neo-nationalists, remained because it was guaranteed by the Constitution. Following up on these reforms after 1966, the Union Nationale government created a system of public secondary schools and turned many of the classical colleges and convents into a system of regional *Collèges d'enseignement générale et professionnelle* (CGEPs). It also set up a provincial system of French-language universities in major urban centres to compete with the established ones of Montréal, Laval, and Sherbrooke. These reforms greatly expanded access to post-secondary education and contributed to the expansion of the Francophone middle class. A great many of the new Francophone graduates were absorbed by the expansion of the state bureaucracy and dozen of agencies and crown corporations where they became active and determined supporters of state-building at all levels of Quebec society.

Indeed, two crucial and highly symbolic areas of state building involved the areas of health and social welfare. Ever since the inception of the national social service state in 1940 the unemployment insurance programme, Quebec nationalists and politicians resented the federal government's intrusion into areas of provincial jurisdiction. Prominent neo-nationalist ministers, like René Lévesque and Eric Kierans, and many deputy ministers were determined that the province of Quebec should acquire exclusive control over all social and health programmes intended for its citizens. In 1961, the Lesage government joined the national hospital insurance programme inaugurated in 1957 thereby making hospitals accessible to all of its citizens without additional fees being charged. The provincial government also took control over all health institutions and social welfare agencies from the various Churches and private organizations. Following heated negotiations with federal cabinet ministers and senior bureaucrats, the Quebec government was allowed to create its own pension plan in 1965 as long as it remained compatible with the Canada pension plan. It was not long before successive governments were able to draw upon the lucrative pension fund to finance numerous provincial programmes and projects.

The next important area of state building involved Quebec's abundant natural resources. Pushed hard by René Lévesque and George Emile Laplame, a reluctant Premier Lesage consented to calling an election in 1962 in order to seek a mandate to nationalize with full compensation. The Liberal Party won re-election on its 'Masters in our own house' campaign and then passed legislation allowing Hydro-Quebec to take over all the private production and distribution companies in Quebec. Over the next three decades Hydro-Quebec would develop into the largest public hydro corporation in North America. In a similar fashion, the Lesage government set up dozens of crown corporations and state agencies to undertake economic planning, to reorganize and underwrite Francophone corporations, to create steel, forestry, and mining industries. The government's objectives were to rationalize and maximize the exploitation of the provinces resources, to develop a Francophone big bourgeoisie, and to provide employment for hundreds of thousands of Francophone post-secondary graduates eager to pursue careers in their own language. This process of state building was both disruptive and very expensive and drove the premier to seek additional taxing powers as well as revenues from the national government.

No sooner was the government of Jean Lesage elected to office in June, 1960 than tensions began to increase between the Quebec and the national governments of PM Diefenbaker and then, after 1963, of PM Pearson. Former premier Duplessis had kept the traditional nationalists at bay by setting up in 1953 a Royal Commission to study Quebec's relationship with Ottawa. The very conservative Tremblay Commission Report recommended against the creation of a Quebec social welfare state. Quebec could avoid having such a social welfare state imposed upon it by Ottawa if the province could acquire either a constitutional 'special status' giving it more powers than the other provinces or if there was a constitutional devolution of responsibilities and taxing powers to all the provinces. Beginning in the mid-1950s, Ottawa responded to Quebec's increasing demands for more powers by granting all the provinces a share of personal and corporate tax revenues. Paradoxically, Premier Lesage adopted the Tremblay Commission Report as his guide on Quebec/Ottawa relations. He used it to push hard for a greater share of personal, corporate, and succession duties in every federal/provincial conference. The pressure paid dividends as PM Pearson, in the context of his policy of cooperative federalism, granted the provinces the right to opt-out of a wide range of federal-provincial programmes in return for personal and corporate tax points. Premier Lesage remained a moderate and pragmatic neo-nationalist. Initially, premier Lesage seemed agreeable to the Fulton-Favreau complex constitutional amending formula that had been arrived at by Ottawa and the provinces in 1964. He was forced to withdraw his support when vocal neo-nationalists inside and outside his government denounced the lack of a formal veto for Quebec in the formula and asked that the matter be put off until Quebec could obtain a new division of powers in its favour. By 1965 lesage became concerned that the militant neo-nationalists in his cabinet, like René Lévesque, were trying hard to convince colleagues and party faithful to support the concept of a constitutional 'special status' for Quebec. Reasserting his control, Lesage personally conducted the provincial election of 1966 and the 'Thunder Team' was left on the sidelines. This decision contributed to the defeat of the government and the subsequent department of many of the neo-nationalist Liberals.

A revived Union Nationale, under the leadership of Daniel Johnson regained office with a minority of the ballots but a slight majority of the seats thanks to the support of rural, small town constituencies which, despite electoral reform, continued to be over-represented in the Legislature. These rural electors felt alienated by many of the reforms and increased taxation associated with the Quiet Revolution. This election saw the emergence of small right-wing and left-wing separatist parties whose candidates collected 9 per cent of the newly enfranchised 18-21-years-old voters, mostly in Francophone working-class constituencies in east-end Montreal. Ironically, Premier Daniel Johnson responded to this development by aggressively pursuing the central objective of the Quiet Revolution which was to create a modern, Francophone-dominated Quebec state. His government moved ahead with the social, economic and political reforms introduced by his predecessor further alienating Union Nationale's voters and its financial backers in the business community. On the matter of Quebec's relationship with Ottawa, Premier Johnson adopted a more militant stand which he characterized as 'Equality or independence'. He envisaged a bi-national federation between Ottawa and Quebec and demanded a systematic devolution of powers to his province. The national government, led by a new Minister of Justice from Quebec, Pierre Elliott Trudeau, denounced the separatist agenda of premier Johnson and refused to contemplate further transfer of revenue or tax points to the provinces. Following Premier Johnson's death in 1968, the Union Nationale went into decline only to recover momentarily in the mid-1970s and then disappear as a party.

The political vacuum was filled by the emergence of a more powerful separatist, the *Parti Québécois,* in 1968. At its head was René Lévesque who had left the Liberal Party after the electoral defeat of 1966 because it refused to endorse his concept of sovereignty-association for Quebec. The *Parti Québécois* was a coalition of right-wing and left-wing separatists but its leader was committed to a society based on the principles of political and social democracy. Lévesque believed that, with the support of a respectable majority of Quebec's citizen's a P.Q. government could undertake to negotiate a new constitutional arrangement with Canada whereby Quebec would gain full political control over its territory while remaining economically associated with the rest of Canada.

In this rapidly changing political context, Lesage resigned in 1969 and was replaced as leader of the Liberal Party by a youthful and inexperienced Robert Bourassa, an economist and natural resources technocrat. The Liberal Party was returned to power in 1970 with 45 per cent of the vote and 72 seats. The official opposition was the Union Nationale with 17 seats but a smaller percentage of votes than the rising *Parti Québécois* which garnered only seven seats. Premier Bourassa promised to hold the line on tax increases by limiting the growth of the state. He also promised to create much needed jobs for thousands of newly-educated baby-boom Francophones in the private sector. The state bureaucracy was saturated and government financial resources were increasingly limited causing intensified disputes with militant and radicalized public and para-public sector labour unions which had been granted the right to strike under a new labour code proclaimed in 1965. Most often, Bourassa's government vacillated in its bargaining with the public sector unions while providing very little support to municipalities, hospitals, and school boards in their struggles with these very demanding unions. Premier Bourassa set in motion several very expensive public work projects such as super highways, Montreal's stunning 1976 Olympic facilities, and the massive James Bay hydro-electric project, all of which were geared to create employment in the construction and manufacturing industries. The 1970s were marked by rising inflation and the unions continually went on strike for increased salaries and benefits to keep ahead. The government joined the national health insurance system, modernized Quebec's health system, set up community social service and health centres, created small claims courts and legal aid fund, consumer protection legislation, and a provincial Charter of Rights.

Beginning in 1963 sporadic incidents of left-wing, separatist terrorism erupted in Quebec. An inexperienced premier hesitated when confronted with the sudden outburst of a more militant and violent terrorist movement, the FLQ, in October 1970. Fearing a political coup led by René Lévesque and other well-known journalists like Claude Ryan of *Le Devoir* for failing to resolve quickly through negotiations the kidnapping of the British High Commissioner, James Cross, premier Bourassa called upon Ottawa to send in the Canadian Armed Forces. This development, in what came to be called the October Crisis, provoked the kidnapping and subsequent murder of his labour minister, Pierre Laporte. The Army eventually found the perpetrators who were either jailed or exiled to Cuba. Both the Bourassa and Trudeau governments were denounced by the *Parti Québécois* and the labour unions for having jailed over 400 suspects without due process or proper trials to clear their names, all under the sweeping powers of the War Measures Act.

In the interim, the new premier having promised an era of 'profitable federalism' agreed to participate in the negotiations between Ottawa and the provinces on the renewal of the Canadian constitution. In 1968, the Pearson government had proposed partition of the Canadian constitution with an amending formula and a Charter of Rights and Freedoms which included protection for Canada's two official linguistic communities. Some of the leading provinces like Ontario and British Columbia, taking a cue from Quebec's Union Nationale, brought to the table often-conflicting shopping lists of powers they wanted transferred to them. PM Trudeau, insisting that the agenda be limited so that an agreement that would not eviscerate the national government could be achieved, convened the premier to a federal/provincial constitutional Conference in Victoria in June 1971. Premier Bourassa agreed in principle with the Victoria Charter package which incorporated a revised amending formula giving Quebec a veto, the entrenchment of official bilingualism and its extension to some provinces, and a limited Charter of Rights. Upon returning to his province, Bourassa encountered visceral and vocal opposition from the neo-nationalists in his cabinet, his caucus, the Liberal Party and most of the nationalist-oriented Francophone media. He informed PM Trudeau that his government would not ratify the Victoria Charter thereby forcing the constitutional issue to the back burner until the late 1970s. PM Trudeau lost all respect he had for the young premier and the federal Liberal Government and party did little to support the Bourassa government, allowing it to go down to defeat at the hands of the PQ in 1976.

Premier Bourassa's mishandling of the growing linguistic crisis merely confirmed Trudeau's severe judgement of his abilities. The linguistic crisis erupted in 1968 in the town of St. Léonard, just north of Montreal, when its school board, under pressure from neo-nationalists campaigning for a unilingual Quebec, insisted on enrolling all children of immigrant families, predominantly Italian in this case, into French-language schools. Neo-nationalist hostility and public protests erupted when the Union Nationale government of J.J. Bertrand passed Bill 63 promoting the teaching of French to all immigrants but confirming freedom of choice in schooling matters for all parents. To placate the neo-nationalists, premier Bertrand created a royal commission of study and report on the matter of the future of the French language in Quebec. The Bourassa government procrastinated in addressing the linguistic issues involved in education and the workplace and allowed the *Parti Québécois,* which became the official opposition in the election of 1973, to exploit this sensitive and explosive issue very successfully. Premier Bourassa, awaited the lengthy report and innumerable recommendations of the Gendron Commission on the matter. In 1974, ignoring most of the Reports' findings and recommendations, his government passed its language law, Bill 22, making French the only official language of the province and all its public institutions and agencies, forcing all children to pass English-language tests or be enrolled in French-language schools, but merely encouraging the private sector to use more French. In the interim, the *Parti Québécois* had gained public support for a much tougher stand on the linguistic rights, especially in the field of education. Looking for another issue to divert public attention from chaos on the home front, premier Bourassa called an early election for November 15, 1976 on the grounds that Quebec had to forestall a unilateral move by the national government of PM Pierre Trudeau to reform the Canadian Constitution.

Having easily defeated the separatist *Parti Québécois* twice, premier Bourassa badly underestimated the widespread dissatisfaction with his government, especially among Anglophone and immigrant Quebeckers who turned to a revived Union Nationale to express their outrage. He also overlooked the shrewd tactics and strategy of the separatists. Pressured by its constitutional *guru,* Claude Morin, the *Parti Québécois* neutralized the impact of its commitment to political independence by promising to refer the matter of Quebec's constitutional future of its citizens in a future referendum. The P.Q. assembled an excellent team of candidates in all constituencies and promised solid, progressive government. In so doing, René Lévesque won the support of the militant labour unions, most of the Francophone new middle class eager to push on with more reforms, and the rural notables and voters who were promised that the PQ would devote attention to their problems. The *Parti Québécois* won the election, setting in motion a train of events that would destabilize Quebec/Ottawa relations until the present-day.

The PQ government proceeded to provide solid and efficient government by implementing legislative measures what were popular with its supporters. It began by addressing the controversial linguistic question. The 1977 Charter of the French Language, introduced as Bill 1 was amended and reintroduced as Bill 101. It made French the only official language of Quebec's National Assembly, Crown corporations, agencies, and provincial courts. It streamed all immigrants and Canadian citizens from other parts of Canada into French-language schools regardless of their knowledge of English. Finally, following strong pressure from the business community it renewed and extended the policy of persuasion in the private sector rather than impose coercive measures as Bill 1 initially proposed. The French Charter was popular among the Francophone majority but it resulted in the out-migration of thousands of English-speaking citizens as well as many large and small companies because the Bill outlawed bilingual commercial signage and increased the level of government intervention in their operations. Bill 101 would face several challenges in the courts and some of its provisions pertaining to education rights for English-speaking Canadians and commercial signage would eventually be struck down by the Supreme Court.

In the economic arena, the PQ government nationalized the asbestos mining companies retained control over Québecair, reasserted its control over all crown corporations and agencies, strengthened the Francophone small and medium manufacturers and the co-operative movement with capitalization, finance and export subsidies. In the social field, the PQ created no fault state automobile insurance programme, stronger protection for consumers, provisions to enhance the equality to women, and a range of labour legislation including a higher minimum wage, the abolition of the use of strike-breakers, and better health and job security measures. The government, hoping to restore social peace in the public and para-public sectors and reap the returns in its proposed referendum, raised substantially the wages and salary scales for all these categories of workers. Plagued by a sharp recession in the early months of its second mandate following the election of 1981, the PQ government was forced to make drastic cuts to all programmes, services, wages, and salaries while turning hard to the right on all matters of economic development. Having lost the referendum of May 1980 and refusing to participate in the renewal of the Canadian federation in 1981-82, the *Parti Québécois* went into decline. The moderates, led by René Lévesque and Pierre-Marc Johnson, abandoned the party's commitment to independence, and the militants led by Jacques Parizeau stormed out of the party. Inevitably, the PQ lost the 1985 provincial election to a revived Liberal Party under a 'recycled' Robert Bourassa eager to rebuild the economy of the province around a reinvigorated private sector.

The central purpose of the *Parti Québécois* was to achieve political independence for Quebec. This ensured that the constitutional question, which had been dropped after the failure of the Victoria Charter, would resurface following the Quebec referendum promised by René Lévesque in 1976. The PQ government delayed the referendum until the defeat of the Trudeau government in 1979 believing that the new Conservative Government of PM Joe Clark would not dare enter the debate. But when PM Clark's ill-fated minority Conservative Government went down to defeat in the House of its first budget, Trudeau was convinced to come out of retirement. The Liberals easily won the federal election of 1980 and the PQ had to face PM Trudeau during the referendum of May 1980. The PQ lost the referendum, 40 to 60 per cent, on its soft question asking Quebeckers if they would give the government a mandate to negotiate sovereignty-association with Ottawa. PM Trudeau clearly indicated that Ottawa would not negotiate with the PQ government. Furthermore, Trudeau promised to set in motion immediately a process to renew the Canadian Constitution along the lines that his government had proposed in Bill C-60 placed before the House of Commons in 1978.

PM Trudeau then reintroduced his constitutional proposals hoping to gain the support of some or all of the provinces for the partition of the BNA Act, the Victoria Charter amending formula based on regional vetoes, and a comprehensive Charter of Rights and Freedoms with educational guarantees for the official linguistic minorities. After several months of political and court battles with the provinces and public parliamentary hearings, Ottawa and nine provinces agreed to the Constitution Act, 1982. The Canada Bill, subsequently debated and passed by the Canadian and British Parliaments, entailed the partition and renaming of the British North America Act, 1867, the Vancouver amending formula giving all provinces a veto over certain crucial matters, a comprehensive Charter of Rights and Freedoms modified with a 'notwithstanding' clause, and, finally, a reaffirmation of the provincial jurisdiction over natural resources. Only the separatist premier of Quebec, René Lévesque, refused to sign the new arrangement and called upon the Quebec National Assembly to condemn the Constitution Act, 1982 and pass legislation nullifying the application of the Charter's provisions in the province.

As the *Parti Québécois* self-destroyed following its defeat over the referendum and its abandonment of its separatist and social-democratic ideals,

Robert Bourassa resumed leadership of the Liberal Party at its convention in October 1983. He rebuilt the party as a coalition of old and new Liberals and disaffected moderate nationalists who had abandoned the PQ. He promised that his government would focus on rebuilding Quebec's shattered economy thereby putting Quebeckers back to work. He also promised to seek a constitutional reconciliation with Ottawa via his friend and ally, Brian Mulroney, Canada's new Conservative Prime Minister whom he and his party helped get elected in the federal election of September 1984. His approach was rewarded with victory in the provincial election of 1985, 56 per cent of the vote and 99 to 122 seats.

His government set about restoring sound financial and administrative management of the province. It created social peace by signing new collective agreements with the public and para-public sector unions. It offered inexpensive hydro-electricity to high technology companies wishing to invest in the province. With the cooperation of the national Conservative government, Quebec's brand name pharmaceutical companies acquired patent legislation protecting all their research and drug patents for twenty years. Montreal also won the transfer of Canada's space research centre from the Ottawa region as well as the maintenance contract for the Armed Forces' CF-18s returning from Europe. The government restructured the regula-tions governing financial institutions hoping thereby to encourage greater participation of Francophone firms in this sector. It also removed many regulations governing business and privatised a number of crown corpora-tions including Québecair. Over time the deficit was reduced and personal and corporate taxes were brought into line with those of Ontario. Indeed, premier Bourassa became a convert to the PQ's longstanding proposal of restructuring Quebec's low wage, low value-added, low productivity, light industrial economy into high wage, high value added, productive high technology industries by gaining access to markets in the United States via a comprehensive free trade agreement. By developing greater trade links with the United States, the Bourassa government hoped that the Quebec economy would become less dependent upon trading links with Ontario.

The Bourassa government's achievements on social, educational and linguistic issues were not as impressive. A continued decline in funding for health and social welfare services prompted the government to appoint the Rochon Commission to analyse the situation and make recommendations. The Rochon Report called for a sweeping overhaul of the system and some of the recommendations, such as user fees, went against the terms of the Canada Health Act thereby engendering a political conflict with Ottawa. The Bourassa government showed little interest in undertaking an evaluation of the many problems confronting the primary and secondary levels of the education. The long debate over restructuring the confessional systems along linguistic lines continued to work its way through the judicial system. By the time the Supreme Court granted the Quebec government the right to proceed with this restructuring provided it respected the constitutional rights, the Bourassa government showed little determination to push forward and would soon come to the end of its second term in office. During the election of 1985, Bourassa had promised to reconcile the English-speaking communities by attenuating the most discriminatory aspects of Quebec's Charter of the French Language, Bill 101. While his government did pass Bill 142 which guaranteed health and social services in English, premier Bourassa procrastinated and then caved in to pressures from the nationalists, inside and outside the government on his promise to amend Bill 101 thereby allowing commercial signage. Despite a reasoned Supreme Court ruling in favour of bilingual commercial signage, the Bourassa government used the 'notwithstanding' clause 33 of the federal Charter of Rights and Freedoms to circumvent the decision. Bill 178 denied Quebec businesses the right to use exterior bilingual signage while severely restricting the nature and amount of interior bilingual signage. Far from achieving reconciliation, premier Bourassa, by siding with the nationalists, had accentuated the linguistic and ethnic polarization of the Quebec society.

By the mid-1980s it appeared that the threat of separatism was over for another generation. Little did people realize that the disarray within the *Parti Québécois* when combined with the political realignment occurring at the national level in the mid-1980s would contribute in a major way to the re-emergence of separatism with a vengeance in the early 1990s. The seemingly permanent determination of Quebec's technocrats, an important segment of its political class, and its Francophone intelligentsia to achieve greater powers for their province either through a reformed federalism, special status, devolution of powers to all the provinces, sovereignty-association, or outright independence, became a destabilizing and ultimately destructive obsession.

In the mid-1980s, most Canadians were concerned with overcoming the effects of the recession and paid no attention to the constitutional question. Few realized that both Brian Mulroney and Robert Bourassa had promised Quebec voters in their respective elections of 1984 and 1985 that they would work together to reintegrate Quebec back into the constitutional family with 'honour and enthusiasm'. Having become PM and Premier, Mulroney and Bourassa worked quietly behind the scene to cajole the remaining nine premiers to accept Quebec's constitutional demands in return for signing the

Constitution Act, 1982. This Mulroney/Bourassa alliance produced the Meech Lake Constitutional Accord of 1987 which incorporated the Quebec government's five minimum demands—a distinct society clause, three judges on the Supreme Court, complete control over immigration, restrictions of Ottawa's spending powers, and a veto over changes to national institutions. Initially all ten premiers supported the Accord. But when three premiers were subsequently defeated in provincial elections, the new premiers of New Brunswick, Newfoundland and Manitoba refused to grant the Accord the unanimity it required to become part of the Constitution. These three premiers did not like Quebec's Bill 178 outlawing full bilingual commercial signs and Bourassa's recourse to the 'notwithstanding' clause to shield it from a court challenge. If Bill 178 was Bourassa's interpretation of how a 'distinct' Quebec society would function, they wanted none of it. When premier Bourassa refused to renegotiate certain aspects of the Meech Lake Accord with these new premiers, it lapsed on June 22, 1990 in an atmosphere of political crisis and recrimination. Quebec nationalists, the majority of whom had denounced the Accord as too little too late, blamed 'English Canada' for its demise and portrayed its defeat as an insult to all Francophone Quebeckers.

With PM Mulroney's tacit consent, Premier Bourassa attempted to channel the nationalists' and separatists' resentment toward a bi-nationally restructured federal system along the lines of the European community. He set up a constitutional committee within the Liberal Party as well as establishing a constitutional commission under the auspices of the National Assembly. His intention was to use the public support galvanized by these organisations as well as their radical recommendations to pressure Ottawa, the provinces, and the Canadian public to accept Quebec's constitutional demands as presented in the Meech Lake Accord. It was in this context that PM Mulroney agreed to reopen the constitution debate in the fall of 1991.

Several months of negotiating efforts were undertaken in order to fashion a constitutional reform package which responded to the constitutional aspirations and demands of Quebec seeking the substance of the Meech Lake Accord, the Western provinces eager for immediate Senate reform, and the aboriginal communities seeking the entrenchment of the inherent right to self-government. The Bourassa government refused to participate in the process until it was made clear that Quebec's constitutional demands were not being undermined by the other provinces or the aboriginal organizations. In the summer of 1992, in Ottawa, the nine premiers, and aboriginal leaders arrived at a constitutional package they felt satisfied with and offered it to Quebec. Premier Bourassa agreed to return to the negotiating table in

August. Under enormous pressure to meet the Quebec government's October date for a referendum on Quebec's future in the federation, all parties produced an incomplete 'rough draft' agreement of basic principles dubbed the Charlottetown Consensus Report in September. PM Mulroney put this incomplete constitutional package to the Canadian people in a national referendum on October 26, 1992. The controversial, underdeveloped constitutional package was rejected by 55 per cent including a majority of Quebec's citizens who were convinced by the 'NO' campaign headed up by the *Parti Québécois* that the five minimum demands of Quebec outlined in the Meech Lake Accord of 1987 had been undermined by the inherent right of self-government for the aboriginal communities and the concept of the equality of the provinces represented by the new Senate based on six elected or appointed senators from each province.

His credibility in shreds, plagued by poor health and exhausted from years of effort devoted to the intractable constitutional issue, premier Bourassa resigned late in 1993. He was replaced by Daniel Johnson, an avowed federalist and brother to former PQ premier, Pierre-Marc Johnson. His government had only a few months to convince the recession-ravaged electorate to give the Liberals a third mandate. Most *pundits,* including some in the national Liberal Party and government, predicted a devastating defeat for Johnson in the September 1994 provincial election at the hands of the revived *Parti Québécois* led by hardline secessionist Jacques Parizeau. Johnson promised economic renewal and warned Quebeckers that the PQ intended to trigger the process of secession the moment it took office by calling upon the National Assembly to make a solemn declaration indicating Quebec's intentions to secede and then setting up a travelling Commission to create a new constitution for the republic of Quebec. Parizeau responded to the Liberals attack by assuring Quebeckers of solid and efficient government and by promising that secession matter would be settled in a referendum due to held before the end of 1995. Parizeau, nevertheless, declared that PQ was sovereignist before, during and after the election and indicated that his government would interpret a PQ's victory as a mandate to begin negotiating Quebec's withdrawal from the federation. The Quebec electorate, anxious for a change of government but still opposed to separation, voted out the Liberals and gave a lukewarm nod to the *Parti Québécois.* The *Parti Québécois* won 77 seats with only 44.7 per cent of the vote while the Liberals retained 47 seats with a very surprising and respectable 44.3 per cent of the vote. Premier Parizeau was given a mandate to provide effective and efficient government but not to trigger prematurely the secession process. It remains to be seen whether a majority of Quebeckers will be convinced by the *Parti*

Québécois to vote for an ethnic nation/state or whether will chose continue
to enjoy the cultural security and economic benefits of one of the globes'
longest surviving and most prosperous multi-national federations.

BIBLIOGRAPHY

Industrial Capitalism and Social Change to 1930

Copy, Terry. *The Anatomy of Poverty: The Condition of the Working Class in Montreal, 1897-1929.* Toronto: McClelland & Stewart, 1974.

Dales, John H. *Hydroelectricity and Industrial Development: Quebec 1898-1940.* Cambridge, Mass.: Harvard University Press, 1957.

Dickinson, John A., and Brian Young. *Brève histoire socio-économique de Québec.* Sillery, Québec: Septentrion, 1992.

Hamelin, Jean et Yves Roby. *Histoire économique du Québec, 1851-1896.* Montréal: Fides, 1971.

Linteau, Paul-André, René Durocher, and Jean-Claude Robert. *Histoire du Québec Contemporain. Da la Confédération à al crise (1867-1929).* Montréal: Boréal Express, 1979.

Little, J.I. *Nationalism, Capitalism, and Colonization in Nineteenth-Century Quebec. The Upper St. Francis District.* Montreal/Kingston: McGill-Queen's University Press, 1989.

Rouillard, Jacques. *Les syndicats nationaux au Québec, 1900-1915.* Québec: Les Presses de l'Université Laval, 1974.

Roy, Fernade. *Progrès, harmonie, liberté: le libéralisme des milieux d'affaires Francophones au tournant du siècle.* Montréal: Boréal, 1988.

Rudin, Ronald. *Banking en français. French-Canadian Banks, 1835-1925.* Toronto: University of Toronto Press, 1985.

Young, Brian. *Promoters and Politicians: The North Shore Railways in the Province of Quebec, 1854-85.* Toronto: University of Toronto Press, 1978.

Politics and Political Institutions to 1930

Bélanger, Réal. *Wilfird Laurier. Quand la politique devient passion.* Québec: Les Presses de l'Université Lavel/Les Enterprises Radio-Canada, 1986.

Neatby, Blair. *Laurier and a Liberal Quebec.* Toronto: McClelland & Stewart, 1973.

Levitt, Joseph. *Henri Bourassa and the Golden Calf: The Social Programme of the Nationalists of Quebec (1900-1914).* Ottawa: University of Ottawa Press, 1972.

Silver, A.I. *The French-Canadian Idea of Confederation, 1864-1900.* Toronto: University of Toronto Press, 1982.

Vigod, Bernard L. *Quebec Before Duplessis. The Political Career of Louis-*

Alexandre Taschereau. Kingston and Montreal: McGill-Queen's University Press, 1986.

Young, Brain. *George-Etienne Cartier, Montréal Bourgeois.* Montreal and Kingston: McGill-Queen's University Press, 1981.

Economy and Society in Transition, 1930-60

Behiels, Michael D. *Quebec and the Question of Immigration: From Ethnocentrism to Ethnic Pluralism, 1900-1985.* Ottawa: Canadian Historical Association, 1991.

Linteau, Paul-André, René Durocher, Jean-Claude Robert, and François Ricard.*Histoire du Québec contemporain. Le Québec depuis, 1930.*Montréal: Boréal Express, 1986.

Lévesque, Andrée. *Virage à gauche interdit.* Montréal: Boréal Express, 1984.

Rouillard, Jacques. *Historie de la CSN, 1921-1981.* Montréal: Boréal Express, 1981.

Roy, Jean-Louis. *La marche des québécois. Le temps des ruptures (1945-1960).* Montréal: Leméac, 1976.

Political Parties and the Political Process under Seige, 1930-60

Behiels, Michael D. *Prelude to Quebec's Quiet Revolution. Liberalism versus Neo-nationalism, 1945-1960.* Kingston and Montreal: McGill-Queen's University Press, 1985.

—. *Québec Since 1945: Selected Readings.* Toronto: Copp Clark Pitman, 1987.

Black, Conrad. *Duplessis.* Toronto: McClelland & Stewart, 1976.

Boismenu Gérard. *Le duplessisme. Politique économique et rapports de force, 1944-1960.* Montréal: Presses de l'Université de Montréal, 1981.

Dion Léon. *Québec 1945-2000 Tome II Les intellectuels et le temps de Duplessis* Sainte Foy. Québec: Les Presses de l'Université Laval, 1993.

Dirks, Patricia. *The Failure of L'Action libérale nationale.* Kingston: McGill-Queen's University Press, 1991.

Quinn, Herbert F. *Union Nationale: A Study in Quebec Nationalism.* Toronto: University of Toronto Press, 1963.

Creating the Modern State, 1960 to the Present

Cook, Ramsay. *Canada and the French-Canadian Question.*Toronto: Macmillan, 1966.

Daigle, Gérard, and Guy Rocher, eds.*Le Québec en jeu. Comprendre les grands défis.* Montréal: Les Presses de l'Université de Montréal, 1992.

Fraser, Graham.*PQ René Lévesque and the Parti Québécois in Power.* Toronto: Macmillan of Canada, 1984.

Jones, Richard. *Community in Crisis.* Toronto: McClelland & Stewart, 1972.

Guindon, Hubert. *Quebec Society: Tradition, Modernity and Nationhood.* Toronto: University of Toronto Press, 1988.

McRoberts, Kennth. *Quebec. Social Change and Political Crisis,* third edition. Toronto: McClelland & Stewart, 1988.

Thomson, Dale C. *Jean Lesage & the Quiet Revolution.* Toronto: Macmillan of Canada, 1984.

Challenging Canadian Federalism: The Politics of Neo-nationalism and Separatism

Balthazar, Louis, and Guy Laforest et Vincent Lemieux, *Le Québec et la restructuration du Canada, 1980-1992: enjeux et perspectives.* Sillery: Septentrion, 1991.

Behiels, Michael, ed. *The Meech Lake Primer. Conflicting views of the 1987 Constitutional Accord.* Ottawa: University of Ottawa Press, 1989.

Coleman, William. *The Independence Movement in Quebec, 1945-1980.* Toronto: University of Toronto Press, 1984.

Gagnon, Alain-G., and Mary Beth Montcalm. *Quebec: Beyond the Quiet Revolution.* Scarborough, Ont.: Nelson, 1990.

Johnson, William. *A Canadian Myth: Quebec, Between Canada and the Illusion of Utopia.* Montréal/Toronto: Robert Davies Publishing, 1994.

Trudeau, Pierre Elliott. *Federalism and the French Canadians.* Toronto: Macmillan of Canada, 1968.

Russell, Peter H. *Constitutional Odyssey. Can Canadians be a Sovereign People?* Toronto: University of Toronto Press, 1992.

REFERENCES

Rouillard, Jacques, ed. *Guide d'Historie du Québec du régime français à nos jours. Bibliographie commentée.* Montréal: Editions du Méridien, 1991.

Trofimenkoff, Susan Mann. *The Dream of Nation. A Social and Intellectual History of Quebec.* Toronto: Macmillan of Canada, 1982.

6

Ontario: Confederation to the Present

MICHAEL J. PIVA

Ontario has since Confederation been Canada's largest and wealthiest province. As so many have observed, Ontario is the engine which drives the national economy, yet the province has always played a confusing and at times contradictory role. Political rhetoric in other provinces and regions contends that Ontario is too powerful. Too often, many commentators suggest that the interests of other regions have been sacrificed to the interests of the centre. Although Ontarians have generally supported regional development programmes designed to redress the imbalance between an overly powerful centre and less economically advantaged regions, many Ontarians have adopted a condescending, almost arrogant, attitude toward the political expression of regional discontent in the Maritimes, Québec or the west. Other Ontarians have adopted an aggressive regional rhetoric of their own observing that Ontario frequently is forced to pay for regional development programmes which always favour other provinces. Indeed, Ontario's aggressive provincialism explains much about the federal nature of the political union which came into being in 1867. Confederation, we too often forget, witnessed the creation of only two new governments, Ontario and Québec, and of the two, Ontario was the more insistent on its desire to partially divorce its partner in the old Province of Canada.

Modern Ontario occupies over 400,000 square miles between the 42nd and 56th parallel of latitude and the 74th and 95th parallels of longitude. The Canadian Shield, that mass of precambrian rock stretching from the Mackenzie Valley in the Northwest Territories, sweeping down into south central Ontario and Québec and on to the Atlantic Coast, occupies most of this immense territory. The ancient rock formations of the Shield have been ground down by the advance and retreat of massive ice formations which have left in their wake countless lakes and channels. Low temperature, moderate rainfall, irregular drainage, and slow evaporation produced over millions of years an environment of numerous lakes, streams, channels, bogs and swamps. Often glacial action left bear rock exposed. Elsewhere soils are thin and acidic. It is an environment which has dictated the primary economic activities of all residents of northern Ontario from native peoples to later immigrants.

Boreal forests stretch for 6500 kilometers over all of this huge territory. The Boreal forests of the Canadian Shield can be divided into three distinct bands: (1) a pine-hemlock belt in the south, (2) a spruce/fir belt in the central regions, and (3) a taiga zone where spruce and fir trees become increasingly dwarfed until they disappear into tundra. These forests, despite severe climatic limitations, are home to a wide variety of flora and fauna. Large Boreal mammals, particularly caribou and deer, supported Algonquian and Iroquoian hunting peoples while smaller mammals, in particular beaver, marten and ermine, provided the basis for commercial exploitation by European traders. The Eastern White Pine of the south, the largest of the Boreal conifers, together with Red Pine and other hardwoods later provided the basis for a thriving timber trade, while the White and Black Spruce of the more northerly regions would eventually provide the resource base for a pulp and paper industry. Still later large mineral deposits throughout the Shield gave rise to an expansive mining and industrial economy both in the north and in the south.

Early settlers, however, came not to the Shield but to the rich fertile lands of southern Ontario. The bulk of Ontario's population has always lived in a geographically smaller region bounded in the west and south by Lakes Huron, Erie and Ontario, in the east by the St. Lawrence and Ottawa rivers and in the north by the precambrian Shield. The Shield runs south-east from Georgian Bay to the St. Lawrence valley with a small spur, the Frontenac Axis, cutting across the St. Lawrence just east of Lake Ontario. South of this line and in the Ottawa and St. Lawrence River valleys the Boreal forest gives way to a transitional forest of conifers and deciduous hardwoods and softwoods. Soils in this region are less acidic, deeper, and far richer. Rainfall in the transitional forests is higher than in the north as is the evaporation rate. This combination provided ideal growing conditions for most field crops. Soil fertility, however, is not uniform. The best lands lay to the south-west, and as one moves to the north-east, particularly in the narrow band of the Ottawa valley, the quality of land, although still relatively good, deteriorates. In the nineteenth century this primary resource—rich arable land—insured rapid population growth in southern Ontario concentrated in the south-western peninsula bounded by the Great Lakes. Organized politically in 1793 as the Province of Upper Canada, Ontario emerged as Canada's most populous province by 1867.

PART 1: CONFEDERATION AND THE BIRTH OF A PROVINCE

The Province of Canada which joined the older colonies of Upper and Lower Canada in 1840 never achieved the legislative union intended by the Colonial Office. Although the new province had a single legislature, the older sections, now renamed Canada West and Canada East, were given equal representation. Designed to thwart colonial demands for greater self-rule, the largely English-speaking Protestant political leaders from Canada West joined with the largely French-speaking Catholic political leaders from Canada East to remake the Union in their own respective images. By 1848 responsible government gave political control over domestic policies to the colonial legislature and recognized the quasi-federal administrative nature of the Province. Henceforth, both French and English would be official languages while other differences between the two sections became institutionalized. By 1854 the 'legislative' union had become a 'federal' union in all but name.

As sectional differences became ever more entrenched so too did sectional rivalry. During the 1840s and early 1850s the provincial government aggressively pursued development policies designed to promote more rapid settlement and economic growth. Economic dislocations in the late 1850s, however, forced the government to become increasingly selective with its aid. The Grand Trunk Railway, headquartered in Montreal, continued to receive support despite loud protests from Canada West. Similarly, in 1858 and again in 1859, the government raised import duties which explicitly favoured the port of Montreal. Ontario's Liberals, led by George Brown, argued that the government had become both extravagant and corrupt while promoting policies which favoured Canada East at the expense of Canada West.

Canada West's Liberals felt aggrieved on the cultural front as well. The leading political voices in the 1850s came to support Liberal leader George Brown's call for religious 'voluntarism' and a complete separation of church and state, particularly in education. Liberals demanded the creation of non-sectarian public schools while the Catholic minority in Canada West continued to insist on public funding for its own separate schools. Equal representation of the two sections guaranteed that the Catholic minority in Canada West could count on the support of the large Catholic majority in Canada East. This support guaranteed the continued expansion of the separate school system despite the ever more vociferous protests of the large majority within Canada West.

By 1859 the Liberals of Canada West, who continued to win large electoral majorities in their section, demanded constitutional reform in order, as they believed, to free themselves from the dominance of Canada

East. Some politicians and journalists suggested a return to the pre-1840 reality of separate political jurisdictions in Upper and Lower Canada. Others, however, worked to tie Ontario's regional discontent to broader concerns about economic development of the St. Lawrence system and the need to extend commercial activities beyond the St. Lawrence drainage basin. Thus the drive for Confederation in Ontario began as an attempt to achieve cultural autonomy within a larger and expanding economic union.

At mid-century Canada West's economy, based as it was on agriculture and forest industries, seemed incapable of generating sufficient growth to meet the needs of an ever expanding population. Timber which had long dominated the export sector had diversified from its original base in the squared timber trade with Britain into a sawed lumber industry aimed primarily at the American market. Although farm products produced less by way of foreign earnings in export markets, agriculture employed many more people. The strength of the Ontario economy throughout the nineteenth century lay in its agricultural potential.

Although rich and productive, Canada West's agricultural sector was, nonetheless, facing serious difficulties by the 1850s. Most of the province's arable land had been alienated; suddenly the relative scarcity of available new land for settlement slowed population growth. More importantly, families now faced new difficulties providing land for their offspring. Increasingly Ontarians looked to the North-west—what is today the province of Manitoba and the prairie beyond—as the answer to their land needs. British North American union meant the annexation of the sparsely populated prairie region and the restoration of a expanding agricultural frontier for both the children of Canada West's agriculturalists and new immigrants from abroad.

Canada West's economy had been changing in other ways as well. Canal and railway construction during the 1840s and 1850s provided construction jobs and later helped generate additional manufacturing employment. Tough economic times of the late 1850s encouraged all railways to reduce their dependence on expensive capital-goods imports by developing their own manufacturing and repair facilities. This, combined with the expanding consumer market provided by a relatively prosperous agricultural sector, insured that manufacturing industries began to emerge alongside the largely commercial concerns in the largest towns and cities. Urban commercial and manufacturing interests, like the province's agriculturalists, recognized the need to promote continued economic growth which could best be achieved by British North American union.

The need for economic growth and expansion became even more pressing during the American Civil War. Political relations between both Britain and the United States on the one hand and Canada and the United States on the other deteriorated rapidly during the war. Then in 1865 the United States announced that it would not renew the 1854 Reciprocity Treaty which had helped promote continental trade. Fearing that the loss of Reciprocity posed a significant threat to export markets, many Canadians came to believe that British North American union provided their only viable economic alternative.

Driven by economic necessity British North American union also required a solution to the political tangle of constitutional reform. Federalism provided such a solution; Confederation provided an expanded central government with sweeping economic powers and at the same time left individual provinces with a large degree of cultural autonomy. Civil law, language and, most importantly, schools, lay within the provincial jurisdiction.

PART 2: ONTARIO'S ARDUOUS DESTINY

A. *Political Developments*

A powerful political coalition of both Liberals and Conservatives—the 'friends of Confederation' as their leaders referred to themselves—steered Confederation to a successful conclusion in 1867 and formed the first government of Ontario under the leadership of former Canadian Prime Minister John Sanfield Macdonald. This government faced the daunting task of creating new political institutions appropriate for the province and repassing those statutes of pre-Confederation Canada which now fell within the provincial jurisdiction. This included the entire civil code, legislation creating the provincial court system, and the school system as well as all municipal and social legislations. With time this necessary but relatively non-partisan effort gave way to a return to more traditionally partisan activities.

Despite Sanfield Macdonald's claims, his government came to resemble more and more closely the pre-Confederation Conservative party. Ontario's Liberal Party, which had traditionally commanded a majority within the western section of the older Union, coalesced in opposition patiently waiting the next election. When that election came in 1871 the Liberals, campaigning as if the opposition were the Conservative government in Ottawa, swept to power. Edward Blake became the new Premier initiating a period of unbroken Liberal dominance which would last until 1905. Blake himself preferred a political career in Ottawa. He remained Premier only long enough to convince Oliver Mowat to leave the judiciary and return to active politics as Ontario Premier. Mowat would hold the Premiership for almost a quarter century.

A lawyer trained in the office of federal Prime Minister John A. Macdonald, Mowat had been an active politician in pre-Confederation Canada. He had attended the Charlottetown and Québec conferences, but then resigned from the cabinet in late 1864 to become a judge. Although intensely partisan, Mowat was no ideologue. He often commented that Ontario required careful 'management'. As Premier of an historically factious province, Mowat was a man of the political centre who carefully avoided extremist positions of all kinds. A liberal in his political views, Mowat was conservative enough to stay very much in tune with the innate conservativism of the province. His political roots, and the traditional strength of Ontario's Liberal party, lay in the agricultural regions of the province. Mowat carefully cultivated the rural constituencies whose electors rewarded him with majorities in every election he fought as leader of Ontario's Liberal Party.

When confronted with a controversy Mowat usually sought compromise, although never at the expense of basic principals. This is best exemplified in his treatment of the province's Catholic minority and their always controversial right to separate religious schools. The granting of jurisdiction over schools and language to the new provinces of Ontario and Québec had been the *sine qua non* of Confederation. But, in exchange for control over schools and languages issues, the two provinces also agreed to guarantee those minority rights which 'existed in law and in practice' at time of Confederation. There would be no expansion of Ontario's separate school system but neither could the system be abolished. Ontario's more militant Protestant organizations, the Orange Order, the Protestant protective Association and late the Equal Rights Association, campaigned constantly for the elimination of Catholic schools. Mowat always resisted such demands. Catholic-Protestant conflicts heated up in the 1880s as a result of events outside the province.

Western expansion had been a primary goal of Confederation, and Ontarians saw the prairie region as a natural extension of their own province. In the Red River, however, the Métis, the children of mixed marriages between European fathers and native mothers, resisted any inclusion in Canada unless their communal rights were first recognized. The federal government in turn passed the Manitoba Act in 1870 which not only created a new province but one which was bilingual and included both public and separate Catholic schools. This decision frustrated many Ontarians and the repercussions of the Manitoba Act would reverberate in the Province for the next quarter century in two distinct ways. It would fuel extremist Protestant political movements and it would create the opening volley in a series of constitutional disputes between Ontario and the federal government.

During the Red River resistance Thomas Scott, an Orangeman from

Ontario, had been executed by the provisional government headed by Louis Riel, the French-speaking Catholic leader of the Red River Métis. Many Ontarians believed Riel to be a rebel and a murderer, and the Ontario government gave in to the popular clamour by issuing a warrant for his arrest. Shortly after becoming Premier in 1871, Blake offered a $5000 reward for Riel's arrest. In the short-term Riel left the country, but the controversy resurfaced in 1885 when Riel returned to lead the abortive rebellion of Métis and native people in Saskatchewan. This time Riel would be tried and hung for treason.

Riel's execution set off a chain reaction of events in both Ontario and Québec. To many *Québeçois* the Métis rebellion represented the struggle of all French speakers to protect their rights in the face of English 'aggression'. In a hugh demonstration in Montreal Wilfred Laurier, the future Prime Minister of Canada, roused the crowd with his claim that he too would have shouldered a rifle had he been on the Saskatchewan. Latter in the provincial election a wave of nationalist resentment swept Honoré Mercier to power.

Although elected in the aftermath of the Riel execution, a number of other concerns preoccupied Mercier. In particular he moved to solve the long festering problem of the Jesuit Estates which had been seized shortly after the British conquest in 1760. Although Mercier, like all previous governments, refused to return the Estates, he offered the Jesuits compensation. The income from the Estates themselves would continue to be used to finance education within the province. Mercier then named the Pope to arbitrate the distribution of moneys between the Catholic and Protestant school systems. The arbitration award itself was imminently reasonable and few in Québec felt any cause for complaint. Protestant extremist in Ontario, however, loudly condemned this papal intrusion into Canadian domestic politics.

Soon a new wave of protestant extremism swept Ontario. The Protestant Protective Association decided to run its own candidates in the 1886 provincial elections. Conservative leader E.R. Meredith, meanwhile, decided to make the continued existence of Catholic schools in the province his major campaign issue. Mowat remained true to his moderate principles of compromise and tolerance. No great friend of Catholicism, Mowat insisted that the rights of the minority guaranteed by the Confederation agreements must be respected.

Mowat won the 1886 election, although with a reduced majority. The Protestant Protective Association gave way to the even more militant and outspoken Equal Rights Association which soon added linguistic intolerance to its staple of religious intolerance. Yet, despite continued agitation, Mowat's victory seemed complete. Protestant extremism had not been eliminated, but it had clearly been relegated to the political periphery. Even the Conservative Party moved to improve its relations with the Catholic minority, particularly after James P. Whitney assumed the leadership of the provincial party during the 1890s.

The Manitoba Act, meanwhile, set off an equally important constitutional chain reaction that would have an even greater long-term impact on both Ontario and Canada as a whole. The boundary between Rupert's Land, as the Hudson's Bay Company called its domain, and Canada had already been a source of much dispute. The Manitoba Act now shattered Ontarians' initial assumption that the prairie region represented a western extension of their province. No sooner had the Manitoba Act been passed than the federal and provincial governments opened talks to resolve the issue of Ontario's northern and western boundary. Unable to reach an agreement, the two parties sent the question to a two person arbitration panel, but the arbitrators failed to agree and submitted separate reports. During the mid-1870s, the two governments agreed to submit the issue to a single arbitrator who then ruled in favour of Ontario. Unfortunately, a change in government in Ottawa led to a federal rejection of the principle of arbitration. This federal action set the stage for a final test of wills between the federal Conservative government of John A. Macdonald and the Ontario Liberal government of Oliver Mowat.

More was at stake than arcane interpretations of old treaties and constitutional documents. The Ontario boundary dispute was intensely partisan and involved as well fundamental issues of economic development and public finance. Timber licenses and royalties on mineral exploitation were a major source of provincial revenue. Under the terms of the British North America Act crown lands and natural resources fell to the provinces, but under the Manitoba Act these powers remained with the federal government. The area in dispute was mainly boreal forest with enormous timber and mineral potential. Should the territory fall within in Ontario then Ontario would control economic development and benefit from the revenue. Similarly, should the disputed territory lay within North-west Territories the federal government would control development and increase its revenue. Moreover, the establishment of municipal government, the granting of liquor licenses, and the appointment of judicial and other officials represented an important source of political patronage which could be used for partisan purposes. Little wonder that both sides saw in the boundary dispute a critical test. Oliver Mowat took a direct interest in the dispute and personally argued the provincial case in the court. When the Judicial Committee of the Privy Council finally ruled in favour of Ontario in 1884 over 50,000 people greeted Mowat on his triumphal return from London.

The Ontario boundary dispute helped rally those who believed that Confederation had created a largely decentralized federation. Mowat, as a 'Father of Confederation', had laboured during the Confederation debates to insure the autonomy of all provinces, not just Ontario. In addition to the boundary dispute, Mowat argued four other precedent setting cases before the Privy Council. He won all four thus establishing once and for all uncontested provincial jurisdiction over questions of property and civil rights. His successful prosecution of court cases also helped limit the federal power to disallow provincial legislation. Together these cases confirmed the older liberal view of a decentralized federalism in which each province was sovereign within its constitutional jurisdiction. John A. Macdonald's desire for a more centralized Canada received a severe set back in the 1880s at the hands of an aggressive Ontario ready to assert provincial rights at every opportunity.

B. *Economic Developments*

Much of the intensity of the provincial rights movement drew its strength from the continued belief that Ontario's economic interests were not being adequately represented by the central government. Such attitudes often stemmed from partisan prejudices rather than analysis of economic reality, yet there were a number of issues where it seemed as if Montreal's interest drove federal policy while Ontario's interests took a back seat. The long tussle over the continental railway to the Pacific coasts, for example, saw the contract awarded to the Canadian Pacific with its headquarters in Montreal. The route for the railway headed west from Montreal through northern Ontario thus by-passing all the major population and production centres in the province. South central Ontario, including the major manufacturing centres of Toronto and Hamilton, remained without direct rail connections to the Canadian west until the early twentieth century. This insured that whatever economic benefits came from western development rebounded to the advantage of Montreal.

Similarly, the federal policy to promote industrialization by import substitution adopted with the National Policy tariffs in 1879 brought mixed reviews in Ontario. The thrust of the National Policy was to promote east-west trade along the new railway system, and this clearly favoured Montreal which acted as the hub between the Canadian Pacific heading west and the Intercolonial, a nationally-owned line, heading east into the Maritime provinces. Maritime interests found protection not only in the publicly-funded and operated Intercolonial railway, but in the new tariffs on raw

materials, particularly coal, provided by the National Policy. Ontario industries, dependent upon coal and other raw material imports to supply its
growing manufacturing industries, now found themselves at a disadvantage
as their production costs increased sharply. Although industrial interests in
Ontario eventually emerged as the most vociferous defenders of the National
Policy's tariff structures, in the short-term most of the opposition to the
policy came from Ontario.

Protests over federal economic policies, however, were always muted.
Even if railway and tariff policy, as many believed favoured other provinces,
Ontarians found compensation in the province's relative wealth and economic strength compared. Relative prosperity, however, could not disguise
the general economic malaise. Ontario's economic growth from the early
1870s to the late 1890s disappointed all British North Americans who had
believed, perhaps too naively, in Canada's 'unlimited' economic potential.

In 1873 a major depression which affected the Atlantic economies in both
Europe and North America initiated a period of commodity price declines
which would continue for much of the rest of the century. Dependent on
export markets for its agricultural and the forest industries, the province
faced severe difficulties. Agriculture, aided by government programmes,
adapted reasonably and quickly to the new economic realities, but at a cost.

Oliver Mowat once commented that 'I could never do too much for
agriculture'. The provincial Department of Agriculture was easily the largest
government ministry. The Department spent thousands each year research-
ing the newest developments in agricultural technology and disseminating
the latest information to the province's farmers. The government established
a new Agricultural College at Guelph to supplement the efforts of numerous
Agricultural Societies throughout the province funded in part by provincial
grants. Ontario's progressive farmers, or at least those who could afford to
keep pace with technological innovation, responded to government prod-
ding. Farmers not only maintained their level of productivity but actually
increased the value of the their agricultural output through this period of
declining agricultural prices.

Productively was maintained through the rapid mechanization of production during the last decades of the century. Mechanization involved high
initial costs for capital equipment, but for those who could afford the initial
outlay the advantages of the economies of scale made possible by mechanized production generated cost savings which more than offset the price
squeeze which followed in the wake of the 1873 depression. The price
squeeze reinforced the trend toward mixed farming already apparent in the
1860s. Dairy farming, meanwhile, took on greater and greater importance.

Initially stimulated by growing urban demands, both milk and butter soon became major cash earners for farmers. Aided by the provincial government, Ontario farmers also began to develop additional export markets for butter which in turn provided a major catalyst for the development of a cheese industry exporting to both the United States and Great Britain. The rapid expansion of both butter and cheese exports insured that the value of agricultural exports from Ontario continued to grow despite the general economic stagnation of the last third of the century.

These economic gains had, however, come at a price. Mechanization required capital investments beyond the reach of many marginal farmers, particularly those in the eastern Ontario who occupied less productive land. The increasingly tight economic squeeze between rising cost and declining prices for production reduced profit margins. Although most could adapt, the new agricultural economics forced some farmers out of the industry. In addition, individual farmers became increasingly rich in capital, but poor in cash and thus unable to purchase land for all of their offspring. The net result of these various trends was both an absolute as well as a relative decline in the rural population despite the continued growth in productivity within the agricultural sector. By 1911, 152,000 fewer people lived in rural Ontario than in 1881 despite the general increase in province's total population. Although agriculture continued to prosper during the late nineteenth century, the industry was unable to provide sufficient employment for Ontario's growing population. The forest industry, the second pillar of the economy, suffered even greater losses following the depression of 1873.

Both the total output and the value-added of Ontario's manufacturing industries, meanwhile, grew at a very moderate rate during the 1870s and a somewhat more rapid rate in the 1880s. Between 1890 and 1900, however, output increased only to 0.7 per cent from $240 million to $242 million, while the value-added of manufacturing output actually declined by 7.5 per cent. During the last three decades of the century there was, then, insufficient growth to compensate for the general stagnation in the province's primary industries.

General assessments of both the provincial and the national economy during the last third of the nineteenth century emphasize the long-term stagnation. The economy grew during these years but growth failed to generate sufficient employment for the growing population. Following 1873, each year witnessed a net loss in population as emigration exceeded immigration. This reality, however, disguises as much as it illuminates. We have already seen how diversification and mechanization in agriculture led to rapid increases in the value of production despite rural depopulation. In manufacturing, too, there were critical economic developments. The last third of the century witnessed increasing concentration in population, in productive units and business organization. This concentration insured that when conditions in the world economy improved at the end of the century, Ontario was positioned to take maximum advantage of the new opportunities presented.

During the last third of the century Ontario's population became increasingly concentrated in fewer and fewer places. At the time of Confederation four of every five Ontarians lived in rural areas; by 1911 a majority lived in cities. This shift was not simple result of either rural depopulation or urban expansion. The largest cities grew at the most rapid rate while smaller towns and villages failed to grow at all. Ontario's demographic restructuring followed the process of industrial restructuring as manufacturing production became increasingly concentrated.

In 1871 Ontario's industrial landscape was characterized by a wide dispersal of very small 'manufacturing establishments', as the census called shops and factories. Saw milling and blacksmithing, Ontario's two largest aggregate employers of labour, proved typical. Only rarely did sawmills or blacksmith shops employ more than five workers. Of the twenty-five major manufacturing industries only eight employed on average more than 10 workers per establishment. Of these eight, only two employed more than 25 workers per establishment. Only in railway works and textiles did manufacturing establishments resemble large factory production rather than small shops.

Primary manufacturing industries, meanwhile, tend to locate near the source of raw materials while secondary manufacturing tends to locate near major markets. In 1871 most of Ontario's manufacturing industries were in primary production which further encouraged the wide dispersal of small shops and factories throughout the province. The high cost of marketing products in a province with poor roads and few branch railway lines in turn tended to inhibit large-scale secondary manufacturing. Inadequate transportation gave small producers an advantage within their small regional markets; this advantage slowly began to disappear, however, during the 1880s and 1890s.

The main trunk railways lines had been completed prior to Confederation. Now new branch lines began to criss-cross the province helping to integrate economic activities over wider areas. Access to larger provincial markets provided by improved transportation facilities created opportunities for aggressive entrepreneurs; it also ended the protection provided to small producers within local markets. Some companies managed to capitalize on expanded markets to achieve economies of scale which allowed them to further expand their operations.

Growth for some frequently meant bankruptcy for others as competition intensified sharply during the 1890s. In 1891 the census reported 32,500 manufacturing establishments in Ontario employing 166,326 people. In 1901 employment in manufacturing had increased only marginally to 166,619 people. These workers, however, were employed in only 6,500 manufacturing establishments. During the decade employment in manufacturing had increased by less than .2 per cent while the value-added in manufacturing declined by 7.5 per cent. The number of manufacturing enterprises, meanwhile, declined by fully 80 per cent during the decade. Often this produced deindustrialization of small town Ontario as larger and more competitive factories located primarily in the largest urban centres.

Transportation improvements gave manufacturers, already strategically located in major urban centres, a competitive advantage. The initial advantages of central location became further enhanced as urban growth provided a catalyst for investment in secondary manufacturing industries which tended to locate near primary consumer markets. These trends always favoured Toronto. An ever increasing proportion of total productive capacity as well as employment came to be centred in the city. In 1881 Toronto was a city of only 86,000, yet 30 per cent of all manufacturing workers in the province already lived in the city. By 1911 the population had mushroomed to 384,000 or over 15 per cent of the provincial total. Fully 70 per cent of all manufacturing workers in the province, meanwhile, lived in Toronto by that year.

The increasing concentration of population and the even greater concentration of manufacturing production in the largest urban centres was also accompanied by increasing concentration in business organizations and structures. Again, the 1890s were the critical decade. Agricultural implements, one of Ontario's most important manufacturing industries during the late nineteenth century, provides a classic example of the process.

Relatively prosperous farmers eager to achieve the economies of scale made possible through mechanization of their farm operations provided a strong market for manufacturing industries which produced the necessary capital inputs for agriculture. At Confederation inadequate infrastructure insured that the agricultural implements industry exhibited the typical Ontario pattern of wide geographic dispersal of small production units, often little more than upscale blacksmithing shops producing a wide assortment of goods. In 1881 Ontario's implements sector had 144 manufacturing establishments; most were small companies scattered in small towns. Small family-owned companies such as those founded by Hart Massey and Alanson

Harris dominated the industry. Massey had grown through aggressive marketing and by 1890 it was even exporting some of its production to Britain. Harris, on the other hand, was the innovator. Among the company's many developments was the open-ended binder which by 1890 provided state of the art machinery to Ontario farmers. Harris, however, did not have the extensive marketing network necessary to fully exploit the competitive advantage provided by his innovation; Massey did. In 1890 the two firms merged with the two families sharing control of the enlarged operations. One consequence of the merger was the decision to concentrate production in a new and much larger factory in Toronto.

The merger gave Massey-Harris an overwhelming competitive advantage in the Ontario market. The competition responded with mergers of their own, including Patterson Brothers and J.O. Wisner and Sons who merged their operations only six months after the Massey-Harris merger. It proved too little, too late. Within the year Massey-Harris took over Patterson-Wisner and consolidated production in Toronto and Brantford. Between 1892 and 1910 Massey-Harris continued to absorb smaller producers, including on occasion a number of American-based companies, and became Canada's largest producers of a wide range of agricultural implements exploiting extensive overseas as well as domestic markets. Within Canada Massey-Harris faced serious competition only from International Harvester, a company which was itself the product of a similar merger in the United States. Having established itself as the dominant American producer, International Harvester jumped the Canadian tariff wall by opening a branch plant in Hamilton.

Although a number of smaller companies continued to produce a limited range of products, the market had come to be dominated by only two corporations whose production was highly concentrated in the Toronto-Hamilton region. Ontario's other industrial sectors exhibited a similar pattern of merger and concentration during the 1890-1910 period. Most of Canada's major corporations emerged during these decades through mergers, as in the case of Massey-Harris and the Steel Company of Canada, through the establishment of branch plants, as in the case of International Harvester, or both as in the case of General Motors Corporation. Despite the absence of significant growth in manufacturing as measured by increases in GDP, output or value-added, many Companies had consolidated their holdings, concentrated their production, and achieved a competitive advantage through the economies of scale by the turn of the century. Many doubted, however, if such economic advances had produced corresponding social benefit for the population.

C. *Social Developments*

The rapid expansion of the factory system not only concentrated population in the larger cities, it altered the very nature of work. Often skilled artisans working in the small manufacturing shops which dotted Ontario's industrial landscape exerted considerable control over the labour process. The increasing division of labour together with the introduction of 'labour saving' machinery, however, began slowly to undermine the workshop of skilled artisans. Rural depopulation, meanwhile, forced greater numbers into the cities where job opportunities were often limited. Rural depopulation together with the de-skilling of artisans increased the pool of unskilled labourers—roughly 25 per cent of the urban population in 1860—originally attracted to the province by the unskilled jobs in canal and later railway construction.

The nature of the Canadian economy further exacerbated the social problems faced by waged workers. The long hard Canadian winter insured that many jobs were seasonal in nature. The construction industry which employed about 25 per cent of the urban work force shut down during the winter months. Employment in transportation picked up significantly during the late fall but declined precipitously during the long winter months. Employment in food canning was concentrated into a three month period at the end of the growing season. Even in industries such as agricultural implements production slowed during the late summer, fall and early winter. Canada, as Leonard Marsh observed in the 1930s, had an eight-month economy.

The distinguishing characteristic of the Canadian labour market, then, was insecurity and, increasingly, the loss of control over the labour process. Skilled workers reacted to slow the deterioration in labour conditions by organizing trade unions. This first wave of trade union agitation would culminate in the 1872 strike of Typographers in Toronto.

Those unions which existed in the 1860s and early 1870s were small local organizations, often locals of either British- or American-based international unions. The desire to reduce the work-day to nine hours led at the end of the 1860s to a decision within labour circles to attempt both legislative action as well as industrial action. Legislative lobbying in turn promoted the organization of labour councils in Hamilton, Ottawa and Toronto between 1869 and 1871. The Typographers, meanwhile, had demanded a nine-hour day, and a 54-hours week with no reduction in take-home pay, during their contract negotiations in both 1870 and again in 1871. In March 1872 the union went on strike to support their demands. The Toronto Labour Council as well as the Hamilton Nine-Hour League and other labour organizations through the province threw their support behind the Typographers, and the strike soon become a critical test of union strength. It also became a highly political strike.

The employers, led by George Brown, former Liberal leader and publisher of the *Globe,* the most important Liberal paper in the province, organized themselves into the Master Printers Association in an attempt to break the union. One dissenting paper, the *Leader,* granted the union's demand and continued to publish throughout the strike. The *Leader* was the major Conservative paper in Toronto, and never missed an opportunity to berate its partisan rival, George Brown, for his authoritarian and anti-labour activities. The federal Conservatives, meanwhile, were facing a tight election in 1872.

Soon the tension and the rhetoric escalated. George Brown and the Master Printers Association went to the courts and twelve strike leaders found themselves charged for conspiracy to restrain trade, a common law offense. Conservative Prime Minister John A. Macdonald immediately saw an opportunity to score political points against an old rival and introduced into the House of Commons the Trades Unions Act of 1872. Modelled on British legislation, this Act exempted collective bargaining from the common law and led to the immediate release of the strike leaders. The striking Typographers received a critical boost to their morale, and the union went on to win the strike and establish the nine-hour day in the printing industry. It proved a major, if somewhat pyrrhic, victory for organized labour in Ontario.

The Trade Union Act is frequently cited as labour's *magna carta,* but its significance proved far more symbolic than real. Although collective bargaining would never again be treated as conspiracy in restraint of trade, the Act assumed that most unions would incorporate under the civil law. Incorporation, however, made unions vulnerable to civil suites for damages; too often courts ruled that business lost as a result of strikes should be recoverable through civil action. Since the system of collective bargaining relied upon economic sanction—either the strike or lockout—the effect of such rulings would be to negate the process entirely. Unions, as a result, refused to incorporate. Many employers in turn rejected, in principle, collective bargaining of labour 'contracts' which could not be enforced in civil courts.

In addition to failing to grapple with the basic issue of liability, the Trade Unions Act also defined as criminal offences a number of standard union practices including picketing during a strike. Such criminal provisions were only rarely employed, but when employed had the effect of severely limiting the effectiveness of labour's only economic weapon, the strike. A symbolic victory, the Trades Unions Act did little to improve deteriorating industrial relations in the province.

Nor did the Typographer's achievement of the nine-hour day help other workers in other industries. Many unions demanded the same concession but with little success. The labour market contracted in 1873 as depression took hold. Unions faced a sharp decline in membership and municipal labour councils collapsed under the pressure of depression and unemployment. Not until the end of the decade, when the economy showed some signs of real growth, did the trade union movement begin to recover.

As the 1880s opened new unions of skilled workers re-appeared in most manufacturing industries. Heeding the call of the Toronto Trades and Labour Council various municipal labour councils organized a special convention in 1883 to discuss the need for a new national federation of labour. Although all agreed on the desirability of such organization, no effective action was taken until 1886 when a second convention put the Trades and Labour Congress (TLC) of Canada on a permanent footing. Limited initially to unions in Ontario, the TLC soon included most labour organizations throughout Canada.

A second organization, the Knights of Labour, burst upon the scene as well in 1886. Local branches of the Knights had been organized at the end of the 1860s but not until 1886 did the explosive growth of the Knights of Labour create a labour management crisis in the province. The Knights were unlike other trade unions in a number of critical ways. Trade unions of skilled workers played upon the pride and 'respectability' of craft, often arguing that the possession of skill was property and thus gave the skilled workers an equal right to participate in the decision-making process in a property-based capitalist economy. The Knights, by contrast, questioned capitalism as a system. Often their social critique of capitalism mixed romantic notions of a pre-capitalist world of independent commodity producers with more modern ideas anticipating both the cooperative and socialist movements of the twentieth century. The Knights rejected the emphasis on skill so central to the trade unions and often organized 'mixed locals' which included all workers within a community regardless of skill or industry. In the context of the 1880s the Knights posed a serious challenge to the emerging industrial order.

In the end Knights' rhetoric promised far more than these organizations could deliver. The ideology of the Knights was not only confused and inconsistent, it often stood at odds with organizational reality. Although the Knights called for the organization of women and other unskilled labourers, most locals included more traditional groups of skilled, male workers. Although Knights' rhetoric condemned strike action, Knights' locals became involved in numerous work stoppages. Those strikes produced few concrete results and led in turn to disillusionment among members. Renewed economic recession in 1887 did the rest. The Knights disappeared as suddenly as they had appeared on the Ontario labour scene. By 1889 there was only a skeleton organization with a corporal's guard for membership.

The sudden burst of labour militancy in 1886, meanwhile, caused middle-class Ontario to sit up and take notice. Newspaper editorialist worried aloud about the 'class question' and the meaning of the new labour militancy. John A. Macdonald also took notice; the federal government created the Royal Commission on the Relations of Labour and Capital to investigate the social problems of the emerging industrial order.

Labour organizations had complained for years about deteriorating social conditions which accompanied industrialization. Although most influential Ontarians considered such complaints exaggerations, the Royal Commission would prove otherwise. After three years of exhaustive investigations the weight of the evidence proved overwhelming. The Royal Commission, despite the conservatism of its methodology, discovered that average wages were well below the poverty line. It reported as well on the excessively long hours which were the norm for most workers, particularly for the growing number of women and children taking manufacturing jobs. The Commission uncovered extensive evidence on the overcrowding of workrooms, the absence of proper ventilation, and the failure of employers to consider the health and safety of employees. Most Ontarians were both shocked and genuinely surprised by the appalling conditions now laid bare by the three-year federal investigation.

By the time the Royal Commission delivered its final report in 1889 there was no longer much debate about the seriousness of the social problems faced by industrial workers. No such agreement existed on what to do to meet this social crisis. One fundamental problem proved to be Canadian federalism. The Royal Commission had been appointed by and reported to federal government. Labour, as Ontario had always insisted, was a civil matter and therefore within the provincial jurisdiction. It remained for the province to act.

Mowat had been as sensitive as Macdonald to the rising cacophony of labour agitation. While Macdonald organized his Royal Commission, Mowat introduced two specific legislative reforms to try to address labour's concerns. The Employers' Liability Act of 1886 attempted to regularize and improve the system by which injured workers could recover some compensation from employers, but this only marginally improved the lot of injured workers. The new legislation consolidated existing practice into a single statute without altering that practice. Although historians sometimes portray the 1886 legislation as Ontario, first 'compensation' law, the Employers Liability Act remained simply a reworked liability statute.

Mowat's second legislative initiative in 1886 also provided few concrete improvements. The Ontario Factories Act restricted the employment of children, limited the hours of labour for both women and children, and made a number of pronouncements designed to improve working conditions in factories and shops. Although a critical legislation precedent, the standards set in this first Factories Act often simply confirmed existing inadequacies. For example, boys under 12—later raised to 14—and girls under 14 could no longer work in province's factories and shops, but very few children this young held jobs. Those few industries which did employ large numbers of children under 14 received exemptions. The food canning industry, to cite the obvious case, employed large numbers of young children for relatively short periods of time; the law specifically exempted the industry during July, August and September. Similarly, women and children under 18 could not be required to work longer than 10 hours per day or 60 hours per week. This did little as the 10 hour-day and the 60 hour-week were standard in most industries by the mid-1880s. Employers, moreover, could request an exemption so long as such exemptions totalled no more than two months during any 12 month period.

Enforcing regulations governing working conditions presented additional difficulties. The Act provided a long series of requirements that, among other things, factories be kept clean, that workrooms be ventilated, that sanitary facilities be provided, and that safety guards be installed on all dangerous machinery. Such clauses were vague and provided no standard against which conditions could be measured. Sanitary facilities could mean a single outdoor privy to serve the needs of several hundred employees. No one had authority under the Act to determine which machines were dangerous, what safety devices needed to be installed, the amount of room space per worker in workrooms, or the amount of air circulation. With depressing regularity factory inspectors investigated and reported on inadequate conditions but in the end the Act proved unenforceable.

Nor is it clear that the province ever intended to enforce the Factories Act; the government appointed only three inspectors for the whole province. Although this number increased to 10 by the first decade of the twentieth century, the Factory Inspection Branch remained understaffed and underfunded. Inspectors, meanwhile, believed that more could be gained through 'education' and public reporting than through prosecutions. Despite the ever-increasing volume of their reports not a single employer was ever prosecuted for a violation of the Factories Act during the nineteenth or early twentieth century. Even in cases where inspectors found underage children working parents rather than employers would be prosecuted. The government had established its right to regulate the conditions of labour with the Factories Acts, but then the government chose not to exercise that right to achieve real reform.

There were few reform programmes to deal with other social problems associated with rapid industrial and urban growth. The dominant liberal ideology prevalent in the province reinforced *laissez faire* attitudes; governments and most citizens continued to believe that social programmes to deal with poverty must be private rather than the public concerns. Poor relief, for example, had traditionally been a public responsibility, but the new municipal legislation passed after Confederation made such programmes optional. No municipality in Ontario enacted a poor relief programme.

Social programmes were private activities usually controlled by various religious denominations. The division of the Protestant community into a wide variety of sects insured that control would be far more indirect than in the Catholic community. Among Protestants, ministers, wardens, deacons and others from several denominations served together on Boards of Directors of various charitable organizations. Religious notions as a result dominated the evolution of social programmes in the province. Two notions in particular impeded the evolution of social policy.

Christians in late nineteenth century Ontario commonly believed that poverty was a punishment for sin. Such beliefs found support among social Darwinists who insisted that hierarchal social structures and economic inequality were part of the natural order of things. Thomas Conant, a well-known and respected Ontario publicist, asked rhetorically in 1898 "Is it wise to foster the growth of the class of persons whose filth and foul disease are the result of laziness and their own vice?"[1] So long as most Ontarians believed that welfare rewarded those whose immorality was the primary cause of their plight there would be few reform initiatives.

Ontario's Christians, However, faced a serious dilemma since most also believed firmly that charity was a Christian duty. One did not want to reward sin, yet many were in need through no fault of their own. Resolving this dilemma explains much about social reform and welfare in the nineteenth century. Those who controlled social welfare institutions always distinguished between the 'deserving' and the 'undeserving' poor. Opponents of public programmes argued that public officials were less able than religious leaders to properly distinguish between the deserving and the undeserving.

[1]Thomas Conant, *Upper Canada Sketches.* Toronto, 1898, p. 195.

Since most of the poor were undeserving, there were few programmes and institutions. Those programmes which did exist were aimed at the 'deserving' poor, most frequently children and women, who could be most easily identified as 'victims'. In this way social welfare ideology reinforced highly discriminatory ideas about 'women's role' and 'men's role' which in turn reinforced other deeply rooted forms of inequality.

The provincial government recognized some responsibility in 1874 with the Charities Aid Act which provided public subsidies to private charities. Yet as late as 1907 the Toronto City Council rejected labour's demands for public programmes to deal with high unemployment with the by now standard argument that:

> There seems to be a mistaken idea abroad that for some reason it is the duty of the Corporation [of the City of Toronto] to provide work for those desiring it, and that the Corporation is responsible for the care of those who are destitute. The City Council is constituted for totally different purposes.... It cannot take the place of private benevolence, nor relieve citizens of their private duties and obligations.[2]

What social programmes and institutions did exist, and they are few, remained private.

The turn of the century, meanwhile, would bring fundamental change. Rapid economic growth combined with accelerated urban growth placed enormous strains on the social fabric on the province. As social conditions deteriorated older notions of *laissez faire* could no longer contain demands for reform. The problems had become so serious they could no longer be ignored.

PART 3: THE MAKING OF INDUSTRIAL ONTARIO, 1896-1945

A. *Economic Developments*

The turn of the century witnessed the start of a remarkable period in the economic history of Ontario which in turn produced a number of fundamental changes. By 1945 Canada emerged as a modern industrial state—a member of the 'Group of Seven' most industrialized economies in the world. As Canada's most heavily industrialized province, Ontario provided the economic engine for the nation.

The last decades of the nineteenth century provided a strong base from which to build; favourable changes in the world economy—the end of economic stagnation in the Atlantic community, the rapid increase in capital

---

[2]Toronto, *Minutes of the Proceedings of the Council of the Corporation of the City of Toronto, 1908,* Appendix A. Toronto, 1909, p. 1596.

accumulation within the western economy, and technological changes which provided incentives for investment of that capital in Canada—created strong economic growth during the first half of the twentieth century despite the major set backs during the 1930s. The traditional sectors of Ontario's economy—agriculture, forestry, and primary manufacturing—all expanded. In addition, new industries—mining and secondary manufacturing—were added to the mix.

The opening of the burgeoning mining sector in 'new' Ontario proved particularly important. Large and productive mineral deposits within the expansive land mass of precambrian rock known as the Canadian Shield were first located and then exploited producing not only a boon in exports but substantial growth of primary manufacturing of non-ferrous metals. The development of the sulphite process in paper-making, meanwhile, breathed new life into Ontario's forest industries which had stagnated since the beginning of the 1873 depression. Although the emergence of a newsprint and other paper-products industries were more significant in Quebec, Ontario too contributed to the boon in Canadian exports. Neither mining nor paper-making, however, proved as significant as the development of the hydroelectric industry.

Ontario's industrialization had always suffered as a result of the province's lack of coal or other sources of cheap energy. Manufacturers imported all of their coal and most other raw materials from American suppliers. The introduction of high protective duties on industrial inputs in 1878 sharply raised the costs of production which was only partially offset by the equally sharp increase in tariffs of the province's industrial output. Ontario needed a cheap source of domestic energy if it was to emerge as a major manufacturing centre. The development of high tension wires which allowed hydroelectricity to be transported cheaply and efficiently from generating stations to industrial cities provided that energy.

Ontarians always referred to hydroelectricity as 'white coal'. Not only did hydroelectricity free Ontario manufacturers from their dependence upon expensive imported energy, it was clear and non-polluting. So important was this new resource to the economic health of the province that many believed it must be publicly controlled. Socialists, urban progressives and Tory businessmen all demanded that the province take control of the province's generating and distribution systems. This debate ended with the province assuming control of the industry. In 1908 the Conservative government of James P. Whitney established Ontario Hydro as a crown corporation.

A boom in the Atlantic economy which stimulated Canadian exports to Europe and North America, the opening of the mining frontier in Northern

Ontario, the growth of the newsprint and paper-making industry, and then hydroelectricity explain most, but not all, of the new economic activity of the early decades of this century. Between 1896 and 1914 immigration increased sharply, the population expanded rapidly, the prairies were settled, and the wheat economy emerged. These developments insured a sustained growth in the domestic market for consumer goods, particularly consumer durables. Ontario's industrial economy was well suited to take advantage of such developments.

Manufacturing industries of all kinds expanded rapidly after the turn of the century leading to an equally impressive expansion in employment. The clothing industry was the largest employer of labour in Toronto and Hamilton during the first decade, but fell to second place during the 1910s. Secondary iron and steel industries quickly assumed the dominant position within the industrial sector; by 1911 iron and steel industries employed more workers than any other sector in all Ontario cities. Increased mechanization and the adoption of labour-saving machinery, meanwhile, led to a stabilization of the work force despite continued growth in the volume and value of production. This extraordinary growth was interrupted in 1913 with the onset of a major depression, but war in Europe soon ended this temporary economic slump. Between 1916 and 1918 the Imperial Munitions Board awarded over $1 billion in contracts for war material in Canada, much of it in Ontario. Such extensive investments even revitalized the industrial base in many small Ontario towns which had remained economically dormant at the turn of the century. Peace in 1919 brought a delayed economic slump in 1921 which, although acute, proved short-lived. But the 1920s the Ontario economy entered another period of sustained growth dominated this time by the emergence of durable good industries.

Between 1896 and 1921 prosperity intensified the demographic trends which were already so pronounced. Production continued to be concentrated primarily in south central Ontario, particularly in Toronto and the surrounding region—the 'golden horseshoe' as Ontarians began to call the arc of territory extending from Hamilton to the west and Oshawa to the east. Concentration of production in turn helped concentrate population; industrial jobs attracted migrants both from abroad and from the surrounding countryside. In the process south-central Ontario also became Canada's single largest consumer market which acted like a magnet for yet more investment.

In the 1920s two industries, electrical appliances and automobiles, played a disproportionate role in generating continued growth in Ontario. Both were classic examples of consumer durables industries which located near primary markets and which came to be concentrated as a consequence in south-central Ontario. Of the two, the automobile industry was the most important because of its extraordinary capacity to generate jobs, not only directly in the manufacture of vehicles but also in primary steel production, in parts production, and in the servicing of vehicles. These were, moreover, good jobs. Automobile production, more than most secondary manufacturing industries, added high value to products which in turn sustained relatively high wages. By the end of the decade automobile production had clearly emerged as Ontario's single most important industry.

Three decades of sustained economic growth ended abruptly in 1929. The expansion of the domestic consumer market during the first three decades of this century had resulted more from population growth than from any increase in the disposable income of individual families. This insured that between 1900 and 1929 the expansion of the consumer market had not kept pace with the more pronounced expansion in the capacity to produce goods. Economic dislocations on both sides of the North Atlantic, meanwhile, led to a sharp decline in the volume and value of Canada's exports. The collapse of export markets and the subsequent decline in employment in export driven industries further restricted the consumer market. The economic ripples generated by the decline in export prices soon became a series of tidal waves as they reverberated through the economy. As consumer spending, already too limited to absorb increased production, declined, manufacturers faced growing inventories of unsold products. They, in turn, cut production and laid off additional manufacturing workers. This produced another contraction in consumer spending leading to another round of production cut-backs and sometimes bankruptcies.

Ontario fared better than most Canadian provinces. The province enjoyed the enormous advantage of having Canada's most diversified economy which helped soften somewhat the economic blows. This remained, however, the single most severe economic reversal ever faced by Ontarians. In terms of the magnitude of the economic disaster and its duration, previous depressions in 1873, 1893, 1913 or 1921 paled in comparison. By 1933, four years after it began, the Great Depression finally bottomed out with fully 25 per cent of Ontario's industrial work force unemployed.

Although the economy slowly began to recover after 1933, growth brought little relief from the economic gloom of the decade. The number of business failures and personal bankruptcies fell and investment slowly began to revive. Commodity prices stabilized and then increased marginally. Although corporate profits recovered, unemployed declined only slightly and wages recovered not at all. Between 1933 and 1937 General Motors Corporation of Canada, for example, reported five consecutive years of record-breaking profits. The corporation also cut wages paid to its employees in each of these years. Despite some measurable growth and high corporate profits, everyone understood only too well that the Great Depression had not yet ended, it had only eased.

A decade after it began, the outbreak of war in Europe, finally ended the depression. As in 1914, the influx of investment capital which accompanied the transition to wartime production reinvigorated the sluggish economy and immediately generated new employment opportunities. By 1943 Ontario came closer to the ideal of full employment than at any other time in its history. Even more importantly new technologies, particularly in chemical and metal industries, insured a geometric explosion in productivity. Although the federal government imposed wage and price controls in 1941, incomes increased as sharply as productivity. By 1945 Ontario entered a new era of affluence with the birth of consumer society.

B. *Social Development*

The consumer society of the second half of the twentieth century stood in sharp contrast to the Ontario of the first half of the century. Although the half century between 1896 and 1945 witnessed, despite the economic set backs of the 1930s, unprecedented economic expansion, there had been no corresponding increase in the standard of living of most Ontarians. Poverty had been the lot of large numbers of Ontarians at the turn of the century; little had changed by the eve the second European war.

The 1889 Report of the Royal Commission on the Relations of Labour and Capital demonstrated that average wages paid to working people fell well below the requirements of a family. The Royal Commission and later the Department of Labour made a number of efforts to establish a minimum budget to maintain 'health and decency' for a family of five yet the reality remained unaltered: very few manual workers earned enough to meet this minimum. Only among skilled workers in the running trades on the railways—locomotive engineers, conductors, firemen and brakemen—did incomes exceed the government's estimated minimum.

Not only were wages well below the poverty line, real incomes declined during the first decades of the century, particularly after 1917 when war-time inflation accelerated. By 1920-21 average wages for adult male wage earners represented less than 75 per cent of what was required to meet the costs of the Department of Labour's 'health and decency' budget. Real incomes recovered their pre-war level during the first half of the 1920s before stabilizing. During the depression wages declined, but so too did the cost of living. For those who kept their jobs throughout the 1930s real incomes actually rose slightly, but with unemployment hitting 25 per cent by 1933 few were so lucky. The standard of living as measured by real wages had, at best, improved only marginally during these four decades. Real wages, however, do not tell the whole story for there had been other improvements in the standard of living for most Ontarians during these years.

Although available statistical data do not allow precise calculations, family incomes probably increased more—if only marginally more—than wages. This resulted from a number of developments including the reduction of hours of work and changes in the structure of the labour force which shifted a large portion of the work force from lower paying jobs to higher paying jobs.

At the turn of the century the standard work week was 10 hours per day, six days per week. Slowly the hours of labour for a minority of workers in a limited number of industries began to decline to 10 hours per day with a 'half-holiday' on Saturday. Then during the war the trend accelerated dramatically. Employers, encouraged by government studies, factory inspectors and trade unionists, came to recognize that industrial fatigue seriously inhibited productivity. A number of experiments with reduced hours were conducted, the most famous at the large Massey-Harris factory in Toronto. Massey-Harris found that shorter hours reduced fatigue and improved moral which in turn improved productivity. Between 1917 and 1919 the company reduced the work-week in their Toronto factory from 60 to 54 and then to 48 hours without any decline in production.

Massey-Harris' experiments with shorter hours proved a classic example of 'welfare capitalism'; reform, employers discovered, was profitable. By 1920 the standard work-week in virtually all industries had been reduced to 48, and in a few industries it had been reduced further to 44 hours. Real wages may not have improved but workers spend far less time in the factory to earn those wages. Moreover, a little overtime increased incomes as workers were paid time-and-a-half. Welfare capitalism produced other imporvement as well.

Factory inspectors had been arguing for years that investments in improved working conditions—better safety measures, improved ventilation, less crowded workrooms—would pay dividends in the form of higher productivity. Although few employers listen prior to 1914, the war brought new reform voices including the Canadian Manufacturers Association. Major employers led the way introducing new programmes designed to promote efficiency and productivity. The reform drive addressed the traditional issues of overcrowding, ventilation and safety, as well as more innovative programme such as lunchrooms, midday meals at cost, and pension plans designed to tie workers to their jobs and thus reduce the cost of labour turnover. Although much remained to be done, the appalling working conditions which existed at the turn of the century no longer prevailed in the province's factories and workshops.

Reform was not limited to the workplace. The first two decades of the century witnessed the emergence of a wide variety of reform impulses; the most dramatic achievements came in public health. The population of Ontario cities had grown far more rapidly than the increase in housing stock or the expansion of basic urban services. The result was an alarming growth of urban slums with their overcrowded housing conditions and low public health standards. As late as 1909 Toronto's infant mortality rate, always the single most sensitive measure of general health standards, stood at over 179.7 per 1000 live births. By comparison, Rochester New York, a city of comparable size and economic structure on the opposite side of Lake Ontario, had an infant mortality rate only half that in Toronto.

Although possessing the power to intervene in the case of communicable disease, public intervention invariably came as a result of a crisis rather than in anticipation of potential difficulties. The reactive posture of both the provincial and local Boards of Health proved inadequate to deal with medical problems which often were the direct result of the failure to provide modern urban services to mushrooming industrial neighbourhoods. Toronto, for example, dumped raw untreated sewage directly into the harbour then pumped this same water back into the city's water system without treatment of any kind.

Reform demands finally produced results particularly after 1908. In that year Toronto undertook the reconstruction of its water and sewage systems. The water intake was moved, and the water itself was first filtered and then chlorinated before delivery to citizens. The city moved its sewage outfall four miles down the shore of Lake Ontario and then built new sedimentation tanks to provide primary treatment. By 1910 the city no longer poisoned its drinking water with its own sewage outflow.

Both the provincial and local Boards of Health adopted a new posture in 1910-11. An increasing number of medical reformers campaigned for new programmes based upon principles of preventive medicine. Reformers insisted that Boards of Health must intervene before crises erupted in order to prevent the outbreak of disease. As reform voices became stronger the movement triumphed when advocates of preventive medicine became Chief Medical Health Officers both at the Provincial Board of Health and at the Toronto Board of Health. Both convinced governments to commit increasing public resources to protecting the public health. In 1911 alone Toronto's

City Council doubled the budget of the Local Board of Health.

Aggressive new programmes followed. The most sweeping of these dealt sanitation and with the relationship between the city's milk supply and infant mortality. In 1913 the city ordered new and more rigorous standards for its milk inspection programmes and ordered that only pasteurized milk could be sold. Over the next five years the infant mortality rate fell dramatically. In the same year a new aggressive campaign of inspection of the housing stock began. The Board condemned increasingly large numbers of slum houses as 'unfit for habitation'. More importantly, the Local Board decided that outdoor privies would be eliminated. Such a programme required an extensive public works programme to insure that sewage and water facilities would be available to every house in the city. By 1920 the Local Board had succeeded in eliminating all open privies within Toronto's city limits.

Toronto's Local Board of Health was the province's largest and most progressive. Its efforts received the enthusiastic support of the provincial Board of Health which in turn encouraged other municipalities to follow Toronto's lead. Public health reform thus gathered momentum, and by 1920 public health standards, as measured by infant mortality, mortality and morbidity rates, were as good as anywhere in North America.

Reform in public health represented aggressive state intervention. In other areas of social policy, however, the government maintained the *laissez faire* inheritance of the nineteenth century. What reforms were achieved came as a result of private effort.

During the nineteenth century religious beliefs commonly stressed the perceived link between personal immorality and poverty; the notion that poverty was the 'wages of sin' limited charity to the deserving poor. At the turn of the century new religious thinkers reversed this cause/effect relationship. Reformers began to argue that low wages, unemployment, overcrowded housing conditions, poor public health and other evidence of the deteriorating social conditions in Ontario's burgeoning industrial cities bred immorality as surely as these conditions bred disease. Religious reformers came to believe that improving social conditions was a prerequisite for improving public morality. The 'Social Gospel', as the movement came to call itself, quickly developed a new definition of missionary activity. Henceforth religious 'missions' would expand those service which later formed the basis of Ontario's social welfare system.

Social Gospel volunteers helped expand the limited poor relief institutions such as the Houses of Industry which dispensed financial assistance to indigent families. They also created new facilities with the Young Men's and Young Women's Christian Association (YMCA/ YWCA) as well as the various University Settlements built in all major cities. These institutions provided recreation activities for neighbourhood children. They provided relatively cheap meals for the neighbourhood poor. They provided as well a wide variety of programmes and classes to help the poor do more with less and to help women, children and men acquire new skills which might translate into better jobs.

The various efforts of social gospellers increased the number of welfare agencies and expanded their activities. These efforts touched thousands of lives, yet much remained to be done. All of these initiatives remained private, although most received small subsidies from governments. The state refused to expand public programmes, and reformers preferred their own private efforts to public programmes. By the war, however, interest in private reform initiative began to wane. Increasingly social reformers came to focus their efforts on one of the two specific objectives: prohibition and women's suffrage.

There had never been much debate that Ontarians drank large quantities of alcohol or that alcohol was linked to crime and other social problems. Every crossroads in the province had a tavern; most did a booming business. Most urban arrests were for crimes related directly or indirectly to bars, tavern and drinking establishments. Among the poor, meagre wages were often spent on drink leaving even less to cover basic necessities. There was far less consensus on the responsibility of the state for public morality.

During the last half of the nineteenth century a temperance movement gathered strength in all areas of the province, particularly among farm families. Temperance advocates demanded at least moderation if not voluntary abstinence. Toward the end of the century zealots came to demand that the state intervene to prohibit the manufacture, sale, and consumption of alcohol. The Liberal government responded to public pressure in 1889 and organized a provincial plebescite followed by legislation instituting a local option on the liquor question. Although a number of municipalities banned the sale of alcoholic beverages within their boundaries, the local option satisfied no one.

Prohibition appealed to the basic ideology of social gospellers as few other issues could. Drunkenness was an issue of public morality; social gospellers were concerned particularly with moral redemption, with achieving a 'New Jerusalem'. Prohibitionists argued that alcohol was a contributor to poverty and other social problems; the outstanding characteristic of the social gospel was its belief that slums and poverty provided the necessary preconditions which bread immorality. Prohibitionists promised this simple act would eliminate public drunkenness, would reduce crime, would ease poverty and would improve social conditions of the poor. Social gospellers quickly became the backbone of the prohibitionist movement. Prohibition, in turn, nearly took over the social gospel movement as this single issue received more and more attention. With the beginning of the war prohibition dominated the reform agenda. It became a dominant issue in provincial elections as well.

The feminist movement underwent a similar process prior to the war. A paternalist society, Ontario recognized few rights for women. During the early Victorian period the situation grew worse. The right to vote in municipal elections, for example, was tied to the ownership of property; new post-confederation legislation took that right away from female owners of property. Although most women had little choice but to acquiesce to discriminatory legislation, slowly a feminist movement emerged to challenge patriarchy. The movement initially addressed a range of issues including the right of a woman to attend university, to gain access to professional training, and eventually the right to practise their profession. Some progress, if slow and grudgingly conceded, was made, particularly in medicine, yet little could be expected so long as women's voices were politically silenced by the denial of the basic democratic right to vote. With good reason the attention of the women's movement came to focus on this most basic of political rights.

Although suffragist concentrated their initial arguments for the vote on civil and political rights, activists were frequently involved in the temperance, later prohibitionist, movement and other social gospel reform efforts. The Women's Christian Temperance Union (WCTU), for example, became one of the largest and best organized lobbyist for the suffrage cause. This organizational overlap of suffrage, prohibitionist, and social gospel groups insured an ideological intermingling as well. 'Maternal feminists', as historians refer to this particular construction of feminism, suggested that granting women the right to vote would help make the political process more caring, more maternal. This in turn would make the state more receptive to reform ideas and more willing to initiate reform programmes. The participation of suffragists in the prohibition and other reform movements reinforced such beliefs. The social gospel, prohibition, and suffrage movements, working together, achieved their greatest influence and success during the immediately following the war. Women exercised their right to vote in Ontario's affairs for the first time in October 1919 when the province held both a referendum on prohibition and a provincial election on the same day. Prohibition won a majority and a new 'Progressive' party won the election. Ontario, it appeared had veered onto a new political path.

C. *Political Developments*

In 1896 Oliver Mowat had accepted an invitation to join the new Liberal cabinet in Ottawa under Prime Minister Wilfred Laurier. He left behind a Liberal Party already in serious decline. Industrialization and urbanization seemed to favour the Conservatives who had traditionally enjoyed the support of urban Ontarians, particularly the urban middle-class. Despite this disadvantage the Liberals survived a very close election in 1902, but then complaints of scandal and corruption undermined their credibility. James P. Whitney, the Conservative leader, focused his criticisms on a variety of charges which, if taken in isolation, were relatively minor. Such complaints, however, began to have a cumulative effect. In the 1905 provincial election Whitney focused all of his attention on the issue of government corruption and Conservative integrity and won an overwhelming victory reducing the once powerful provincial Liberals to a corporal's guard in the legislature. Whitney would win three more elections before his death in 1914. He left behind a still powerful Conservative government in control of the legislature.

The Conservative government, openly pro-business and pro-development, proved highly innovative and at times progressive. Whitney showed particular concern for the expansion of mining activities in the north and always portrayed the Conservatives as the party of 'New Ontario'. Similarly, Whitney supported the various municipalities in the province concerned that private power monopolies might come to dominate the critically important hydroelectric industry. In 1908 the government acted decisively with the creation of Ontario Hydro; public ownership solidified Whitney's reputation as a progressive. That reputation would be further enhanced in 1914 when, working closely with employers, he responded to trade union demands and enacted a new Workmen's Compensation Act. Unlike Mowat's 1886 legislation, Whitney went far beyond employer's liability to provide automatic compensation to injured workers through a government administrative fund controlled by a public board. Less progressive was Whitney's reworking of the older conflict over separate schools into a renewed educational confrontation over language.

When Whitney became party leader he worked hard to improve relations with the Catholic community, relations which had been strained by the party's traditional opposition to separate schools. Whitney insured that a number of high-profile Catholic candidates were recruited for the 1905 election and later included in the cabinet.

During the last years of the nineteenth century, meanwhile, large numbers of French Canadians had been settling in the Ottawa Valley and in parts of northern Ontario. In areas where they were a majority, Franco-Ontarians transformed local separate schools into bi-lingual separate schools. The provincial Ministry of Education investigated these schools in 1912 and judged them to be substandard, particularly in term of teacher training and English-language instruction. Rather than working with the Franco-Ontarian community to improve the standards of French-language instruction, the Whitney government introduced Regulation 17 prohibiting the use of French in Ontario's schools. The Franco-Ontarian community vigorously protested and in some School Boards in the Ottawa region defied the provincial regulation. Regulation 17 and similar provincial legislation in the western Canada contributed to a marked deterioration in French-English relations which culminated in the conscription crisis during the war.

Whitney's overwhelming electoral victories, no doubt, resulted more from his identification with programmes which promoted economic growth than his staunch opposition to French language instruction in Ontario's schools. The disarray of the provincial Liberal Party also contributed substantially to Conservative dominance. The Liberals proved unable to find a viable leader or a viable issue. Between 1905 and 1914 internal party squabbling twice led to the resignation of the party leader in the middle of a provincial election. Then in 1914 the Liberals campaigned as if prohibition were the only issue. The demise of the once powerful Liberal machine came in 1917 when N.W. Rowell, the provincial Liberal leader, resigned in order to join the 'coalition' government in Ottawa headed by Conservative Prime Minister Robert Borden. Those who opposed the Conservative government would have to find another political option to express their views.

Following Whitney's death in 1914 the premiership fell to William Hearst, the most prominent cabinet minister from northern Ontario. Hearst, an ardent imperialist, wholeheartedly supported the war effort and deferred to the federal government which assumed the lead in organizing Canada's domestic war effort following the passage of the War Measures Act. Although they never translated into significant opposition to the war, federal policies generated popular resentment in many parts of Canada. Once peace returned in late 1918, pent up wartime frustration and opposition to federal programmes rebounded on the provincial Conservatives. In October 1919 the Hearst government fell to an unlikely combinations of agrarian progressives and urban labour organizations. Some newspaper editorialist commented that Ontario was experiencing a political 'revolution' at the hands of discontented voters.

Political protest, already apparent before the war, intensified under the pressures of the war economy. Farmers' had long faced difficult economic times as the costs of production rose far faster than the prices received for their products. Farm leaders blamed government policies such as protective tariffs which kept costs high and farm incomes low. Both traditional political parties, farmer leaders argued, represented the interests of urban business. With jurisdiction over banking, railways and tariffs, federal policies in particular promoted, in the eyes of farmers, high interest rates, high freight rates, and expensive manufactured goods. This perception gained currency in 1917 when Conservative Prime Minister Robert Borden named Ontario's Liberal Party leader, Newton W. Rowell, to the cabinet in a new coalition Union government in Ottawa. Farmers needed an alternative party to represent agrarian interests. The United Farmers of Ontario (UFO), the largest farm organization in the province, called for direct intervention in electoral politics. In 1919 the UFO nominated its own candidates and won 44 seats in the provincial legislature. The UFO suddenly became Ontario's largest party.

Industrial workers too saw their standard of living deteriorate during the war as costs increased far more rapidly than wages. Labour leaders too argued that both traditional parties represented the interest of urban businessmen. Like the UFO labour named its own candidates and elected most of them in 1919. Although they ran far fewer candidates and elected only eleven members, the Independent Labour Party (ILP) won huge majorities in virtually every city in the province outside Toronto. Inside Toronto factional squabbling had divided the labour vote and severely limited the party's electoral chances.

With 55 seats between them, the UFO and the ILP formed a 'Progressive' coalition government under E.C. Drury. The 'political revolution' which brought the Progressives to power, however, provoked far less change than might have been expected. The Drury government never coalesced into an effective administration. The Progressives proved rudderless and, in the end, never articulated a clear vision nor a consistent policy. The problems involved conflicts within both the UFO and the ILP as well as difficulties in maintaining relations between these organizations.

After electing so many of its members to the legislature, the UFO immediately questioned the wisdom of a coalition with labour. At the first convention held after the election, the UFO condemned Drury's plans to merge the two parliamentary caucuses into a single Progressive party. Similarly the trade unions, although accepting the necessity of working in cooperation with the UFO, also condemned Drury's plans. Labour became even more disillusioned when Drury refused to concede the 8-hour day to striking workers at Ontario Hydro. Farm and labour leaders were not the only Ontarians who became quickly disillusioned with Drury's Progressives.

Social reformers had pinned their hopes on the success of prohibition. The elimination of alcohol would lead, reformers promised, to improved public morality and an end to other social ills. Nothing of the kind happened. Enforcement was always difficult and inconsistent as too many Ontarians defied the law. By the end of the 1920s Ontario abandoned its efforts at prohibition and opted instead to government control of the sale of alcoholic beverages. Female suffrage achieved far more but proved no less disillusioning.

The right to vote was a basic right finally granted to the province's women. Suffragists had, however, promised more than the acquisition of the vote; the vote would lead, most believed, to improvements in the social and economic conditions for women and others. Voting women, however, continued to face systemic discrimination, particularly in the labour market. Women workers remained ghettoized in a limited number of low wage and low status occupations. Women were frequently the last hired and the first fired, and were paid substantially less than their male co-workers even in sectors where they worked beside men doing the same job. The lack of improvement in the labour force frustrated reform effort on the social and political issues of concern to women.

Although the social reform and feminist movements lost much of their earlier vigour, neither entirely disappeared. The same could not be said for the Progressive government of E.C. Drury. The Progressives were already weakened by continuing conflicts between, on the one hand, the labour and farmer members of the coalition and the disagreements between, on the other hand, the coalition and both the UFO and the trade unions. By 1923 it was clear that Ontario's Farmer-Labour government had lost both momentum and credibility. It surprised no one when in 1923 the Conservative party under G. Howard Ferguson was swept back into power.

Ontario's 'Big Blue Machine', as the Conservative party organization was known continued to deliver electoral majorities until finally overtaken by the depression during the early 1930s. In 1934 a disgruntled electorate, tired of four years of depression and unemployment, turned to the Liberals under Mitchell Hepburn. Hepburn portrayed himself as a social reformer, a friend of labour and the poor. The labour movement in particular soon came to regard the premier as an aggressive reactionary.

D. *The Rise of Organized Labour*

Trade unions had been in retreat for a decade when the depression began. The rise of mass production industries after the turn of the century undermined the economic position of skilled workers; trade unions organized on the basis of craft skills found themselves stripped of their bargaining strength, unable to defend the economic interests of their members. Industrial unions attracted some mass-production workers, but threatened craft unionists. Throughout the 1910s conflicts which erupted between craft and industrial unions often paralleled other struggles between socialists and liberal unionists. Increasing militancy during the war favoured socialists and industrial unionists whose influence increased as the labour movement expanded. New organizing drives and demands for collective bargaining rights culminated in 1919 when virtually all industrial sectors in Ontario's major manufacturing centres were swept up in a wave of labour unrest and strikes action. Few of those strikes, however, resulted in collective agreements.

In general the new initiatives to organize industrial unions failed to achieve concrete results while the new political initiatives, as we have seen, produced short-term success but long-term frustration. In the aftermath of the 1919 upheavals in labour-management relations most of the emerging industrial unions disappeared. The growth of mass-production industries then accelerated further restricting the field for the older craft unions. By 1923 organized labour seemed to be in full retreat. Membership declined sharply, most industrial unions collapsed, and the craft unions adopted a conservative stance desperately trying to defend the interests of a shrinking membership.

The depression threatened the very survival of trade unionism in Ontario. With unemployment hitting 25 per cent of the work force trade unions desperately worked to keep losses to a minimum. There would be little advantage resisting wage cuts too vigorously if the alternative was unemployment. Similarly unions already hard pressed to protect what they had saw little value expending limited resources on new organization drives which would likely to fail. Hard times thus reinforced the conservativism of the existing craft unions.

The depression also encouraged the growth of more radical movements ranging from the moderate socialists who coalesced under the banner of the Cooperative Commonwealth Federation (CCF) to the more radical communists. Both socialists and communists looked to the trade union movement as the primary organization to defend the social and economic interests of industrial workers. Both deprecated the conservatism of the existing craft unions, and both called for a new organization drive among mass production workers. CCFers and Communists joined forces with advocates of industrial unionism inside the labour movement to force major changes in organized labour in North America.

The Roosevelt administration in the United States provided a catalyst for the rebirth of the labour movement when it introduced new legislation which required all employers to bargain collectively with unions. Shortly after Roosevelt's New Deal was announced, major strikes at Autolight in Cleveland, among teamsters in Minneapolis and among Longshoremen on the Pacific coast signalled the rising tide of militancy among industrial workers in North America. The craft dominated American Federation of Labour (AFL) reacted by expelling its militant industrial unions which then organized themselves into the Congress of Industrial Organizations (CIO) in 1935. Led by John L. Lewis of the United Mine Workers, the new CIO launched major organization drives in the steel, automobile, rubber and electric industries. By 1937 the CIO had made significant gains and had clearly established itself as a major force in labour-management relations.

Canadian unionists had a strong attachment to international unionism. Indeed, the majority of unions in Ontario were local branches of AFL unions headquartered in the United States. The sudden success of the CIO in the United States immediately spilled across the border as Canadian workers began to organize their own CIO unions. The irony would be that these were not CIO organizing drives in the usual sense of the term. The American based unions sent no organizers across the border nor did they pay the costs of organizing efforts. Rather, Canadian unionists did all the work and paid all the bills. Often Ontario unionists used the CIO name without even consulting CIO headquarters in the United States.

After 1934 economic conditions improved somewhat, yet social conditions remained bleak. Many companies, particularly large multinational corporations, began reporting increased profits only to reduce wages still further. By 1936-37 it was clear that the struggle to establish industrial unionism and collective bargaining would be joined in Ontario, Canada's most industrialized province and centre of most of the nation's mass production industries. The most famous battle occurred at the General Motors plant in Oshawa.

In the 1920s GM had bought out the McLaughlin Carriage Works and then expanded the facilities in Oshawa, making it the largest GM assembly plant in Ontario. In early 1937 GM Canada simultaneously announced a fifth year of record profits, a fifth wage cut in the last five years, and new medical examinations which seemed to threaten the jobs of older workers. Led by Charles Millard the workers downed their tools and a spontaneous strike swept through the factory. The local organization then telephoned the headquarters of the United Automobile Workers (UAW) in Detroit and asked for assistance. The UAW dispatched Hugh Thompson to advise the local Oshawa union.

Thompson's initial advise was to return to work. He did not believe much could be achieved by disorganized, spontaneous strike action. Local unionists needed time to plan their strategy and coordinate their efforts. The Oshawa union organized itself as Local 222 of the UAW, established a negotiating committee, formulated more concrete demands and notified GM of their intention to negotiate a collective agreement. GM in the United States had already fought a long and bitter strike with the UAW at its plants in Flint, Michigan which ended in union recognition and collective bargaining. GM Canada seemed prepared to follow suit when suddenly Ontario's Liberal Premier Mitch Hepburn intervened. Hepburn opposed the establishment of any CIO union in his province. With the Premier on the side of management talks broke down, and in April 1937 4000 GM workers in Oshawa downed their tools.

Hepburn's actions surprised many. In the provincial election he had portrayed himself as the friend of labour, and he had appointed a number of pro-union liberals to his cabinet. He had, however, a number of close personal friends among the province's mining entrepreneurs who in turn were major financial backers of the Liberal Party in general and Mitch Hepburn in particular. Ontario's mining magnates feared CIO organizing drives in the north. Hepburn seems to have come to the conclusion that labour difficulties in the province's mining industries might be avoided if the CIO could be prevented from establishing a foothold in the auto industry. Hepburn took the lead in GM's confrontation with the UAW.

The Oshawa strike also led to a squabble between the provincial and federal wings of the Liberal Party. Hepburn, against the advice of the mayor of Oshawa, dispatched a detachment of provincial police to Oshawa. This action provoked the resignation of two cabinet ministers: the now former Minister of Labour, David Croll, commented that he preferred to walk with the workers than ride with General Motors. Hepburn then demanded the federal government send an RCMP unit to strike-bound Oshawa. Prime Minister W.L. Mackenzie King refused. Although members of the same political party, Hepburn and King had never been close. They now became embattled rivals within the party.

The strike in Oshawa, meanwhile, proceeded without incident while negotiations shifted to Toronto and the offices of the provincial Premier. Both the union and GM wanted a settlement; both compromised on Hepburn's modified terms. The union gained recognition, collective bargaining, a wage increase and other benefits. GM got its assembly plants reopened. Hepburn got a symbolic victory: neither the UAW nor the CIO was mentioned by name in the contract. Hepburn could claim that he had prevented the CIO from entering Ontario; everyone else recognized that the UAW-CIO was the union of choice of GM employees. The next contract, negotiated without a strike, made this explicit.

Other breakthroughs in collective bargaining proved more difficult to obtain. The partial economic recovery of the mid-1930s ended in 1937 as economic stagnation again gripped the province. Organizing drives in Ontario's other mass production industries faltered until the outbreak of war brought economic recovery. By 1940 the labour movement was well placed to launch a new organizing drive. This time there would be no turning back.

As in the first war, the federal government took the lead in organizing Canada's domestic war efforts. Mackenzie King had become Liberal leader in 1919; he was as a result very sensitive to the political disaster which befell the party between 1917 and 1919. In his view the two critical threats to stability were conscription which could undermine French-English unity and inflation which could undermine everyone's standard of living and might, as in 1918-19, lead to widespread social unrest. King dedicated his government to avoiding the mistakes of first war; his government paid particular attention to managing successfully the conscription controversy and managing the economy.

King was convinced that the difficulties of regional economic imbalances and inflation could only be avoided through the careful management of economic resources. He assembled an impressive team of hard-nosed managers in the cabinet. Led by industry minister C.D. Howe government procurement of war material preceded smoothly with few hitches. When inflation threatened to get out of hand in 1940-41 the government imposed wage and price controls. Imports insured that some inflation was inevitable, but the government regulators proved flexible and allowed prices to rise in a controlled fashion. Similarly government regulators allowed wages to rise either to predepression levels or to industry standards. Wages were also allowed to keep pace with inflation through the awarding of cost of living bonuses. Indeed, wages rose faster than prices during the war as a result of both government policy and a marked increase in productivity.

Labour unions pressed their advantages organizing mass production workers during these years. When a wave of strikes over union recognition threatened to disrupt the war-time production, King again intervened. A special War-time Labour Board investigation recommended in later 1943 that the government introduce compulsory collective bargaining; the King government then passed appropriate legislation in February 1944. Collective bargaining led to further, substantial gains for industrial workers.

In sharp contrast to the first war, real incomes and standards of living improved markedly during the war. In 1939 seven of every 10 urban families lived below the poverty line. When peace returned in 1945 the number had dropped to only one family in four. The age of affluence had begun.

PART 4: AFFLUENT ONTARIO, 1945-90: THE CONSUMING SOCIETY

A. *Economic Development, 1945-80*

The post-war period witnessed an extraordinary economic boom in the Western world. Various *pundits* talked of the birth of a 'consumer society' a new 'age of affluence'. By the end of the war the majority of Ontario families earned incomes high enough to cover all of the basics of life; they spent the surplus on an impressive range of durable and semi-durable consumer goods and services. This spending generated yet more growth. The numbers tell the story.

Between 1940 and 1950 personal disposable income in Canada increased by an impressive 64 per cent. Once launched, the inertia of growth carried the economy forward as personal income increased by 50 per cent between 1950 and 1960 and then by another 76 per cent between 1960 and 1975. Ontario, as Canada's largest province, shared in this extraordinary boom as growth in per capita personal increase acceleration between the 1950s and the 1970s (see Table 1). By 1971-76 the rate of growth in per capita disposable income was nearly as great as during the 1940s.

Spending on consumer durables fuelled this extraordinary growth. Personal expenditures on durable commodities increased by 93 per cent between 1945 and 1960. During the same period there was a 64 per cent increase in expenditures on non-durable commodities. Although the rate of growth slowed somewhat between 1960 and 1975, durables continued to expand more rapidly than non-durables: 79 per cent and 70 per cent respectively. Such patterns of personal expenditures benefitted Ontario disproportionately.

TABLE 1

Increase in Per Capita Personal Income, Ontario, 1941-76

Year	Percentage Increase	
1941-51	53	per cent
1951-56	18	
1956-61	12	
1961-66	27	
1966-71	33	
1971-76	46	

By far the most important of these consumer durables was the automobile, the assembly of which was concentrated in the province. Even more than before the war the auto industry played the key economic and industrial role by generating high paying jobs and sustaining the consumer economy. The federal government stepped in to protect Ontario's critical automobile industries by negotiating the Auto-pact Agreement with the United States in 1965. This agreement opened the entire North American market to Canadian production. As the industry rationalized its production on a continental scale, specific content regulations protected Canada's share of production. The Auto-pact helped maintain growth in the auto industry which in turn helped maintain growth in other industrial sectors.

In the 1970s the rate of growth slowed somewhat, although prosperity was maintained. The oil crisis following the Yom Kipper War in 1973 increased fuel costs which in turn helped open the North American market to smaller, more fuel efficient automobile imports from Europe and Japan. American producers were slow to respond and began losing market share to the imports. This slowdown in industrial growth, however, was taken up by the growth of service industries which became the dominant creator of new jobs in the 1970s and 1980s. Increasingly, however, the growth of public service industries—health, education, and welfare—increased government expenditures without a corresponding increase in revenues. When technological change, the growth of off-shore manufacturing, and the adoption of free trade in 1988 brought a severe economic recession at the beginning of the 1990s, all governments found themselves facing major budgetary deficits resulting from collapsing revenues. By 1990 the Ontario economy remained large and prosperous. Yet, it was equally clear that four decades of rapid expansion were over. Four decades of sustained prosperity sustained as well the Conservative party, Ontario's 'Big Blue Machine'.

B. *Politics and the Challenge from the Left*

Mitch Hepburn's anti-Labour policies during the late 1930s encouraged the emergence of a socialist alternative in Ontario. The remnants of the old labour and farmer's parties of the early 1920s had begun to re-emerge during the depression both in Ontario and in the west. By 1935 the Canadian Commonwealth Federation (CCF) began to make inroads in Saskatchewan while in Ontario activists threw themselves into the CIO organization drives in mass production industries. Although Hepburn initially won re-election in 1937 on the basis of his anti-labour policies, the war led to substantial growth in labour organizations and collective bargaining. By 1941 the various CIO unions came together to form a new national federation, the

Canadian Congress of Labour (CCL), which then endorsed the CCF as the party of organized labour. The CCF drew support away from the Liberals and made Ontario a genuine three-party system.

The new Conservative leader, George Drew, responded to the perceived swing to the left by assuming the new appellation of 'Progressive Conservative' and announcing a 'Twenty-two Point Programme' of reform. In the 1943 provincial election the Liberals were reduced to third place, and Drew's Progressive-Conservatives managed to win only four more seats than the CCF. Drew formed a precarious minority government. In the spring of 1945 Drew's Progressive-Conservatives lost a vote in the Legislative Assembly and immediately called a new provincial election. Drew emphasized the 'Progressive' in his Progressive-Conservative party and successfully played to fears of 'state socialism' of the CCF. The CCF won only eight seats, and Drew had his majority.

Drew's major concerns in 1945 revolved around the difficult problem of demobilization and the transition to a peace-time economy. During the war the King government in Ottawa had invoked the War Measures Act. Under the Act's authority King expanded the federal jurisdiction over all forms of taxation while pressurising the provinces to share other jurisdictions. Many observers hoped that the shift in power would prove permanent.

During the depression some of the essential economic and fiscal weaknesses of the Canadian federal system had been laid bare. The federal government had far greater financial resources, but the provinces had jurisdiction in labour and social policies. This mismatch of money and jurisdiction severely hampered the government's capacity to respond to the economic crisis; unemployment insurance, for example, required a constitutional amendment to enact. During the final years of the 1930s a federal Royal Commission on Dominion-Provincial relations became a forum for centralists who advocated an expansion of the federal jurisdiction at the expense of the provinces. The war which erupted just as the Royal Commission delivered its report provided the opportunity for centralists to carry their ideas into practice. Although centralists hoped there would be no turning back, Quebec and western provinces clearly opposed the new centralizing tendencies. At the end of the war all eyes turned to Ontario. Canadians did not have to wait long to hear George Drew's answer.

The King government called a Conference on Reconstruction in 1945 and 1946 to deal with the demobilization of Canada's war-time economy. Federal civil servants, the strongest centralists in the country, did much to prepare the ground for the federal government's initial position that various war-time financial arrangements be retained during the post-war period.

Although by March 1945 Drew had not yet met with the Quebec government, he had already been approached by a number of other provincial governments wishing to explore the possibility of a common provincial position. Despite these discussions the Conference opened in August with no clear united front among the provinces, although it was clear most provincial governments, particularly Quebec, would like to argue in favour of a return to the constitutional *status-quo ante-bellum*.

Despite the assumption that Quebec would assume the lead, it was the federal Prime Minister and the Ontario Premier who staked out their respective ground. Mackenzie King opened the conference with a call for a new 'co-operative' effort led by the federal government. Drew insisted that 'powerful argument could still be made in favour of the decentralized governmental system'.[3] As the conference proceeded Drew reasserted Ontario's traditional insistence on provincial autonomy. In the process Ontario stymied the wartime drift toward a more centralized Canada. Drew transformed the conference agenda of tax transfers and social policy into a fight for the older federalism of Oliver Mowat.

Although Ontario would later adjust its position on federal-provincial cost-sharing programmes, this initial victory against a centralizing Ottawa helped consolidate Drew's hold on power in the province. Not only did he establish the tone for post-war federal-provincial relations, he set the tone for three decades of Tory government. Drew's Conservative successors, Leslie Frost, John P. Robarts, and William Davis, followed the formula Drew had initiated. Progressive Conservative governments between 1945 and 1985 were 'progressive' but cautious. They avoided intervention in the economy and preferred to allow the market to assert itself. They 'managed' economic and financial policies with a view to making Ontario attractive for private investment. They recognized the need for new social programmes to protect more effectively Ontarians from the vagaries of the market, but they always feared going too far. Ontario's handling of the language issue illustrates these tendencies.

C. *New Social Realities*

Post-war Québec had witnessed sweeping social and economic changes which in 1960 found political expression in the Quiet Revolution ushered in by the Liberal electoral victory under Jean Lesage. A new assertive, secular French Canadian elite associated with the Liberals intended to use the

[3] National Archives of Canada, MG 32 B 5, Brook Claxton Papers, vol. 142, file "Reconstruction 1", Dominion Provincial Conference 1945, *Proceedings*, 9, cited in Marc J. Gotlieb, "George Drew and the Dominion-Provincial Conference on Reconstruction of 1945-6", *Canadian Historical Review*, LXVI, 1985, 33.

provincial government to achieve 'Maitres chez nous'. They intended as well to insure that Québec's place within Canada topped the federal agenda as well. Advocates of Bilingualism and Biculturalism insisted that the federal government must open itself to the full participation of both 'founding peoples'. Foremost on the agenda was the creation of a bilingual federal bureaucracy to guarantee French-language services in all federal institutions.

John Robarts and Jean Lesage were personal friends. This relationship insured a sympathetic response in Ontario to many of Quebec's demands including linguistic equality in the federal system. In August 1968 Robarts made a decisive gesture when he announced in a speech to *l'Association canadienne des educateurs de langue française,* that Ontario would establish and fund new French-language secondary schools, both public and separate, in Ontario to bridge the gap between French-language primary and university education. Robarts' successor, William Davis continued the process by slowly expanding French-language services throughout the province. Yet, despite these important gestures, the Conservatives held back on the recognition of official Bilingualism for Ontario.

Franco-Ontarians recognized the importance of French-language secondary schools, yet they continued to complain about the failure of the Conservative government to respond adequately to their needs. Progress may have been dramatic when viewed from the government benches at Queen's Park, but when viewed from the perspective of the Franco-Ontarian minority Tory efforts were piecemeal and grudgingly given. The Tories generally supported the Royal Commission on Bilingualism and Biculturalism and subsequently Prime Minister Pierre Elliott Trudeau's Official Languages Act (1969). Yet, Robarts, Davis and later David Peterson, continued to argue that official bilingualism in their province would provoke an English backlash and put other reforms at risk. Yet despite the failure to enact official bilingualism, French-language services provided by all Ontario government agencies expanded substantially.

In other areas of social policy progress, if slow and piecemeal, proved equally substantial. After the war Ontario had opted for a welfare state. A decade and a half of depression and war between 1930 and 1945 illustrated the inadequacy of the old structures of publicly subsidized private charity to deal with the concrete problems of a modern industrial society. In the short term, the federal government took the lead with the development of new programmes such as unemployment insurance in 1940 and mother's allowances in 1945. Welfare, however, lay within provincial jurisdiction. The provinces moved to replace the older system of private relief by a system of publicly-controlled and administered welfare agencies. Provincial governments provided most of the funds through transfer payments to municipalities which administered programmes. Government concerns about fiscal conservatism, meanwhile, insured chronic underfunding of the welfare system. Ontario's Progressive Conservative government resisted, but could not block, the expansion of the welfare system demanded by a majority of voters. The obvious case in point was medicare.

After the Saskatchewan government implemented Canada's first medicare programme in 1961-62, the federal government of Lester B. Pearson committed itself to medicare at a federal-provincial conference in July 1965. Federal legislation in 1966 and 1968 provided federal funds to cover 50 per cent of the costs of provincial health programmes. Ontario's Progressive-Conservatives, however, were slow to take advantage of this federal cost sharing programme. Not until 1972 did the Davis government create the Ontario Health Insurance Plan (OHIP). Now all Ontario residents paid small regular premiums for medical insurance against virtually all hospital and doctor bills up to a minimum standard of care. In 1989 the Liberal government of David Peterson replaced individual premiums with a new employers tax.

Under OHIP the level of care and the insurance coverage for most people expanded rapidly. So too did doctor's incomes as they were now guaranteed payment on a fee for service basis. OHIP, together with rapid advances in high-technology medicine, also increased government expenditures exponentially. By the late 1980s the provincial government's attempts to hold the line on costs led to a breakdown in negotiations over fee schedules and a short doctor's strike. The economic recession of the 1990s which undermined provincial revenues and led to a mushrooming provincial deficit. Public debt has now made medicare reform a dominant concern.

A similar story unfolded in education. Prosperity and the changing nature of Ontario's economy insured that the Progressive Conservatives turned their attention to the province's schools and universities. During the heady days of economic prosperity of the 1960s the system not only expanded rapidly but become increasingly diverse. Local Boards built new primary and secondary schools and diversified programmes within those schools. By the 1980s many local public school boards offered a variety of programmes including French emersion and alternative education. The Separate School Boards expanded just as rapidly often with both French and English sections. In addition, separate high schools began receiving provincial funds during the 1980s while French-language Boards emerged within the public school system. Linguistically and culturally mixed communities, such as metropolitan Ottawa, had no less than six local school boards by 1990.

The expansion of the primary and secondary system was minor compared to the extraordinary expansion in the province's university system. The Robarts government committed itself to providing access to University for all residents no matter where they lived. Old institutions, such as the University of Toronto, expanded rapidly. Private institutions, such as the University of Ottawa, became publicly funded. New institutions such as Laurentian and Lakehead were created to serve northern Ontario. Supervising it all was Education Minister William Davis who in 1971 succeeded Robarts as Premier.

The rapid expansion of the system, as in the case of medicare and welfare, proved a fiscal burden, and during the 1970s the government moved to contain costs. Although transfer payments to the universities continued to increase in absolute terms, per capita funding for the system fell dramatically. By 1980 the system was seriously underfunded relative to other provinces.

The fiscal pressures on the universities and other social services eased somewhat during the last years of the 1980s. A booming economy insured that social services, particularly the medical system, could expand without large government deficits, prosperity, however, ended in 1990. The economic recessions, tied as it was to the new Canadian-American Free-Trade Agreement, insured that Ontario would be hit harder than other provinces. As manufacturing jobs disappeared by the thousands, welfare roles rose just as fast. Revenue collapsed even more rapidly when the federal conservative government of Brian Mulroney froze federal transfer payments to Ontario.

The New Democratic Government of Bob Rae convinced itself that the public debt was growing out of control; the government reacted to the revenue crisis by introducing massive cut in public spending. Among those cuts was a new 'Social Contract' programme designed to reduce compensation paid to public sector workers by $2 billion. The story of the early 1990s quickly became the cycle of lay-offs, fiscal crisis, budget cuts and more lay-offs. The irony of a 'labour/socialist' government cutting social programmes put in place by Progressive-Conservative governments was not lost on many voters. By the 1990s labour had lost its preeminent position within the NDP as new social concerns headed the party's reform agenda.

D. *The Roots of Social and Political Change in Contemporary Ontario*

The success of the suffrage movement during the first war led, as we have seen, to a period of relative quiescence for the women's movement in the 1920s and 1930s. Although always present, women activists often subordinated their particular interests to other broader concerns. The CCF and the labour movement, for example, attracted many women who toiled tirelessly for the cause. Although often frustrated in their efforts to achieve recognition within these organizations, these women activists pushed hard to achieve specific objectives such a equal pay for women workers or greater representation for women within the governing structures of trade union locals or riding associations within the party. Their voices could not be ignored forever. Substantial change came slowly; World War II marked a turning point.

The war witnessed a dramatic increase in the participation of women in the work force. Unlike the First World War which also witnessed a sharp increase in participation, large numbers of married women with children worked for wages in the 1940s. To accommodate working mothers the government launched new child care and other programmes. At the end of the war, however, the government dismantled many of these support programmes and actively encouraged married women to abandon their jobs in favour demobilized soldiers. Although many individual women did leave their paid jobs in favour of the more traditional unpaid labour of housekeeper, the participation rate fell only slightly and never returned to the pre-war level. The increase in female participation then accelerated in the 1950s and 1960s. In 1941 less than 1 in 5 workers in the paid labour force was a women. By 1961 it was more than 1 in 3.

There had also been a marked change in the jobs held by women. Prior to the war women had been rigidly ghettoized in a small number of occupations; the war saw women assuming jobs traditionally held exclusively by men. Although the pattern of rigidly gendered occupations returned in the late 1940s, the range of occupations available to women had, nonetheless, expanded greatly. By 1971 with women occupying one in every three jobs, changes in the labour market came far more rapidly. Not only did the participation rate continue to increase rapidly, women demanded access to occupations still reserved for men.

The feminists movement regained much of its lost vitality in the 1970s. Activists succeeded in forcing new issues such as day care and abortion onto the political agenda. Feminists demanded greater recognition of their rights and an end to all forms of systemic and individual discrimination which blocked their path to social, political and economic advancement.

By the 1980s increasingly greater numbers of women could be found occupying positions of power and influence, and from these positions they helped accelerate the pace of change. As an example the Ontario government has passed a series of acts and regulations forcing both the private and the public sector employers to achieve both employment and pay equity. Some of these initiatives have fallen short of their stated objectives, and much remains to be done, particularly on issues such as violence against women. The current NDP government, meanwhile, has waffled on many labour issues but continues to pursue an active reform programme to insure gender equality in the province. This same government has shown itself to be as concerned with racism as it has been with sexism.

Ontario has always been a destination for large numbers of immigrants. During the nineteenth century those immigrants came primarily from the United Kingdom. Although the United Kingdom continued to provide 40 per cent of all new immigrants during the first decades of this century, large numbers of people began to arrive from continental Europe. The two groups, British and non-British European immigrants, distributed themselves very differently among Canada's various regions. Non-British European Immigrants settled in the main in northern Ontario and in the prairie west; many British immigrants came to the industrial cities and towns of central Canada, particularly cities like Toronto and Hamilton. As late 1921, for example, immigrants accounted for fully 40 per cent of Toronto's burgeoning population; three out of every four of those immigrants came from the United Kingdom.

The sharp rise in immigration before the war, then, reinforced the essentially British flavour of Ontario culture. Ontario continued to be both a province of immigrants and overwhelmingly Anglo-Protestant in its ethnic mix. The exception to the provincial rule were the sparsely populated mining and timber regions in the north. For Canada's largest and most populous province, substantial demographic change would not come until after World War II.

After the war immigration to Canada increased sharply from only 22,000 arrivals in 1945 to 282,000 in 1957. Although immigrant arrivals fell to 93,000 by 1963, the late 1960s witnessed more than 150,000 new arrivals annually. As was the case during the first decades of the century, these immigrants were a highly diverse group, most arriving from continental Europe. This flood of new immigrants fundamentally altered the demographic complexion of Canada, most particularly the relative decline in the percentage of the population which was ethnically British. Historically the majority, British Canadians declined from 55 per cent of Canada's population in 1921 to only 45 per cent in 1971.

By 1971 one in four Canadians was neither British nor French. Unlike the early twentieth century wave of immigration, post-war arrivals from continental Europe and elsewhere settled in the largest numbers in the industrial cities of southern Ontario. Toronto in particular became the destination of choice for increasingly large numbers of immigrants.

During the 1970s and 1980s the number of immigrant arrivals remained high, and their cultural backgrounds became even more diverse. Large numbers of people arrived from developing nations in Asia—China, India, Sri Lanka, Pakistan and Vietnam—the Caribbean, and the Middle East. As with other post-war immigrants, many settled in the large industrial cities of southern Ontario. Change has been most visible and most dramatic in Toronto. Long dominated by English, Irish and other British ethnic groups with their reputation for social conservativism and reserve, Toronto has become one of North America's most cosmopolitan cities.

Ontario's capital long enjoyed the reputation of 'Toronto the Good'. The social ambience of the city was much like that of the province as a whole. Toronto, and Ontario, were conservative, safe and staid. As with most stereotypes, numerous contradictions challenged this image. Toronto was home to the original Group of Seven who made an indelible mark on Canadian painting. It was home as well to world class musicians of whom Glenn Gould was but the most famous. As Canada's publishing capital, Toronto attracted a vibrant literary community which made its mark on the city, on the nation, and on the larger world beyond. Yet despite the long litany of literary and artistic achievements of its citizens, the enduring image of the city and the province was not its artistic production but its continuing ban on Sunday shopping and its highly restrictive liquor laws. Nearly all visitors could agree that the city as well as the province in general was both safe and clean, and this no doubt provided a major tourist attraction. But Toronto and the rest of Ontario was also homogeneous and dull.

Not any more. Toronto has become truly cosmopolitan. Throughout the city one can find a bewildering array of ethnic shops, groceries and restaurants. In Many neighbourhoods one confronts a babel of languages and customs. Each community presents its own face to the city in celebrations ranging from Chinese New Year to Caribbean carnival. The social fabric of Ontario has been, as a result, enriched by this diverse cultural mix. New social tensions, unfortunately, have also appeared.

Ontario has witnessed the emergence of new nativist and racist groups which, if isolated, remain vocal and visible. Perhaps more significantly, an undercurrent of racism within the province has made life difficult for many members of Ontario's multicultural community. Most of Ontario's social and economic institutions from Boards of Directors of major corporations, to labour unions, to local police forces continue to be dominated by the older English stock which long dominated the province. Increasing pressure is now being mounted to insure that such institutions present a multicultural face to an increasingly multicultural community.

Although there certainly have been increased racial tensions in contemporary Ontario, traditions of accommodation, tolerance, and compromise remain as strong as ever. All three political parties remain committed to various multicultural programmes as well as to a strong human rights tribunal able to investigate abuses and impose remedial action. In the aftermath of recent racial rioting in Toronto, the government was quick to appoint Stephen Lewis, Canada's former ambassador to the United Nations, to investigate racism in the province. The current NDP government has been equally quick to endorse his various recommendations.

Perhaps even more importantly, a recent public opinion poll showed that a large majority of Ontarians were concerned about a perceived increase in racism in the province and wanted their government to intervene with programmes to counter such developments. Accommodation and compromise remain at the core of Ontario's political culture.

Conclusion

A quarter-century ago A.R.M. Lower, one of the province's outstanding historians, posed an odd question in *Ontario History* and provided an even odder answer. Lower asked: 'Ontario, does it exist?'[4] He answered 'no'. Lower was neither the first nor the last to wonder if Ontario was anything more than 'a space on the map, …a legal entity administered from Toronto'. When Peter Oliver, one of only a handful of committed 'Ontario' historians, penned a 1975 essay entitled 'On being an Ontarian', he too concluded that, in effect, it remained 'Yours to Discover'.[5] In Canada there is no lack of evidence pointing to strong and potent regional loyalties in the Maritimes, in Québec and in the West, but Ontario, as Lower observed, is different. No one doubts Ontario is a region of sorts, yet its regionalism, as Oliver laments, has been neither investigated nor analyzed. No doubt Lower's question and Oliver's lament result primarily from the tendency among Ontarians to see their province not as a region, but as the Canadian heartland. Not without reason Ontario's many historians usually write 'Canadian' history and often fail to distinguish between the story of their province and that of their nation.

Since 1867 Ontario has been the most populous, economically the most powerful, and always the most influential province in the Canadian federation. The immigrants who settled the land, and built its roads, bridges, railways, factories, towns and cities, also constructed political institutions which, although modified to suit changing circumstances, have endured.

[4]A.R.M. Lower, 'Ontario—Does It Exist?', *Ontario History*, LX, 1968, 65-69.
[5]'Your to Discover' is the provincial motto which appears on automobile license plates.

Perhaps more importantly than the institutions themselves, Ontarians created a political culture which was essentially conservative in orientation, yet contained many liberal elements. Socially and politically conservative, Ontarians place a high value on social order and political compromise.

The province's conservative heritage insured a clear recognition of the importance of the community as well as the individual. This has allowed various governments to remain committed to open markets and private initiative while also pursuing interventionist programmes in the economic and eventually the social life of the province. In the nineteenth and early twentieth centuries state activism most frequently occurred in the province's economy. The province jealously guarded the principle of public ownership of resources while allowing those resources to be developed by individual entrepreneurs and private corporations upon payment of royalties. Those royalties supported other government programmes designed to promote economic development. On occasion the public interest would require public ownership and operation of particular industries; Ontario Hydro remains the outstanding example of such enterprises. State intervention, however, was kept to a minimum; as the economy developed and became increasingly strong, intervention declined. During recent decades state intervention has occurred more frequently in social legislation. The outstanding examples of these trends are the rise of the welfare state after the war and the more recent creation of a publicly-funded medicare system. Although state intervention has been less dramatic and less extensive than in many Western European nations, it remains far more significant than in the United States.

An even more striking characteristic of Ontario's political culture is its respect for and tolerance of social diversity. Throughout its history Ontario has witnessed any number of conflicts between its largely English Protestant majority and its various minorities. There were long and often bitter struggles over Catholic schools, equally bitter confrontations over the linguistic rights of Franco-Ontarians, and, more recently, painful episodes of conflict between the province's dominant English culture and various visible minorities, South Asians and African-Canadians in particular. Yet through it all there has been an equally strong tendency to seek compromise and promote tolerance. Extremist political movement has always been more vocal than effective. The ruling political party of the day has more often than not moved to recognize and protect—if sometimes grudgingly—the political, religious, linguistic and cultural rights of minorities. Ontario's political culture has served it well as recent immigration creates a richer cultural and social mosaic within the province.

Ontario now stands at crossroads of sorts with its powerful economy severely shaken by the recent recession. Long reliant on large manufacturing industries, the province has witnessed severe losses of industrial jobs. Although the economy has recently shown signs of recovery, it has been a jobless recovery. No doubt Ontarians will adapt to changing world conditions, but adaptation has proven more painful than expected. For the first time in a half century a fiscal crisis threatens Ontario's extensive social 'safety net'. Ontario's challenge during the rest of the 1990s will be to find the ways to adapt to a post-industrial world and the means to maintain those social programmes which all Ontarians have come to value so highly. Ontario, no doubt, will remain the economic engine driving the Canadian economy; as such Ontario's challenge will be Canada's challenge.

BIBLIOGRAPHY

General

Bishop, Olga et al., eds. *Bibliography of Ontario History, 1867-1976: Cultural, Economic, Political, Social,* 2 vols. Toronto: University of Toronto Press, 1980.

Bothwell, Robert. *A Short History of Ontario.* Edmonton: Hurtig Publishers, 1986.

Bray, Matt, and Earnie Epp, eds. *A Vast and Magnificent Land: An Illustrated History of Northern Ontario.* Thunder Bay: Lakehead University, 1984.

Fryer, Mary Beacock, and Charles J. Humber, eds. *Loyal She Remains: A Pictorial History of Ontario.* Toronto: United Empire Loyalists, Association of Canada, 1984.

Gentilcore, R. Louis, and C. Grant Head. *Ontario's History in Maps.* Toronto: University of Toronto Press, 1984.

Hall, Roger et al., eds. *Patterns of the Past: Interpreting Ontario's History.* Toronto, Ontario Historical Society, 1988.

Keane, David, and Colin Read. *Old Ontario: Essays in Honour of J.M.S. Careless.* Toronto and Oxford: Dundurn Press, 1990.

Piva, Michael J., ed. *A History of Ontario: Selected Readings.* Toronto: Copp Clark Pitman, 1988.

Russell, Victor L. *Forging a Consensus: Historical Essays on Toronto.* Toronto: University of Toronto Press, 1984.

Schull, Joseph. *Ontario Since 1867.* Toronto: McClelland & Steward, 1978.

White, Randall. *Ontario: A Political and Economic History.* Toronto: Dundurn Press, 1985.

Political History

Armstrong, Christopher. *The Politics of Federalism: Ontario's Relations with the Federal Government, 1867-1942.* Toronto: University of Toronto Press, 1981.

Humphries, Charles W. *"Honest Enough to be Bold": The Life and Times of Sir James P. Whitney.* Toronto: University of Toronto Press, 1985.

Macdonald, Donald C. *The Government and Politics of Ontario.* Toronto: Macmillan of Canada, 1975.

—. *The Government and Politics of Ontario,* 2nd ed. Toronto: Van Nostrand Reinhold, 1980.

—. *The Government and Politics of Ontario,* 3rd ed. Scarborough, Ont.: Nelson Canada, 1985.

McDougall, Allan K. *John P. Robarts: His Life and Government.* Toronto: University of Toronto Press, 1985.

Oliver, Peter. *G. Howard Ferguson: Ontario Tory.* Toronto: University of Toronto Press, 1977.

—. *Public and Private Persons: The Ontario Political Culture, 1914-1934.* Toronto: Clark, Irwin & Company, 1975.

Swainson, Donald, ed. *Oliver Mowat's Ontario.* Toronto: Macmillan of Canada, 1972.

Economic History

de Visser, J., R. Sallows, and J. Carroll. *The Farm: A Celebration of 200 years of Farming in Ontario.* Toronto: Methuen, 1984.

Drummond, Ian M. *Progress without Planning: The Economic History of Ontario from Confederation to the Second World War.* Toronto: University of Toronto Press, 1987.

McDowall, Duncan. *Steel at the Sault: Francis H. Clergue, Sir James Dunn, and the Algoma Steel Corporation, 1910-1956.* Toronto: University of Toronto Press, 1985.

McInnis, R. Marvin.*Perspective on Ontario Agriculture, 1815-1930.*Ganaoque: Ontario, Langdale Press, 1992.

Nelles, H.V. *The Politics of Development: Forests, Mines and Hydro-electric Power in Ontario, 1849-1941.* Toronto: Macmillan of Canada, 1974.

Rea, K.J. *The Prosperous Years: the Economic History of Ontario, 1939-1975.* Toronto: University of Toronto Press, 1985.

Social History

Action, Janice, Penny Goldsmith, and Bonnie Shepard, eds. *Women at Work: Ontario 1850-1920.* Toronto: Canadian Women's Educational Press, 1974.

Akenson, Donald Harman. *The Irish in Ontario: A Study in Rural History.* Kingston and Montreal: McGill-Queen's University Press, 1984.

Backhouse, Constance. *Petticoats and Prejudice: Women and Law in Nineteenth-Century Ontario.* Toronto: The Osgooda Society, 1991.

Craven, Paul, ed. *Labouring Lives: Work and Workers in Nineteenth-Century Ontario.* Toronto: University of Toronto Press, 1995.

Gaffield, Chad. *Language, Schooling, and Cultural Conflict: The Origins of the French-Language Controversy in Ontario.* Kingston and Montreal: McGill-Queen's University Press, 1987.

Gagan, David. *Hopeful Travellers: Families, Land and Social Change in Mid-Victorian Peel County, Canada West.* Toronto, University of Toronto Press, 1994.

Greenhill, Pauline. *Ethnicity in the Mainstream: Three Studies of English-Canadian Culture in Ontario.* Montreal and Kingston: McGill-Queen's University Press, 1994.

Kealey, Gregory S. *Toronto Worker's Respond to Industrial Capitalism, 1867-1892.* Toronto: University of Toronto Press, 1980.

Struthers, James. *The Limits of Affluence: Welfare in Ontario, 1920-1970.* Toronto: University of Toronto Press, 1994.

Valverde, Mariana. *The Age of Light, Soap and Water: Moral Reform in English Canada, 1885-1924.* Toronto: McClelland & Stewart, 1991.

7

Canada's Aboriginal Peoples: 1760 to the Present

LINDA KERR

In September 1760, the French army surrendered to the British at Montreal. For the next three years, until the peace treaty was signed, New France would be held under military rule. In 1763, Britain, by the terms of the peace, gained permanent control of the what had been New France.

The 'conquest' of Canada ushered in a new era in European-Amerindian relations. Where the French had long recognized the importance of trade and military alliances with the native population, the British had a far different approach. To understand this more fully it is important to look at both the French and English and examine their aims in this territory. In brief, the French had always been interested in maintaining a good working relationship with Amerindians because at first their goal was trade and then, after 1701 because of their interest in New France as a strategically important area in their global wars with England over territory. Both France and England were committed to the goals of a mercantilist policy. The country with the most bullion and the most colonial territory from which to extract resources and sell manufactured goods too, would be the most powerful. Thanks to their trade, marriages and political alliances in the interior of New France, the French were able to, in European eyes at least, control or claim to possess the interior of the continent. After the conquest, the French presence in much of this interior, was ended. This change posed fundamental problems for Amerindians because the intent of the British was different. Theirs was not to be trading empire in the West, it was a settlement empire. The British government was interested in land, and lots of it. Possession meant physically moving onto the land. As historian Olive Dickason has noted, in the final analysis Europeans believed that because they had explored for a Western route to China and found another land mass in their way, that this land belonged to them. The French had never recognized aboriginal sovereignty so they are hardly less culpable in this matter than the English.

The Meaning of the Conquest for Amerindians

To understand the impact of the conquest of Canada on its native people it is necessary to consider the impact first, of British policy and secondly, of the American Revolution on Amerindians. To look at it from a less familiar angle, it is necessary to examine the impact of Amerindians on the British post-conquest settlement in Canada.

The British had a host of problems to deal with in Canada after the conclusion of the peace. Many of the issues they were faced with were bound up with the territory itself. First, the settlers there were French-Canadian Catholics with their own religious, political and legal institutions. Secondly, this was a colonial possession and like the rest had to be financially stable, preferably a net exporter of goods. For any chance of a healthy export-import trade there had to be an undisrupted trade with the interior. Thirdly, it had a native population which had, historically been allied with the French, at times against the English and which was well versed in the techniques of guerilla warfare.

French Canadians were lucky, the English believed that it was important to gain their loyalty. This group was allowed to retain its laws and system of landholding as well as the practice of its Catholic faith. All of these concessions became legal with the Quebec Act of 1774.

Amerindians had a somewhat different experience. Their status and rights were defined in a settlement called the Royal Proclamation. Although long heralded as the *Magna Carta* of Amerindian rights this was a document which acted primarily as the general settlement for all the new North American territories which came within the British sphere as a result of the Seven Years War. However, it would be fair to say that it was passed quickly, partly in response to Amerindian unrest in the interior and, that over time it came to apply to all of the West, laying the basis for modern land settlements.

Why was there unrest in the interior? It had much to do with the general British military attitude towards Amerindians and to the cost factor. Although the British government had gone deeply into debt to fund and win the war it had put the brakes on military spending as soon as it was over. 'Gifts' to Amerindians, the basis of trade and military alliances, came under the knife of budget cuts. These types of expenditures were to be avoided at all costs. To be fair, the British garrison at Quebec was paid only once in specie from 1760 to 1766 and the Governor in Chief, James Murray never at all. The economic crisis in the colony caused a mutiny at the Quebec garrison in 1764.

The military attitude and the problem of military expenditure meant an end to the traditional practice of gift-giving to cement alliance between Europeans and Amerindians. The British considered gift-giving as akin to bribery and had no use for it at all. What the British did not seem to realize was that interruption of custom led to unrest and unrest affected trade. Unrest was not long in coming because what had been strictly regulated in the past, trade to the interior, now became free for all as traders poured into Amerindian territory charging extortionate prices and disrupting traditional channels of trade. Settlers soon followed, an indication that for the British all of North America would be a settlement frontier.

The question raised in 1763 was, if the British claimed possession of the interior could they hold it? The odds did not look good unless the Amerindian nations were on their side. Amerindians believed that they had allowed the English to 'take over' French posts in the interior but that was all. To the English it was a different story, they had won the battle for New France and all of this territory was now theirs. Europeans never recognized Amerindians as sovereign peoples. Why? They were not settled, most were still no Christian and therefore it was felt that they had no rights in the land. When the British followed the Dutch lead in purchasing land from Amerindians they did so to legitimize the land transfer with the European community and as a way to avoid costly wars over territory. This was changed by the Royal Proclamation.

To the British Government the Proclamation seemed a fair settlement for the Amerindian communities but it caused much trouble among the settlers in the Thirteen colonies and with the small English-speaking community at Quebec because it shut them off from the interior, from fur trade country. That part of the Proclamation which applied specifically to Quebec saw the boundaries of the colony reduced in the East and in the West. The western hinterland, where the fur trade had been fully operational, was now closed to settlement and could be entered for trade purposes only with a licence and a bond of good behaviour worth twice the value of the trade goods, bound into the interior.

What is of greatest interest in the Proclamation is the huge western territorial block set aside for Amerindian communities. It was the old 'interior' that the French had held with a string of posts from Quebec to Louisiana. The most vital component of the Proclamation is that through it, the British agreed that they had no claim of ownership to this territory and therefore no right of colonization without purchase. There were to be no more private purchases; all sales had to be made directly to the crown at a public forum of all persons or groups involved. This policy would continue in Upper Canada in the Loyalist period and even later again in the West as Canada sought to gain control of the prairies. Amerindians would not hold this land in freehold tenure, with a few exceptions this land would be held communally. The underlying intent was that the land was British controlled and would provide space, in the long-term, for expansion without war.

The event which had precipitated this hastily passed Proclamation was the spontaneous rising in the interior by many Amerindian peoples but which is commonly referred to as Pontiac's rising. Pontiac was an Odawa whose people had fought on the French side until near the end of the Seven Years War. Shortly after the end of hostilities in North America it became clear that the British did not intend to continue to supply their Amerindian allies with guns, ammunitions and other necessaries. Trade to the interior was disrupted and the gift-giving ceremonies were cut back. Even the man in charge of Indian Affairs, William Johnson, recognized as early as 1762 that there was trouble brewing and tried to persuade the British Commander-in-Chief to allow for the customary exchanges of gifts but this was forbidden. In 1763 the tensions in the interior erupted into open warfare. Between May and September, Amerindians managed to take nearly all of the key British posts in the interior, but, word that the French had reached an agreement with the British, a lack of guns, the outbreak of smallpox and the onset of winter ended this initially successful campaign. A series of negotiations concerning the Amerindian position continued until 1769 but although the Proclamation had been the initial hurried response to hostilities it would remain the only response. This document did not cover the Mi'kmaq and Abenaki to the East and, although proclamations of 1761 and 1762 covered their rights, these proclamations were generally ignored and the aboriginal land base was quickly eroded. Even in Central Canada, treaties would be singed from 1764 onwards alienating parcels of land to the crown but the key land transactions came in two spurts just after the American Revolution and after the War of 1812.

Position of Amerindian Peoples in Canada, 1763-1830

The ever growing number of land transfers in the wake of 1763 brings us back to the question of the weakened position of Amerindians in this period. This was undoubtedly a period of crisis for the Amerindian population of the interior. From the American Revolution to the War of 1812, the status of native people was eroded. By the signing of the Treaty of Ghent in 1814, Amerindians had ceased to pose a military threat to either the British or the Americans. One of the most serious and long-term consequences of this was their increased marginalization in the countries which had been theirs for centuries.

An examination of three of the crisis periods and the impact of each on the Amerindian groups involved the American Revolution, Battle of Fallen

Timbers and, the War of 1812. After the American Revolution the flow of Loyalists north to Quebec and Nova Scotia is estimated at approximately 50,000. The majority of these refugees went to Nova Scotia increasing the pressure on the Mi'kmaq and Malecite.Many others came to Quebec where Governor Haldimand was quick to move them away from French Canadians. He approached the Mississauga in 1781 who, in return for 300 suits of clothing, sold their land four miles deep along the full length of the Niagara river. These Niagara purchases continued over the next few decades. Huge numbers of people moved into this western territory. This number included about five thousand Iroquois under the leadership of Joseph Brant who had been loyal to the British. Brant and his people were given the Six Nations reserve on the Grand River. An examination of the Iroquois experience can best help to explain the weakening of the Amerindian position. The Six Nations are the Cayuga, Seneca, Mohawk, Onondaga, Oneida, and Tuscarora. William Johnson, Commissary of Indian Affairs, worked with the Mohawk in the post-conquest period and tried to keep them loyal to the British. But another factor was at work which eventually would break apart the solidarity of the Six nations. That factor was the missionary activity of Samuel Kirkland.

When the American Revolution began Kirkland, through his work with the Oneida and Tuscarora, managed to gain their support for the American side while Johnson, working with Joseph Brant a Mohawk educated at an Anglican school, was firmly attached to the British and convinced the Cayuga and Mohawk to fight on the British side. Members of the Seneca and the Onondaga could be found on both sides. The American Revolution broke the Great White Tree of peace, the unity of purpose first established in the fifteenth century by founder of the Iroquois League, Deganawideh. Because of their participation on the British side, American frontiersmen retaliated with vigour against Amerindians in some savage encounters, not stopping to ask which side the Amerindian villagers were on. In 1779 the Americans set out to bring the Iroquois to heel. The main invasion of Iroquoia was undertaken by General John Sullivan who laid waste village after village, destroying crops and the sustenance base of the people. This caused a northern movement of about 5000 Iroquois into the Niagara area. This did, however, not end Iroquois participation in the Revolution, if anything they became more active and impassioned about their participation. The Amerindian war against the Americans was going so well that they were surprised to find that the British had lost. The result of the American Revolution for the Iroquois was that some of them were displaced to Canada, their homeland and traditional hunting territories destroyed and their land soon overrun by American settlers. Their experience is typical of other communities in the interior except that many moved further west rather than north.

The Peace of Paris signed in 1783 was a disastrous treaty from the Amerindian perspective. Because the British had been forced to sue for peace and they were not able to dictate terms, Amerindians were consequently ignored and no provisions were made for the protection of their lands and the Americans were in no mood to be forced into deals. But, at the same time the American government, through cash purchases of land, had recognized that it did not own title to the land. Congress even recognized that Indian tribes were distinct political entities that had to be dealt with as separate nations. Once again Amerindian communities were the victim of a power play between the English proper and the English abroad. Although lip service was paid to the idea of keeping settlers out of Amerindian lands, it was clear even to the British by 1784 that the Americans were not going to be held back. To maintain some influence in the interior the British held on to their four posts in the western territory. They did not vacate these until an agreement was reached by the terms of Jay's Treaty in 1794. The evacuation took place in 1796. In the meantime, Joseph Brant led his followers up to the Six Nations reserve.

In 1784, the Iroquois signed a treaty with the American government (Stanwix) relinquishing their claims to lands north-west of the Ohio. This was followed by a series of treaties which further eroded their land base. In the end, this increased tensions in the interior led to many open battles headed by Chief Little Turtle and by Blue Jacket. These smaller battles, mostly won by Amerindians, culminated in the Battle of Fallen Timbers in 1794, the same year as Jay's Treaty saw the British relinquish their hold on the west. The Amerindians were decisively defeated at Fallen Timbers. Their military successes until then now counted for nought. With their unity of purpose shattered and their land base eroded Amerindians were experiencing serious difficulties by the late 1790s. Into this unstable and uncertain environment came the man who would gather the fold back together and lead them on a final assault against the outsiders who sought to destabilize their lives. This man was called Tecumseh (Shooting Star). Tecumseh was a Shawnee by birth but he considered himself an Amerindian first and foremost. He threw all of his efforts into creating a Pan-Indian confederacy which would have its own territorial state. Because of the high profile of Joseph Brant, Tecumseh did not really burst on to the political scene until after Brant's death in 1807. He had, by this time, seen his people pushed off their hunting territory taken over by Americans. He had watched as one tribe after another had given their land away bleeding the Amerindian peoples as a whole. He had some personal experience of this process as well because the Shawnee had supported the British during the American Revolution and perhaps in retribution, their lands were flooded with settlers. After the Battle of Fallen Timbers, Tecumseh refused to accept the treaty signed the following year which saw most of the Ohio Valley surrendered to the Americans.

After 1807, along with his brother the Shawnee Prophet, Tenskwatawa, Tecumseh urged an end to inter-tribal warfare. He believed that Amerindian land belonged to all Amerindian peoples and, that no one chief could sell any part of it. He rallied tribe after tribe to block American government acquisitions of their land through purchase and warned of resistance if the government tried to seize the land they wanted by force. The Americans were not long in responding and the two sides met at Tippecanoe in 1811. The Americans won. The conflict was not yet over because in 1812 the Americans declared war on Britain and invaded Canada. Isaac Brock of Upper Canada called on Amerindians to assist him promising them help after the war was over. In fact, the successes on the Canadian side were a direct result of Tecumseh's forces and his own military genius. Tecumseh's involvement brought the Six Nations to the British side as well. But, the death of Tecumseh at the Battle of Moraviantown on October 5, 1813 signalled the beginning of the end for the concept of an Amerindian confederacy. There was no real winner here but although no territory changed hands at the Treaty of Ghent which ended this war in 1814, the boundary between Canada and America would soon be set at the 49th parallel and the geographic unity of the West was broken. The British did not want to see a repeat of the 1783 treaty and tried to negotiate for an independent state for Amerindians, but their efforts came to nought. The Americans called for a return to the pre-war status quo but soon began their old policy of land transfers concluding an important series of treaties between 1815-30.

For Amerindians in Canada, the War of 1812 also marked the end of an era. As long as the colonial wars lasted, Amerindians still had some power but now their role was diminished. By being forced to choose sides time and again their land base had been eroded and their numbers diminished. Yet, the colonial powers whom they had fought for gave them little in return.

In fact this was to be the beginning of a new era where Amerindian peoples were no longer a military threat. The aim of government policy was now to 'civilize', and Christianize Amerindians on territory reserved for their use. Responsibility for their welfare was even shifted from the military to the civilian side of government. This was a fundamental change. Amerindians were now seen as superfluous and the treatment of them had a distinctly reformist edge. There was one group further West which had a slightly different relationship with the Europeans, a community born of the fur trade and still deeply tied to that trade and called the Métis.

The Métis

The word Métis comes from the word *to mix*. When did the first Métis appear? Some historians say it was nine months after the first European stepped ashore, others claim that the word Métis refers to a socio-cultural mix and should be applied primarily to the Great Lakes and the Red River area (around modern day Winnipeg). Whichever definition is accepted, this 'new people' were a result of the needs of the fur trade. Such alliances between European men involved in the fur trade and native women, were formed; for commercial and political reasons, for companionship and for survival. By the mid-eighteenth century there was a large encampment of French Métis families at the forks of the Red and Assiniboine Rivers. Two groups were there by the late eighteenth century, the country born who were the offspring of English or Scotsmen working for the Hudson Bay Company (HBC) and the Métis, children of Frenchmen or Scotsmen working for the North West Company (NWC).

Red River was special because the mixed-blood or Métis population were the majority in the area and eventually retired fur traders would settle there with their Amerindian families. The situation at Red River became strained in the early nineteenth century as fierce competition between the HBC and the NWC to control the fur trade led to the Métis of Red River being caught in the middle of this corporate struggle. Their position further deteriorated when Lord Selkirk, a majority shareholder in the HBC asked for and was granted 116,000 square miles of land in the area. He had plans to relieve some of the pressure on Scots families dispossessed in the Highland Clearances by resettling them in a new land. His idea was to found an agricultural colony yet he made no attempt to secure the agreement of the Cree or the Métis to this plan until the crisis of 1817. The first party of settlers arrived in 1812 and had a dismal time of it. They would not have lasted the winter without the help of the local Métis community which provided them with meat from the buffalo hunt.

In the nineteenth century the buffalo hunt reached new proportions. In the early decades of the century about 500 participated in the two seasonal hunts but by 1860 this number had increased to just under three thousand. Much of the strength in their way of life came from the organization of the hunt. The hunt was organized democratically and its rules were strictly enforced because of the danger from the Sioux. The Battle of Grand Coteau in 1851 which gave the victory to the Métis over the Sioux gave the Métis control over the southern plains.

Although there was an uneasy peace between these new settlers and the Métis population the actions of the Governor of the colony, Miles Macdonnell led to outright hostilities. One of the chief economic activities of the Métis was to harvest the buffalo herds and make pemmican from the dried meat by mixing it together with melted fat. The mixture was placed into buffalo skins in bags weighing 90 lbs each. This pemmican could be kept for years and therefore was invaluable to the fur traders and explorers attempting to move further west. The Métis of Red River provided the NWC with its pemmican supplies. In 1814 the Governor tried to establish an embargo on foods exported from the area and an end to the running of the buffalo. These two proclamations were direct attacks on the livelihood of the Métis and on the ability of the NWC to function. At the insistence of the NWC the Métis, for the first time, concerned themselves with the question of land ownership in the Red River area. By 1815 they were upset enough to order the settlers to leave. The next Governor, Robert Semple arrived that same year with more settlers and the NWC responded by enlisting the help of Métis leader and NWC employee Cuthbert Grant to raise the standard. The ensuing confrontation, the Battle of Seven Oaks, saw the settlers lose 20 including the Governor whereas the Métis lost only one. This event has been viewed by some as far more than just a local battle. It has been seen by many historians as the birth of a Métis consciousness, the rise of a New Nation. Within a few years the HBC and the NWC merged retaining the name of the former. Within a few short decades the Métis population had also managed to break the fur trade monopoly of the Company and trade became free in the Red River colony. From mid-century on ties between Red River and American traders in the St. Paul region were strengthened. Members of the Métis community were even appointed to the Council of the Assiniboia. Out of this Red River community would come Louis Riel who would bring the area to national prominence when he formed a provisional government to prevent the sale of the area to the Canadian Government without the agreement of and consultation with the local Métis and Amerindian population. Let us turn back for the moment to Government policy towards Amerindians in the nineteenth century.

The Design and Administration of British Amerindian Policy

The responsibility for Indian affairs was transferred to the civil arm of government and overhauled. There was an immediate decrease in the number of honours and gifts granted. This is not to say that interest in native people dropped off. If anything, it increased, fuelled by the humanitarian societies' sense of responsibility as seen in the abolitionist movement, and by others, who wished to, 'protect and civilize' native populations throughout the empire. In the written word and the European settlers' imagination, Amerindian peoples made a comeback, not as the cruel savage capable of unspeakable deeds, but as the 'noble' savage.

The 1830s were a time of great reforms in Britain which included the Reform Act of 1832 and a parliamentary inquiry into the plight of native peoples from one end of the empire to the other. This inquiry resulted in 1837 in a report which led ultimately to the Crown Lands Protection Act of 1839. Its intention was to stem the negative impact of settler expansion onto Amerindian lands. In more general terms through, the British government considered at least two alternatives; segregation or integration and eventual assimilation. In this, as in other parts of the Empire, the British chose the former rather than the latter. The British did not anticipate making full citizens of its subject people. 'Civilizing', in the nineteenth century meant settling down to work the land, becoming Christian, receiving the education that would instill you with civic virtues and casting off the old ways and the beliefs which had sustained natives in the face of such rapid change. To be 'civilized' was to be a carbon copy of British society, in thought, word and deed. What remained to be seen was how the government planned to have such a policy unfold in Upper and Lower Canada. British territory in Quebec was divided into two separate areas in 1791, Upper and Lower Canada, after the influx of Loyalist from what had become the United States of America. The two areas would remain separate until the Union of 1840. In each area the governors suggested the establishment of model farms and villages to make Amerindians self-sufficient. One such village was at Credit River in 1825-26, where Reverend Peter Jones (Sacred Feathers), a Mississauga-Scots Methodist minister, supervised the building of one such model village. Officials had provided a 20 house village and 4000 acres of land to Jones and his Methodist followers. Although land clearing was going well and Jones had been made chief, the government refused to hand over the deed because the feeling was that Amerindians were not ready yet for such responsibility. The story did not end there for, along with the Six Nation they established New Credit in 1847 near Hagersville Ontario. However, many other villages were established until, in the 1830s, the Lieutenant-Governor of Upper Canada, Francis Bond Head, wrote the experiment off as a failure and switched to a policy of isolation, 'in the best interest of the Indians'. He arranged two land cessions involving the Manitoulin islands chain in return for its protection as Indian territory. In the face of inevitable European settlement on their lands, the natives were helpless to resist, and exchanged millions of acres of good land for a chain of barren isolated islands and the promise of protection. Amerindian policy continued to be administered from London but there was little in the way of infrastructure at the colonial level to actually make and carry out policy. It was typically in the hands of one person and his primary goals were at odds with one another; to look after the interests of Amerindians and to transfer Indian lands to the crown through the Crown Lands department. Although Indian affairs were transferred to the civil wing of government in 1830, it was not until 1860 that the responsibility for Amerindians would be handed over to the colony. This happened at a time of political deadlock and a growing obsession in the province of Canada with the idea of Confederation. From 1830 to 1845 administering Indian policy onwards it would be the job of the Lieutenant of Upper Canada and the military secretary in Lower Canada. In this period, Amerindians were paid annuities for lands handed over to the crown instead of a one-time only cash settlement. But this had more to do with the financial difficulties experienced by colonial assemblies than with any beneficial plan to provide long-term assistance to the native population east of Lake Superior. After the Union of the Canadas, however, provisions for the payment of these annuities was overlooked and it took another four years to remedy the situation. In general, the native population was to suffer from *too much* rather than *too little* interest in their future role within the expanding Canadian state. For example, the Colonial Office did develop regional plans for dealing with the native population in the province of Canada and in the Atlantic provinces covering the wide range of options from isolation to amalgamation. Whether or not these were in their best interests is debatable. In 1842-44, the Bagot Commission, named after Governor Charles Bagot, investigated the plight of Amerindian peoples in the new province of Canada. The commissions findings recommended; centralized control rather than regional planning and endorsed the position taken in the Proclamation of 1763 that Amerindians had 'user rights' to the land and should be given compensation for land surrenders. But this commission went one step further, calling for deno-minational schooling for native children, the teaching of modern land management skills to native adults, and the registration of all title deeds. On the negative side, the recommendations also included the wish to see Amerindian peoples sell land which was surplus to their needs, and to be given the opportunity of selling land amongst themselves. The ultimate goal of these suggestions was to speed up the process of civilizing, i.e., integrating, Amerindians by forcing them to treat land the same way the Europeans did by making the idea of private property acceptable to them. Once they were 'civilized' they would be ready to take clear title to their land. Landowners made good citizens with little need for state support.

As a result of the work of this commission, and the growing sense of urgency among government officials, two acts were passed in 1850 which directly affected the native population. The first was "An Act for the Better Protection of the Lands and Property of the Indians in Lower Canada" and "An Act for the Protection of the Indians of Upper Canada from Imposition, and the Property Occupied and Enjoyed by them from Trespass and Injury." One of the consequences of passing such acts was that it now became necessary to define exactly who was an 'Indian'. At no point were the various Amerindian communities consulted on this matter. These two acts were passed in reaction to loggers who were exploiting Amerindian lands illegally and keeping the benefits for themselves. These acts excluded Amerindians from taxation and made provisions for them to receive compensation when their land was exposed to railroad construction and the like. Also in 1850, a new post was created called the Commissioner of Indian Lands while the following year 142,000 acres of Crown land were set aside for Amerindians.

Lower Canada was the first to take a crack at defining 'who is an Indian'. The result was a sweeping and inclusive definition, so liberal that it had to be modified within the year. This initial definition included; all persons of Indian blood living among their own people on Indian lands, anyone intermarried with such an Indian, anyone living with an Indian tribe whose parents on either side were Indian or anyone adopted by Indians and living with them, and of course, their descendants. The following year, another definition aimed at excluding Canadians living among Indians and non-natives married to Indian women was passed. Now 'Indianness' was to be traced through the male line and marriage would only provide this if a non-native woman married a native man. Amerindian women married to a non-native kept their status but could not pass it on to their children. The precedent was now set for who was Indian and who was not, or, who was a Federal responsibility and who was not. By the late 1850s there was even more interest in shaping the path of Amerinidan travels. Because the policy of settling Amerindian communities in isolated areas had not seemed to work, a change in tactics seemed necessary and it was now thought that bringing Amerindian communities closer to Canadian settlements might 'show them the way' by example. This was an approach as old as European travels to North America, remember the example of the Jesuits in Huronia. In a sense it could be argued that this really meant a change in the long-term goals of the dominant society, for Amerindians were now to be reshaped in the image of Europeans.

Two Commissioners were given powers to investigate the position of the Amerindian communities in Canada and they reported to John A. Macdonald (later to become Prime Minister of Canada). One result of their work was the 'Act for the Gradual Civilization of the Indian Tribes of the Canada', passed in 1857. This act laid the foundation for the final prize-enfranchisement. Any Amerindian male over twenty-one, who could read and write in French or English, was free of debt and was of good moral character was eligible. This act defined who was an 'Indian' and so, in the very instant when Canadians had decided that they had the power and the wherewithal to phase out this particular cultural group, they insisted on proof that each had the ability to leave it and join the dominant society. The level of proof was too difficult for most. The Gradual Civilization Act proved to be the first step in the tearing down of Amerindian independence because it also involved holding land in the European way, the introduction of the concept of private property. Land would, over time, no longer be held by the community. As each male was enfranchised he would receive 20 hectares of land, reserve land! Accepting the franchise meant of course giving up the status of 'Indian', this was asking a lot.

Why was there such a fierce need on the part of Canadians to break the traditional bond of Amerindian peoples to the old ways? It has a lot to do with the definition of civilization. It was believed that it was only if people accepted the idea of freehold tenure that they would be industrious and make the land productive; this was the test, and the prize was the franchise. The trouble was, that Amerindian communities did not want to see their lands chipped away at, and resisted these attempts. The other problem was that the standards had been set too high. Canadian society at large was generally not functionally literate, and to expect this from one group was simply too much to ask. There was also the underlying question of whether or not this was all strictly legal. Under the provisions of the Proclamation of 1763, colonial legislatures were not allowed to involve themselves in 'Indian Affairs' and this would remain the case until these powers were handed to the Dominion Government at the time of Confederation in the British North America Act (BNA).

Despite these problems it would be well to ask how many Amerindian men sought and were accepted to receive the franchise. Between 1857 and 1876 only a handful applied and only one in fact was successful. By 1920 the number of such men who had received the franchise was still to be counted in the low hundreds.

Another change wrought upon Amerindian peoples in the period just before Confederation was the 'Act for Civilization and Enfranchisement' passed in 1859. The Act allowed intervention on a more personal level including a ban on the sale of liquor to Indians. In 1860 this Act was followed by the 'Management of Indian Lands and Properties Act' which handed·over the administration of Indian affairs from the Colonial Office in London to a Superintendent of Indian Affairs. The pattern had long been set and as usual there was no consultation with the people most affected when changes to Indian policy and administration were made.

The Dominion Government Develops an Indian Policy

Under the terms of the BNA Act [91(24)], Amerindians were declared a federal responsibility and were clearly in the position of wards rather than citizens. Still, there was some improvement as the Department of the Secretary of State was given the responsibility for Amerindians but within five years the Department of the Interior took over this portfolio. Both departments had found it difficult to get a sense of the regional disparities in the treatment and condition of Amerindian peoples so they began by reviewing the existing legislation. In 1868 the department increased the sweeping power of the 1857 Act in an attempt to speedily assimilate Indians with the steadily growing number of settlers. It is not unusual to find government departments working at cross purposes and this appears to be one of those occasions.

One of the primary goals of the Fathers of Confederation was to extend the land holdings of the new dominion westward and fill the region with settlers who would make the land productive. This goal involved the transfer of lands from Amerindian communities to the crown and this was best accomplished not by the old policy of the protection of Amerindians and their land but by the assimilation of Amerindians into mainstream society. To further this aim, another act was passed in 1869 'An Act for the Gradual Enfranchisement of Indians'. This act signalled an increase in the level of government intervention in the lives of Amerindian peoples. Government officials decided that the desire for enfranchisement was there, but it was being suppressed by the chiefs, therefore, the chiefs became the next target of government intervention, as those in charge of policy decided to abolish hereditary chieftainships and make that position and the positions on the band councils elective. In this way, the person in charge of Indian Affairs, the Superintendent General could shape the agenda of these councils and have more impact on decisions made there. By using an elective body, the superintendent could also see to it that obstructive councillors were removed from office. This act also introduced the blood quantum test, to be an 'Indian' it was necessary to prove one-quarter Indian blood. The interesting part of this act is that it introduced something called the location ticket to push Amerindian communities into accepting the European style of land holding. The reserves were to be surveyed and then measured plots were to be assigned individually. Location tickets were handed out and after three years probation the successful individual received the title to the land and was handed the franchise. It was also possible to receive a location ticket and the franchise by going to university. Again the purpose of this was to end the traditional native ideas of land use and to replace them with more modern ways. But this time it was to sweep away the reserves themselves because as more location tickets were handed out and title granted the reserve itself would wither and eventually disappear.

The culmination of the newly created country's attempts to codify its Indian policy brought the 'Indian Act' of 1876. This act tried to centralize and consolidate all the pre-Confederation legislation in a nationwide framework. Its aim was clear; to assimilate Amerindian peoples. Even the definition of 'Indian' was altered to cover anyone registered as an Indian or entitled to be registered and, anyone of Indian blood belonging to a band. It gave more powers to elective band councils. Over the next few decades amendments to the act came to include prohibitions on various aspects of Amerindian culture including a ban on potlatches and on the Sun Dance.

Further developments came with the Act of 1880 which created separate administration for Indian Affairs within the Department of the Interior which would continue until well into the twentieth century. This administration then *imposed* the elective band system, to eat away at traditional Amerindian political systems based on cooperation and consensus. The Minister of the Interior also held the position of superintendent general. In 1884 the 'Indian Advancement Act' was passed granting more power to elected band councils and to the superintendent general to intervene in band affairs. To encourage more bands to accept this elective system, Amerindian peoples of Eastern Canada were given the franchise in Dominion elections in 1885 but their lack of participation led to withdrawal in 1896.

By the turn of the century it now seemed to government officials, that what was really holding native people back from becoming Canadians, was the reserve system itself. It was thought by some department officials that if reserve life remained much as it was, then perhaps the movement off them would turn from a trickle into a flood. While this was never expounded as general government policy it appears to have figured in the actions of some government servants such as D.C. Scott. From the 1880s until the mid-twentieth century the government intervened more and more in the lives of Amerindian communities and the provinces began to interfere with treaty rights. For instance, in 1890 Manitoba decided to make its game laws take precedence over treaty rights. An amendment was passed in the 1890s to allow the government to offer cash for land in order to then free this land up for settlement. It was not, of course, fair market value that was offered. The amendment also made it possible for the lease of Indian land for mineral exploration, railways and other uses. In 1898 a measure was introduced for moving native people off reserve land which was next to a town. This was followed in 1911 by an amendment allowing the superintendent general to seize reserve land for public use. In this and many other ways the government hoped to steadily decrease the holdings of reserves and move native people into towns and farming communities as functioning members of society. Amendments also spoke to changing culture, the ban on the wearing of aboriginal dress and on the performance of traditional dances was just the beginning. This also came to involve the compulsory education of native children in government-funded, church administered schools to aid the process of assimilation.

In the interwar years the Canadian government faced many problems not least of which was coping with Great Depression. In this period Amerindian peoples and the policy of assimilation were pushed into the background. In 1936 the responsibility for Indians was passed to the Department of Mines and Resources. This unofficial policy of neglect ended after the war in part because of the high level of native participation in the army. There was also recognition of the increased birth rates and survival rates on reserves and the emergence of the social welfare state in Canada. Ottawa could not champion social welfare for Canadians while excluding Amerindian communities for which it had a clearly defined fiduciary responsibility. The government also did not have far to look to see the abuse of human rights in the Indian Act and its many amendments. Veteran groups were just one of the many voices calling for a radical reassessment of the condition of Amerindian peoples in Canada in terms of their civic rights. In 1946 a Joint Committee of the Senate and the House of Commons was set up to look at the condition of native people in Canada. The Committee's report called for a revision of all sections of the Indian Act but it did not question the goal of the act and the many amendments to it — the acculturation of Canada's native peoples. The result was the revised Indian Act of 1951 which reduced the powers of the Minister to a supervisory role but left him with the power of veto. It introduced the secret ballot, increased the powers of the band council and gave women the vote in council elections. Acculturation was still the goal but the coercive measures of the past were no longer acceptable. In reality this revision to the Indian Act had quite the opposite effect. In 1963 UBC Anthropology professor Harry B. Hawthorn was appointed by the Federal Government to look into the position and status of Amerinidan communities across the country. Hawthorn's report was published in 1966 and contained some startling findings and offered some novel suggestions for change. Hawthorn commented on the poor level of education received by young Indian children and suggested that they should be taught in their own language, that the language used to describe them in Canadian history texts should be far less pejorative and that a change in the way they were taught would show a better path for their future. The report also refused to accept that Amerindian peoples should give up their own cultures and traditions in favour of the culture of the dominant society. The Department of Indian Affairs was targeted for not offering enough active assistance and advice to bands. The Hawthorn report was a real departure in terms of its suggestions that Bands should govern on their own terms not ours, that they should have control of their own monies and that education was the way of the future, their way out of dependency. The report of 1966 paved the way for the White Paper of 1969.

In 1969 what was thought to be the final step, was taken by the Federal Government, when it put forward its White Paper which would have set the stage for *an end to the reserve system* and an end to the *legislative* differences between Natives and Non-natives in Canadian society. This brought a wave of protest from the native communities in Canada and it was quickly withdrawn. In the 1990s, the call has again been heard for an end to the Indian Act but this time it has come from the Native community itself and does not involve any loss of identity, in fact, quite the reverse. It involves self-government on their own terms, including the return to traditional modes of aboriginal decision-making for some communities.

The Impact of Nation-building on Native Peoples in the West

Part of the reason for Confederation was the wish of expansionists in Ontario to gain control of the fertile lands of the West but a number of things stood in the way, the first was the need of the Dominion Government to gain control of Rupert's Land and the second was to come to some arrangement with the native populations as far West as the Rocky Mountains. A brief examination of the government's attempt to buy Rupert's Land brought the first crisis in the West. The key settlement in this Hudson Bay territory, which covered all the territory which drained by river into Hudson Bay, was at the Red River settlement but in all there was about 100,000 widely scattered throughout the land. In our discussion of the West we noted the small but vocal Métis community at Red River, and the growing aspirations of expansionists to make the area part of Dominion territory. Assuming they had no rights in the land neither the Native nor the Métis community was consulted about the land transfer. But the Métis were interested in the survival of their way of life. They were particularly worried about the Canadians in their midst who had established a local paper called the *Nor Wester* which called for annexation with Canada. George Brown's *Globe* also called for annexation of the West. On Dr. Schultz used the *Nor Wester* as the voice of the pro-Canadian party at Red River.

The Dominion Government opened negotiations around the same time with the HBC for these lands. Two million square miles of land was involved, the vast territory which drained by numerous rivers into Hudson Bay, the agreement made was that the HBC would surrender its territory for 300,000 in sterling, funds the Dominion Government would borrow from London. Because it was not sure exactly what it had purchased, the Dominion Government passed a temporary act for governing the territory until surveyors could be sent out. The arrival of government surveyors precipitated the crisis among the settlers. The transfer was set to take place before the end of 1869 and the paperwork completed before the Métis at Red River realized fully the import of events taking place. They had reason to be concerned for the Ontario expansionists who had nothing but contempt for them and their way of life and made it clear that great changes were afoot.

Besides this direct political threat to their community, the Red River was experiencing a number of economic difficulties in the 1860s. These included a fur trade in decline, ever shrinking buffalo herds to harvest, and the sudden appearance of government surveyors who began to divide up the land into square lots contrary to the traditional long river lot arrangement of the Métis. Lastly, the crop failures of 1868-69 brought further uncertainty to the community. It was a highly volatile situation and the return of Louis Riel to Red River community of his father brought matters to a head. People looked to him to lead them out of their difficulties. He was the best educated man in Red River, understood politics, had knowledge of the law and could speak English, French and Cree. Riel became the leader of the resistance to this Euro-Canadian expansionist drive for internal empire.

As a historical character Riel is a complex study, a man of great complexities and ambiguities Riel was a Métis, born in 1844 in the Red River area. He was a smart child, picked out by the Bishop as someone with the potential to enter the priesthood. He was sent to Quebec and educated at the College Classique in Montreal. He left in 1865 without taking his degree and with no intention of entering the priesthood. Instead, he worked briefly in law offices in Montreal, Chicago and St. Paul, and then returned to Red River in 1868. As one of the best educated people in the colony, able to move in both Métis and

Canadian circles, he was the natural choice to lead the resistance to the government's decision to annex the territory without consulting the local population.

Without going into too much detail, the important thing to keep in mind about the 1869 Rising, was that Riel was equally concerned about the welfare of the Métis and the Amerindian population of the area.

A National Committee was organized under the effective leadership of Riel and the committee moved quickly to prevent the entry of the Canadian Governor William McDougall into this territory. The Métis would have to be consulted before any agreement could be reached or cooperation given. Following this plan, Riel seized Fort Garry, and the new Governor was held to the American side of the border. Meanwhile, Riel called for a representative council of 12 English-speaking and 12 French-speaking settlers to form a Provisional Government to replace the Council of Assiniboia. On 1 December 1896 McDougall forged a proclamation appointing himself Lieutenant Governor, crossed the border, read the declaration and fled back to the American side. This was an unfortunate move for the Dominion because once McDougall had acted and then left, the *de jure* government was absent and a *de facto* government could be set up in the meantime. Riel's provisional government was just that and would continue to run the territory until a settlement with the Dominion Government could be reached. Riel and his government sought to negotiate the terms under which their region entered Confederation. To this end, the Provisional government prepared a Bill of Rights and opened negotiations.

In January 1870 Donald Smith, later Lord Strathcona, was sent to the Red River to open talks and he promised that the Dominion would negotiate in good faith, respecting their right to negotiate. The community then elected a 40 man national convention to discuss Smith's proposals and by March a Red River delegation was en route to Ottawa. One of the reasons that Ottawa was so open to negotiations was that this crisis had occurred over the winter when it was virtually impossible to send troops to quell any unrest. Another factor was that there was some concern in Ottawa that the Americans might take advantage of the situation and seize control of the area or annex it. But while the government negotiated in good faith throughout the spring it also readied troops to send to the area at the first thaw. Just as things had seemed to be moving along quite nicely an incident occurred which changed the whole tone of the situation. The Canadian expansionists at Red River tried to re-take Fort Garry and were jailed and one particularly nasty prisoner, Thomas Scott, was tried for treason and shot. Scott's death would drive Riel into exile. It was the one blunder Riel made and the reaction in Ontario was near hysteria. Still, negotiations resumed and a settlement was reached and the *Manitoba Act* was passed, giving the area around Red River the status of province, self-government and federal representation. Most importantly, the Act provided a land settlement for the Métis, about 1,400,000 acres of land were set aside, each head of household would receive 160 acres or the equivalent in cash. There was even a verbal promise of amnesty for Riel, which Bishop Tache had asked for, but the strength of public opinion made Macdonald renege on the deal. An armed expedition, the Wolseley expedition was sent to the area to seize Riel. It took the military three months to reach Red River only to discover that Riel was gone. Wolseley encountered no resistance. The *Manitoba Act* did not solve the problems the Métis faced. While they received their land in individual plots, many did not remain in the area long enough to even collect their land script. In the face of Ontario expansion and settlement the Métis began slowly moving further west to Prince Albert and Batoche. Their frustration with the Dominion Government would explode again in 1885 and they would again look for a leader and find him in an older and much changed Riel.

Once the Dominion Government gained title to the lands in the West, it was vital that the territory attract settlers for farming. The Macdonald government's great obsession was to join the country from one coast to the other by laying down a railroad. Before this could be done the government had to come to terms with the many groups of Native people on the Prairies. The government sent treaty commissioners West to negotiate, in an attempt to make the West safe for settlement. The settlements agreed to go a long way towards explaining some of the problems native people have experienced up to the modern period.

The government wanted to settle the West. It had the political and economic will to proceed with this goal but it had to ensure the safety of the settlers. To begin, the federal government needed to gain title to the West. The men the government chose to negotiate these treaties were expansionists. The government's goals included: gaining title to the land, settling it peaceably, keeping the cost of westward expansion low and avoiding costly conflicts, halting American expansion into the area, and lastly, responding to Amerindian communities' requests for treaties.

This last point is particularly interesting and of course begs the question why treaties? The answer may lie in the nature of Amerindian-European contact since the sixteenth century. Most of the contact experience had occurred through the framework of the fur trade. The West in particular had been dominated by contacts between the NWC and the HBC. There was a certain protocol which had been followed in trade relations between Europeans and Amerindian communities. This brings us to the next point. What did the Amerindian communities of the West believe that they were negotiating for in the treaties?

There were a number of reasons why the first nations people of the plains found themselves in a very difficult position. First there was trouble with the food supply. The rapid spread of American settlers moving westward, and the great profit to be made in the buffalo robe trade, coupled with overhunting in some regions increased the pressure on the food supply. In 1800, a rough estimate gives a buffalo population of 50 million, by 1865 this had dropped to just over 1 million, and by 1875 the number was negligible. Buffalo herds had disappeared from the Canadian Plains and were in danger of extinction on the American Plains in the face of population movements and overkill.

Secondly, this became a period of increased warfare among Amerindian nations as traditional enemies were forced from sheer necessity, to hunt in the same territory. The Sioux moved into Blackfoot territory and the Cree began hunting in the neutral zone which had until then, separated them from their traditional enemy the Blackfoot. A series of treaties kept the peace between Cree and Blackfoot until the mid-1860s but by 1869 a state of war again existed. In 1870, Cree peacemaker, Maskepetoon set off for Blackfoot territory to sign another peace and he was killed during the negotiations.

Thirdly, two epidemics swept through the plains in the decade following 1865, and estimates give up to a 50 per cent loss of life. Fourthly, the movement of American Whisky traders into Canadian territory had a further negative impact on an already unsettled atmosphere. These traders were dug in at the Old Man district, and, the alcohol which they dispensed so freely brought more violence. For an example of this let us examine the Cypress Hills Massacre. Cypress Hills was a meeting place for hunters and traders but it was also part of the Blackfoot-Cree traditional neutral zone. American whisky traders frequently set up shop there. In the winter of 1872/73 there were two such posts and an Assiniboine band was camped near the posts. The traders claimed that one of their horses had been stolen and the American wolvers visiting the post decided to take matters into their own hands. They attacked the Assiniboine camp nearby, killing over twenty and partaking in unspeakable acts against the women in the camp. This was the first and the last time that such lawlessness would occur in the Canadian West.

That same year the Dominion Government passed an act creating the NWMP (North West Mounted Police). Within a year the NWMP were out West policing the area. Forts Macleod, Walsh and Calgary were quickly established to give the force a physical presence in the area and men such as James Macleod played key roles in the treaty signing that soon followed.

Taken together the loss of food source, impact of disease, unregulated movement of traders and increased inter-tribal warfare meant that the position of Amerindians on the Prairies was precarious. They needed assistance and, when the Dominion Government approached them they agreed to negotiate the way they were accustomed to, by the form of treaty.

Historians are divided over the issue of the treaties. Some believe that Amerindians on the prairies were victims of the biggest land grab in Canadian history, that they had no understanding of the meaning or intent of the treaties, that the translations provided by the Métis interpreters were less than reliable because even between these two groups there was a different understanding of land and land transfers. Other historians believe that the treaties were equitable agreements because it was Amerindian communities who chose the treaty as the form of agreement. The works of Jean Friesen and Arthur Ray have demonstrated that Amerindians were sophisticated traders and had centuries of experience dealing with Europeans therefore they knew how to get a fair deal. But the question remains, did they bargain well in the 1870s and did both sides bargain for the same thing? The answer to these questions is more ambiguous.

Since the rise of ethnohistory and the understanding among historians that reliance on the written record is simply not enough when dealing with the history of a people who relied on the oral tradition, it has become clear that it is also necessary to give full weight to the Amerindian side of their history as it has been passed on through the oral tradition. From the written record of treaty it is painfully clear that the government had in fact been negotiating for land, and that it believed that such a sale or transaction had occurred. From the cultural perspective of Amerindians, land could not be bought or sold, only used. They were the guardians of the land and it in turn ensured their survival. The Cree understood from the treaty that the land had been borrowed not bought.

Even the form of treaties is of interest. The Dominion Government wanted everything written down of course and then believed themselves bound by that document. Amerindian communities were, of course, not interested in the written word but in the oral part of the treaty process. To them the oral preamble was the key part of the negotiations and they committed it to memory. They seem to have been well aware that the negotiators wanted their land but time after time they refused to agree to transfer it. In fact, they repeatedly declared, 'this is our land'. Amerindians were willing to grant access to their land and their resources but the price which they insisted on in return was full economic security for their people. We can see that this recognition of their future needs in some of the different provisions from one treaty to the next. For Instance, by Treaty #6 the recipients received a medicine chest while by Treaty #3 the recipients negotiated for larger plots of land. Historians such as Friesen argue that native people knew what they were doing because they used the terminology of kin in the treaties and kinship entailed obligation.

The intense discussion over the meaning of treaties and the question of why Amerindians signed and what they hoped to gain points to a far greater problem within the historical discipline. It shows that historians have been torn between their traditional outlook of Amerindians as children, wards, incapable of influencing let alone shaping policy, to the newer approach which no longer thinks of European-Amerindian relationships in terms of victim-oppressor but views Amerindian peoples as active participants and agents, in the historical process. As we move further away from the 'victim' mentality it is harder to view Amerindians as dupes in the process of treaty making. Instead, it is possible to see them as peoples who recognized that they were in a difficult position, that the world was changing around them and that they actively needed to make some choices to meet the new challenges they faced. This does not mean that we must accept that there were no misunderstandings at the treaty negotiations but that perhaps the spirit of the treaties was sound but the manner in which they unfolded was unexpected. There were some indications that the Treaty Commissioners were not consistent at each of the negotiations and they may have sent different signals to different groups. For example, in the Elders interviews undertaken in the 1970s for TARR, the Cree Elders of Treaty #6 agreed that the treaty was an agreement to let the Canadians use the land for farming. For the Treaty #7 Elders the situation was different. They believed that neither the sale nor the borrowing of the land had been mentioned, instead in return for keeping the peace. The treaty was not an instrument of land surrender but a peace treaty. The two treaties of great importance in the West, dealing with the Cree and Blackfoot aboriginal communities within present-day southern Alberta and the central portion of Saskatchewan boundaries are Treaties #6 & #7. The area involved was extensive and soon to be settled by immigrants brought in by Laurier and Sifton. During the negotiations, Poundmaker, who would later become chief made a famous speech about the land, "This is our land it is not a piece of pemmican to be cut off and given in little pieces back to us. It is ours and we will take what we want." In 1876 negotiations were heated and the participants were promised aid and rations in the event of famine. This 'famine clause' would soon become a source of discord between the Amerindian communities and the Government with the disappearance of the buffalo. The following

year, Treaty #7 was concluded because the government badly needed to
reach an agreement with the Blackfoot. Fortunately for the government,
Crowfoot was on friendly terms with and trusted James Macleod of the
NWMP and this influenced him at the signing. One of the missionaries
present at the signing speculated that Crowfoot and the others had not
signed a treaty in order to hand over their lands and their rights in the lands
but because he and his people had been dealt with kindly by the authorities
in previous treaties or agreements. Crowfoot hoped that the treaties would
simply give them food and clothing whenever the need arose. Red Crow, on
the other hand, believed that the treaty would keep the Métis and the Cree
out of Blackfoot territory and stop them from following Blackfoot buffalo.
In fact, quite the reverse occurred.

In contrast to this, the politicians back in Ottawa were not particularly
interested in the fate of the participants. It was expected that they would,
in all likelihood be placed on reserves and trained in agriculture. Instead
they expected to continue with their traditional lifestyle while being able to
turn now to the government in time of crisis. Neither side saw the crisis
coming. It was the disappearance of the buffalo which brought matters to
a head. The completion of the Union Pacific railroad in 1869 had cut the
herd in two and a massive slaughter began. By 1879 virtually no plains
bison remained. This led to a crisis for the Plains Indians who had to go
further and further south. The presence of Sitting Bull and his Sioux
followers to the south only made matters worse. Faced with certain starvation,
thousands of Amerindians crossed the border to go on the hunt. Those left
behind faced the threat of famine and the years from 1878 to 1880 were the
worst in Amerindian history. People were reduced to killing horses and
dogs. At Fort Macleod thousands were fed everyday from a small amount
of rations. The situation was critical and the government fearing an Indian
rising rushed supplies to the region. Still it was not enough. In 1880 the
Indian department was formed to take control of Indian policy and its first
priority was to place Amerindians on reserves where their activities could
be monitored. This policy was not successful in the Alberta region at first
because many remained south of the border. But, as the misery continued
the majority of people agreed to take up their reserve. This was the
beginning of a policy of restriction and wardship.

Just a few words in general about life for the Cree and Blackfoot after
the rebellion. The best source for this is Sarah Carter's *Lost Harvests*. In it
Carter examines the restriction placed upon Amerindians involved in
agriculture on the prairies in the late nineteenth century. Carter argues that
the Cree were generally unsuccessful at farming for a complex blend of

reasons, none of which have to do with laziness, etc. First she noted that they had done quite well in the decade following treaty, buying farm equipment, participating in agricultural fairs and the like. They had pooled their resources and farmed the land in common. Then the Department of Indian Affairs decided that it would promote individualism and break this tribalism that they believed held back the process of assimilation.

These changes bore their fruits under Hayter Reed, Indian Commissioner from 1889-97. Reed believed that Indians should be kept like subsistence peasant farmers. This meant that they could only plough what their family could harvest by itself. There was to be no farm machinery of any sort involved unless homemade, because machinery made people lazy (he neglected to admit aloud that machinery also made farmers competitive). Indians were not to grow cereal crops because that would put them in direct competition with the new settlers who were already fighting over a limited market. Reed introduced the ban on machinery and the pass system to restrict the movement of people and goods. He also upheld the ban on raising investment capital from outside sources.

Of course all of this was well in line with public opinion, which when it thought at all about Indians, thought that they should be assimilated and the reserves broken into separate landholdings. There was also a general feeling that man had progressed through several stages of development to reach his present lofty position and that the Indians could not be allowed to 'skip' a stage by adopting modern technology immediately. This was a common theme in both America and Britain in the late 1880s and was often applied to the working classes as well (Chamberlain in 1885 election— Dawes Act of 1887 in America). By the early 1890s the Indians began direct petitions to Ottawa but Reed was able to explain it all away by saying that these people were chronic whiners and complainers, so no one paid them much attention. They were sacrificed at the high altar of immigration.

Carter argues that it was Reed's policy which undermined the development of agriculture on the reserve and promoted instead the good of settlers.

Coming to Terms with Western Settlement

There was little to do but to resign themselves to what they hoped was better than it seemed, but the taking of reserves was followed, under Edgar Dewdney, by a virtual policy of starvation in an attempt to bring recalcitrant Cree leaders like Big Bear, into line. There were occasional moments of tension usually caused by the shortage of food. Commissioner Macleod wrote in his official correspondence with Ottawa that hunger was a dangerous element and something which should be avoided if possible in the interests of peace on the plains. When stories of starvation and deprivation made their way to Ottawa the government acted promptly and supplies were rushed to the western forts but, the government insisted that this was merely a temporary measure. Edgar Dewdney had been appointed as the first Indian Commissioner and given sweeping powers to control policy in the North-west. Dewdney met with the leading chiefs and tried to persuade them to settle on their reserves making them self-sufficient in as little time as possible.

Although Dewdney also made it clear that the government's assistance was temporary, he was also careful to point out that no one would starve, in this early phase of settling in on the reserves. At the same time, in 1882, the Mounties force was almost doubled, to 500 men. They had a huge, un-manageable jurisdiction over 350,000 square miles of territory but this strengthening of the force was seen as necessary because there were approximately 27,000 starving Indians in the area and trouble was anticipated. The boom in land values had also just begun along the CPR route through the prairies, and there was a boom in settlement, for instance, the population of Winnipeg doubled in a twelve month period. One of the first difficulties came with trying to control the thousands of railway workers in the western territory and with them, the unregulated appearance of alcohol and the violent crimes associated with its use.

The building of the Canadian Pacific Railway (CPR), had quite a dramatic effect on the government's Indian policy. The government wanted all of the reserves to be moved north of the track and out of the Cypress Hills area, to stop their movement south across to the USA. There was of course heated resistance to this, and Cree leader, Piapot, uprooted the survey stakes and camped his people in front of the construction crews. The Mounties could not deny them the right to hunt through tracts of surrendered land but the fact that many Indians were destitute by now and allowed police to bribe them away from the Fort Walsh area, and by the spring of 1883 most Cree were escorted north, Fort Walsh was torn down and Regina made the new headquarters. Slow starvation and a bitter winter had brought the Cree to this sorry condition where they could be pushed about by government officials. The Blackfoot too were in strained circumstances, reduced to boiling moccasins and rawhide in water for sustenance. Times were worse than they had ever been and the Blackfoot threatened to kill the government men if not given proper tools or seed and if rations were not increased. There were many instances of resistance as the police force tried to stop the Sun Dance and other traditional celebrations.

In 1883 there was an outbreak on the reserve of Poundmaker, 2000 Indians assembled for the annual thirst dance, a modified version of the Sun Dance. The local farm instructor was assaulted at one point during the gathering and the local Mounties were sent for. On their arrival they were surrounded by an angered crowd and forced to hand out rations. This was the only action that could offset further violence. Still there was no general uprising and if anyone had the grievances to justify rebellion it was the native population.

When the rebellion came however, it was as a result of Métis complaints stemming from the settlement of 1870 and their movement westward in the face of a fast moving settlement frontier. Sadly enough it was the Cree and Blackfoot who came up the losers in this conflict as well. What the 1885 rebellion shows, is that the Canadian Government's attempt to settle the Western lands, and to deal for them through land script and treaty, had solved nothing. The Manitoba Act, and Treaties One through Seven, had not addressed the reality of the changes taking place on the prairies. As life deteriorated for the Cree, Blackfoot and Métis, new tensions erupted under the pressure of a wave of settlers crowding into areas formerly closed to them. An examination of the Rebellion of 1885 raises a number of interesting questions; was it the last stand of Amerindians and Métis, both worried about their physical and cultural survival? Did it happen because of government indifference to their plight or because of the figure of Louis Riel who once again played a central role in the history of the first nations struggle against the government? To answer this we need to look first to Riel. After the 1869 rising, Riel led an interesting lie, ending up as a school teacher on a reserve in Montana. During this period he had either a deeply moving religious experience or a bout with insanity. In 1884 he was asked by a delegation of Métis to once again represent their interests and he accepted. Riel believed that this was a call from God and, after his return to Canada he gradually began to reveal his religious doctrine. His followers accepted his new religion but it did not outlast the rebellion. The central focus of this religion was Riel himself. He often used the signature 'Prophet' and modelled himself on David in the *Old Testament*. According to Riel the Métis had a mission but religion played no role at all in his contact with the Cree. The Métis were God's chosen people. The Métis were the mingling of the first chosen people (the Indians, descended from the wandering Hebrew tribes), with the French (great missionary people of the Christian era). The Métis were the chosen people and, would continue to expand and perfect the evangelical vision of New France. This new religion was to spread around the world and the Métis would be the vanguard. The Métis would be first to break with the Catholic Church. Riel felt that he was inaugurating the last phase of human history before Christ returned. He would create a theocracy; fusion of church and state.

While Riel had been out of the political scene the North-west had obtained its own Lieutenant Governor in 1875. The capital became Battleford in 1877. David Laird was the first appointee, replaced in 1881 by Edgar Dewdney, a Macdonald man (Indian Commissioner for two years prior to that). But there were three groups of inhabitants in the North-west and each group had its own grievances which the government in Ottawa seemed slow to address. Canadian settlers complained that the homesteading process was much too slow and they were upset by the relocation of the CPR to a more southerly route. The settlers also had political demands for better representation in Ottawa. The Métis settlers were upset because of the introduction of square lots rather than their traditional river lot arrangement. The Amerindian communities of the West, especially the Plains Cree had been unable to persuade the government to set their reserves adjoining each other. By the early 1880s, the promised government assistance for this period of transition had simply not materialized. Big Bear spent much of 1879 trying to marshal support for an Indian Confederacy, but, he had little success. Big Bear then tried to get a large block reserve near Cypress Hills, in effect creating an Indian territorial base but the government refused to sanction this. A new policy was even started whereby Indians would have to work for their rations. Until 1882 Poundmaker did not grumble or threaten Indian department employees. But when the promised aid was not forthcoming and the rations were cut in the winter of 1882-83 Poundmaker was as discouraged as anyone.

On the government side, the biggest problem came in the spring of 1883 when a large gathering of Cree met near the border at Cypress Hills. As long as Big Bear, Little Pine, Lucky Man and Piapot remained in the Cypress Hills, they attracted large numbers of Cree who had already taken reserve. The Cree relied on Fort Walsh for sustenance so, the only thing to do was to close the fort. Only after this action did the Cree agree to move North.

These diverse communities in the North-west needed to take some action which would make the government take notice of them. A delegation was appointed to get Riel and arrived at St. Peter's Mission, Sun River, Montana in the summer of 1884. Riel agreed to accompany them to Canada. He felt that he had to be there in person to help. He returned faster than anyone expected, 5 July and immediately made overtures to the English Métis. He was invited to speak to the business community at

Prince Albert and pressed for a grand coalition. The settlers, Amerindians and Métis were to petition Ottawa to establish provinces in the North-west. Riel also wanted the land laws amended to better suit the rapid settlement of the country and speed up the process of gaining title.

Throughout the fall Riel worked on drafts of the petition to send to Ottawa. The petition, sent on 16 December 1884, called for free title to the land for settlers, making homesteading process easier, guaranteeing the rights of all pre-survey tenants, two million acres of land for the Métis, a 240 acre grant for each Métis and finally for the distribution of proper rations to the Indians. While this action was being taken out in West the government in Ottawa passed an Order-in-Council, in January 1885, authorizing the Minister of the Interior to appoint a three man commission to make a list of all half-breeds. No mention was made of their grievances and only a vague promise was given, to investigate their claims. Riel's measured response came on 8 March when he announced his intention to proclaim provisional government. At a meeting that day he passed a ten-point *Bill of Rights,* similar to the earlier document sent to Ottawa. Riel was trying to duplicate the Red River rising of 1869. But there were differences this time: 500 Mounties; the CPR; and thousands of white settlers. The Métis formed themselves into companies of 10 men and one captain, modelled on the organization of the hunt and formed a council. Government troops moved out of Fort Carlton to oppose Riel on March 26 without waiting for reinforcements. Both sides met at Duck Lake. The battle lasted 30 minutes and at the end 9 volunteers and 3 Mounties lay dead. On the other side the toll was 5 Métis and Indians. Riel intervened to prevent further slaughter. Fort Carlton was abandoned but fire destroyed most of its buildings. The effect of the victory was that the Duck Lake Cree joined Riel. News of the government defeat spread rapidly, and terror seized the little Prairie communities. Many abandoned their farms and fled to Prince Albert and Battleford. The rebellion lasted until May with battles taking place at Battleford, Fish Creek and Cutknife Hill. The final confrontation took place at Batoche when the Métis were overwhelmed by the sheer numbers and artillery ranged against them.

Riel gave himself up to the authorities on 15 May 1885. The question now was what to do with Riel? After some deliberation the government decided that the Canadian and Métis settlers had not rebelled on their own but had been pushed into it by Riel. They ignored the fact that he was an American citizen and tried him for High Treason (status of Edward III, 1352). The trouble was that his trial could only go ahead if he were sane at the time of the rebellion, and a few people had their doubts. In the end this was not a problem because Riel refused to plead insanity in case Métis grievances would therefore not be taken seriously. He defended the Métis cause from the dock but was still found guilty, although the jury recommended mercy. When the news of the verdict reached Quebec there was pandemonium. Two appeals delayed the inevitable for a time but, on 16 November 1885, Riel was hanged by the neck until dead. Speeches given by Laurier in support of Riel would, within a short time, catapult him into the office of Prime Minister. Laurier said that Riel was not the cause of the rebellion, rather, the government was. Outside of this most of the government's time and effort went into persecuting the Cree Chiefs, One Arrow, Big Bear and Poundmaker who each received three year sentences for their part in the rebellion on very tenuous evidence.

The rebellion produced a dramatic change in Western Canada. First of all, the NWT did get representation in Parliament. Secondly, a Half-Breed commission was set up to hand out land scrips. Thirdly, a rebellion losses committee was set up to re-imburse settlers. But no crops went in for a year or two, it continued to take too long to settle claims and, the Métis were broken as a political force creating the conditions for their final dispersal. Many left for Montana and the Dakotas, others moved to The Pas in Manitoba to take to the trap lines, and still others came West to St. Albert, Lac La Biche and further north to the Mackenzie River area and the southern tip of the modern day North-west Territories. Most had found themselves the victims of land speculators after 1885, selling their land scrips.

Meeting the Challenge of an Urban/Industrial Society

By the turn of the century it was clear that Canadians saw Indians as obstacles to progress, a people that would either become Canadian or disappear as a cultural force in their own right. When neither happened, the politicians and bureaucrats were at a loss. It would take nearly seven decades for politicians to come up with a 'new' approach. Prime Minister Trudeau provided this in the late 1960s but its only success was that it focused the leadership of the Amerindian community and they emerged with their own vision of the future for their people. Since the 1970s this has developed into a political strategy that will see them take over the running of their own affairs and, participate in the constitutional affairs of Canada. When the newly elected house began to sit in January of 1994, the Minister of Indian Affairs promised that the talks for self-government would start immediately. How did the course of Amerindian affairs change so dramatically from the restrictive ward system at the turn of the century to the state of affairs in 1993 when four groups (speaking on behalf of a variety of status and non-status peoples) were represented at constitutional talks with the Conservative Government and negotiated for recognition of the First Nations inherent right to self-government?

The first real sign that Amerindians were not going to fade into the background came with a demographic change. By the 1930s the Amerindian birth rate was increasing faster than any other group in the country but this had a negative side because it also brought overcrowding on the reserves and led to a certain restiveness within native communities. On the government side there was by the interwar years increasing doubt that the residential schools and Industrial schools had not accomplished their original goals of civilizing and assimilating young native children. Amerindian communities were in poor shape. The government had recognized that its policy of separating children from their families and cutting them off from their spiritual belief systems and culture was counterproductive but there was little or no attempts at reform because the country was focusing its energies on other issues. Amerindians, especially in the West, found their lands encroached upon, their diets poor, and their susceptibility to European diseases, especially to tuberculosis, worrying and devastating. Disease ran unchecked through the residential schools in the early decades of the century giving mortality rates of 50 per cent in some schools. But the trend towards population decline was halted in the 1920s and in the decade following, for the first time, their numbers increased. In the 1930s their numbers climbed over the 110,000 mark and another boom in population came again in the 1950s. This decade then marks real change in Amerindian communities' attitudes towards their own future and a change in attitude in the population at large.

Pressures for Change

Within Amerindian communities nationwide there were attempts to gain redress for past grievance. The province where this activity was most vocal and at first most successful was British Columbia, the very region which for a variety of historical circumstances had signed very few treaties. By the time British Columbia entered Confederation its government had been loathe to recognize land claims of its Amerindian communities although they proclaimed that the lands belonged to them because their aboriginal title had never been extinguished. In 1864 British Columbia had refused to make treaties and to hand over reserve lands and at the time of Confederation and after, the government in Ottawa had been busy elsewhere and not insisted on a transfer of territory to Amerindian peoples. It was hoped that this would be rectified in 1888 when the Privy Council recognized that Amerindians did have land rights but the provincial government refused to acknowledge what it considered to be outside interference. The issue went to a Royal Commission in 1912 and by 1915 some new reserve lands were indeed handed over. This gave encouragement to other Amerindian communities experiencing difficulties with provincial governments. What made the struggle in British Columbia very interesting was that, with a few exceptions, they had never surrendered their lands to the Crown. In 1902 a number of tribes petitioned to the Monarch and formed an organization which was known as *The Indian Tribes of the Province of British Columbia* and began issuing land claims petitions. As early as 1906 as the provincial and federal government argued over Amerindian land rights, Joseph Capilano, Chief of the Squamish, ignored both and appealed directly to the British Crown. By 1927 the federal government was forced to set up a Joint Committee on Indian claims and it found that Amerindian groups in the province had not established a claim to their lands based on aboriginal title. After this, the Department of Indian Affairs amended the Indian Act to make it a criminal offence to raise funds to put in a land claim without their prior permission. This was not dropped until the 1950s.

There had been some political activity outside of British Columbia as well. This first congress of the *League of Indians of Canada* was held in 1919. It protested against the pass system, pressed the government for better schooling, called for a protection of Amerindian culture and for the spirit of the treaties to be followed. It would later break into two groups. After WWI and the creation of the League of Nations, Amerindians made their presence felt in the halls of power there where they fought for freedom from the oppression of the Indian Act and, after 1930, from a lack of recognition of treaty rights by provincial governments.

This nascent political action came to a head in the years following the Great Depression and can best be seen by looking at some of the new political organizations founded. Two of these organizations were the *Indian Association of Alberta* (1939) and the *Federation of Saskatchewan Indians* (1944). The leaders were graduates of the old residential schools, Eugene Steinhauer in Alberta and John Tootoosis in Saskatchewan. Later came the *Native Brotherhood of British Columbia* who, despite the Indian Act, continued to petition for land claims and who spoke before the parliamentary committee of 1946-48 set up to discuss changes to the Indian Act. In the decade after the end of WWII, Canadians seemed to cross that bridge between seeing the need for reform and actually doing something about it. The post-war era saw Canadians take the first steps towards a policy that seemed to promise a chance of success, although the long-term goal of assimilation was never really dropped. A joint committee was set up to consider changes to the

Indian Act and it received submissions from a variety of these new political organizations but never seemed to listen to what it heard. The final result was that the coercive elements of the Act were tempered but the long-term goal remained. This approach was acceptable to the Liberal Government and the Indian Act was amended to this effect in 1951. Not much had changed.

For northern peoples, their status in the new dominion had been uncertain from the beginning. In 1924, the Indian Act was amended to include them within the jurisdiction of the Federal Government. This meant that the Eskimo (or Inuit) were under the direct control of the government through the Department of Indian Affairs and there they remained until the 1930s. In the late 1930s, the Premier of Quebec, Maurice Duplessis, took Ottawa to court over the issue of responsibility for the native peoples of northern Quebec. On anthropological evidence the Federal Government made the case that these Inuits were not really Indians at all and therefore should be the responsibility of the provincial government. But, the Supreme Court of Canada ruled that, for administrative purpose, the Inuits were Indian and therefore a Federal responsibility. Although the government accepted this 1939 ruling, it later gave authority for the Inuits to the Minister of Resources and Development and excluded them from the revised Indian Act of 1951. As government and business became interested in the exploitation of the north and making sure that Canada's sovereignty in the North could be sustained, (especially from the Diefenbaker era onwards) a change was called for in the structure of Indian affairs. The result was the amalgamation in 1966, of the Indian administration and northern resource management into the department of Indian Affairs and Northern Development (DIAND). This new department was reorganized again in the late 1980s to act as an advocate for native initiatives and is called Indian and Northern Affairs Canada (INAC). The rights of the Inuit to be considered as aboriginal people has since been entrenched in the constitution which was patriated in 1982. The mandate of INAC is to help native people to move quickly towards self-government, to aid in economic development and to protect the special relationship that exists between native people and the federal government. INAC has been involved in the process of transferring control to bands and away from the federal government and is at the present time in the first stage of being dismantled. Because of the political activity in the north, there have been some dramatic changes which have involved the formation of a North-west Territories and a Yukon government with some Inuit representation and with government headquarters in the region. This increased recognition of the need for direct political involvement in the north has also brought to fruition an ideal which has been a dream of the Inuit for decades. Thanks to

the work of political organizations such as Tapirisat, we have in 1994, passed
into legislation, the framework for the creation of a new territory called
Nunavut which will be run by the Inuit. Nunavut received royal assent in
June 1993 and will have redrawn the Political map of Canada by 1999.

There have been other changes since the 1950s especially on the thorny
issue of Amerindian rights to the land. Action now began on land claims
because suddenly the peripheral areas that they had been shunted off to were
found to contain a wealth of minerals, out West this was especially true after
the major oil finds. The resource boom in the West meant the penetration of
marginal areas again by business and government. Conflict would continue
to occur over and over again from the Pacific Coast to Central Canada.
Businessmen wanted to see land claims settled one way or the other so that
these mineral resources could be harvested and pressure was now applied to
the Federal government so that the Canadian economy would not be held
back.

In terms of external influences on attitudes towards native people, this
was the era of global decolonization, European powers getting out or being
thrown out of Africa, the Middle East, India, and Latin America. Canadian
native groups were also affected by a politically radical movement in
America, part and parcel of the activism of the 1960s. This was AIM, the
American Indian Movement. Social conditions on U.S. reserves were generally
very poor and blame was put upon the Bureau of Indian Affairs which was
responsible for federal policy towards Indians. AIM was founded in the late
1960s by Dennis Banks and George Mitchell. At first its purpose was simply
to ease the transition from reserve to urban life but through this work they
became aware of the depths of the social problems their people faced. The
organization turned militant and its spokesmen called for the restoration of
tribal lands, for better social welfare programmes and for more vigilance in
the protection of the civil rights of Indian people. AIM and other groups were
involved in political demonstrations such as the Broken Treaties Caravan
which moved on Washington in 1972, and the occupation of the village of
Wounded Knee the following year. Canadian native organizations while
seldom so militant, could not help but be influenced by the struggle of Indian
people to the south. The question being asked in Canada was, did Canadians
intend to continue forever treating aboriginal communities like little colonies
inside the country, controlling their political and economic life? This line of
questioning had an impact on Pierre Trudeau who, as part of his *Just Society*
platform answered No! They should be just like any other Canadians. He
was also, no doubt, influenced by the *Hawthorn Report* on Canadian Amerindians issued in the mid-1960s which illustrated that native people in this

country were in a miserable state indeed. Harry B. Hawthorn was asked in 1963 to head an investigation into the position of Amerindians in Canada and the North. His report, published in 1966, gave 151 recommendations. Hawthorn found that the condition of Amerindian communities and individuals in the country left much to be desired. He supported modifications to the Indian Act which would allow for greater levels of political independence, and, more importantly he claimed that Amerindians should not be forced to accept the values of the dominant society. Hawthorn highlighted the need for Indian Affairs to play a more active role (advocacy) in setting the groundwork for future self-government. He saw a stronger commitment to education as one of the necessary tools for achieving political independence. He also noted that the bands had very little control over the monies held in trust for them and pointed out that without an economic base there could be no lasting political autonomy.

Changes in the federal approach towards Amerindians also came because of the rise of a number of articulate leaders from within their own communities who framed their plight in Canada in terms of the Third World. They identified strongly with the colonial world and some of the abuses therein.

Besides regional groups, there have been a number of active national groups, among them are the North American Indian Brotherhood which represented all non-treaty Indians until its demise in 1969. There was also the National Indian Council (NIC), founded in 1960 and funded by the Secretary of State. It lasted only until 1968 because of the incompatibility of the aims of its membership. In 1968 it divided into the National Indian Brotherhood (NIB) which represented status Indians, and the Native Council of Canada (NCC) which represented non-status Indians and the Métis.

The NCC has been recognized by the Federal Government since 1982 and has participated in the constitutional debate which has dogged Canadian political life since then. In 1983, however, this organization has seen a substantial number of its members leave and create a new group, the Métis National Council which focuses not on the call for re-instatement as status Indians (as the NCC did) but on aboriginal rights and Métis self-government.

The NIB maintained its focuse on acting as an advocate for status Indians but it was thrown on to the centre of the political stage by the introduction of the government White Paper in 1968. The position taken by the Liberal government of the day forced the NIB into the position of spokesmen for all native concerns. The leadership of the NIB became Ottawa-based lobbyists. They were successful in raising the awareness of Canadians on this issue. By 1980 the organization was showing some signs of strain as it moved into action to guard aboriginal rights as the constitution was patriated. By late 1981 it was no longer seen as representative enough and as it ground to a halt, another organization came to take its place, the Assembly of First Nations. The Assembly (AFN) concentrates on constitutional issues and the issue of self-government. It has worked closely with the federal government and fought successfully to win representation at the constitutional talks. The AFN has a Council of Elders and a national chief. Ovide Mercredi has just been elected to a second term in office as national chief. The AFN is an organization developed by chiefs to gain respect for the sovereignty of the *First Nations*. Since the creation of this organization, the term 'First Nations' has become part of the Canadian vocabulary. Although it is a politically charged term, it is likely the most commonly used, replacing Amerindian, Native and Aboriginal in common usage. The AFN position is that the First Nations have an inherent right to self-government and that aboriginal rights have never been extinguished. The AFN has its critics but it has been successful in coping with the challenge of representing people with a great diversity of condition and needs.

One of the most dramatic changes which have occurred in the native community since the 1960s is the struggle of native women for some redress of their grievances. Change began in the late 1960s with the Royal Commission on the Status of Women. This commission was charged with the responsibility of finding the types of inequalities that existed and providing recommendations for change. In 1968 Mary Two-Axe Early, a non-status Mohawk, presented her case to the commission. She had married a non-native and under law lost her status. What brought her to the commission was a related matter. Her parents had left her a house on the reserve and in 1967 the band informed her that as a non-status Indian she could not hold property on the reserve. When native women married non-natives they lost their status and privileges but when non-native women married native partners they gained full rights as status Indians. Two other separate cases were brought through the courts in the early 1970s (Bedard and Lavell) and reached the Supreme Court in 1973. The women lost their case 5 to 4 on the grounds that the Canadian Bill of Rights did not overrule the Indian Act. Taken together, these cases, supported by feminist groups, saw the emergence of a national body of native women, The Native Womens Association of Canada (1971). Within a few years it was lobbying both the NIB and NCC and was called to make presentations to a house subcommittee. The association believed that women should not lose all their rights through marriage. A Maliseet woman (Lovelace) brought her case before the United Nations Human Rights Commission in Geneva. She too had lost her status upon marriage and although separated from her husband found herself barred from returning to her reserve. The Canadian government promised to pass an amendment to the Indian Act to remove any discrimination based on gender. Subsequent changes to the Act have removed the discriminatory clauses. The result is Bill C-31, passed in 1985. Bill C-31 was an amendment to the Indian Act which redefined who was an Indian and tried to reinstate some groups excluded in the past such as women who had married non-natives and lost their status. The Federal government used its power to make bands reinstate women who had lost their status through marriage. This was seen as a victory by native women but has brought a court case against the government by Walter Twinn of the Sawridge band of Alberta. Band councils have pointed out the drain that this will cause on their resources since 20,000 or more women nationwide are eligible to reapply. In fact, by 1991 almost 70,000 people had successfully applied to regain their status but only a small number are back on their reserves.

The political activity of these native organizations throughout the last three decades has been able to offset and then redirect some of the paths of action proposed by the federal government. The federal government under Lester B. Pearson had seemed committed to revising the Indian Act but the election of P.E. Trudeau in 1968, temporarily halted any change. Pierre Trudeau could not be seen to concede special status to Indians when the Quebec government was breathing down his neck for exactly the same thing and he was unwilling to concede to its demands. There was to be no legislation giving anyone special status! Trudeau felt that the best way to stop French Canadians and Amerindians being treated as second class citizens was to make everyone equal under the law and not to have any group in a treaty situation. He refused to accept the argument that in the historical sense, successive governments, had treated the native peoples of Canada badly and therefore that they needed special help to catch up. Despite this belief, he continued the government's consultation with native political organizations especially the National Indian Council (NIC).

NIC leaders called for economic assistance from the government. They wanted Ottawa to set up a claims commission to settle the steadily growing number of land claims. The organization believed that it was part of a meaningful process of consultation yet, within two months of the Trudeau victory in 1968, Jean Chretien rose in the house and presented the *White Paper*. This statement of intent implied that the policy contained in it had been formulated after a year of consultation with native leaders. It came as a shock to the NIC. In summary the White Paper said that Indians were disadvantaged because they had a different legal status from other Canadians. The problems of poverty which they faced and the fact that they were marginalized within the national economy could all be resolved by changing the law. The first step therefore that needed to be taken was to abolish Indian status, transfer control of Indian communal lands to them, repeal the Indian Act and make them just one more part of the multi-ethnic society that was Trudeau's vision for Canada. All of this was to be phased in over a five-year period.

It is clear that some of the philosophy behind this was tied into the larger world outside of Canada, decolonization for example, and it does have its own internal logic. Native leaders were stunned by this latest direction in government policy. To those who cried foul, Chretien maintained that the White Paper had been framed in consultation with native leaders and that it was not right for countries to have internal treaty agreements with segments of its population. The White Paper was a slap in the face to native leaders because it had ignored Indian proposals for advancement without assimilation and was a clear sign that the government did no want to fulfil its part of the treaty responsibilities. It was also a very handy solution for the government because this would let it off the hook for the pile of land claims petitions piling up the nation's capital. The White Paper dismissed the idea of aboriginal title and dispensed of the need for a claims commission. Part of the problem for the new government may have been that Trudeau wanted quick action and decided to circumvent the usual channels such as the Department of Indian Affairs. He believed in individualism and equality of opportunity and disliked dealing with collectivities. The NIC did not take the White Paper as the final word on the future of its peoples. Instead, its leaders fought back. Ironically, the government's policy revitalized the political agenda of the NIC by providing a focus for joint political action.

The Alberta Chiefs led this political rallying, arguing that the treaties were moral as well as legal obligations and called, ironically, for the Indian Act and the Department of Indian Affairs to be retained. Their worry was that an acceptance of the White Paper would mean a loss of special status and a loss of federal protection. Harold Cardinal, Cree representative from the Indian Association of Alberta and later the author of *Unjust Society,* tore the government's position to shreds and accused it of a deliberate policy of the extermination of Indian culture. By June, 1970, the Chiefs of Alberta had drafted a response called *Citizen Plus,* more commonly referred to as the Red Paper. This response from the native community called for amendments to the Indian Act rather than outright abolition. It also looked to education as a way to improve the socio-economic position of native communities and called for the creation of an Indian Education centre which would prepare children for life in Canada without having to relinquish their traditional way of life. This was not followed up on by the government but education would become the rallying point for native communities from one end of the country to the other and both the NIB (National Indian Brotherhood) and the AFN (Assembly of First Nations) would spend much of their energies in the 1970s and 1980s on plans for Indian control of Indian education. This has now become a reality with over 80 per cent of status Indians receiving an education which is band controlled and culturally appropriate. Within a year, the government had to retract the White Paper and covered its tracks by claiming that it had only been up for discussion and was not government policy. Native leaders were not only concerned about education they were also concerned about other political issues in the 1970s and 1980s. One of the political actions which had the most potential for affecting native communities was the Trudeau government's patriation of the constitution. The constitution amendment bill was introduced in 1978 and although the government arranged for native organizations to attend the First Ministers Conferences on this issue, they were to attend as observers not participants. The National Indian Brotherhood, the Native Council of Canada and the Inuit Committee on National Issues were all present but their worry was that only vague reference to their people had been made in the lead up to the conference. The NIB continued, albeit unsuccessfully, to demand voting privileges. By 1980 the NIB protest had paid off. The Trudeau government gave each of the native organizations $400,000 to research and make their presentations on constitutional reform and aboriginal peoples. Still, when the First Ministers conference met in 1980, aboriginal issues were not on the table and the native organizations attended only as observers. The native response to this was dramatic, a mini conference was held and then a lobby group was sent to London where they also took out advertisements in the *London Times* stating their concerns over the protection of their rights with a patriated constitution. The following year the federal government added a section protecting the rights of all aboriginal peoples and promised a First Minister conference dealing with aboriginal issues. But, when the 1982 accord emerged, it had no clause recognizing aboriginal or treaty rights and an Aboriginal Rights Coalition emerged. When the constitution was finally patriated section 35 of the constitution act enshrined aboriginal rights, section 25 ensured that aboriginal rights would not be affected negatively by the charter of rights and freedoms and section 32 required that the federal government hold more First Minister conferences to deal with aboriginal issues. While the final stages of patriation were ongoing, the National Indian Brotherhood gave way to a new organization, the Assembly of First Nations and while the government continued to talk of aboriginal rights the native community responded with their own change in terminology 'First Nations'.

What the native community had won in the patriation process was recognition of 'existing' aboriginal rights but there was not definition of exactly what that meant. It is still a problematic term for governments today. But, to the AFN, aboriginal rights meant land rights, self-government, control of land resources and sovereignty. One of the great steps forwards for aboriginal communities was that the Métis and the Inuit were now also recognized as aboriginal people.

The government honoured its obligation and a number of First Ministers Conferences on aboriginal issues were held from 1983 to 1987. The first stalled because provincial premiers were not happy with the First Nations plan of self-government in the forseeable future and there was some dissension within the native community over what self-government actually meant. The Penner Report was also published in 1893. It was an all party parliamentary report on aboriginal self-government. The report supported First Nations aspirations and called for self-government of a style of their own choosing which would be entrenched in legislation. In other words, Penner said that self-government was an aboriginal right. In June 1984 Bill C-52 was introduced in House, *An Act Relating to Self-Government for Indian Nations,* but parliament ended and the bill died. The next session however, saw the introduction of Bill C-93 which was based on Bill C-52. The AFN was not happy with this bill because it did not recognize sovereignty, it merely delegated its authority to native communities at the band level. In 1984 the Liberal Government was voted out of office and replaced by the Conservative Party led by Brian Mulroney. The First Ministers Conference of that year had ended in frustration with few provincial premiers supporting the concept of self-government and, to make matters worse, the Nielson report, which showed that the Conservative Government was going to slash budgets and follow a narrow intrepretation of its fiduciary obligations to aboriginal groups, was made public. A legal challenge was immediately launched and in 1985 the Supreme Court of Canada upheld the fiduciary responsibility of the Federal Government. The promised First Ministers conferences continued until 1987 but the definition of self-government was still not clear and premiers continued to disagree that native people in Canada had an inherent right to self-government. There were some gains in the 1980s. The Cree-Naskapi Act of 1984 in Quebec was seen as the first piece of self-government legislation and took on the responsibilities for programmes that, until then, were administered by the Department of Indian Affairs. This was followed by the Sechelt Indian Band Self Government Act of 1986 in British Columbia. Advances were made in another key area when Bill C-31 removed any sexual discrimination from the Indian Act.

In 1987, the political scene in Canada found new life, when Prime Minister Brian Mulroney put forward his plan to bring Quebec back into the constitutional fold by proposing that Quebec should be recognized as distinct and given special status. This became known as the Meech Lake Accord and it was signed by all the premiers and was to be ratified within three years. With their wishes for self-government still yet unrecognized the AFN and other native groups were opposed to the 'special status' for Quebec when the premiers had refused it over the decade for them. The AFN was also opposed to Meech Lake because it perpetuated the myth that Canada was the creation of two national groups, French and English and gave no recognition to First Nations people. As the final deadline drew near and the Accord began to slowly unravel it fell to Elijah Harper, a native and backbencher in the Manitoba Legislature to end the accord. As the self-imposed deadline of the Mulroney government approached only New Brunswick and Manitoba had still to ratify the deal and Newfoundland remained opposed. The premiers of New Brunswick and Manitoba agreed to present the Accord in their legislatures and Newfoundland said it would no longer oppose it if the other two provinces ratified the accord. Harper, a Cree chief from Red Sucker Lake opposed the deal and it collapsed in June 1990. In the last few years the Conservative Government once again sought constitutional change and this time the AFN was actively engaged in the process. The latest attempt, known as the Charlottetown Accord, was also a failure. The Charlottetown accord would have written the right of First Nations people to govern themselves, into the constitution. It was not rejected because of this but because it tried to be all things to all people and in the end it failed.

The Conservative Government was defeated in the last election and the Liberal Government of Jean Chretien has been active in native issues since its election in late 1993. In January 1994, the new Minister of Indian Affairs, Ron Irwin promised native self-rule within six months. He has agreed that the Liberal Party recognizes that the inherent right to self-government exists. Because of this he sees no need to re-open the constitutional debate and have this written in, but Ovide Mercredi, Grand Chief of the Assembly of First Nations, still maintains that this will be necessary in case aboriginal rights are challenged in court. The process of moving from federal to aboriginal control has already begun in Manitoba. The process is being watched with great interest. In March 1994, Ron Irwin announced that the first steps were being taken to dismantle Indian Affairs in Manitoba, that the pace would be set by the native community and that the government would maintain its responsibilities to the aboriginal community. It is hoped that the Manitoba case will provide a model for the rest of the country. In August 1994, at a special assembly of Manitoba Chiefs on self-government, it was agreed that there is now a framework in place for the process to continue based on the working plan *Towards Manitoba First Nations Governments,* and a memo of understanding has been signed between the Manitoba chiefs and the Minister of Indian Affairs. It may not be self-government in six months but it has certainly brought us closer than ever before to closure in the political struggle of Canada's First Nations for a recognition of their inherent right to self-government.

BIBLIOGRAPHY

Amerindian Life to 1830
Barman, J. et al., *Indian Education in Canada: The Legacy.* Vancouver, 1986.
Dickason, Olive Patricia. *Canada's First Nations.* Toronto, 1992.
Frideres, James S. *Native Peoples in Canada,* 4th edn. Scarborough, 1993.
Miller, J.L. *Skyscrapers Hide the Heavens.* Toronto, 1989.

The Métis
Barron, F.L., and Waldram, James B. *1885 and After Native Society in Transition.* Regina, 1986.
Beal, Bob, and Macleod, Rod. *Prairie Fire. The 1885 North-West Rebellion.* Edmonton, 1984.
Bowsfield, Hartwell. *Louis Riel Selected Readings.* Toronto, 1988.
Flanagan, Thomas. *Louis "David" Riel: Prophet of the New World.* Toronto, 1979.
Peterson, J., and Brown, J.H.S., eds. *The New Peoples: Being and Becoming Métis in North America.* Manitoba, 1985.
Sealey, D. Bruce, and Lussier, Antoine S. *The Métis: Canada's Forgotten People.* Winnipeg, 1975.
Sprague, D.N. *Canada and the Métis, 1869-1885.* Waterloo, 1988.

British North American Amerindian Policy
Dickason, Olive Patricia. *Canada's First Nations.* Toronto, 1992.
Frideres, James S. *Native Peoples in Canada,* 4th edn. Scarborought, 1993.
Miller, J.L. *Sweet Promises. A Reader on Indian-White Relations in Canada.* Toronto, 1991.
Smith, D.B. *Sacred Feathers the Revered Peter Jones and the Mississauga Indians.* Toronto, 1987.
Tennant, Paul. *Aboriginal People and Politics. The Indian Land Question in British Columbia, 1849-1989.* Vancouver, 1990.
Titley, E.B. *A Narrow Vision: Duncan Campbell Scott and the Administration of Indian Affairs in Canada.* Vancouver, 1986.

The West
Buckley, Helen. *From Wooden Ploughs to Welfare.* Montreal, 1992.
Carter, Sarah. *Lost Harvests: Prairie Indian Reserve Farmers and Government Policy.* Montreal, 1990.
Dempsey, H.A. *Crowfoot: Chief of the Blackfeet.* Edmonton, 1972.
Dempsey, H.A. *Big Bear. The End of Freedom.* Vancouver, 1984.
Getty, I.A.L., and Lussier, A.S., eds. *As Long as the Sun Shines and the Water Flows.* Vancouver, 1978.
Getty, I.A.L., and Smith, D.B. *One Century Later.* Vancouver, 1978.
Miller, J.L. *Sweet Promises. A Reader on Indian-White Relations in Canada.* Toronto, 1991.
Price, R. *The Spirit of the Alberta Indian Treaties.* Edmonton, 1987.
Tennant, Paul. *Aboriginal Peoples and Politics. The Indian Land Question in British Columbia, 1849-1989.* Vancouver, 1990.
Titley, E.B. *A Narrow Vision: Duncan Campbell Scott and the Administration of Indian Affairs in Canada.* Vancouver, 1986.

Challenges of Urban/Industrial Society and the Pressure to Change
Asch, Michael. *Home and Native Land. Aboriginal Rights and the Canadian Constitution.* Toronto, 1984.
Assembly of First Nations. *Breaking the Silence.* Ottawa, 1994.
—. *Tradition and Education: Towards a Vision of Out Future.* Ottawa, 1988.
Canadian Journal of Native Education. Supplement to volume 18, 1991. Edmonton, 1991.
Cardinal, Harold. *The Unjust Society.* Edmonton, 1969.
Cassidy, Frank, ed. *Aboriginal Self-Determination.* Lantzville, 1991.
Coates, Ken, ed. *Aboriginal Land Claims in Canada a Regional Perspective.* Toronto, 1991.
Department of Indian and Northern Affairs. *Statement of the Government of Canada on Indian Policy, 1969.* Ottawa, 1969.
Frideres, James S. *Naive Peoples in Canada,* 4th edn. Scarborough, 1993.
Friesen, John, ed. *The Cultural Maze Complex Questions on Native Destiny in Western Canada.* Calgary, 1991.
Gomme, Graham, and Kirk Camerson. *The Yukon's Constitutional Foundations,* vol. 2. Whitehorse, 1991.
Government of Canada. *Towards Manitoba First Nations Government.* 1994.
Government of the Northwest Territories. *Learning Tradition and Change in the Northwest Territories.* Yellowknife, 1982.
National Indian Brotherhood. *Citizens Plus.* Ottawa, 1970.

Ponting, J. Rick. *Arduous Journey. Canadian Indians and Decolonization.*
    Toronto, 1989.

Richardson, Boyce. *People of Terra Nullius.* Vancouver, 1993.

Silman, Janet. *Enough is Enough, Aboriginal Women Speak Out.* Toronto,
    1992.

Wotherspoon, Terry, and Vic Satzewich. First Nations. Scarborough, 1993.

Wuttunee, William I.C. *Ruffled Feathers Indians in Canadian Society.* Calgary,
    1971.

York, Geoffrey. *The Dispossessed Life and Death in Native Canada.* Toronto,
    1993.

8

Immigration and Ethnic Relations Since 1867

JEAN BURNET

Canada has from the beginning been a country of immigration with an ethnically, culturally, and linguistically diverse population. The vast and varied territory that is now Canada was at the time of first contact with Europeans inhabited by heterogeneous peoples, who although they had myths of originating in the land are generally believed to have migrated thousands of years ago across the Bering Strait from Asia. Europeans added at first a few and then a considerable number of new elements. Lately immigrants and refugees have been received from all parts of the globe. What is recent is not diversity, but recognition of diversity, and since 1971, with the policy of multiculturalism, recognition of diversity as both advantageous and a permanent aspect of Canadian society.

I. *Defining Ethnicity's Components*

According to the 1991 census, the Canadian population was approximately 27,000,000. The number of ethnic groups and the size of each are impossible to determine with precision. An ethnic group is described by Milton Gordon as characterized by a sense of peoplehood. Members of an ethnic group, according to Robert Schermerhorn, believe that they have a common ancestry, whether in fact they do or not; they have memories of a shared past; and they have certain badges, physical or cultural or both, which enable them to identify one another and to exclude outsiders. Because it involves subjective factors, ethnicity is hard to gauge. Further, ethnicity is not fixed or certain. The boundaries of a people may alter from time to time, shrinking or expanding. In Canada, for instance, people who once thought of themselves as Galicians or Ruthenians came to consider themselves Ukrainians. Membership in an ethnic group used to be considered to be ascribed at birth: "If it is easy to resign from the group it is not truly ethnic group", wrote sociologist Everett Hughes in the 1940s.[1] Now it is recognized that ethnic

[1]Everett C. Hughes, *The Sociological Eye: Selected Papers,* Chicago, 1971, p. 154.

identity can change, although not easily, and individuals, especially those of multiple origins, can at the same time or over a period of time identify with more than one ethnic group, depending upon the situations in which they find themselves. Peoples who in Canada call themselves Hungarian may when travelling abroad claim to be Canadian. Immigrants may have had little consciousness of ethnic identity in their homelands, but many acquire one in their new country.

The Canadian census has from the beginning been concerned with the origins of the population. It has not asked people their ethnic self-identification, but rather their racial or ethnic origin, which was assumed to be outside of North America and until 1971 to be traced through the male line, except for Native Peoples. Since 1971 the census had dropped the reference to the male line, and has begun taking account of multiple ethnic origins: by the 1991 census 20 per cent of the population claimed multiple origins. The wording of the question concerning origin asked by the census has varied over time, partly in response to criticism (for example, the term 'racial' was dropped in 1951), and the results have been by no means precise. People whose ancestors have been in Canada for many generations may not know their origin or origins, or if they do their origin may have no significance for them. On occasion a group has been urged to boycott the census, or to give misleading responses to the origin question—in 1961 it was suggested that French Canadians answer Negro to the question about ethnic origin—and the census returns have indicated that the urging has had effect. When a particular origin has become unpopular, as for example German during the two world wars, the number claiming it has shrunk. However, the ethnic origin figures from the census have been the index most often used in estimating the size of various groups. Tables 1, 2, and 3 give the population by ethnic origin, 1871-1991.

If figures about ethnic origin are not precise, neither is information about the number and strength of the various cultures represented in Canada. Culture is concerned with the organized system of understandings shared by a people; it includes beliefs, values, institutions, rituals, and manners. The boundaries between cultures in the modern world are hard to determine. Indeed, some scholars, including the renowned Canadian sociologist, John Porter, talk of the convergence of cultures, or say that culture has become a myth. Ethnic groups are frequently thought of as the bearers of cultures, but ethnic groups unless territorially isolated—and few are in the modern world —do not have totally distinct systems of institutions, beliefs, and values, but partial or truncated cultures. They have symbols of their ethnic identity or peoplehood, but some of the symbols, such as the Scot's kilt and bagpipes, the German's sauerkraut and Oktoberfest, the Pole's polka, and the Ukrainian's decorated Easter eggs, are readily adopted by others. Further, people of a particular origin as defined by the census or even a particular ethnic identity may have adopted another culture, usually the dominant one in the community where they live.

TABLE 1 A

Ethnic Origin of the Canadian Population, 1871-1991[1]

	1871	1881	1901	1911	1921	1931
Total[2]	3,485,761	4,324,810	5,371,315	7,206,643	8,787,949	10,376,786
British	2,110,502	2,548,514	3,063,195	3,999,081	4,868,738	5,381,071
French	1,082,940	1,298,929	1,649,371	2,061,719	2,452,743	2,927,990
Dutch	29,662	30,412	33,845	55,961	117,505	148,962
German	202,991	254,319	310,501	403,417	294,635	473,544
Italian	1,035	1,849	10,834	45,963	66,769	98,173
Jewish	125	667	16,131	76,199	126,196	156,726
Polish			6,285	33,652	53,403	145,503
Russian	607	1,227	19,825	44,376	100,064	88,148
Scandinavian	1,623	5,223	31,042	112,682	167,359	228,049
Ukrainian			5,682	75,432	106,721	225,113
Other European	3,830	5,760	23,811	97,101	214,451	261,034
Asiatic	4	4,383	23,731	43,213	65,914	84,548
Indian & Eskimo	23,037	108,547	127,941	105,611	113,724	128,890
Other & not stated	29,405	64,980	49,121	52,236	39,727	29,035

Source: Censuses of Canada.

[1]Data for 1871 and 1881 are incomplete, particularly in the treatment of small numbers of those from central Europe, 1891 is omitted because of insufficient data.

[2]For 1871 includes the population of the four original provinces of Canada only: Nova Scotia, New Brunswick, Quebec, and Ontario. Newfoundland is excluded until 1951.

[3]Calculated from 1991 Census, Catalogue 93-315. Data for British includes single origin and multiple origin British only.

[4]Multiple origins' category first listed in 1981 Census.

Languages are part of culture, and often though not always the most cherished badge of ethnic identity. Some ethnic groups, like Canadians, Americans, and Australians, do not have distinctive languages—although they have some distinctive words and phrases—and some, like the Dutch, place more emphasis upon another cultural trait, such as religion, than they do on language. Language does, however, provide another objective index that census-takers can use. It is important in Canada because in recent decades it has been the chief marker used by the two dominant groups in Canada, the French Canadians and the English Canadians. In addition to knowledge of the official languages of Canada, English and French, the Canadian census records mother tongue, that is, the first language learned in childhood and still understood, and the language used in the home.

TABLE 1 B

Ethnic Origin of the Canadian Population, 1871-1991[1]

	1941	1951	1961	1971	1981	1991
Total[2]	11,506,655	14,009,429	18,238,247	21,568,310	24,092,500	26,944,045
British	5,715,904	6,709,685	7,996,669	9,624,115	9,674,245	7,595,170
French	3,483,038	4,319,167	5,540,346	6,180,120	6,439,100	6,146,600
Dutch	212,863	264,267	429,679	425,945	408,240	358,180
German	464,682	619,995	1,049,599	1,317,195	1,142,365	911,560
Italian	112,625	152,245	450,351	730,820	747,970	750,055
Jewish	170,241	181,670	173,344	296,945	264,025	245,840
Polish	167,485	219,845	323,517	316,425	254,485	272,810
Russian	83,708	91,279	119,168	64,475	49,435	38,220
Scandinavian	244,603	283,024	386,534	384,790	282,795	174,370
Ukrainian	305,929	395,043	473,337	580,655	529,615	406,645
Other European	281,790	346,354	711,320			
Asiatic	74,064	72,827	121,753	285,535	464,470	1,607,230
Indian & Eskimo	125,521	165,607	220,121	295,215	413,380	470,615
Other & not stated	64,202	188,421	242,509	1,066,60	1,574,760	2,206,620
Multiple origins					1,838,615	5,810,130

Source: Censuses of Canada.

[1]Data for 1871 and 1881 are incomplete, particularly in the treatment of small numbers of those from Europe, 1891 is omitted because of insufficient data.

[2]For 1871 includes the population of the four original provinces of Canada only: Nova Scotia, New Brunswick, Quebec, and Ontario. Newfoundland is excluded until 1951.

[3]Calculated from 1991 Census, Catalogue 93-315. Data for British includes single origin and multiple origins British only.

[4]'Multiple origins' category first listed in 1981 Census.

Every Canadian language except the two official languages, English and French, declines from generation to generation. A number of Native languages have died out and other now have few speakers. In immigrant languages by the third generation fluency is virtually extinct. But the adoption of English or French does not necessarily mean assimilation into English-Canadian or French-Canadian culture. Someone of French Canadian stock who speaks perfect English may still have an outlook and values that are distinctly French Canadian.

TABLE 2 A
Ethnic Origin of the Canadian Population (percentages), 1871-1991[1]

	1871	1881	1901	1911	1921	1931
Total[2]	100.00	100.00	100.00	100.00	100.00	100.00
British	60.55	58.93	57.04	55.49	55.41	51.86
French	31.07	30.03	30.71	28.61	27.91	28.22
Dutch	0.85	0.70	0.63	0.78	1.34	1.44
German	5.82	5.88	5.78	5.60	3.35	4.56
Italian	0.03	0.04	0.20	0.64	0.76	0.95
Jewish	*	0.02	0.30	1.06	1.44	1.51
Polish			0.12	0.47	0.61	1.40
Russian	0.02	0.03	0.37	0.61	1.14	0.85
Scandinavian	0.05	0.12	0.58	1.56	1.90	2.20
Ukrainian			0.10	1.05	1.21	2.17
Other European	0.11	0.13	0.44	1.35	2.44	2.51
Asiatic	*	0.10	0.44	0.60	0.75	0.81
Indian & Eskimo	0.66	2.51	2.38	1.46	1.29	1.24
Other & not stated	0.84	1.51	0.91	0.72	0.45	0.28

Source: Censuses of Canada.

[1]Data for 1871 and 1881 are incomplete, particularly in the treatment of small numbers of those from central Europe, 1891 is omitted because of insufficient data.

[2]For 1871 includes the population of the four original provinces of Canada only: Nova Scotia, New Brunswick, Quebec, and Ontario. Newfoundland is excluded until 1951.

*Percentage lower than 0.01.

Religion is also part of culture, and often very important. More than one religion, and numerous denominations, may be represented within a single ethnic group. But in some cases religion has become the basis of a sense of peoplehood. Jews are frequently still considered to be Jews even when they have adopted another religion than Judaism, or have ceased to practice any religion. Jewish is listed both as an ethnic origin and as a religion in the Canadian census. Mormonism, Mennonitism, and Islam are listed only as religions and not as ethnic origins, but they also are associated with distinctive ways of life and feelings of identity. They are unlike Judaism, however, in that they engage actively in proselytizing.

The meaning of the terms race and racial have changed radically since the first half of the twentieth century, when virtually every ethnic group was considered to be a race, with distinctive physical features and also distinctive mental, moral, and emotional characteristics. As late as 1947 a Canadian historian and anthropologist, A.G. Bailey, presented a paper to the Canadian Historical Association arguing that French Canadians were not physically distinct from English Canadians. Now the term 'race' is used with caution to apply to broad, physically distinctive, divisions of humankind, considered to be three or four in number and to be distinguishable by skin colour.

TABLE 2 B

Ethnic Origin of the Canadian Population (percentages), 1871-1991*

	1941	1951	1961	1971	1981	1991
Total	100.00	100.00	100.00	100.00	100.00	100.00
British	49.68	47.89	43.85	44.6	40.2	28.1
French	30.27	30.83	30.38	28.7	26.7	22.8
Dutch	1.85	1.89	2.36	2.0	1.7	1.3
German	4.04	4.43	5.75	6.1	4.7	3.4
Italian	0.98	1.09	2.47	3.4	3.1	2.8
Jewish	1.48	1.30	0.95	1.4	1.1	0.9
Polish	1.45	1.57	1.77	1.5	1.1	1.0
Russian	0.73	0.65	0.65	0.3	0.2	0.1
Scandinavian	2.12	2.02	2.12	1.8	1.2	0.6
Ukrainian	2.66	2.82	2.59	2.7	2.2	1.5
Other European	2.45	2.47	3.90			
Asiatic	0.64	0.52	0.67	1.3	1.3	6.0
Indian & Eskimo	1.09	1.18	1.21	1.4	1.7	1.7
Other & not stated	0.56	1.34	1.33	4.9	6.5	8.2
Multiple origins					7.6	21.5

Source: Censuses of Canada.

II. *Immigration and Immigration Policy, 1867-1920*

The first census after Confederation covered the four original provinces of Canada only—Nova Scotia, New Brunswick, Quebec, and Ontario— even though Manitoba entered Confederation in 1870 and British Columbia in 1871. The population was 3,485,761; 2,110,502 or 60.6 per cent were of British origin, and 1,082,940 or 31.1 per cent were of French origin. Of the British, the English numbered 706,306, the Irish 846,414, the Scots 549,946,

TABLE 3

Population by Ethnic Origin, for Canada,
1991 Census—20 per cent Sample Data*

Single origin	19,199,790
British origins	5,611,050
French origins	6,146,600
European origins	4,146,065
Western European origins	1,355,485
Northern European origins	213,600
Eastern European origins	946,810
Southern European origins	1,379,031
Other European origins	251,140
Asian and African origins	1,633,660
Arab origins	144,050
West Asian origins	81,660
South Asian origins	420,295
East and Southeast Asian origins	961,225
African origins	26,430
Pacific Islands origins	7,215
Latin, Central and South American origins	85,535
Caribbean origins	94,395
Black origins	224,620
Aboriginal origins	470,615
Other origins	780,035
Multiple origins	7,794,250
British only	1,984,120
British and French	1,071,880
British and Canadian	116,530
British and other	2,516,840
British, Canadian and other	40,160
French only	12,065
French and Canadian	20,825
French and other	425,190
French, Canadian and other	5,280
Canadian and other	58,030
British, French and Canadian	13,545
British, French and other	680,235
British, French, Canadian and other	13,560
Other multiple origins	835,990

* *Source:* 1991 Census—Cat. no. 93-315, Ethnic Origin.

and others—including the Welsh—7,773. The French included the Acadians of New Brunswick and Nova Scotia and the French Canadians of Quebec and Ontario. There were 202,991 of German origin, 29,662 of Dutch origin, 23,037 of Native Indian and Eskimo (Inuit) origin, and 21,496 of Negro (Black) origin.

People from continental Europe often landed in British North America during the nineteenth century, but usually only on their way to the United States. While its neighbour was receiving vast numbers of immigrants, Canada was attracting few people. About the time of Confederation, however, the settlement of the Canadian West was beginning, in part by eastern Canadians, British, and Americans but also by Europeans. In the 1870s Mennonites and Icelanders settled in Manitoba, and a little later Polish and Russian Jews, fleeing pogroms in eastern Europe, were assisted to set up agricultural colonies; these were an experiment, and though some failed a few succeeded.

The government of Canada as it emerged after 1867 was concerned with developing industry in central Canada, building a transcontinental railway, and settling western Canada. All of these required people:

> But in the years immediately following Confederation, and in fact up to the end of the century, progress was slow, spasmodic, uncertain. Instead of the anticipated immigration of desirable settlers, Canada was flooded with unemployed British craftsmen and unskilled labourers, together with destitute emigrants from Germany and the Scandinavian countries.[2]

Not until the late 1890s did mass immigration begin. It required the coincidence of many factors to begin the peopling of the West on a large scale. These included the end of a long depression, the completion of the Canadian Pacific Railway and the building of other lines, the quelling of the second Riel insurrection, the closing of the American frontier, and the launching of an aggressive immigration policy by a dynamic Minister of the Interior, Clifford Sifton. Sifton directed his efforts at recruiting people eager to go on the land and equipped for rural life, whom he considered to be found in the United States and in Europe, especially eastern and central Europe. Sifton's most famous phrase concerning immigrants was contained in an article in *Maclean's* magazine in 1922: "I think a stalwart peasant in a sheep-skin coat, born on the soil, whose forefathers have been farmers for ten generations, with a stout wife and a half-dozen children, is good quality."

Although he was succeeded by Frank Oliver in 1905, Sifton's name is given to the first major wave of Canadian immigration of the twentieth

[2]Norman Macdonald, *Canada: Immigration and Colonization, 1841-1903,* Toronto, 1968, p. 92.

TABLE 4

Immigration to Canada by Calendar Year, 1867-1991*

Year	Number	Year	Number	Year	Number	Year	Number
1867	10,666	1898	31,900	1929	164,993	1960	104,111
1868	12,765	1899	44,543	1930	104,806	1961	71,689
1869	18,630	1900	41,681	1931	27,530	1962	74,586
1870	24,706	1901	55,747	1932	20,591	1963	93,151
1871	27,773	1902	89,102	1933	14,382	1964	112,606
1872	36,578	1903	138,660	1934	12,476	1965	146,758
1873	50,050	1904	131,252	1935	11,277	1966	194,743
1874	39,373	1905	141,465	1936	11,643	1967	222,876
1875	27,382	1906	211,653	1937	15,101	1968	183,974
1876	25,633	1907	272,409	1938	17,244	1969	161,531
1877	27,082	1908	143,326	1939	19,994	1970	147,713
1878	29,807	1909	173,694	1940	11,324	1971	121,900
1879	40,492	1910	286,839	1941	9,329	1972	122,006
1880	38,505	1911	331,288	1942	7,576	1973	184,200
1881	47,991	1912	375,756	1943	8,504	1974	218,465
1882	112,458	1913	400,870	1944	12,801	1975	187,881
1883	133,624	1914	150,484	1945	22,722	1976	149,429
1884	103,824	1915	36,665	1946	71,719	1977	114,914
1885	79,169	1916	55,914	1947	64,127	1978	86,313
1886	69,152	1917	72,910	1948	125,414	1979	112,096
1887	84,525	1918	42,845	1949	95,217	1980	143,117
1888	88,766	1919	107,698	1950	73,912	1981	128,618
1889	91,600	1920	138,824	1951	194,391	1982	121,147
1890	75,067	1921	91,728	1952	164,498	1983	89,157
1891	82,165	1922	64,224	1953	168,868	1984	88,239
1892	30,996	1923	133,729	1954	154,227	1985	84,302
1893	29,633	1924	124,164	1955	109,946	1986	99,219
1894	20,829	1925	84,907	1956	164,857	1987	152,098
1895	18,790	1926	135,982	1957	282,164	1988	161,929
1896	16,835	1927	158,886	1958	124,851	1989	192,001
1897	21,716	1928	166,783	1959	106,928	1990	212,166
						1991	228,557

**Source:* Employment and Immigration Canada.

century, from the turn of the century until the outbreak of the First World War. Oliver did not share Sifton's views concerning men in sheepskin coats: he favoured immigrants from the United Kingdom and eastern and central Canada above others, and tightened regulations against eastern and central Europeans. But the wave once started could not be stemmed. In 1913 the number of arrivals was 400,870, a number never again approached.

The British and the Americans were the immigrants generally considered ideal, although Sifton had doubts about British townspeople. Between 1901 and 1914 a million and a quarter immigrants from the United Kingdom and nearly a million immigrants from the United States entered Canada. But many of the Americans were of other origins than British and were required to claim those origins by the Canadian census. In addition many immigrants—about 800,000—came directly from continental Europe, including Germans, Scandinavians, and Dutch, already represented in the Canadian population, but also Ukrainians, Poles, Hungarians, and Russians.

The Ukrainians, then called Ruthenians or, after the provinces from which most of them came, Galicians and Bukovynians, were impoverished peasants. A little earlier, in the late 1870s, Ukrainians had migrated to the mines, foundries, and factories of the United States. In Canada, however, they took up farms in the parkland north of the prairie in the western provinces. The prairie, which was seen as very fertile and because it was free of forest capable of being brought under the plough immediately, had been homesteaded by earlier arrivals—eastern Canadians, British, and American—and in any event the Ukrainians were attracted to bush country and wooded lands where they could have wood to build their homes and to supply fuel.

The Poles, fewer in numbers than the Ukrainians, were not dissimilar in background. Having been neighbours of the Ukrainians in eastern Europe, they settled in small groups among Ukrainians. Some intermarried, learned Ukrainian, changed their names to Ukrainian ones, and became assimilated to Ukrainians. Hungarians had come to the West through the efforts of the colourful Count Paul Esterhazy in 1885 and 1886. Peasants in Europe, they had found work in the mines and foundries of Pennsylvania hard, dangerous, and ill-paid. Consequently they welcomed the chance to farm in Manitoba and Saskatchewan. They attracted fellow countrymen from Europe, and established eight colonies in Saskatchewan before the First World War.

The Russians included 7,000 or 8,000 Doukhobors, who first settled in Saskatchewan. After brushes with the authorities many moved to British Columbia. Their history was turbulent for many years, especially since the Sons of Freedom sect of Doukhobors resisted the schooling of their children and inflicted arson and dynamiting upon Doukhobors who did not share their views.

Although the settlement of the West attracted attention, as many immigrants went to the cities of central Canada, to British Columbia, and to the railway, mining, and construction camps of the north, which were burgeoning to supply the needs of the homesteaders. Sifton wanted to attract farmers, but those, he considered undesirable, also came: urban dwellers from the United

Kingdom and the United States, Italians, Jews, and in smaller numbers Greeks, Macedonians, Syrians, Lebanese, and Armenians. By 1914 Montreal had the second largest Jewish community in the British Empire, exceeded only by that of London, and a large and growing Italian community.

The first immigrants were usually young men, helped to migrate by members of their families. They were expected to repay their passage money and to contribute to the welfare of the family by assisting other young men to migrate also. Many of them thought of themselves as sojourners rather than settlers. It was only when they were joined by their wives and sweethearts, or found wives in Canada, that permanent ethnic communities began. On farms the labour of wives and children was essential, and in towns and cities women ran boarding houses and contributed to such family enterprises as grocery stores and bakeries. Single women were welcome to immigrate as domestic servants. According to Marilyn Barber, in the ten years before the First World War 90,000 British domestics came, 60 per cent of them from England, 29 per cent from Scotland, 10 per cent from Ireland, and 1 per cent from Wales. Being on the Pacific rim, British Columbia drew large numbers of Asians. Chinese had come to British Columbia at the time of the Gold Rush, and later had been brought in to build some of the most difficult parts of the Canadian Pacific Railway. Those who survived work on the railway—many did not—were not assisted to return home afterward. Other Chinese joined them, in spite of severe discrimination, including a head tax that by 1903 had risen to $500 and agreements that they should not be hired to work on the other transcontinental railways. Japanese also came in large numbers, until after riots in Vancouver in 1907 against Chinese and Japanese, the Canadian and Japanese governments limited immigration by a series of 'gentlemen's agreements'. South Asians had become acquainted with Canada when a contingent of soldiers and officers from Hong Kong, including a small number of Sikhs, had crossed Canada on their way to and from celebrations of Edward VII's coronation in 1902. About five thousand South Asians, chiefly Sikhs, entered from 1905 to 1908 to work on the railway and in logging and lumbering. They became the targets of the same racist attitudes as the Chinese and Japanese, and, in spite of being British subjects, from 1908 on new South Asian immigrants were excluded by an order-in-council requiring that immigrants come by a 'continuous journey' from their country of origin, an impossibility for people from India. In 1914 an enterprising Sikh, Gurdit Singh, hired a Japanese steamer, the *Komagata Maru,* to test the requirement for a continuous journey, but 354 would-be immigrants were denied entry and after two months in Vancouver harbour the ship had to return to Asia.

Since Asians were not wanted as permanent settlers, they were discouraged from bringing in women and setting up families. The Chinese and South Asian groups were largely male, and set up all-male households. The first Chinese woman had arrived in Victoria in 1860. By 1885 there had been 53 Chinese women to 1,495 Chinese men, and between 1885 and 1894, 34 women had entered. Between 1911 and 1914 many more women came, but they and the Canadian born were far from enough to balance the sex ratio. According to Edgar Wickberg, although most of the Chinese women were wives and fiancees of immigration men, Canadian society often regarded them as prostitutes. A few South Asian wives were grudgingly admitted before the First World War, but by Norman Buchignani and Doreen Indra's account as late as 1925 there were no more than 40 women, all married to immigrant men. The Japanese, however, considered that the immigration restrictions in the 'gentlemen's agreements' did not apply to wives; consequently most Japanese immigration after 1908 was of women and the Japanese sex ratio began to move toward balance.

Although the net gain in population was great, the years of heavy immigration were also years of heavy emigration. For many, Canada was a second choice, after the United States, and if an opportunity came to move to the United States they seized it. Others, disappointed with the new land, returned home. From the 1860s to the end of the nineteenth century Canada lost more people by emigration than it gained by immigration. Among the emigrants were thousands of French Canadians who moved into New England to work in the sawmills, brickyards, and textile mills. The generally accepted estimates of the number of Quebeckers who emigrated to the United States during the nineteenth century ranged from 500,000 to 525,000.

From 1900 to 1914 the tide of immigration was strong. Nonetheless, between 1901 and 1911 while immigration totalled 1,759,000 emigration is estimated to have been 1,043,000, and between 1911 and 1921 while immigration was 1,612,000 emigration is estimated at 1,381,000.[3]

III. *Immigration and Immigration Policy, 1921 to the present*

The outbreak of the First World War cut short the flood of immigrants. So long as it lasted, new arrivals were few and almost all came from the United States. After the end of the war, as early as 1919, a new wave of immigrants began, directed rather to the cities and to the industrial, mining, and pulp and paper towns of Quebec, Ontario, and British Columbia than

---

[3]There are no official records of emigration. The estimates are based on official reports of immigrants entering the United States who gave Canada as their birthplace or their last place of permanent residence.

to the wheat-growing Prairie Provinces. Again, immigrants from the United Kingdom and the United States predominated. In 1919, 1920, 1922, and 1923 more than half the immigrants were of British origins, and for the rest of the 1920s special assistance from both the British and Canadian governments brought substantial numbers of Britishers. But many immigrants came also from continental Europe, especially after the government entered into agreements with the two continental railways in 1925 authorizing them to bring in agriculturalists, agricultural labourers, and domestic servants. The United States was restricting immigration, and many who would have gone there came to Canada instead. The ethnic groups were much the same as earlier, except that those of Russian origin now included Mennonites and Hutterites, two sects of German origin many members of which had moved to Russia at the time of Catherine the Great. The Hutterites had migrated to the United States, but came to Canada after having been treated harshly during the war because of their pacifism. Jewish war orphans and refugees were admitted, to the number of 48,500 between 1920 and 1930. The Italians had their immigration cut off by the Italian government after the accession to power of the fascist party in 1923. Chinese were virtually excluded by the Canadian government's Chinese Immigration (Exclusion) Act of 1923. Regulations against South Asians were relaxed somewhat: they were allowed to bring in wives and children after 1919. From 1920-21 to 1929-30, 422 South Asians came, 90 of them adult males, 144 adult females, and 188 children.

In the 1920s, as before, most of the immigrants were men, and many of them were unable to bring out their wives or sweethearts when the Depression struck. But as before domestic servants were encouraged to come, to serve as hired girls on the farms or as helpers in urban households. During the 1920s some 80,000 came from Britain, and an increasing number from continental Europe. In particular, of 37,000 Finns who entered Canada in the 1920s about 40 per cent were women, and many were single domestics who prided themselves on their reputation for hard work, cleanliness, and independent spirit.

The second wave of immigration came to an abrupt end in 1929 with the Great Depression. The Railway Agreement was terminated in 1930, and during the 1930s immigrants were restricted to members of the immediate families of men already established in Canada and farmers with enough money to begin farming at once. The number of British immigrants became less than the number from the United States, many of whom were returning Canadians, and the number of others was negligible. The government was not even moved by compassion to admit Jewish victims of Nazism, although some Sudeten Germans were admitted. Many people were deported, either as indigents or radicals, and some people were voluntarily repatriated. Between 1921 and 1931 the number of immigrants had been 1,198,000; between 1931 and 1941 the number was 149,000 and emigration exceeded immigration.

During the Second World War Germans were treated with more discretion than during the First World War, but some were interned as were about 18,000 Italians. However, the greatest sufferers were the Japanese Canadians. At the outbreak of the war there were 23,000 Japanese Canadians, of whom 22,000 were in British Columbia; of those in British Columbia 13, 300 were Canadian born, 2,900 were naturalized Canadians, and most of the remainder had been Canadian residents for twenty-five years or more. Anti-Japanese interests in British Columbia used the attack on Pearl Harbour to call for the removal of the Japanese Canadians from the coast and the confiscation of their fishing boats, which were rumoured to be used for spying for Japan. They were removed to relocation centres, and much of their property was confiscated. At the war's end about 4,000, over half of them Canadian born and two-thirds of them Canadian citizens, were 'repatriated' to Japan. Of those who stayed in Canada, many did not return to British Columbia, and since the end of the war there has been little Japanese immigration.

Within a few years after the end of the Second World War a new wave of immigration began, which was to bring almost 4,000,000 people to Canada by 1971. Many came to put distance between themselves and their families and threats of another war, others to take part in the economic expansion that occurred in Canada in the 1950s and 1960s. A third of the immigrants were British; the other origins most strongly represented were Italian, German, Dutch, Polish, and Jewish. Most of the newcomers settled in the cities, especially Toronto and to a lesser extent Vancouver and Montreal.

Early arrivals were war brides and their children. About 45,000 of them were British, 1,900 of them Dutch, 650 Belgian, and 100 French. In the case of the Dutch, the war brides were the first comers of more than 160,000 immigrants who came by 1960.

The war brides were followed by thousands of European displaced persons and refugees. They included well-educated people with professional training, artistic talents, linguistic skills, and experience in business, government, the military, or a skilled trade. Some 4,500 veterans of the Polish Free Army; Dutch farm workers; Maltese immigrants, and thousands of Estonians, some of whom made their way across the Atlantic in small boats, Latvians and Lithuanians were among those who came in the late 1940s. Others were economic migrants, who came to fill labour shortage in the booming economy. Some had skills for which training was unavailable in Canada; others brought willingness to do work that the Canadian born shunned. They included Germans and Italians, who had been enemies of Canada during the war, Greeks, Portuguese, and many others. A quarter of a million Italians arrived between 1951 and 1961. Many came under contracts as agricultural labourers, track workers, woodworkers, and miners; more came as sponsored relatives through chain migration. In 1958 the number of Italian immigrants surpassed the number of British immigrants— the first time that British immigration had been second to that from another European source. The bulk of the Italians, Greeks, and Portuguese brought little education and few skills, and started off in entrance-status occupations, but through hard work by both men, many of whom worked in construction, and women, who worked in the needle trades, the food industry, and domestic service, prospered.

The revulsion against racism after the Second World War, and the demands of an expanding economy, led to the end of the 'white Canada' policy. From the late 1940s onward the special restrictions on Asians at entry and within Canada began to diminish. In 1951 regulations permitted 150 Indians, 100 Pakistanis, and 50 Ceylonese (Sri Lankans) to enter each year, as well as the immediate families of Canadian citizens resident in Canada from India, Pakistan, and Ceylon. In 1957 the Indian quota, the only one that had been consistently filled, was raised to 300, and in 1958 the range of relatives that could be sponsored by Indians was broadened.

In the 1960s Canadian immigration policy was changed to eliminate racial discrimination, which after the Second World War and the growth of the United Nations had become unacceptable. Universalism and non-discrimination were enshrined in the Immigration Act of 1976. Thus the post-war wave of Immigration can be divided into two parts, in the first of which from 1945 to 1970, the chief sources were in Europe, and in the second of which Asia, the Caribbean, Africa, and Latin America became increasingly important sources. Asians went from being 13 per cent of Canadian immigrants in 1968 to being 45 per cent in 1987. Chinese and South Asian arrivals in particular increased markedly, immigrants of South Asian origin coming not only from India, Pakistan, and Sri Lanka but from Uganda, Kenya, South Africa, Tanzania, Guyana, Trinidad, Fiji, Mauritius, and Great Britain. There had been a trickle since 1955 of immigration from the Caribbean in the form of a programme for the admission of a limited number of women domestics; now there was a flood. Included in it were French-speaking Haitians, who settled in Quebec.

After 1970, refugees became a regular portion of the immigration stream.

From the war on Canada had been a leading receiving country for refugees, but Hungarians in 1956, Czechs and Slovaks in 1968, Tibetans in 1970, Ugandan Asians in 1972, and Chileans in 1973 had been admitted on an *ad hoc* basis. By the early 1970s, the government recognized that the problem of refugees was permanent, and the Immigration Act (1976) included provisions for admission not only of those conforming to the United Nations refugee convention—Convention Refugees—but of others in a *de facto* refugee situation—Designated Classes. The Immigration Act came into force in 1978, between the flight in 1975 of Vietnamese and Vietnamese Chinese, of whom 6,500 were admitted to Canada as political refugees, and the coming of the 'boat people' from Vietnam, Laos, and Kampuchea between 1979 and 1981. More than 80,000 boat people entered Canada, sponsored either by the government or by private groups and churches. In the late 1980s, Canada was awarded the Hansen medal for its humanitarianism regarding refugees. Generally, however, Canada evoked criticism for its selection of the young, healthy, and well-educated men among refugees, rather than the most needy.

The change in sources of immigrants and the admission of refugees from Asian, African and Latin American countries resulted in a growing number of Canadians who were considered to be non-white. The term 'visible minorities' became current to describe them, and attention began to be paid to the problems of discrimination that they faced. Since they included many able and educated people, from Asia and Africa in particular, they could lobby effectively, using Canadian and international human rights legislation. Two important national studies concerning their situation appeared in 1984: *Equality Now!*, Report of the Special Committee of the House of Commons on Visible Minorities in Canadian Society, and *Equality in Employment*, by the Abella Commission. The studies found unemployment, underemployment, and income discrimination among immigrant numbers of the visible minorities, both men and women.

Since the Second World War more women than men have immigrated, especially from the United Kingdom, the United States, and the Caribbean. There is now a slight surplus of women both among the foreign born and in the population as a whole. According to the 1991 census the sex ratio—the number of men per hundred women—was 98. Major factors have been the removal of racial discrimination and the emphasis on family unification in immigration policy, which have enabled men to bring in their wives. Recently there has been recognition that the bulk of people in refugee camps are women and that women refugees face special hardships, and a programme, Women at Risk, was set up late in 1987 to facilitate their entry.

The numbers admitted under the programme have, however, been small.

In 1991, ethnic origins other than British and French were reported by 31 per cent of the population, 28 per cent giving a single ethnic origin and 3 per cent giving multiple origins. Of those giving a single origin, 8.5 per cent gave Asian or African origins. In 1991 the 10 leading sources of immigrants were Hong Kong, Poland, China, India, the Philippines, Lebanon, Vietnam, the United Kingdom, El Salvador, and Sri Lanka.

Since the Second World War immigrants have settled mainly in the three largest metropolitan areas of Canada, Toronto, Vancouver, and Montreal, although they have also fanned out into smaller cities, towns, and rural areas. Their intended occupations have been predominantly in the manufacturing, professional and technical, and service and recreational categories. Those admitted as independent immigrants have a higher average level of formal education than the Canadian born. Illegal immigrants probably on the average have less education, are located in the same metropolitan areas, and occupy lower occupation categories.

Canada used to have high birth rates, Quebec one of the highest in the Western world, but all rates have fallen drastically since the mid-1960s. At present it is realized that without immigration Canada's population would begin to shrink early in the next century. As a result, an annual level of immigration, including refugees, of 250,000 has been adopted. To attain this level, Asian, African, Caribbean, and central and south American sources will have to the tapped. Declining birth rates, social welfare programmes, and in some countries prosperity have diminished the number of people in Canada's traditional European source countries who are eager to try their fortune in North America.

IV. *Ethnic Relations: Trials and Tribulations*

The immigration policy of the Federal Government reflected the attitudes of British Canadians, the dominant group in Canada. Until the end of the nineteenth century, those of British stock were confident in their entitlement to special rights and privileges in Canada, in the superiority of their 'race' and institutions, and in assimilation to the British model as a worthy goal for immigrants. Other peoples were ranked as desirable or undesirable according to their similarity to the British and their presumed assimilability: British and Americans of British origins first, then in descending order other northern and western Europeans, eastern, central, and southern Europeans, Jews, Asians, and Blacks. During the 1920s the confidence of the British was somewhat shaken as the British Empire declined and Canadian nationalism flourished. Emphasis was placed on Canada and Canadianization. Since the

Second World War as Britain again declined and as the numerical dominance of those of British origins in Canada decreased so too did the notion that British Canadians have special virtues and rights.

Blacks had been part of the population from early times, and had been objects of prejudice and discrimination. There were Black slaves in New France before 1760. After the American Revolution, Blacks entered British North America as Loyalists and slaves of White Loyalists. Large numbers of fugitive slaves arrived in Canada in the 1850s and 1860s. But at the time of Confederation, which occurred a few years after the end of the American Civil War, many Blacks returned to the United States. The number of Blacks in Canada declined, and did not begin to grow again until 1921. Because they were few and decreasing in number, they attracted little attention until the late 1960s, when a substantial immigration from the Caribbean and Africa began.

Jewish immigrants had also been part of the population for a long time. The first comers were English and German Jews, and were well accepted. Because of their small numbers and their cultural similarities to English immigrants they posed no threat to the dominant group. Henry Nathan of Victoria, who was Jewish, was elected to Parliament in 1867. But by the end of the nineteenth century, with the advent of large numbers of Jews from central and eastern Europe with a much different culture, there was evidence of antisemitism in virtually all parts of Canada, especially the large urban centres.

A small number of individuals of various European origins had come to Canada, often after a sojourn in England or the United States, with values so similar to those of the majority that they had been quickly absorbed. The Pole Casimir Czowski, for example, had learned English and married an American before moving to Upper Canada in 1842, where he enjoyed success as an engineer and in military, educational, and religious activities. Another Pole, Alexandre-Edouard Kierzkowski, was elected to Parliament in 1867.

In the late nineteenth century and the early years of the twentieth century immigration was accepted as an economic necessity. The population of British origins had declined only to 57 per cent by 1901 and British immigration remained high; the population of French origin and the population of German origin had remained stable at 31 per cent and just under 6 per cent respectively from 1871 to 1901. The bulk of those of French origin and a substantial proportion of the Germans—the Mennonites and Amish—were rural, familial, pious people who aimed at self-sufficiency and bothered little with political or other outside affairs. Thus the British and the Americans of British stock dominated, and were so secure in their domination that they paid little attention to those Canadians not blessed by British ancestry. In the economy they held the top positions, and even working-class British and American immigrants were given better jobs than 'foreigners'. In politics they had a virtual monopoly, except for places allocated to French Canadians.

Although many Canadians shared Sifton's conviction about the economic necessity of settling the West, they did not consider eastern and central European immigrants to be acceptable neighbours. Germans, Swiss, and Scandinavians were considered to be literate, skilled, hard-working, and clean, and could therefore work with and for the Canadians and British immigrants as equals. The eastern and central Europeans, though their labour was welcome, were faced with suspicion, scorn, and discrimination: Orest Subtelny quoted newspapers that called the Ukrainians, for example a 'mass of human ignorance, filth and immorality', 'Ignorant and vicious foreign scum', and 'the dregs of Europe'.[4] The small numbers of Asians and Blacks who managed to enter the country suffered even harsher treatment, and even more injurious stereotyping.

In the railway and mining construction camps 'white men'—French and English Canadians, British and American immigrants, Scandinavians, and Finns—held all of the jobs considered to be good, and 'foreigners' engaged 'in the mucking and heavier tasks'.[5] Asians were rare in the camps: after doing some of the hardest and most dangerous work on the Canadian Pacific Railway, the Chinese were excluded from work on the Grand Trunk. Other non-Whites were also unwelcome.

In the towns and cities some of the ethnic groups were invisible, in that they were insignificant in mainstream economic development, politics, and cultural and social life. They provided a labour force for heavy and dirty jobs, such as those in construction and in the stockyards, but they avoided government officials, met their own needs and wants in their boards houses and small shops, and when they needed to go outside their group went to members of ethnic groups they had known in the Old Country, often Germans or Jews, for goods and services.

British Columbia, as well as an exceptionally large Native population, had an Asian population—Chinese, Japanese, and South Asians (called Hindoos, although they were chiefly Sikhs)—of 9 per cent in 1881 and 11 per cent in 1901. The attitude of the British Canadians to them was hostile. The hostility was expressed not only in the pressure exerted upon the Federal

---

[4]Orest Subtelny, *Ukrainians in North America: An Illustrated History*, Toronto, 1991, p. 58.

[5]Edmund W. Bradwin, *The Bunkhouse Man: Life and Labour in the Northern Work Camps*, Toronto, 1972, p. 105.

Government to restrict immigration, but in harassing and discriminatory legislation and popular behaviour directed against Asians in the province. That the Asian immigrants were almost wholly male exacerbated the situation, since the Canadians of British origins feared that the Asians would have sexual relations with non-Asian women. One of the frequent charges brought against the Chinese in particular was that they participated in 'the White slave trade'.

French Canadians were even less happy about new arrivals, who included few French. The Canadian government claimed that the French government would not permit the recruitment of immigrants, but French Canadians believed that the Canadian government was not putting enough effort into recruiting in France and Belgium. It was anticipated, correctly, that most of the immigrants who spoke neither French nor English would be assimilated by the English Canadians, and therefore French-Canadian nationalists, notably Oliver Asselin and Henri Bourassa, railed against immigration. The clergy put their faith in the birth rate and in the creation of colonies in the North and the West for the repatriation of emigrants from New England. One of their grievances was that while immigrants were given inducements to come from Europe, French Canadians were not being assisted to move to the West.

Within Quebec, Jews were a special target for hostility and fear. They were too numerous in Montreal to be ignored: by 1914 they were about 6 per cent of the population. The nationalists and the Montreal press depicted Jewish immigrants as a threat to the French-Canadian 'race' and the Roman Catholic religion.

Non-British immigrants were not expected to be active in politics. It was felt that except for the Germans and Scandinavians they were ignorant of democratic institutions, and had to be educated before they could take an intelligent part in political life. Germans in the Waterloo area of south-western Ontario, some of them descendants of United Empire Loyalists, were politically active by the mid-nineteenth century. The Icelanders—'natural politicians'[6]—were wooed by both parties, and began participating in Canadian elections a few years after their arrival in western Canada in the late 1879s and 1880s. Early in the twentieth century they had two members in the Manitoba legislature.

In the Prairie Provinces those of other than British, French, or Native origin constituted by 1911 a third of the population. They could therefore not be ignored at election times. The Conservative and Liberal parties were ready

[6]J.S. Woodsworth, *Strangers within our Gates or coming Canadians*. First published 1909, reprinted, Toronto, 1972, p. 80.

to buy their votes, directly and through the support of newspapers that presented the points of view of the parties, but they were less ready to have them stand as candidates. The Conservatives were especially disdainful of the immigrants, and this fact, as well as the espousal of their coming by the Liberal Clifford Sifton, inclined most of the immigrants toward the Liberals. Where they were concentrated, the immigrants began to field their own candidates, either as independents or an Liberals, and as early as 1913 a Ukrainian was elected to the Alberta legislature.

A minority of Jews and Ukrainians and a majority of Finns in central and western Canada espoused socialism, and for this drew governmental repression and popular fear and hatred. In British Columbia Sikhs also turned to socialism, as well as agitation against British rule in their homeland, in the Ghadar (Mutiny) Party. Organized in 1913 in the United States and Canada, its aim was to promote Indian independence by means of violent revolution. Shortly after the Komagata Maru incident and the outbreak of the First World War, many of its leaders returned to India, where they were jailed or confined to their villages. The harsh treatment meted out to the leaders was considered sometimes to be the cause of their political radicalism, and sometimes to be justified by it. The Ghadar Party died out during the First World War; it was revived during the 1920s and 1930s, but did not become strong .

The First World War brought hardship to one of the oldest and previously favoured ethnic groups, the Germans, and to others who were considered to be 'enemy aliens' Germans, who had been preferred immigrants for much of Canada's history, now were made to register, were in some cases interned, and were often subjected to discrimination. Even the playing of music by German composers led to protests. Other enemy aliens also had to register and sometimes were interned, including those like Ukrainians who had been reluctant members of the Austro-Hungarian empire. But when labour shortages developed many of the internees were released. The Wartime Elections Act of 1917 disenfranchised people who were of enemy alien birth or customarily spoke an 'enemy alien language' and who had been naturalized after 31 march 1902. Naturalization of all aliens was suspended during the war, and by an Act passed in 1919 for ten years after the war; the Act was rescinded in 1923.

Almost immediately after the First World War ended, in May and June 1919, the Winnipeg General Strike greatly increased fear of 'foreign radicals'. Ukrainians, Finns, Russians, and Jews were prominent in left-wing labour ranks. The leading manufacturers, bankers, and politicians of Winnipeg blamed the strike on 'alien scum'. Many of the participants had been British working men and some of the prominent supporters of the strike were intellectuals of British origins; however, some of the apparent leaders of British stock were put in prominent positions in order to refute the charges of foreign radicalism.

After the war the Canadians and British immigrants remained wary about the non-British immigrants in their midst. Hence in the 1920s the drive to Canadianize the immigrants, which had begun before the war, intensified. The schools were the instrument that was considered most appropriate for 'civilizing' newcomers.

Canadianizing and civilizing required the English language. While in the nineteenth century another language, usually French or German, was the language of instruction in schools in regions where most of the population shared that language, and while Manitoba had had bilingual schools from 1897 to 1916, from then on instruction was in English only and punishment was meted out for using another language in school. In the Prairie Provinces some groups felt acutely that this was unfair, and the regulations were defied when teachers of other than British origins presided over schools in which their own group predominated.

As well as the English language, British values permeated school curricula. The stories, essays, and poems in school readers and the songs taught in music classes all were designed to inculcate British values and loyalty to the British crown. Canada had no flag of its own, and the British Union Jack was displayed in schools and pictured in school readers.

In the 1920s the Ku Klux Klan, a white supremacist organization from the United States, made a brief incursion into Canada, and attracted followers in Ontario, British Columbia, Alberta, and Saskatchewan. The targets of the Klan were different in the different provinces: in Ontario, Blacks and Roman Catholics; in British Columbia, Asians or Orientals; in Alberta and Saskatchewan, central and eastern European immigrants and Roman Catholics. Only in Saskatchewan did the movement gain any strength. There it played an important part in the provincial election of 1929, but faded immediately afterward. Presumably many of the Klansmen were of British origins.

In the 1930s there was an increase in anti-immigrant and antisemitic demonstrations, with immigrants being blamed for unemployment and both immigrants and Jews for radicalism. Although they never became powerful, a number of fascist movements appeared. Perhaps the best known was in the province or Quebec, led by Adrien Arcand, and violently antisemitic journalist and founder of a short-lived National Social Christian Party. Among the middle class, restrictive covenants on residences and vacation properties became popular. The brochures of holiday resorts carried the phrase 'select clientele', which was understood to mean that no Jews or Blacks were admitted. Training courses—such as nurses' training—were often closed to Blacks. Hotels and clubs refused admittance even to Blacks of international fame, and barber shops refused to cut the hair of Blacks: the Granite Club in Toronto rebuffed the noted Black American singer Marion Anderson, and the Black Canadian jazz pianist Oscar Peterson was refused barber services in the city of Hamilton.

A number of European countries took an interest in their nationals in Canada. Both the German National Socialist and the Italian fascist consuls attempted to gain support. Some Germans were attracted, as were some non-Germans, but the majority were not. Many of those of German origin had not come from Germany itself; many had been in Canada too long to identify with the German cause; many belonged to religious sects that kept aloof from politics. The Italian cause was more successful, partly because during the 1930s fascism was approved by many English Canadians. Italian Canadians saw fascism as having prestige and conferring prestige upon them.

The Second World War caused a revulsion against racism and antisemitism. In the 1940s it was still possible for politicians to talk of the Canadian population as being of the White race, and for the Prime Minister, Mackenzie King, to say in his statement concerning immigration policy in 1947 that the government "opposed 'large-scale immigration from the Orient', which would certainly give rise to social and economic problem".[7] But scholarly knowledge and popular understanding of race and desire to observe the conventions of the United Nations that Canada had signed began to alter attitudes. Fair employment practices acts, pay equity acts, fair accommodations practices acts, and human rights codes began to be adopted in all the provinces, and federally the Canadian Bill of Rights of 1960 attempted to reduce discrimination.

The changes were not immediately evident in the everyday life of members of minorities and immigrants. But as those who came under contracts fulfilled their obligations and found work in the expanding economy and as other immigrants and second and third generation Canadians of other than British or French origins used their education and skills to enter or to start enterprises in commerce, industry, and finance the other ethnic groups began to spread throughout the society.

The 1960s was the decade during which ethnic issues became salient in Canada, as well as many other parts of the world, and those of non-British stock became assertive. An issue that was ethnic as well as political erupted

[7]*House of Common Debates,* vol. 3, May 1, 1947, pp. 2644-47.

in Quebec. Premier Maurice Duplessis and the Union Nationale Party that he led had ruled the province from 1944 in a paternalistic and conservative fashion. On Duplessis's death in 1959 protest erupted against what the people of Quebec considered the sources of their subordination in the province and the country: the Church and the English. In 1960 a new Liberal Government launched the Quiet Revolution, a period of rapid social and economic change directed by the government. Separatist movements gathered strength, and from 1963 to 1970 there was a flare-up of terrorism, carried out by militants in the *federation de la liberation due Quebec* (FLQ).

In order to cope with the turbulence in Quebec, in 1963 the Federal Government set up the Royal Commission on Bilingualism and Biculturalism, which was mandated

> to inquire into and report upon the existing state of bilingualism and biculturalism in Canada and to recommend what steps should be take, to develop the Canadian Confederation on the basis of an equal partnership between the two founding races, taking into account the contribution made by the other ethnic groups to the cultural enrichment of Canada and the measures that should be taken to safeguard that contribution....[8]

The original intention of the commissioners was to fulfil their mandate regarding the other ethnic groups in a perfunctory fashion by having members of ten or twelve of the groups, write essays on their contribution to the cultural enrichment of Canada and by paying some attention to the part the other ethnic groups—which in the linguistically oriented discussions of the timer were dubbed allophones—were playing in French-English relations. However, news about the commission and its terms of reference led to oral and written briefs protesting the treatment of the other ethnic groups, and the staging of highly publicized conference at which demands were made for attention to the situation of the other ethnic groups.

A sociological study described important aspects of that situation. In 1965 Porter published The Vertical Mosaic: An Analysis of Social Class and Power in Canada, which quickly became a bestseller. Its theme was that elites composed of Canadians of British origins maintained themselves in positions of wealth, prestige, and power, excluding all others except, in a few areas, French Canadians, by magnifying the cultural differences between themselves and the others. Those cultural differences were in fact, according to Porter, mythical. Culture was based on science and technology, and American science and technology were fast becoming universal. Nonetheless, statistics showed that the ethnic origin categories in Canada formed a vertical mosaic,

[8]Royal Commission on Bilingualism and Biculturalism, *Report,* Ottawa, 1969.

with the British at the top. Porter drew the conclusion that ethnic differences should be ignored, in the interests of equality.

Members of the other ethnic groups were impressed by *The Vertical Mosaic,* but the conclusion they drew was that they should receive state support to maintain their cultures, as did the Canadians of British origin and the French Canadians. And by the time Porter wrote, members of the other ethnic groups were rising, in part by taking part in high-risk enterprises such as construction and real estate. As Jeffrey Reitz demonstrated, inequality among ethnic groups in job status and income was decreasing, and occupational status becoming less dependent than it had been upon ethnic ancestry. Members of the other ethnic groups were becoming active politically, and holding both elective and appointed offices. Ethnic organizations were claiming for their members a certain proportion of appointments—to the senate, for example—as a right. It was the mobility of individual members of non-British ethnic groups and the consequent increased status of the groups themselves that gave them confidence to press for recognition and made the government yield to the pressure. The Royal Commission devoted a section of its report to the other ethnic groups, and two years after its publication, on 8 October 1971, the government proclaimed a policy of multiculturalism within a bilingual framework.

V. *The Policy of Multiculturalism*

The policy of multiculturalism within a bilingual framework was the first formal policy on ethnic relations adopted in Canada. Previously, since the 1920s, the dominant metaphor for ethnic relations had been the mosaic, in contrast to the American melting-pot, but little or no support had been given to ethnic groups to maintain their institutions. Instead, there was a policy, in good part implicit, of assimilation to the British Canadian model. The new policy, which was closely linked to policies of immigration, citizenship, and human rights, had four aims:

First, resources permitting, the government will seek to assist all Canadian cultural groups that have demonstrated a desire and effort to continue to develop a capacity to grow and contribute to Canada, and a clear need for assistance, the small and weak groups no less than the strong and highly organized.

Second, the government will assist members of all cultural groups to overcome cultural barriers to full participation in Canadian society.

Third, the government will promote creative encounters and interchanged among all Canadian cultural groups in the interest of national unity.

Fourth, the government will continue to assist immigrants to acquire at least one of Canada's official languages in order to become full participants in Canadian society.[9]

In order to implement the policy, programmes were developed to give grants to meet certain needs or wants of cultural groups, study the relation of language to cultural development, secure histories of various ethnic groups in Canada, explore the possibility of establishing one or more centres of Canadian ethnic studies, discuss with the provinces mutually acceptable forms of federal assistance towards the teaching of the official languages to school children, and enable federal cultural agencies—such as the Canadian Broadcasting Corporation, the Canadian Radio and Television Commission, the National Film Board, the National Museum, and the Public Archives—to respond to recommendations of the Royal Commission on Bilingualism and Biculturalism's Report. Several provinces also proclaimed policies of multiculturalism, with their own programmes.

The policy contained ambiguities. The name of the policy of multi-culturalism implied that it had to do primarily with the retention of cultures. But only one of its four aims, the first, had to do with cultural retention, and that aim was the only one for which a rationale was thought to be necessary: that multiculturalism would create confidence in one's identity, out of which could grow respect for the identity of others and a willingness to share with them ideas, attitudes, and assumptions. Thus the intent of the policy was to affirm Canada's respect for and pride in all of the various ethnic groups that are part of the population, and to assure those who belonged to the groups that if, while participating in the work force, educational institutions, and social life generally in English or in French, they wished to maintain their language and other symbols of their ethnic identity the government would encourage and support them. Since culture, including language, can be maintained and developed only when it is fully employed in all areas of life, it can hardly have been the intent of the framers of the policy to promote multiculturalism; rather it was to endorse polyethnicity or ethnic pluralism.

There were several reasons why the term multiculturalism was used. As Howard Palmer has pointed out, given that the policy was responding to reports of the Royal Commission on Bilingualism and Biculturalism the term multiculturalism was probably inevitable. Also, even among social scientists culture and ethnicity were often confused, although one had to do with systems of behaviour and the other with a sense of peoplehood. The term culture was more familiar than the term ethnic, though hardly better understood; the term ethnic was often in popular speech and epithet,

[9]Canada, *House of Commons Debates,* 1971, pp. 8545-46.

signifying foreigner; and ethnic identity was sometimes taken to emphasize origin and hence to be immutable. In the research division of the Royal Commission the word ethnic had been outlawed, except in the phrase ethnic origin category, and it was similarly outlawed among the framers of the response to the commission's report.

Pressure for a policy concerning ethnic groups had come from the spokespeople for ethnic organizations in groups that had arrived in Canada before the First World War from central and eastern Europe, and that had received small numbers of immigrants after the Second World War. Chief among them were Ukrainians, 82 per cent of whom were born in Canada by 1971. In that year, ethnic organizations were estimated to have between 30,000 and 60,000 members, out of a Ukrainian population of 580,000. Newcomers found that Canadian-born generations were uninterested in learning and using their ancestral languages and customs, and looked to government to shore up their cultures. The spokespeople for the organizations representing established White ethnic groups considered that it was their pressure that had forced the government to proclaim the policy of multiculturalism, and that the aim of the policy was their aim, the support of cultural retention.

Being from central and eastern Europe from which emigration was extremely difficult during the Cold War, the spokespeople were little interested in immigration, although one of the four aims of the policy, having to do with teaching one or both of the official languages to newcomers, was directed toward immigrants. The spokespeople indeed looked upon teaching Canada's official languages as injurious to them, as it swelled the English and French linguistic communities at the expense of others. The First Annual Report of the Canadian Consultative Council on Multiculturalism, a body set up to advise the minister responsible for multiculturalism, excoriated multicultural centres because all groups could participate in their programmes "only through use of a common language, presumably either French or English".[10]

Groups that were largely composed of recent immigrants, such as the Italians, 46 per cent of whom were foreign born in 1971, were not greatly interested in the policy of multiculturalism, nor were the advocates of the policy much concerned about them. The advocates were also unaware of the change in sources of immigration that were occurring even as the *Report of the Royal Commission on Bilingualism and Biculturalism* was being written and the government's response to it was being framed. The

---

[10]*First Annual Report of the Canadian Consultative Council on Multiculturalism,* Ottawa, 1975, p. 20.

newcomers, many of them members of the visible minorities, were less immediately concerned with loss of language and culture than they were with discrimination. Some of them had English or French as a mother tongue or a second language—people from the Caribbean, for example, some Hong Kong Chinese, some South Asians and Vietnamese—and were not greatly concerned about the one aim of the policy of multiculturalism most clearly directed at immigrants. Discrimination was another matter. A member of a European group—a Pole, say, or a Lithuanian—cannot be quickly identified by physical characteristics. Blacks or Asians can usually be, though with no great precision, singled out for special treatment, and since they have suffered such treatment in the past, they are highly sensitive to it, and see it where outsiders might not. Further, they cannot shed their colour or other distinguishing features. Hence what are of most importance for some at least of the new immigrants are what are called human rights rather than the collective rights that are claimed under the policy of multiculturalism.

By 1975, the government had become aware that the outstanding issue in ethnic relations in Canada was not the retention of languages and cultures but racism directed against the immigrants from south, south-east, and east Asia and from the Caribbean—the visible minorities. The minister responsible for multiculturalism, John Munro, therefore attempted to change the emphasis of the policy of multiculturalism from cultural retention to group understanding and the combating of discrimination, which were also, as was clear from the prime minister's statement introducing the policy, important aims. Immediately the spokespeople for the organizations of white ethnic groups, led by the Canadian Consultative Council on Multiculturalism, protested vituperatively, alleging that Munro was betraying multiculturalism. It was an indication of the power that the groups and the Council possessed that Munro failed to obtain cabinet approval for the change he had announced.

In 1977 the new Citizenship Act abolished preferential treatment previously accorded to British subjects who applied for Canadian citizenship, putting all applicants for citizenship on the same level for the first time. Also in 1977 the Canadian Human Rights Act outlawed discrimination on grounds of race, national or ethnic origin, or colour, or a number of other factors, within the federal area of legislative competence.

A few years later, as the visible minorities continued to increase and as racial incidents, including cross-burnings by the Ku Klux Klan in Ontario and British Columbia, began to multiply, another minister responsible for multiculturalism, James Fleming, was able to create a race relations unit within the Multiculturalism Directorate and to commission studies of racism in a number of cities across the country.

Finally, the Charter of Rights and Freedoms in the Constitution Act of 1982 contained two clauses designed to entrench both the individual and the collective aspects of the policy of multiculturalism:

15. (1) Every individual is equal before and under the law and has the right to equal protection and equal benefit of the law without discrimination and, in particular, without discrimination based on race, national or ethnic origin, colour, religion, sex, age or mental or physical disability.

(2) Subsection (1) does not preclude any law, programme or activity that has as its object the amelioration of conditions of disadvantaged individuals or groups, including those that are disadvantaged because of race, national or ethnic origin, religion, sex, age or mental or physical disability....

27. This charter shall be interpreted in a manner consistent with preservation and enhancement of the multicultural heritage of Canadians.[11]

The policy won endorsement from all national political parties, and it continued to receive support when the Federal Government changed from Liberal to Conservative in 1984. In 1988 a Multiculturalism Act was passed, and three years later the Multiculturalism Directorate, under the aegis of a minister of state, was replaced by a full-fledged Ministry of Multiculturalism and Citizenship.

But all along there had been criticism as well as praise for the policy. The Quebec government in the 1960s, having become aware of a drop in the birth rate to below replacement levels, had changed its attitude toward immigration. From being hostile Quebec had become eager to recruit immigrants who would join the French-speaking linguistic community. It had set up a Quebec immigration service in 1965 and a department of immigration in 1968, and had entered into an agreement with Ottawa to have Quebec officials in federal immigration offices to help select suitable immigrants for Quebec. However, both the provincial government and some of the leading intellectuals of Quebec opposed the policy of multiculturalism. Almost as soon as it was announced, it was denounced as destructive of the hardly won status of French Canadians as one of the two charter-member groups in the Canadian federation. It was seen as backward-looking, and designed to preserve the privileges of the British elites. Spokesmen for ethnic organizations decried the policy as insufficient, in

[11]*A Consolidation of the Constitution Acts 1867 to 1982,* Ottawa, 1989.

that it did not give to their languages the massive support that French received under the Official Languages Act (1969). Political opponents of the Liberal Government considered it a cynical political attempt to play off the other ethnic groups against the French Canadians and to buy the chimerical ethnic vote.

While academics, politicians, and journalists criticized, the public for several years was unaware of the policy. A survey carried out between November 1973 and March 1974 found that only about 20 per cent of those included in a national sample knew of the policy. There was, however, a generally positive attitude toward it, although there was also "convert concern and reluctance to accept ethnic diversity".[12]

As time went on and people from outside the country—including Queen Elizabeth II and the Pope—praised multiculturalism, the desirability of ethnic diversity as an aspect of Canadian society became generally accepted. The term multiculturalism entered into popular speech: a person of other than British origin, especially a member of a visible minority, began to be referred to as a multicultural person. The policy of multiculturalism, however, was interpreted as doing little but providing public funds for the retention of cultures, and many people had misgivings concerning this. It was thought to be conducive to ghettoization or balkanization, and inimical to national unity. That the policy also had aims of equality and respect for others went unnoticed.

Criticism of the policy of multiculturalism increased during the consultations preceding the vote in October 1992 on the Charlottetown Consensus Report—an agreement concerning the constitution which the Federal Government hoped would be accepted by a majority of Canadians in all the provinces and territories, but which was overwhelmingly rejected by a plebiscite. During the campaign, the Reform Party, a Conservative Party originating in Alberta which spread rapidly in the early 1990s, pledged to abolish the policy of multiculturalism. The two aspects of the policy that drew most fire were the encouragement of cultural retention, which was only one part of the policy, and the cost of the policy, which was by governmental standards low. As the Reform Party spread and began to threaten the party in power, it is probably not coincidental that two statutes foreshadowed in the Multiculturalism Act of 1988, the Canadian Race Relations Foundation Act and the Canadian Heritage Languages Institute Act, though they received royal assent in 1991 have not yet, at the start of 1994, been proclaimed in force. The Act to create a Department of

[12]John W. Berry, Rudolf Kalin, and Donald M. Taylor, *Multiculturalism and Ethnic Attitudes in Canada,* Ottawa, 1977, pp. 240-48.

Multiculturalism and Citizenship to replace a Multiculturalism Directorate under a minister of state did come in force in 1991, but in 1993 the new department was rolled into a ministry of Canadian heritage, along with culture, the arts, broadcasting, parks and historic sites, and sport.

The Current Situation

By the 1990s, the white ethnic groups that had long thought of themselves as minorities were well on the way to equality and inclusion in the mainstream. The Ukrainians, once extremely vocal about their minority status, approximated the total Canadian population in socio-economic status, and could point to a Ukrainian-Canadian minister of finance, Governor-General, and member of the Supreme Court. They were revising their history to omit any mention of sheepskin coats, and to deny illiteracy and dire poverty. Other European groups similarly had advanced in occupational and income levels, and begun to share in honorific economic and political appointments. The differences in social and economic status among the groups of European stock had dwindled. In a study carried out in 1991 of Canadian attitudes toward immigrant and ethnic groups by John Berry and Rudolf Kalin, the groups of European origins were all rated positively, and just about equally so, by respondents of British and other ethnic origins, although the ratings by respondents of French origin were lower and more varied. With acceptance, those of European origins were marrying with Canadians of British and other origins more and more frequently. That does not mean that symbolic markets of ethnic identity were necessarily disappearing. The policy of multiculturalism was not simply to allow but to celebrate diversity and pluralism. The holidays and holy days of many religions and ethnic groups were hailed in Canadian media, and Christian holy days, such as Christmas, were deprecated, even though 84 per cent of the population claimed Christianity as their religion. (The next largest groups, 12.6 per cent, claimed no religion.)

The people who are grouped together as visible minorities vary considerably in social and economic status: Chinese business and professional men from Hong Kong, for example, or wealthy Iranian immigrants are in very different positions from Haitian or Somali refugees. Generally, however, immigrants belonging to visible minorities fare less well than White immigrants or Canadian born Whites. Salaries of non-Whites tend to be less than those of Whites of similar qualifications. A study by Frances Henry and Effie Ginzberg in Toronto found that white job applicants were treated fairly and courteously, and received job offers and second interviews more often than non-Whites. Members of visible minorities reported harassment by the police, managers of shopping malls, and others.

But the visible minorities are in many instance, though not always, far different from the peasants who came to Canada in the late nineteenth and early twentieth centuries. They are familiar with city life, with industrial, commercial, and financial occupations, and with professions. They are able to use the human rights and multiculturalism policies, and the media, adeptly to reduce their disadvantages. When promotion to high-status jobs is denied human rights commissions or ombudsmen are appealed to. Immigrants have always improved their economic position quite quickly after coming to Canada, and the members of visible minorities are doing so.

They are able even to seek redress from the government for past discriminatory actions against them. The Japanese Canadians, after years of effort, obtained a symbolic acknowledgment of their wartime mistreatment in 1988; Chinese and South Asians were emboldened to seek redress also, for the head tax and the Komagata Maru incident, along with Ukrainians (for internments during the First World War) and Italians (for internments during the Second World War).

Whether the visible minorities will join the British, French, and other White ethnic groups in the pluralistic mainstream is hard to predict. Some indications are that they will. In the study of contemporary Canadian ethnic attitudes by Berry and Kalin, the Chinese, who had earlier been subjected to much discrimination and then for twenty-four years virtually excluded from Canada, and Native Canadian Indians, who had also suffered greatly from discrimination, were ranked as positively as the European groups. West Indian Blacks, Arabs, Muslims, Indian-Pakistanis, and Sikhs ranked lower, but still fairly positively. Intermarriage is often taken as the ultimate sign of acceptance, and once visible minority, Japanese Canadians, has in the third generation or sansei been said to have an intermarriage rate of 85 or 90 per cent.

In the 1980s the names that symbolized wealth and economic power in Canada included such non-British names as Frank Stronach, Thomas Bata, the Bronfmans, the Reichmans, the Belzbergs, and the Ghermazians. The fact that their success had been achieved in areas where risks were high resulted in almost all of them encountering difficulties during the recession of the early 1990s, but by 1993 several had begun to regain lost ground.

Women belonging to visible minorities, including refugee women, have occasionally done better economically than men belonging to the same group, but generally have fared less well. They have tried to get support from women's organizations in order to obtain a less dependent immigration status and to gain greater access to language and job training. Domestic workers have worked and lobbied hard to improve their positions. The women's organizations have provided a few jobs for middle-class immigrant women, but there is little evidence concerning the degree to which they have improved the lot of working-class women.

In politics the increased numbers and the residential concentration of visible minorities, especially in large cities, have drawn the attention of all political parties. During the 1980s Toronto's visible minorities were marshalled by candidates to participate in nomination meetings. The members of the minorities quickly saw the advantages of running for election in ridings where they formed a substantial portion of the population. The federal election of October 1993 involved many parties and many candidates, and they were of highly diverse backgrounds. Those elected included people of many origins, including visible minorities—Chinese, South Asians, Guyanese, and West Indians.

On the other hand, small racist groups have continued to appear in various parts of the country. In the 1970s and 1980s the Ku Klux Klan and several other organizations reappeared in the major cities, although they never drew many followers. While they attracted some Canadians of British origin many of the leaders were immigrants of European origins, German, Dutch, Serbia, and Latvian among them. They drew attention by such measures as hate messages on the telephone directed against minorities and immigrants, vandalism in Jewish synagogues and cemeteries, and graffiti and vandalism directed against Sikh temples, the homes of South Asians, and schools with South Asian students. Usually they received notice in the media for a short period and then disappeared from view, to reappear, with some of the same individuals involved, ten or fifteen years later. Recently—in the 1990s—the organizations have attempted to recruit members among teenagers, but young people have banded together against them, and the anti-racist groups have drawn far more support than the racist groups.

Two incidents that drew much attention in the 1980s became widely known as the Zundel affair and the Keegstra affair. Ernst Zundel was a German immigrant who came to Canada in 1958, and took as mentor the fascist Adrien Arcand. Moving to Toronto in the mid-1960s, he associated with various neo-Nazi groups and became a publisher of antisemitic literature, which among other things denied that the Holocaust had never happened. Tried on a charge of spreading false news knowingly, he was convicted, he appealed, after a second trial was again convicted, and again appealed. James Keegstra was the son of immigrants from the Netherlands and a high school teacher in the small town of Eckville, Alberta. He was charged in 1985 of willfully promoting hatred against the Jewish people by means of his

teaching. He also was convicted, but the Supreme Court of Alberta overthrew
the conviction. The Court took the case to the Supreme Court of Canada,
which upheld the constitutionality of the law under which Keegstra had been
convicted. The Alberta government decided that a new trial was necessary;
Keegstra was again convicted, and again appealed.

Conclusion

When the term vertical mosaic was applied to Canadian society, the
ethnic origin categories that were considered to form the mosaic, most of
which had been present in the country for upwards of fifty years, were almost
all White. They had originally been visible, because of their costumes—
sheepskin coats, for example—and their accents, but not because of physical
traits. Now the White groups have become much more equal to the once-
dominant British and each other and have merged, retaining symbolic
markers of their origins only if they so wished. In the last quarter of a century,
because of the elimination of racism from the country's immigration policy,
the visible minorities have increased greatly. They are still not fully equal to
other Canadians except in law, but in spite of the permanence of their marks
of difference some at least of them are advancing toward equality much more
rapidly than their predecessors.

BIBLIOGRAPHY

Defining Ethnicity's Components
Bailey, Alfred G. "On the Nature of the Distinction between the French and
    English in Canada: An Anthropological Inquiry", *Report of the Annual
    Meeting of the Canadian Historical Association,* 1947, pp. 63-72.
Epp, Frank. "The Mennonite Experience in Canada", in *Religion and
    Ethnicity,* ed. Harold Coward and Leslie Kawamura. Waterloo: Wilfrid
    Laurier University Press, 1978, pp. 21-35.
Gordon, Milton M. *Assimilation in American Life.* New York: Oxford
    University Press, 1963.
Halli, Shiva S., Frank Trovato, and Leo Driedger, eds. *Ethnic Demography:
    Canadian Immigrant Racial and Cultural Variations.* Ottawa: Carleton
    University Press, 1990.
Hughes, Everett C. *The Sociological Eye: Selected Papers.* Chicago: Aldine-
    Atherton, 1971.
Mauss, Armand L. "Mormons and Ethnics: Variable Historical and Inter-
    national Implication of an Appealing Concept", in *The Mormon Presence
    in Canada,* ed. Brigham Y. Card, Herbert C. Northcott, John E. Foster,

Howard Palmer, and George K. Jarvis. Edmonton: University of Alberta Press, pp. 332-52.

Parry, Keith. "Mormous as Ethnics: A Canadian Perspective", in *The Mormon Presence in Canada,* ed. Brigham Y. Card et al. Edmonton: University of Alberta Press, pp. 353-65.

Porter, John. *The Vertical Mosaic: An Analysis of Class and Power in Canada.* Toronto: University of Toronto Press, 1965.

—. "Bilingualism and the Myths of Culture", *Canadian Review of Sociology and Anthropology* 6:2, May 1969, pp. 111-18.

—. "Dilemmas and Contradictions of a Multi-Ethnic Society", *Transactions of the Royal Society of Canada* 4: 10, October 1972, pp. 193-205.

—. "Ethnic Pluralism in Canadian Perspective", in *Ethnicity: Theory and Experience,* ed. N. Glazer and D.P. Moynihan, Cambridge, Mass.: Harvard University Press, 1975, pp. 267-304.

Schermerhorn, Robert A. *Comparative Ethnic Relations.* New York: Random House, 1970.

Immigration and Immigration Policy, 1867-1920

Barber, Marilyn. "Sunny Ontario for British Girls, 1900-1930", in *Looking into My Sister's Eyes: An Exploration in Women's History,* ed. Jean Burnet. Toronto: Multicultural History Society of Ontario, 1986, pp. 55-73.

Ferguson, Ted. *A White Man's Country: An Exercise in Canadian Prejudice.* Toronto: Macmillan of Canada, 1975.

Hayne, David M. "Emigration and Colonization: Twin Themes in Nineteenth Century French Canadian Literature", in *The Quebec and Acadian Diaspora in North America,* ed. Raymond Breton and Pierre Savard. Toronto: Multicultural History Society of Ontario, 1982, pp. 11-22.

Jin Guo: Voices of Chinese Canadian Women. Toronto: Women's Press, 1993.

Johnston, Hugh. *The Voyage of the Komagata Maru: The Sikh Challenge to Canada's Colour Bar.* Delhi: Oxford University Press, 1992.

Macdonald, Norman. *Canada: Immigration and Colonization, 1841-1903.* Toronto: Macmillan of Canada, 1968.

Troper, Harold. "Immigration", *The Canadian Encyclopedia.* Edmonton: Hurtig Publishers, 1985, p. 863.

Wickberg, Edgar, ed. *From China to Canada: A History of the Chinese Communities in Canada.* Toronto: McClelland & Stewart, 1982.

Immigration and Immigration Policy, 1920 to Present

Abella Irving, and Troper, Harold. *None is Too Many: Canada and the Jews of Europe, 1933-1948.* Toronto: Lester & Orpen Dennys, 1982.

Abella, Rosalie. *Report of the Commission on Equality in Employment.* Ottawa: Supply & Services, 1984.

Barber, Marilyn. "The Women Ontario Welcomed: Immigrant Domestics for Ontario Homes, 1870-1930", *Ontario History* 72:3, September 1980, pp. 148-72.

Buchignani, Norman, and Indra Doreen M. with Ram Srivastava.*Continuous Journey: A Social History of South Asians in Canada.* Toronto: McClelland & Stewart, 1985.

Canada, Special Committee of the House of Commons on Visible Minorities in Canadian Society. *Equality Now!* Ottawa: Queen's Printer, 1984.

Hawkins, Freda. *Canada and Immigration: Public Policy and Public Concern.* Montreal: McGill-Queen's University Press, 1972.

—. *Critical Years in Immigration: Canada and Australia Compared.* Montreal: McGill-Queen's University Press, 1989.

Horn, Michael. "Canadian Soldiers and Dutch Women after the Second World War", in *Dutch Immigration to North America,* ed. Herman Ganzevoort and Mark Boekelman. Toronto: Multicultural History Society of Ontario, 1983, pp. 187-95.

Lindström-Best, Varpu. *Defiant Sisters: A Social History of Finnish Immigrant Women in Canada.* Toronto: Multicultural History Society of Ontario, 1988.

Simmons, Alan B. " 'New Wave' Immigrants: Origins and Characterics", in *Ethnic Demography: Canadian Immigrant Racial and Cultural Variations,* ed. Shiva S. Halli, Frank Trovato, and Leo Driedger. Ottawa: Carleton University Press, 1990.

Ethnic Relations: Trials and Tribulations

Avery, Donald. *"Dangerous Foreigners": European Immigrant Workers and Labour Radicalism in Canada, 1896-1932.* Toronto: McClelland & Stewart, 1979.

Bradwin, Edmund W. *The Bunkhouse Man: A Study of Work and Pay in the Camps of Canada, 1903-1914,* first published 1928. Toronto: University of Toronto Press, 1972.

Brown, Michael. "From Stereotype to Scapegoat: Anti-Jewish Sentiment in French Canada from Confederation to World War I", in *Antisemitism in Canada: History and Interpretation,* ed. Allan Davies. Waterloo: Wilfrid Laurier University Press, 1992, pp. 39-66.

Canada. *House of Commons Debates,* vol. 3, 1 May 1947, pp. 2644-47.

—. Royal Commission on Bilingualism and Biculturalism. *Report.* Ottawa: Queen's Printer, 1967-70.

Reitz, Jeffrey G. *The Survival of Ethnic Groups.* Toronto: McGraw Hill Ryerson, 1980.

Subtelny, Orest. *Ukrainians in North America: An Illustrated History.* Toronto: University of Toronto Press, 1991.

Winks, Robin W. *The Blacks in Canada: A History.* Montreal: McGill-Queen's University Press, 1971.

Woodsworth, James S. *Strangers within our Gates or coming Canadians,* first published 1909. Toronto: University of Toronto Press, 1972.

The Policy of Multiculturalism

Berry, John W., and Jean A. Laponce, eds. *Ethnicity and Culture in Canada: The Research Landscape.* Toronto: University of Toronto Press, 1994.

Berry, John W., Rudolf Kalin, and Donald M. Taylor. *Multiculturalism and Ethnic Attitudes in Canada.* Ottawa: Ministry of Supply and Services, 1977.

Canada. *House of Commons Debates,* 1971, pp. 8545-46.

—. *A Consolidation of the Constitution Acts 1867 to 1982.* Ottawa: Department of Justice, 1989.

First Annual Report of the Canadian Consultative Council of Multiculturalism. Ottawa: Canadian Consultative Council on Multiculturalism, 1975.

Frideres, James S., ed. *Multiculturalism and Intergroup Relations.* New York: Greenwood Press, 1989.

Palmer, Howard. "Reluctant Hosts: Anglo-Canadian Views of Multiculturalism in the Twentieth Century", in *Multiculturalism as State Policy.* Conference Report, Second Canadian Conference on Multiculturalism. Ottawa: Ministry of Supply and Services, 1976, pp. 81-118.

Rocher, Guy. "Multiculturalism: The Doubts of a Francophone", in *Multiculturalism as State Policy.* Conference Report, Second Canadian Conference on Multiculturalism. Ottawa: Ministry of Supply and Services, 1976, pp. 47-53.

The Current Situation

Barrett, Stanley R. *Is God a Racist? The Right Wing in Canada.* Toronto: University of Toronto Press, 1987.

Berry, John W. "Multicultural and Ethnic Attitudes in Canada: Contemporary views about the Multicultural Policy and Ethnocultural Groups", unpublished paper presented at Nordiske Migrationsforskerseminar, Esbjerg, Denmark, 16-19 September 1993.

Betcherman, Lita-Rose. *The Swastika and the Maple Leaf: Fascist Movement in Canada in the Thirties.* Toronto: Fitzhenry & Whiteside, 1975.

Henry, Frances, and Effie Ginzberg. *Who Gets the Work: A Test of Racial Discrimination in Employment*. Toronto: The Urban Alliance on Race Relations and the Social Planning Council of Metropolitan Toronto, 1985.

Luciuk, Lubomyr, and Stella Hryniuk, eds.*Canada's Ukrainians: Negotiating and Identity*. Toronto: University of Toronto Press, 1991.

Richmond, A.H. "The Income of Caribbean Immigrants in Canada", in *Ethnic Demography: Canadian Immigrant Racial and Cultural Variations*, ed. Shiva S. Halli, Frank Trovato, and Leo Driedger. Ottawa: Carleton University Press, 1990.

9

Women in Canada[1]

WENDY MITCHINSON

Introduction

1867 is a meaningless date in Canadian women's history. It focuses attention on the political creation of the Domination of Canada but does not address the day-to-day lives of Canadian people. Life the day after Confederation continued much as it had the day before. This perception has been one of the contributions of women's history to the general field of Canadian history. Dates and events which have traditionally loomed large in the received version of the nation's development appear less significant when seen through the lens of women's experience; other events previously ignored take on added significance.

Women's history in Canada is a product of the women's movement which emerged in the late 1960s and early 1970s. Many young women had entered the university system and discovered that their past was not being taught, indeed was not even recorded. They queried what history was if it could ignore half the population? They questioned whether the generalities which historians made about the Canadian people really described the experience of women. Some historians had assumed that women in the past had been largely passive and thus not a subject for historical investigation; there was a sense that women's world was the private sphere and the conviction that history should focus its attention on the public arena where it was believed women had not participated; when there was an admission of agency, historians had assumed that the experiences of men and women differed little from one another. What twenty years of research into women's history has revealed is how erroneous such assumptions were. Women in the past were anything but passive, their experience differed from those of men in many respects, and all Canadians, both men and women, lived and worked in the

---

[1]Much of the interpretation of this chapter comes from my work with Alison Prentice, Paula Bourne, Gail Cuthbert Brandt, Beth Light, and Naomi Black in writing *Canadian Women: A History,* Toronto, 1988.

private and public worlds, indeed the overlap between the two is such that it is difficult to separate them.

Women's history takes as its premise that the role of women in historical events or the absence of women from them must be recognized and assessed. Historians of women ask the question what would the past be like if women were placed at the centre of inquiry.[2] They argue that gender roles have been ascribed on the basis of social choice rather than nature and therefore it lies within the historians' competence to study them. But it is not an easy task. Women compose half the population and consequently are difficult to generalize. They have been excluded from power but as wives, daughters, etc., they often were closer to actual power than many men. They were exploited. Women were members of families, citizens of different regions, economic producers just as men were but how they experienced these roles was different. One can't talk of the status of woman in the singular but must do so in the plural—personal, familial, legal, economic, and political.

As with all areas of historical scholarship, women's history after twenty years of research has a historiography. The first literature on women was biographical and laudatory—the great woman theory of history. The tendency was to stress those aspects of women's lives in which they succeeded like men. Following this was the victim approach, viewing women as an oppressed group and dealing with their struggles against their oppressors. But treating women as victim places them in a male-defined conceptual framework; it makes them passive. The limitations of the victim approach and its essentially negative overtones led historians to seek a more positive interpretation. In recent years, they have been concentrating first on women's culture and secondly on the way in which the world of men and women interact. Race, class, ethnicity, and sexual orientation are also becoming more integrated into the historical analysis leading to the differences between women being recognized and stressed as well as the similarities.

Trying to be inclusive is not easy; it often leads to 'add-on' history, that is, history where a different group's experience is simply added to the narrative but doesn't really change the interpretation. Perhaps the reason for this stems from the profile of historians in Canada. Most tend to be white, middle-class, and until recently male. We tend to write from a Euro-centric perspective which places those not from that tradition on the periphery. Even the native Canadians who lived on the land for thousands of years before the coming of the Whites are marginalized. There is an insider/outsider element to most history, whether acknowledged or not,

---

[2]Gerda Lerner, *The Majority Finds Its Past: Placing Women in History,* New York,1979, pp. 162, 168-80.

and it does colour interpretation.

Also distorting the history of women is the element of relationship. We cannot study women without studying men; they are present as fathers, sons, husbands, employers, and fellow workers, even when not discussed. We cannot study the concept of womanhood without the concept of manhood existing in the background. The tendency to classify groups of people involves comparison with other groups so that we cannot study women of colour without being aware of White women; working-class women without addressing the social construction of middle-class women, etc. Historians of women are trying to cope with these realizations and in doing so have made women's history an incredibly stimulating field.

Women in Victorian Canada: At Home

When examining the day-to-day lives of women over time, what is striking is the theme of continuity and change. The nature of human existence incorporates both and some periods of history are characterized by more or less of one or the other. For the native women in Canada this was certainly true. By mid-century, many natives in the northern and far western reaches of the country were continuing the lifestyle that had been theirs for centuries. Where food was abundant, more settled life occurred but where it was scarce a nomadic way of life was crucial for survival. Each tribe or grouping was individual, just as the nations of Europe varied one from another, but were also bonded together by general principles and beliefs. For some tribes in Canada, the matrilineal line was that which identified a person's heritage, for others it was the male line. In some tribes women appeared, at least from the European perspective, beasts of burden whereas in others, usually the more agricultural tribes such as the Iroquois, women had a status which European men found disconcerting. In whatever situation, women were vital for the survival of the tribe in helping to provide the food the tribe ate, the clothing it wore, and in bearing the children so necessary for its continuation.

While existence could be extraordinarily harsh in the traditional way of life, harder still was the experience of those native women who had come into contact with European settlers. In eastern Canada and the southern parts of central Canada, numbers by mid-century were winning out— natives were being usurped from their ancestral land. The new settlers had an insatiable thirst for land and whereas the need for native/European military alliances had previously kept the Europeans in check, this need had by mid-century disappeared. Colonial and imperial governments now viewed the natives as an encumbrance, obstacles to progress. Natives found

themselves placed on reserves set aside for them, more often than not, on
agriculturally unproductive land. While this was a process which began in
central and eastern Canada it eventually moved West. Those most intimately
involved with natives were convinced that in order to survive the natives
would have to be assimilated. In part, assimilation meant that those tribes
who proffered high status, power, and recognition to women would have
to learn that woman's place was subordinate to man, not equal to man. As
Sylvia Van Kirk has detailed, the coming of the Europeans meant a lowering
of status for many native women. In those areas of western Canada where
the fur trade was still strong at mid-century and where alliances had
occurred between the traders and native women, the coming of White
women meant too often the throwing off of native wives. White women
were unwilling to accept native women as their equals despite the fact that
both shared the challenges of living in a world in which the wildness
surrounded them. For women of native ancestry this had been true from
time immemorial. For European women, leaving the confines of settled
communities, for what they saw as an uncivilized land, was a new and at
times terrifying experience made easier in some cases by feeling superior to
the native women they found living there.

Feeling superior to others may have helped psychologically, but it could
not negate the physical hardships experienced by White women settlers. At
Confederation, many Canadians were still experiencing a pioneer way of
life. In fact, in parts of the country this has continued to the present. At
mid-century, pioneering often involved significant dislocation for families
and individuals. People left one part of the country to settle in another or
people left their native country to emigrate and begin a new life in Canada.
In either case, women as well as men were on the move. For those emigrating
to Canada, often from Britain, the journey could be horrendous—long,
tedious, sometimes life-threatening. For many women such a move was
made without their consent; their husbands had presented them with a *fait
accompli*. In such cases, the resentment added to the physical problems of
relocation must have been overwhelming. One individual recalled her/his
trip to the Canadian West and what happened when the family arrived.

And finally you were out on the prairie. In a sod house and where were
you? Nowhere. Your nearest neighbor, the Jacksons or the Meltons, miles
away across the prairie and every sound outside at night was a grizzly bear.
Some women couldn't stand it. What happened I don't know, but after
about a year my mother had to go home. She couldn't take it and somehow or other we raked up the money and she went back to England with

the baby. Dad and the rest of us stayed; we never saw her or the baby again.[3]

For women who voluntarily came, either on their own or with their families, what kept them going throughout the harshness of travel was the hope that they were helping to build a better future for themselves and their loved ones. For some emigration enthusiasts, these women represented the tangible bonds of Empire, a way of expanding Britain's rule. Significant by the turn of the century were the many single women who were coming to Canada, driven by lack of opportunity in Britain, faced with the reality of a future without family because of the dearth of men.

Even more significant for Canada's future were the 500,000 non-English-speaking immigrants coming to Canada from southern, central, and northern Europe or from Asia. The adjustment problems of trying to learn a foreign language and to understand and integrate into a foreign culture were mind boggling especially when Canadians, including Canadian women, were not all that welcoming. Those who were non-White, even if English-speaking, were deemed especially unsuitable. Earlier in Canada's history, Black women loyalists had been discriminated against by White women and Blacks fleeing the slavery of the United States at mid-century in hopes of finding freedom in Canada found a very mixed welcome. Freedom they found but not equity. Neither were prospects better for the Chinese 'slave girls' and the Japanese 'picture brides' of the early twentieth century. But Canada needed immigrants and all could be of some use—married women because they would bear future Canadians and single women as servants in the homes of White, middle-class families. Well into the twentieth century, Canadian officials when they were trying to block the entrance of certain classes and groups of male emigrants, were willing to accept single women if they claimed they were domestic servants.

Women who came to Canada to homestead with their families found the challenges of pioneering had just begun. One of the conditions which was most difficult to accept was the isolation. One woman recalled here experience. "Life was very monotonous in the winter, and very lonely." One year she did not see another women outside her own family for even months.[4] The harsh Canadian winters in much of the country added to that sense of being cut off from all that women had known in their former homes. This physical isolation was accentuated by the fact that for many

[3]Barry Broadfoot, *The Piooner years 1895-1914: Memories of Settlers Who Opened the West,* Don Mills, 1978, p. 204.

[4]Linda Rasmusse et al., *A Harvest Yet to Reap: A History of Prairie Women,* Toronto, 1976, p. 62.

farming families contact with the outside world was limited because of cost of pens, ink, paper, stamps, books, and magazines.

While many women felt lonely, they certainly did not have time on their hands. The work which women did on the farms was crucial to the survival of the farm family. Commentators often made the point that single men could not make it on the farming frontier—there was too much work to do. A man needed a wife and children. The simplicity of economic and social organization concentrated a variety of essential activities on the woman and her family. Two aspects insured that women were important—the immediate necessity of her work and the fact that it was never ending. They cooked, sewed, cleaned, butchered, gardened, and bore children. And some of these responsibilities increased. By mid-century many farm homes had gone beyond the large open central fire place which heated the homes and over which the meals were cooked. The introduction of the iron box stove meant that huge logs were no longer needed for heat but that smaller pieces of wood would suffice. This lessened the work of men who had traditionally been in charge of wood gathering and often placed the burden of this chore on women and children. In such a way technology lessened labour but not necessarily everyone's labour. These new stoves expanded the variety of food women could and thus were expected to cook. The stoves were time consuming to clean as well. One study of domestic life has described the multitude of tasks required in caring for an iron range in the 1880s.

... remove the covers and brush the soot free from the top of the oven into the fire-box then clean out the grate; and if the stove have conveniences for so doing sift the ashes, save all the old coal and cinders. Put in shavings or loose rolls of paper, then fine pine kindlings, arranged crosswise, and a layer of hard wood leaving plenty of air space between the pieces. Be sure the wood comes out to catch the end of the fire-box. Put on the covers; and if the stove needs cleaning, moisten some pulverized stove polish with water, and rub the stove with a paint brush dipped in the polish. When all blackened, rub with a dry polishing brush until nearly dry. Open the direct draught and over damper, and light the paper, as a slight heat facilitates the process of polishing. When the wood is thoroughly kindled, fill the fire-box with coal even with the top of the oven. Brush up the hearth and floor, empty the tea kettle and fill with fresh water. Watch the fire and push the coal down as the wood burns away, and add enough more coal to keep it even with the top of the fire-bricks.[5]

[5]Una Abrahamson, *Domestic Life in Nineteenth Century Canada,* Toronto, 1966, p. 85.

As the century passed, housekeeping books advised women how to do their work. One recommended work schedule was washday, followed by ironing day, at least 2 baking days, and a mending day. Standards were being created. As well as the daily chores of housekeeping, which were necessary in all homes, women living in isolated areas were expected to serve as physicians and teachers to their families. They had to learn what the medicinal plants were in a new environment and to be able to make up medicines for times when family members fell ill.

Pioneering women and other farm women in the early years often generated the only income a farm family might see. This they did through the sale of butter and cheese which they made and eggs gathered from the chicken they raised. All members of a farm family worked hard but what did seem to be the case was that the work of women overlapped that of the men but that of men did not overlap the work of women. At harvest time, women could be found in the fields but seldom did men help with the domestic chores. Man's focus was on the outside world, his goal was growing a cash crop. His work would create the future comfort of the family whereas the woman's work of taking care of the home, the kitchen garden, and raising the small livestock ensured their survival until that day come. Any excess money the family had, went to support the husband's work, not the wife's. As Marjorie Cohen has argued, the most significant sector in the pre-industrial period in terms of number of people working the level of production was agriculture. In this sector, waged labour was considerably less important to the production process than the non-wage labour of family members. Each member had a different role and women's role was critical to capital accumulation for the family. "To the extent that woman's efforts sustained the family in its basic consumption needs, male labour was free to engage in production for exchange on the market...; to the extent that the total income from market production need not be expended on consumption, accumulation of capital in the family's productive unit could occur."[6]

What did all this mean for women? The harshness of life led to dependence on men just as many men were dependent on their wives and daughters. Prestige originated in the family not the individual and the outside world viewed the man as the head of the family. Any accumulation of capital was his. The existence of the family economy emphasized the importance of fertility and thus the image of woman as mother was central. At mid-century, women would have given birth to 7 to 8 children and

---

[6]Marjorie Cohen, *Women's Work, Markets, and Economic Development in Ninteenth-century Ontario*, Toronto, 1988, p. 8.

families probably averaged 5 to 6 surviving children. But such figures gloss over what these births meant for women. Statistics from the 1851 census, for example, indicate that of deaths among women aged 15 to 50, two in ten were related to bearing children. Childbirth could also lead to ill health but no statistics for maternal morbidity exist. Unless she died, a woman's childbirth experience did not become public.

As farms became more prosperous over time, women often found their work less central than it had been. Sons' work was crucial as farmers expanded their land holdings. The traditional work of women in raising livestock and making butter and cheese, however, declined—not because it was less important but ironically because it became more important. When cheese and butter production became viable commercially, it came under the domain of men. Cheese factories were set up which only hired male workers despite the fact that women had been the traditional cheese makers in society. Dairying increased and the herds placed under the control of men. The money that women had brought in was no longer as significant for the family as it once had been. Outside the home, the opportunities for young women in the farming communities were non-existent and so many had no choice but to leave and search for a future elsewhere.

For those young women whose position had been usurped on the farms and for those many single women immigrants coming to Canada on their own, the city provided opportunity. Thus it was that in the cities and more settled provinces of central and eastern Canada, women congregated. Certainly the census of 1881 and 1891 reveals this gender imbalance. The old saying of 'go west young man go west' may have been more gender specific than was realized. By 1921 adult women between the ages of 15 and 19 outnumbered men in most urban centres in Canada. Most of these young women would eventually marry and raise their families there facing the similar challenge of their rural counterparts—providing for their children.

In the decades after mid-century, women in urban homes were struggling to make do on very little. Certainly paid employment of consistent nature was scarce for married women. Like their rural sisters, married women focused on the day-to-day survival of their families. They could add some money to the family coffers by taking in boarders, raising animals until public health regulation forbade it, keeping a small garden, or taking in sewing or laundry. They save money by stretching the family budget in any way that they could. Their work in the home was so crucial for family that if a second wage earner was needed (and in most working-class families this was the case) then the children were sent out, often into the new factories emerging by mid-century. Even middle-class women were hardpressed to keep up appearances. Money often went to provide for the accoutrements of middle class existence such as a servant girl instead of providing for the education of daughters or for the easing of domestic work.

The Popular Image of Woman

The irony of woman's experience on the farm and the city home was its relationship with the public perception of what women should be doing. At one level, most Canadian women were where they were supposed to be—in the home; on another level, the reality of that place hardly met the conditions of the domestic ideology. Women in Canada at mid-century and beyond lived in a society which had strong views about how they were to behave. This idealization of women placed limits on their activities, led to conformity, created a certain stability in keeping actions under control, and was a measuring rod for change. It influenced how women looked at themselves. The strength of this stereotype should not be underestimated for most Canadian women felt called upon to make homage to it even those who could not or would not conform to it. The idealized view of women was delineated in the religious press, the secular press, through sermons, medical advice literature, and through the educational system. Nevertheless, native peoples and many of the non-White, immigrant groups had a different view of woman, their own idealized conception but one that differed from that espoused in mainstream society. Historians are only beginning to realize the existence of alternative views of womanhood and to understand that the accepted view was as socially constructed by race, class, and sexual orientation etc., as it was by gender.

As mentioned above, the central tenet of the domestic ideology was that woman's place was in the home. Man was head of the household, provider for his family and its defender. As for woman, "Woman's first and only place is her home. She is destined by Providence to make her home a... cloister wherein one may seek calm and joyful repose from the busy, heartless world.... The land she governs is a bright oasis in the desert of the world's selfishness."[7] Woman's place in the home had been ordained by God. She was to remain isolated from the world, her husband acting as buffer; he was active, she was less so. The good woman was to be submissive to her husband. She was dependent on him. She was never to question this dependence—it was natural and it was her duty to submit. Her submissiveness was part of a larger order, man's submissiveness to God. For some *pundits,* this hierarchy—God, man, woman—was supported by both religion and science.

[7]"Woman's Sphere", *The Harp,* December, 1874, p. 25.

Canadians saw woman as the upholder of religion. Woman was the strength of the Church, for men had little time as they increasingly focused their attention on worldly pursuits. It is not difficult to see why Canadians perceived women as naturally more religious than men. Religion in the mid-nineteenth century was found on an 'other worldly' concept. It was not concerned with the condition of society but with spiritual matters. Thus for women, who were to leave worldly affairs to men, religion appeared merely an extension of their role in the home. It did not involve them in the temporal aspects of life. The only exceptions to this were the nuns of the Catholic (and Anglican) Church, many of whose orders did engage their members in the world of helping others, usually through nursing and teaching. Being a nun was the only other option to being a wife deemed worthy of respect.

The ideal women was of course, a virtuous woman. This stemmed from a moral intuitive sense rather than a rational one. Female virtue was essential, for women were the child-bearers and rearers of children and nineteenth-century Canadians believed strongly in the power of màternal impressions, that is, the thoughts and feelings of a pregnant women could determine the moral characteristics of the child she bore. Many believed that women were morally superior to men and from that superiority they gained prestige. So strong was the belief in this that when a woman transgressed the boundaries of moral behaviour it was tantamount to a crime. Indeed, magistrates were more willing to incarcerate women who transgressed moral standards than they were men for, in women it seemed more serious, going against their very nature.

Motherhood was woman's chief glory. As Canada's foremost suffragist, Nellie McClung, made clear, 'every normal woman desire children'.[8] Mother love was a redemptive influence on mankind when all else failed. Hardened criminals, fallen women were known to weep at the mention of the word 'mother'. Maternity was a qualitative difference which separated women from men. Childbirth placed women's lives in jeopardy but women were not to question this—maternal instinct overrode all. A woman's concern for her children extended as well to the home. Woman was the domestic force in society; but home was not just of interest to woman. Home was a visual and concrete sign of independence for a man, that he had become successful enough to marry, support a family, and establish a home. All three went together in the middle-class lexicon of respectability.

The consequences of such an idealized view of women were far reaching.

[8]Candace Savage, *Our Nell: A Scrapbook Biography of Nellie L. McClung*, Saskatoon, 1979, p. 40.

For one, it restrained their actions. In her autobiography Nellie McClung tells of her experience as a young girl when in her own home there was a discussion concerning the Riel Rebellion. She wanted to speak and entered the debate. "Then came the ordeal, when the silence fell on the room. I have faced audiences who were hostile since then and encountered unfriendly glances, but the antagonism here was more terrible being directed not as much against what I had to say, as against the fact that I dared to say anything."[9] If women stepped outside their roles they could face ridicule, hostility, and at times violence. Society did not encourage women to develop their potential. Rather it tried to isolate women from temporal activities. Woman was to be an observer not a participant. Women who did not conform, such as single women, widowed women, women of colour, disabled women, and working women were outside the limits of respectability as defined by the ideal. It didn't seem to matter that the ideal was not a reflection of the reality of most women's lives. It was how many Canadians of British origin wanted reality to be.

Historians have debated the reasons for the existence of the ideal. Certainly for centuries women had been told what to do and how to behave. The details of the vision might change but the control it imposed on actions seldom did. However, in the mid-to-late nineteenth century, there did seem to be a resurgence of concern about woman's place in society. There are a multitude of reasons for this. There was a desire for stability in society and a fear of disorder. Although the nineteenth-century farming community exudes an image of stability, what historians are discovering is the great transiency rates which existed. Canadians were a people on the move. Many farmers failed and moved to another area to try again, some moved to expand their holdings, immigrants moved to Canada and even within towns and villages people were constantly in flux. In such a society stability becomes a longed-for condition. If there was agreement on what women were to do, the acceptance that the characteristics deemed female were dictated by nature, there was a force for stability in society.

Instability also existed because of the changing determination of status in society. Whereas the early nineteenth century ascribed status on the basis of birth, whose one's family was, by mid-century status was conditional more on what one did and how one behaved. As Alison Prentice has argued, "Where pre-industrial thought made much of multitudinous and fixed 'orders' of human society, and assumed considerable contract and dependency between people of differing ranks, many nineteenth century people were beginning to think of the world as divided into two increas-

[9]Ibid., p. 12.

ingly alien camps: the respectable, proprietary or 'middle' classes on the one hand and, on the other, the propertyless lower classes or the labouring poor."[10] Behaviour was one way the new middle class could separate itself out from the lower orders.

Structural changes occurring in society bolstered the delineation of woman's sphere. The economic structure had altered so that increasingly place of work and place of residence were separating, at least in the urban centres. Women who once had been involved, to an intimate degree, with the work of their husbands were now left at home as more men sought wage labour. This lessened the visibility of woman's economic role. Her husband was paid for his work outside the home but she was not paid for her work in the home. Unpaid work became associated with non-productive work even though the existence of pioneer farming was still within memory of all Canadians and being experienced by many others.

While the world of home and family encompassed that of most adult women in Canada, the experience of it was altering. From mid-century to the end of the First World War, the life events by which many women measured the passage of time was shifting. Puberty was declining somewhat, the age of marriage was increasing and the percentage of women not marrying was similarly increasing from 8.2 in 1851 to 11.1 in 1921. In addition, by the end of the century, women were outliving men and so the experience of widowhood was being felt by more women. Children were staying at home longer as compulsory education laws and child labour laws prevented them from assuming adult work roles. Thus woman's role as child rearer was extended even as the birth rate among women declined. All this created unease among many Canadians and made some cling to rigid gender roles even more vehemently.

The separation of spheres which the ideology espoused was a socially constructed one, and one not completely linked to reality. As already evident in the work which married women did in the home, their economic contributions made them part of the public world. But historians have sensed in looking at women in the past, that while they could not help but be part of the world, their relationship to it was often different than man's, they had carved out a somewhat separate culture. Margaret Conrad, for example, has pointed out that the concept of time and space was different for women. Women tended to look inward to family and men outward to market. There was a sense of family time characterized by a woman's role of daughter or wife and women's time measured by events such as menstruation and childbirth.

[10]Alison Prentice, *The School Promoters: Education and Social Class in Mid-Nineteen Century Upper Canada*, Toronto, 1977, p. 67.

The reality of existence in Canada created a separate woman's culture. And it was difficult for Canadians to perceive the distinction between 'the what was' of that reality and 'the what should be'. Because women stayed at home and took care of their children, people assumed it was natural for them to do so. For the Victorians what was natural was what was right. And what alternative did married women or even single women have but to remain at home or to hope for a home in which to remain? Women's lives were such that breaking out of that prescribed role was difficult.

Other Realities of Women's Lives

Underlying the idealized view of women was the assumption that women's bodies dominated them and were deficient when compared to men's bodies. This view was given credence by the medical profession and was widespread within the society. For example, in 1890 the *Globe* on the physical abilities of woman declared, "She can swim, she can dance, she can ride; all these things she can do admirably and with ease to herself. But to run, nature most surely did not construct her." Like the domestic hen which at times attempts to fly, woman when she runs displays "a kind of precipitate waddle with neither grace, fitness nor dignity."[11] Women were in a no win situation. Physicians viewed almost every aspect of women's lives as physically or biologically problematic—menstruation, childbirth, menopause. They believed that bodies were endowed with a limited amount of energy and that dissipation of that energy would weaken the individual. Unfortunately for women, doctors also believed that their complex reproductive system absorbed more energy compared to men's and thus women had to live a life which would limit the energy they lost. Thus doctors advised women not to engage in physical games, not to attend dances and late night parties, and not to weaken their systems at a crucial age by going to school. Conveniently ignored was the harsh physical labour which women did in factories, on farms, and in the home. Apparently that kind of expenditure of energy was not debilitating. Ignoring this reality underscored the class-based nature of the ideology. Also ignored or certainly not approved was the increasing involvement of women in sports, organized and otherwise.

According to the ideology of true womanhood, women did not have rights but privileges. Rights were based on power, usually physical and since women were seen as weak, they could not defend 'rights'. Women had privileges granted to them not as individuals but as a group set apart—wives, mother, daughters—something that did not happen to men. Men were

---

[11]Wendy Mitchinson, *The Nature of Their Bodies: Women and Their Doctors in Victorian Canada,* Toronto, 1991, p. 14.

deemed individuals—not solely husbands, fathers, sons—and individuals had rights. Native women especially were hurt by this perspective for they actually lost status with the creation of the new Dominion. In the Indian Act of 1869 an Indian was defined in male terms. Women achieved status only through their relationship to men. According to the Act, native women were to be subject to their husbands as were other women. Their children were *his* children; ideally women were not to own and transmit property and rights to their children. This, of course, violated traditional Indian notions of kinship, particularly in matrilineal and matrilocal societies. Until 1951, the Indian Act also deprived native women of any formal political rights. Band councils consisted only of men and were elected by men. These too were set up in the nineteenth century and went against tradition. A native woman who married a non-Indian was deprived of her legal right to hold land on the reserve, her children would not have Indian status, although she could still be on the band list and collect her annuity unless she chose a lump sum payment. In 1951 even this was removed. While the Indian Act did not question the validity of native marriages, their more open divorce customs were.

Non-native women also faced legal hurdles. They certainly had very few public rights. Married women were often considered not as individuals but as adjuncts to their husbands. For example, a woman's very citizenship depended on that of her husband. An alien woman could marry a British subject and thereby immediately become a British citizen whereas a Canadian woman who married a foreigner lost her British citizenship unless she specifically petitioned against it. Not until 1946 when the Canadian citizenship Act came into force did a Canadian woman have a citizenship status of her own. Beginning in the 1870s through the 1890s, women did gain the municipal franchise if they were owners of real property rated on the assessment roll to the specified amount. But this did not acknowledge women's right to vote but the right of their property to be represented. Such was woman's public or political rights that she was not even considered a *person* within the meaning of the British North America Act until 1929 when the Judicial Committee of the Privy Council in England overruled a Supreme Court of Canada decision that women were not persons. This 1929 ruling enabled women to sit in the Senate of Canada.

Economically women were legally disadvantaged. While women were important economically on the farm, they were under the control of men legally. Daughters seldom inherited much and a widow at times had her actions monitored according to the wishes expressed in a dead husband's will. Not until the 1930s were women on a par with men in gaining homesteading rights in the three Prairie Provinces. In some provinces women were not allowed to keep their own earnings if married. In 1900, the National Council of Women of Canada (NCW) summarized the situation as it existed in Nova Scotia and Prince Edward Island. "In Nova Scotia the written and filed consent of the husband is necessary in order for a married woman to be entitled to her earnings from any business, and in Prince Edward Island she is not entitled to them in any case, except a separation has taken place between the spouses."[12] Nonetheless, advances were made and by 1907 all common-law provinces had passed Married Women's Property laws so that married women had full powers over their own property. This meant women, if they had some financial security, could maintain it separate from their husbands. No longer would they be totally dependent upon the good graces of their spouses. It is necessary to remember, however, that few women had such financial security. These were laws to protect the 'have', not the 'have nots' of Canadian society.

The law reflected the idealized image of woman as an individual who would be protected by a man be it her husband, father, or brother. But even in the areas where the conventional wisdom accepted woman's preeminent role it would seem that women had little protection. As a wife, woman was to be protected and cherished by her husband. He was to honour her. Yet in 1900 according to the NCW, "A husband has still to a limited extent custody and control of his wife's person. There custody lasts now only till he has been guilty of cruelty or a separation has taken place between them. He can commit a rape upon her and is not liable to an action even although he communicate to her a disease of a most loathsome nature. The restraint must not endanger her life or health...."[13]

Not surprisingly, given the importance of marriage for both men and women in society, marital dissolution was not easy. The Maritime provinces had their own divorce courts and granted divorce on the same grounds to both men and women. Quebec and Ontario had no divorce courts and only a private bill of Parliament could grant a divorce to residents of these two provinces and Parliament only recognized one cause—adultery. In some cases, if a wife committed adultery, the husband could sue the lover for damages and, in other cases, an adulterous wife was not allowed to see her children, although this was not so in the case of the husband. In the provinces of Manitoba, British Columbia, Alberta, and Saskatchewan, a man could obtain a divorce on the grounds of adultery but a divorce was granted

---

[12]*Women of Canada: Their Life and Work*, National Council of Women of Canada, 1975, p. 40.

[13] Ibid., p. 40.

to a woman only if she could prove that her husband had been guilty of incestuous adultery, bigamy with adultery or if he was convicted of rape or sodomy. This legislation was not changed until 1925 and reflected the double standards in law. For a woman to commit adultery was much more reprehensible than for a man.

As mothers, woman were sacred symbols of purity and the most important influence in their children's lives. Yet they had few rights over them. Generally women were not the guardians of their own children. British Columbia in 1917 was the first province to grant equal guardianship rights to both parents. As for woman's highly prized virtue and purity, it was only protected if she 'was of previously chaste character'. Even then the laws of seduction and rape were very difficult to implement. They were impossible if the woman had 'fallen' even through no fault of her own.

Examining the law in Canada could very easily lead to the conclusion that women, especially married women, had few rights. The law simply was not set up to see women as individuals. Married women especially would appear to have been disadvantaged. Yet the reality was that most women in Canada married. They sought the approval of all around them by conforming to what was perceived as 'natural' for them to do. They sought the companionship and love of working with a spouse to raise a family and improve their future. Few alternatives existed for women. The life of the single woman—unless as a religious—had little prestige. And the economic realities almost ensured that single women would live a subsistence existence.

Educational opportunities, too, limited what options were open to women other than marriage. Canadians valued education and believed that all citizens should be able to read and write. This meant that public or elementary education was generally open to all and by the end of the nineteenth century was compulsory and free in most provinces. But education beyond this level had a purpose which was to prepare an individual for her/his place in society. Since for women that place was the home, few Canadians were interested in seeing women proceed to the higher levels of education. Middle-class parents were concerned that their daughters have access to high schools but university was beyond the expectations of most Canadians of either sex. Yet this did not stop some women from dreaming of what might be. "One of my day-dreams, which I feel to be selfish, is that of going to school.... I do so long to go. And here I go again, once begin dreaming of the possibilities and I become half daft over what I know will never come to pass. Oh, to think of studying with other girls! Think of learning German, Latin, and other languages in general. Think of the loveliness of thinking that it entirely depended on myself whether I go on, and that I had the advantages I have always longed for...."[14] Maud Abbott achieved her dream and more, going on to medical school and becoming a world expert in diseases of the heart.

Due to the perseverance of individuals such as Abbott, the higher levels of education slowly opened to women beginning in the 1870s; by 1900 women totalled 11 per cent of Canadian college students. Universities were generally loath to open their doors to women but in need of paying students and rationalizing education for women as a way of creating better wives and mothers, they did so. Mount Allison in New Brunswick in 1875 became the first institute of higher learning in Canada and in the British Empire to grant a degree to a woman, Grace Annie Lockhart. She and other early women graduates received much opposition, especially when they enrolled in faculties traditionally thought of as male. For example, when Elizabeth Smith in the late 1870s was applying to be accepted as a medical student her best friend wrote her, urging her not to take that step, "to lay aside those silly thoughts...Lizzie....You can never repay your father and mother for all they have done for you...if you cannot help that in any way then I say go and earn your own living but do not, I beseech you, do not be a Doctor, is there no other occupation more womanly than this?"[15] But the occupations more womanly than being a doctor were hardly ones to attract bright ambitious women. Indeed, when the paid work which women did in the late nineteenth and early twentieth centuries is examined, it is clear that women worked because they had to, for economic survival. Their options limited, it is no wonder that many women would see marriage as a way out, a form of upward mobility in a society which offered little to women.

Women in Paid Labour

The ideal view of women suggested that they should not be in paid employment. They were to be protected and supported by men but the reality was that many women worked for wages. By 1901, 16.1 per cent of adult women were so engaged. In 1912, 35 per cent of all women between the ages of 15 and 34 worked. Such figures were official ones and ignored the income-generating work of farm and urban mothers because such work was not steady or full time. The official figures were conservative estimates of women's involvement in paid labour but even they revealed that this phenomenon was increasing. To explain it, Canadians told themselves that women were simply working in temporary positions until marriage, that

[14]Mitchinson, *The Nature of their Bodies,* p. 87.
[15]University of Waterloo, Doris Lewis Rare Book Room, Elizabeth Smith Shortt papers, Maud Service to Elizabeth Smith, Sept. 1877.

work would keep them from being frivolous until then, that women were not working for survival as men were but for pin money, and that the training they gained through paid employment would help them run a household better. Given such rationales, there was little sympathy for working women. As a result wages were low and lower than men's in all employment. In 1889 the Annual Report of Ontario Bureau of Industries provided the following wage and cost of living figures for female workers.[16]

Female Workers over Sixteen Years of Age without Dependents

Average number of hours/week worked	54.03
Average number of days/year worked	259.33
Average wages/year from occupation	$216.71
Extra earnings aside from regular occupation	
Total earnings/year	$216.71
Cost of clothing	$67.31
Cost of board and lodging	$126.36
Total cost of living	$214.28
Surplus	$2.43

Female Workers over Sixteen Years of Age with Dependents

Average number of dependents	2.10
Average number of hours/week worked	58.52
Average number of days/year worked	265.43
Average wages/year from occupation	$246.37
Extra earnings aside from regular occupation	$23.05
Earnings of dependents	$16.48
Total earnings/year	$285.90
Total cost of living	$300.13
Deficit	$14.23

Is it any wonder that many young girls saw marriage as a way out of their economic plight? The situation did not seem to be improving either. Technology did not help—even when machines took over the hard physical work which was deemed unsuitable for women, jobs did not open up for women. Women were not considered skilled enough to work on machines. Their strengths were inherent in their femaleness and thus discounted. Thus wage discrepancies continued. In 1911 the average annual wage for a man was $593, for a woman $313. In 1921 it was $1057 for a man and only $573 for a woman.

[16]Lori Rotenberg, "The Wayward Worker: Toronto's Prostitute at the Turn of the Century", in Janice Acton et al., ed., *Women at Work: Ontario 1850-1930,* Toronto, 1988, pp. 48-49.

The major employment sector of women was domestic service. In 1891 servant made up 41 per cent of the female work force followed by dressmakers. In 1901 servants still headed the list. Only in 1921 did clerical work usurp the lead position of service as the major employment area for women. What was it like to be a servant in the late nineteenth century and early decades of the twentieth? Most servants were young and lived in. This resulted in long hours, being on call 24 hours a day, with little time to call your own. It meant living an isolated life. The pay was poor, although commensurate with factory work and the work was physically hard and demanding. There was little privacy and the servant was always aware of her lower class position *vis-à-vis* her employer. The work had little prestige and left a girl open to sexual exploitation by her employer. There were no standards of work—conditions varied from home to home. If fired, a servant not only lost her job, but wages which were often held back to ensure good behaviour. In addition, she lost her home and at times found herself on the streets with nowhere to go. The result was that many in such a situation were forced to turn to prostitution in order to survive.

Other areas of employment were not much better. Waitressing demanded long hours, hard physical labour, and provided low pay. Even work in sales, while perhaps allowing the woman to remain clean was still characterized by long hours of standing, low pay, and the added demands of a certain wardrobe to bolster the image of respectability which store owners were trying to portray. Factory work at mid-century had opened up new areas of employment for women; in 1871, 42 per cent of Montreal's industrial work force and 34 per cent of Toronto's were women and children. While factory work provided more independence than domestic service, the conditions could be appalling. In the garment trade, for example, which was the major industry which hired women in 1901, a woman was discovered working at rates equivalent to 2 cents an hour. Work in this and other industries was often seasonal and done according to piece work. Fines charged for on-work mistakes were often high. The physical environment was dirty, dangerous, and posed severe health hazards. Concerned about the future child-bearing capabilities of such women, provinces towards the end of the nineteenth century instituted factory legislation to try to offset the worse of the abuses. They limited the hours of work to 60 a week, forbade night work for women, and insisted on separate washroom facilities for women.

As reported by the Royal Commission on the Relations of Labour and Capital in 1889, male workers were ambivalent about what female labour meant to them. As head of households, they realized that the wages paid to daughters and wives could be essential for a family's survival; as union members they wanted to see all workers receive adequate wages; yet there was still a sense that if society functioned as it should and if men were paid a family wage, then women would not need to work. Perhaps for this reason, unions were not that sympathetic about organizing women workers. In the late nineteenth and early twentieth centuries, union organizers complained that women were not interested in joining unions. Despite this perception, women did organize themselves and at times had to fight not only their employers but the enmity of male unionists. In 1907, for example, Bell Telephone workers in Toronto went out on strike and revealed their willingness to stay out, to help fellow workers who were in worse financial shape, and to do so with little assistance. While there was not a clear victory for the workers in that their union was not recognized, Bell did institute some work reforms which eased the conditions under which the women had been working.

One profession which was open to women and deemed respectable, even for middle-class women, was teaching. From mid-century on, Canadians witnessed the feminization of the teaching profession at the elementary level and by the end of the century next to domestic service, it was the major employer of women. The reason for this was twofold. With the expansion of education and the belief in its importance for the future of the country, local communities were forced to bear an increased cost. One way to lessen the burden was to hire teachers who would accept low rates of pay—women. As women replaced men as teachers of younger children, men became the teachers at institutes of higher learning which catered to older students. Men held the jobs which society viewed as most prestigious. Women were accepted as teachers for young children because they could act as surrogate mothers. So great was this trend that by 1904 women teachers in public schools represented 82 per cent of teachers in Nova Scotia, 74 per cent of those in Ontario, and 55 per cent of those in Manitoba. Yet women teachers were always paid lower wages than men with equal qualifications, a discrepancy which existed in all provinces.

Nursing, too, expanded due to the increased numbers of hospitals and the tendency for the sick poor and later for middle-class Canadians to be treated there rather than at home. In 1874 the first training school for nurses opened in St. Catherine's which emphasized high moral character in its graduates; while it tried to attract middle-class women, because of the work involved nursing was essentially a working-class occupation. It certainly would be difficult to call nursing a profession at this time; the work involved was no less menial and physically demanding than factory work. In 1889 a trained nurse at the Montreal General earned $12 to $15 a month whereas the hospital rat catcher earned $20. Student nurses worked 12 hours a day with their training lectures coming afterwards. Such nurses provided cheap labour for the hospitals; when they graduated the hospitals did not hire them but rather the nurses had to seek employment opportunities as private duty nurses and in essence became high class domestic servants.

In 1897 the Victorian Order of Nurses (VON) was created by the National Council of Women to celebrate Queen Victoria's Jubilee. Originally designed to include midwives and as a help to women in the isolated reaches of the country, the VON had to limit its sights due to the opposition of the medical profession which feared the nurses as competition. Consequently the midwifery aspect was removed and the nurses were trained as helpmeets for physicians. Still they did admirable work and were relatively independent when situated in areas where they did not have to worry about local physicians. Early in the twentieth century, the larger cities were beginning to hire nurses as part of their social outreach efforts and such nurses shared with the VON a semblance of independence. Nurses were well aware of their low status and poor working conditions and tried to alter both. Early attempts at organization were occurring by the end of the century and in 1919 the first nursing degree programme opened at the University of British Columbia in an attempt to professionalize nursing. But it would be many years before this goal was even being approached let alone attained.

Other professions simply did not attract many women, largely because they were seen as 'male' occupations and because of opposition, legal and otherwise. Women could not be trained in Canada as physicians until the 1870s; until the 1890s it was not even legal for a woman to practise law in Ontario and in 1900 it was still illegal in Nova Scotia and Quebec. In the latter province, women could not practise law until 1941 even though they could graduate in law as early as 1914. The law also did not recognize women as chartered accountants until 1919. Nonetheless, women were breaking new ground. Many more of them were entering journalism, photography, writing novels, plays, poetry, and becoming artists both visual and performance.

Women and Reform

Unless women conformed or at least tried to conform to the ideal, and unless they were fortunate to be among the privileged sector of society, life could be very harsh in Canada. The situation in which many women found themselves did not go unnoticed. Some women wanted to ameliorate the situation they found themselves in or if not in need themselves to help those women who were. In either case, the desire was to reform the system rather than change it in any fundamental way. The women most involved in reform tended to be White, middle-class, and of Anglo-Celtic heritage, who had the time to commit to reform activities and the education to convince politicians and the public of the need for change. They were often influenced by religious teachings and many of the leaders had been touched by an evangelical cast which stressed the responsibility of Christians to help those around them. They were central to what became known as the Social Gospel movement which was a religious based effort to apply Christ's teachings to the material world. Such women worried about the problems that came with urbanization and industrialization such as poor sanitary conditions or the difficulties faced by young working women. They felt that they could not protect their own families without engaging in the world outside the home and trying to alter that world or at least control some of its worst abuses. But what could women do by themselves? Very little, but they did have the experience of women's charitable and religious organizations on which to build.

Women had long been involved in charitable activities, attempting to help those in need in a very direct way. They had come together to build orphanages, refuge homes for women, and to build hospitals. They had been the supporters of their local churches through women's auxiliaries. In the last decades of the nineteenth century and early decades of the twentieth, these endeavours expanded. Within the church, women became involved in missionary work, forming women's missionary associations to support women missionaries overseas and at home. Underlying such activities was an imperial orientation, the desire to make other women be more like themselves in the belief that they were representative of what it meant to be a woman. Less dogmatic were church groups which were very specific about helping their own communities. For example, in Nova Scotia, black Baptist women in Halifax organized in 1914 to support education for their community through the development of an industrial and moral school. A few years later they formed the worker's Missionary Society to continue other activities of a social development nature.

Women not only expanded their charitable and self-help endeavours but through such organizations as the Young Women's Christian Association (YWCA) also struggled to help working women attracted to the cities. They worried about the kind of dislocation which alcoholism caused families, especially the innocent wives and children of drunkards. The Women's Christian Temperance Union (WCTU) was a new departure in women's organizations. Previously, women had helped those in need simply because they were in need. WCTU women were interested in discerning why people and families were needy and to eradicate the cause of the problem. They were reformers. When appealing to men to forgo alcohol did not succeed, many determined to bring the state into the fray and began to support prohibition through mixed temperance societies and through the all-women WCTU. Organizations such as the charity, church, and reform groups mentioned were joined by a proliferation of other women's associations emerging in the 1890s, many of them affiliated through the umbrella organization the National Council of Women of Canada (NCWC) formed in 1893. Designed to be non-sectarian and non-partisan, by 1900 the NCW claimed to have federated five to six hundred societies.

Women's organizations in Canada varied in size but some were quite substantial. In 1900 active membership in the WCTU was over 10,000. By 1922 it was over 18,000. In 1921, Alberta alone had 330 Women's Institutes (WI). Women's Institutes were rural women's organizations, first formed in 1897 and designed to bring the advantages of easier and better living to farm families. In 1919, when they federated, they had 100,000 members in 2000 locals. In 1913 the YWCA had over 18,000 members. The total women involved in organizations in 1911 was 250,000, thus one out of every 8 women between the ages of 15 and 80 was a member. The number does not perhaps seem as large as it should after quoting membership statistics, but the explanation is simple, women seemed to become involved in more than one organization at a time. The woman's club movement was one to rival any other in Canada.

Such organizations provided safe, group activity, and little time commitment unless a woman wanted to commit herself fully to them. They provided women with a forum to express their concerns and out of them was manifested the middle-class desire to control those who lived differently from themselves. They provided women with the chance to learn administrative skills, they unified women, they taught women. They also were comfortable for the women who joined them. Often exclusionary through their assumption of what values were best and at times overtly racist, they nevertheless taught many women the power of organization. They forced women to come face to face with their own powerlessness as many discovered that, although they believed that much needed to be changed in society, not all agreed. Certainly male politicians seemed reluctant to undertake any reform activities on behest of an unenfranchised group. Women slowly began to learn that without the vote they had little concrete power with which to accomplish their goals. The irony of their efforts was that the motivation behind their work was often traditional—the protection of their families and the protection of other women and children. Too often historians have accepted to reform women's views of themselves as quintessential nurturers, an image while not totally without merit, hides the harsher reality of them as the beneficiaries of a class-based and Euro-centric society. But whatever their motivation, these women were trying to help as best they could and often justified their actions on traditional grounds, leading many historians to refer to such women as material feminists. Their activities, however, changed the accepted norms of female behaviour. Canadians became accustomed to seeing and hearing women talk about the issues of the day. They also became accustomed to seeing, although not always comfortable with, women agitating for the vote.

In Canada, the vote was neither a right as it was in the United States, bolstered by the theoretical concept of the equality of all people, or a privilege as it was in Great Britain where it was dependent on property ownership which few could attain. Not surprising, influenced as Canada was by Britain, the mother country, and the United States, its nearest neighbour, the vote in Canada fell somewhere in between being a right and a privilege. While by the 1890s there was general manhood suffrage (except for certain groups such as native men and Japanese men), opposition to women's suffrage was well entrenched. Goldwin Smith, political commentator and man of letters, made it clear where he stood on the issue. Votes for women would lead 'to national emasculation'.

The struggle for the women's franchise began essentially with the Toronto Women's Literary Club formed by Emily H. Stowe in 1877. Born in 1831, Stowe was a forceful woman, who had been compelled to support her family when her husband became ill with tuberculosis. She was a teacher at the age of 15 and when denied entrance to the University of Toronto she went to Normal School and eventually became the first woman principal in Ontario. She then decided to become a doctor; medical training for women not being available in Canada, she went to the United States after leaving her family in the care of her sister and graduated in 1868 and returned to Toronto to practise. It was then that she began the literary club which met weekly and provided a forum for women to discuss the issues of the day. In 1881 they sent a deputation to the provincial government asking for suffrage and in 1882 the members saw their first success when unmarried women with property were given the vote on municipal by-laws. In British Columbia this right had been granted to both married and unmarried women as early as 1873. In 1883 the club became the Toronto Woman's Suffrage Club and in the same year the Ontario Medical College for Women was formed and Stowe's daughter Augusta Stowe became its first graduate. Despite some of the successes of the Club, enthusiasm lagged and complacency with the gains made set in. To reinvigorate the group, Stowe brought in lecturers such as Anna Shaw and Susan B. Anthony from the United States and also courted the press.

Meanwhile the work went on. In 1886 the University of Toronto opened its doors to women. Also many petitions were sent to the legislature asking for suffrage and the municipal franchise for married women. In 1889 the Dominion Women's Enfranchisement League was formed and, although it had branches throughout Ontario and in some provincial capitals, it never attained dominion-wide support. It was essentially a Toronto-based organization. Nonetheless, it did accomplish publicity and education of the public and expressed the ambition of a handful of women to create a nation-wide movement. Elsewhere in their country, the suffrage work was going on as well. Between 1883 and 1900 private members of the British Columbia legislature alone had introduced some 10 or 11 suffrage bills. In 1894 the Manitoba Equal Franchise Club was established and in the province Icelandic women were organizing to get the vote, something which they had in their home country. In the Maritimes organizations existed but were weak.

By the early 1890s, the energy of the suffrage movement had shifted away from those women whose primary aim was the vote to the maternal feminists who were interested in the vote largely as a means to an end, that is, to give them clout in order to implement their reforms. Although, it is easy to make the distinction between the two groups supporting votes for women, when individual women are examined it is difficult to impose labels. Suffragists were often involved in reform organizations and many of the maternal feminists also believed that women should have the vote for its own sake. Canadian women tended to be pragmatic in their work rather than purists in their ideology. This was just as well, for on their own marginalized suffrage groups could do little. They somehow had to involve more women. One of the more activist groups was the WCTU and when formed in 1873, their president, Letitia Youmans had taken great care not to associate her organization with women's rights. However, it gradually became clearer to the temperance women that without the vote they would never accomplish their aims. In 1891 the WCTU officially endorsed suffrage. The importance of this was that the WCTU was organized on a national basis with locals in small towns. It reached women the suffrage organization could not. In 1909 The International Council of Women met in Toronto and approved suffrage and the following year the NCW came out and did the same. When the leading women's organization in the country, not noted for taking controversial stands, endorsed suffrage, observers knew that the enfranchisement of women had come of age.

Although a great deal of activity was occurring on the suffrage front, there was not unanimity among women. Not all women believed they should have the vote, arguing that it was man's responsibility and that separate sphere was a natural and healthy state of affairs. Even among women supporting the vote, unanimity was not always possible. At times suffragists and maternal feminists disagreed over tactics and goals, most suffrage organizations were middle class and did not involve working women. Indeed, many were anti-labour. The national organizations tended to be dominated by central Canadians and this caused dissension especially among western farm women who probably, correctly, felt that the problems of farm women and western farmers in general were not a high priority for easterners. This was unfortunate, for the western farm women's organizations had an energy that was often missing in the eastern women's groups. They also seemed to have more support from men than did eastern women perhaps because of the tendency of farmers to see the world not only in terms of gender but also class-based economic activity. It was difficult to see women as inferior when the work they were doing to help carve settlements out of the wilderness was right before their eyes. One of the most energetic women in the western movement was Nellie McClung who could talk to both rural and urban women. Raised on a farm in Manitoba, teaching at 15 or 16 after only a few years of formal schooling herself, she was the closest Canada came to a suffrage leader. She entered the movement in full stride, attacking the establishment, especially their complacent women who were comfortable, happily married, and who had little awareness of the reality faced by most women.

Support for suffrage gradually increased and World War I gave women a new weapon. Most women supported the war by reorienting their volunteer organizations to the war effort. By 1916, Canadian women had raised between $40 million and $50 million for war-related activities. Household Leagues, which women had formed at the end of the century, made government more aware of the need to regulate prices and to control food production and distribution so individuals would be less able to exploit the wartime scarcity. Women were entering the work force in unprecedented numbers to replace men going overseas. This opened new areas of employment to women such as work in heavy industries, particularly munition factories, but also in white collar and clerical work in banks. While the former jobs disappeared at the end of the war, banking remained a significant employer of women, although usually at the most junior levels. Women were also taking over even more responsibilities for farm work. But most significant they were sending their sons overseas, knowing the risks of them being killed. Women, too, were at risk; nurses were part of the Army Medical Corps and during the war, 2504 of them were involved in duty overseas, 46 of whom died in the service of their country. All this and yet their country did not think that women were deserving of the vote. It was a situation that would not last. Success when it came, came quickly: Manitoba granted women the vote in January 1916 followed by Alberta and Saskatchewan; British Columbia and Ontario in 1917; Nova Scotia in 1918; New Brunswick in 1919; Prince Edward Island in 1922; but not until 1940 in Quebec. The federal government granted the franchise in 1918 but not graciously. In 1917 it had allowed nurses serving in the war and then the wives, widows, mothers, sisters, and daughters of servicemen to vote— this was not an acknowledgment of women's rights but a political manoeuvre on the part of the Union government to get re-elected on a conscription platform. Once these women had the vote, the government had little choice but to give it to other women.

World War I was a turning point for Canadian women as it was for the country as a whole but not for the same reasons. For women, World War I had seen the granting of the vote to most women (Japanese and native women were excluded, for example) in Canada, it had also seen the arrival of one of their most long sought after reforms—prohibition granted at a national level as a wartime expedient. Women could look back with a great sense of accomplishment. Although they had not overtly challenged male hegemony in any direct way, through their efforts they had demanded that it be shared.

The reasons for the latter are caught up in Canada's ongoing challenge of trying to incorporate different groups within its structure without destroying the individuality of those groups, that is, to provide equality while acknowledging difference. Granting the vote to women did not signal a lessening of the domestic sphere as women's arena; it recognized its importance. Women were equal to men but different. This effort to combine equality with different was not and is not easy to accept. It was especially problematic for the province of Quebec. For French Catholic Quebec, women's suffrage represented a foreign reform, one that was based on an individualist tradition and antithetical to the collective orientation espoused by the Catholic Church. Leading French-Canadian nationalists such as Henri Bourassa were vehemently opposed to such a change in Quebec society. As a result, the early efforts to engage in the suffrage movement were made by English-speaking women who felt cut off from their own traditions in Quebec. Only slowly did French-speaking women come to endorse suffrage. It perhaps took them longer because of the cultural issue referred to above but also because they did not have a strong lay tradition of involvement behind them as existed in English-speaking Canada. In Quebec, many of the reforms that focused on the welfare of people were controlled by the Church which dominated education, health care, and even parts of the labour movement.

One of the first significant lay women's organizations to form in Quebec was the *Fédération Nationale Saint-Jean Baptiste* (FNSJB). Similar to the NCW in that it brought French-Canadian women together, it began in 1907 and emerged from women's work with the Montreal Local Council of Women. It brought together 22 isolated groups with a membership of 12,000 and formed them into 3 sections: charitable, educational, and economic. It introduced women to the issues of maternal feminism such as the well-being of children, preserving the home, temperance, and the White slave trade. Concerned that women on their own might be led astray, the Bishop of Montreal appointed a chaplain over the FNSJB to ensure that activities followed Church doctrine. For this reason and others, the FNSJB became more conservative, dominated by Catholic social doctrine, and oriented toward philanthropy rather than reform. As a result, it experienced a decline in the 1920s.

In 1922 the Provincial Franchise Committee (later the League of Women's Rights) was formed with a dual leadership of French and English. Unfortunately, the Committee was rebuffed by premier Taschereau and the Church pressured the French Canadian leader to resign thus weakening the organization. In 1927 a split within the group occurred and *L'Alliance Canadienne pour le Vote des Femmes du Québec* formed, more committed to the working class and energized to do more than the Committee. The Committee, however, was not destined to remain moribund. One of its leaders was Thérèse Casgrain who had become involved in politics through campaigning in the federal election of 1921 on behalf of her husband. This was a daring thing to do in Quebec and thus brought her to the attention of others who supported women's rights. Following the Church's veto of suffragist activity, the leadership of the movement in Quebec passed to a younger generation of women like Casgrain and Mlle. Saint-Jean (founder of *L'Alliance*) who were willing to face ecclesiastical disapproval. Their energy reinvigorated the feminist forces and by the late 1920s they instituted an annual visit to the Quebec legislature to see their suffrage bill presented and defeated.

To appease the feminist forces, the Quebec government in 1929 introduced a major reconsideration of the civil status of women in the province. The Commission on the Civil Rights of Women or the Dorion Commission, however, while making some important changes such as giving women the right to control their salaries and property brought into a marriage, did little to alter the real inequities between the sexes in the province of Quebec. As a result, Quebec women continued their efforts and as their English-Canadian counterparts had done before them resorted to the media, in this case the radio with a programme by Casgrain called Femina. All this activity kept the issue of votes for women before the public and reminded people that Quebec was the only province not to have granted women the vote. The final victory began in 1938 when the provincial Liberal Party invited 40 women delegates to its convention. The convention endorsed suffrage for women and in 1939, due to political manoeuvring over a wartime issue, the provincial Liberals won the Quebec election. Despite continued opposition of the Church, the enfranchisement of Quebec women went ahead.

The Interwar Years

With the success of the suffrage movement in most of Canada by the end of the war, women turned their attention to other concerns. Although Agnes Macphail became the first women to be elected to Parliament in 1921, women generally did not use their vote to elect one another in large numbers. Nonetheless, they were successful in pressuring various levels of government to implement changes for which the women had been agitating for years. Immediately after the success of the suffrage campaign, politicians, not knowing how the new woman electorate would vote, were more than sympathetic to their wishes. One of the reforms which many of the middle-class organizations had been demanding was a federal department of Health and this was created in 1919 and included a Child Welfare Division. In the 1920s the Department's interest expanded to include efforts to lessen the high material mortality rates in the country.

Eventually it became clear to politicans that women voters did not act as a block and with this realization, their willingness to sympathize with the women's demands lessened. Perhaps for this reason, historians had initially viewed the period after the suffrage success as a denouement, a decline in the activism of women. More research has revealed that reform efforts still took place; they were simply focused on different issues and no longer was there an overriding agreement on a single reform as had been the case with the vote. For many women who had been working for decades in organizations, it was now time to retire from the fray. Others, however, were still anxious to engage in the fight for change. Organization such as the WCTU continued to pursue their efforts to maintain prohibition but in the 1920s this seemed to be a losing battle as province after province rescinded war-time prohibition legislation. During the interwar period, many women became involved in the international peace movement through the Canadian League of Nations Society, the Canadian Women's Peace Party, and the Women's International League for Peace and Freedom. Farm women's organizations continued and, unlike some women's groups, increased in strength as farmers continually felt that politicians and non-farm people did not sympathize with the needs of the farming community. These farm groups were especially strong in western Canada. In Quebec the conservative *Cercles de Fermières,* which was the equivalent of the Women's Institutes, also expanded as did the Institutes themselves. In fact the Women's Institute example was so successful that in 1933 the Associated Country Women of the World was formed.

For younger women, the priorities of their mothers and grandmothers were not always theirs. Organizations such as the WCTU, the NCW and even the reinvigorated peace movement seemed not to speak to their concerns. Younger women were anxious to take advantage of some of the advances which had been won for them such as educational opportunities and openings in the work force. The Federation of Medical Women of Canada, for example, formed in 1924 to represent the specific interest of this small group. In addition, other career-oriented associations, such as the Canadian Nurses' Association and the Canadian Women's Press Club, felt it was necessary to represent the concerns of their constituents rather than to broaden their interests as the maternal feminists had. One aspect that did not change with these various women's organizations was the lack of minority groups in them. When thought of at all, women of colour, non-Christian women, and working-class women were not particularly welcomed. Such women formed their own associations. For example, Lillian Rutherford, a Montreal woman, organized the Phyllis Wheatley Art Club in 1922 for young black women. This club eventually was reconstituted as the Negro Theatre Guild of Montreal in the mid-1930s.

Religion in the form of the Social Gospel had underlay the pre-war reform movement, but in the 1920s this was no longer the case. Many Protestant women instead turned their attention to the newly formed United Church of Canada. Yet the United Church was not particularly open to them except as unsung workers. In 1926 Lydia Gruchy first applied to be ordained a minister and eight years later the church reluctantly agreed to allow unmarried women to enter the clergy. Married women had to wait until 1946. Other churches were even more inhospitable. The Roman Catholic Church continued to press women to continue their traditional homemaker roles and even set up *écoles ménagères* to insure that domestic science would be taught to young girls. Later these schools were reorganized and in the wider community referred to as 'schools for happiness'.

As the above indicates, the interwar period was one of continuation. In the world of fashion, however, the emphasis was on change as skirts in the 1920s became shorter, hair was cut, and some respectable young women seemed willing to be seen in public drinking and smoking. The media hype advised women that to attract a man they had to be physically attractive and if nature had not endowed them then the cosmetic industry would come to their assistance. Admonitions to stay slim abounded. Real flappers in Canada, however, were a minority. Most young women did not flaunt authority and those who did were viewed as outcasts whether they saw themselves that way or not. Some women refused to marry and identified themselves in loving partnerships with other women. Unwed mothers were particularly vulnerable, although some Finnish servant women in Montreal seemed willing to accept the responsibilities of single motherhood. Unlike most young women, they may have made a conscious decision to become mothers since indications are that their average age was 37.

While the image of young women seemed to be changing in some respects, in others it remained the same. Young girls were still socialized into feminine roles. Domestic science training, which had begun in the late nineteenth century, rapidly expanded in the 1920s with the efforts to make housekeeping scientific. Students taking such courses faced middle-class injunctions that the way their mothers cooked and kept house was incorrect. They were taught to use utensils and appliances which many would never be able to afford and cook foods they would never buy for themselves. The ideal of what a home should be and the reality of it for many was not bridged in the classroom. Nonetheless, Canadians still viewed education as positive and women continued their education as never before. In 1920, 13.9 per cent of college students were women and in 1929 this percentage rose to 23.5 per cent. In graduate school it was over 25 per cent. This percentage was not to be reached again for many decades. The depression of the 1930s intervened and when money became tight parents favoured the education of their sons over that of their daughters. Even in the 1920s many young girls who were needed at home or where entering the work force in their mid-teens could not pursue their educational dreams. Neither could they take advantage of the youth culture which garnered so much publicity in the 1920s. They could not join the Girl Guides, the Canadian Girls in Training, or the other myriad of orgnizations developed to ensure that Canadian youth kept to the straight and narrow.

Some people have referred to the interwar period as the Golden Age of sports for women in Canada as individual and team activities flourished.

Young women had some incredible role models to prove that there was little that women could not do if they put their minds and bodies to it. Perhaps no women athletes captured the Canadian imagination more than the Edmonton Grads. Made up of graduates from a local high school, this basketball team won four world championships and in the period 1915 to 1940 only lost 20 games, winning 502. No other team had duplicated its record. On university campuses, as well, women were demanding better facilities for their athletic endeavours. They wanted equality with their male colleagues, not necessarily to play sports with them but to have their own teams, and be given the kind of respect and financial support men's athletic efforts attracted.

Most young women had little time for sports as they entered the work force. The area of clerical, white-collar work continued to attract increasing numbers of women. Domestic service, which had been the major employer of women in the late nineteenth and early twentieth centuries, declined in importance in the 1920s. It also changed its nature. The live-in servant of yore gave way to the cleaning woman, often married and usually non-British. In the 1930s, the strange irony of the economy was such that as long as one had a decent salary the decline in cost of consumer items meant that many families who previously had been unable to afford domestic help could now do so. And many more women, out of jobs themselves or whose husbands were unemployed were willing to do housework for others. Thus the economic plight of some women was of benefit to other women.

Although more women were entering the paid labour force—in 1921, 15 per cent of the labour force was female and in 1931 it was 17 per cent—who these women were had not changed significantly. They were still over-whelmingly single. In both the 20s and the 30s there was a sense that marriage and employment could not be combined. In the more prosperous 20s, the concept of the family wage was becoming the reality for some men, although certainly not the majority. The reality for the majority of Canadians on the eve of the depression was that 60 per cent of Canadian men and 82 per cent of women who worked earned less than the minimum needed to support a family of four. The Federal Government finally acknowledged this reality in 1944 when it introduced the family allowances scheme which assured every child in Canada payment independent of the means of his/her parents.

Wages were still low for women in comparison to men, 54 to 60 per cent, even though the country saw minimum wages for women established. The minimum wage first appeared in Alberta in 1917 and by the end of the 1920s only New Brunswick and Prince Edward Island lacked such legislation. But the minimum wage, while seemingly protective in impulse, did not always help women workers. For one, it undermined their competitiveness.

Employers often hired women because they could pay them less than men and once this was not possible, the incentive to hire women receded. Also there were many loopholes which businesses could use to escape paying the minimum wage and not enough ways to call such business owners to account. Even more serious, the minimum wage too often degenerated into the maximum wage.

If women had not reached their working utopia in the 1920s, the depression of the 1930s dashed their hopes entirely. Due to its dependence on exports, Canada was among the hardest hit of any industrialized country in the depression. Various jurisdictions forbade the hiring of married women in the hopes of providing work for unemployed men. Overlooked was the fact that rarely did men and women work in the same areas and that many married women were the sole support of their families. While the government of Canada introduced programmes to help unemployed young men get back to work, ignored were young women. They were viewed as a surplus of no consequence who could be called upon in good times but who were dispensable when times were bad. In the 30s, the economic situation was so bad that many men were undercutting the minimum wage legislation as it applied to women. When it became clear that this was occurring, various provinces began to apply the legislation to male workers in an attempt to keep male wages at a level that could support them. Thus protective legislation for women eventually worked to the benefit of men.

To help cope with many of the problems they faced in both decades some women were taking responsibility for their own working lives and trying to improve them through association. But unions were still not very accepting of women and many white-collar workers who associated unions with a decline in status resisted any attempts to organize them—the result was that only about 1 per cent of female workers were actually unionized. Those who were interested in the labour movement could be quite militant. Women were among the first workers to walk off their jobs in the Winnipeg General Strike of 1919. In 1924, workers at the E.B. Eddy factory in Hull, Quebec also walked off their jobs as a protest against the firing of a woman supervisor and management's efforts to change the nature of their work. They were not particularly successful in gaining what they wanted but perhaps received some satisfaction, illusory though it might have been, by attacking the plant manager.

Porfessional women, still predominatly teachers and nurses, had their own problems which they hoped joining together would help alleviate—in the teachers case to raise their benefits to those of male teachers and in the nurses to raise the status of their work. Nurses were in a particularly awkward position. In attempting to professionalize themselves through higher education, they created a rift in their ranks between those nurses who were trained at a university and those trained in the traditional way and thus weakened joint efforts. And despite the assertion of professionalism, many nurses still remained glorified domestic servants as the majority of them, even in 1929, were private duty nurses.

While increasing numbers of women were in paid employment leading to an acceptance of single woman working, married women were still the major child nurturers and continued to be seen as the centre of the family and home. The ideals of home and family, however, had begun to shift. Whereas in the nineteenth century, man was deemed head of the household in law and custom, in the 1920s a new ideal was emerging. The ideal of a marriage between equals, a more companionate relationship, began to hold sway. This equality between spouses was reflected in the federal 1925 Divorce law which allowed divorce to a woman on the same grounds as that granted to a man— specifically adultery. Women in the home were no longer producers of items as they had been; instead they were the main purchasers for the family, making their way through all the competing advertising and prices. Managers were increasingly applying scientific management principles to the workplace in an effort to make workers more productive and thus profits higher, and these principles also found a place in the domestic sphere as middle-class housewives, especially, were inundated with publicity about the best way of keeping the home in the most up to date and scientific way. Labour militancy even had a way of entering the domestic sphere. In 1932 Jewish housewives in Toronto picketed kosher butchers whose religious monoploy kept prices higher than in gentile shops; in 1938 the Housewives' Association of Toronto boycotted dairies that had raised milk prices.

Despite all the glory housekeeping garnered in women's magazines and all the appliances advertised, many families could not meet the expectations. In western Canada, women's agrarian groups raised the issue of lack of household amenities and that too often the house was beggared for the barn. Such women were still waiting for running water and rural electrification. In 1941 almost 70 per cent of houses were electrically wired but mostly in central and eastern Canada and in urban centres. Housing could still be primitive. In 1921, 68 per cent of Saskatchewan's housing in rual areas was 4 rooms and under; in 1931 it was 64 per cent; and in 1941 it was still 61 per cent. These crowded conditions became the norm for many families in the 1930s as people took in lodgers. In 1931, 10.4 per cent of rural and 17.5 per cent of urban home owners rented out accommodation. One aspect that had changed was the decrease in the isolation of women due to radios and telephones. But other appliances were not so postitive. As in the previous century, technology was often two edged. While those women who could afford the electric refrigerator and washing machine were no doubt thankful for the relief they gave them, it did alter what was expected of them. Standards of food consumption increased as food could be kept longer and standards of cleanliness increased with the ease of cleaning. Indeed, the medical profession demanded cleanlines and lectured women against the insidious onslaught of germs into their domestic sphere.

In Newfoundland, the economy always seemed to go from bad to worse. The concept of family wage was simply not a reality to a people who were largely dependent on their own efforts in the fishing industry. There, wives were still accustomed to bring in what money they could, whether it was through berry-picking or other work. For many working wives in the 1930s, the pressures of home life became unbearable. Husbands were often out of work and some, too ashamed of a situation for which they were not responsible, left in search of work which did not exist, leaving their wives to carry on somehow and keep the families together. Not all women succeeded but most did and did so in ingenious ways.

Responding to all these various pressures, the lifecycle of women shifted. Women were having fewer babies and having them over a shorter period of time. In 1921, the mean age of child-bearing was 25.8 years, but 1931 it has dropped to 25.1 years and in 1941 to 24.7 years. Experts bombarded women with advice on how to raise the fewer children. They admonished parents not to be too affectionate to their children or else their children would grow up spoiled. This was far removed from the traditional native way of childrearing which encouraged the immediate response of any adult to the needs of a child. Mothering was to be a full time job, one to which a woman was to devote herself. But it could be dangerous work. While infant mortality rates had been declining, maternal mortality rates were still unacceptably high. In 1925, it was 5.6 per 1000 live births only surpassed by the U.S. at (6.6), Scotland (6.2), and Belgium (5.8) of 14 western nations studied. The result of such statistics was an active campaign spearheaded by the NCW, the medical profession, and governments to introduce an extensive prenatal care system into the country. Pregnancy and childbirth became increasingly monitored and more births occurred in hospitals as medicine idealized the scientific birth.

The trend to smaller families was not one that was new in Canada. Indications came as early as the late nineteenth century that families were limiting their size. The birth rate had declined by 44 per cent in Ontario between 1871 and 1901 and 21 per cent in Quebec between 1851 and 1921.

Most historians believe that the change from a rural agricultural existence to a more urban industrial one partially explains the desire to have fewer children. In the former, children could always be of economic use and were not a drain on the family finances. With industrialization and the change in attitudes concerning child labour and desire for more universal and compulsory education, children were a cost which some families, for whatever reason, did not feel warranted in incurring. Historians agree that the methods used to control conception were numerous. Some women prolonged the length of time they breastfed; some used effective spermicides which had been available for centuries; others depended on the rhythm method endorsed by the Catholic Church. For those women whose attempts at contraception were unsuccessful abortion was sometimes resorted to and for the most desperate infanticide was an option.

Birth control, though illegal, was a private act. It only became a public issue when those on the left advocated it early in the twentieth century. But they were few in number and did not always agree on why they supported it. Mainstream society did not endorse birth control publicly because many of the middle class associated it with racial suicide. As more non-English-speaking immigrants came to the country, the old stock worried that such people had a higher birth rate than themselves. The future appeared evident. Unless people of Anglo-Celtic heritage continued to reproduce at a high rate, they would eventually be outnumbered. Pro-natalist views were particularly strong after World War I. Many *pundits* argued that a high birth rate was needed to replace the 60,000 lives lost in the war. The irony, of course, was that these arguments may have made sense on a theoretical level but the reality was that most Canadians did not want to have more children and in private, decisions taken within the family were the against large families.

Not until the 1930s when the economic plight of many families became evident and when middle-class Canadians were struggling to find ways to lessen the public burden of those on welfare was birth contol advocated publicly. Many young people were delaying marriage and those who married delayed having children. Indeed the absolute number of children born in the 1930s actually declined for the first time since records began to be kept in 1851. The idea that those who could not support children should have the option of not having them became more respectable than it had been.

A central figure in the birth control movement was A.R. Kaufman, a Kitchener industrialist, who discovered the high birth rate among his discharged workers in 1929. As an aid to them and others, he established the Parents' Information Bureau which through visiting nurses distributed low cost contraceptives to the poor and socially dependent. Underlaying Kaufman's concern was his belief that birth control (and sterilization of the unfit) was a solution to poverty, social unrest, and racial decline. At the same time birth control clinics were emerging in various centres of the country, usually run by women who saw birth control as a woman's issue and part of the right of women to decide when they should bear children.

In 1936 one of Kaufman's visiting nurses was arrested for disseminating birth control devices when canvassing a French Catholic suburb of Ottawa. In the ensuing court case, the defence and prosecution put forward arguments for and against birth control. The judge found in favour of the defendant on the grounds that she has been disseminating birth control information and contraceptives for 'the public good'. Such a decision did not make birth control legal but it did send a signal to the police that it was going to be difficult to get a conviction against those involved in the movement. Birth control did not become legal in Canada until 1969.

World War II and After

Many Canadians suffered as a result of the depression and, as already mentioned, women in the work force were particularly singled out. This happened as well in WW II but in a different way. Due to the labour shortage caused by men going overseas, the government and media encouraged women, indeed told them, it was their patriotic duty to enter the work force. Most Canadians still did not like to see women in the work force. They were accustomed to seeing single women working before marriage and had come to terms with this but married women—no—and married women with children—most definitely not. Desperation, however, can bring about change and for the good of the war effort even married women with children were recruited. The Federal Government attracted them through tax benefits and in the provinces of Quebec and Ontario by the setting up of joint federal-provincial day nurseries, although most of the nurseries existed in Ontario due to the opposition of Quebec to the conscripted war effort and to Catholic Quebec's continued opposition to married women working in paid employment.

The result of the war time emergency was that tens of thousands of women—255,000 working in war industries or related by 1943—were entering the work force for the first time and many others were changing their jobs from the traditional ones associated with women to ones which only men had done. They were even accepted into all three armed services, not as combatants but to relieve men for active duty. Rates of pay for women increased but seldom reached those of men. Nonetheless, the image of women during the war years changed. The glamorous woman became the war worker, familiar in advertisements wearing coveralls or pants, something only the very daring had previously worn. Despite all the publicity about the war and the patriotic duty of women to participate, most entered the labour force not because of patriotic feelings but because of economic need. Of married women over 35.9 per cent said they entered for patriotic reasons but 59 per cent said it was the desire to supplement family income and 32 per cent said it was for personal needs. Whatever the reasons, their work was essential.

Especially crucial was the agricultural labour which they did. While Canada needed war workers, it also needed farm workers for there was increased demand for agricultural products to feed armies at the same time that there was a shortage of manpower in the agricultural sector. In 1940, an average of 9.2 sons from every 100 farms left the areas for industrial employment or the armed forces; this increased to 14.5 in 1941. The volunteer work which women did was also crucial in raising money and in collecting items for recycling.

All this effort on the part of women did not signal any major shift in ideology toward them. Even the armed forces were careful to assure Canadians that the women in the three services were there to help men, that they were doing traditional work, familiar to women, and that their femininity and morality were not being jeopardized. However, many women discovered that they enjoyed working and would like to continue after the war, especially in the non-traditional areas which paid better than the so-called women's occupations. The government was not particularly supportive. Fearing a return of the depression and aware of the danger of returning veterans if they found themselves unemployed the government took away the incentives to women's labour force participation that it had introduced. After a certain amount of pressure, it was willing to include women in a study by the Advisory Committee on Reconstruction but there is little evidence that government officials ever read the specific report dealing with women. They certainly did not act on many of its recommendations. As far as government was concerned, and as far as many Canadians were concerned, including many women, Canada should return to normal after the war and for them normal meant women, especially married women, should return to the home.

For some women this simply was not possible. Part of the war strategy had resulted in the dilocation of Japanese-Canadian families from the west coast and placement in the interior or in internment camps. Often separated from their husbands, the women had to cope on their own. This internment was a reminder that not all women would see the war years in the same way. After the war, they and their families were forbidden to return to the west coast and had to begin their lives elsewhere in Canada. Once the hysteria over the supposed war-time threat they had posed died down and the shame of how they had been treated was realized, the government was willing to make some amends and in 1951 granted Japanese-Canadians the vote.

While for Japanese-Canadian women normalcy was going to be difficult, the media assumed for most women it would be a welcome and easy transition. The media reinforced this by inundating women through their magazines, newspapers, and radio shows with the image of the 'happy homemaker'. And it would seem that women were learning the lesson. Certainly participation rates of women in the labour force in 1946 indicated a drastic reduction. In 1945 women were 31.4 per cent of the work force but in 1946 they were 22.7 per cent. That reduction, however, proved to be only a peacetime adjustment. Equally illusory was the shift in the birth rate from a decline to what was popularly known as the baby boom. In some areas, women did not go back to pre-war conditions but actually regressed further. For example, the advances which women had made in physical activities before the war seemed to have been lost. The press ignored women's team sports. The athletic heroines of the post-war period were Barbara Ann Scott who won the Olympic, World, and European figure skating titles in 1948, and Marilyn Bell who at the age of sixteen swam across Lake Ontario, the first person ever to do so. While their efforts revealed the strength of women's bodies and their abilities, what was focused on was the feminine nature of both young women. The media defined them by their gender not by their accomplishments.

If the press image of Canadian women in general in the 1950s is examined, it would appear that women were content in their homes, raising their families. Advice manuals assured women that motherhood was their natural destiny. At the same time, behaviourists and medical experts were telling women that they did not know how to raise their own children scientifically. But books abounded to assist them. Even in rebellion, women were told what to do. Experts were behind the new movement for natural childbirth which challenged the medical establishment control over birth. But natural childbirth was natural only in the absence of instrumental and medical aids. Births still took place in a hospital with a woman surrounded by people telling her what to do.

Underneath the surface veneer of conformity, changes were occurring which in the late 1960s and 1970s would explode into the second women's movement. The shifts were there for those astute enough to see. Women were marrying earlier. In 1940, the average age was 24.4 years and in 1961 it was 22.9 years. In 1941, 56 per cent of women under 45 had their first child before they reached 25 whereas 70 per cent did in 1961. The birth rate, too, altered from 22.2/thousand in 1941 to 31.7/thousand in 1959. In actual fact, the peak year was 1956 and after that fertility declined. Coupled with increased life expectancy, it meant that being a mother became simply one short phase of a woman's life. Women who followed the 'traditional' path and stayed home with their children faced much of their lives before them after their children no longer needed immediate supervision. For many, employment seemed the answer both to boredom and to fulfilment. For Many married women, the luxury of choice was not theirs— employment was a necessity—a necessity unrecognized by society. Child care was not viewed as a state responsibility but a parental one—in fact maternal one.

In 1931, only 10 per cent of women workers were married, in 1941, 12.7 per cent, in 1951, 30 per cent and by 1961 over 47 per cent. Another way of looking at this is to note that between 1951 and 1961, the percentage of married women who worked had doubled. The jobs that married women occupied revealed why they worked. Almost 57.4 per cent of married female workers in 1951 and 58.9 per cent in 1961 were occupied in clerical, sales, and service employment. More than unmarried women, they found themselves in lower paying jobs. Nonetheless, the income they earned was crucial for the well-being of the family. In 1959, a family's income had to be over $8000 year in order to meet middle-class expectations. Thus in many families, the wife had to choose between taking on either the burden of a double day or a low standard of living. For the new wave of immigrants coming to Canada after the war, the contribution of wives was vital simply for their survival. Although who the immigrant women were had changed— Asians, West Indians, and Latin Americans making Canada a multi-cultural and multi-racial society—the work they tended to do was the traditional domestic service work that immigrant woman had been doing throughout Canada's history.

Many Canadians were not appreciative of the economic push which was driving married women into paid employment. Returning veterans especially could not get used to the idea of women working. They feared that married women working would create 'an artificially high standard of living'. Luxury was suspect and there was a sense that the wise should produce most of the goods and services consumed by the family. Neither did all the advice manuals approve of the phenomenon of the working wife. For example, some worried about the decline in masculinity when married women seemed to be usurping the husband's responsibility. Easily forgotten was the long history of married women contributing to the family's coffers. Image for such *pundits* was truth not reality.

Although more women entered the work force they still remained largely unorganized, perhaps because they were not able to enter the sectors where unions were traditionally strong, that is, in manufacturing. Nonetheless, as in previous periods women did try to protect themselves. One unsuccessful attempt began in 1946 when the Retail, Wholesale and Department Store Union undertook to unionize the predominantly female work force of the T.E. Eaton Company in Toronto. Complicated because of the high rate of turnover and company tactics, the drive eventually failed and the effort ended in 1952.

The Turbulence of the 1960s and After

By the 1960s the working woman had become a reality that many Canadians could not ignore, no matter how much they may have wanted to. The image of women was changing. Working women were part of the norm, although married women were still viewed as problematic. But it was not any single working woman who was the media's delight. By the end of the 1960s, it was the young professional woman. She represented the first of the post-war baby boomers who had finished their education, and this generation more than any before continued on to university. Such university-trained women were not accepting of the traditional jobs which were open to women. They wanted whatever employment opportunities were available to their brothers as well. If what was happening in the 50s had remained unacknowledged, the phenomenon of the late 60s and early 70s was analyzed constantly. And there was much to analyse. By 1971, women were over one-third of the work force and by 1983 were over 40 per cent of the labour force. The young women entering the work force were tending to stay in it longer, even after they married, and after the mid-1980s even when they had young children. By 1981, the majority of married women were in the paid labour force.

This change did not come without cost. Married women with children who entered the work force often felt guilty about not being full-time mothers. In 1970, 15 per cent of Canadains were against married women with no children taking a job and in 1973, 62 per cent of males and 57 per cent of females felt that women's participation in the work force had a harmful effect on family life. Also in 1970, 80 per cent of Canadians believed that if a woman had young children at home she should not work.

But given the kinds of jobs which most women held, it is clear that they worked because they economically had to.

Few women were able to meet the new ideal that emerged of having it all—career, marriage, and family. Most women did not have careers, they had jobs. The work which women did had not really altered. According to Statistics Canada's research, the top female areas of employment in 1986 were: secretaries and stenographers; sales clerks and sales persons; book-keepers and accounting clerks; tellers and cashiers; nurses; waitresses; elementary and kindergarten teachers; general office clerks; receptionists and information clerks; and janitors, charworkers and cleaners. Not only were they in traditional jobs but many were doing double duty in that while the average male had only one job, married women who worked outside the home had two since they bore responsibility for children and the home. Day care facilities had expanded but nowhere met the demand.

Despite the phenomenon of women entering the work force in unprecedented numbers, the cruel reality of Canada was and is that the poor are largely women and children. In 1970 two-thirds of all welfare recipients were women and two-thirds of these were widowed, separated, or divorced and more than 50 per cent had small children. Throughout the 1980s, women never went below being 55 per cent of the total poor of *any* age in Canada. Part of this is accounted for by the wage differential between men and women. In 1971, income for full-time women workers as a percentage of men's was 42.1 and in 1987 it was 56.3. Because women did not earn what men did; their pensions were lower. They also were and are dependent on them more since women live longer than men. By 1971 women's life expectancy was 76 years whereas men's was only 69.

The age of marriage was still decreasing. In 1971 it was only 22.6 years for women and 24.9 year for men. Young women of the early boomer generation were better educated than their mothers; yet they still were marrying and at younger ages. Continuting a trend begun in the 1950s, many were moving out to the suburbs to escape the crowded conditions of the urban environment. There they were able to take advantage of the strong economy which let them purchase homes. Isolated, however, from the mainstream of society many of these young mothers who remained in the home joined together to form formal and informal groups—almost survival enclaves. Advice manuals told these women to spend more time on raising children but these women were having fewer and fewer of them— the average in 1971 was 1.7. Ironically given the concerns of many Canadians about being outnumbered by immigrants and their families, immigrant groups were having even fewer children. Especially significant was the decline in the birth rate of Quebec. Between 1959 and 1969 it declined by 50 per cent. What this meant was that Quebec began to feel that its future in Confederation was not assured. Immigrants coming to Quebec were not learning French and were not being integrated into the French culture. In an effort to assure Quebec's cultural survivals, the Quebec government instituted language laws which would enforce French as the language of use within the province. Such laws often put pressure on the oftentimes fragile relationship between Quebec and the rest of Canada.

One group which was running counter to this fertility decline was native women. The native birth rate was increasing and with better access to health care, more of those babies were surviving. This would have important ramifications for native/white relations. It underlay a resurgence in native strength and demands on the largely White community to recognize the native reality. However, the birth rate of native women could not hide the fact that their lives and those of their children were often lived in squalor and while their babies might have a better chance of survival than previously, the native infant mortality rate was still significantly higher than that of other Canadians and the life expectancy rate much lower.

The general decline in birth rates indicated that legal or not, Canadians continued to use birth control. By the 1960s, the pill had become a method of choice for many women and only years later did they discover that long use could lead to detrimental side effects. Men increasingly were sharing the burden of birth control and many were voluntarily having vasectomies. The law clearly needed to be changed to catch up to reality and in 1969 this finally occurred when birth control was made legal. In 1984, Statistics Canada revealed that for women aged 18 to 49, the contraception method followed was female sterilization (35.3 per cent), male sterilization (12.7 per cent), the pill (28 per cent), the IUD (8.3 per cent), and the condom (9.1 per cent). Abortion, however, was carefully controlled by the medical profession and access was difficult except for medical reasons and for women who had access to doctors who would support them in their requests. These woman tended to be married, White, and middle class.

In that same year, the divorce laws of Canada were made more open in recognition of the changing nature of marriage and the number of people who were divorcing. This law essentially recognized marital breakdown with no blame attached to either partner. While divorce has increased significantly since 1969, the repercussions on women have been serious. Women are most often given custody of the children of a marriage and while child support payments were usually imposed, they are often inadequate to maintain an acceptable standard of living. Even worse, the vast majority of child support payments are defaulted on with the result that women and their children become part of the increasing number of poor in Canada. Perhaps this reality has jaded young women. Age of Marriage since 1973 has been increasing, reaching 24.7 in 1987 and at the same time, marriage rates (marriage per 1,000 single, widowed, and divorced women aged 15 and over) have declined from 70.6 in 1972 to 45.5 in 1987. More and more couples chose to live common law marriages.

The Women's Movement

With all the tremendous changes taking place in the lives of women, women's organizations continued to press for reform. Many of those created in the late nineteenth century and in the inter-war period persevered in fighting for improvement in women's experience and treatment. They were the link between the modern period and the first women's movement. The Business and Professional Women's Clubs pressured the various governments to open up opportunities to women especially in the federal Civil Service. They and other women's groups also managed to get equal work legislation passed by the federal and most provincial governments. However, they soon discovered that equal pay was difficult to achieve when men and women essentially did different kinds of work. The legislation was effective only when men and women were doing the same work and so could be compared. In Quebec, in the 1960s the legal restrictions on wives were lessened so they could participate in a profession on their own and sign contracts. One of the most significant groups to form in the early 1960s was the Voice of Women, an organization concerned about the escalation of the Cold War. They were especially incensed when the Liberal Government under Lester Pearson decided to have nuclear weapons on Canadian soil. They also questioned the increasing ties with the United States which seemed to limit the sovereignty of Canada. Such activism was often overlooked by the wider society.

Women continued to support the arts in Canada. They were responsible for the formation of the Royal Winnipeg Ballet, The National Ballet of Canada, and Les Grands Ballet Canadiens. Minority women organized to ensure the continuation of their own cultural heritage so that it would not disappear in the ocean of North American cultural hegemony. In literature, too, Canadian women made a name for themselves and their country. Margaret Laurence, Margaret Atwood, Alice Munro, Gabrielle Roy, Marie-Claire Blais and Anne Hebert dominated the literary scene.

The activism and the accomplishments of women coupled with their participation in the paid labour force were at odds with the image which was protrayed of them in the popular media. When this occurs, the image needs to give way and society is challenged to catch up. In the mid to late 60s this happended. Women's organization began a resurgence. In 1966, in Quebec, many existing groups joined the *Féderation des femmes du Québec,* a coalition which focused first on housewives and in time broadened their interests. In the same year, Laura Sabia, president of the Canadian Federation of University Women, formed the Committee for the Equality of Women in Canada to press for a Royal Commission on the Status of Women (RCSW). Realizing the danger of the government coopting such a commission and the historical tendency for Royal Commissions in Canada to be ignored, these women still felt it was necessary to raise public awareness and force politicians to face the fact that all was not right for Canadian women. Reluctantly the government agreed and the next year created the Commission. It held public meetings and while some groups of women were not represented on the Commission, many voices were heared, Indeed, it was the public meetings of the Commission which captured the imagination of the press. Initially sceptical, journalists became overwhelmed by the predicament and injustices faced by many women in the country. The Commission reported in 1970 and its 167 recommendations became the platform of the feminist movement.

Four principles underlay the report: "women should be free to choose whether or not to take employment outside their homes; ...the care of children is a responsibility to be shared by the mother, the father, and society; ...society has a responsibility for women because of pregnancy and childbirth, and special treatment related to maternity will always be necessary; and ...in certain areas women will for an interim period require special treatment to overcome the adverse effects of discriminatory practices."[17] To put pressure on the government to implement the recommendations, an Ad Hoc Committee of the Committee on Equality was formed and eventually transformed itself into the National Action Committee on the Status of Women, an umbrella organization of many women's groups, representing over 5,000,000 women in the country.

The largely White, middle-class, and middle-age women behind the RCSW were not the only women who were beginning to insist on a hearing. In 1972 the Ontario Native Women's Association began to look at the sections of the Indian Act which meant that native women who married non-native men lost their position as status Indians. Despite pressure by this group and other native women, the federal government refused to act even when the United Nations Human Rights Committee found the government in breach of the International Covenant on Civil and Political Rights. In this

[17]Prentice et al., *Canadian Women*, 349.

refusal to move, the government was supported by many native men.

At odds with the mainstream women's organizations were the young educated women who came out of the student movement and the counter culture philosophy of the 1960s. Referring to their efforts as 'women's liberation' in identification with the liberation of other colonized peoples and nations, they aligned themselves with the rhetoric and analysis of Marxism and socialism. They argued that women would not be free until the capitalist system itself was eradicated. For their part, radical feminists maintained that it was not the economic system which was at the root of the inequities faced by women but rather the oppression of women by men. Both these groups were more committed to including non-mainstream women in their groups than the traditional women's groups had been. Attempts were made to support working-class women in their efforts to improve their working situations and with immigrant women to gain the same kind of rights which immigrant men were given on entry to Canada, specifically access to job-training and language instruction. They challenged the system as never before. These radical groups had a separatist orientation taken furthest by the lesbian movement which through the women's movement found a public voice. Most of the new groups had a 'hands on' philosophy. They demanded that women's studies courses be taught in universities, they set up women's shelters to help battered women, they set up health clinics, and feminist presses.

The new women's association attracted young women, often college and university students. Certainly women were becoming a force. According to Statistics Canada, in 1970 they were almost 37 per cent of full time college and univerity undergraduates; by 1987-88 they were 50 per cent. These and other young women articulated a series of grievances and beliefs which became a guiding ideology for feminists. Certainly the time was ripe for this. The feminists provided the point of view around which to organize. They could appeal to other women for whom the problems of women sounded a familiar note—those women in the work force facing discrimination and many homemakers frustrated by the lack of respect accorded to them in society. In addition, the time for change seemed to be present. The late 60s and early 1970s was a period of challenge in Canadian society, particularly in the protests by youth against what they saw as an entrenched conservative establishment. Influenced by the student revolts in other countries, Canadian youth were questioning the kind of world they had inherited and the value system underpinning that world. Everything seemed open to question— morality, religion, capitalism—why not the relationship between the sexes?

Out of the women's liberation movement, certain key concepts emerged:

consciousess raising; sexism; male chauvinism; and feminism. Feminists tried to run their groups in a non-elitist, non-hierarchical way. They demanded an end to job discrimination, repeal of Canada's abortion laws, and establishment of day care facilities. They argued that girls were stereotyped from the time that they were born. Few young girls had positive role models. Parents did not encourage their daughters to continue their education to the same extent as their sons feeling somehow education would be wasted if their daughters married and raised a family, perhaps indicating the esteem in which such a role was held. Feminists worried about how girls were socialized. There was increasing concern about violence against women in society, particularly the way in which rape was treated. The law still seemed to reflect long held attitudes that rape was a sexual act, rather than an act of violence and one of power. They were concerned about sexist language and how much of it excluded women. They raised the hidden issue of sexual harassment on the job. How all this was going to be rectified was what separated feminists. Some believed the system could be adjusted to conform to the equity principles it espoused. Others believed that underlying capitalism was a patriarchal system which needed to be removed. Others claimed that a revolution in sex relations had to be overcome before any change for the better occurred.

This first generation of modern feminists tended to be White and middle-class women. They overemphasized the benefits of being in the labour force and the oppression felt by many women in the home. In doing so, they often antagonized homemakers who rightly felt proud of what they were doing. This first generation was also not as sympathetic as they might have been to working-class women and women of colour. In the early years, they ignored the problems of disabled women and lesbian women. They had an inclusive ideology but one which was not always practised. Their concerns were not the concerns of all women, at least not in the way in which they often phrased them. But despite the myriad of groups and splinter groups, many of the activist women were able to join together when the common interests of women were at stake.

The changes brought about by the feminist movement have been significant. They introduced the concept of equal pay for work of equal value to overcome the problems of implementing equal work legislation. They have been able to get property laws changed so that on the dissolution of a marriage the assets are more equitably distributed. Underlying this change was the acknowledgment that much of the work which women do in the home allows the husband to concentrate on the development of his business or work and that, as a result, the wife is entitled to the family assets as much as he. Due to their activism, women have been more visible in politics than even before. Many commentators have argued that in the crucial 1980 Quebec referendum on the Constitution that women were instrumental in the victory of the yes side, that is, the side that supported continued participation with Confederation. In 1993 Canada saw the succession of Kim Campbell to the leadership of the Conservative Party and consequently to the Prime Ministership of Canada, an event which in 1960 would have been unthinkable.

Perhaps nothing else illustrated the coming of age of women and the problems they had to face than the revamping of the Canadian Constitution with its Charter of Rights and Freedoms in 1980-81. Section 15 of the charter assured equal benefits and protection to all Canadians under the law. Section 28 supported that by stating "Notwithstanding anything in this Charter, the rights and freedom referred to in it are guaranteed equally to male and female person." When strong opposition from certain provinces seemed to put Section 28 at risk, thousands of women mobilized and engaged in a lobbying campaign which forced the premiers and the federal politicians to reinstate Section 28. Canadian women had won a significant constitutional victory. It was only because of their own vigilance, not because the white male politicians of Canada had been sensitive to the implications their actions would have on women.

Much still needs to be done. Women in Canada compose over half the population and so they cannot be generalized. Not all women are united. The creation of Real, Equal, Active, for Life (REAL) women remains evidence of this. While supporting the role of women in the home, and against publicly funded childcare, they also endorse job-sharing, extending maternity leaves, tax credits for homemakers. They oppose what they think NAC stands for, but the irony is that many of their demands reflect the influence of the feminist movement. Many women are against abortion rights, a major plank among feminists and, while some would certainly not sympathize with the other aspects of the feminist movement, those among them who feel themselves feminist are torn over an issue about which they feel strongly. The striking down of the abortion law in Canada by the Surpreme Court in 1988 did not end the abortion debate. It still continues and to date there seems to be no way of reconciling the two opposing groups. But both extremes are in minority positions. The majority of Canadians do believe in equal access to abortion but not abortion on demand. Divisions within the feminist movement also exist between women who are concerned about the repercussions of the proliferation of pornography and the connection between it and violence against women and those women who feel that any censorship, even against pornography, would infringe on the civil liberties of Canadians. Lesbian women often feel disaffected from heterosexual women. Young women feel that feminism is an outdated concept and many refuse to use the term. Nonetheless, they still want the equality for which many of their mothers, grandmothers, and even great-grandmothers fought. Women are separated by class, colour, ethnicity and at times such have precedence in their lives over gender.

Women's experience is continually changing and those changes will bring their own demands. Since the mid-1980s women's lives are no longer characterized by three phases of work, child-bearing, and work. Childbearing and paid employment are integraded. The so-called traditional family of mother staying home and father going out to work is not the norm. Marriage is certainly not forever for many women. The work situation for women is still not as good as it might be especially in the recent recession. Women in the public sector and in other white collar jobs have been unionizing but in recent years unions have not been particularly strong in the face of layoffs and the restructuring of the economy which has occurred in the wake of an increasing global economic network and the Free Trade Agreement negotiated with the United States.

Young women are still too much influenced by the popular media portrayals of women which has led to the phenomenon of anorexia and bulimia. Childbrirth has become more subject to interference by the medical profession, although due to pressure by women's groups midwifery is making a resurgence. New reproductive technologies pose a real challenge to what has been central identification of women — motherhood. Increasingly, medical science seems to be able to separate the process of conception and development from the body of woman. We live in an age when a child can have five parents, 3 mothers (biological, gestational, and social) and 2 fathers (biological and social). The future is upon us and the challenge which it presents may make the changes of previous 150 years seem simple by comparison.

BIBLIOGRAPHY

Abrahamson, Una. *Domestic Life in Nineteenth Century Canada.* Toronto: Burns & MacEachern, 1966.

Acton, Janice et al., eds. *Women at Work: Ontario 1850-1930.* Toronto Women's Educational Press, 1974.

Arnup, Katherine et al. *Delivering Motherhood: Maternal Ideologies and Practices in the 19th-20th Centuries.* London: Routledge, 1990.

Arnup, Katherine. *Education for Motherhood: Advice for Mothers in Twentieth-*

Century Canada. Toronto: University of Toronto Press, 1994.

Bacchi, Carol Lee. *Liberation Deferred? The Ideas of the English-Canadian Suffragists, 1877-1918*. Toronto: University of Toronto Press, 1983.

Backhouse, Constance. *Petticoats and Prejudices: Women and Law in Nineteenth-Century Canada*. The Osgoode Society, 1991.

Bradbury, Bettina. "Pigs, Cows, and Boarders: Non-Wage forms of Survival Among Montreal Families, 1861-91", *Labour/Le Travail* 14 (1984), pp. 9-46.

Brouwer, Ruth. *New Women for God: Canadian Presbyterian Women and India Missions, 1876-1914*. Toronto: University of Toronto Press, 1990.

Brown, Jennifer. *Strangers in Blood: Fur Trade Company Families in Indian Country*. Vancouver: University of British Columbia Press, 1980.

Casgrain, Thérèse. *A Women in a Man's World,* translated by Joyce Marshall. Toronto: McClelland & Stewart, 1972.

Cleverdon, Catherine L. *The Woman Suffrage Movement in Canada*. Toronto: University of Toronto Press, 1974.

The Clio Collective, *Quebec Women: A History*. Toronto: The Women's Press, 1987.

Coburn, Judi. " 'I See and Am Silent': A Short History of Nursing", in Acton et al., *Women at Work,* pp. 127-63.

Cohen, Marjorie. *Women's Work, Markets, and Economic Development in Nineteenth-Century Ontario*. Toronto: University of Toronto Press, 1988.

—. "The Decline of Women in Canadian Dairying", *Histoire Sociale/Sociale History* 17, 34 (November, 1984), pp. 307-34.

Comacchio, Cynthia R. *Nations are Built of Babies: Saving Ontario's Mothers and Children*. Montreal and Kingston: McGill-Queen's University Press, 1993.

Connelly, Patricia. *Last Hired, First Fired: Women and the Canadian Work Force*. Toronto: Women's Educational Press, 1978.

Conrad, Margaret. " 'Sunday Always Makes Me Think of Home': Time and Place in Canadian Women's History", in Veronica Strong-Boag and Anita Clair Fellman, eds., *Rethinking Canada: The Promise of Women's History*. Toronto: Copp Clark Pitman, 1991, pp. 97-112.

Crowley, Terry. *Agnes MacPhail and the Politics of Equality*. Toronto: James Lorimer & Co., 1990.

Danylewycz, Marta. *Taking the Veil: An Alternative to Marriage, Motherhood, and Spinsterhood in Quebec, 1840-1920*. Toronto: McClelland & Stewart, 1987.

Dubinsky, Karen. *Improper Advances: Rape and Heterosexual Conflict in Ontario, 1880-1929*. Chicago: University of Chicago Press, 1993.

Frager, Ruth A.. *Sweatshop Strife: Class, Ethnicity, and Gender in the Jewish Labour Movement of Toronto 1900-1939*. Toronto: University of Toronto Press, 1992.

Gagan, Rosemary. *A Sensitive Independence, Canadian Methodist Women Missionaries in Canada and the Orient, 1881-1925*. Montreal: McGil-Queen's University Press, 1992.

Iscovetta, Franca, and Mariana Valverde, eds. *Gender Conflicts: New Essays in Women's History*. Toronto: University of Toronto Press, 1992.

Jackel, Susan, ed. *A Flannel Shirt and Liberty: British Emigrant Gentlewomen in the Canadian West 1880-1914*. Vancouver: University of British Columbia Press, 1982.

Kealey, Linda, ed. *A Not Unreasonable Calim: Women and Reform in Canada 1880-1920*. Toronto: Women's Educational Press, 1979.

—, and Joan Sangster, eds. *Beyond the Vote: Canadian Women and Politics*. Toronto: University of Toronto Press, 1989.

Lavigne, Marie, Yolande Pinard, and Jennifer Stoddart. "The Federation Nationale Saint-Jean-Baptiste and the Women's Movement in Quebec", in Linda Kealey, ed., *A Not Unreasonable Calim: Women and Reform in Canada, 1880s-1920s*. Toronto: The Women's Press, 1979, pp. 71-87.

Lerner, Gerda. *The Majority Finds Its Past: Placing Women in History*. New York: Oxford University Press, 1979.

Light, Beth, and Veronica Strong-Boag. *True Daughters of the North: Canadian Women's History: An Annotated Bibliography*. Toronto: OISE Press, 1980.

Lindstrom-Best, Varpu. *Defiant Sisters: A Social History of Finnish Immigrant Women in Canada*. Toronto: Multicultural History Society of Ontario, 1988.

Lowe, Graham S. *Women in the Administrative Revolution*. Toronto: University of Toronto Press, 1987.

Luxton, Meg. *More than a Labour of Love: Three Generations of Women's Work in the Home*. Toronto: The Women's Press, 1981.

Martin, Michèle. *"Hello, Central?": Gender, Technology, and Culture in the Formation of Telephone Systems*. Montreal: McGill-Queen's University Press, 1991.

McLaren, Angus, and Arlene McLaren. *The Bedroom and the State: The Changing Practices and Politics of Contraception and Abortion in Canada, 1880-1980*. Toronto: McClelland & Stewart, 1986.

Mitchinson, Wendy L. *The Nature of Their 'Bodies': Women and Their Doctors in Victorian Canada*. Toronto, Buffalo, London: University of Toronto Press, 1991.

National Council of Women of Canada, *Women of Canada: Their Life and*

Work. National Council of Women of Canada, reprinted, 1975.

Parr, Joy. *The Gender of Breadwinners: Women, Men, and Change in Two Industrial Towns 1880-1950*. Toronto: University of Toronto Press, 1990.

Pedersen, Diana. *Changing Women, Changing History: A Bibilography of the History of Women in Canada*. Toronto: Green Dragon Press, 1992.

Pierson, Ruth Roach. *They're Still Women After All: The Second World War and Canadian Womanhood*. Toronto: McClelland & Stewart, 1986.

Potter-MacKinnon, Janice. *While the Women Only Wept: Loyalist Refugee Women in Eastern Ontario*. Montreal and Kingston: McGill-Queen's University Press, 1993.

Prentice, Alison et al. *Canadain Women: A History*. Toronto: Harcourt, Brace, Jovanovich, 1988.

—. *The School Promoters: Education and Social Class in Mid-Nineteenth Century Upper Canada*. Toronto: McClelland & Stewart, 1977.

Rasmussen, Linda et al. *A Harvest Yet to Reap: A History of Prairie Women*. Toronto: The Women's Press, 1976.

Razack, Sherene. "Schools for Happiness: Instituts Familiaux and the Education of Ideal Wives and Mothers", in Katherine Arnup, Andree Levesque, and Ruth Roach Pierson, eds., *Delivering Motherhood: Maternal Ideologies and Practices in the 19th and 20th Centuries*. London and New York: Routledge, 1990, pp. 211-37.

Rooke, P.T., and Schnell, R.L. *No Bleeding Heart: Charlotte Whitton, A Feminist on the Right*. Vancouver: University of British Columbia Press, 1987.

Sangster, Joan. *Dreams of Equality: Women on the Canadian left, 1920-1950*. Toronto: McClelland & Stewart, 1989.

—. "The 1907 Bell Telephone Strike: Organizing Women Workers", *Labour/ Le Travail*, III (1978), pp. 109-30.

Savage, Candace. *Our Nell: a Scrapbook Biography of Nellie L. McClung*. Saskatoon: Goodread Biographies, 1979.

Silverman, Elaine Leslau. *The Last Best West: Women on the Alberta Frontier, 1880-1930*. Montreal: Eden Press, 1984.

Snell, James. *In the Shadow of the Law: Divorce in Canada 1990-1939*. Toronto: University of Toronto Press, 1991.

Statistics Canada. *Women in Canada: A Statistical Report*. Ottawa: Ministry of Supply & Services, 1990.

Strong-Boag, Veronica. *The New Day Recalled: Lives of Girls and Women in English Canada, 1919-1939*. Toronto: Copp Clark Piman, 1988.

—. *The Parliament of Women: The National Council of Women of Canada 1893-1929*. Ottawa: National Museum of Canada, 1976.

—, and Anita Clair Fellman, eds. *Rethinking Canada. The Promise of Women's History.* Toronto: Copp Clark, 1986.

Sufrin, Eileen. *The Eaton Drive: The Campaign to Organize Canada's Largest Department Store 1948 to 1952.* Toronto: Fitzhenry & Whiteside, 1982.

Swyripa, Frances. *Wedded to the Cause: Ukrainian-Canadian Women and Ethnic Identity 1891-1991.* Toronto: University of Toronto Press, 1993.

Thompson, Joanne Emily. "The Influence of Dr. Emily Howard Stowe on the Woman Suffrage Movement in Canada", *Ontario History* 54, 4 (December, 1962), pp. 253-66.

Trofimenkoff, Susan Mann, and Alison Prentice, eds. *The Neglected Majority: Essays in Canadian Women History.* Toronto: McClelland & Stewart, 1977.

—. *The Neglected Majority: Essays in Canadian Women History,* vol. 2. Toronto: McClelland & Stewart, 1985.

Van Kirk, Sylvia. *Many Tender Ties: Women in Fur Trade Society, 1670-1870.* Winnipeg: Watson & Dwyer, 1980.

—. *Towards a Feminist Perspective in Native History.* Toronto: Centre for Women's Studies, Ontario Institute for Studies in Education, Occasional Paper no. 14, 1987.

Vipond, Mary. "The Image of Women in Mass Circulation Magazines in the 1920s", in Susan Mann Trofimenkoff and Alison Prentice, eds., *The Neglected Majority: Essays in Canadian Women's History.* Toronto: McClelland & Stewart, 1977, pp. 116-24.

10

The Expansion of a Nation: 1867-1990

Michael D. Behiels

I. Forging the Nation, the Macdonald Era, 1864-96

A. *Convergence of Interests—Economic and Political*

Having achieved and practised internal self-government during the late 1840s and 1850s, the governing political and economic elites of the British North American Colonies were pressured by external and internal factors in the 1860s to restructure, yet once again their constitutional arrangements. During September and October 1864, representatives of these colonial elites came to a meeting of minds beginning in Charlottetown then on through Halifax, Saint John, Fredericton to end up finally in Quebec City. There they hammered out the 72 resolutions which would form the basis of a new constitutional arrangement. The end result of three years of further deliberations among the colonial elites would be the inauguration on July 1, 1867 of a semi-autonomous, federation called the Dominion of Canada. The founding provinces of Nova Scotia, New Brunswick, Quebec and Ontario, were joined eventually by Manitoba in 1870, British Columbia in 1871, Prince Edward Island in 1873, Alberta and Saskatchewan in 1905, and Newfoundland in 1949.

To internal political and economic pressures, especially in the Colony of Canada where railway construction debts and political deadlock prevailed, were added very crucial and determining external pressures. Great Britain's governing classes were eager to cut escalating expenditures on the colonies. They were particularly fearful of having to come to the defence, yet once again, of their British North American colonies against the growing commercial, industrial and military colossus to the South. Many United States politicians expressed manifest destiny ambitions, especially toward the Hudson Bay Territory in the Northwest. The U.S. Federal Government did little to dissuade the Irish Nationalists, known as Fenians, from launching terrorist raids across the border into New Brunswick and Ontario. Only if united in some form of new political entity would the colonies be able to deal adequately with their respective debt problems, assure the security of their borders while preparing to enter the industrial era.

It was primarily under the guidance of the ambitious, astute, yet at times lazy, Prime Minister J.A. Macdonald, that the Canadian nation-state experienced its formative stages of development. The classical federal system of equal but coordinate sovereign entities which emerged by the 1890s was not the quasi-unitary state envisaged by J.A. Macdonald in 1864. Neither was it the decentralized confederal system of equal provinces and two founding nations sought by proponents of the ascending provincial rights school or the French-Canadian castor/rouge nationalists like Henri Bourassa. At the time of Macdonald's passing in 1891, the Canadian federal system was, in the estimation of most observers, then and now, a genuine reflection of the complex geo-political and socio-economic realities of the country. Canada's governing elites had learned early on not to be overly constrained by a narrow construction of the constitution. Instead, by their deeds and actions they created a dynamic constitution capable of adjusting to new realities as these emerged. Indeed, the founders' dream of a distinctive nation-state north of the 49th parallel had weathered several difficult political and economic crises through imagination and foresight. As a result, Canada was well-positioned to enter the new century with renewed zeal and expansive aspirations.

Given the highly distinctive natures and outlooks of these scattered colonial societies, the process of nation-state building would prove to be both arduous and prolonged. Fortunately, it was relatively easy for the authorities in the British Colonial Office and in the various colonial offices to forge the necessary accommodation of what appeared on the surface to be competing interest because the colonial political and economic elites of both linguistic communities shared common social, cultural, economic, and political values and interests. It would be a much greater challenge for these elites to forge in the minds and hearts of Canada's new citizens a shared sense of nationhood. In reality, the new constitutional arrangement of 1867 was in many ways a watershed event. The BNA Act symbolized the end of last phase in the prolonged and somewhat uneven maturation of the various colonial societies. Yet, it also marked the beginning of a series of somewhat more difficult phases of nation-state building that would severely test the fibre and endurance of governing elites at all levels in the Canadian society.

In fact, the colonial elites were, most assuredly, not unanimous in their outlook. Their social, economic and political interest and problems often diverged as much as they converged. The pro-confederation forces comprised those elites in the various colonies who supported a more rapid transition to financial, commercial and industrial capitalism as symbolized by the development and expansion of railways. The anti-confederate forces were generally led by those elite whose constituencies were involved in primary production, namely agriculture, fishing, timber, and related industries such as shipbuilding and sawmilling.

Yet, even this divergence was not always clear cut. In Canada East, the Conservative or Blue Party of Etienne-Pascal Taché and George-Etienne Cartier had its primary political base in the innumerable French-Canadian rural constituencies while garnering strong support among the predominantly English-speaking and rapidly-industrializing urban constituencies on Montreal Island and in urban centres such as Sherbrooke and Trois Rivières. For Cartier's hybrid Blue Party, industrialization and urbanization were essential to the commercialization of Quebec's severely depressed agricultural economy and the retention of the growing surplus of the rural Francophone population in the colony. Thus Cartier and his colleagues supported a new constitutional arrangement which would accelerate all forms of economic development while ensuring the French-Canadian political elite control over all local affairs. For Cartier and his colleagues, the Francophone elite's control over an autonomous province within the new federation marked the end of Lord Durham's strategy of assimilation via French-Canada's political subordination within the legislative union of the Canadas.

The anti-clerical and nationalistic Rouge party, which held a few predominantly Francophone ridings in Montreal east and north, denounced urbanization, industrialization, and the railroad mania because its leaders claimed that these developments enhanced the power and development of the Anglophone bourgeoisie and its constituencies at the expense of the farming communities. Instead, the urban, petty-bourgeois Rouges favoured the regeneration of agriculture and the retention of the rural way of life for the vast majority of French Canadians. The Rouges vigorously opposed the new constitutional arrangement because it was not a true Confederation, that is a dual compact of provinces and two nationalities. The central government in Ottawa, dominated by British Canadians, would have too much economic and political power whereas the majority Francophone province of Quebec would not have exclusive control over all matters of language and culture and would have to endure the presence of a constitutionally-entrenched powerful, predominantly Protestant British-Canadian minority.

In Canada West, the situation was both analogous and divergent from that in Canada East. J.A. Macdonald's Liberal-Conservative Party which lead, jointly with various leaders of the Blue Party, several administrations under the Union represented primarily the interest of the established financial and commercial elites of Canada West. This association assured Macdonald's party of solid financial support but produced relatively few seats, a situation which contributed to the political deadlock of 1864. On the other hand, George Brown's Victorian Liberal Party, formerly the republican-inspired Clear Grit movement, had its roots in the innumerable rural constituencies comprising yeomen farmers and their families and the various trades and retail shopkeepers in the local and regional villages and towns. Yet, Brown's Liberal Party shrewdly defended the interests of an important segment of Toronto's ambitious financial, and commercial elites, of which he was a prominent member, who wished to turn their city into a powerful financial and industrial rival to that of Montreal. They hoped to achieve their ambition by separating from the Union of the Canadas and then annexing the Northwest territory, still under Hudson Bay control, to the new province of Ontario. The vast region west of Lake Huron stretching to the Rockies and to the northern tundra would become the resource rich hinterland of metropolitan Toronto as well as an outlet for Ontario's surplus population and any future immigration from the British Isles.

The development of the governing elites in the Maritime provinces was not as advanced as that in the Canadas. The region's economy remained overwhelmingly tied to resource development, primarily agriculture and timber, while the manufacturing sector, comprising mainly shipbuilding, was intimately linked to the complex but lucrative business of Atlantic shipping involving trade among the colonies as well as with and between the New England States, Great Britain and the Caribbean Islands. By the 1860s, a small but growing segment of this business community was eager to make the transition to the age of industry and railways. Following the failure of the initial negotiations with the politicians and businessmen from the Canadas over the building of an intercolonial railways, the governing elites of Nova Scotia and New Brunswick, led by Conservative Party premiers, Charles Tupper and Samuel Tilley, flirted with Maritime Union only to be convinced that they could achieve their objectives of defence security and economic diversification by joining forces with the elites from the Canadas to create a federation of all the British North American colonies. The price they exacted was an intercolonial railroad to be built and operated by the Canadian government. The price Tupper paid for refusing to allow a legislative vote on the new constitution was political defeat at the hands of Joseph Howe's strong anti-confederate movement which swept the Conservatives out of office and sent a merry band of anti-confederate MPs to Ottawa in 1867. Howe desperately sought repeal of the Union in Great Britain in 1868 but the British authorities flatly rejected the notion of an autonomous Nova

Scotia and pressured him to make a deal with Tupper. Howe agreed to join Macdonald's cabinet as secretary of state for the provinces in return for better financial terms for Nova Scotia. Albeit reluctantly, Howe understood in the twilight of his political career that Nova Scotians had to make the transition from the glorious age of wind, water and sail to the compelling age of the factory, the iron horse, and the steel hulled steamships if they were to keep their sons and daughters at home.

The Constitution Act, 1867

The British parliament passed the British North America Act in April 1867 thereby creating, effective July 1, the Dominion of Canada, a country consisting of some 3½ million citizens scattered throughout Nova Scotia, New Brunswick, Quebec and Ontario. What was the nature of the constitutional arrangement hammered out by the representatives of the various colonial societies under the watchful eye of the British Colonial Office? The BNA Act, now referred to as the Constitution Act, 1867, was an ingenuous hybrid. It married the British Parliamentary system of representative responsible government with the concept of a federation comprising central and provincial governments. The federal concept allowed the Maritime legislatures to remain in place while providing both sections of the Canadas, renamed Quebec and Ontario, with provincial legislatures of their own in Quebec City and Toronto. The former capital of the Canadas, Ottawa, primarily a lumber town at the confluence of the Ottawa and Rideau rivers, was chosen as the capital of the newly created Dominion.

The Provincial Legislative Assemblies were granted, under section 92, exclusive powers over all local matters including municipal government, the levy of direct taxes, public lands and all natural resources, all social and health matters, the administration of justice, the licensing and regulation of provincial commerce and industry, property and civil rights. Under section 93, the provinces had exclusive control over education as long as Ontario respected its existing Catholic separate schools and Quebec its dissentient schools for its Protestant and English-speaking Catholic minorities. If not, Ottawa had the power to impose remedial legislation. Of the four provinces, only Quebec chose a bicameral system in creating an appointed Legislative Council in order to temper the republican thrust of representative democracy. For both similar and different reasons, the Parliament of Canada was also bicameral, with an appointed Senate based on the regional representation and an elected House of Commons.

The Parliament of Canada was empowered to "make Laws for the Peace, Order, and good Government of Canada". Contrary to the initial U.S.

constitution, Ottawa was granted exclusive legislative authority over all matters not assigned in whole or in part to the provincial legislatures. In part, Ottawa's legislative authority extended to defence matters, banking and currency, trade and tariff policies, interprovincial trade and commerce, the native people, postal services, navigation and shipping, and fisheries. These were considered areas essential for a successful process of nation building. The provinces had neither the desire nor the resources to administer them effectively. Localism and regionalism were powerful forces in nineteenth century society. To ensure that the provinces could not derogate from, or add to, their constitutional authority, Ottawa was empowered to disallow provincial legislation and to appoint the provincial lieutenant governors and Supreme Court judges. Indeed, until the late 1930s, Ottawa exercised its powers of disallowance on many occasions. These provincial actions and Ottawa's reactions engendered a political/constitutional debate over the appropriate roles of both levels of government thereby helping create conventions, that is, unwritten rules which became incorporated into our understanding and interpretation of the Constitutional text.

Manifest Destiny: Ottawa Style

J.A. Macdonald became Canada's first PM once his Liberal-Conservative/Blue Party won 101 of the 181 seats in the House of Commons. His government's major priority, aside from setting the new governmental and bureaucratic institutions, was to negotiate quickly with the British government and the Hudson Bay Company for the acquisition of the vast north-west territory. Rupert's Land, as it was called, was home to some 60,000 Indians. At the heart of the buffalo hunt and the fur trade were nearly 10,000 French-Catholic and English-Protestant Métis, the Bay's employees, and a small outpost of Canadians all of whom were clustered at the confluence of the Red and Assiniboine rivers near Fort Garry. The Canadian people acquired the North-west Territories in return for granting £300,000, one-twentieth of the lands of the fertile belt, and a fur trading monopoly to be Hudson Bay Company. The transfer was to take effect on December 1, 1869. The PM's lack of appreciation for the complex and volatile situation in Red River colony would both delay and alter his government's plans for the region.

Once word reached the Red River colony of the deal, the small band of Canadian land speculators celebrated. Meanwhile the French Métis, led by Louis Riel, took action to protect their economic and political interests and their way of life. His men blocked entry of the new governor, William McDougall, captured Fort Garry, and imprisoned a few of the boisterous Canadians. When the Canadians tried to retake Fort Garry, Thomas Scott, an Irish Protestant from Ontario, was caught, tried, and put to death on Riel's orders. Support by the English-Protestant Métis, Riel appointed a provisional government to open negotiations with Ottawa on the terms of the Red River's entry into Confederation. Furious at Riel and his rebels, but unable to impose his government's will without considerable bloodshed and very eager to open the west for business, the PM assigned Cartier to negotiate with Riel's delegates in the Spring of 1870. The outcome of these difficult negotiations was the creation of a small province of Manitoba centred on the Red River Colony. Under the terms of the Manitoba Act, effective from 15 July 1870, Métis would receive just over a half-million hectares of land, while the new province, like Quebec, would have a bilingual legislative Assembly, and Council as well as judicial system. At the insistence of the Bishop for Rupert's Land, A.A. Taché, supported by Cartier, Manitobans were assured of state-funded denominational schools. Yet, in a very significant way, Manitoba's provincial status was unique, or as W.L. Morton preferred to call it, biased. As with the remainder of the North-West territories, the Federal Government retained exclusive control over all Crown lands in order to use them to entice settlement under the terms of the Dominion Lands Act and as a lucrative subsidy for any prospective railroad company undertaking to build a transcontinental railway. Fearing for his life from those seeking revenge for Scott's death, Riel fled to the U.S. once a British military expedition found its way into the region. He would only return fifteen years later to lead a second much more fateful Métis uprising in the Batoche region of the North-West.

On the verge of bankruptcy, the colony of British Columbia was virtually driven into Confederation after the collapse of the Gold rush. The British Colonial Office was eager to rid itself of this liability and send out a new governor, Anthony Musgrave, in 1869 to entice the 10,000 non-native residents to enter Confederation. Macdonald was eager to make a deal and British Columbia was offered and accepted generous terms. On July 20, 1871, Ottawa assumed the colony's heavy debt load, provided an annual subsidy, undertook a public works programme, and to begin construction of a railway line within three years and complete it within a decade. British Columbians acquired responsible government and six members in the House of Commons. The recession of the 1870s threatened to jeopardize the transcontinental railway project but after much protest British Columbians were able to reach central Canada via the CPR in 1885.

The Garden of the Gulf, Prince Edward Island, was cause of some concern to the PM. The colonists were desperate to resolve the issue of the absentee landlords while the ruling elite rebuffed the initial terms of union offered by Cartier and Tilley in 1869 seeking instead a reciprocity agreement with the United States. A flurry of railroad construction after 1870, based on public credit, put the colony into financial hardship. When the Colonial Office refused further guarantees for Island bonds and British financial institutions withdrew, PEI politicians were driven to plead with the Canadian government to join the federation. In 1873, Canada agreed but on less generous terms than were offered to BC. The railway debt was assumed, a subsidy was granted, a commitment was made to resolve the absentee landlord issue, a communications link to the mainland was guaranteed, and the Island gained six seats in the House of commons. But 1873, the fledgling Dominion was a vast, uncharted, unpopulated territory stretching from the Atlantic to the Pacific. Its leaders faced the enormous challenge of turning the dream of a modern nation-state into a reality.

Economic Nationalism, Railways, and Industrialization

The key to meeting this challenge was the creation of vibrant, integrated economy capable of generating profits for investors, jobs for Canadians, and revenues for public services. Standing at the cutting edge of the revolution were the railway and the Iron Horse. The exploitation of Canada's immense natural resources, the commercialization of agriculture, the settlement of the fertile belt of the North-West, and the development of large-scale manu-facturing, required an integrated system of nation and regional modes of transportation, including canals, waterways and the railways. As with the British and colonial governments, Canadian governments maintained and expanded the canals and waterways while focusing much of their energy and public resources on the rapid expansion of railways.

The Canadian government pushed ahead, at considerable cost of taxpayers, with the construction of the publicly-funded and administered intercolonial railway to the east coast. It could not afford the same approach with the transcontinental to the west coast. In 1972 Cartier was mandated to strike a deal with a private sector consortium by offering attractive public incentives in the from of land grants, subsidies, and loan guarantees. Two syndicates, one in Toronto led by Senator David MacPherson and a second in Montreal led by Hugh Allan, competed vigorously for the lucrative contract, $30 million in public funds and 20 million hectares of land, to build the Canadian Pacific Railway to the west coast. Unfortunately for the Macdonald government, which received a second razor thin majority of six seats in the election of 1872, the CPR project was implicated in scandal. His government was charged by the Liberal opposition of granting the lucrative CPR charter to the Montreal syndicate of Hugh Allan in the Fall of 1872, in return for

$320,000 of contributions to the Conservative Party during the election. A Royal Commission confirmed the charge and revealed that the syndicate's principal investors were American. Allan relinquished the Charter and PM Macdonald, facing a vote of non-confidence in the House, resigned on November 5, 1872.

The Interim Liberal administration of Alexander Mackenzie, comprised of pro- and anti-confederate Liberal and Rouges, easily won the election of 1874. The Liberal Government's railway policy, in reality though not in theory, differed little from that of the Conservatives. The intercolonial was completed, linking Halifax to the Grand Trunk system at Rivière du Loup by 1876. Given the severity of the recession in which exports, imports, and government revenues and corporate profits declined sharply, no syndicate came forward to build the CPR. The government concentrated on the completion of a railway/waterway system from the head of Lake Superior to Winnipeg and postponed the line to the west coast. Following vigorous protest from British Columbia and pressure from London, PM Mackenzie administration only agreed to extend the deadline to 1890 in return for building the Esquimalt and Nanaimo railways.

By 1878, the Mackenzie government experienced growing pressures from the Canadian manufacturing interests experiencing relentless competition for U.S. firms dumping their products on the Canadian market. Even Liberals were asking the government to increase tariffs to offset the decline in revenues but PM Mackenzie remained wedded to his Liberal principles of free trade and non-intervention in the economy. Sensing a great political opportunity, the Conservative Party responded to the crisis during the election of 1878 by offering Canadian voters the National Policy, that is, tariffs set at a rate sufficiently high to prevent foreign dumping and to encourage domestic foreign investors to create a fully-developed, self-sufficient Canadian industrial economy based on the U.A. model. Other dimensions of the Conservative agenda of economic nationalism entailed a promise to complete forthwith the CPR and to use the railway and the offer of free public land to attract immigrants to settle in the North-West and turn the region into the bread basket of Canada and the world. Disgruntled voters agreed and returned the Conservatives to office where they remained until the mid-1890s.

Two aspects of the national policy were relatively easy to implement. Tariffs were raised to between 20 and 35 per cent depending upon the product setting off an investment binge in manufacturing in the four original provinces. Thousands of jobs were created preventing the need for Canadians, established and recently-arrived, to seek their fortune south of the border.

Federal Government revenues rose dramatically allowing it to invest more heavily in public infrastructure. PM Macdonald pursued aggressively the completion of the CPR. In February 1881 a new charter was granted to a syndicate headed up by two railway tycoons, George Stephen, president of the Bank of Montreal, and Donald Smith, chief factor of the Hudson's Bay Company. In return for completing the transcontinental railway, the CPR syndicate received a subsidy of $25 million, 10 million hectares of fertile Prairie land, and government-owned sections of railways in Ontario and BC valued at $30 million. CPR property was free of taxation in perpetuity and no competitor was allowed to run South-East of its line. Before the American contractor, William Van Horne, could complete the project, the syndicate, despite howls of protest from both sides of the House, demanded and received a $30 million dollar loan guarantee and further subsidies from the Federal Government. In return, the government had to subsidize regional lines in Quebec and the Maritimes and the CPR had to make Quebec City and Saint John termini. Unplanned, the CPR became Canada's first transcontinental corporation.

The cost to taxpayers was enormous yet appeared justified when the CPR enabled Ottawa to rush troops to the far North-West territories to quell the second Riel Rebellion in the Batoche region during March, April and May, 1985. Many of Manitoba's disgruntled and disinherited Métis had settled along the banks of the South Saskatchewan river and intended to link up with starving Cree Bands of the North Saskatchewan river area to rid the region of the Ottawa's presence, namely government officials and the North-west Mounted Police. Some 8,000 men were sent West via the CPR to re-establish law and order in the region. Riel and the Cree leaders, Poundmaker and Big Bear, upon surrendering were tried. The Cree chiefs were jailed and eight rebels were hung. Riel, the messianic leader, was found guilty of high treason and was hanged in Regina on November 16, 1885. This violent suppression of the Indian and Métis communities was devastating. Along with the destruction of the buffalo herd and the reservation system, the end of the rebellion ushered in a long period of decline and destitution of these visibly proud and self-reliant peoples.

PM Macdonald and his cabinet did what they had to do for reasons of the fledgling nation's security. Yet, there were political ramifications for his government and party in Ontario and Quebec. British-Canadian Protestant opinion leaders in Ontario and the Maritimes applauded Macdonald's aggressive response to the rebellion and rejoiced at Riel's hanging, sweet and justified revenge for Scott's murder they claimed. French-Canadian Catholics, portraying Riel as a defender of the beleaguered French-Canadian Catholic nationality in the West, pleaded for royal clemency for Riel on the grounds of insanity. French-Canadian nationalists, journalists, Church officials, and the public pressured French-Canadian cabinet ministers to resign but to no avail. The hanging of Riel constituted one more nail in the coffin of the once powerful Quebec Conservative party. In 1887, Honoré Mercier's minority provincial Liberal Government gained office thanks to the support of Ultramontane Conservatives who had bolted their party over the Riel affair. By 1891, Wilfrid Laurier's National Liberal Party absorbed into its ranks many disgruntled moderate Conservatives, thereby setting the stage for the Liberal Party's takeover of Quebec and Laurier's becoming PM in 1896. Socio-economic, demographic, and ideological transformations in the Ontario and Quebec societies contributed to the slow but inevitable decline of the once dominant Macdonald/Cartier Conservative Party.

Canadian-American Relations

The fact that Canada was created in defiance of the North-South thrust of the continent's geography and the 'manifest destiny' imperative of Americans' rather bellicose nationalism meant that, at the very least, the relationship with our southern neighbour would be frought with tension. This was especially so given that Ottawa had no jurisdiction over foreign diplomacy and trade issues. Outstanding matters related to the civil war, boundary disputes, and fishing rights had to be discussed via the British foreign office in London and the British High Commission in Washington. In 1871, PM Macdonald was invited to join the British delegation involved in a joint British/US commission to negotiate the Treaty of Washington. Macdonald's objective was to get a new reciprocity treaty in return for US access to the Canadian fisheries. The British, eager to withdraw their troops from Canada and restore good relations with the United States, were very conciliatory with the Americans at Canada's expense. Macdonald returned home virtually empty handed while Americans gained access to the fisheries and unimpeded navigation of the St. Lawrence River. Ottawa agreed to ratify the lopsided deal only when the British agreed to provide compensation for the costs involved.

Despite the national policy, Macdonald remained wedded to his objective of obtaining limited reciprocity with the United States, especially in primary products, in return for American access to the Maritime fisheries. When the United States refused to negotiate, the PM authorized in 1886 and 1887 the seizure of hundreds of American fishing boats. The U.S. President threatened to terminate all trade with Canada. The Americans and the British set up a Joint High Commission in 1887 to resolve the matter but, once again, Canada's interests were sacrificed on the altar of British-American diplomacy. There would be no reciprocity in primary products. The Americans would withdraw from the inshore fishery while Canadians could sell fish in the U.S. market in return for granting Americans access to Canadian ports. Yet, Macdonald did not give up. When the new Republican Government introduced even higher tariffs on farm products in 1890, the PM lobbied the American administration via the British Ambassador for a free trade agreement. When the public and irate Republican Congressmen became aware of the secret negotiations, Washington quickly withdrew. This left Macdonald with no option but to defend vigorously his National Policy and the Canadian state from the protectionist Americans and from the Liberal free traders.

A fascination/paranoia syndrome characterized Canadians perceptions of the United States during these formative years. A young Wilfrid Laurier, inherited in 1887 the leadership of a Liberal Party that was deeply divided over fundamental economic policies, especially the issue of free trade with the United States. Edward Blake, leader between 1880 an 1887, had become reconciled to the National Policy. Meanwhile Richard Cartwright from Ontario and J.W. Longley from Nova Scotia championed a concept of 'commercial union', that is free trade, with the United States with a common set of trade barriers against the rest of the world, including Great Britain. Mackenzie and Blake objected that 'commercial union' opened the Liberal Party to the charge of disloyalty from the Conservative Party. The ardent free traders then adopted the policy of 'unrestricted reciprocity' with the United States. Laurier accepted this new policy in time for the 1891 election but he and his colleagues had great difficulty in convincing sceptical Canadians that 'unrestricted reciprocity' was not just a stepping stone to 'commercial union' and then to political annexation with the United States. Backed by the major beneficiaries of the National Policy, the CPR and the Canadian Manufacturing Association, the moribund Conservative Party wrapped itself in the rhetoric of loyalty to the British Empire. Strong Loyalist sentiment in the Maritimes and Ontario won the election for the Tories. The Liberal defeat allowed Blake to denounce his party's policy of unrestricted reciprocity. The ambitious and increasingly pragmatic Laurier worked hard over the next two years to convince the party to abandon, in practice if not in theory, its quest for free trade with the United States.

Provincial Rights on the March

During the formative years, Canada's national political and economic leaders were preoccupied with turning the dream of a nation-state into reality. Little attention was paid to the needs and aspirations of the provincial political and economic elites. Yet, it was only a matter of time until those elites would begin to pursue an interpretation of the constitutional rules of 1867 which would benefit both themselves, their electorates, and provincial institutions. In theory, with its control over the Lieutenant Governors, the judicial system, transfer payments, and its extensive power of disallowance, the national government was greater than the sum of its provincial parts. By the 1890s, the highly centralist Macdonaldian constitution had been laid to rest. As a result of political, socio-economic and juridical developments, it had been replaced by a more decentralized federal system, one in which both the central and provincial governments where sovereign entities within the fields of jurisdiction assigned to them by the British North America Act. This development did not end federal/provincial disputes but rather ensured that those disputes would become institutionalized within a framework of federal/provincial diplomacy.

Oliver Mowat's Ontario, the largest and most prosperous of the Canadian provinces, would lead the way in this process of province building during the 1870s and 1880s. Premier Mowat had three objectives: increase the territory of the province to incorporate the vast region north of the Great Lakes all the way to James Bay and Manitoba; exercise sovereignty over all the areas of provincial jurisdiction and have, if necessary, that sovereignty confirmed by the courts; and curtail the role of the Federal Government so as to limit its need to tax Ontario's citizens. A Commission appointed by PM Mackenzie recommended in 1878 that the territory of the Hudson's Bay should be amalgamated to Ontario. Macdonald, returning as PM that year, refused to accept this proposal and stalled. The matter was referred to the Judicial Committee of the Privy Council in London which supported Ontario's well-documented arguments for annexation. The province's potential economic wealth and political power had grown enormously.

Mowat pressed his growing advantage by legislating in a wide range of areas. Initially, Ottawa disallowed much of the legislation and its actions were upheld by the courts during the 1870s. But, in a series of important decisions during the 1880s, the JCPC irrevocably changed the nature of federal/provincial relations. To begin, decisions in 1881 and 1882 severely curtailed Ottawa's ability to regulate trade and commerce with provincial boundaries. Then, the JCPC, in the Hodge v. The Queen decision of 1883 and expanded upon in subsequent cases, ruled that the provinces were sovereign entities within areas of their own jurisdiction. A highly centralized federation in theory evolved into a form of quasi-classical federalism of equal and coordinate sovereign entities. Province-building had acquired juridical sanction and it was not long before provincial political elites exploited that advantage.

In 1886, Nova Scotia's fiscally hard-pressed Liberal Government of W.S. Fielding, seeking a re-election issue, passed a motion sanctioning secession from Confederation. The Liberals handily won re-election in 1886 but Fielding, finding little sympathy in official London for secession, and having no constitutional secessionist mechanism to invoke, simply procrastinated until the economic situation improved. Nova Scotia's political clout was marginal at best and Ottawa need only to temporize while the province became increasingly integrated into the federal structure.

Province-building in Quebec was delayed momentarily by the fact that the National Conservative Party and government controlled their provincial counterparts. This situation came to an end in 1886 when the longstanding division between the Conservative Party's moderate pro-business and ultramontane pro-Catholic Church wings erupted into a full-blown schism. Honoré Mercier, the Liberal leader, formed the *Parti National* in 1886 hoping to capitalize on Riel's hanging and attract disgruntled conservatives into the fold. Mercier who won a plurality of the seats in the election was only able to form a *Parti National* government in 1887 with the support of a handful of successful ultramontane candidates who exacted a price for their support. Pressured by these *nationalistes* and eager to gain better financial terms and greater control over judicial appointments, Premier Mercier convened the first interprovincial conference in 1887 to rally support of other disaffected provincial governments. Liberal Premiers from Nova Scotia, New Brunswick, Ontario, and Quebec, along with the Conservative Premier of Manitoba, discussed common grievances and issued a declaration. They called for the abolition of Ottawa's power of disallowance, provincial control over appointments to the Senate and provincial courts, and substantially improved financial arrangement for the revenue starved provincial treasuries. PM Macdonald simply denounced this exercise of provincial solidarity as one of political partisanship and ignored the legitimacy of the provincial resolutions. Yet, it was clear by the late 1880s that the process of province building was well under way and would only gain political momentum as demographic and economic developments worked in their favour. Ottawa, henceforth, would have to exercise its circumscribed constitutional powers more diplomatically while learning and applying the complex federal/provincial game of divide and rule. Indeed, Ottawa would find just the right leader for that exercise in Wilfrid Laurier.

II. The Nation Transformed, Laurier and Borden, 1896-1920

Mastering the Discipline of Power

The national election of 1896 came to symbolize a major watershed in Canadian political history. The Conservative Party, in constant disarray following the death of Macdonald in 1891, was swept from office after exercising power, except for one term, ever since 1867. A handsome, charming, eloquent, and aristocratic-looking Wilfrid Laurier, formally confirmed as leader of the Liberal Party by delegates attending the first national political party convention held on June 20, 1893, became Canada's first French-Canadian, Catholic Prime Minister with a comfortable 30 seat majority. Under his skilful guidance, the Liberal Party finally achieved the stature of a national party, one capable of representing and mediating between competing interests from all parts of the country. Under Laurier' watchful eye, his national government would quickly master the discipline of power thereby ensuring four consecutive administrations for him and the Liberal Party.

Over time, the Laurier era became synonymous with the demographic, social and economic transformation of Canada. Yet, perhaps because of this remarkable restructuring of the Canada's economy and its social fabric, PM Laurier became quintessentially conservative in his social values and outlook. He firmly considered procedural liberalism as the best means of resolving old cleavages involving religion, regionalism, cultural and linguistic diversity, and new cleavages around emerging gender and class differences. With Quebec as the political bastion and power base of the Liberal Party and government, PM Laurier made his peace with the Catholic Church. He did so by respecting its hard-won authority over all education and social matters and by using his enormous influence to keep successive Quebec provincial Liberal Governments from becoming too socially progressive and economically interventionist.

The first clear indication of Laurier's skills as a conciliator came with the thorny Manitoba schools question which remained unresolved since it erupted on the national scene in 1890. A strong supporter of provincial autonomy, Laurier rejected the Conservative government's proposed remedial legislation forcing Manitoba to restore public funding to Manitoba's Catholic schools. Instead, once he was PM he negotiated an agreement with the Liberal Greenway government of Manitoba whereby the Public School Boards would have to hire Catholic teachers for every 25 Catholic students in rural schools and 40 Catholic students in urban schools. If there were 10 students who spoke French or any other language than English, instruction had to be provided in that alternate language. Finally, students would receive religious instruction in the last half hour of the school day. While Manitoba's largely rural French-Canadian Catholics were satisfied with the compromise, Catholic Church leaders in Manitoba and Quebec were furious that state-funded Catholic School system had not been restored and appealed to the Papacy for support. Laurier's emissaries convinced the Papacy to accept the Manitoba settlement as the best one possible under the circumstances and the papal encyclical *Affari Vos* so advised a reluctant French-Canadian clergy. As a result, many continued to mistrust Laurier for his former membership in the radical Rouge party which was committed to separation of Church and State. Still Laurier managed to develop an effective working relationship with the French-Canadian Catholic Church through Bishop Bruchési of Montreal.

The matter of tax-supported denominational schools emerged again in 1905 when Ottawa created the provinces of Saskatchewan and Alberta out of the Northwest Territories. Concerned with placating the Catholic Church and opening the west to French-Canadian settlers, PM Laurier attempted to restore in the new provinces the public Catholic and Protestant School systems which successive territorial governments had replaced with a public system. While certain members of Cabinet threatened resignation, the Minister of the Interior, Clifford Sifton, did resign. A shaken Laurier allowed Sifton to amend the Autonomy Bills restoring only those minority rights which existed in 1901. The French-Canadian clergy, backed by the outspoken nationalist leader, Henri Bourassa and the newly-formed *Ligue nationaliste,* denounced the compromise as an insult to one of Canada's two founding peoples because it placed them on the same level as the immigrants. On other divisive social issues such as prohibition and the Lord's Day, Laurier either temporized or side-stepped. When the 1898 plebiscite on prohibition revealed the gulf between English and French Canada, Laurier ignored the results. Pressured to pass a Lord's Day Act in 1906, he shrewdly passed its administration over to the provinces. Laurier's 'sunny ways' style of politics helped his government retain office in the elections of 1900, 1904, and 1908. Soon thereafter, his approach became a liability as more Canadians polarized around competing French-Canadian and British-Canadian nationalisms representing divergent domestic and foreign visions of Canada.

Prometheus Unbound: The Twentieth Century Belongs to Canada

In theory, the Laurier Liberal Party remained loyal to economic *laissez faire* principles of non-intervention and free trade in order to retain the support of farmers and natural resource producers. Canadians, envious of what their southern neighbours had managed to accomplish through the industrial revolution, were determined to emulate American economic nationalist policies in order to replicate their success. Consequently, the quest for material progress forced Laurier's government to keep the National Policy of tariffs for protection of manufacturers, Canadian, British and American, firmly in place. It also meant that the Laurier government would promote aggressively, thanks to state financial and land incentives, the two other dimensions of the national policy, namely the rapid settlement of the western region via immigration and the construction of two more national transcontinental railways.

Laurier's 'cabinet-of-all-talents', replete with members of the rising bourgeoisie and reflecting linguistic, religious and regional cleavages, was overwhelmingly protectionist, sending a huge sigh of relief through the fledgling boardrooms of central Canada. The Minister of Finance, W.S. Fielding, retained the existing tariff structure with modest concessions to the farmers. To appease free traders and British Canadian nationalists, in 1897 he introduced legislation granting a 12.5 per cent, increased to 25 per cent the next year, tariff preference to countries offering Canada reciprocal rates. British manufacturers, because of the United Kingdom's free trade policies, qualified immediately for the preferential duties allowing them to compete more effectively with American imports. An intermediate schedule of tariffs was introduced in 1907, prompting the signing of limited reciprocal trade deals with Japan, Italy and France. The government retained the allegiance of its free traders while keeping the National Policy in place.

"Railways, and more Railways!" became the clarion call of western farmers who distrusted the monopoly of the CPR and who were anxious to get their bumper wheat crops to markets in Great Britain and western Europe. While governments at provincial and municipal levels helped fund local and regional lines with land grants and bond guaranteed, the Laurier government felt similarly pressured to underwrite the construction of, not one, but two national transcontinental railways. Flush with surplus revenues and determined to expedite the rapid expansion of the Western cereal grain production destined for foreign markets, Laurier's government helped William Mackenzie and Donald Mann extend their Canadian Northern Railway, running from central Canada to Winnipeg, all the way to the Pacific coast. The long-established Grand Trunk corporation also wished to get into the transcontinental business in order to protect its market share of freight and passenger service in central Canada. The Grand Trunk Pacific was granted a charter to build a railway from Winnipeg to Prince Rupert, British Columbia. In return the GTP received a government guarantee of 75 per cent on its bonds and the right to lease at 3 per cent of its cost per annum the government constructed railway stretching 3,000 km from Winnipeg to Moncton, New Brunswick via Quebec City.

Virtually every interest group including the farmers, the manufacturers, the retailers and wholesalers, the railway corporations and contractors, the largely immigrant labour force, and the politicians benefited from this railway mania. It was the taxpayers who were left to pay the lion's share of the costs for decades. Yet, the vast majority supported the policy believing that Canada could only prosper economically and survive politically if it built an integrated east-west economy. Neither line was completed by 1911 and both faced bankruptcy by the end of the war thanks to rampant corruption and flagrant mismanagement. The Borden government, fearing the impact of any railway default on its financial position, felt compelled to amalgamate and nationalize both lines into the Canadian National Railways network which expanded dramatically throughout the 1920s.

On the other hand, the Laurier government's approach to financial and industrial capitalism was strictly *laissez-faire*. Corporate taxes were minimal and capital-gains and personal income taxes non-existent. Canada's increasingly large chartered banks, thanks to rapid consolidation, and other financial institutions expanded topsy-turvey as did their profits. Investment in manufacturing and the output of production easily surpassed a billion dollars each by 1910. In order to temper excessive competition while generating lavish profits for themselves and investors, a new generation of financial *gurus,* lead by Montreal's Max Aitken, later Lord Beaverbrook, carried out a series of mergers and cartels in all the major manufacturing sectors from construction materials to food processing. The government made a largely futile gesture to curtail the formation of monopolies and restore meaningful competition through the Combines Investigation Act, first introduced in 1889 and redrafted in 1910. Unfortunately from Labour's perspective, the Act was virtually unenforceable. As a result of this unfettered capitalism, inflation increased substantially by 1910 thereby robbing the largely non-unionized industrial workers, especially the unskilled women and children, of any gains in wages over the decade. The Liberal Government continued the tradition of undermining the fledgling union movement by sending in the militia to break up strikes, illegal or otherwise, whenever requested by the provinces or the corporations on the pretext of protecting private property and maintaining law and order. Faced with an increased number of prolonged and, at times violent strikes, the Laurier government passed the Industrial Disputes Investigation Act in 1907 to ban strikes and lockouts in mines and public utility corporations until a three-person commission had made a report to both parties and the government. Mediation and conciliation, accepted only reluctantly by business, rather than compulsory arbitration, favoured by organized labour, characterized the government's approach to labour/corporate conflict during this era of industrial expansion. The corporate sector was considered to be government's partner in nation building and could not be unduly restrained in its efforts to create jobs and wealth.

Robert Borden and the Politics of 'Progressive' Conservatism

The Laurier era was brought to an end in the tumultuous election of 1911 by an ambitious Nova Scotia Lawyer turned seasoned politician, Robert Borden. The task was far from easy. Starting in 1900, Borden remade the stodgy, ineffectual Conservative party over into his image of a 'progressive', business-oriented political machine capable of attracting support from the emerging provincial Conservative governments, as well as a wide cross-section voters experiencing profound economic and social dislocation. He did so by forging, over time, a loose coalition of French-Canadian and British-Canadian nationalist movements, the feminist organizations, the prohibition movement, as well as a wide range of other social reform groups which had come of age during this era of frenetic organization, secularization, and professionalization.

Responding to the public's growing distaste for the entrenched politics of patronage in all its forms, Borden committed his party to cleaning up the system of bribes and kickbacks for government construction contracts, procurement of goods and services, and civil servant positions. Borden formulated quite 'progressive' proposals in his Halifax programme of 1906 drawn up after consulting selected MPs, certain business people and Conservative premiers. He promised to end the system of patronage and replace it with a cost effective business style system of government which issued tenders for goods and services and was staffed by civil servants appointed on the merit principle. Other proposals included the need for government regulation of certain services such as telephones and, government nationalization of natural resources to ensure the public a fair return on its property. Borden wanted a reorganized Conservative party and a government to be operated on modern business principles and practices to ensure that they serve the interests of all the citizens rather than those of business and industry. This was heady idealism. Yet Borden's determined gamble paid off as more and more Canadians voted for Conservative candidates in every election beginning in 1900. It was the age of business as management and social progressivism in North America and Borden tapped into both streams and reaped all the political rewards.

In 1911, PM Laurier hoped to achieve a fifth consecutive electoral victory by offering Canadian voters a tangible financial gain in the form of a free trade agreement with the United States. Cheaper farm equipment and foodstuffs would benefit both farmers and urban workers hard-pressed by inflation and ever-rising prices. A reciprocity treaty would allow Laurier to ride above the divisive socio-economic issues generated by an open-door immigration policy and untrammeled industrial/urban expansion. Initially, even Borden despaired at the thought of yet another Laurier victory. Sensing a ground swell of opposition to freer trade from pro-British business and organized labour communities in central Canada, Borden and his caucus prevented the ratification of the Reciprocity Treaty before Laurier was forced to adjourn Parliament so he could attend the Imperial Conference in London.

The opposition forces, represented by the Canadian Home Market Association, the Canadian National League, 18 Toronto 'former-Liberal' entrepreneurs, four Conservative Provincial Premiers, and the nationalist/ Tory alliance of Henri Bourassa and Frederick Monk in Quebec, had gained two months of precious time to coalesce around Borden's leadership and his 'progressive' Conservative Party. It was an impressive political machine when compared with the aging and dispirited Liberal political party, especially in Ontario where British-Canadian nationalist sentiment over Laurier's detested Reciprocity and Naval Service Acts was running rampant thereby encouraging a great many moderate Liberals to switch sides. Indeed, Borden used the debate over Reciprocity to reassert his control over reluctant old-line Tories in the Caucus and the party. He went into the election confident of becoming Prime Minister. Laurier soon realized that gains in the newly-created Western provinces were not enough to offset the expected lose of seats—16—in Quebec to the Bourassa/Monk alliance nor the expected greater loss of seats—25—in Ontario. Borden's 'progressive' Conservative coalition scored a stunning victory with a comfortable majority of 134 seats and reducing the once powerful Liberals to 87 seats, the large majority from Quebec. The great transformation of the Laurier years has produced a momentary political realignment. The challenge facing Borden was whether or not he would be able to consolidate that realignment so that he could govern for as many terms as Laurier.

Unlike any other Prime Minister, Borden's political leadership skills would be put to the test more often and more severely during his nearly ten years as PM. Out of office for fifteen years, many stalwart Conservatives clamoured for every conceivable government job or contract thereby making a mockery of Borden's promise of clean and efficient government. Civil service reform and the curtailment of patronage would not come until the conditions of war enabled him to override opposition in caucus and cabinet.

Indeed, forming his cabinet quickly brought home the message that politics is always the art of the possible. He was compelled to name the nationalist Tory Frederick Monk, a lightweight with little influence in his own province, to the Ministry of Public Works. W.T. White, one of renegade Liberal members of the Toronto 18 businessmen, became Minister of Finance. Colonel Sam Hughes, a blustering incompetent who had backed Borden through thick and thin, became Minister of Militia and Defence, and would undermine severely the government's war effort with his cronyism and prejudice toward French Canadians and Catholics. Borden's attempts at reforming the tariff and sorting out the railway mess were stalled but he did manage to set up the Board of Grain commissioners to regulate the grain trade. By the fall of 1913, when immigration peaked at some 400,000 arrivals, the government was faced with the most serious recession since the 1890s. It was triggered by the rapid withdrawal of British investment, a development that would accentuate during and after the war forcing Canadian businesses to look increasingly to the United States for investment capital. The invisible economic ties that had long bound Canada to the Empire were being eroded. There appeared little that Borden or anyone else could do to reverse this trend which would accelerate dramatically in the 1920s

Laurier, Borden and the Imperial Connection

To strengthen Canada's economic ties with the Empire, in 1897 Laurier's Finance Minister, William Fielding, instituted a preferential tariff of 25 per cent for British Manufacturers as a gesture of gratitude for its free trade policy toward Canadian agricultural products. Unfortunately, many British manufactured products were poorly designed for the Canadian context and Canadians relied increasingly upon domestic and American branch-plants to fill their expanding requirements. Laurier's eagerness to strengthen economic ties with Great Britain was driven by self-interest and not by any desire for closer political and military ties. Laurier was a strong Canadian but he was not convinced, unlike his Quebec colleague Henri Bourassa, that time was ripe for Canada to seek the status of an independent nation-state outside the Empire. Neither did Laurier believe that Canada should seek to play a greater role in world affairs through the Empire as suggested by Borden and the British-Canadian nationalists. As long as a consensus eluded Canadians, it was preferable for their government to retain the status quo.

Laurier appeased the British Canadian nationalist by participation in the ceremonial trappings of the Empire such as Queen Victoria's Golden Jubilee

Celebrations in 1897. Similarly, he bowed to the concerns of the French-Canadian nationalists by adroitly resisting any formal involvement in Imperial affairs. When in 1899 the British government requested Canadian troops to help them defeat the Boers in South Africa, the Laurier government responded with an offer to raise and transport 1,000 volunteers to South Africa where they would fight under British officers and be paid from the British treasury. British Canadian nationalists denounced Laurier for doing too little. Henri Bourassa resigned from the cabinet because he believed the war against the Boers was unjust and the decision to send some 7,000 volunteers created a serious precedent for further involvement in Imperial wars.

In conference after conference Laurier rejected Joseph Chamberlain's—the colonial secretary—centralizing schemes for an expanded Royal Navy with grants from the colonies and an imperial Federation Parliament to hash out a common foreign and defence policies. The Laurier government's defeat over the issue of the Alaska boundary in 1903, thanks to the decision of the British appointee, Lord Alverston, to support the American claim, merely confirmed Laurier's view that Imperial foreign and defence policy would always be dictated by British priorities and not by those of the colonies. When the race between Britain and Germany for naval superiority escalated in 1908-09, Laurier once again faced enormous pressures from both the British authorities and the British-Canadian public to make an emergency contribution to the dreadnought construction programme. Instead, in 1910 Laurier responded with his Naval Bill whereby Canada would acquire a Navy of five cruisers and six destroyers that could, with the approval of Parliament, be put at the disposal of the British Royal Navy in times of war.

The compromise enraged both nationalist movements. In Quebec Henri Bourassa was the uncontested leader of a growing nationalist movement. He created a newspaper, *Le Devoir,* to denounce imperialism in general and the Laurier government's sell-out of Canadians to British interests. In concert with the nationalist Tory, Monk, he demanded that such an important issue as the Naval Bill be put to Canadians in a referendum. Laurier was put on the defensive in his home province as was shown by the defeat of the Liberal candidate in the 1910 Drummond Arthabaska by-election by a unknown nationaliste candidate. Borden, emboldened by Tory premiers and a jingoistic press, supported the creation a Canadian navy but demanded that Canada also make an emergency contribution to the dreadnought programme. Borden's approach appealed to both moderate and extreme British-Canadian nationalists across the land. He was amply rewarded with their votes in the election of 1911.

In fact, Borden had no more luck than Laurier in addressing the Imperial question. Borden was driven by British-Canadian nationalist belief that greater Canadian participation in the military affairs of the Empire would bring Canada a greater role in the determination of imperial defence and foreign policy. Canada would achieve its independence through the Empire. Responding to a new request from Britain for an emergency grant for the construction of dreadnoughts, Borden visited Britain and received representation on the Imperial Defence Committee but only when matters concerning Canada were being discussed. Upon receiving secret reports of the crisis facing the British navy from the German fleet, Borden introduced his Naval Aid Bill to the House in December 1912 granting Britain $35 million for the construction of dreadnoughts. After five months of bitter debate in the House the government was forced to use closure, the first time in Canadian history, to bring the Bill to a vote on May 15, 1913. It was all a waste of time and energy since the Naval Aid Bill was duly defeated in the Liberal dominated Senate. On the verge of the World War I, the prolonged and bitter debate over Canada's relationship with the British Empire had not been resolved to the satisfaction of either the French-Canadian or British-Canadian nationalists. The war would tip the balance in favour of the latter group.

The Crucible of War: A Nation is Born

Thousands of British Canadians went to war in October 1914 with high enthusiasm as members of a quasi-colony of the British Empire. Those fortunate enough to return home in 1918-19 did so as proud citizens of a full-fledged member of a bloodied but mature nation-state. The hundreds of thousands of Canadians who fought the war on the home front in a variety of ways could also take credit that their efforts had made the sacrifices of the 60,000 dead and 173,000 wounded, out of a total force of some 650,000 men and women, somewhat easier to accept if not totally comprehend.

The political unanimity in favour of Canadian participation obscured the reality that Canada was ill-prepared to send its poorly-trained and ill-equipped young citizen-soldiers off to do battle on the smelly, muddy and nightmarish killing fields of northern France and Belgium. Under the direction of the self-righteous and interfering Sam Hughes, minister of militia, Canadian volunteers were gathered and trained at a new camp built at Valcartier, Quebec. Distrusting all regular officers, Hughes recruited largely British-Canadians, first generation and recent immigrants, through the local militia units spread across the country. The first contingent of men was organized into the Canadian Division under a British Officer, Gen.

E.A.H. Anderson. Following further training in England, Canadian soldiers experienced the full brunt of trench warfare in April 1915 at Ypres when they faced, along with the French, the first of many German gas attacks. While the German attack was eventually repelled, over half of the Canadian 2nd and 3rd brigades were wounded, killed or taken prisoner. It was not a very auspicious beginning but it did not seem to put a damper on recruitment.

By the December of 1915, Canada had three divisions at the front organized into a Corps initially under Gen. Anderson and then commanded by Lieut-Gen. Julien Bying after the difficult battle of St. Eloi Craters in April 1916. By August a fourth division joined the Corps putting 80,000 men in direct action while a fifth division was kept in reserve in Britain. In all, some 500,000 men and women were enlisted in the Canadian army by mid-1916 with the number reaching over 650,000 by the end. Canada's citizen-soldiers performed remarkably well considering Sam Hughes's sloppy administration of the Department of Militia and Defence and the constant interference of his spies into the army's General Headquarters in England. Despite hundreds of complaints about the unreliability of the Ross Rifle, it jammed constantly when conditions were bad, Hughes refused to consider replacing it with the British Lee-Enfield. Only after the high casualties of the battle of St. Eloi Craters did the cabinet overrule Hughes and provided the soldiers with Lee-Enfields. Despite his loyalty to Hughes, Borden was forced to strip him of his powers by creating a Ministry of Overseas Military Forces in London under the Canadian High Commissioner. Hughes resigned in November 1916.

Following the ferocious, deadly, and ineptly planned battles of the Somme campaign in the summer and fall of 1916, Canadian officers and politicians finally realized the lack of imagination and originality of the Imperial General Staff led by Gen. Sir Douglas Haig. The campaign had produced over a half million casualties with virtually nothing to show in terms of concrete results. By the spring of 1917 the nature of warfare began to alter as tanks and aircrafts were introduced into the battles and officers abandoned trench warfare for well-planned lightning strikes into enemy territory. After months of planning and preparations, the Canadian Corps participated in the comprehensive April 9, 1917 assault on the seemingly impregnable Vimy Ridge long held by the German forces allowing them to dominate the region. The massive barrage of very accurate artillery fire and the determination of the Canadian soldiers enabled them to take Vimy Ridge at a cost of over 10,000 casualties, one-third of their assault force. Canadian Military historians contend that this was the moment that the Canadian Forces gained confidence in themselves and their tremendous abilities.

Recognizing this achievement, the British promoted the brilliant tactician and 1st Division commander, Arthur Currie, to commander of the Canadian Crops. The well-deserved victory at Vimy Ridge, along with several more which came during the successful fall campaign of 1918, did much to accelerate Canada's transition from colony to nation.

The War on the Homefront

The war brought about a fundamental shift in that attitude of Canadians toward the role of the state. Through its War Measures Act, Ottawa gave itself a comprehensive range of powers which it eventually applied to all the social, economic and political aspects of Canadian life. The press was heavily censored as were communications between the front lines and the home front. Canadians would learn about all the gruesome aspects of modern warfare and the bungling of the British officers only when the disgruntled soldiers returned home. Ottawa interned over eight thousand enemy aliens for the duration of the war without as much as a single complaint from a politician. Nationalist hysteria prevented clear thinking on most issues and rendered all critics of the government suspect of working for the Kaiser.

At the outset the families of soldiers were looked after through a charitable organisations called the Canadian Patriotic Fund while the non-military needs of men overseas were attended to by organizations such as the YMCA. Soon, government agencies had to supplement the valiant efforts of these agencies. The major preoccupation of the government was to ensure the smooth supply of foodstuffs and munitions to the war effort. When it became clear that the Shell Committee, because of poor administration and corruption, could not meet the demand for munitions, it was replaced by the Imperial Munitions Board presided over by the Toronto pork-packing magnate Joseph Flavelle who ran the operation like a czar. Eventually the IMB owned and operated factories across Canada producing every conceivable weapon of war. Wages were fixed, working conditions were difficult, unions were not recognized or were ignored. When severe labour shortages developed in 1916, some 30,000 lower paid women were recruited and quickly trained to take over jobs traditionally restricted to men.

Shortage of supplies of food and fuel, additional revenues to fund the war, and rampant inflation forced the government to intervene in the economy and in society in ways that no one could have imagined prior to the war. Prices of staples such as floor, meat, bacon, sugar and fuel were first regulated and then supplies were rationed by food and fuel controllers. Responding to a demand from Western farmers Ottawa set up a Board of Grain Supervisors to buy and market all cereal grains. Strong demand and labour shortages had pushed up all commodity prices. The government aggravated the inflationary cycle because its large borrowing via the sale of domestic and foreign bonds drove up interest rates. By 1916 Ottawa was forced to impose corporate taxes to raise revenues and curtail excess profit taking. The next year the government imposed taxes on personal incomes over $2000 per year, a programme the Minister of Finance promised would end once the war was over. When it became painfully clear by the spring of 1917 that both the Canadian Northern and the Grand Trunk Pacific Railways were in the verge of bankruptcy, PM Borden's cabinet authorized the purchase of all the railways except the CPR and founded the Canadian National Railways. The demands of war and economic stability had allowed Borden to implement one of his cherished progressive goals.

The most controversial intervention of the state into the lives of Canadians occurred in the May of 1917 when Borden, fresh from a visit with soldiers in Britain and at the front, decided that conscription was required if Canada was going to fulfil its commitment to a total war effort. Voluntary recruitment had declined throughout 1916 and into 1917. If the Canadian Corps's five divisions were to be sustained Borden was convinced that it could only be done through conscription. He also feared the impending collapse of the Russian front which would allow the German army to launch a massive counter-offensive on the Western Front which, in fact, it did in 1918. The Military Service Act, debated through the summer, became law in late August 1917 with many English-Canadian Liberals from Ontario and the Western provinces voting with the government against their leader, Laurier, who had refused to endorse conscription for fear of turning Quebec over to Bourassa and the nationalists.

Clearly, conscription was driven by more than military imperatives. PM Borden could not ask for a third extension of the life of his government. The only way to ensure political victory for his government was to appeal to the hearts of the majority of British-Canadians on the primordial issue which involved the government's determination to win the war at all costs thereby obtaining British recognition of Canada as an equal in the Empire. British-Canadian nationalism, with its vision of Canada as an English-speaking, protestant melting pot, reached its zenith during 1917-18 and Borden was determined to use it to his political advantage. Yet, more than ideology and emotion were required to guarantee electoral victory. Borden, with the help of his ambitious solicitor general, Arthur Meighen, decided to implement two highly undemocratic legislative measures thereby raising the art of political gerrymandering to new heights. The Military Voters Act enfranchised all male and female members of the armed forces and allowed that soldier's votes be cast for or against the government rather than specific candidates. Unless a solider could stipulate his own riding, his vote could be counted in any riding chosen by the electoral officer. The Wartime Elections Act enfranchised female kin and daughters of soldiers and disenfranchised conscientious objectors and all the immigrants from enemy countries who had arrived in Canada since 1902.

Opposition from French Canadians was expected but the government did very little to quell the fears of parents concerned over the future of their sons or to dispel the widespread belief that conscription was aimed primarily at their nationality for having shirked its duty. The refusal of the Borden government to help restore French language instruction in Ontario's Catholic schools did much to confirm this belief that the majority simply wanted to impose its will on the weak minority. Henri Bourassa's influence soared when he denounced Catholic Church leaders for having been duped by PM Borden's promise of no conscription. Opposition from English Canadian farmers, organized labour, and some elements of the women's movement was more worrisome. Fortunately for the government, the vast majority of women and workers placed their nationalism ahead of gender or class preoccupations. When it became apparent that farmers would vote against government candidates, Borden promised exemptions for agricultural labourers two weeks before the vote only to withdraw those exemptions after the election.

Putting his country before his party, Borden decided to ensure his political victory and the subsequent implementation of conscription by enticing disgruntled Ontario and western Liberal MPs fearful of loosing their seats as well as provincial Liberal Premiers to join his coalition Union Government. The Laurier Liberal caucus was reduced to a rump of MPs from Quebec. Borden enhanced the attractiveness of this coalition by promising prohibition, the vote for women, and civil service and tariff reform. Given all this gerrymandering, the outcome of the 'conscription' election of December 17, 1917 was a foregone conclusion. Borden and his Unionist team won 152 seats nearly forty of which were Unionist Liberals mostly from the West. Thanks to the backing of Bourassa's nationalists, 62 of Quebec's 65 ridings remained loyal to Laurier and the Liberal Party.

PM Borden moved to implement prohibition, granted votes to women, instituted extensive regulation of business, set up a veterans affairs department, and created the Civil Service Commission. The government did little to appease hard pressed workers and organized labour and angered the farming community by refusing to lower the tariff and by cancelling the exemptions promised to farm labourers. Labour militancy and the number of wildcat strikes increased while the farmers began to look actively for another political party to represent their interests. Having switched their political allegiance once, farmers were quite ready to do so again. The German assaults between March and June of 1918 took a heavy toll in lives and injuries on both sides but the Canadian Corps, once reunited under General Currie, helped the Allied Forces successfully repel the German mobile attacks and put their forces on the run by August of 1918. The Kaiser stepped down and the German Social Democratic republican government sued for an armistice which was arranged for November 11 at 11:00A.M. 1918. The Great War had come to an end but its short- and long-term consequences would reverberate around the world.

The Challenge of Peace

PM Borden had drawn Canadians into an all-out war effort, including a divisive policy of conscription, on the belief that Canada would emerge as an equal within a reconstituted British Empire. During the Imperial War Cabinet in 1917 Borden had extracted an agreement, in theory, from the British that Canada and the dominions would be consulted on foreign policy and defence issues. In 1918 after denouncing the incompetency of the British military leaders, Borden and other Dominion representatives were allowed to participate in the development of the Imperial forces war strategy. Once the war was over, PM Lloyd George, backed by the U.S. President Woodrow Wilson, attempted to back down on the agreement to grant the Dominions equal status. Borden insisted that each Dominion be granted full represen- tation in the peace-making process. Canada had two delegates at the Paris Peace Conference which set the terms of the peace settlement and created the League of Nations. Canada sought and was granted a seat on the League's general council as well as on the League's International Labour Organization. In reality Canada played little role in the peace settlement and the British were too preoccupied with reconstruction to address the issue of Canada's role in the Empire.

An exhausted PM Borden returned home in late May 1919 to encounter continuing frustration and anger amongst the returning soldiers many of whom had not been able to find employment or proper share of compensation for their injuries. Furthermore, organized labour, kept under control by the War Measures Act, was on the verge of exploding. PM Borden's eager and ambitious self-appointed successor, Arthur Meighen, felt there was little need to appease the disgruntled farmers of Ontario and the Prairie Provinces as they prepared to back T.A. Crerar's efforts to build a farmers' party. Meighen was a staunch supporter of the National Policy and had the backing of the manufacturing interests in Quebec, Ontario and Winnipeg. On the other hand, Meighen was very quick to help the political and business elites of Winnipeg to crush the General Sympathetic Strike which had started peacefully on May 15, 1919. While labour militancy persisted in the mining industry in Cape Breton and British Columbia, it would take over a decade and a prolonged depression for the labour movement to rebuild and revitalize itself.

III. THE FEDERATION CHALLENGED: KING AND BENNETT ERAS, 1920-48

Canada emerged from the war a prouder, more confident nation but one which could not deliver on the oft-repeated promise of prosperity and peace for all. Over the next quarter of a century, Prime Minister King and Bennett would face the challenge of guiding the country through a serious post-war recession, the social turmoil associated with rapid yet uneven economic expansion in the mid-twenties, the comprehensive crisis generated by the prolonged Depression of the 1930s, and the upheaval created by the Second World War, more devastating and global than the Great War. PM King, a wily politician of few principles, would thrive on many of these challenges to become one of Canada's most successful Prime Ministers. PM Bennett, a hard-nosed man of orthodox principles, survived for one term and retired to Great Britain in obscurity.

The Rise and Fall of Sectional Politics

While the militant wing of organized labour would endure a crushing defeat in the aftermath of the war, farmers' organizations, on the rise for over a decade, abandoned their ties with both traditional parties in favour of farmer-controlled political parties and governments. They felt betrayed by Borden who drafted their sons and then abolished the Wheat Board when prices crumbled. Farmers' Platform, published as the New National Policy, called for the abolition of the tariff and government intervention and control over most areas of the economy crucial to agriculture such as transportation and the grain trade. The United Farmers of Ontario, in the coalition with labour, held office from 1919 to 1923, the United Farmers of Manitoba helped to reduce the Liberal Government of T.C. Norris to a minority in 1920, and the United Farmers of Alberta swept the Liberal Government out of office in 1921 and remained there until 1935. Maritime farmers coalesced around the 'Maritime Rights' movement which found a political home in the rejuvenated provincial Conservative parties and soon-to-be governments.

Yet, it was on the federal election of 1921 that the upstart National Progressive Party, formed in late 1920 by T.A. Crerar, a disgruntled western

Liberal Unionist agricultural minister, had its most spectacular impact. The Conservative Party, led by the orthodox National Policy supporter, Arthur Meighen, was reduced to a rump of 50 seats and no longer functioned as national party. The Liberal Party, led by a young, relatively unknown Ontario politician by the name of William Lyon Mackenzie King, obtained a plurality of 116 seats. The spoiler was the Progressive movement which garnered 65 seats, 21 in Ontario and 38 on the Prairies. The two-party system faced the threat of extinction if Crerar could hold his fragile party together long enough for it to acquire the discipline of power.

A young, inexperienced PM King, heading up the first minority government since 1867, was just determined to do everything within his power to entice the 'Liberals in a hurry' Progressives back into the fold. King perceived of himself as the great conciliator and mediator having learned these skills working for the Rockerfeller Foundation and his boss' serious labour problems in the Colorado coal mines during the war. Former Minister of Labour in the Laurier government, King had remained loyal to his leader throughout the difficult conscription crisis of 1917 and was rewarded with the support of the French-Canadian delegates during the 1919 leadership convention. In a minority situation with only three Liberals elected on the Prairies, PM King has no choice but to adopt policies which addressed the problems, perceived and real, of the western farmers. Wooing a majority of the Progressives back into the fold would prove less difficult than he imagined. Meighen wrote them all off as a bunch of cranks and he defended his cherished National Policy and the central Canadian manufactures, the CPR, and the large banks who benefited from the policy. King's task was made easier by the fact that the Progressives were deeply divided. First, there were the classical Liberals, like Crerar, who wanted to abandon all protective tariffs and the ties with big business. His was a people's developmental Liberalism which found favour among most of the heavily commercialized and prosperous farmers. Second, there were the Christian socialist-leaning 'populist' Progressives, like Henry Wise Wood, who wanted government to be based on occupational or class groups functioning along cooperative rather than competitive principles. This philosophy of government found support among the less-well-off mixed farming community located in Alberta where many American Progressive farmers had settled. This split prevented the Progressives from creating a genuine national party organization, from choosing a leader and, from accepting the role of Her Majesty's official opposition.

PM King had merely to play on these divisions and lure the 'liberal' Progressives with pragmatic economic and transportation policies rather than would reinforce national unity. Given the importance of the protective tariff to industrial economies of central Canada, PM King kept tariff structure in place while allowing many piecemeal modifications to the schedules. King delivered balanced budgets and continuously refused to embark on expensive unemployment or social welfare schemes needed by the urban working poor but shunned by the agricultural class. His government did underwrite the wholesale expansion of the Canadian National Railroad system which served the northern Prairies and, after much wrangling, King restored a modified Crows Nest Pass Agreement under which farmers continued to receive subsidized freight rates. Once cereal grain markets and prices returned to war-time levels by the mid-1920s most prairie farmers abandoned their flirtation with the Progressives and turned their attention to electing farmer-Controlled provincial governments. The one important political grievance remaining was Ottawa's continued control over the natural resources of the Prairie Provinces. After protracted negotiations, Ottawa handed control over natural resources to the Prairie Provinces by 1930. The inherent bias of Confederation had been removed but the benefits would not flow until after the Depression.

PM King, not convinced of the need to address the grievances of the Maritime provinces, got a rude awakening in the October 1925 election. Arthur Meighen's Conservative Party swept Ontario and the Maritime region winning a plurality of 116 seats. King's Liberals were reduced to 99, mostly from Quebec, while the Progressives retained a rump of 24 seats and Independent labour held 6 seats. The Prime Minister, who had lost his own seat, formed a government convinced that the Progressives would support his administration rather than allow Meighen's pro-tariff Conservatives to take over. He promised the Independents an old-age pension scheme. Hoping to recover the setback in the Maritime region, PM King set up the Duncan Commission to inquire into the region's grievances. The Duncan Report called for modest measures and King eventually agreed to restore some measure of subsidized freight rates to the region. Little was done to address the region's structural economic problems but King had shrewdly dissolved the glue that had held the movement together.

Meanwhile, the Conservatives, aggrieved at being denied the opportunity to form the government, launched a concerted and ultimately successful attack on the government with revelations of a juicy scandal involving widespread smuggling in booze and other commodities which was being aided and abetted by officials in the Customs Department. PM King, trying to avoid censure by a Committee of the House, requested that Governor-General Byng dissolve Parliament and call an election. The Governor-

General refused and called upon Meighen to form a government. Since the PM and his cabinet had to be re-elected before taking office, PM Meighen tried to govern from the parliamentary gallery by using the device of an 'acting ministry'. Meighen's second tenure as PM was cut short when his 'acting ministry' lost the motion on its legality by one vote when a Progressive member got confused and forgot to rise during the roll call! An angry Governor-General Byng was forced to send the parties back to the hustings. Wrapping himself in the flag, King thundered on about the unconstitutionality of Lord Byng's actions which, he claimed, posed a most serious threat to responsible government. With no platform except the defence of the tariff and privilege, Meighen denounced the Liberals for their unbridled patronage as well for condoning wanton corruption in the Customs Department. In the 1926 election, King was returned to office with 128 seats while the Tories managed to hang on to only 91 seats with an increased popular vote. Once again, more Progressives shifted to the Liberals reducing the party's presence to a mere 20 seats. The two-party system had been restored, at least, momentarily.

From Colony to Nation

After functioning as a quasi-colony in matters external for over half a century, Canada was long overdue by the early 1920s to achieve complete autonomy over its relations with other nation-states. Continuous bickering over Canada's role in the British Empire had done grievous harm to national unity and PM King wanted the issue resolved once and for all. Unlike Laurier, King believed that it was crucial for Canada to obtain, as soon as possible, full control over its foreign affairs. He hoped to prevent Canada's entanglement in any British adventures which had even the remotest possibility of undermining national unity. He quickly abandoned Borden's and Meighen's policy of trying to achieve nation-state status within the British Empire on the grounds that common economic, military or foreign imperial policies were a chimera because they would always be formulated by the British to serve their national interests. Like Laurier, King's most favoured defence against the intrusions of British Imperialists was to proclaim that only the Parliament of Canada could decide the nature and extent of Canadian involvement in all matters of foreign, defence, and trade policy.

Two incidents allowed King to act on his conception of a new Canada-British relationship. One involved the Chanack crisis in September 1992 when the British government requested and expected Canadian troops to be sent to help the British defend the demilitarized zone of the Strait of the

Dardanelles against an imminent Turkish attack. PM King, who read about the conflict and the request in the papers, was furious at the arrogance of the British request which treated Canada like a colony, one obliged to jump every time the master called. Following discussion of the matter in Cabinet, he informed the British Prime Minister that his government would not be recalling Parliament to address this request. Meighen, the arch-imperialist, was furious but he found little support among the Canadian public for sending troops to the under-belly of the Balkans. The second incident entailed the King government's decision to send Earnest Lapointe to Washington in March 1923 to sign the Halibut Treaty with the United States without notifying the British in advance. The Imperial Conference of 1923 marked the end of the second British Empire and heralded the beginning of the British Commonwealth of nations as King and his supporters from some of the other dominions like Ireland and South Africa rejected any and all notions of a common imperial foreign, defence and economic policies and institutions. This great leap forward was formally proclaimed in the Balfour Declaration issued at the end of the 1926 Imperial Conference which recognized the emergence of a new Common-wealth of autonomous and equal Dominions in both domestic and foreign policy. The Statute of Westminster of 1931 put all of these changes into formal constitutional language. In the interim the King government established Canadian legations in Paris, Washington and Tokyo and welcomed the British High Commissioner to Ottawa. While Canadians could easily unite behind the high symbolism of nationhood, PM King was determined not to allow Canada to become embroiled in the disputes brewing at the League of Nations. He and his government fought long and hard to rid the League of Nations Charter of Article 10 pertaining to collective security arrangements for the League's members. King feared that Article 10 would automatically drag Canada into military disputes involving far-flung parts of the globe where no Canadian interest was involved. As witnessed by Canada's weak responses to the Manchurian and Ethiopian crises of the 1930s, the vast majority of Canadians were neither prepared nor willing to help strengthen the collective security powers of the League of Nations. That was highly regrettable but understandable given that the United States was not a member of the League. It is highly unlikely that a more aggressive stance on Canada's part would have had much effect. It would take the experience of WW II before Canadians would consent to exercise effective responsibilities and influence in world affairs. Until then, most Canadians savoured their newly-won status as an independent if not too venturesome nation-state.

478   *Michael D. Behiels*

The Great Depression

The most serious challenge to Canadian federalism came in the form of a prolonged and agonizing depression which began with the Crash on Wall Street in New York on October 29, 1929. Virtually every sector of the Canadian economy, except for precious metals, went into a tailspin and did not recover until the early 1940s. The comprehensive collapse of the Canadian economy resulted from developments during the late 1920s. In those heady boom years both the private and public sectors had over-invested in expensive infrastructure thereby entering the 1930s with excess productive capacity and very high levels of debt, often at fixed interest rates and in foreign currency. For those corporations and companies which survived the economic hurricane, there were very few profitable industries requiring new investment in plant and equipment. With a precipitous decline in both demand for, and prices of, Canada's abundant raw and semi-processed resources, entire communities of working people and farmers were left to fend for themselves or rely on the haphazard and inadequately funded private and public social welfare agencies. Single unemployed men were not eligible for assistance and rode the rails from town to town in search of illusive work. The high level of unemployment, reaching as high as 30 per cent in 1932-33, curtailed dramatically the purchase of goods and services thereby putting even more people out of work and on the dole. The construction industry, easily the largest and most widespread employer, simply ground to a halt by the mid-1930s after existing projects were completed and governments at all levels either could not, or refused to, borrow more funds for public works projects. The widespread economic deprivation would be seared into the hearts and minds of an entire generation of Canadians.

Canada's political leaders were ill-prepared, psychologically and intellectually, to deal with the magnitude of the social and economic problems facing Canadians. PM King, a fiscal conservative and a political procrastinator, firmly believed that the economic downturn was temporary. The Federal Government's only responsibility was to balance the budget by cutting expenditures to the bone. Social problems were the responsibility of the provinces and it was up the premiers to raise the revenues to provide the basic minimum of social assistance to the eligible poor to ensure that they did not become overly dependent upon the state. This would be King's guiding philosophy throughout the crisis despite his reputation as a progressive thinker. The economic theories of John Maynard Keynes, calling for counter-cyclical financing and budgetary deficits during economic recessions, were anathema to King and the leader of the opposition. R.B.

Bennett, a brash and blustering self-made millionaire, real-estate speculator, and lawyer from Calgary, became leader of the Conservative Party in 1927. During the federal election of 1930 he proclaimed confidently that he could resolve the crisis by granting $ 20 million for public works projects and blasting Canada's way into the markets of the world by raising tariffs to unprecedented levels.

Promising action in contrast to Kings' temporizing and receiving the full backing of several conservative premiers, Bennett easily won the fall 1930 election with 137 seats leaving King as leader of a demoralized Liberal opposition of 91 members. King, sensing that the crisis was going to be longer and more severe than he had predicted, was not displeased with the results. He could sit back and watch the new Prime Minister politically self-destruct as he struggled with intractable problems. If PM Bennett failed to alleviate the depression it was not for the lack of effort and sincerity. Over-confident in his abilities, he rarely delegated important tasks especially in the departments of finance and external affairs. His government provided $20 million for public relief projects but this barely made a dent in unemployment levels while adding to the debt. He raised tariffs to unprecedented levels but this merely drove countries, like our largest trading partners the United States and the United Kingdom, to emulate Canada. Canada's trade surpluses and revenues from customs and excise taxes quickly vanished. The policy also allowed the protected industries to maintain or raise prices thereby increasing their profit margins while curtailing their labour forces.

At the Imperial Economic Conference, held in Ottawa in 1932, Bennett attempted to regain markets for Canada's primary products by obtaining approval for the creation of an imperial customs union. Britain made a few concessions but the idea of an imperial trading block was rejected. Responding to widespread criticism from prairie farmers and small businessmen about the unscrupulous foreclosure practices, high interest rates, tight money, and seemingly high profits of the chartered banks, Bennett created the Bank of Canada in 1934 but left it firmly under the control of the chartered banks. Few Canadians were impressed and most perceived the banks as part of the problem not the solution and PM Bennett as their stooge. Branch managers on the Prairies often had their lives threatened and they and their families were socially ostracized.

The development which Bennett feared the most was the political radicalization of the large numbers of single unemployed men roaming the country from East to West. Even the Minister of Labour, Gideon Robertson, was convinced that measures of social control had to be implemented to

ensure that law and order would prevail. The government ordered the
Department of Defence to set up dozens of work camps far from towns and
cities where the young men were given room and board and 20 cents a day
in return for busy work. Protesting their incarceration, thousands of these
men set out from Vancouver in the On-to-Ottawa Trek. The PM ordered,
the trains stopped in Regina while he arranged to meet their leaders in
Ottawa. He denounced them as communist rabble rousers and ordered the
Mounties and police to clear the trekkers out of Regina. A violent clash
ensured resulting in one death, dozens of injuries, and 130 arrests. Canadians,
normally a peaceful people, had been pushed to their limit. The PM had
lost all credibility as he appeared to have run out of any constructive
solutions to the prolonged crisis.

The PM failed to heed the warnings of his minister of trade and
commerce, H.H. Stevens, to the effect that unscrupulous industrialists
were price-fixing and mercilessly exploiting their workers. Stevens quit the
cabinet and founded his own Reconstruction Party supported by thousands
of small businessmen. Hoping to recover some of his credibility and fend
off certain defeat at polls in the 1935 election, PM Bennett announced on
radio, without consulting his cabinet colleagues, his government's decision
to offer Canadians a modest version of President F.D. Roosevelt's progressive
New Deal. A deeply demoralized and divided cabinet and caucus reluctantly
voted for legislation setting minimum wages and hours of work, creating
an unemployment scheme, and allowing the government to regulate business
practices, determine marketing conditions and set prices. Voters were not
convinced that Bennett had converted when it came time cast their ballots
in mid-October 1935. As King predicted, the government was self-destroyed
as 400,000 Conservatives voted for the Reconstruction Party. The Liberals,
promising little except tariff reductions, a trade agreement with the U.S.,
and the slogan 'King or Chaos' won a landslide victory of 173 seats
reducing the Tories to a rump of 40 seats.

The King government acted quickly on its two promises. It then
nationalized the Bank of Canada and focused its energies on balancing the
budget by closing the hated work camps and cutting back on relief grants
to the indebted four western provinces pushing them even closer to
bankruptcy. Bennett's infamous New Deal legislation was referred to the
courts which declared the measures unconstitutional because they dealt
with provincial responsibilities. Ottawa's hands were tied and the provinces
had neither the political will nor the money to act. In 1937 King's response
was to create a Royal Commission to analyse the dilemma confronting
federal/provincial relations. In the interim, King faced increased political

pressure coming from the premiers of Alberta, British Columbia, Ontario, and Quebec, some of whom objected to the Federal Government's inaction while others condemned Ottawa's interference in their affairs. As the depression worsened through the winter of 1937-38, a small coterie of like-minded political advisors, ministers, and bureaucrats finally convinced the Prime Minister that a modest degree of economic pump priming was necessary to rebuild confidence in the Canadian economy and alleviate the prolonged suffering of many destitute Canadians. It had taken nearly a decade of severe hardship and debate to convince Canadians and their national government that it was essential for the state to take measures to ensure economic stability and to provide a modest safety net for Canadians thrown out of work through no fault of their own.

Much of the pressure for rethinking the role of the state came from the third parties, both on the right and the left, which emerged during the 1930s. Much of the militancy on the left came from the newer elements within the normally conservative labour movement. Thanks to a determined underground campaign of the communist Workers' Unity League in Ontario, many workers turned to the concept of industrial unionism, especially in the innovative automobile industry. Many labour leaders were also keen on creating a new party to represent the interests of working people across the land. J.S. Woodsworth, Independent labour MP since the early 1920s, was considered the ideal candidate to head up a formal coalition of numerous labour, farm, and socialist organizations. The Cooperative Commonwealth Federation was born in Calgary in 1932 and formalized with the publication of the Regina Manifesto in 1933. The party platform entailed a clarion call to all Canadians to join forces in the construction of a comprehensive social democratic society based on the principles of cooperation and sharing rather than competition and profit. The CCF, more a movement than a party, had modest political success at the provincial level forming the official opposition in BC and Saskatchewan in the 1930s and eventually in Ontario in 1943. In 1935 CCF candidates polled nearly 400,000 votes and won seven seats yet its long-term influence was far greater than these meagre results might suggest. J.S. Woodsworth and the CCF acted as the conscience of the nation and focused attention on the need to extend equality of opportunity as well as greater equality of conditions to individual Canadians and to all classes and regions of the country.

The prevailing conception of the role of the state was also challenged by the Social Credit Party. It emerged in Alberta between 1932 and 1935 under the dynamic yet authoritarian leadership of 'Bible Bill' William Aberhart, a Calgary School principal and founder of the fundamentalist Bill Institute.

Aberhart popularized the social credit theories of a British engineer named Major C.H. Douglas. There was 'poverty in the midst of plenty' because there was never enough cash to enable consumers to purchase the seemingly unlimited production of goods and services. The shortage of purchasing power could be remedied by the state granting every adult citizen a monthly 'social dividend' or cash payment. This was justified since the public had a right to its share of wealth generated by the abundant natural resources granted by God, resources which were monopolized and exploited by the financial and industrial capitalists for their personal profit. It was the state's responsibility to guarantee that the public received its fair share of this social credit so that the capitalist system could function to the benefit of all citizens. Aberhart's Social Credit movement took off like a prairie brush fire during a scorching summer day and quickly absorbed the militants and the party structure of the corrupt UFA. Aberhart's movement won 63 of the 70 seats in the Alberta legislature in the 1935 election. Pressured by a small but vocal group of militants, the Aberhart government passed a few fiscal and monetary social credit measures only to see them overturned by the Supreme Court. Efforts were made to take the Social Credit party and its philosophy into national politics but it remained a sectional party which thrived on a sense of western alienation and anti-establishment feelings which prevailed in Alberta.

A National Gears up for War

Throughout 1937-38, PM King, following PM Chamberlain's strategy of appeasement, hoped somehow to forestall the inevitable. While he believed that Canadians, for a second time in a generation, would be dragged into a messy and costly European war, he shrewdly refused to make a public declaration to that effect or to tip his hand by allowing British pilots to be trained in Canada. When British declared war on German in September 1939, the PM convened Parliament which decided within a week to enter the fight against Hilter and the Axis forces. Yet King was determined to avoid a replay of the Great War which had left Canadian unity and the Borden government in utter shambles.

The nature of warfare had changed quite dramatically. Indeed, both the air force and the navy would play pivotal roles until 1944 when the allied armies invaded Italy and western Europe. This suited King fine because, as he believed wrongly, large casualty rates could be avoided. His government promised French Canadians that in return for their support for the war effort there would not be conscription for overseas service. Second, King adopted a policy of 'limited liability' focusing Canada's contributions on foodstuffs, materials, and munitions of all kinds in an effort to rebuild its flagging economy. While most Canadians concurred, the Premiers of Quebec and Ontario did not agree with this approach.

Since the best defence is often a strong offence, King decided to attack these two critics head on. Maurice Duplessis called a premature election in the Fall 1939 hoping to remain premier on the grounds that he was French Canada's only defence against conscription. King's French-Canadian colleagues reacted swiftly to the challenge and threatened to resign if French Canadians returned Duplessis to the premiers office thereby leaving the government in the hands of the Anglophone majority. The national Liberal Party intervened massively in the provincial campaign and ensured the election of a Liberal Government led by Adelard Godbout. Concerned French-Canadian nationalists, fearing that Godbout was a puppet of Ottawa, created the *Bloc Populaire Canadien* to fend off conscription and defend the autonomy of Quebec.

Ontario's Premier Mitchell Hepburn, a long time political foe of PM King on many issues, had his legislature pass a motion condemning the Federal Government's lukewarm support for an endangered Great Britain. King dealt Hepburn a serious political blow by calling a snap election seeking public approval for his government's war policies. He received an overwhelming endorsement when the Liberal won 181 seats while the Conservatives were reduced to 40 seats and the CCF a mere 8 members. The conscriptionist forces in Ontario had been momentarily kept in check but they would soon find another politician to lead their cause. The King government would not have to return to the electorate before the war had been won.

The PM was fortunate in being able to put together one of the strongest cabinets since 1867. His War Committee included his trusted Quebec lieutenant, Ernest Lapointe, and Colonel J.L. Ralston as Minister of Defence, along with Chubby Power as Air Minister and Angus Macdonald in charge of the Navy. On the economic side there were the Minister of Finance and superb administrator, J.L. Ilsley, and the indefatigable, C.D. Howe, Minister of Munitions and Supply, who would use the state's enormous purchasing powers to modernize the industrial heartland of Canada. These men turned Canada into a veritable arsenal for democracy. One of Canada's most elaborate endeavours was the British Commonwealth Training Programme which trained 132,000 aircrew—73,000 Canadians—costing the taxpayers $1.6 billion. Canadian pilots, navigators, gunners and maintenance men participated in the battle in the skies over Britain and in the very dangerous bombing raids into the heart of Germany. The Royal Canadian Navy, greatly expanded in terms of ships and personnel, helped to win the battle of the North Atlantic against Hitler's U-boats by escorting nearly 1,500 convoys comprising thousands of ships carrying supplies and men.

King's best laid plans went awry by the spring and summer of 1940. The phony war ended when the powerful German *Blitzkrieg* rolled over Norway, Denmark, Holland, Belgium and then all the way to Paris forcing the Allies to organize a brilliant and timely evacuation at Dunkirk. By the end of 1941, the Soviets had joined the Allies and Japan had joined the Axis powers. Canada, inadvertently, found itself in the vortex of the world's first truly global total war, one which would alter both its domestic and its foreign relations. In 1940, the National Resources Mobilization Act was passed empowering the government to conscript men for home defence, called Zombies, thereby freeing up thousands of regular soldiers for overseas duty. Since Canada could no longer rely on the British Royal Navy to defend its lengthy Atlantic and pacific coastlines, PM King and F.D. Roosevelt signed the Ogdensburg Agreement establishing a Permanent Joint Board of Defence to plan and coordinate the protection of North America. Henceforth, Canadians lived under the umbrella of fortress America. Canada's purchase of millions of dollars of American parts for the construction of arms and ammunition intended for Great Britain greatly added to its trade deficit to the United States, a deficit normally offset by our trade surplus with Great Britain but which had all but vanished by 1941 because the U.K. was broken. Again King and Roosevelt worked out an arrangement at the president's Hyde Park residence whereby Canadian purchases of components required to fulfil British orders would be added to the British account under the American Lend-Lease agreement. Assured of numerous contracts, the economy boomed enabling Canada to afford to grant Britain billions in loans in aid. The war confirmed that the economic ties between Canada and Britain had been severed and that the United States had become Canada's dominant trading partner and source of capital and technology.

Unlike 1914-18, the war on the home front, apart front the internment of the Japanese Canadians, was managed very professionally. While the government had sound reasons to fear for the lives of some 23,000 Japanese Canadians living in coastal communities in British Columbia, there was no justification for stripping them of their homes, their businesses, and their belongings without full compensation. Neither can the government's post-war campaign to pressure many of them to return to Japan be justified under international law. The incident was a shameful stain on Canada's claim to be a tolerant, open society.

On other fronts, C.D. Howe converted dozens of peacetime industries into highly productive and profitable war materials industries, a few of which such as the aircraft industry, became permanent fixtures in the economy. The state created hundreds of crown corporations to manufacture a wide assortment of necessary products from petro-chemicals to uranium and plutonium required for the secret construction of nuclear weapons in the United States. The government monitored the availability of labour through its National Selective Service system and kept inflation under control through the wartime prices and Trade Board. When Labour unrest threatened production, cabinet issued the National War Labour Code permitting workers to unionize and forcing employers to bargain with the new unions. By the end of the war nearly three-quarters of a million workers held union cards.

Only a small fraction of these unionized workers were women despite the fact that over one million women worked full-time in war industries and the service sector by late 1944. Nearly as many toiled on farms across the land. Their wages, while considerably better than in their traditional jobs, were still only two-thirds those given the men. Yet, overall total family income increased quite substantially during the war and most of the increase was set aside in the form of forced savings through Victory Bonds. Many women were eager to participate more directly in the war effort. Nearly five thousand served as nursing sisters while close to fifty thousand joined the ranks of the Canadian Women's Army Corps, the RCAF's Women's Division, and the Women's Royal Canadian Naval Service. At the end of the war the vast majority were demobilized but the precedent had been set. Similarly, the vast majority of women in the paid labour force set down their tools to get married, have children and tend to their families. Many of these women would return to the work force later in life as well as encouraging their daughters to pursue full-time careers.

War and Conscription

Total war also precipitated a political crisis for the King government by allowing the pro-conscription forces in Toronto, lead by the new leader of the Conservative Party, Arthur Meighen, to pressure the government to amend the NRM Act to allow conscription for overseas service. While PM King remained steadfastly opposed to conscription he was determined not to allow Meighen any ground on which to build a mass movement. Following Lapointe's death by cancer in the fall of 1941, the government announced its decision to hold a plebiscite on April 27, 1942 asking Canadians to release it from the promise not to impose conscription for overseas duty. French-

Canadian nationalists, led by a young André Laurendeau, fought a brilliant 'NO' campaign throughout Quebec while most of King's cabinet colleagues sat on their hands. As a result, 73 per cent of voters in Quebec said 'NO' while 80 per cent of voters in the nine provinces said 'YES'. The PM amended the NRM Act but reassured Canadians that his government opposed conscription and would only resort to it if absolutely necessary. King also undermined the conscriptionist movement by ensuring that Meighen was never elected to Parliament. He ordered that a Liberal candidate not run in the North York by-election in 1942. A respectable but unknown CCF candidate, Joseph Noseworthy, defeated Meighen who was, in due course, replaced by the former premier of Manitoba, John Bracken as leader.

Firmly convinced that he had circumvented brilliantly the issue of conscription, the PM was devastated when it re-emerged to haunt his government just as the war was entering its final phase in late 1944 with the Allies confident of victory. The Canadian army had suffered humiliating defeats in battle over Hong Kong in December 1941 and in the poorly planned and executed disastrous assault on the French port of Dieppe in August 1942. Yet, the various divisions of the Canadian army were well-trained, well-equipped, and professionally lead for the major assaults on the Axis powers throughout the spring and summer of 1944. A Canadian division participated in the assault on Italy via Sicily and encountered ferocious opposition from the German soldiers and officers who preferred to die rather than surrender. Finally Rome was captured in June 1944 setting the stage for long-awaited attack on western Europe via the beaches at Normandy beginning on June 6.

The First Canadian Army, lead by General H.D.G. Crerar of WW I fame, and reinforced with Polish and British contingents, occupied the left flank of the Allied onslaught. Exhausted but brave Canadian soldiers liberated many French ports, including the infamous Dieppe, and pushed on up through Holland and the Schledt estuary. Casualties were very high and experienced replacements were soon at a premium given the high ratio of supporting to fighting troops in the Canadian army structure. Expecting more casualties in the spring 1945 offensive, Canadian Officers requested that experienced NRMA soldiers be conscripted for overseas services. Colonel Ralston, having visited the troops at the front in September 1944, agreed. He pressed the PM to abide by his commitment of conscription if necessary and indicated that he and other supportive cabinet ministers were prepared to resign on the issue. King, refusing to agree that conscription was necessary for the Allies to achieve victory, accepted Ralston's resignation and called upon General McNaughton, the popular former army commander, to see if he could persuade a good percentage of the 68,000 NRMA troops to volunteer for overseas service. Furious at the PM for having conscripted them in the first place and angry at the shabby treatment by their regular officers, the Zombies refused the General's entreaties. King, facing a political revolt from within the cabinet, and firmly convinced that he had to head off a military conspiracy to destabilize his government, reluctantly agreed to the conscription of 16,000 of the NRMA soldiers. Barely 2,500 reached the front before the war was over.

The PM's strategy of procrastinating to the bitter end paid political dividends. He managed to maintain the unity of his cabinet, his caucus, and the Liberal Party. French-Canadian voters protested, not by electing the progressive nationalist *Bloc Populaire canadien,* but by returning the traditional nationalist Maurice Duplessis to power in August 1944. The Liberal Party suffered a mild rebuke in the 1945 election, but PM King remained in office with 127 seats, 53 from Quebec, while the Tories remained in opposition with 67 seats having campaigned for conscription for the Japanese war when all Canadians wanted a return to normalcy. The CFF, which had come on strong in opinion polls in 1943-44, managed to obtain only 28 seats as the Liberals had stolen much of its platform.

IV. THE NEW FEDERALISM: FROM ST. LAURENT TO DIEFENBAKER, 1945-63

The Making of a Modern Social Security State

In the two decades following WW II, Canadian society was transformed to a degree that would have been unimaginable to those who experienced the Great Depression. Accelerated industrialization and urbanization brought on by high birth rates, a new wave of immigration, and unprecedented levels of domestic and foreign investment, broke the back of the remaining traditional social, cultural and religious values and institutions. By the 1960s, the vast majority of Canadians lived in some twenty medium to large urban centres and worked in a wide variety of occupations increasingly in the expanding private and public service sectors of the economy. Energized by a new-found confidence in themselves, Canadians dramatically altered the role that the state played in their lives.

As increasing numbers of Canadians supported the CCF party which formed the official opposition in Ontario in 1943 and the government in Saskatchewan in 1944, the Soviet Union formed part of the Allied force and social democracy was no longer rejected out of hand. By late 1944, the Liberal Government in Ottawa realized the urgent need for reconstruction planning so as to ensure a smooth transition of the economy to peacetime and provide employment for the returning members of the Armed Forces. Leonard Marsh, a McGill social scientist, prepared a comprehensive *Report on Social Security for Canada* in 1943 for the government. But, it was the senior bureaucrats in the Department of Finance, all converts to the theories of Keynesian economics, who convinced the Prime Minster that only an activist Federal Government could ensure economic stability and high employment. These goals would be achieved by combining a selection of fiscally responsible social welfare programmes with major public works projects most likely to create jobs throughout all parts of Canada.

Following the Depression and the publication of the Rowell-Sirois Report in 1940, Ottawa and the princes had agreed to a constitutional amendment empowering Ottawa to administer a contributory unemployment insurance programme. Just in time for the 1945 election, PM King delivered a family allowance programme whereby mothers received monthly cheques to help purchase family necessities which ensured a growing demand for consumer products. The CCF leaders were furious that the Liberals had moved to the left while the so-called Progressive Conservatives denounced the scheme because, they claimed, that it favoured the larger French-Canadian families of Quebec. Ottawa stimulated the economy by providing grants to corporations to transform their production from war to peacetime commodities, by setting up a Central Mortgage and Housing Corporation to provide families with low-cost, insured mortgages thereby setting off a housing construction boom that lasted for a decade, by providing Veterans with a whole range of programmes from medical coverage and to a choice between land and housing or post-secondary education.

Hoping to capitalize on Canadians hard-won sense of national pride, Ottawa attempted, during two federal-provincial conferences in 1945-46, to convince the provinces to accept its Green Book proposals calling for a restructuring of the federal system along the lines recommended in the Rowell-Sirois Report. Ottawa argued that an effective implementation of Keynesian economic theories for achieving economic stability and full employment required that it have exclusive control over all corporate and personal income taxes as well as succession duties. In return, the provinces would receive increased unconditional subsidies. Ottawa would use its revenues to fund large scale public works projects, for an expanded old-age pension scheme, universal for those over seventy and meanstested for those 65 to 69 to be cost-shared with the provinces, as well as a health insurance system. The premiers, especially Duplessis from Quebec and Drew from Ontario, rejected outright Ottawa's attempt to undermine provincial autonomy and create a more centralized federation. Ottawa's only option was to renew the tax-rental agreements with seven provinces on a bilateral basis while awaiting a more opportune time to implement other social security measures. Ottawa pressed on with its pension plans and managed to convince the provinces in 1951 to accept a constitutional amendment to empower Ottawa to create a universal old-age security programme for Canadians over seventy and to cost-share a meanstested pension plan for seniors between 65 and 69 with cooperating provinces. It took longer for Ottawa to hammer out an agreement with the provinces for a hospital insurance scheme. By 1957 Paul Martin, the Minister of National Health and Welfare, received approval from a majority of the provinces for a 50/50 shared-cost programme covering basic in-patient services. The Hospital Insurance and Diagnostic Services Act took effect on July 1, 1958. Unrelenting pressure from their citizens eventually forced all provinces, even Quebec, to join this very popular programme.

Ottawa did not always win these federal provincial battles. The political war over taxing powers gained momentum in the 1950s as the provinces were hard-pressed to meet the growing demand for expanded and improved health, social security and educational facilities and services. By 1952 Ontario's new Premier, Leslie Frost, joined the tax-rental agreement scheme leaving Quebec isolated. French-Canadian nationalists, backed by the Tremblay Commissioners, convinced the Duplessis government to implement a provincial sales tax of 15 per cent and to press Ottawa to allow Quebec taxpayers to deduct this amount from their federal income tax. After months of verbal jousting, the St. Laurent government met with Premier Duplessis in October 1954 to indicate that Ottawa would reduce its personal income rates by 10 per cent for any provinces wishing to impose their own personal income tax schemes. During the 1956 federal-provincial conference Ottawa offered the provinces a choice between a new five-year tax-rental programme to take effect in 1957 or a share of all direct tax revenues—10 per cent of personal and corporate income taxes and 50 per cent of succession duties—coupled with equalization grants for those provinces whose taxing base produced revenues lower than the averages of the two wealthiest provinces. Initially only Ontario and Quebec accepted the tax-sharing option. But, eventually, the remaining provinces would abandon the tax-rental option and pressure Ottawa to offer them an ever-increasing proportion of lucrative direct taxes. Consequently, Ottawa's ability to regulate the Canadian economy via its fiscal policy measures would be diminished.

In the interim, the Canadian economy, and along with it the vast majority of Canadians, prospered as never before. Gross domestic production expanded by 166 per cent from nearly $ 12 billion in 1945 to nearly $ 32 billion by 1957 while the average weekly wage for a male factory worker rose by 103 per cent from nearly $31.00 to $65.00. There are several reasons for these developments. Technological innovation, spurred on by the war and the cold war, produced better and more efficient machinery, construction materials, and consumer products. The Canadian population, thanks to the phenomenal post-war baby boom and the influx of some 1.7 million refugees and immigrants between 1945 and 1957, reached the 18 million level by 1961 up from 11 million in 1941. Much of the economic growth was made possible by unprecedented levels of domestic and foreign investment, especially American investment which reached $ 8 billion by 1952. The renewal of Canada's trading links with Europe and other parts of the world, thanks to Canada's willingness to extend credit to Britain and western Europe and to General Agreement to Tariffs and Trade in 1947, provided much needed markets for its abundant renewal and non-renewable natural resources. But it was the United States which absorbed 60 per cent of all Canada's exports and sent it over 70 per cent of Canada's total imports by 1957. These developments took place in rapidly evolving system of global geo-politics.

Taking on Responsibilities: Canada in a Changing World

Canada's role in WW II enabled a coterie of brilliant and dedicated senior mandarins in the Department of External Affairs to transcend Mackenzie King's foreign policy based on the struggle for, and achievement of, full nationhood status. Instead, these officials formulated a foreign policy based on the necessity of Canada exercising certain important international responsibilities that were in accordance with its capabilities and resources. A 'golden age of Canadian diplomacy', 1945 to 1956, was ushered in by Hume Wrong, Norman Robertson, Lester Pearson, and Escott Reid, all strong pragmatic idealists who wanted Canada to act upon its hard-won status. During the war, Wrong developed the functional principle to justify a significant participation of Canada in the councils of the Great Powers which were prosecuting the war as well as planning for post-war reconstruction. Middle powers like Canada, Wrong argued, had specialized resources and knowledge in areas such as agricultural and mineral production and transportation which justified their participation in such organizations as the Combined Production, the Resources Board and the Combined Food Board and the United Nations Relief and Rehabilitation Administration. In 1945, Canadian representatives at the founding conference of the United Nations in San Francisco attempted to apply the functional principle to acquire a greater role for middle powers in the creation and operation of the new organization but with no direct results.

Following the discovery of a Soviet spy network in Canada, thanks to the Christmas, 1945 defection of Igor Gouzenko a clerk in their embassy in Ottawa, relations between Canada and the Soviet Union deteriorated rapidly. The Cold War took on a new significance when the Red Army invaded Czechoslovakia in 1948 and established a puppet regime. Since the Soviets and the Chinese exercised veto power over the Security Council of the United Nations, Canadian foreign policy planners, lead by Escott Reid, were convinced that a European collective security organization had to be established to keep the Soviet Union in check. Once the British and the Canadian Prime Ministers convinced a reluctant President of the United States of the urgency of the matter, the North Atlantic Treaty Organization was created in April 1949. In due course, Canada played an active role in the NATO alliance by stationing an army brigade and a dozen air force squadrons in occupied Germany where they remained until the early 1990s.

Taking its UN responsibilities seriously, the Canadian government agreed in 1950 to send a brigade to help a United Nation's force, dominated by the American military, repel the invasion of the democratic regime of South Korea by the Soviet- and Chinese-backed Communist regime of North Korea. Some 22,000 Canadians served in Korea with over 300 loosing their lives while 1200 returned home wounded before a cease-fire, drawing a permanent border between North and South Korea, was achieved. Canada's finest moment in diplomacy came in 1956 when Lester Pearson, the secretary of state for external affairs, negotiated a deal between President Nasser of Egypt, who repossessed the Suez canal by military force, and the British, French, and Israeli governments' stated intention to reclaim control over the canal by military force. The conflict threatened to undermine NATO because the Americans were furious at the British and the French for destabilizing the Middle East. It also threatened the Commonwealth because Canada was siding with the Americans in opposing the British and the French invasion plans. All-out war was averted when the participants accepted Pearson's proposal of a United Nation's peacekeeping force, including Canadian logistics troops, to interpose itself between the combatants and preserve the fragile truce. War was averted in the Middle East and Pearson received the Nobel Peace Prize which enhanced his political profile immensely.

The Governing Party: From Hegemony to Opposition

PM King stepped down in 1948 and was replaced by Louis St. Laurent, a genuinely affable former corporate lawyer from Quebec City who knew how to gather excellent men of action around the cabinet table. Post-war prosperity, the powerful Liberal Party electoral machine, a Tory Party under the leadership of the not-so-progressive George Drew, and $40.00 pensions for everyone over 70, ensured that the Liberals easily won re-election in 1949. PM St. Laurent received a strong majority of 193 seats while the Conservatives remained mired in opposition with 41 seats with the CCF holding 13 seats. Continued prosperity and the end of the Korean war solidified the Liberal Party's hold on power. The Massey Commission Report of 1951 had recommended federal grants to universities in order to help them accommodate the rapidly growing demand for professional and graduate degrees. PM St. Laurent responded immediately by providing per capita grants, first directly to the universities, and then via the provinces, for post-secondary education. Responding only much later to another of the Report's recommendations, the St. Laurent government used the taxes from two lucrative estates to create in 1957 the Canada Council to fund a wide range of arts organizations, to provide grants to individual artists, and graduate scholarships to ambitious and talented students. The 1953 election saw the Liberals returned to office with 171 seats while both the Conservatives and the CCF each picked up ten additional seats.

By the mid-1950s the Liberal Government's political arrogance was beginning to wear a little thin. The Conservative opposition's favourite target was C.D. Howe, known as the 'Minister of Everything' because he ruled over a variety of high spending portfolios related to defence and post-war reconstruction. In 1955, when Howe attempted to have Parliament renew the Defence Production Act of 1951, with its extensive powers, the opposition filibustered until PM St. Laurent agreed to a four year limit on the legislation. In 1956, the opposition, led by a brash, ambitious Red Tory from Prince Albert, Saskatchewan, John Diefenbaker, decided to attack C.D. Howe, the Minister of Trade and Commerce, for the legislation pertaining to the construction of the Trans-Canada Pipeline to transport Alberta's huge supplies of natural gas to the markets of central Canada. The legislation offered the beleaguered Trans-Canada Pipeline corporation, an American-Canadian consortium, a government loan to complete the western section of the pipeline within a set deadline. The Conservatives denounced this gift to a predominantly American-owned corporation which would control a valuable natural resource. When they set in motion another very effective filibuster, Howe received permission from the PM to impose closure on various stages in the Parliamentary debate so as to ensure that the company received its funds in time to meet the construction deadline. The Liberals won the legislative battle but lost the public relations war.

Increasing numbers of Canadians were becoming frustrated and uneasy with PM St. Laurent's lack of leadership and the arrogance of his Ministers and senior members of the bureaucracy who appeared to have lost all sense of impartiality.

George Drew stepped down as leader of the Conservatives in late 1956 to be replaced by the outspoken, highly partisan, and charismatic John Diefenbaker at a noisy leadership convention which saw a new guard of 'outsiders' from the Western and Atlantic regions win control over the Progressive Conservative Party. The Liberal Government and the media paid scant attention to this momentous transition. When an exhausted and somewhat despondent PM St. Laurent called the June 1957 election few politicians and *pundits* expected the government to be defeated. And yet, that is exactly what transpired. Prime Minister Diefenbaker found himself at the head of a minority government with 112 seats to the 105 held by the Liberals. The balance of power was in the hands of the 25 CCF and 19 Social Credit members.

Not wanting to rely on the Social Credit members, PM Diefenbaker set the stage for another election before the demoralized Liberals could get reorganized. He reached out to disgruntled Tories and many Canadian nationalists by promising, during the Commonwealth Conference, to rebuild relations and expand trade with Great Britain. He raised the levels of assistance to the unemployed, to prairie farmers, and to Maritimers. When the new Liberal leader, Lester Pearson, called upon the government to resign he was easily ridiculed and humiliated. Diefenbaker responded by calling a snap election which his party won with a landslide of 208 seats. The Liberals were reduced to a rump of 49 seats and the CCF, almost obliterated, held on to 8 seats. Thanks to the machinations of Premier Duplessis, fifty Union National conservative Tory MPs were elected in Quebec. Diefenbaker galvanized the imagination of the voters in all regions of the country with his roads to resources 'Northern Vision', his commitment to redressing growing regional inequalities, and his 'One Canada' speeches which emphasized the need to integrate the large numbers of recent immigrants into the mainstream of a refurbished British-Canadian society.

The Diefenbaker Vision: Trials and Tribulations

The change of government raised expectations in the hinterlands where Canadians had not experienced the post-war prosperity that had swept over Central Canada. The St. Laurent government had focused on the restructuring and recapitalization of the farm, forestry and fishing industries of the Atlantic region but this approach threatened to undermine family businesses and the smaller communities. Robert Stanfield, Premier of Nova Scotia, attempted to shore up the rural communities by providing grants and loans to entrepreneurs to set up small- and medium- scale companies throughout the province. The Diefenbaker government supported this approach by providing $ 25 million adjustment grants annually to the Maritime provinces. This was followed up with the Agricultural and Rural Development Act, a shared-cost programme to accelerate the modernization of agriculture throughout economically depressed rural regions of Canada. These regional development programmes were costly and not always very effective in raising the standard of living or in preserving the traditional lifestyle. Yet, the funds allowed a less painful transition of the people of these economically disadvantaged regions into the larger urban-industrial centres where education and employment opportunities were greater. PM Diefenbaker cemented the political allegiance of the prairie farmers when his government put new life into the depressed wheat economy by signing profitable contracts for wheat sales, first with China and then with the Soviet Union. The government also cost-shared in the construction of the huge Diefenbaker Dam project in Saskatchewan which alleviated the reoccurring water shortages while creating much appreciated recreational opportunities in the region.

Despite Diefenbaker's sympathy for provincial autonomy, his government soon found itself in conflict with certain provinces. Interminable discussions between Ottawa and the Social Credit of the government of British Columbia delayed for several years the signing of the treaty between Canada and the United States for the construction of the lucrative Columbia River Dam project. The treaty was finalized in 1964 with the Pearson Liberal Government. It was the battle with the 'Quiet Revolution' and Liberal Government of Quebec which destabilized federal-provincial relations in the early 1960s. Diefenbaker's vision of 'One Canada' based on the monarchy, British parliamentary institutions, an unhyphenated citizenship, and a Canadian Bill of Rights allowed little space for the recognition of the French-Canadian nationality located predominantly in Quebec. Diefenbaker did not understand the aspirations of the secular new middle-class nationalists who abandoned the Catholic Church in droves to build a modern social security state in Quebec. They also wanted all federal institutions and crown corporations to welcome Francophones by becoming bilingual and for Ottawa to help the minority Francophone communities spread across Canada to gain access to public services in their language and to be able to control and manage Francophone schools for their children. PM Diefenbaker cavalierly rebuffed all of these requests thereby ensuring the demise, once again, of the Conservative Party in Quebec.

The government, faced with a recession and rising unemployment, found itself in conflict with James Coyne, the Governor of the Bank of Canada. Concerned with the rising levels of American investment, the Governor tried to increase Canadian savings levels by raising interest rates and reducing the money supply. Canadian businesses and economists reacted negatively as did the government. All wanted to accelerate economic expansion and create jobs. The government's attempt to deal with Coyne by introducing a Bill calling for his resignation created a public relations scandal which, ironically, resulted in more rather than less autonomy for the Governor of the Bank of Canada. Eventually, the government opted for a policy of inflation by allowing the Canadian dollar to float, that is until the middle of the 1962 election when the speculators forced the government to peg the currency at 92.5 cents American. The Liberals and the cartoonists ridiculed the government's vacillation.

Foreign and Defence Policies

PM Diefenbaker was determined to restore trade and political ties with Great Britain in order to offset Canada's increasing reliance on the United States for investment and markets. Yet, he managed to alienate the British government by openly denouncing its attempts to join the European Economic Community and by insisting that South Africa be expelled from the Commonwealth. Diefenbaker agreed with the Walter Gordon Report on Canada's Economic Prospects' concern over the high levels of American control over certain sectors of the Canadian economy but his government's concern over job creation prevented it from implementing economic nationalist policies.

It was in the area of defence policy that the Diefenbaker government ran afoul of Canadian public opinion. Like his Conservative predecessors, Diefenbaker was critical of the Liberal Government's participation in a scheme of continental defence controlled by the United States military and political leaders. One area where Canada had the lead over the Americans was in the design of a supersonic fighter, the CF-105 Arrow. It was a very costly research and development programme but the lack of foreign sales threatened to derail production of the prototype. The government procrastinated for months on end before deciding to cancel the project putting thousands of high skilled aeronautics workers out of work. The decision accelerated the integration of the Canadian and American defence industries and Canada ended up purchasing American fighter planes.

In fact, the Diefenbaker government quickly ratified the North American Air Defence Agreement, NORAD, negotiated by the Liberals soon after taking office in 1957 without asking any tough questions about its contents. In 1962, when the Cuban missile crisis erupted, President Kennedy placed the American Defence Forces on high alert expecting that the Canadian government would do the same. Not willing to accept that a crisis existed, PM Diefenbaker refused to authorize a full alert. Kennedy felt betrayed and was visibly upset. Canadians were left confused and worried because the extensive media coverage had convinced them that nuclear war between the superpowers was a distinct possibility. Canadian-American relations deteriorated further when Diefenbaker, ignoring the terms of the NORAD agreement, refused to arm the Bomarc missiles with nuclear warheads. When his Minister of National Defence, Douglas Harkness, resigned over the issue in February 1963, public outrage was enough to provoke the three opposition parties into defeating the government on a non-confidence motion.

The demise of the Diefenbaker government occurred in two stages. The government's indecision over domestic issues precipitated a sharp decline in public support, especially in the large urban centres. Diefenbaker was truly an outsider, a 'renegade in power' to use the term of a celebrated journalist, who had failed to gain and hold the confidence of Conservative stalwarts in Ontario and the sympathy of the national media. When the results of the 1962 election were in, the Tories were reduced to a minority government with 116 seats from the Maritime and western provinces and rural Ontario. Conservative, small-town, and rural voters in Quebec abandoned the Conservative Party to join Réal Caoutte's populist Social Credit movement which elected 26 MPs thereby denying Diefenbaker his majority. The weakened and disoriented Diefenbaker government bungled its foreign and defence policies and brought down upon its head the wrath of the popular President Kennedy. Educated, urban, middle class Canadian voters were only too happy to be given another opportunity to elect a government which reflected their concerns and aspirations. The Liberal Party opted to accept nuclear warheads for the Bomarc missiles and to expand the social security system with improved pensions and universal health insurance. Yet, underestimating Diefenbaker's tenacity and ability to fight back and mismanaging their own campaign badly, the Liberals under Lester Pearson won 128 seats, just enough for a minority government. The Social Credit and New Democratic Parties held the balance of power while Diefenbaker's remarkable performance allowed him to retain the leadership of the bruised but not beaten Conservative Party to fight another election.

V. CONFEDERATION CHALLENGED: PEARSON AND TRUDEAU, 1963-84

Governing a Divided Nation

PM 'Mike' Pearson, as he preferred to be called once he gained the knack of politics, much to his regret governed for five years without ever achieving a majority. Social, economic, linguistic, ethnic and regional cleavages came to the fore during the heady years of the 'counter-cultural' and the Quebec not-so-quiet revolutions of the 1960s. While the political elites were born before the Great Depression, increasingly the voters, products of the Depression, the War, and the baby-boom phenomenon, had a very different outlook on the world. They were less deferential toward authority of all kinds and they were eager to replace the traditional political culture with a more open, participatory form of democracy. As a result, the mid-1960s was a period of political turmoil as well as a transition between the old guard and the rising new guard. PM Pearson's experience as a diplomat was both an asset and a liability. Hoping to avoid conflict and to keep his government in office, he often resorted to some dubious and costly compromises, especially with the nationalistic Premier Lesage of Quebec. His diplomatic abilities helped him manage effectively his unruly caucus and cabinet and maintain Canadian-American relations on a even keel during the difficult years of the Vietnam war.

Undoubtedly, Pearson's greatest achievement was his government's completion of a universal, accessible, and portable social security system, a goal which had eluded his predecessors. Prosperity returned by the mid-1960s, the government at all levels felt they could indulge the voters. In 1965, the government implemented the Canada Assistance Plan whereby Ottawa cost-shared with the provinces a wide-range of income support, social security, and retraining programmes. Following heated discussions with the provinces, especially Quebec, Ottawa established the universal and contributory Canada/Quebec Pension Plans for everyone over 65. Benefits for widows and dependents were to be supplemented by a federal Guaranteed Income Supplement for the elderly who did not qualify for the CPP/QPP. The most expensive, controversial programme was that of comprehensive medical insurance. The Saskatchewan NDP government blazed the trail in 1962 following a bitter strike with the doctors. Pearson, during the 1963 election, promised that the Liberal Government would create a national plan. Overcoming strong opposition from the doctors and provinces like Ontario, Ottawa offered to cost-share a comprehensive, universal, and portable medicare system. By the early 1970s, voters pressured all the provincial governments to join the programme. Within a decade, medicare and other social security measures became central pillars of the Canadian identity, setting Canadians apart from their neighbours to the south. Responding to the rapid increase in university enrolment, the Pearson government increased its grants to the provinces for post-secondary education to $5.00 per capita in 1965 and then decided in 1967 to share half the cost of post-secondary programmes, a move that it soon regretted because the cost escalated well beyond what any federal bureaucrat or politician had dreamed.

The Pearson Liberal Government found itself facing a rising tide of neo-nationalist and even secessionist sentiment in the province of Quebec. Premier Lesage successfully pressured Ottawa to allow all the provinces, to opt-out of many of the shared-cost programmes in return for a greater share of the personal and corporate tax revenues. After long months of tedious negotiations to hammer out the complex Fluton-Favreau constitutional amending formula, Premier Lesage refused to put it to his cabinet and legislature for ratification. Much to Pearson's credit, he did respond to pressures from leading neo-nationalists like André Laurendeau to make all federal institutions and crown corporations functionally bilingual. He created the Royal Commission on Bilingualism and Biculturalism in 1963 to offer concrete recommendations as to how this might be done. Against strong opposition inside and outside Parliament, his and successive governments moved slowly but systematically in this direction and accelerated the progress with the passing of the Official Languages Act in 1969. Over the next decade a veritable transformation took place in all federal institutions, agencies and crown corporations as was demonstrated by the sharp increase of French-speaking civil servants working at all ranks of the bureaucracy, in and outside Ottawa. Yet, the expansion of the Quebec separatist movement gained momentum when Charles de Gaulle made his "Vive le Québec! Vive le Québec libre" declaration from the balcony of Montreal's city hall during Expo 67. Within a year the various right and left wing separatist movements came together in the *Parti Québécois* led by René Lévesque, a former minister in the Liberal Government of Jean Lesage.

The Pearson government fed the spirit of Canadian unity by adopting a new flag, the Canadian maple leaf between two red borders, by funding a wide variety of centennial celebration projects across the land and, by helping Montreal fund Expo 67, truly first class world's fair. Thanks to television many of these events were broadcast throughout Canada and to the world in living colour. The Liberal Government also accentuated the social transformation of Canadian society by liberalizing the immigration criteria thereby preventing discrimination in the selection of immigrants based on race, ethnicity, religion, or colour. Within a decade, the major points of origin for

immigrants arriving in Canada shifted from Great Britain and Europe to all
of the major Third World countries transforming Montreal, Toronto, and
Vancouver into multicultural, multilingual, cosmopolitan metropolises.

Canadian-American Relations

PM Pearson's diplomatic skills would be severely tested in several areas of
Canadian-American relations. The Finance Minister, Walter Gordon,
prepared his 1963 budget which intended, in part, to address the public's
growing concern over the rapid escalation of American direct investment in
Canada. A series of discriminatory takeover and withholding taxes were
popular with nationalist voters but enraged both Canadian and American
business leaders. A besieged PM insisted that his Minister of Finance
withdraw the offensive and impractical measures. Yet, Gordon pressed
forward again in his 1965 budget with a measure preventing Canadian
companies from receiving tax-exemptions for advertising in foreign magazines.
Two corporate magazine giants, *Time* and *Reader's Digest* successfully
lobbied the Prime Minister for exemptions. The PM was not immune from
the wrath of American political leaders. As the war in Vietnam escalated and
the Americans adopted a questionable strategy of carpet bombing North
Vietnam, the normally discrete PM threw caution to the wind. During a
convocation address in Philadelphia, he called upon the US to halt the
bombing as a prelude to negotiations. The intemperant and boisterous
President Lyndon B. Johnson forcefully and physically unbraided PM
Pearson for meddling in the internal affairs of its largest trading partner.

Indeed, the President was rudely reminding Pearson that the Canadian
and U.S. economies were inextricably linked and that many Canadian
companies benefited from contract for U.S. military suppliers. One valuable
economic sector which benefited greatly from closer cooperation was the
booming automobile and truck industries. After long and arduous
negotiations, Canadian and American politicians ratified the 1965 Auto Pact
which opened the vast American market to Canadian-made vehicles while
allowing the big three, GM, Ford, and Chrysler to completely integrate their
plants north and south of the border. Continental integration further
Americanized the Canadian automobile industry but productive and efficient
Canadian plants and workers gained a sizeable share of the North American
market. The spin-offs for the Ontario economy were tremendous.

Trudeaumania: Rise and Fall

His minority government teetering on the brink of defeat, plagued by
political scandal and, harassed almost daily by a frustrated and vindictive

John Diefenbaker, PM Pearson, exhausted and exasperated, decided to step aside late in 1967. There were several political veterans, including Paul Martin and Robert Winters, who believed that it was their time to lead the Liberal Party to a victory. Instead, a young, dynamic, rising political star by the name of Pierre Elliott Trudeau was encouraged by the PM and his close friends, mostly outside the party and Ottawa's official circles, to join the leadership race. As Minister of Justice, Trudeau had piloted the controversial Abortion and Divorce Acts through the House of Commons. As a constitutional specialist sitting at the side of PM Pearson during the 1968 federal-provincial conference on the constitution, he dramatically and successfully challenged the nationalist-separatist Premier Daniel Johnson's doctrine of 'equality or independence' for Quebec. Indeed, Trudeau would devote the rest of his life to fighting the Quebec secessionist movement. Trudeau's brash, iconoclastic style gave him instant recognition as his daily utterances were beamed into family living rooms via television. To the despair of his opponents and the surprise of the *pundits,* the Trudeaumania bandwagon swept aside all public scepticism concerning this eligible bachelor who promised nothing more than to devote himself as the people's servant to pursuing 'the Just Society', in all its variants. Backed by Jean Marchand, Gérard Pelletier, Mitchell Sharp, and a majority of the delegates, Trudeau won the leadership convention and called a snap election. Neither Robert Stanfield, the Conservative leader, nor Tommy Douglas, the NDP leader, could challenge directly Trudeau's style or his pledge to create a truly 'open city' based on participatory democracy and a Charter of Rights and Freedoms. The Liberals achieved their first majority government since 1953 with 155 seats but less than 50 per cent of the votes.

PM Trudeau's first term in office would almost terminate his nascent career as a politician. Until he mastered the discipline of power, that is, until he transformed himself into a political leader rather than a philosopher and political theorist in politics, he would not relate to citizens on terms which they understood. Much time and energy was wasted in trying to reorganize and rationalize the decision-making process in the Prime Ministers' Office, in the Privy Council, and in Cabinet. The flows charts were a beauty to behold but the government faltered in the execution of many of its programmes.

The government embarked on a wide-ranging re-evaluation of foreign and defence policy which raised expectations and fears but produced very few tangible results. PM Trudeau's fist valiant effort to patriate the British North America Act, 1867 with an acceptable amending formula and a Charter of basic rights and freedoms failed miserably and left him despondent.

In 1969, following the introduction of the White Paper on Indian Affairs calling for the eventual dismantling of the 'special status' of Canada's status Indians, the government was forced to beat a hasty retreat and then deal with the rising tide of aboriginal nationalism sparked by the White Paper. In October 1970, Trudeau found his government dragged into the search for the *Front de Libération du Québec* terrorists, one group who kidnapped the British High Commissioner, James Cross, while a second group kidnapped and then murdered Pierre Laporte, the Quebec Minister of Labour. Trudeau invoked the War Measures Act only to watch its extensive powers widely abused by the Quebec Provincial Police who rounded up 400 supporters and sympathizers of the secessionist *Parti Québécois,* all harmless suspects who had not proven connections with the terrorists. Swift action and extensive intelligence work by the RCMP brought an abrupt halt to terrorism in Quebec but the incident added to the martyr complex so vital to the separatists' cause. All of these incidents explain why the Trudeaumania bubble burst, and the Liberals were reduced to a minority government, 109 seats for the Liberals compared to 107 for the Conservatives and 31 for the NDP, in the election of 1972. Rather than resign, Trudeau, with the cooperation of the NDP, decided to learn the difficult art of politics.

Building the Just Society

Having promised little in terms of specifics during the 1968 election, PM Trudeau government set out to expand or develop a Federal Government presence in many areas of provincial jurisdiction such as employment training, urban development, municipal renewal, and environmental policy. A full range of programmes, administered by the Department of Regional Economic Expansion (DREE), was created to modernize the infrastructure and create good-paying employment opportunities in the economically-depressed regions of the country. PM Trudeau's minority government situation, 1972-74, prompted him to seek and retain the support of the New Democratic Party caucus by expanding on many of these very costly but seldom effective programmes. A modest prosperity was experienced in many of the remote rural regions of Atlantic Canada, Quebec, Northern Ontario and the Prairies, a momentary phenomenon which allowed many communities and families to adjust to the increasingly harsh realities of technological change and global economic competition. The programmes slowed but did not reverse the tide of rural depopulation and socio-economic decline of these regions.

The government faced a far more extensive problem involving the need for accelerated job creation in all the rapidly-growing metropolitan centres in order to absorb all the well-educated baby-boomers entering the labour force throughout the 1970s. Aggravating this increased unemployment was increased inflation produced by raising incomes, easier credit and a demographically-driven demand for homes, cars, and private and public offices and services. The government increased unemployment insurance benefits, as well as family allowances and pensions which were also partially indexed along with the income-tax rates. Inflation rose to over 10 per cent when after 1973, the Organization of Petroleum Exporting Countries (OPEC), acting like a cartel, doubled then tripled the price of oil sending every country scrambling for alternate sources of energy as well as to find ways to make their economies more efficient. Fearing the impact of excessive inflation and the social costs of cartel prices, the Trudeau government opted for a two-price system for oil. All the provinces east of the Ottawa river which relied on expensive off-shore oil would receive subsidies while the price for Alberta oil available in the rest of Canada would be maintained below the artificial OPEC price. Ottawa would obtain the revenues to finance this very expensive two-price system by imposing an export duty on Alberta oil and gas going to the energy hungry United States. Consumers, especially in Central and Atlantic Canada were grateful for the two-price system but Alberta's Premier Peter Lougheed denounced Ottawa for its economic imperialism and for robbing Albertans of their rightful heritage. The sense of political alienation in Western Canada grew dramatically destroying any possibility of Liberals getting elected in that region. Prepared to meet Canadians as an experienced politician, PM Trudeau deftly engineered the defeat of his government.

During the 1974 election, Robert Stanfield, Conservative leader, proposed to address Canada's unemployment and inflationary crises by imposing stringent wage and price controls. Trudeau ridiculed the proposal as unworkable and maintained that cooperation between government, labour, and business could resolve the problems without the need to create a new bureaucracy to supervise a complicated system of wage and price controls. The Trudeau government was returned to office with a majority of 141 seats, thanks to gains primarily in Ontario. Following the election, a better organized and more powerful organized labour movement, dominated by middle-class public sector unions, entered the fray and set off a new round of push-driven inflation through an aggressive round of very successful collective agreements which provided catch-up for past inflation and protection against future inflation. Corporations reacted by laying off employees to protect profit levels. As stagflation—rising inflation and unemployment combined—set in, the Minister of Finance, John Turner, pleaded unsuccessfully with business and labour for voluntary restraint. When Trudeau rejected his request to move to another ministry, Turner resigned. The new Minister of Finance, Donald Macdonald, was given the unenviable task of implementing a three-year system of wage and price controls limiting wage and salary increases to public sector and large corporation employees to a maximum of 10.8, and 6 per cent increases. The majority of Canadians supported the programme, that is, until they realized that it was much easier for the government to control wages and salaries than it was to keep prices in check. Eventually, the collapse of the OPEC cartel coupled with a short, sharp recession in the early 1980s took some steam out of the inflationary cycle. With the fast growing labour force among Western nations, an economy still heavily reliant upon the export of natural resources, and an aging, low-wage, labour intensive manufacturing sector, the Trudeau government had only limited success in devising and executing its economic programmes. One thing was clear by the early 1980s. The growth of the Canadian economy and government revenues at all levels had not kept pace with either rising costs of social welfare, education and health or with the increasing demands made by the corporate sector for lower taxes and wide variety of lucrative subsidies. Increased social justice had come with a hefty price tag of escalating deficits and debts compounded annually by rising interest rates.

Trudeau on the World Stage

Since the early 1960s, especially since Pearson accepted nuclear warheads for the Bomarc missiles, PM Trudeau was very critical of Pearsonian diplomacy and its exaggeration of the Soviet threat. He rejected the term 'middle power' for Canada as well as its vaunted role as 'helpful fixer' in international relations. He believed, incorrectly, that Pearson's approach to Canada's foreign and defence policy was driven exclusively by idealism and altruism. Trudeau argued that foreign and defence policy should be extensions of the priorities of domestic policy. This was spelt out clearly in *Foreign Policy for Canadians,* a review he commissioned and which appeared in 1970. In the meantime, he reduced Canada's commitment to NATO by 50 per cent in 1969 and recommended the withdrawal of Canada's Armed Forces from Germany. Facing much criticism and pressure from NATO members, PM Trudeau backed off. Believing in the need to build bridges between the East and the West, Trudeau, following the lead of France, recognized the communist regime in China, a step which angered the American establishment. Increasingly aware that the greatest gulf was not between the East and the West but rather between the North and the South,

PM Trudeau attempted to divert more foreign aid to Third World countries. Yet much of this aid was premised on the condition that the purchases should benefit the Canadian economy thereby negating its effectiveness for the recipient countries.

The rise of Québécois neo-nationalism and separatism forced the Trudeau government to address the demand of various Quebec governments, federalist and separatist, to play a role in international affairs to the point of signing treaties in areas of provincial jurisdiction. PM Trudeau's response was to give a bilingual mandate to the Department of External Affairs, that is, to complement Canada's relations with members of the English-speaking Commonwealth with similar relations with the French-speaking countries, namely in Africa. Ottawa allowed the Quebec government to participate in a wide range of conferences and even sign comprehensive cultural exchange agreements with Francophone countries and the Francophone Common-wealth but always under its guidance and supervision. Successive Quebec governments pushed incessantly for more jurisdiction over foreign policy and adopted proactive roles by establishing an expensive formal presence in many countries hoping to spread the gospel of Quebec independence.

In many ways, Trudeau's greatest challenge was to maintain a strong working relationship with the United States and the State Department. This was difficult, at times, because his government pursued after 1973 a strategy of economic nationalism reflected in the establishment of the Foreign Investment Review Agency. The government was concerned that the American dominated oil and gas industry located in western Canada would use its windfall profits, accumulated thanks to the OPEC cartel, to monopolize Canada's energy supply and to buy up other important high-technology, high value-added sectors of the Canadian economy. The FIRA scrutinized all major foreign investments or takeover attempts to see if they were in Canada's long-term interests. The process infuriated the American corporate leaders and politicians who charged that PM Trudeau was a closet socialist who posed a serious threat to the security of the United States. The agency only managed to slow the growth of American investment in Canada while turning Canadian and American businessmen against the government. This opposition was consolidated when the Trudeau govern-ment introduced in 1980 its National Energy Policy which set a goal of 50 per cent Canadian ownership of the oil and gas industry. When Petro Canada, the national oil and gas producer and distributor, was guaranteed an automatic 25 per cent of the discoveries made by the private companies, the American government protested loudly and vigorously. These tensions diminished, but only slightly, when the OPEC cartel collapsed and along with it the economic basis for the NEP. PM Trudeau infuriated the Washington elite when he decided to focus on developing a more meaningful dialogue between the wealthy industrial nations of the northern hemisphere and the underdeveloped Third World nations of the southern hemisphere. He also tried to use his influence to temper the rising Cold War rhetoric coming out of Washington by stressing the need for disarmament and greater world peace. American political and corporate leaders had grown to respect but distrust PM Trudeau and were not displeased with his January 1984 decision to retire from politics. Whatever one might think of Trudeau's lack of success in the economic realm, he raised to a new level the discourse about what it meant to be a Canadian in a volatile and changing world.

Trudeau and the Constitutional Question

PM Trudeau was driven into national politics in 1965 by his concern over the rising tide of secessionist nationalism in Quebec and, in particular, by the Liberal Government of Jean Lesage's decision to use nationalism to acquire 'special constitutional status' for Quebec. Ottawa's concessions on the Canada/Quebec pension plan and a one-way cooperative federalism whereby Quebec opted out of many shared-cost programmes in return for additional taxing powers were considered by Trudeau as *de facto* special status that should be curtailed. In response to the Ontario-sponsored 1967 Confederation of Tomorrow Conference, Ottawa opened constitutional negotiations with the provinces on a wide variety of issues. After two years of intense negotiations, a consensus emerged on a small package of reforms including a four-region based amending formula, a modest Charter of Rights, entrenchment of official bilingualism in federal institutions and in certain provinces, and greater control by the provinces over social programmes. The new premier of Quebec, Robert Bourassa, gave Ottawa and the provinces the assurance that his government would ratify the 1971 Victoria Charter. Once he returned, he succumbed to intense pressures from Neo-nationalist cabinet colleagues like Claude Castonguay and journalists like Claude Ryan who insisted that Quebec obtain exclusive control over all social programmes with the necessary taxing powers before it would accept any amendments to the constitution. Bourassa so informed PM Trudeau who concluded that he was a political weakling, a conditional federalist who could never be trusted to bargain in good faith. The breach between the national and Quebec Liberal parties opened to a full chasm as the latter increasingly fell under the intoxicating lure of a secular, State-building neo-nationalism.

In the interim, the Trudeau government endeavoured to enhance the allegiance of French Canadians to their central government by accelerating the expansion of bilingualism at all levels and in all areas of its activities and services. Under the aegis of the Official Languages Act, 1969, millions of dollars were spent on second language training for English-speaking and French-speaking civil servants. By the end of the 1970s, nearly 25 per cent of the civil servants were Francophones occupying positions at all levels and in most departments, agencies and crown corporations including the RCMP and the Armed Forces. The Secretary of State spent millions funding improvements to education for the two official linguistic minority communities as well as second language immersion training for English-speaking children from coast to coast. Support for official bilingualism was fragile at the best of times during the early stages. A crisis erupted in 1976 over the extension of bilingualism to air traffic controllers working traffic into and out of Quebec's regional airports. English-speaking air traffic controllers fearing for their jobs, supported by the pilots and a majority of Canadians, decided to call a strike during the hectic summer season. They contended that passenger safety would be jeopardized if the use of French was allowed in the sky over Quebec. The Government was forced to placate fears and get the planes flying again by appointing a commission of inquiry which reported in 1979 that bilingualism was a benefit rather than a threat to safety. Yet, the political damage had been done and the *Parti Québécois* benefited from the incident.

The Bourassa government saw Ottawa's language policy as an intrusion into the field of education, an area of exclusive provincial jurisdiction. The separatists in the *Parti Québécois* denounced the policy of official bilingualism as a feeble, misguided attempt to buy off moderate Quebec nationalists thereby undermining the province's push for more powers, and for some, independence. Beginning in 1974, the Quebec state introduced its first comprehensive language law. Bill 22 forced children of immigrant families, if they did not pass an English-language exam, into French-language schools while calling upon large businesses to voluntarily make French the working language of their operations. The *Parti Québécois*, in power following the election of November 1976, introduced a more coercive language law, Bill 101, which streamed all immigrant children as well as children of families moving into Quebec from any part of Canada, into French-language schools. PM Trudeau, rather than disallowing Bill 101 as many suggested, decided to fund court challenges to specific elements of the law while preparing his own package of constitutional amendments which would restore freedom of choice for Canadian citizens.

Hoping to undermine the *Parti Québécois* chances in its promised but postponed referendum on sovereignty-association, PM Trudeau attempted to kick-start the constitutional renewal process by issuing a position paper entitled *A Time for Action* and by introducing Bill C-60 into the House of Commons. He invited the Premiers to respond and then join him at the negotiating table. Neither the voters, concerned with rising unemployment and inflation, nor the Premiers, busy drawing up lengthy constitutional shopping lists, were eager to embark on a new round of negotiations. The Liberals had lost a series of by-elections and the Premiers sensed defeat for Trudeau. So did Joe Clark, Conservative Party leader and ardent supporter of a decentralized federation, and Ed Broadbent, NDP leader who decried Trudeau's focus on defeating his arch-rivals, the Québécois neo-nationalists and separatists. The May 1979 federal election brought an end to sixteen years of uninterrupted Liberal rule when Joe Clark's Conservative Party won a minority government with 4 per cent fewer votes than for the Liberals who took all but one seat in Quebec and lost all but three seats west of Ontario. Not one of the three national parties could claim to speak on behalf of all regions of the country. Trudeau, uncomfortable as leader of the opposition resigned the leadership of the Liberal Party prompting a race for his job. This development lulled a naive PM Joe Clark into believing that his government could function as if it had a majority. Little did he realize that the Trudeau loyalists had no intention of loosing their leaders and their chances at regaining power.

Indeed, the opposition parties were handed a golden opportunity to defeat the unstable Joe Clark government over the issue of taxes. The Finance Minister, John Crosbie's budget imposed, in the name of deficit reduction and 'short term pain for long term gain', a 4 cent per litre tax on gasoline. Consumers, who had been absorbing steady increases in gasoline prices thanks to the OPEC cartel, quickly denounced this tax grab and supported the opposition parties' decision to defeat the budget and the government. The Liberal Party, ahead by 20 per cent in the polls, enticed Trudeau to return as leader with the argument that he would have one more opportunity to resolve the constitutional crisis posed by the upcoming Quebec referendum on sovereignty-association. Believing that PM Joe Clark lacked the discipline of power and that Trudeau was better equipped to deal with the Quebec separatists and the aggressive Western Premiers, voters returned the Trudeau Liberals to office in the February 1980 election. His government held every seat except one in Quebec, made important gains in urban Ontario but was almost completely blocked out of the four western provinces. The country was polarized along deep-seated cultural and regional faultlines.

PM Trudeau acted like a leader determined to live up to the high expectations long held by the majority of Canadians. His government introduced the National Energy Policy, the most extensive intervention of any national government in the economy, which resulted in a negotiated settlement with Premier Lougheed of Alberta whereby domestic oil and gas prices would rise in stages to international prices. Despite the accommodation, western political leaders never forgave Trudeau for his government's aggressive bargaining tactics and strategy. They became even more determined than ever to obtain political and constitutional changes that would curtail severely the powers of the national government. If an alliance with Quebec was necessary to achieve this objective then such an alliance would be established.

Indeed, neither would Premier René Lévesque and the Quebec political elite and chattering class forgive Trudeau's determination to use a reformed constitution to build a stronger Canada and undermine their drive for secession. Unlike former PM Clark, Trudeau did not believe that the referendum was a matter to be left in the hands of Quebec's politicians. His government turned its full attention and resources to ensuring a resounding defeat for the separatists in the May 20, 1980 Quebec referendum based on the nebulous concept of political sovereignty with economic association. Trudeau convinced Claude Ryan, leader of the Quebec Liberal Party, to set aside his 'beige paper' proposals for constitutional renewal based on extensive decentralization to the provinces with additional powers for Quebec. When the NO campaign fell behind in the early stages, Trudeau sent in his federal emissaries led by Jean Chrétien to take charge. He then gave four well-timed speeches in which he demonstrated the impracticality of sovereignty-association and then promised that his government would proceed quickly with constitutional renewal if a majority of Quebeckers voted NO. Sixty per cent of the voters put their confidence in PM Minister Trudeau by voting NO, thereby denying Premier Lévesque a mandate to begin to dismantle the federation.

Striking while the iron was hot, Trudeau, after consulting with the Premiers to see if a consensus could be achieved on a limited number of reforms, decided that unilateral action by Ottawa was the only way the fifty-year constitutional logjam was going to be broken. The Canada Bill, including patriation, an amending formula, and a Charter of Rights and Freedoms, was introduced into the House of Commons on October 2, 1980. This action precipitated political and legal struggles with Joe Clark, the leader of the opposition, and several Premiers, all of whom challenged the unilateral nature of the process all the way to the Supreme Court. Much to PM Trudeau's eternal chagrin, the Supreme Court ruled that Ottawa's unilateral procedure was perfectly legal but nevertheless violated a Canadian constitutional convention requiring substantial support from the provinces.

Trudeau convened a federal/provincial conference in November 1981 to see if Ottawa could entice a majority of the provinces representing a majority of the population to support the Canada Act. Since the outset, the 'gang of eight', comprising all the provinces except Ontario and New Brunswick, had signed an agreement to derail the Canada Bill for a variety of reasons. Some premiers feared that the Charter of Rights and Freedoms would undermine parliamentary supremacy. The secessionist premier of Quebec, René Lévesque, could not accept any constitutional amendments which could reinforce the federation. The Alberta, British Columbia and Newfoundland Premiers wanted a much more decentralized federation. Ottawa's challenge was to break the 'gang of eight'. Trudeau accomplished this task by offering the Premier of Quebec a referendum on the amending formula if a consensus could not be achieved within two years of patriation. Premier Lévesque accepted the offer of a referendum but in doing so he alienated his fellow premiers. Fearing that an unamended Canada Act would be ratified by referendum, some of them approached Ottawa to hammer out a deal. Pressured by the Premier of Ontario, PM Trudeau agreed to accept the provinces' Vancouver amending formula—seven of ten provinces with 50 per cent of the population—and a 'notwithstanding' clause which allowed legislatures to override for five-year terms certain sections of the Charter of Rights and Freedoms. All of the premiers, except René Lévesque, accepted the Canada Act as amended.

Following a noisy ratification by the British Parliament, Canadians acquired, at-long-last, control over their constitutional evolution. The Constitution Act, 1982 was bitterly condemned by the Quebec government, and the highly nationalistic political elites and the chattering classes. Yet polls indicated clearly that a majority of Canadians, including Quebeckers, felt proud of patriation and were favourably disposed to the Charter of Rights and Freedoms which gave citizens the judicial power to challenge discriminatory legislation and regulations of their increasingly interventionist governments. Trudeau would leave office believing that he had accomplished his primary political objective, the patriation and the renewal of the Canadian constitution, a feat that had eluded every Prime Minister since the 1920s. He also believed that the Quebec secessionist movement had been dealt a heavy blow and would not recuperate for some time. Little did he suspect that his successor, Brian Mulroney, would succumb to the sirene song of the Québécois nationalists and secessionists.

VI. CANADA BESIEGED: THE RISE AND FALL OF BRIAN MULRONEY, 1984-93

The Politics of Ambition

Brian Mulroney, the second Quebec Tory Prime Minister since Arthur Meighen in 1920, achieved office in 1984 in a flurry of accolades for his party's breakthrough in Quebec and his rash promise to renew the socio-economic and political fabric of the nation. Little went right and much went awry for this most ambitious and opportunistic of Canadian Prime Ministers. A very old-fashioned, glad-handing, back-room politician who demanded respect rather than earning it, Brian Mulroney would be driven from office nine years later by an irate and angry citizenry. Canadians felt deeply betrayed by ongoing patronage scandals, by his dramatic and unexpected change in heart about free trade with our largest trading partner and neighbour, and especially by two ill-conceived, elitist, but ultimately unsuccessful constitutional deals which seriously threatened the nation's prospects for survival into the new century. What had started out as a watershed election rivalling the defeat of the Macdonald Tory party by the Laurier Liberals in 1896, ended in the political destruction of the Tory party. PM Mulroney's serious political misjudgments, stemming primarily from his being out of touch with the new Canada, gave birth two destructive sectional parties, the secessionist Bloc Party from Quebec led by Lucien Bouchard and the western-based Reform Party led by Preston Manning. And who says that Canadian history is dull!!

During the leadership convention of 1976, a young Albertan politician formed in the crucible of Diefenbaker conservatism, Joe Clark defeated the slick front runner from Baie Comeau, Quebec, a well-connected businessman by the name of Brian Mulroney. This romantic blunderbuss believed that ungrateful delegates had conspired to deny him the brass ring and he was determined to try again the moment an opportunity presented itself. Within three years of the humiliating defeat of the Clark government in 1980, Brian Mulroney carried out a well-planned coup to replace Joe Clark in a leadership campaign that he need never have called. Joe Clark, humiliated once again but determined to remain close to power, threw his support behind Mulroney because he believed, correctly, he had the political savvy and personal connections to break the Liberal stranglehold over the Quebec electorate.

Determined to deliver on his promise, Mulroney fashioned a loose coalition of nationalistic Conservative, Union Nationale, provincial Liberal and disillusioned *Parti Québécois* militants, all of whom despised the federal Liberal Party and its retiring leader, Trudeau. To cement this alliance during the election of 1984, Mulroney, coached by a loyal friend, fellow lawyer and PQ supporter, Lucien Bouchard, promised to reintegrate Quebec into the Canadian constitutional family with 'honour and enthusiasm'. In a moment of pure but misguided ambition, Mulroney promised to amend the Constitution Act, 1982 so as to make it acceptable to Quebec's highly nationalistic political and intellectual elites. Up against a wooden and lackluster John Turner who succeeded Trudeau at the head of the Liberal Party, Mulroney easily won a landslide victory with 211 seats. The once-dominant Liberal Party was reduced to a rump of 40 MPs, nearly half from English-speaking ridings in Quebec. The first stage in the political realignment had been achieved. Mulroney would attempt to consolidate this process by delivering on his promise to the Québécois nationalists in all parties. Yet, he would rue the day that he ever made this promise with his friend who, when it appeared that Mulroney could not deliver, resigned from the cabinet to become leader of the secessionist *Bloc Québécois* in the House of Commons.

During the television debate PM Mulroney scored big points with the voters when he denounced Turner for accepting a series of patronage appointments by the outgoing Trudeau. Yet, he made a principled stand on patronage knowing all-too-well that he intended to reward every card-carrying, influential Tory, especially his long list of friends, who approached him for a lucrative government contract, a judgeship or a seat in the Liberal-dominated Senate. Responding to their leader's none-too-subtle cue, many members of the Tory caucus and party quickly immersed themselves in an old-fashioned political culture described in telling detail by one well-informed journalist as 'On the Take'. Mulroney's government soon faced a 'scandal a month' and the public, forced to chose between his rhetoric of clean government and the reoccurring reality of scandal and patronage, came to perceive their Prime Minister as an old-fashioned Irish 'political boss' doling out extravagant goodies to his cronies at public expense. It did not help his image when he and his wife, Mila, paraded around in the latest and most expansive garb and refurbished the official PM's residence at great expense. By tying the Conservative Party's electoral success directly to himself, PM Mulroney was able to demand and receive total and unquestioned loyalty from his caucus and the party. No prominent Tory ever dared question his political judgement or his decisions throughout his two terms as Prime Minister.

Competing in the Global Economy

The Canadian business community backed the rise of Brian Mulroney in the belief that his government would address the problem of ballooning deficits and an ever-increasing national debt. They also hoped that he would curtail state intervention in the economy, reduce taxes on business, cut back on social welfare expenditures, and seek a comprehensive free trade agreement with the United States. Mulroney promised action on all these fronts except for free trade. As president of the Iron Company of Canada, a subsidiary of Hollinger Mines of the United States, he favoured freer trade but believed it was political suicide for a Tory Party historically associated with the protectionism of J.A. Macdonald's National Policy.

Ironically, PM Mulroney would disappoint his business supporters on every issue but free trade and lower corporate taxes. A believer in the market economy, yet Mulroney was no Ronald Reagan or Margaret Thatcher neo-conservative. Rather than undertaking a wholesale down sizing of the Keynesian-inspired social service state, PM Mulroney stood firmly in the centre of the political spectrum and was satisfied with tinkering around the edges. Fulfilling a promise made to the Albertan government, PM Mulroney quickly dismantled the Trudeau government's National Energy Policy, a move that was rendered easy by the collapse of the OPEC cartel. He then offered Newfoundland control over the potentially lucrative but costly to develop off-shore Hibernia petroleum field. Warming the cockles of the boardroom *gurus* both North and South of the 49th parallel, he turned the Foreign Investment Review Agency into Investment Canada, an agency soliciting increased foreign investment. His government put in place a plan to privatize aging and inefficient Crown corporations but took action in only a few cases. By the 1970s, the manufacturers' sales tax had become an impediment to industries in Canada competing for business in the United states. Despite widespread opposition, the Mulroney government had the courage to replace it with a national 7 per cent goods and services tax that, his Finance Minister claimed, would bring in additional revenue to help reduce the deficit. While fine in theory, in practice the unprogressive tax irritated consumers and did not provide the expected windfall revenues once a recession took hold in 1990.

The Tory government disappointed business when it decided to subsidize the expansion of a Quebec-based pulp and paper Company, Domtar in return for job creation. While the government put an end to universal family allowances, it quickly backed away from wholesale cuts to social welfare, health, and pensions as soon as it faced angry protests from senior citizens, poverty organizations and the women's movement. The task of addressing the rising costs of a wide variety of entitlements would be left up to the Chrétien Liberal government after 1993. In the interim, the government was forced to raise substantially personal income taxes as well as other taxes just to prevent the deficit from expanding any further while ever higher interest rates dictated by the Governor of the Bank of Canada in the early 1990s added billions to both the public and private debt.

Facing continued high levels of unemployment and the prospect of increased protectionism from the United States which absorbed 80 per cent of Canada's exports, PM Mulroney who had become a close friend of President Reagan gambled on the free trade option. He was convinced by business organizations, economists, senior bureaucrats, and numerous academics, who produced the voluminous 1985 Report by the Royal Commission on the Economic Union and Development Prospects for Canada that a free trade agreement with the United States was the best way to restructure and modernize the Canadian economy thereby creating high-paying jobs and high value-added industries capable of competing successfully in the global economy. While the Mulroney government's motive was primarily defensive, the business community, especially in Quebec, sought greater access to the U.S. market and stronger constraints on state intervention in the economy. For its part, the United States was eager to eliminate all restrictions on investment in Canada while obtaining guaranteed access to Canada's immense natural resources, especially energy and water. It was relatively easy to agree on the reduction of traditional tariff and non-tariff barriers over ten years. The negotiations were very complex and the United States, which had the upper hand, drove a very hard bargain especially on the question of countervailing duties, that is, the right to penalize imports that they considered to be unfairly subsidized by governments. Canada gave in on this point in return for disputes resolution mechanism to address this issue and other disagreements which might arise. Both parties agreed to defer the definition of 'unfair subsidies' to a later date.

The Prime Minister simply intended to have Parliament ratify the most comprehensive Canadian-American trade agreement ever but fierce opposition from the Liberal and NDP leaders forced him to take the FTA to the Canadian public in the general election of November 21, 1988. Lining up behind the FTA with plenty of fiscal and human resources were a number of powerful and influential business organizations from the Canadian Manufacturers Association to the Business Council on National Issues, a right-wing lobby group funded by some of Canada's largest corporations. They promised that free trade, by attracting increased foreign investment and opening the large U.S. market to Canadian products and services, would create ever-increasing number of high-skilled lucrative jobs to replace the low-skilled, low-paying positions. They orchestrated a very slick and very expensive advertising campaign in the home stretch of the election to convince concerned Canadians that the FTA was essential to the economic prosperity of Canada.

Opposing the FTA was an informal coalition of the Liberal and NDP parties, a few prominent businessmen, and their various allies in the labour, women's poverty organizations as well as the economic and cultural nationalist movements. They contended, with some justification, that the comprehensive integration of the Canadian and U.S. economies would destroy what little remained of Canada's economic sovereignty. It would not be long, they argued, before the U.S. government would force Canada into bringing its full range of domestic and foreign policies into line with those of the United States. Organized labour feared, again with some justification, that many of the smaller and less productive U.S. branch plants in Canada would be shut down by their parent companies and production shift south of the border. The NDP feared that greater restrictions on state intervention would make it virtually impossible for a social democratic government to nationalize, in the public's interest, certain industries or services or to provide incentives for regional development programmes. Women's and social justice organizations argued that the FTA would compel Canadian companies to reduce wages, working conditions, and benefits in order to make them more competitive with their U.S. competitors. Prominent leaders in Canada's cultural industries fought strenuously to keep their industries off the table and were displeased with the vaguely worded exemption in the FTA.

A first it looked like the FTA's powerful advocates in the business community and among the provinces like Alberta and Quebec were going to re-elect the Mulroney government. That is until the television debates in which John Turner denounced, with great effect, the PM for selling out Canada and the heritage of its citizens to the Americans for a mess of potage. Shell-shocked, the Conservative Party and its business allies launched a massive advertising campaign attacking and undermining with considerable success the personal integrity of John Turner. Thanks to PM Mulroney's Quebec-Alberta alliance, strong business support in south-western Ontario, and a politically divided opposition, the Tories garnered 170 of the 295 seats with only 43 per cent of the vote. The FTA became law on January 1, 1989 just as the country's economy entered a long and deep recession in which thousands of Canadians lost their jobs, mostly in Ontario's industrial heartland. The results seemed to prove that the FTA's critics were right yet the government felt obliged to negotiate and then ratify the North American Free Trade Agreement—NAFTA—which incorporated Mexico in order to protect the gains made in the FTA. Despite this constant catering to the corporate agenda, by the time PM Mulroney left office in early 1994, he had lost much of his personal credibility and political capital within the business community whose support had been essential to his political victories in 1984 and 1988. His government had failed miserably in addressing the ballooning annual deficits and the national debt.

The Constitutional Pandora's Box

PM Mulroney squandered most of his political capital and destroyed any prospect of consolidating the political realignment he had initiated in 1984 when he 'rolled the dice' by reopening the constitutional pandora box. Not wanting to appear too cosy with separatists government of René Lévesque, PM Mulroney waited until 1985 when Robert Bourassa's Liberal Party was elected to office. Quebec's Minister of Justice and Intergovernmental Affairs, Gil Rémillard, with Ottawa's full support and cooperation, began a series of secret negotiations to convince the Premiers, that his government would sign on to the Constitution Act, 1982 if they accepted five conditions. When it appeared that the negotiations were going to fail, PM Mulroney convened the premiers to a 'taking-stock' session at the government's Meech Lake retreat in Gatineau Park on April 30, 1987. He then proceeded, during an all-day bargaining session during which no advisors were allowed, to badger the premiers one-by-one into accepting Quebec's five conditions. The provinces eventually accepted Quebec's demands because the PM agreed that four of those conditions would be extended to all the provinces.

The fragile, seamless-web deal almost collapsed under its own weight, that is, until former PM Trudeau denounced PM Mulroney as a wimp for betraying his responsibility to defend the integrity of the national government and the Premiers as a bunch of 'snivelling eunuchs'. On June 3rd, during a meeting at the Langevin Block in Ottawa, Trudeau's scathing condemnation of the accord emboldened the first ministers, whatever their concerns and reluctance, to put their signature on the legal version of the Meech Lake Constitutional Accord. The stage had been set for a destructive mega-constitutional and political battle that would endure for over five years and push the country closer to political and economic disintegration.

Via a comprehensive interpretative clause, the Accord recognized Quebec as a distinct society. All the provinces would receive a veto over a wider range of matters in the constitution including the creation of new provinces and the reform of the Senate. All provinces would be granted, if they so desired, increased control over immigration, the right to opt-out of shared-cost programmes in areas of their jurisdictions with financial compensation, and the right to send lists of names to Ottawa for appointments to the Supreme

Court. The Accord also stipulated that there would be annual meetings of the
Premiers and the Prime Minister on the Constitution thereby granting the
premiers endless opportunities to remake the federation in their image and
to their benefit.

Much to the private consternation of Premier Bourassa and the incredu-
lity of constitutional experts and observers, what began as the 'Quebec
Round' was turned very deftly into the 'Provincial Round', by the self-
serving premiers taking advantage of PM Mulroney's desire for a 'deal at any
cost'. Almost no one recognized this striking development during the initial
period of euphoria and self-congratulatory rhetoric. Yet, it was exactly this
transition that eventually destroyed the Meech Lake Constitutional Accord.
Eventually Canadians came to understand that the Accord's entrenchment
of the contradictory 'provincial' and 'two nations' compact theories would
render the federation virtually ungovernable. The Accord's demise set off a
momentous political crisis which precipitated a highly divisive referendum
on the ill-conceived Charlottetown Consensus Report in October 1992 and
culminating in the nearly fateful Quebec Referendum of October 1995 in
which the bungling federalist forces snatched the narrowest of victories from
the jaws of defeat.

Fortunately for the federation, the unanimity among the premiers soon
vanished when Premier Hatfield of New Brunswick called an election and
was soundly defeated by the ambitious Frank McKenna. Leader of the
Liberal Party, McKenna feigned opposition to the Accord, confusing
momentarily its critics while increasing his bargaining power with Ottawa
for better financial terms. In Manitoba, whose NDP Premier had been one
of the last holdouts in Meech, the Conservative Party led by an astute and
cautious Gary Filmon came to office in 1988. Pushed by the NDP and
Liberal leaders, Gary Doer and Sharon Carstairs, as well as his own caucus,
Premier Filmon deftly used the opportunity provided by Premier Bourassa's
Bill 178, which restored in amended form the unilingual signage provision
of Bill 101 in contravention of the decision of the Supreme Court, to demand
changes to the Accord before the June 1990 deadline. Otherwise, he warned,
his government would not proceed with ratification.

Filmon's opposition was emboldened when he was joined by the newly-
elected Liberal Premier of Newfoundland, Clyde Wells, who managed in
very short order to become the lightning rod for widespread opposition from
ordinary Canadians to the Accord. A staunch believer in the principle of the
constitutional equality of the provinces and a powerful advocate for the
Triple "E" Senate, Premier Wells saw clearly the central flaw in the Accord.
There was a direct conflict between the principle of the equality of the

provinces and the interpretative distinct society clause which would, over time, allow Quebec to achieve via Supreme Court decisions greater powers than the other provinces. Backed by Trudeau and a great many disgruntled Liberals, as well as by numerous anti-Meech critics across the land, including Senate reformers in western Canada, aboriginal organizations who felt excluded from the process, women's organizations and the unions whose leaders denounced the abolition of national standards for social welfare and health programmes, and avid Charter supporters who feared that certain of its provisions would be undermined by the distinct society clause, Premier Wells rescinded the ratification of the Accord in the Newfoundland Assembly. Not surprisingly, Premier Wells became the whipping boy of the Québécois nationalists and secessionists.

Wells gambled that this action would convince the Prime Minister and Premier Bourassa that appropriate amendments needed to be made to the Accord before the June 1990 deadline if it was to survive. Little did he realize that when the PM reconvened the premiers in early June, the decision had been taken to stonewall the three recalcitrant premiers and literally badger and, if need be, threaten them into signing an unamended Accord with merely the promise of a second round of negotiations. After a week of intense pressure during long closed door sessions followed by media sound bites, the recalcitrant but broken premiers signed on. Premier Well's condition was that his government be given the opportunity to consult the people of Newfoundland in a referendum if possible. In the interim, the Accord ran up against a procedural obstacle in the Manitoba Legislature where unanimity was required to alter the agenda and introduce debate and a vote on the Accord. A Native MP, Elijah Harper, pressured by Assembly of First Nations and the provincial Aboriginal and Métis organizations, refused consent thereby preventing what would have been a divisive vote on the Accord. Watching developments in Manitoba, Premier Wells shrewdly decided to call off the free vote in the Assembly thereby, incurring the full wrath of the Prime Minister and his point man, Senator Lowell Murray, as well as further vilification by the hypocritical Québécois nationalists and separatists who had opposed the Meech Accord at every stage. There was great irony in the fact that PM Mulroney had contributed to the demise of the Meech Lake Accord by bragging to a couple of journalists that he had forced the recalcitrant premiers onside by 'rolling the dice' at the most strategic moment before the deadline. His crass political opportunism and gerrymandering gave Premier Wells every reason not to do anything that might restore the declining political capital of a universally despised Brian Mulroney.

Premier Bourassa was outraged, vowing that the Quebec government would henceforth only negotiate constitutional reforms with Ottawa and not with the province because two had reneged on their signatures. The Accord's demise put fresh wind into the flagging sails of the secessionist movement as its protagonists heaped scorn on what they referred to as a monolith and imperialistic English Canada which had, once again, humiliated the entire Quebec nation. Believing he could channel this outrage to his political benefit, Bourassa created the Bélanger-Campeau commission to study Quebec's constitutional options. The Premier fell ill with skin cancer and the Commission's proceedings were quickly monopolized by the secessionists who took the opportunity to whip up support for their cause across a broad spectrum of Quebec society. The Bélanger-Campeau report recommended that the Quebec government prepare for a referendum on independence. Trying to retain some semblance of control over events, Bourassa had the National Assembly pass Bill 150 which set up a referendum for October 1992 with the question to be either on independence or a package of acceptable constitutional proposals from Canada. Canadians wondered if Premier Bourassa had finally joined the camp of the secessionists.

Clearly, the ball was back in PM Mulroney's court. To buy time, the PM called upon Keith Spicer to head up a Citizens's Forum on Canada's Future as a way of dissipating the growing resentment towards Quebec's political class and its incessant demands. He also wanted to test the waters for a second run at entrenching and amended version of the Meech Lake Accord. Instead, ordinary Canadians turned their wrath on PM Mulroney for his constant attempts to appease the Québécois nationalists and separatists while forgetting the rest of the country and its troubled economy. In his introduction to the *Report to the People and Government of Canada,* Spicer had no choice but to place most of the blame for 'a crisis of identity, a crisis of understanding, a crisis of leadership', squarely on the shoulders of PM Mulroney. Refusing to heed this ominous warning, the PM renewed his ill-fated alliance with Premier Bourassa in the fall of 1991 by initiating a new round of mega-constitutional negotiations with the government's constitutional proposals entitled *Shaping Canada's Future Together.* Indifference, scepticism and outright hostility to the joint parliamentary committee which was set up to discuss these proposals almost derailed the process.

The process was partly salvaged by Joe Clark, the Minister of Federal-Provincial Relations, who hastily arranged a series of televised yet highly-orchestrated regional constitutional conferences to give ordinary Canadians the impression of having input into the process. In the interim, the Beaudoin-Dobbie Committee's February 1992 report *A Renewed Canada,* advanced recommendations that were eminently acceptable to the game plan agreed upon by the PM and Premier Bourassa. It set the stage for a return to the 'closed door' executive federalism of the Meech Lake Accord. A volatile series of Multilateral Meetings on the Constitution involving Ottawa, nine provinces, and the four aboriginal organizations culminated in the elaborate but fragile Person Accord on July 7, 1992. While Bourassa was clearly displeased with two of its central proposals, an equal Senate and the inherent right to self-government for aboriginal peoples, PM Mulroney convinced him to return to the bargaining table with the premiers and the aboriginal organizations with assurances that appropriate amendments would be made to the document. After several long days of negotiations, Bourassa managed to get modest yet important changes written into the renamed Charlottetown Consensus Report by September. Pressured by the opposition parties, PM Mulroney was forced to call a national referendum for October 26, 1992. The changes proved insufficient for Bourassa to retain the support of the *nationaliste* wing of the Liberal Party which joined the secessionists, Jacques Parizeau and Lucien Bouchard, in the Quebec 'NO' camp. The changes, especially those pertaining to Senate reform and a guarantee of 25 per cent of the seats in the House of Commons for Quebec, also undermined the support of the Western Premiers and their constituents, for the amended package.

While the weary public's response to the Charlottetown Consensus Report was initially favourable, it soon became apparent that the Mulroney/ Bourassa alliance had, yet again, dug its own political grave. The Quebec nationalists and secessionists denounced Bourassa for having accepted a circumscribed version of the Meech Lake Accord while the aboriginal organizations had managed to extract for themselves a form of sovereignty-association denied to the Quebec political class. Dozens of 'NO' groups in Western Canada, of which the strongest and best funded was Preston Manning's Reform Party, denounced the Charlottetown Consensus Report for giving too much to Quebec while denying westerners their dream of a genuine Triple 'E' Senate. The entire range of groups which had contributed to the demise of the Meech Lake Accord also joined the eclectic, under-funded, yet strangely dynamic 'NO' campaign. By late September, the polls indicated that the tide had turned against the new Accord.

Once again, former PM Trudeau entered the debate denouncing the Charlottetown deal as 'A Mess that deserves a big NO', thereby accelerating the move to the 'NO' side. The 'YES' side, championed by the PM with little support from the opposition parties and his allies, the premiers, ran an extravagant $12 million campaign, funded by governments and large corporations, based primarily on fear mongering. The PM ripped up the lengthy yet incomplete draft version of the deal in an attempt to shock Canadians into voting for the accord while holding their noses or watch the breakup of Canada. The Majority of Canadians felt repulsed by the PM's politics of desperation. They were no longer easily persuaded into deferring to authority, especially when Ottawa and the provinces could not even agree on a final legal draft before the vote and there remained some fifty political accords to be negotiated.

Premier Bourassa's strategy of an October 1992 referendum on a new deal or decision had forced the parties to the bargaining table. Yet, the strategy back-fired because there was simply not enough time to hammer out the details for what was the most complex and revolutionary restructuring of the federation since its inception in 1867. The Aboriginal communities had managed to win support for a separate constitution within the Canadian constitution while the provinces, led by Quebec, had set in motion a process of decentralization that had no bottom line. While the popular vote was close, 54.4 per cent 'NO' and 44.6 per cent 'YES' the accord was soundly defeated in Nova Scotia, Quebec, and the four western provinces as well as by the native peoples on the reserves. Even in Ontario the 'YES' forces watched their enormous lead dwindle to a pathetically narrow victory. While the Canadian economy did not collapse as predicted by the doomsayers, the political fall-out from this second failed attempt to alter the first principles under which Canadians are governed was dramatic and comprehensive. PM Mulroney's life-long ambition, with the help of Québécois nationalists in all parties, was to carry out a political realignment rendering the province of Quebec a Tory fiefdom with him at the helm. His monumental, tragic gamble exploded like a modern day cluster bomb politically-wounding everything within reach. Deeply despised, even hated, and ultimately rejected by a large majority of Canadians, PM Mulroney was forced to step down as PM and leader of the Tory party in 1993. He was a quintessential nineteenth century politician/boss whose thoughts and actions belied a political culture that was foreign to the majority of Canadians, many of them recent arrivals from distant lands seeking democratic, liberal governance capable of protecting individuals and genuine minorities from the omnipresent state dominated by nationalist-imbued majorities.

The most significant fall-out from the Mulroney regime was the destruction of the once-proud National Conservative Party of J.A. Macdonald and G.E. Cartier. Mulroney's replacement, PM Kim Campbell, a naive and inexperienced leader with no time to rebuild a demoralized government and party, courageously took the brunt of the public's wrath in the October 1993 national election. The Conservative Party was virtually destroyed, reduced from 169 to 2 seats in the House and from 43 per cent to 16 per cent in the polls. In its wake, two regional and potentially destructive political movements emerged on the national scene. Preston Manning's neo-conservative, populist Reform Party, with its roots deep in the political culture of western alienation and new-found ambition, elected 52 MPs mostly from British Columbia and Alberta. In Quebec, Lucien Bouchard's secessionist Bloc Québécois won 54 of the province's 75 seats destroying both the old Liberal fiefdom and Mulroney's fragile, explosive, nationalist/separatist Tory coalition.

The Liberal Party, under Jean Chrétien, a recycled political boss from the Trudeau years, took power with a majority government. The Liberal Government, as per its campaign Red Book, was committed to creating 'Jobs, Jobs, Jobs', to putting an end to the extravagant and expensive patronage of the Mulroney years, and to never raising the dreaded 'C' word, that is, the constitution. The majority of Canadians wanted a kinder, gentler form of American neo-conservatism and they believed that a cautious, experienced PM Chrétien would guide the nation through its darkest hour. The challenge was daunting and many observers wondered if a politician from another time and another age could lead Canadians united into the truly global village of the 21st century.

BIBLIOGRAPHY

Forging the Nation, the Macdonald Era, 1867-96
Armstrong, Christopher. *The Politics of Federalism: Ontario's Relations with the Federal Government, 1867-1942*. Toronto, 1981.
Brown, R.C. *Canada's National Policy 1883-1900: A Study of American-Canadian Relations*. Princeton, 1964.
Dales, John. *The Protective Tariff in Canada's Development*. Toronto, 1966.
Flanagan, Thomas. *Louis 'David' Riel: Prophet of the New World*. Toronto, 1979.
Forsters, Benjamin. *A Conjunction of Interests: Business, Politics and Tariffs, 1825-1829*. Toronto, 1986.
Morton, W.L. *The Critical Years: The Union of British North America 1857-1863*. Toronto: McClelland & Stewart, 1964.
Owram, Douglas. *Promise of Eden: The Canadian Expansion Movement and the Idea of the West, 1856-1900*. Toronto, 1980.
Silver, A.I. *The French-Canadian Idea of Confederation*. Toronto, University of Toronto Press, 1982.
Stanley, G.F.G. *The Birth of Western Canada*. Toronto, 1936.
Waite, P.B. *Canada 1878-1896: Arduous Destiny*. Toronto: McClelland &

Stewart, 1971.

—. *The Life and Times of Confederation*. Toronto, 1964

The Nation Transformed, Laurier and Borden, 1896-1920

Babcock, Robert. *Gompers in Canada: A Study in American Continentalism before the First World War*. Toronto, 1974.

Berger, Carl. *The Sense of Power: Studies in the Ideas of Canadian Imperialism, 1867-1914*. Toronto: University of Toronto Press, 1970.

Brown, Robert Craig. *Robert Laird Borden: A Biography*, vol. 1, 1854-1914; vol. 2, 1914-1937. Toronto: Macmillan of Canada, 1975.

—, and Ramsay Cook. *Canada 1896-1921: A National Transformed*. Toronto: McClelland & Stewart, 1974.

Clippingdale, Richard. *Laurier: His Life and World*. Toronto: McGraw-Hill Ryerson, 1979.

English, John. *Borden: His Life and World*. Toronto: McGraw-Hill Ryerson, 1977.

—. *The Decline of Politics: The Conservatives and the Party System, 1901-1921*, 2nd ed. Toronto: University of Toronto Press, 1993.

Granatstein, J.L., and J.M. Histman. *Broken Promises: A History of Conscription in Canada*. Toronto: Oxford University Press, 1977.

Morton, Desmond. *Marching to Armageddon: Canadians and the Great War 1914-1919*. Toronto: Lester & Orpehn Dennys, 1989.

Neatby, Blair H. *Laurier and a Liberal Quebec: A Study in Political Management*. Toronto: McClelland & Stewart, 1973.

Stacey, C.P. *Canada and the Age of Conflict: A History of Canadian External Policies*, vol. 1, 1867-1921. Toronto: University of Toronto Press, 1981.

The Federation Challenged: King and Bennett Respond, 1920-39

Finkel, Alvin. *The Social Credit Phenomenon in Alberta*. Toronto: University of Toronto Press, 1989.

Glassford, Larry. *Reaction and Reform: The Politics of the Conservative Party Under R.B. Bennett*. Toronto: University of Toronto Press, 1991.

Graham, Roger. *Arthur Meighen: A Biography*, vol. 2, And Fortune Fled. Toronto: Clarke Irwin, 1963.

Granatstein, J.L. *Mackenzie King: His Life and World*. Scarborough: McGraw-Hill Ryerson, 1977.

Laycock, David. *Populism and Democratic Thought in the Canadian Prairies, 1910-1945*. Toronto: University of Toronto Press, 1990.

Morton, W.L. *The Progressive Party in Canada*. Toronto: University of Toronto Press, 1950.

Neatby, Blair H. *William Lyon Mackenzie King. The Lonely Heights*, vol. 2,

1924-1932. Toronto: University of Toronto Press, 1963.

—. *William Lyon Mackenzie King. The Prism of Unity,* vol. 3, 1933-1939. Toronto: University of Toronto Press, 1970.

Owram, Douglas. *The Government Generation: Canadian Intellectuals and the State, 1900-1945.* Toronto: University of Toronto Press, 1986.

Stacey, C.P. *Canada and the Age of Conflict,* vol. 2, 1921-1940, The Mackenzie King Era. Toronto: University of Toronto Press, 1981.

Thompson, John Herd with Allen Seager. *Canada 1922-1939. Decades of Discord.* Toronto: McClelland & Stewart, 1985.

The New Federalism: St. Laurent and Diefenbaker, 1940-63

Creighton, Donald. *The Forked Road, Canada 1939-1957.* Toronto: McClelland & Stewart, 1976.

Douglas, W.A.B., and Bereton, Greenhous. *Out of the Shadows: Canada in the Second World War.* Toronto: Oxford University Press, 1977.

English, John. *Shadow of Heaven. The Life of Lester Person,* vol. 1, 1897-1947. Toronto: Lester & Orphen Dennys, 1989.

Granatstein, J.L. *Canada 1957-1967. The Years of Uncertainty and Innovation.* Toronto: McClelland & Stewart, 1986.

—. *Canada's War: The Politics of the Mackenzie King Government, 1939-1945,* 2nd ed. Toronto: University of Toronto Press, 1990.

—, and Desmond Morton. *A National Forged in Fire: Canadians and the Second World War, 1939-1945.* Toronto: Lester & Orphen Dennys, 1989.

Newman, Peter C. *Renegade in Power: The Diefenbaker Years.* Toronto: McClelland & Stewart, 1963.

Robinson, Basil. *Diefenbaker's World: A Populist in Foreign Affairs.* Toronto: University of Toronto Press, 1989.

Stursberg, Peter. *Diefenbaker. Leadership Gained, 1956-1962.* Toronto: University of Toronto Press, 1975.

—. *Diefenbaker. Leadership Lost, 1962-1967.* Toronto: University of Toronto Press, 1976.

Thomson, Dale, *Louis St. Laurent: Canadian.* Toronto: Macmillan of Canada, 1967.

Confederation Challenged: Pearson and Trudeau, 1968-84

Clarkson, Stephen, and Christina McCall. *Trudeau and Our Times,* vol. 1, The Magnificent Obsession. Toronto: McClelland & Stewart, 1990.

English, John. *The Worldly Years. The Life of Lester Person 1949-1972.* Toronto: Alfred A. Knopf Canada, 1992.

Granatstein, J.L. *Canada 1957-1967. The Years of Uncertainty and Innovation.* Toronto: McClelland & Stewart, 1986.

—, and Robert Bothwell. *Pirouette. Pierre Trudeau and Canadian Foreign Policy.* Toronto: University of Toronto Press, 1990.

Gwyn, Richard. *The Northern Magus: Pierre Trudeau and Canadians.* Toronto: McClelland & Stewart, 1980.

—. *The Shape of Scandal: A Study of a Government in Crisis.* Toronto: Clarke Irwin, 1965.

McCall, Christina, and Stephen Clarkson. *Trudeau and Our Times,* vol. 2, The Heroic Delusion. Toronto.

Radwanski, George. *Trudeau.* Toronto: Macmillan of Canada, 1978.

Simpson, Jeffrey. *Discipline of Power. The Conservative Interlude and the Liberal Restoration.* Toronto: Macmillan of Canada, 1980.

Sheppard, Robert, and Michael Valpy. *The National Deal: The Fight for a Canadian Constitution.* Toronto: Fleet, 1982.

Stursberg, Peter. *Lester Pearson and the Dream of Unity.* Toronto: Doubleday, 1978.

—. *Lester Pearson and the American Dilemma.* Toronto: Doubleday, 1980.

Canada Beseiged: The Rise and Fall of Brian Mulroney, 1984–93

Armstrong, Joe C.W. *Farewell the Peaceful Kingdom. The Seduction and Rape of Canada, 1963 to 1994.* Toronto: Stoddart, 1995.

Behiels, M.D. *The Meech Lake Primer. Conflicting Views of the 1987 Constitutional Accord.* Ottawa: University of Ottawa Press, 1989.

Cameron, Stevie. *On the Take: Crime, Corruption and Greed in the Mulroney Years.* Toronto: MacFarlane, Walter & Ross, 1994.

Cohen, Andrew. *A Deal Undone. The Making and Breaking of the Meech Lake Accord.* Toronto: Douglas & McIntyre, 1990.

Delacourt, Susan. *United We Fall. The Crisis of Democracy in Canada.* Toronto: Viking, 1993.

Doern, Bruce, and Brian W. Tomlin. *Faith and Fear: The Free Trade Story.* Toronto: Stoddart, 1991.

Fraser, Graham. *Playing for Keeps: The Making of a Prime Minister, 1988.* Toronto: McClelland & Stewart, 1989.

Johnson, William. *A Canadian Myth: Quebec, Between Canada and the Illusion of Utopia.* Outremont, Que.: Robert Davies, 1994.

Martin, Lawrence. *Pledge of Allegiance: The Americanization of Canada in the Mulroney Years.* Toronto: McClelland & Stewart, 1993.

McQuaig, Linda. *The Quick and the Dead: Brian Mulroney, Big Business and the Seduction of Canada.* Toronto: Penguin, 1991.

Sawatsky, John. *Mulroney: The Politics of Ambition.* Toronto: Mcfarlane, Walter & Ross, 1991.

Index